Hellenistic and Biblical Greek

This Hellenistic Greek reader is designed for students who have completed one or more years of Greek and wish to improve their reading ability and gain a better appreciation for the diversity of the language. The seventy passages in this reader reflect different styles, genres, provenances, and purposes and are arranged into eight parts according to their level of difficulty. Grammatical support and vocabulary lists accompany each passage, and a cumulative glossary offers further assistance with translation. Students are led to a deeper understanding of Hellenistic Greek and a greater facility with the language.

- Includes canonical and non-canonical Christian texts, Septuagint (prose and poetry), Jewish pseudepigrapha, inscriptions, and Jewish and Hellenistic literary Greek.
- Includes a Web component with more than thirty additional readings for classroom and independent use.
- Offers a glimpse into the everyday life of Hellenistic Greeks, with themes such as sexuality, slavery, magic, apocalypticism, and Hellenistic philosophy.

B. H. McLean is Professor of New Testament Language and Literature at Knox College, University of Toronto. He is the author of *Biblical Interpretation and Philosophical Hermeneutics* (Cambridge University Press, 2012), *New Testament Greek: An Introduction* (Cambridge University Press, 2011), *An Introduction to the Study of Greek Epigraphy of the Hellenistic and Roman Periods from Alexander the Great Down to the Reign of Constantine (323 BCE–337 CE)* (2002), and *Greek and Latin Inscriptions in the Konya Archaeological Museum* (2002). Using a variety of textbooks, he has taught introductory New Testament Greek for more than twenty years in four institutions and serves as the Greek examiner for biblical doctoral candidates at the Toronto School of Theology.

Hellenistic and Biblical Greek

A Graduated Reader

B. H. McLean

Knox College, University of Toronto

CAMBRIDGE
UNIVERSITY PRESS

CAMBRIDGE
UNIVERSITY PRESS

32 Avenue of the Americas, New York, NY 10013-2473, USA

Cambridge University Press is part of the University of Cambridge.

It furthers the University's mission by disseminating knowledge in the pursuit of education, learning, and research at the highest international levels of excellence.

www.cambridge.org
Information on this title: www.cambridge.org/9781107686281

First published 2014

A catalog record for this publication is available from the British Library.

Library of Congress Cataloging in Publication data
McLean, Bradley H. (Bradley Hudson), 1957–
Hellenistic and biblical Greek : a graduated reader / B. H. McLean.
  pages cm
Includes bibliographical references and index.
ISBN 978-1-107-02558-5 (hardback) – ISBN 978-1-107-68628-1 (paperback)
1. Greek language, Hellenistic (300 B.C.–600 A.D.) – Readers.   2. Greek language, Hellenistic (300 B.C.–600 A.D.) – Grammar.   3. Greek language, Biblical – Readers.   4. Greek language, Biblical – Grammar.   5. Bible. New Testament – Language, style – Problems, exercises, etc.   I. Title.
PA617.M34   2014
487'.4–dc23   2014002029

ISBN 978-1-107-02558-5 Hardback
ISBN 978-1-107-68628-1 Paperback

Additional resources for this publication at www.cambridge.org/Greekreader

Contents

Online Materials

Additional resources for this publication are available at www.cambridge.org/
9781107686281

Part 8

List of Illustrations

Guide to Abbreviations and Grammar

I. EDITORIAL ABBREVIATIONS

√	verbal root
>	alternative/variant/dialectical form of
abbrev.	abbreviation
acc.	accusative case
act.	active voice
adj.	adjective/adjectival
adv.	adverb/adverbial
Aeol.	Aeolic dialect
¹aor.	first aorist
²aor.	second aorist
apoc.	apocopated
approx.	approximately
art. inf.	articular infinitive
assim.	assimilation
Att.	Attic dialect
attr. rel.	attraction of the relative pronoun (to the case of its antecedent)
1st attrib. pos.	modifier in first attributive position
2nd attrib. pos.	modifier in second attributive position
3rd attrib. pos.	modifier in third attributive position
BCE	before the Christian era = before Christ (BC)
btw.	between
ca.	*circa* (Lat.), about
CE	Christian era = *Anno Domini* (AD)
cf.	*confer* (Lat.), compare
cogn. acc.	cognate accusative (i.e., same root word as the verb governing it)
col.	column
conat. impf.	conative imperfect (expressing an action attempted in the past)
cond.	conditional

conj.	conjunction
contr.	contracted / contraction
cust. impf.	customary imperfect (expressing habitual action)
dat.	dative case
ὁ δεῖνα	"So-and-so"
dep.	deponent
dim.	diminutive
disc. syn.	discontinuous syntax
Dor.	Doric dialect
ed.pr.	*edition princeps* (Lat.), the first editor of a text
e.g.	*exempli gratia* (Lat.), for example
emph. fut. neg.	emphatic future negation
encl.	enclitic
Ep.	Epic dialect
epex. gen.	epexegetic/explanatory genitive
epith.	Epithet
esp.	especially
euphem.	Euphemism
fig.	figurative/figuratively
fm.	feminine gender
fr.	from
freq.	frequently
fut.	future tense
gen.	genitive case
gen. absol.	genitive absolute
gen. comp.	genitive of comparison
Heb.	Hebrew
HGr	Hellenistic Greek
hist. pres.	historic present
hort. subj.	hortatory subjunctive
i.e.	*id est* (Lat.), that is
impers.	impersonal
impf.	imperfect tense
impv.	imperative
incept. impf.	inceptive imperfect (expressing the beginning of a past action)
ind.	indicative mood
indecl.	indeclinable
inf.	infinitive
instr.	instrumental
intens.	intensive
interrog.	interrogative

intrans.	intransitive (refers to verb not taking a direct object)
Ion.	Ionic dialect
irreg.	irregular (heteroclite)
iter. impf.	iterative imperfect
κ.τ.λ.	καὶ τὰ λοιπά = *et cetera* (Lat.)
l. / ll.	line(s)
Lat.	Latin
lit.	literally
loanw.	loanword
LXX	Septuagint
m.	masculine gender
mid.	middle voice
mod.	modern-day
ms./mss.	manuscript(s)
MT	Masoretic text (of the Tanakh)
naut.	Nautical
n.b.	*nota bene* (Lat.), note well
neg.	negative
neol.	neologism
nom.	nominative case
nt.	neuter gender
NW	Northwest group of dialects
obj.	object
obj. gen.	objective genitive
obsol.	Obsolete
OG	Old Greek version
opt.	optative mood
pass.	passive voice
passim	very frequently attested
periph.	periphrastic construction
pers.	person
pf.	perfect tense
²pf.	second perfect (no κ)
pl.	plural
pleon.	pleonastic
plpf.	pluperfect tense
poet.	poetic
poss.	possession, possessive
postpos.	postpositive
pred. pos.	predicate position
prep.	preposition
pres.	present tense

prob.	probably
prog. impf.	progressive imperfect (expressing continuing past action)
prolep.	prolepis (word brought forward for emphasis out of its normal syntactical order)
pron.	pronoun
ptc.	participle
rel.	relative pronoun
sc.	*scilicet* (Lat.), implied but not written
sg.	singular
subj.	subjunctive mood
superl.	superlative
trans.	translated; translation
uncontr.	uncontracted
v./vv.	verse/verses
var.	variant
voc.	vocative case
w.	with
w/o	without
Y^1 hyp.	Y^1 hyperbaton: [modifier] + intervening word(s) + [substantive]
Y^2 hyp.	Y^2 hyperbaton: [substantive] + intervening word(s) + [modifier]

II. ABBREVIATIONS OF TEXTS CITED IN THE GLOSSARY

Acts	Acts of the Apostles
Acts Andr.	Acts of Andrew
Acts Paul	Acts of Paul and Thekla
Acts Thom.	Acts of Thomas
Aesch.	Aeschylus
Amos	Amos
Apoc. Pet.	Apocalypse of Peter
Ar.	Aristophanes
Barn.	Epistle of Barnabas
1 Chr	1 Chronicles
2 Chr	2 Chronicles
CIJ	J. B. Frey (ed.), *Corpus Inscriptionum Iudaicarum: Recueil des inscriptions juivres qui vont du IIIe siècle avant J.-C,* 2 vols. (Rome: Pontificio istituto di archeologia Cristiana, 1936–1952)

Col	Colossians
1 Cor	1 Corinthians
2 Cor	2 Corinthians
Dan^{OG}	Book of Daniel, Old Greek version
DanTh	Book of Daniel, Theodotion version
Dem.	Demosthenes
Deut	Deuteronomy
Did.	Didache
1 En.	1 Enoch
Eph	Ephesians
Epict. *Diatr.*	Epictetus, *Diatribai (Dissertationes)*
Epicurus, *Her.*	Epicurus, *Letter to Herodotus*
Epicurus, *Men.*	Epicurus, *Letter to Menoeceus*
1 Esd	1 Esdras
Esth	Esther
Eur. *Med.*	Euripides, *Medea*
Exod	Exodus
Ezek. Trag.	Ezekiel the Tragedian
Gal	Letter to the Galatians
GDI	H. Collitz and F. Bechtel (eds.), *Sammlung der griechischen Dialekt-Inschriften*, 4 vols (Göttingen, 1884–1915); rpt. Nendeln/Liechtenstein, 1973; II, 2. *Die delphischen Inschriften* (nos. 2087–2342), ed. J. Baunack, 1896
Gen	Genesis
Gos. Mary¹	Gospel of Mary Magdalene (POxy 3525)
Gos. Mary²	Gospel of Mary Magdalene (PRylands 463)
Gos. Pet.	Gospel of Peter
Gos. Thom.	Gospel of Thomas (POxy 654 / POxy 1 / POxy 655)
Heb	Epistle to the Hebrews
Herm.	Shepherd of Hermas
Herod. *Hist.*	Herodotus, *Histories*
Hos	Hosea
I Eph II	C. Bürker and R. Merkelbach (eds.), *Die Inschriften von Ephesos*, vol. II (nos. 101–599) (Bonn, 1979)
I Eph VI	R. Merkelbach and J. Nollé (eds.), *Die Inschriften von Ephesos*, vol. VI (nos. 2001–2958) (ed. Bonn, 1980).
IG II²	Johannes Kirchner, ed. *Inscriptiones Atticae Euclidis anno posteriors*, 4 vols. (Berlin, 1913–40)
IG IV²/1	F. Hiller von Gaertringen (ed.), *Inscriptiones Epidauri* (Berlin, 1913)

IG V/1	W. Kolbe (ed.), *Inscriptiones Laconiae et Messeniae*, pars 1 (Berlin, 1913)
IG IX/1²	G. Klaffenbach (ed.), *Inscriptiones Acarnaniae*, pars 1, fasc. 2 (Berlin, 1957)
IG X/2	C. Edson (ed.), *Inscriptiones Thessalonicae et viciniae*, pars 2, fasc. 2 (Berlin, 1972)
IG XI/4	P. Roussel (ed.), *Inscriptiones Deli: Decreta, foedera, catalogi., dedicationes, varia* (Berlin, 1914)
IG XII Suppl.	F. Hiller von Gaertringen (ed.), *Supplementum* (Berlin, 1939)
IG XIV	G. Kaibel (ed.), *Inscriptiones Siciliae et Italiae, additis Graeci Galliae, Hispaniae, Britanniae, Germaniae inscriptionibus* (Berlin, 1890)
IJudDonateurs	Baruch Lifshitz, *Donateurs et fondateurs dans les synagogues juivres. Répertoire des dédicaces grecques relatives à la construction et à la réflection des synagogues* (Paris, 1967)
IMagn-Mai	O. Kern (ed.), *Die Inschriften von Magnesia am Maeander* (Berlin, 1900); rpt. Berlin, 1967
IMilet	A. Rehm (ed.), *Milet, Ergebnisse der Ausgrabungen und Untersuchungen seit dem Jahre 1899: VI. Der Nordmarkt und der Hafen an der Louwenbucht* (nos. 187–192) (Berlin, 1922)
IPriene	F. F. Hiller von Gaertringen (ed.), *Inschriften von Priene* (Berlin, 1906); rpt. Berlin, 1968
Isa	Isaiah
Jer	Jeremiah
JMIB	E. Leigh Gibson, *The Jewish Manumission Inscriptions of the Bosporus Kingdom* (Tübingen, 1999)
Job	Book of Job
1 Kgdms	1 Kingdoms (1 Samuel)
1 Kgs	1 Kings
L.A.E.	Life of Adam and Eve (Apocalypse of Moses)
Lev	Leviticus
LiDonnici	Lynn R. LiDonnici, *The Epidaurian Miracle Inscriptions: Text, Translation and Commentary* (Atlanta, 1995)
LSCG	F. Sokolowski, *Lois sacrées des cités grecques* (Paris, 1969)
LSCG Suppl.	F. Sokolowski, *Lois sacrées des cités grecques: Supplément* (Paris, 1962)
Luke	Gospel of Luke
1 Macc	1 Maccabees
2 Macc	2 Maccabees
4 Macc	4 Maccabees

MAMA	W. M. Calder, E. Herzfeld, S. Guyer, and C. W. M. Cox (eds.), *Monumenta Asiae Minoris Antiqua* (London 1928–1993)
Mark	Gospel of Mark
Mart. Pol.	Martyrdom of Polycarp
Matt	Gospel of Matthew
NewDocs I–V	G. H. R. Horsley, *New Documents Illustrating Early Christianity* (North Ryde, Australia, 1981–1992)
NewDocs VI–IX	S. R. Llewelyn, *New Documents Illustrating Early Christianity* (North Ryde, Australia, 1992–2002)
Num	Numbers
PChBeatty 46	Papyrus Chester Beatty
PEnteuxeis	O. Guéraud (ed.), *ENTEUXIS: Requêtes et plaintes addressées au Roi d'Egypte au IIIe siècle avant J.-C* (Cairo, 1931)
1 Pet	1 Peter
PGL	G. Vitelli and M. Norsa (eds.), *Papiri greci e latini* (Florence, 1917)
PGM	Karl Preisendanz (ed.), *Papyri Graecae Magicae: Die Griechischen Zauberpapyri* (Leipzig/Berlin, 1928)
Philo, *Alleg. Interp.*	Philo of Alexandria, *Allegorical Interpretation*
Philostr. *VA*	Lucius Flavius Philostratos, *Vita Apollonii*
Phlm	Philemon
Pl. *Rep.*	Plato, *Republic*
PMich	A. E. R. Boak, *Papyri from Tebtunis*, Michigan Papyri, vols. II and V (Ann Arbor, 1933–1944)
Poim.	*Poimandres*, Hermetic Writings
Prot. Jas.	Protoevangelium of James
Ps	Psalm
Rev	Revelation of John
Rom	Paul's Letter to the Romans
SEG	*Supplementum Epigraphicum Graecum*
SIG³	W. Dittenberger, *Sylloge inscriptionum graecarum*, 3rd ed., 4 vols. (Leipzig, 1915–1924)
Sir	Sirach (Ecclesiasticus)
Song	Song of Songs (Canticles)
Soph.	Sophocles
T. Levi	Testament of Levi
T. Reu.	Testament of Reuben
1 Thess	1 Thessalonians
2 Thess	2 Thessalonians
1 Tim	1 Timothy
Wis	Wisdom of Solomon

III. ABBREVIATIONS OF BOOKS, ARTICLES, AND ANCIENT MANUSCRIPTS

AM
Mitteilungen des Deutschen Archÿauologischen Instituts: Athenische Abteilung

AnatSt
Anatolian Studies, Journal of the British Institute of Archaeology at Ankara

ANRW
Aufstieg und Niedergang der römischen Welt

BCH
Bulletin de correspondance hellénique

BDAG
W. Bauer, F. Wm. Danker, W. F. Arndt, and F. W. Gingrich, *A Greek–English Lexicon of the New Testament*, 3rd ed. (Chicago, 2000)

BE
Bulletin épigraphique (published in *REG* 1888–); issues of *BE* by J. and L. Robert published separately in 10 vols. (Paris, 1972–1987) with 5 vols. of indices (Paris, 1973–1983)

Bernhard
Andrew E. Bernhard, *Other Early Christian Gospels: A Critical Edition of the Surviving Greek Manuscripts* (London, 2006)

Buck
Carl Darling Buck, *Greek Dialects: Grammar, Selected Inscriptions, Glossary* (Chicago, 1955)

CIG
Corpus Inscriptionum Graecarum, 4 vols. (Berlin, 1828–1877); rpt. Hildesheim, 1977

CIJ
J. B. Frey, ed. *Corpus Inscriptionum Iudaicarum: Recueil des inscriptions juivres qui vont du IIIe siècle avant J.-C.*, 2 vols. (Rome, 1936–1952)

CIRB
V. V. Struve et al. (eds.), *Corpus inscriptionum regni Bosporani* (Leningrad, 1965)

CMRDM
E. Lane, *Corpus monumentorum religionis dei Menis*, 4 vols. (Leiden, 1971–1978)

Comfort/Barrett
Philip W. Comfort and David P. Barrett (eds.), *The Text of the Earliest New Testament Greek Manuscripts: A Corrected, Enlarged Edition* (Wheaton, IL, 1999)

CR
Classical Review

DGE
E. Schwyzer (ed.), *Dialectorum Graecarum exempla epigraphica potiora* (Leipzig, 1923); rpt. Hildesheim, 1960

Ehrman
Bart Ehrman (ed.), *Apostolic Fathers*, 2 vols., LCL 24–25 (Cambridge, MA, 2003)

GDI
H. Collitz and F. Bechtel (eds.), *Sammlung der griechischen Dialekt-Inschriften*, 4 vols. (Göttingen, 1884–1915); rpt. Nendeln/Liechtenstein, 1973; II, 2. *Die delphischen Inschriften* (nos. 2087–2342), ed. J. Baunack, 1896

GRA	J. S. Kloppenborg and R. S. Ascough, *Greco-Roman Associations: Texts, Translations, and Commentary. I. Attica, Central Greek, Macedonia, Thrace* (Berlin, 2011)
GRBS	*Greek, Roman and Byzantine Studies*
HSCP	*Harvard Studies in Classical Philology*
HTR	*Harvard Theological Review*
IBM III/1	E. L. Hicks (ed.), *The Collection of Ancient Greek Inscriptions in the British Museum: III.1 Priene and Iasos* (Oxford, 1883)
IDelos	*Inscriptions de Délos*, 7 vols. (Paris, 1926–1972)
IEph II	C. Bürker and R. Merkelbach (eds.), *Die Inschriften von Ephesos*, vol. II (nos. 101–599) (Bonn, 1979)
IEph VI	R. Merkelbach and J. Nollé (eds.), *Die Inschriften von Ephesos*, vol. VI (nos. 2001–2958) (Bonn, 1980)
IG II²	Johannes Kirchner (ed.), *Inscriptiones Atticae Euclidis anno posteriors*, 4 vols. (Berlin, 1913–1940)
IG IV²/1	F. Hiller von Gaertringen (ed.), *Inscriptiones Epidauri* (Berlin, 1913)
IG V/1	W. Kolbe (ed.), *Inscriptiones Laconiae et Messeniae*, pars 1 (Berlin, 1913).
IG IX/2	G. Klaffenbach (ed.), *Inscriptiones Thessaliae* (Berlin, 1972)
IG IX/1²	G. Klaffenbach (ed.), *Inscriptiones Acarnaniae*, pars 1, fasc. 2 (Berlin, 1957)
IG X/2	C. Edson, *Inscriptiones Thessalonicae et viciniae*, pars 2, fasc. 2 (Berlin, 1972)
IG XI/4	P. Roussel, *Inscriptiones Deli: Decreta, foedera, catalogi, dedicationes, varia* (Berlin, 1914)
IG XII/5	*Inscriptiones Cycladum*, 2 parts (Berlin, 1903/1909)
IG XII Suppl.	F. Hiller von Gaertringen, ed. *Supplementum* (Berlin, 1939)
IG XIV	G. Kaibel (ed.), *Inscriptiones Siciliae et Italiae, additis Graeci Galliae, Hispaniae, Britanniae, Germaniae inscriptionibus* (Berlin, 1890)
IGE	B. H. McLean, *An Introduction to the Study of Greek Epigraphy of the Hellenistic and Roman Periods from Alexander the Great Down to the Reign of Constantine (323 BCE–337 CE)* (Ann Arbor, MI, 2002)
IGRR I	R. Cagnat, J. Toutain, and P. Jouguet (eds.), *Inscriptiones Graecae ad res Romanas pertinentes: I. Inscriptiones Europae (praeter Graeciam) et Africae* (Paris, 1906); rpt. Chicago, 1975
IGUR	L. Moretti *Inscriptiones Graecae Urbis Romae* (Rome, 1968–1991)

IJO	David Noy, Alexander Panayotov, and Hanswulf Bloedhorn (eds.), *Inscriptiones Judaicae Orientis*, vol. 1 (Tübingen, 2004)
IJudDonateurs	Baruch Lifshitz, *Donateurs et fondateurs dans les synagogues juivres. Répertoire des dédicaces grecques relatives à la construction et à la réfection des synagogues* (Paris, 1967)
IKonya	B. H. McLean, *Greek and Latin Inscriptions in the Konya Archaeological Museum*, Regional Epigraphic Catalogues of Asia Minor, BAR International Series (London, 2002)
IKosHerzog	Rudolph Herzog (ed.), *Heilige Gesetze von Kos* (Berlin, 1952)
ILydiaKP	J. Keil and A. von Premerstein (eds.), *Bericht über eine Reise in Lydien und der sünlichen Aiolis* (1910), DenkschrWien 53/2 (Vienna, 1908–1914)
IMagnMai	O. Kern (ed.), *Die Inschriften von Magnesia am Maeander* (Berlin, 1900); rpt. Berlin, 1967
IMilet	A. Rehm (ed.), *Milet, Ergebnisse der Ausgrabungen und Untersuchungen seit dem Jahre 1899: VI. Der Nordmarkt und der Hafen an der Lÿouwenbucht* (nos. 187–192) (Berlin, 1922)
IPriene	F. F. Hiller von Gaertringen (ed.), *Inschriften von Priene* (Berlin, 1906); rpt. Berlin, 1968
ISardBR	W. H. Buckler and D. M. Robinson (eds.), *Sardis. VII/1. Greek and Latin Inscriptions* (Leiden, 1932)
ISmyrna	G. Petzl (ed.), *Die Inschriften von Smyrna* (Bonn, 1982–1990)
JbAc	*Jahrbuch für Antike und Christentum*
JBL	*Journal of Biblical Literature*
JHS	*Journal of Hellenic Studies*
JRS	*Journal of Roman Studies*
JSNT	*Journal for the Study of the New Testament*
JTS	*Journal of Theological Studies*
Klauck	Hans-Josef Klauck, *The Religious Context of Early Christianity: A Guide to Graeco-Roman Religions*, trans. Brian McNeil (Edinburgh, 2000)
LiDonnici	Lynn R. LiDonnici, *The Epidaurian Miracle Inscriptions: Text, Translation and Commentary* (Atlanta, 1995)
LSAM	F. Sokolowski, *Lois sacrées de l'Asie Mineure* (Paris, 1955)
LSCG	F. Sokolowski, *Lois sacrées des cités grecques* (Paris, 1969)
LSCG Suppl.	F. Sokolowski, *Lois sacrées des cités grecques: Supplément* (Paris, 1962)
LSJ	*A Greek–English Lexicon with Revised Supplement*, comp. Henry George Liddell and Robert Scott, rev.

	and augmented by H. S. Jones and R. McKenzie (Oxford, 1996)
MAMA	W. M. Calder, E. Herzfeld, S. Guyer, and C. W. M. Cox (eds.), *Monumenta Asiae Minoris Antiqua* (London, 1928–1993)
MBAH	*Münsterlische Beitrüge zur antiken Handelsgeschichte*
Michel	C. Michel (ed.), *Recueil d'inscriptions grecques* (Brussels, 1900); rpt. Hildesheim, 1976
NETS	Albert Pietermas and Benjamin G. Wright (eds.), *A New Translation of the Septuagint: A New Translation of the Greek into Contemporary English* (New York, 2007)
NewDocs I–V	G. H. R. Horsley, *New Documents Illustrating Early Christianity* (North Ryde, Australia, 1981–1992)
NewDocs VI–IX	S. R. Llewelyn, *New Documents Illustrating Early Christianity* (North Ryde, Australia, 1992–2002)
NovT	*Novum Testamentum*
OGI	W. Dittenberger (ed.), *Orientis graeci inscriptiones selectee*, 2 vols. (Leipzig, 1903–1905); rpt. Hildesheim, 1970
Pap 30	Papyrus 30 (Oxy 1598), Ghent University (in Andrew E. Bernhard, *Other Early Christian Gospels: A Critical Edition of the Surviving Greek Manuscripts* (London, 2006))
PChBeatty 46	Papyrus Chester Beatty II (ca. 200 CE); in Bernhard, 2006
PEnteuxeis	O. Guéraud (ed.), *ENTEUXIS: Requêtes et plaintes addressées au Roi d'Egypte au IIIe siècle avant J.-C.* (Cairo, 1931)
PGL	G. Vitelli and M. Norsa (eds.), *Papiri greci e latini* (Florence, 1917)
PGM	Karl Preisendanz (ed.), *Papyri Graecae Magicae: Die Griechischen Zauberpapyri* (Leipzig, 1928)
PMich	A. E. R. Boak, *Papyri from Tebtunis*, Michigan Papyri vols. II and V (Ann Arbor, 1933–1944)
POxy	B. P. Grenfell, A. S. Hund, et al. (eds.), *The Oxyrhynchus Papyri* (London, 1986–)
PRyl	*Rylands Papyrus*
RAC	*Reallexikon für Antike und Christentum* (Stuttgart, 1950–)
Rahlfs/Hanhart	Alfred Rahlfs and Robert Hanhart (eds.), *Septuaginta*, ed. altera (Stuttgart, 2006)
RE	*[Paulys] Realencyclopÿaudie der classischen Altertumswissenschaft*, ed. K. Ziegler, rev. G. Wissowa (Stuttgart, 1894–1980)
REG	*Revue des études grecques*

RHR	*Revue de l'histoire des religions*
SEG	*Supplementum Epigraphicum Graecum*
SIG³	W. Dittenberger, *Sylloge inscriptionum graecarum*, 3rd ed., 4 vols. (Leipzig, 1915–1924)
SIRIS	Ladislaus Vidman (ed.), *Sylloge inscriptionum Religionis Isiacae et Sarapiacae* (Berlin, 1969)
Smyth	Herbert Weir Smyth, *Greek Grammar*, Rev. Gordon M. Messing (Cambridge, MA, 1956)
TAM V/II	P. Herrmann (ed.), *Tituli Asiae Minoris: V.2. Regio septentrionalis ad occidentem vergens* (Vienna, 1981–1989)
TLG	*Thesaurus Linguae Graecae* (*www.tlg.uci.edu*), Irvine, CA
White	John L. White, *Light from Ancient Letters* (Philadelphia, 1986)
ZNTW	*Zeitschrift für die Neutestamentliche Wissenschaft*

IV. FREQUENTLY OCCURRING GRAMMATICAL CONSTRUCTIONS

Contents

1. Adverbial Participles

   Temporal Adverbial Participles: 1.1 Present Participle; 1.2 Aorist Participle; 1.3 Perfect Participle

   Non-Temporal Use of Adverbial Participles: 1.4 Causal Adverbial Participle; 1.5 Concessive Adverbial Participle; 1.6 Instrumental Adverbial Particle Expressing Means; 1.7 Expressing Adverbial Purpose; 1.8 Conditional Adverbial Participle

2. Articular Infinitive: 2.1 Prepositions with Articular Infinitive Expressing Purpose; 2.2 Prepositions with Articular Infinitive of Time; 2.3 Articular Infinitive of Cause

3. Attraction of the Relative

4. Attributive Adjectives: 4.1 First Attributive Position; 4.2 Second Attributive Position; 4.3 Third Attributive Position

5. Case Endings Expressing Time: 5.1 Accusative of Time; 5.2 Dative of Time; 5.3 Genitive of Time

6. Counting the Days of the Month

7. Deponent Verbs

8. Emphatic Future Negation

9. Genitive Absolute

10. Genitive of Comparison

1. Adverbial Participles

Temporal Adverbial Participles

Many adverbial participles function temporally, which is to say, they specify the time of an action relative to the action of the main verb. Thus, the tense of a temporal participle is always *relative to the tense of the finite verb of the sentence*:

1.1 A present participle denotes an action occurring *at the same time* as the main verb. This *contemporaneous* action can be expressed by the use of helping words such as "while" or "when" (e.g., "*When the disciples arrived*, Jesus was praying").

1.2 An aorist participle often denotes an action occurring *prior to* the action specified by the main verb. This *antecedent* action can be expressed by the use of the helping word "after" (e.g., "*After the disciples arrived*, Jesus prayed").

1.3 A perfect participle, like the perfect indicative, denotes a present state as a result of past actions.

Non-Temporal Use of Adverbial Participles

Even though adverbial participles often function temporally, especially in narratives, one should not overlook the fact that adverbial participles can have many other meanings, depending on the specific context. Here follow some typical non-temporal uses of adverbial participles:

1.4 *Causal Adverbial Participle ("because")*

The cause of an action or event can be indicated by the use of a participle: for example, "*because he wanted* to justify himself, he said to Jesus" (Luke 10:29).

1.5 *Concessive Adverbial Participle ("although")*

A participle can be used to concede, or admit, a point: for example, "for *although we are walking* in the flesh, we are not fighting according to the flesh" (2 Cor 10:3).

1.6 *Instrumental Adverbial Particle Expressing Means ("by means of")*

A participle can be employed to specify the means or manner by which an action takes place: for example, "*by touching* the ear, he healed him" (Luke 22:51).

1.7 *Expressing Adverbial Purpose ("in order to")*

A participle can specify the purpose of an action: for example, "Elijah is coming, *in order to* save him" (Matt 27:49).

1.8 *Conditional Adverbial Participle ("if")*

A participle can be used to indicate the protasis (i.e., "if" clause) of a conditional sentence: for example, "*if you keep* yourselves from such things, you will do well" (Acts 15:29).

2. Articular Infinitive

When an infinitive is preceded by an article (always neuter), it is termed an "articular infinitive." If the infinitive has an explicit subject, it will be in the accusative case. If there is an object, it will also be in the accusative case.

2.1 *Prepositions with Articular Infinitive Expressing Purpose*

Articular infinitives are often preceded by prepositions. Much of what you learned about the meaning of prepositions is applicable here, though there are important differences. The prepositions εἰς and πρός followed by the articular infinitive (with article in accusative case) express purpose:

(a) εἰς + accusative article + infinitive ("in order to")
(b) πρός + accusative article + infinitive ("in order to")

2.2 *Prepositions with Articular Infinitive of Time*

The articular infinitive in conjunction with various prepositions can express the time of an action:

(a) πρό + genitive article + infinitive, "before" (antecedent time)
(b) ἐν + dative article + infinitive, "when/while" (simultaneous time)

(c) μετά + accusative article + infinitive, "after" (subsequent time)

(d) ἕως + genitive article + infinitive, "until"

2.3 Articular Infinitive of Cause

διά + accusative article + infinitive, "because"

3. Attraction of the Relative

When the antecedent of the relative pronoun is in the genitive or dative case, the case of the relative pronoun is normally "attracted" to the case of its antecedent. In other words, it takes on the same case as its antecedent, *regardless of its grammatical function*. For example, if the antecedent is genitive or dative, the relative pronoun would conform to this case by becoming respectively genitive (οὖ) or dative (ᾧ) regardless of its function in its own clause.

4. Attributive Adjectives

Attributive adjectives directly modify a noun. *An attributive adjective is always preceded by a definite article.* There are three possible configurations, with little difference in meaning:

4.1 First Attributive Position

In this case, the attributive adjective is found *between* the article and the noun, as it often is in English syntax. This is termed the "first attributive position": ὁ ἀγαθὸς ἀδελφός ("the good brother")

4.2 Second Attributive Position

In this case, the attributive adjective *follows* the noun and has its own article. This is termed the "second attributive position": ὁ ἀδελφός ὁ ἀγαθὸς ("the good brother").

4.3 Third Attributive Position

In this case, the attributive adjective follows the noun and has its own article, but the noun lacks an article. This is more common with attributive participles than with adjectives. This is termed the "third attributive position": for example, ἀδελφὸς ὁ ἀγαθός ("the good brother"). This construction is commonly used with proper names.

5. Case Endings Expressing Time

The case endings can be used, without prepositions, to express different meanings of time:

> 5.1 Accusative of *duration* of time: e.g., δύο ἡμέρας (acc. pl.) ("for two days").

> 5.2 Dative of time *when* something happens (i.e., often a specific point in time, e.g., τῇ τρίτῃ ἡμέρᾳ (dat. sg.) ("on the third day").

> 5.3 Genitive of time *within which* something happens (e.g., the thief comes *in* the night): "You must say that his disciples came *during* the night (gen., νυκτός) and stole him away while we were asleep" (Matt 28:13).

6. Counting the Days of the Month

The first day of the month was known as νουμηνία (first day of the lunar month/new moon). The days from 2 to 10 were counted as the "rising" (iJstamevnou) of the month (μηνός), using ordinal numbers (e.g., δευτέρα ἱσταμένου, τρίτη ἱσταμένου, τετρὰς ἱσταμένου, πέμπτη ἱσταμένου, etc.). The second decade (i.e., days 11–19) was counted either by continuing the previous count (i.e., 11th, 12th, 13th, …, 19th) or by recommencing the count with 1 (i.e., 1st, 2nd, 3rd, …, 9th) followed by the term μεσοῦντος (μηνός). The 20th day was known as εἰκάς or εἰκοστή. The third decade (days 21–29/30) was counted in terms of the "dying" or waning of the month (μηνὸς φθίνοντος/παυομένου/λήγοντος/ἀπιόντος/μετ᾽ εἰκάδας).

7. Deponent Verbs

A "deponent" verb is a verb that is middle, or passive, in form but *active* in meaning. The term "deponent" describes the *function* of a word, not its form. For this reason, it should not be used for the parsing of verbs, because parsing is an analysis of *morphology* (i.e., form), not function.

8. Emphatic Future Negation

The aorist subjunctive, preceded by οὐ μή, expresses a very strong denial: for example, "… unless your righteousness exceeds that of the scribes and Pharisees, you *will never* enter (οὐ μὴ εἰσέλθητε) the kingdom of God" (Matt 5:20).

9. Genitive Absolute

The genitive absolute is a special grammatical construction that has no equivalent in English grammar. If you fail to recognize this grammatical structure in the Greek text, you will find yourself unable to translate the sentence correctly. Therefore, you must fully master this construction. The genitive absolute has the following features: (1) a genitive participle is followed by a noun or pronoun in the genitive case, forming an adverbial phrase; (2) the subject of the participle is independent of the subject of the main verb of the sentence; (3) the genitive participle is translated as an adverbial participle (see 1.1–1.8): temporal, causal, concessive, and so on.

10. Genitive of Comparison

When two things are compared with one another, a comparative adjective or adverb is often used, followed by a noun in the genitive. This is termed the "genitive of comparison." In translation, the word "than" must often be supplied (e.g., "more than," "greater than"): for example, πλεῖον τῶν γραμματέων καὶ Φαρισαίων; Farisaivwn (Matt 5:20).

11. Historic Present

When reading the gospels, one often encounters the present tense in contexts where one would expect the past tense. It is used by authors to give a narrative greater vividness. Verbs in the "historic" present tense should be translated as *past tense* verbs (e.g., "Jesus said").

12. Hortatory Subjunctive

The hortatory subjunctive is used to express an imperative in the first person plural: for example, "let us have (ἔχωμεν) peace with God" (Rom 5:1).

13. Imperfect

13.1 Progressive Imperfect

> The progressive imperfect describes an *ongoing* past action (e.g., "he was —ing").

13.2 Customary Imperfect

> The customary imperfect describes a regularly occurring action in the past over an extended period of time (e.g., "he used to ...", "she continually ...").

13.3 Iterative Imperfect

The iterative imperfect describes a *repeated* action in the past over a period of time (e.g., "he repeatedly …").

13.4 Conative Imperfect

The conative imperfect describes an action that was *attempted* but not completed (e.g., 'he tried to … ,' 'she attempted to …').

13.5 Inceptive Imperfect

The inceptive imperfect describes the beginning of an action (e.g., "he began to …").

13.6 Imperfect with Verbs of "Saying"

Verbs of "saying" (e.g., ἔλεγεν) often occur in the imperfect tense, especially if they introduce a speech of some length. In such cases, the emphasis is not on the fact that "such and such" a thing was said, but on the exposition of what was said. These imperfects can be translated as simple past tenses ("he said").

13.7 Imperfect in Indirect Discourse

Indirect discourse in the Greek language preserves the original tense of direct discourse. In contrast, in English, when direct discourse is changed to indirect discourse, a present tense verb must be changed to a past tense verb, the tense also changes. For example, if John says: "I *am going* to the library," and someone asks you what John said, you would reply, "John said that he *was going* to the library." Notice how the present tense verb "am going" is changed to the past tense "was going" in English.

14. Impersonal Use of εἰμί

The third-person forms of εἰμί are sometimes used impersonally, without an implied real subject: ἐστί(ν), "there is"; εἰσί(ν), "there are."

15. Infinitive with ὥστε to Express Result

When ὥστε is followed by an infinitive, the infinitive expresses the result of an action ("so that:): for example, ἡ πίστις ὑμῶν ἡ πρὸς τὸν θεὸν ἐξελήλυθεν, ὥστε μὴ χρείαν ἔχειν ἡμᾶς λαλεῖν τι ("Your confidence toward God has gone out, *so that we have no need* to say anything" [1 Thess 1:8]).

16. *Iota*-adscript

In inscriptions of the Classical period and beyond, the *iota* of the so-called improper diphthongs was *never* written subscript (i.e., -ῃ -ᾳ -ῳ). When written at all, it was written adscript, after the thematic vowel (i.e., -ηι -αι -ωι). Throughout the Hellenistic period, these diphthongs were gradually monophthongized in popular speech and consequently came to be written simply as (-η -α -ω without an *iota*-adscript, because there was no longer any qualitative distinction in terms of pronunciation between these vowels and their corresponding simple vowels.

17. Objective Genitive

This can be explained as follows. As an example, we will use the phrase "blasphemy *of the Spirit* (τοῦ πνεύματος βλασφημία)" (Matt 12:31). Once again, imagine the *non-genitive* noun as a verbal idea. In the case of this example, "blasphemy" implies the verbal idea of "blaspheming." Next, think of the noun in the genitive as the *recipient* (direct object) of this verbal action or that this verbal action is directed toward the term in the genitive. In the case of our example, "*of the Spirit*" implies blasphemy that is "directed toward the Spirit." Thus, "of the Holy Spirit" is an *objective* genitive.

18. Periphrastic Constructions

The term "periphrastic" means a roundabout or indirect manner of doing something. In Greek, the so-called periphrastic construction is composed of an auxiliary verb, εἰμί, followed by a participle. In the formation of a periphrastic construction, no element may come between the auxiliary verb (εἰμί) and the participle, except for terms that complete or directly modify the participle itself. The following three periphrastic tenses are formed with the *present* participle:

present periphrastic	pres. ind. of εἰμί	+	present participle
imperfect periphrastic	impf. ind. of εἰμί	+	present participle
future periphrastic	fut. ind. of εἰμί	+	present participle

The perfect, pluperfect, and future perfect are formed with the *perfect* participle:

perfect periphrastic	pres. ind. of εἰμί	+	perfect participle
pluperfect periphrastic	impf. ind. of εἰμί	+	perfect participle
future perfect periphrastic	fut. ind. of εἰμί	+	perfect participle

19. Predicate Adjectives

In this case, the adjective is *not* preceded by a definite article. As before, the adjective may come before or after the noun it modifies, with very little difference in meaning: (a) first predicate position: ἀγαθὸς ὁ ἀδελφός; (b) second predicate position: ὁ ἀδελφὸς ἀγαθός. Both of these phrases mean "the brother (is) good" or "the brother who is good." Note that in *neither* case is the adjective preceded by an article.

20. Subjective Genitive

This use of the genitive case can be explained as follows. As an example, we will use the phrase "comfort *of the Holy Spirit* (τῇ παρακλήσει τοῦ ἁγίου πνεύματος)" (Acts 9:31). First, imagine the *non-genitive* noun as a verbal idea. In the case of our example, "comfort" implies the verbal idea of "comforting." If the *genitive term* would better serve as the *subject* of the verbal action, in the sense of *initiating* this verbal action, then the genitive term is a *subjective genitive*. Thus, "comfort *of the Holy Spirit*" implies the comfort *given by* the Holy Spirit. Thus, "of the Holy Spirit" is a *subjective* genitive.

Introduction

This Hellenistic Greek reader is designed to meet the needs of those who have completed one or more years of Greek studies and now wish to improve their Greek reading ability and gain a better appreciation for the diversity of Hellenistic Greek. This goal can be accomplished only if one reads through a selection of Greek texts that reflect different styles, genres, provenances, and purposes.[1] The Greek passages in this reader have been arranged into eight parts on the basis of their *level of difficulty*. Each passage is accompanied by grammatical aids and vocabulary lists, as well as other aids to translation. The grammatical information is contained in the footnotes. The vocabulary lists are conveniently positioned below the Greek texts to which they refer.

The provision of these vocabulary lists relieves the translator of the time-consuming work of looking up every unfamiliar lexeme in a Greek lexicon. Of course, much of this vocabulary is not even listed in lexica dedicated solely to early Christian literature[2] or to the Septuagint[3] and can be found only in the Greek lexicon of Liddell and Scott.[4]

Each vocabulary list makes a clear distinction between vocabulary for memorization, *which is printed in boldface type*, and supplementary vocabulary, which

---

[1] This book draws its inspiration from Allen Wikgren's *Hellenistic Greek Texts* (Chicago: Chicago University Press, 1947).

[2] E.g., W. F. Bauer, W. Danker, W. F. Arndt, and F. W. Gingrich, *A Greek–English Lexicon of the New Testament*, 3rd ed. (Chicago: University of Chicago Press, 2000); J. P. Louw and E. A. Nida, *Greek–English Lexicon of the New Testament based on Semantic Domans*, 2 vols. (New York: United Bible Societies, 1988).

[3] E.g., Eynikel J. Lust and K. A. Hauspie, *A Greek–English Lexicon of the Septuagint*, 2 vols. (Stuttgart: Deutsche Bibelgesellschaft, 1992–1996); T. Muraoka, *A Greek–English Lexicon of the Septuagint* (Leuven: Peeters, 2009).

[4] Henry George Liddell and Robert Scott, *A Greek–English Lexicon with Revised Supplement*, revised and augmented by H. S. Jones and R. McKenzie (Oxford: Oxford University Press, 1996).

is not. The vocabulary lists in Part 1 have been designed on the assumption that the translator has previously learned only those Greek words (lexemes) occurring *fifty times or more* in the Greek New Testament.[5] These high-frequency words are not listed in any of the vocabulary lists. However, they have all been included in the final glossary (§10). Thus, the vocabulary lists in Part 1 include *all* the vocabulary occurring in the translation passages themselves, except those words occurring fifty times or more in the Greek New Testament. Within Part 1, the vocabulary for memorization does not build from passage to passage; each vocabulary list in Part 1 is based on the same assumption, namely that the translator is familiar only with those New Testament lexemes occurring fifty times or more.[6]

However, since one of the primary purposes of this graduated reader is to assist the users of this book in expanding their knowledge of Greek vocabulary, they are required to undertake some memory work in order to proceed expeditiously. To help them with this task, the design of the vocabulary lists in Part 2 *does* assume that they have learned the bolded vocabulary in Part 1. The same assumption holds for subsequent parts of the book, with Part 3 assuming knowledge of the bolded vocabulary of Parts 1 and 2, and Part 4 assuming knowledge of the bolded vocabulary of Parts 1–3, and so forth. But if one happens to forget some of this vocabulary, there is always the option of consulting the cumulative glossary at the end of the book (§10).[7] Thus, when a word in one part of this reader is a bolded word for memorization, it will *not* be listed a second time in the vocabulary lists in subsequent parts of the book. Instead, *all the definitions and grammatical forms* needed for subsequent uses of the same lexeme are provided in the *first* listing of that lexeme. By implication, one should endeavor to become familiar with all the definitions and grammatical forms of the bolded vocabulary, even if such information is not needed for the specific Greek passage in question.

Following the main entry of verbs in the vocabulary lists, additional verbal forms are sometimes listed, followed by a number from 1 to 6. These numbers refer to Greek principal parts (2 = future active/middle, 3 = aorist active/middle, etc.). By necessity, the number of words for memorization (printed in boldface type) in each passage are of variable length, owing to the nature of the passages themselves: some passages contain more high-frequency words than do others.

---

[5] For a list of these words consult Bruce M. Metzger, *Lexical Aids for Students of New Testament Greek* (Edinburgh: T & T Clarke, 1990).

[6] The online material is not part of this schema. Thus, one need not necessarily learn any of the (bolded) vocabulary for memorization in the *online* Greek passages to progress from part to part in the printed version of this graduated reader. High-frequency words in the vocabulary lists of the online texts have been set in boldface type to help you build your vocabulary base.

[7] The glossary includes all bolded words (including the bolded words in the vocabulary lists of the online passages), as well as all lexemes occurring fifty times or more in the Greek New Testament.

The vocabulary lists in Part 1 tend to be the longest because this book assumes (rightly or wrongly) that the translator has acquired only a minimal Greek vocabulary base. This being said, most lists of words for memorization are limited to about twenty words each. The footnotes help identity frequently occurring grammatical forms (summarized in §IV of this introduction)[8] and references to the tables of verb paradigms (§9), located at the back of the book, as well as limited textual commentary.

This reader also includes many *non-canonical* Jewish and Christian writings, which may be less familiar than canonical writings and, for this reason, are perhaps of greater interest and educational value. For example, Part 1 includes a representative sample of various gospel genres, including a "sayings gospel" (Gospel of Thomas, §1.4), a "nativity gospel" (Protoevangelium of James, §§1.8, 1.14), and a "passion gospel" (Gospel of Peter, §§1.9, 1.15), as well as the first vision of the Shepherd of Hermas (§1.6), which was one of the most beloved books in early Christian antiquity. Similarly, Part 5 includes selections from the Epistle of Barnabas (§5.6), the Apocalypse of Peter (§5.8), and the Acts of Paul and Thekla (§§5.9, 5.15).

But to refer to such writings as "non-canonical" is somewhat misleading, because many of these texts were indeed considered to be canonical at various times and places. For example, the Shepherd of Hermas was widely considered to be canonical scripture and was often bound with the New Testament. The Epistle of Barnabas is included in Codex Sinaiticus (fourth century) and Codex Hierosolymitanus (eleventh century). The Apocalypse of Peter (§5.8) appears in the canonical lists of the Muratorian Canon and Codex Claramontanus. Likewise, the Acts of Paul and Thekla was widely disseminated in early Christian antiquity and also appears in the canonical list of Codex Claramontanus.

The inclusion of these extra-canonical texts has distinct educational advantages: When one sets out to translate a text from the Greek New Testament, whose English translation is already known, *this familiarity tends to interfere with the translation process.* One may even be tempted to skip over textual difficulties in the Greek text because the English translation of the verse is known in advance, before the translation process begins. In such cases, it is hardly surprising that the translation one produces may be nearly identical with the published English translations of the New Testament. This raises the question, why bother reading the Greek text at all? Thus, the translation of non-canonical texts helps to circumvent this vicious hermeneutic circle.

---

[8] See "Editorial Abbreviations" (§I) for an explanation of all abbreviations. For detailed grammatical information see Herbert Weir Smyth, *Greek Grammar*, rev. Gordon M. Messing (Cambridge, MA: Harvard University Press, 1959); cf. F. Blass and A. Debrunner, *A Greek Grammar of the New Testament and Other Early Christian Literature*, trans. and rev. Robert W. Funk (Chicago: University of Chicago Press, 1961); Maximilian Zerwick, *Biblical Greek Illustrated by Example*, adapted from the Latin by Joseph Smith (Rome: Pontifici Instituti Biblici, 1963).

But there is a second danger: experience suggests that when students are exposed only to passages from the Greek New Testament, they may become dependent upon computer software (e.g., *BibleWorks 9.0*, *Logos 4*), interlinear translations, and parsing guides,[9] all of which can close down the reasoning processes that should accompany the act of translation. Once such unhealthy dependencies have been formed, it can be difficult to break them, rendering one unable to translate Greek texts without the aid of such supports. Thus, from an educational perspective, *the translation of non-canonical texts* (for which such academic resources are generally not available) *provides the most beneficial experience of translating Hellenistic Greek texts.* Indeed, this is the best way to build one's translational skills and confidence over time. Indeed, the ability to translate non-canonical Greek passages is a better indicator of one's translational skills.

1. A GRADUATED GREEK READER

As previously noted, the passages for translation in this Hellenistic Greek reader have been grouped into eight parts primarily on the basis of level of difficulty rather than on the basis of date of composition, style, genre, provenance, or theme. In other words, this is a *graduated* reader. The Greek readings in this book become more difficult as one progresses from part to part. This being said, no Greek text is perfectly homogeneous in terms of level of difficulty. All texts possess certain peculiarities of form, syntax, and vocabulary, and characteristics of the localities in which their respective authors lived. As such, the issue of level of difficulty can perhaps be theorized more profitably if we recognize that different types of Greek texts pose different kinds of challenges. For example, the isometric translational Greek of the Septuagint in Part 2, the Greek inscriptions in Part 7, and the Atticizing and literary Greek texts in Part 8 each pose different kinds of translation challenges.[10]

The contents of the eight parts of this reader can be summarized as follows. Part 1 is comprised of early Christian texts whose Greek is characterized by relatively short sentences, limited vocabulary, minimal participial subordination, and a limited use of syntactical constructions (such as the genitive absolute, articular infinitive, adverbial participles, and periphrastic construction). The

---

[9] E.g., Maurice A. Robinson, *Analytical Lexicon of New Testament Greek*, rev. ed. (Peabody, MA: Hendrickson, 2012); Nathan E. Han, *A Parsing Guide to the Greek New Testament* (Scottdale, PA: Herald Press, 1971); Bernard A. Taylor, *The Analytical Lexicon to the Septuagint: A Complete Parsing Guide* (Peabody, MA: Hendrickson, 1994).

[10] I.e., Hellenistic Greek composition that has modeled itself on the style and idiom of the Attic (Athenian) Greek of the fifth to fourth century BCE.

majority of extracts in Parts 2 and 3 are taken from the Septuagint.[11] The term "Septuagint" designates the Greek translation of the Tanakh (Hebrew Bible or "Old Testament"),[12] which was produced in Alexandria (Egypt) in the third to second century BCE.[13] This translation is one of the undisputed centerpieces of Greco-Jewish literature of the Hellenistic period. It functioned as the liturgical text for innumerable synagogues in the Ptolemaic and Seleucid domains, and later as the "Scriptures" (or "Old Testament") of emerging Christian churches.

The readings in Parts 2 and 3 have been chosen with two specific pedagogical aims. The first aim is to contrast the *translational* Greek of the Septuagint with the compositional Greek of the Christian texts in Part 1. (I use the term "compositional Greek" in reference to texts that were *originally composed* in Hellenistic Greek.) The second, related pedagogical aim is to contrast the *isometric* translational Greek of texts in Part 2 (which is characteristic of *most* of the books of the Septuagint) with the "recensional" Greek of texts in Part 3 (as found in such books as Job, Esther, Daniel, and 1 Esdras). "Isometric" translational Greek is characterized by a high degree of *linguistic interference* from the source language (i.e., Hebrew), resulting in an *almost word-for-word correspondence* between the Hebrew and Greek texts and a corresponding avoidance of the typical literary conventions of Hellenistic Greek. In contrast, the "recensional" translation Greek in Part 3 is characterized by greater assimilation to the standard literary conventions of Hellenistic Greek. These latter texts are more likely to employ typical Greek syntactical constructions, with correspondingly less interference from the Hebrew parent text.

Parts 4–6 take up the study of the compositional Greek of more challenging texts. As previously noted, compositional Greek employs a broad range of typical Greek syntactical constructions and vocabulary. Part 4 begins with the non-literary (so-called documentary) Greek of ancient papyrus letters, introducing the student to the four primary types of ancient Greek letters: letters of introduction (§4.1), letters of petition (§4.2), family letters (§4.3), and memoranda (§4.4). This knowledge of the structure of ancient letters provides our point of departure for reading and interpreting the ancient letters of Paul (§§4.5–11, 4.12-16).[14] For the Greek text of Paul's letters I have used (where possible) the Chester Beatty papyrus (PChBeatty 46), dating ca. 200 CE, which is the earliest extant manuscript

---

[11] The dates for all Christian texts have been assigned on the basis of L. Michael White, *From Jesus to Christianity: How Four Generations of Visionaries & Storytellers Created the New Testament and Christian Faith* (San Francisco: HarperSanFrancisco, 2004).

[12] Which is to say, the "Masoretic text," as published by R. Kittel, K. Elliger, and W. Rudolph, (eds.), *Biblia Hebraica Stuttgartensia* (Stuttgart: Deutsche Bibelstiftung, 1977).

[13] Alfred Rahlfs and Robert Hanhart, (eds.), *Septuaginta*, ed. altera (Stuttgart: Deutsche Bibelgesellschaft, 2006).

[14] Cf. William G. Doty, *Letters in Primitive Christianity* (Philadelphia: Fortress, 1973); Calvin Roetzel, *The Letters of Paul: Conversations in Context*, 4th ed. (Louisville: Westminster/John Knox, 1998); Stanley K. Stowers, *Letter Writing in Greco-Roman Antiquity* (Philadelphia: Westminster, 1986).

of the ten Pauline letters (noting unexpected readings in the footnotes).[15] In contrast to the edited text of the Greek New Testament published by the United Bible Society[16] and Nestle-Aland (which is conjectural in character), the Chester Beatty papyrus is a real, physical, historical text that was actually used and read by churches in antiquity.

Part 5 introduces other early Christian texts that display higher literary aspirations, such as the Acts of the Apostles (§§5.1–3, 5.5, 5.12, 5.13) and the Epistle to the Hebrews (§5.14). Well more than a century ago, Joseph Lightfoot pioneered the study of the "apostolic fathers" in the field of New Testament studies.[17] Drawing inspiration from Lightfoot's legacy, Part 5 introduces a variety of non-canonical texts, including the Epistle of Barnabas (§5.6), the Martyrdom of Polycarp (§5.7), the apocryphal Acts of Paul, Thomas, and Andrew (§§5.9, 5.10, 5.15, 5.16), and the Apocalypse of Peter (§5.8). The account of the burning of the magicians' handbooks in Acts 19:11–20 (§5.3) has been complemented with the remarkable magical handbook (§5.4, cf. §7.3) discovered among the famous Greek magical papyri in Egypt.[18]

Part 6 takes us into the world of Jewish *literary* Greek, as attested in the writings of 2 Maccabees (§§6.1, 6.2), 4 Maccabees (§6.3), and Philo of Alexandria (§6.4). Such Jewish (compositional) Greek is highly literary and makes use of the full expressive range of the Hellenistic Greek language, including discontinuous syntax.[19] Also included in this part is the metrical Jewish tractate of Ezekiel the Tragedian (§6.6), which is remarkable for having been composed in iambic trimeter, which is to say, in the poetic style of ancient Greek tragedy. The imprint of Hellenization is also evident in the Jewish Testament of Reuben (§§6.5, 7), which reflects many ideas found in contemporaneous Stoic philosophical speculation.

Part 7 surveys a representative sample of the primary types of Greek inscriptions, including decrees, sacred laws of voluntary religious associations, healing testimonials, redemption (manumission) inscriptions, and so forth.[20]

---

[15] As published by Andrew E. Bernhard, *Other Early Christian Gospels: A Critical Edition of the Surviving Greek Manuscripts* (London: T & T Clark, 2006).

[16] *The Greek New Testament*, 4th ed., rev. Barbara Aland, Kurt Aland, et al. (Stuttgart: Deutsche Bibelgesellschaft, 2001).

[17] J. B. Lightfoot, *The Apostolic Fathers*, ed. and completed by J. R. Harmer (London: Macmillan and Co., 1891); cf. Bart Ehrman (ed.), *Apostolic Fathers*, 2 vols., LCL 24–25 (Cambridge, MA: Harvard University Press, 2003).

[18] Hans Dieter Betz, (ed.), *The Greek Magical Papyri in Translation including the Demotic Spells*, 2nd ed. (Chicago: University of Chicago Press, 1992).

[19] Discontinuous syntax, or "hyperbaton," often takes the form of the interruption of syntax of the modification of substantives (such as nouns) by modifiers (e.g., adjectives, participles); cf. A. M. Divine and Laurence D. Stephens, *Discontinuous Syntax: Hyperbaton in Greek* (New York: Oxford University Press, 1999).

[20] B. H. McLean, *An Introduction to the Study of Greek Epigraphy of the Hellenistic and Roman Periods from Alexander the Great Down to the Reign of Constantine (323 BCE–337 CE)* (Ann Arbor: University of Michigan Press, 2002).

Louis Robert once described Greco-Roman civilization as "une civilisation d'épigraphie." With such a great profusion of epigraphic writing in antiquity there is virtually no aspect of ancient life upon which epigraphy does not bear. Epigraphic monuments are especially valuable in reconstructing social and religious history of the ancient world, for they are primary witnesses to society's laws and institutions, its social structures, public cults, and private associations, its thoughts and values, and, of course, its language. As long ago as 1908, Adolf Deissmann recognized the immense importance of epigraphical and papyrological texts for the study of the New Testament.[21] Such contemporary publications as *New Documents Illustrating Early Christianity* and the newly published *Greco-Roman Associations* build on this venerable tradition of biblical scholarship.[22] As important as Greek inscriptions may be for understanding the New Testament, they also pose special challenges owing to their particular grammatical constructions, specific functions, and sometimes their dialectical features.

Part 8 brings together a small sample of literary authors of distinction, beginning with Flavius Philostratus, whose *Life of Apollonios of Tyana* (§§8.1, 8.5) is written in Atticizing Greek. "Atticizing" Greek is a style of Hellenistic Greek that is modeled on the literary standards of the Classical Greek of the great Attic authors of the fourth and fifth centuries BCE. Part 8 also includes three samples of philosophical Greek, namely excepts from Epicurus's *Letter to Menoeceus* (§8.2), his *Letter to Herodotus* (§8.6), and an excerpt from the *Discourses* of the Stoic philosopher Epictetus (§8.3). The style and vocabulary of Epictetus are remarkably close to the Greek found in the New Testament. Part 8 concludes with *Poimandres*, the first part of the well-known Hermetic Corpus (§8.4).[23]

With the contents and design of this reader having been summarized, a few additional comments are in order. First, in order to keep the book within publishable limits, it was necessary to exclude much of which might otherwise have been included, such as extensive bibliographies and detailed textual commentary. To compensate for this deficiency, the user of this book should foster the habit of making use of a university library to consult the chief authorities first-hand, instead of relying too implicitly on the limited information supplied by

---

[21] Adolf Deissmann, *Light from the Ancient East: The New Testament Illustrated by Recently Discovered Texts of the Graeco-Roman World*, 4th ed., trans. Lionel R. M. Strachan (New York: George H. Doran Co., 1927); cf. James H. Moulton and George Milligan, *The Vocabulary of the Greek New Testament Illustrated from the Papyri and Other Non-Literary Sources* (Grand Rapids, MI: Wm. B. Eerdmans, 1930).

[22] G. H. R. Horsley, *New Documents Illustrating Early Christianity* (North Ryde, Australia, 1981–1992); S. R. Llewelyn, *New Documents Illustrating Early Christianity* (North Ryde, Australia, 1992–2002); J. S. Kloppenborg and R. S. Ascough, *Greco-Roman Associations: Texts, Translations, and Commentary. I. Attica, Central Greek, Macedonia, Thrace* (Berlin: De Gruyter, 2011), with vol. II forthcoming.

[23] Brian P. Copenhaver, *Hermetica: The Greek Corpus Hermeticum and the Latin Asclepius in a New Translation* (Cambridge: Cambridge University Press, 1992).

this textbook. It must also be stated that the texts included in this reader are not identical to the critical published editions. Minor editorial changes have been made to the texts in order to facilitate rapid reading. Therefore, when employing any of the texts in this book for research purposes, one should always consult the original publications first.

2. PRONOUNCING HELLENISTIC GREEK: THE "HISTORICAL" GREEK PRONUNCIATION SYSTEM

The traditional system for the pronunciation of Hellenistic Greek is known as the "Erasmian" system, so-called because it was developed centuries ago by Desiderius Erasmus (1466/69–1536 CE). This system gives the same pronunciation values to Greek letters as their corresponding Latin "equivalents." It is also based on the *non-linguistic* principle that each letter should be pronounced differently. As might be expected from its origins, this system of pronunciation is *entirely artificial and misleading*. It is merely "classroom" pronunciation that has *never been used by Greeks in any period of their history*. On the basis of thousands of papyri and inscriptions, we now know that this Latinized pronunciation *contradicts* how Greek was actually spoken in the Hellenistic period.

In retrospect, it is indeed surprising that this pronunciation system, invented by a Dutchman living five hundred years ago in northern Europe, who had no real contact with Greek culture, should still be in use in the modern Western university of the twenty-first century. But this is indeed the case. Nevertheless, in our own era, many scholars, following the lead of Chrys Caragounis, are now advocating a return to what he has termed the "historical Greek" pronunciation system (which is a Modern Greek pronunciation). Though I have explained this system in detail in my book *New Testament Greek: An Introduction*, it can be summarized as follows:[24]

		Letter name	*Pronunciation*	*Phonic value*
A	α	**al**fa	father	[a]
B	β	**vi**ta	vat	[v]
Γ	γ	**gha**ma	yet / go	[y] / [g][25]
Δ	δ	**dhel**ta	the	[dh]
E	ε	epsilon	bet	[e]
Z	ζ	**zi**ta	zoo	[z]
H	η	ita	ski	[i]

---

[24] B. H. McLean, *New Testament Greek: An Introduction* (New York: Cambridge University Press, 2011), 1–18 (audio files provided online).

[25] See (c) (iii).

Θ	θ	**thi**ta	*th*ink	[th]
I	ι	**iota**	sk**i**	[i]
K	κ	**ka**ppa	**k**eep	[k]
Λ	λ	**lam**dha	**l**etter	[l]
M	μ	**mi**	**m**oon	[m]
N	ν	**ni**	**n**oon	[n]
Ξ	ξ	**ksi**	o**x**	[ks]
O	ο	**o**mikron	d**o**g	[o]
Π	π	**pi**	**p**ut	[p]
P	ρ	**rho**	**r** (trilled)	[r / rh when initial]
Σ	σ / ς	**sig**ma	**r**ose	[s]
T	τ	**taf**	**t**op	[t]
Y	υ	**ipsilon**	sk**i**	[i]
Φ	φ	**fi**	**f**ind	[f]
X	χ	**khi**	(Scottish) lo**ch** (German) Ba**ch**	[kh]
Ψ	ψ	**psi**	hi**ps**	[ps]
Ω	ω	**o**mega	d**o**g	[o]

(a) Pronouncing Vowels

α	[a]	ἀπό	(a-**po**)
ε	[e]	ἐλπίς	(el-**pis**)
ι	[i]	ἴσος	(**i**-sos)
ο	[o]	ὄνομα	(**o**-no-ma)
η	[i]	μή	(mi)
υ	[i]	κύριος	(**ki**-ri-os)
ω	[o]	φῶς	(fos)

(b) Pronouncing Double Vowels

	Pronunciation	*Phonic value*
αι	bet	[e]
ει, οι, υι	sk**i**	[i]
ου	l**oo**k	[ou]
αυ	*av* before vowels and β, γ, δ, ζ, λ, μ, ν, ρ	[av]
	but *af* before all other consonants	[af]
ευ	*ev* before vowels and β, γ, δ, ζ, λ, μ, ν, ρ	[ev]
	but *ef* before all other consonants	[ef]
ηυ	*iv* before vowels and β, γ, δ, ζ, λ, μ, ν, ρ	[iv]
	but *if* before all other consonants	[if]

(c) Pronouncing Stops and Fricatives

(i) Labials : π, β, φ

π   like *p* in *p*age: e.g., πόλις (**po**-lis)
β   like *v* in *v*an: e.g., βιβλίον (vi-**vli**-on)
φ   like *f* in *f*act: e.g., φίλος (**fi**-los)

(ii) Dentals: τ, δ, θ

τ   like *t* in *t*op: e.g., τόπος (**to**-pos)
δ   like *th* in *th*e [dh]: e.g., δοῦλος (**dhou**-los)
θ   like *th* *th*ink [th]: e.g., θάνατος (**tha**-na-tos)

(iii) Velars: κ, γ, χ

κ   like *k* in *k*een: e.g., κύριος (**ki**-ri-os)
γ   like *y* when followed by *e-* and *i-*sounds (namely, ε, η, ι, υ, αι, ει, οι, υι)

To be more precise:

γι / γη / γυ	*yi*	as in "yeast"	γινώσκω (yi-**no**-sko) / ὀργή (or-**yi**) / γυνή (yi-**ni**)
γε / γαι / γιαι	*ye*	as in "yet"	γελῶ (ye-**lo**) / Αἰγαίος (e-**ye**-os) / ὑγιαῖνος (i-**ye**-nos)
για / γεια	*ya*	as in "yard"	ἁγιάζω (a-**ya**-zo), ὄργια (**or**-ya), ἁγία (a-**ya**) / ἐνέργεια (e-**ner**-ya)[26]
γιο	*yo*	as in "yogurt"	ἅγιος (**a**-yos), λόγιον (**lo**-yon), πτερύγιον (pte-**ri**-yon), σφάγιον (**sfa**-yon)
γ		like *g* as in "go"	(but deeper, from the back of the throat: "gho") before other vowels: e.g., γάμος (**ga**-mos), γάλα (**ga**-la), ἐγώ (e-**go**)
χ		like *ch* in Scottish	*loch*: e.g., χαρά (kha-**ra**), χάρις (**kha**-ris), χρόνος (**khro**-nos)

(iv) Pronouncing Special Groups of Velar Consonants

γγ / γκ	finger	[ng-g]	ἄγγελος	(a[ng]-ge-los)
		[ng-g]	ἀγκάλη	(a[ng]-**ga**-li)

---

[26] Similarly -ιει = *ya* (e.g., ὑγίεια, i-**yi**-ya).

| γχ | | [ng-kh] | ἐλέγχω | (e-**le**ng-kho) |
| γξ | banks | [ng-ks] | ἔλεγξις | (e-**le**ng-ksis) |

(v) Pronouncing Other Consonant Clusters

| μπ | [mb] as in "symbol" | πέμπω | (**pem**-bo) |
| ντ | [nd] as in "end" | ἀντί | (an-**di**) |

(d) Aspiration

Attic Greek *did* use aspiration at the beginning of certain words, though it did *not* use a "rough" breathing mark. However, such aspiration was used for only a relatively brief period, and then only erratically. The other main dialects of Greek, namely Ionic, Doric, and Aeolic, never employed aspiration. *All aspiration in Greek died out prior to the first century CE.*[27] Therefore, there is no good reason to continue using these breathing marks in modern editions of the Greek New Testament. The historical Greek pronunciation system ignores these rough breathing marks. Likewise, one should ignore them when pronouncing Hellenistic Greek words.

In contrast to the Erasmian system, the "historical Greek" (or Modern Greek) pronunciation is a *real*, euphonic system. Some scholars would argue that this pronunciation system does not make absolute phonetic distinctions, but it should be noted that no language limits itself to such rigid consistency. Moreover, the purported benefits of the Erasmian system of pronunciation shrink when one realizes that there is no consensus, even among those scholars who employ it: there are actually *several* Erasmian pronunciations according to whether one learns Hellenistic Greek in the United States, Germany, or Britain. In contrast, learning the historical Greek pronunciation system is not very difficult because it is entirely regular. This feature allows one to master it easily with a little patience and practice. On the basis of its advantages, I strongly encourage the users of this Hellenistic reader to consider adopting this pronunciation system in order to enrich their experience of Hellenistic Greek.

---

[27] This ancient aspiration leaves its mark in the language only in some forms of elision. Breathing marks were *never* written in the oldest New Testament manuscripts.

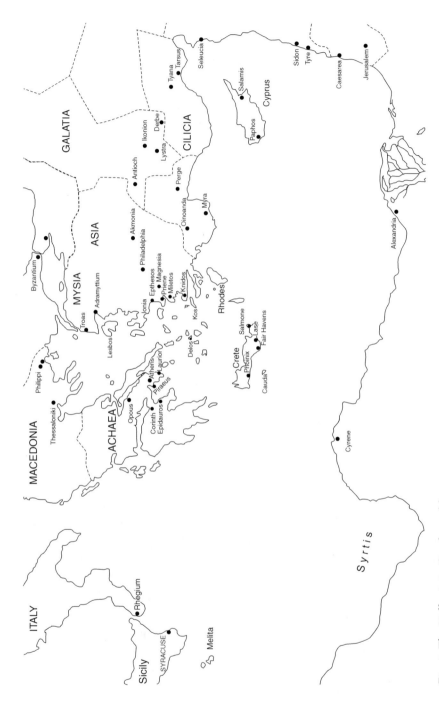

Fig. 1. The Hellenistic Greek world

PART 1

Basic Level: Early Christian Texts

art 1 consists of ten early Christian texts (§§1.1–10) and five more online (§§1.11–15) whose Greek is characterized by relatively short sentences, limited vocabulary, minimal participial subordination, and a limited use of more complex syntactical constructions.[1] Notably, this section also includes some non-canonical writings (or at least texts that are no longer canonical). These texts will be less familiar to many and yet may be of greater interest and educational value because, from a pedagogical perspective, the ability to translate such texts provides a better measure of one's translation ability.

In the vocabulary lists, the words for memorization are in boldface type. The vocabulary so designated for memorization does not build from reading to reading in this section. Instead, each of the vocabulary lists in Part 1 is compiled on the basis of the same assumption, namely that you have learned only those words occurring fifty times or more in the Greek New Testament.[2] These words, as well as all bolded words for memorization throughout the book, have been compiled in the final glossary (§10). (Non-bolded vocabulary is not listed in this cumulative index.) Nonetheless, you should strive to become familiar with as much of the bolded vocabulary as possible in the readings found in §§1.1–8 because this vocabulary will not be repeated in the remaining parts of the book.

---

[1] For example, constructions such as the genitive absolute, articular infinitive, adverbial participles, periphrastic construction, and discontinuous syntax. This is especially common in the case of the interruption of syntax of the modification of substantives by modifiers (e.g., adjectives).

[2] For a list of these words see Bruce M. Metzger, *Lexical Aids for Students of New Testament Greek* (Edinburgh: T & T Clarke, 1990).

1.1.

Didache: The Two Ways Doctrine

(Did 1:1–2, 3:1–10)

Provenance: Syria (or Alexandria).   *Date:* 100–140 CE.

Text: Ehrman, I, 305–333; Aaron Milavec, *The Didache: Faith, Hope & Life of the Earliest Christian Communities, 50–70 CE* (New York: Newman Press, 2003).

The Didache, also known as "The Teaching of the Twelve Apostles," preserves parts of the oldest surviving church catechism and church order. This ancient text was originally part of the Christian canon in some regions (being included in, e.g., Codex Hierosolymitanus). The first section of the Didache (Did 1–6) summarizes the basic character of Christian life in terms of a "two ways" doctrine: a way of life and a way of death.

Related Texts: The final section, Did 16:1–8, contains a brief apocalypse, which is available online (§1.11).

ΔΙΔΑΧΗ ΚΥΡΙΟΥ ΔΙΑ ΤΩΝ ΔΩΔΕΚΑ ΑΠΟΣΤΟΛΩΝ ΤΟΙΣ ΕΘΝΕΣΙΝ

1:1 Ὁδοὶ δύο εἰσί, μία τῆς ζωῆς καὶ μία τοῦ θανάτου, διαφορὰ δὲ πολλὴ μεταξὺ τῶν δύο ὁδῶν. 2 ἡ μὲν οὖν[1] ὁδὸς τῆς ζωῆς ἐστιν αὕτη· πρῶτον ἀγαπήσεις τὸν θεὸν τὸν ποιήσαντά σε, δεύτερον (ἀγαπήσεις) τὸν πλησίον σου ὡς σεαυτόν· πάντα δὲ ὅσα ἐὰν[2] θελήσῃς μὴ γίνεσθαί σοι, καὶ σὺ ἄλλῳ μὴ ποίει. (text continues …)

---

[1] μὲν οὖν, "moreover."
[2] ἐάν > ἄν.

FIG. 2. Carved figures of three men and a woman, in panel with pediment, Kuşça, Turkey (IKonya 130).

Vocabulary
δεύτερος, -α, -ον, second; secondary
διαφορά, ἡ, difference
διδαχή, ἡ, teaching, instruction
μεταξύ (w. gen.), between; next
πλησίον (w. gen.), near, nearby; ὁ πλησίον, neighbor; ἡ, female companion
σεαυτοῦ, -ῆς (reflexive pron.), yourself

3:1 Τέκνον μου, φεῦγε ἀπὸ παντὸς πονηροῦ καὶ ἀπὸ παντὸς ὁμοίου αὐτοῦ. 2 μὴ γίνου[3] ὀργίλος, ὁδηγεῖ γὰρ ἡ ὀργὴ πρὸς τὸν φόνον, μηδὲ[4] ζηλωτὴς[5] μηδὲ ἐριστικὸς μηδὲ θυμικός· ἐκ γὰρ τούτων ἁπάντων φόνοι γεννῶνται. 3 τέκνον μου, μὴ γίνου ἐπιθυμητής, ὁδηγεῖ γὰρ ἡ ἐπιθυμία πρὸς τὴν πορνείαν, μηδὲ αἰσχρολόγος μηδὲ ὑψηλόφθαλμος· ἐκ γὰρ τούτων ἁπάντων μοιχεῖαι γεννῶνται. 4 Τέκνον μου, μὴ γίνου οἰωνοσκόπος, ἐπειδὴ ὁδηγεῖ εἰς τὴν εἰδωλολατρίαν, μηδὲ ἐπαοιδὸς μηδὲ μαθηματικὸς μηδὲ (ὁ) περικαθαίρων, μηδὲ θέλε αὐτὰ βλέπειν μηδὲ ἀκούειν· ἐκ γὰρ τούτων ἁπάντων εἰδωολολατρία γεννᾶται. 5 τέκνον μου, μὴ γίνου ψεύστης, ἐπειδὴ ὁδηγεῖ τὸ ψεῦσμα εἰς τὴν κλοπήν, μηδὲ φιλάργυρος μηδὲ κενόδοξος· ἐκ γὰρ τούτων ἁπάντων κλοπαὶ γεννῶνται.

Vocabulary
αἰσχρολόγος, ὁ, foul-mouthed person
αὐθάδης, -ες, stubborn
εἰδωλολατρία, -ας, ἡ, idolatry
ἐπαοιδός (= ἐπῳδός), ὁ, enchanter, one who uses magical spells and incantations[6]
ἐπιθυμητής, ὁ, one who is filled with desire
ἐριστικός, -ή, -όν, quarrelsome
θυμικός, -ή, -όν, quick-tempered
κενόδοξος, -ον, conceited, boastful
κλοπή, ἡ, theft, pl. acts of robbery
μαθηματικός, ὁ, astrologer
μαρτυρέω, bear witness, testify; speak favorably of; approve of somebody (dat.); pass. gain approval for something, be approved of by somebody
μοιχεία, ἡ, adultery
οἰωνοσκόπος, ὁ, one who obtains omens by interpreting the flight of birds
ὅμοιος, -α, -ον (w. dat.), like, similar to (w. dat. or gen.); subst. τὰ ὅμοια, the same things

---

[3] Cf. table 9.2.4(a); [2]aor. verbs in non-indicative moods have the same endings as the present tense of the same mood.
[4] μηδέ…μηδέ…μηδέ….
[5] In this context, "one who is jealous."
[6] Cf. PGM XIII, 230–334 (§5.4), PGM IV, 1496–1595, XXXVI, 320–332 (§7.3).

ὀργίλος, -η, -ον, inclined to anger, quick-tempered; subst. hot temper, one of
    violent temper
περικαθαίρω, use purification rites of magic for personal gain
πορνεία, ἡ, unlawful sexual practice, sexual promiscuity/immorality
πρόβατον, τό, sheep
ταπεινός, -ή, -όν, humble, lowly, undistinguished
ὑψηλόφθαλμος, -ον, one who directs one's eyes lustfully
φεύγω, 2. φεύξομαι, 3. ἔφυγον: flee, escape; avoid, turn from
φιλάργυρος, -ον, avaricious, greedy; subst. a lover of money
φόνος, ὁ, murder
ψεῦσμα, -ματος, τό, lying

3:6 τέκνον μου, μὴ γίνου γόγγυσμος, ἐπειδὴ ὁδηγεῖ εἰς τὴν βλασφημίαν, μηδὲ
αὐθάδης μηδὲ πονηρόφρων· ἐκ γὰρ τούτων ἁπάντων βλασφημίαι γεννῶνται.
7 Ἴσθι⁷ δὲ πραΰς, ἐπεὶ οἱ πραεῖς κληρονομήσουσι τὴν γῆν. 8 γίνου μακρόθυμος
καὶ ἐλεήμων καὶ ἄκακος καὶ ἡσύχιος καὶ ἀγαθὸς καὶ τρέμων τοὺς λόγους,
οὓς ἤκουσας. 9 οὐχ ὑψώσεις⁸ σεαυτὸν οὐδὲ δώσεις⁹ τῇ ψυχῇ σου θράσος. οὐ
κολληθήσεται ἡ ψυχή σου μετὰ ὑψηλῶν, ἀλλὰ μετὰ δικαίων καὶ ταπεινῶν
ἀναστραφήσῃ. 10 τὰ¹⁰ συμβαίνοντά σοι ἐνεργήματα ὡς ἀγαθὰ προσδέξῃ, εἰδώς¹¹
ὅτι ἄτερ θεοῦ οὐδὲν γίνεται.

Vocabulary
ἄκακος, -ον, innocent
ἀναστρέφω, 6. ἀνεστράφην, fut. pass. ἀναστραφήσομαι: overturn something;
    pass. behave/conduct oneself; associate with (gen.)
ἅπας, ἅπασα, ἅπαν, alternate form of πᾶς, πᾶσα, πᾶν
ἄτερ, without
βλασφημία, ἡ, slander, defamatory speech
γογγυσμός, ὁ, complainer; complaining
ἐλεήμων, -ον, -ονος (gen.), merciful, compassionate
ἐνέργημα, -ματος, τό, experience
ἐπεί, when, after; because, since, for
ἐπειδή, since, because, whereas, after
ἡσύχιος, -ον, quiet, well-ordered
θράσος, -ους, τό, arrogance, insolence
κληρονομέω, inherit, acquire possession of something

---

⁷ Cf. table 9.13.4.
⁸ Note the three successive fut. ind. verbs instead of the expected impv.
⁹ Cf. table 9.8.3(a).
¹⁰ τὰ...ἐνεργήματα.
¹¹ Table 9.5.4; the root of οἶδα originally began with a *digamma*, √ Ϝιδ-, √ Ϝοιδ- or √ Ϝειδ(ε)- (comparable
    to the Lat. word, *vid-eo*); Ϝιδ- became οἰδ- in the pf. ind., and ειδ- in most other tenses, from which the
    plpf., ᾔδειν is derived.

κολλάω, join with, associate with

μακρόθυμος, -ον, patient, forbearing

ὁδηγέω, to guide, lead; to lead to (w. πρός/εἰς)

πονηρόφρων, -ον, evil-minded

πραΰς, πραεῖα, πραΰ, mild, soft, gentle; meek, unassuming

προσδέχομαι, accept; receive, welcome; admit into membership; expect, wait for

συμβαίνω, 3. συνέβην, 4. συμβέβηκα, pf. ptc. συμβεβηκώς: happen; συμβαίνω τί τινι, something happens to somebody; subst. τὸ συμβεβηκός, a contingent attribute ("accident") of something

ταπεινόω, humble, humiliate; bring low, be made low

τρέμω: tremble at (w. acc.), shake in fear, be in awe of

ὑψηλός, -ή, -όν, tall, high; proud, haughty

ὑψόω, lift up, raise; fig. to exalt

1.2.

Gospel of Luke: Jesus' Trial by the Adversary

(Luke 4:1–15)

Provenance: Probably outside of Palestine.   *Date:* 80–100 CE.

The story of Jesus' temptation in the wilderness introduces the character of an "adversary" (διάβολος) who tempts Jesus three times. It is significant that the Septuagintal version of the Book of Job opens with the story of Job's trials at the hands of this same "adversary" (Job 1:6–2:13, §3.4) rather than "Satan" (who is named in the Hebrew version).

Related Texts: Luke's story of Jesus' trial was probably included in the first section of the "Q Sayings Gospel." Its original function may have been to validate Jesus' authority as a teacher of wisdom. This understanding of Jesus as a teacher of wisdom is comparable to the presentation of Jesus in the Gospel of Thomas (§1.4) and Mark 4:10–20 (§1.5), where he is similarly presented as a teacher of enigmatic proverbs and parables.

4:1 Ἰησοῦς δὲ (ὢν) πλήρης πνεύματος ἁγίου ὑπέστρεψεν ἀπὸ τοῦ Ἰορδάνου καὶ ἤγετο ἐν τῷ πνεύματι ἐν¹ τῇ ἐρήμῳ 2 ἡμέρας τεσσεράκοντα² πειραζόμενος ὑπὸ τοῦ διαβόλου.³ καὶ οὐκ ἔφαγεν⁴ οὐδὲν ἐν ταῖς ἡμέραις ἐκείναις καὶ συντελεσθεισῶν⁵ αὐτῶν ἐπείνασεν. 3 εἶπεν δὲ αὐτῷ ὁ διάβολος· εἰ⁶ υἱὸς εἶ τοῦ θεοῦ, εἰπὲ τῷ λίθῳ τούτῳ ἵνα γένηται⁷ ἄρτος. 4 καὶ ἀπεκρίθη πρὸς αὐτὸν ὁ Ἰησοῦς· γέγραπται ὅτι

---

¹   ἐν for εἰς.
²   Acc. of time (cf. IV, 3.1).
³   ὁ διάβολος as "adversary," cf. Job 1:6–7, 9, 12; 2:1, 2–4, 6–7 (LXX) (§3.4).
⁴   S.v. ἐσθίω/ἔσθω.
⁵   Gen. absol. (cf. IV, 9).
⁶   εἰ w. ind. introducing a real condition.
⁷   ἵνα + sub. (γένηται) for inf.

Οὐκ ἐπ' ἄρτῳ μόνῳ ζήσεται ὁ ἄνθρωπος (Deut 8:3). 5 Καὶ ἀναγαγὼν αὐτὸν ἔδειξεν[8] αὐτῷ πάσας τὰς βασιλείας τῆς οἰκουμένης ἐν στιγμῇ χρόνου 6 καὶ εἶπεν αὐτῷ ὁ διάβολος· σοὶ δώσω τὴν ἐξουσίαν ταύτην ἅπασαν καὶ τὴν δόξαν αὐτῶν,[9] ὅτι ἐμοὶ παραδέδοται[10] καὶ ᾧ ἐὰν[11] θέλω δίδωμι αὐτήν· 7 σὺ οὖν ἐὰν προσκυνήσῃς ἐνώπιον ἐμοῦ, ἔσται σοῦ πᾶσα. 8 καὶ ἀποκριθεὶς ὁ Ἰησοῦς εἶπεν αὐτῷ· γέγραπται· κύριον τὸν θεόν σου προσκυνήσεις καὶ αὐτῷ μόνῳ λατρεύσεις (Deut 6:13, 10:20).

Vocabulary

ἀνάγω, 3. ἀνήγαγον, 6. ἀνήχθην: lead up; mid. or pass. be brought to/up; be restored to an original condition; sail away, put out to sea

ἀποδίδωμι, [2]aor. impv. ἀπόδος: give, give back, return; hand over; deliver a letter; pay, repay, reimburse, reward; ἀποδοῦναι λόγον, give account, render financial accounts; to grant; give off (smoke)

διάβολος, ὁ, slanderer, adversary (cf. Job 1:6–2:13, §3.4)

λατρεύω, serve somebody (dat.), worship

οἰκουμένη, ἡ, inhabited world

περίχωρος, -ον, neighboring, surrounding; τὸ περίχωρον, surrounding region

στιγμή, ἡ, point; an "instant" (of time)

τεσσαράκοντα (Att. τετταράκοντα), forty

4:9 Ἤγαγεν δὲ αὐτὸν εἰς Ἰερουσαλὴμ καὶ ἔστησεν ἐπὶ τὸ πτερύγιον τοῦ ἱεροῦ καὶ εἶπεν αὐτῷ· εἰ υἱὸς εἶ τοῦ θεοῦ, βάλε σεαυτὸν ἐντεῦθεν κάτω· 10 γέγραπται γὰρ ὅτι Τοῖς ἀγγέλοις αὐτοῦ ἐντελεῖται περὶ σοῦ τοῦ διαφυλάξαι[12] σε (Ps 91:11) 11 καὶ ὅτι Ἐπὶ χειρῶν ἀροῦσίν σε, μήποτε προσκόψῃς πρὸς λίθον τὸν πόδα σου (Ps 91:12). 12 καὶ ἀποκριθεὶς εἶπεν αὐτῷ ὁ Ἰησοῦς ὅτι εἴρηται·[13] Οὐκ ἐκπειράσεις[14] κύριον τὸν θεόν σου (Deut 6:16). 13 Καὶ συντελέσας[15] πάντα πειρασμὸν ὁ διάβολος ἀπέστη ἀπ' αὐτοῦ ἄχρι καιροῦ. 14 Καὶ ὑπέστρεψεν ὁ Ἰησοῦς ἐν τῇ δυνάμει τοῦ πνεύματος εἰς τὴν Γαλιλαίαν. καὶ φήμη ἐξῆλθεν καθ' ὅλης[16] τῆς περιχώρου περὶ αὐτοῦ. 15 καὶ αὐτὸς ἐδίδασκεν[17] ἐν ταῖς συναγωγαῖς αὐτῶν δοξαζόμενος ὑπὸ πάντων.

---

[8] S.v. δείκνυμι/δεικνύω.
[9] The antecedent of αὐτῶν is βασιλείας.
[10] Cf. table 9.11.5(a).
[11] ἐάν > ἄν.
[12] Art. inf. expressing purpose (cf. IV, 2).
[13] S.v. λέγω.
[14] οὐ w. fut. (categorical prohibition).
[15] Adv. aor. ptc.
[16] Distributive κατά (of places viewed serially).
[17] Iter. or incept. impf. (cf. IV, 13.3, 5).

Vocabulary

ἀφίστημι, ¹aor. ἀπέστησα/²aor. ἀπέστην, ²aor. subj. ἀποστῶ: cause to stand away; keep away from somebody (gen.); withdraw something; mid. go away, withdraw from, abandon; rebel, revolt

διαφυλάσσω, 3. διεφύλαξα: preserve from danger/harm

ἐκπειράζω, put to the test, tempt

ἐντέλλω/ομαι, 2. ἐντελοῦμαι, 3. ἐνετειλάμην, 5. ἐντέταλμαι: command somebody (dat.)

ἐντεῦθεν, from there/here (of place), from then (of time), from that (of cause); ἐντεῦθεν...ἐντεῦθεν..., on this side ... on that side

κάτω, down (adv.)

μήποτε, that ... not, lest

πειρασμός, ὁ, period/process of tempting, trial, test

προσκόπτω, 2. προσκόψω, 3. προσέκοψα: hit against; offend

πτερύγιον, τό, parapet

συντελέω, ¹aor. pass. ptc. συντελεσθείς: bring to an end, finish; carry out, accomplish; arrange, agree upon; pay toward common expenses, contribute; pass. to end; be brought to perfection

ὑποστρέφω, return

φήμη, ἡ, good report, fame

1.3.

Gospel of Luke: Jesus' Inaugural Sermon

(Luke 4:16–30)

In Jesus' inaugural sermon in Nazareth, the key themes of his later ministry (as presented in the Gospel of Luke) are summarized.

4:16 Καὶ (Ἰησοῦς) ἦλθεν εἰς Ναζαρά, οὗ[1] ἦν τεθραμμένος,[2] καὶ εἰσῆλθεν κατὰ τὸ εἰωθὸς αὐτῷ[3] ἐν τῇ ἡμέρᾳ τῶν σαββάτων[4] εἰς τὴν συναγωγὴν καὶ ἀνέστη ἀναγνῶναι. 17 καὶ ἐπεδόθη αὐτῷ βιβλίον τοῦ προφήτου Ἡσαΐου καὶ ἀναπτύξας τὸ βιβλίον εὗρεν τὸν τόπον οὗ ἦν γεγραμμένον·[5]

> 18 Πνεῦμα κυρίου ἐπ᾽ ἐμὲ[6]
> οὗ εἵνεκεν[7] ἔχρισέν με
> εὐαγγελίσασθαι πτωχοῖς,
> ἀπέσταλκέν με
> κηρύξαι αἰχμαλώτοις ἄφεσιν
> καὶ τυφλοῖς ἀνάβλεψιν,
> ἀποστεῖλαι (away) τεθραυσμένους ἐν[8] ἀφέσει,
> 19 κηρύξαι ἐνιαυτὸν[9] κυρίου δεκτόν. (Isa 61:1–2a)

---

[1] οὗ, gen. of ὅς, is also an adv. of place ("where").
[2] Plpf. periphr. (cf. IV, 17); since the pf. of this verb is normally translated as a present tense, the plpf. should be translated as a simple past tense.
[3] Dat. of poss.
[4] The pl. form, τὰ σάββατα, is normally used to express a single Sabbath day.
[5] Plpf. periphr. (IV, 18).
[6] Nominal phrase (supply a form of εἰμί).
[7] εἵνεκεν > ἕνεκεν.
[8] ἐν, instr. ("by means of").
[9] ἐνιαυτὸν...δεκτόν.

4:20 Καὶ πτύξας τὸ βιβλίον ἀποδοὺς[10] τῷ ὑπηρέτῃ ἐκάθισεν· καὶ πάντων οἱ ὀφθαλμοὶ ἐν τῇ συναγωγῇ ἦσαν ἀτενίζοντες[11] αὐτῷ. 21 ἤρξατο δὲ λέγειν πρὸς αὐτοὺς ὅτι σήμερον πεπλήρωται ἡ γραφὴ αὕτη ἐν τοῖς ὠσὶν ὑμῶν.

Vocabulary
αἰχμάλωτος, ὁ, captive
ἀνάβλεψις, -εως, ἡ, restoration of sight
ἀναπτύσσω, 3. ἀνέπτυξα: unroll a scroll
ἀτενίζω, 2. ἀτενίσω: stare at, look intently at (w. dat./πρός)
ἄφεσις, -εως, ἡ, release (fr. captivity); the act of sending away, letting go; a pardon (fr. punishment)
διέρχομαι, go through; come/go toward a destination; cross over
εἴωθα (pf. tense takes the place of an obsol. pres. form, ἔθω), [2]pf. ptc. εἰωθώς, -υῖα, -ός: be accustomed to; nt. [2]pf. ptc. subst., τὸ εἰωθός, a custom
Ἐλισαῖος, ὁ, Elisha
ἕνεκα/ἕνεκεν (w. gen.), because of, for the sake of; in honor of; on account; for this reason
ἐνιαυτός, ὁ, year; κατὰ ἐνιαυτόν, annual, yearly
ἐπιδίδωμι, 6. ἐπεδόθην, pf. ptc. ἐπιδεδωκώς: put into one's hands, give somebody one's hand; surrender, give up control; give back/return; increase, grow in size
θραύω, pf. pass. ptc. τεθραυσμένος, to break, pass. be oppressed, downtrodden
Καφαρναούμ, ἡ (indecl.), Capernaum, a city on Lake Gennesaret
λιμός, ὁ/ἡ, famine
οὖς, ὠτός, τό, ear; pl. τὰ ὦτα, hearing
πτύσσω, 3. ἔπτυξα, roll up (a scroll)
τρέφω, 3. ἔθρεψα, pf. pass. ptc. τεθραμμένος: rear/raise a child; feed
ὑπηρέτης, -ου, ὁ, assistant, attendant; helper
χρίω, 3. ἔχρισα, 4. κέκρικα, 5. κέχριμαι/κέκρισμαι: anoint (with), rub/smear (with)

22 Καὶ πάντες ἐμαρτύρουν αὐτῷ καὶ ἐθαύμαζον ἐπὶ τοῖς λόγοις τῆς χάριτος[12] τοῖς ἐκπορευομένοις ἐκ τοῦ στόματος αὐτοῦ καὶ ἔλεγον· οὐχὶ υἱός ἐστιν Ἰωσὴφ[13] οὗτος;[14] 23 καὶ εἶπεν πρὸς αὐτούς· πάντως ἐρεῖτέ[15] μοι τὴν παραβολὴν ταύτην· ἰατρέ, θεράπευσον σεαυτόν· (and you will say) ὅσα ἠκούσαμεν γενόμενα εἰς τὴν Καφαρναοὺμ ποίησον καὶ ὧδε ἐν τῇ πατρίδι σου. 24 εἶπεν δέ· ἀμὴν λέγω ὑμῖν

---

[10] Cf. table 9.12.4(a).
[11] Impf. periphr. (IV, 18).
[12] τῆς χάριτος, i.e., gracious, pleasing (words).
[13] Ἰωσήφ (indecl.), here gen.
[14] οὐχὶ in questions anticipates the answer "yes" (i.e., "Isn't this … ?").
[15] S.v. λέγω.

ὅτι οὐδεὶς προφήτης δεκτός ἐστιν ἐν τῇ πατρίδι αὐτοῦ. 25 ἐπ' ἀληθείας[16] δὲ λέγω ὑμῖν, πολλαὶ χῆραι ἦσαν ἐν ταῖς ἡμέραις Ἠλίου ἐν τῷ Ἰσραήλ, ὅτε ἐκλείσθη ὁ οὐρανὸς ἐπὶ[17] ἔτη τρία καὶ μῆνας ἕξ, ὡς ἐγένετο λιμὸς μέγας ἐπὶ πᾶσαν τὴν γῆν, 26 καὶ πρὸς οὐδεμίαν[18] αὐτῶν ἐπέμφθη Ἠλίας εἰ μὴ εἰς Σάρεπτα τῆς Σιδωνίας (χώρας) πρὸς (τινὰ) γυναῖκα χήραν. 27 καὶ πολλοὶ λεπροὶ ἦσαν ἐν τῷ Ἰσραὴλ ἐπὶ[19] Ἐλισαίου τοῦ προφήτου, καὶ οὐδεὶς αὐτῶν ἐκαθαρίσθη εἰ μὴ Ναιμὰν[20] ὁ Σύρος. 28 καὶ ἐπλήσθησαν πάντες θυμοῦ ἐν τῇ συναγωγῇ[21] ἀκούοντες ταῦτα 29 καὶ ἀναστάντες[22] ἐξέβαλον αὐτὸν ἔξω τῆς πόλεως καὶ ἤγαγον αὐτὸν ἕως ὀφρύος τοῦ ὄρους ἐφ' οὗ ἡ πόλις ᾠκοδόμητο αὐτῶν[23] ὥστε[24] κατακρημνίσαι αὐτόν· 30 αὐτὸς δὲ διελθὼν διὰ μέσου αὐτῶν ἐπορεύετο.

Vocabulary

δεκτός, -ή, -όν, acceptable, favorable

διέρχομαι, go through; come/go toward a destination; cross over

ἐκπορεύομαι, go away, to come out (of gods/evil spirits)

ἕξ, six

Ἠλίας, -ου, ὁ, Elijah

Ἠσαΐας, ου, ὁ, Isaiah

θαυμάζω, intrans. marvel, wonder, be amazed; trans. marvel/wonder at, admire

θεραπεύω, serve a god, perform a ritual for a god; heal

θυμός, ὁ, soul/spirit (as the principle of life); soul/heart (as revealed by one's feelings and passions); passion, desire; anger, rage

ἰατρός, ὁ, physician

καθαρίζω, purify, cleanse

κατακρημνίζω, throw down a precipice

κλείω, 6. ἐκλείσθην: close up, shut up

λεπρός, -ά, -όν, having a serious skin disease[25]

μήν, μηνός, ὁ, month

οἰκοδομέω, pf. pass. ᾠκοδόμημαι: build, construct; to form, fashion; fig. build up, encourage

ὀφρῦς, -ύος, ἡ, eyebrow; (fig.) edge (of a cliff)

πάντως (adv.), certainly, doubtless; strictly

---

[16] ἐπ' ἀληθείας, "in truth."

[17] ἐπί (w. acc.) expressing duration of time.

[18] Antecedent is χῆραι.

[19] ἐπί (w. gen.), "at the time of."

[20] Ναιμὰν ὁ Συρος, Naaman, the Syrian commander, who was healed by Elisha.

[21] πάντες...ἐν τῇ συναγωγῇ.

[22] S.v. ἀνίστημι.

[23] ἡ πόλις...αὐτῶν.

[24] ὥστε + inf. (instead of ἵνα + subj.) (cf. IV, 15).

[25] Leprosy, or Hansen's disease (as it is now known), originated in the Far East and was not present in the Mediterranean area during the Hellenistic period.

πατρίς, -ίδος, ἡ, homeland; hometown

πίμπλημι, 3. ἔπλησα, ¹aor. inf. πλάσαι, ¹aor. impv. πλῆσον, 6. ἐπλήσθην, fut. pass. πλησθήσομαι: to fill, fulfill; pass. be filled with (w. gen.)

Σάρεπτα, τά, Zarephath, a city on the Phoenician coast between Tyre and Sidon (cf. 1 Kgs 17:9)

Σιδώνιος, -α, -ον, of Sidon, Sidonian (adj.)

Σύρος, ὁ, Syrian

χήρα, ἡ, widow

SELECT BIBLIOGRAPHY

Kimball, Charles. "Jesus' Exposition of Scripture in Luke 4:16–30: An Inquiry in Light of Jewish Hermeneutics." *Perspectives in Religious Studies* 21/3 (1994), 179–202.

1.4.

Gospel of Thomas: The Greek Fragments

(Gos. Thom. 1–7, 27–28, 30–32, 77b / 36–37, 39 and Synoptic Parallels)

Text: Bernhard, 56–78, §§2–23.

In 1897 and 1903, three Greek fragments of the Gospel of Thomas were discovered in an ancient garbage dump near the ancient city of Oxyrhynchos in Upper Egypt (POxy 654, POxy 1, POxy 655). These fragments were subsequently published in 1903. A complete Coptic version of the Gospel of Thomas was subsequently discovered in 1945 in the city of Nag Hammadi, shedding fresh light of the nature and significance of the three Greek fragments as all belonging to an ancient sayings gospel, comparable to the Q Sayings Gospel. Some of the sayings recorded in this document may preserve traditions that are independent of the Synoptic Gospels, though other sayings were added over time.[1] It is now recognized that some of the earliest sayings of Jesus, as recorded in the Gospel of Thomas, actually predate their parallel versions in the Synoptic tradition.

Date: These three papyrus fragments date from 130–250 CE.

Related Texts: The Gospel of Thomas is also representative of the "Thomas tradition" of early Syrian Christianity (in contrast to the Petrine and Pauline traditions). Many Syrian Christians, believing that Thomas was the twin brother of Jesus (Mark 6:3, cf. John 11:16, 20:24, 21:2), came to regard him as Jesus' privileged spokesperson (contrasting the role of Peter in Mark 8:22–9:1, §1.13). This so-called Thomas Christianity was also responsible for the Gospel of Thomas, the Book of Thomas, and the Acts of Thomas (§5.10).

---

[1] Included in the former category are Gos. Thom. 8 (Matt 5:14), 20 (Mark 4:30–32), 34 (Matt 13:47–50).

Prologue: Οὗτοι οἱ λόγοι οἱ ἀπόκρυφοι οὓς ἐλάλησεν Ἰησοῦς ὁ ζῶν[2] καὶ ἔγραψεν Ἰούδας ὁ καὶ[3] Θωμᾶς.

1 καὶ (Jesus) εἶπεν· ὅστις ἂν τὴν ἑρμημνείαν τῶν λόγων τούτων εὑρίσκῃ, θανάτου οὐ μὴ γεύσηται.[4]

2 λέγει Ἰησοῦς· μὴ παυσάσθω ὁ ζητῶν τοῦ ζητεῖν ἕως ἂν εὕρῃ, καὶ ὅταν εὕρῃ θαμβηθήσεται, καὶ θαμβηθεὶς βασιλεύσει, καὶ βασιλεύσας ἀναπαήσεται.

3 λέγει Ἰησοῦς· ἐὰν οἱ ἕλκοντες ὑμᾶς εἴπωσιν ὑμῖν· ἰδοὺ ἡ βασιλεία (is) ἐν οὐρανῷ, ὑμᾶς φθήσεται τὰ πετεινὰ τοῦ οὐρανοῦ· ἐὰν δ᾽ εἴπωσιν ὅτι ὑπὸ τὴν γῆν ἐστιν, εἰσελεύσονται οἱ ἰχθύες τῆς θαλάσσης προφθάσαντες ὑμᾶς· καὶ ἡ βασιλεία τοῦ πατρὸς ἐντὸς ὑμῶν ἐστι κἀκτός.[5] ὅστις ἂν ἑαυτὸν γνῷ[6] ταύτην εὑρήσει· καὶ ὅτε ὑμεῖς ἑαυτοὺς γνώσεσθε, εἴσεσθε[7] ὅτι οἱ υἱοί ἐστε ὑμεῖς τοῦ πατρὸς τοῦ ζῶντος· εἰ δὲ μὴ γνώσεσθε ἑαυτούς, ἐν τῇ πτωχείᾳ ἐστὲ καὶ ὑμεῖς ἐστε ἡ πτωχεία.

Luke 17:20–21 Ἐπερωτηθεὶς δὲ ὑπὸ τῶν Φαρισαίων πότε ἔρχεται ἡ βασιλεία τοῦ θεοῦ (Jesus) ἀπεκρίθη αὐτοῖς καὶ εἶπεν· οὐκ ἔρχεται ἡ βασιλεία τοῦ θεοῦ μετὰ παρατηρήσεως,[8] 21 οὐδὲ ἐροῦσιν·　ἰδοὺ ὧδε ἢ ἐκεῖ, ἰδού, γὰρ ἡ βασιλεία τοῦ θεοῦ ἐντὸς ὑμῶν ἐστιν.

Mark 13:21: (Jesus said) Καὶ τότε ἐάν τις ὑμῖν εἴπῃ· ἴδε ὧδε ὁ χριστός, ἴδε ἐκεῖ, μὴ πιστεύετε.

Vocabulary

ἀναπαύω, [1]aor. mid. ἀνεπαυσάμην, [2]fut. pass. ἀναπαήσομαι: cause to rest; to end, finish; mid. rest

ἀπόκρυφος, -ον, hidden, secret; τὰ ἀπόκρυφα, hidden things

γεύομαι, to taste/eat something (gen.); experience

ἐκτός (w. gen.), outside of, except

ἕλκω, [1]aor. εἵλκυσα: pull an object, attract somebody; stretch something; spin thread

ἐντός (w. gen.), within, among; within (a period of time); inside

ἑρμηνεία, ἡ, interpretation

θαμβέω, be astounded, amazed; pass. w. act. sense

ἰχθύς, -ύος, ὁ, fish

οὐαί (w. dat.), woe/alas (concerning, by reason of)

παρατήρησις, -εως, ἡ, close observation (Luke 17:20)

---

[2] Modifier in 3rd attrib. pos. (cf. IV, 4.3).

[3] ὁ καί, "also called," "also known as."

[4] οὐ μή + aor. subj. (emph. fut. neg., cf. IV, 8).

[5] κἀκτός > καὶ ἐκτός.

[6] Cf. table 9.6.3.

[7] S.v. οἶδα, which has two future forms, εἰδήσω and εἴσομαι.

[8] I.e., in such a way that it can be observed.

παύω, make to end, bring to an end; mid. cease/stop doing something

πετεινός, -ή, -όν, winged; τὸ πετεινόν, bird

προφθάνω, go before

πτωχεία, ἡ, poverty

φθάνω, 2. φθήσομαι, 3. ἔφθασα, 4. ἔφθακα: come/go before somebody, come/go first

4 λέγει Ἰησους· οὐκ ἀποκνήσει ἄνθρωπος παλαιὸς ἡμερῶν[9] ἐπερωτῆσαι παιδίον τῶν ἑπτὰ ἡμερῶν περὶ τοῦ τόπου τῆς ζωῆς, καὶ αὐτὸς ζήσεται· ὅτι πολλοὶ ἔσονται πρῶτοι ἔσχατοι[10] καὶ οἱ ἔσχατοι πρῶτοι, καὶ εἰς ἓν καταντήσουσιν.

> *Mark 10:31* (Jesus said) Πολλοὶ δὲ ἔσονται πρῶτοι ἔσχατοι καὶ οἱ ἔσχατοι πρῶτοι.

5 λέγει Ἰησοῦς· γνῶθι[11] τὸ ὂν[12] ἔμπροσθεν τῆς ὄψεώς σου, καὶ τὸ κεκαλυμμένον ἀπό σου ἀποκαλυφθήσεται σοι·[13] οὐ γάρ ἐστιν[14] (anything) κρυπτὸν[15] ὃ οὐ φανερὸν γενήσεται, καὶ τεθαμμένον[16] ὃ οὐκ ἐγερθήσεται.

> *Mark 4:22* (Jesus said) Οὐ γάρ ἐστιν κρυπτὸν ἐὰν μὴ ἵνα φανερωθῇ, οὐδὲ ἐγένετο ἀπόκρυφον ἀλλ᾽ ἵνα ἔλθῃ εἰς φανερόν.

6–7 ἐξετάζουσιν αὐτὸν οἱ μαθηταὶ αὐτοῦ καὶ λέγουσιν· πῶς νηστεύσομεν; καὶ πῶς προσευξόμεθα; καὶ πῶς ἐλεημοσύνη ποιήσομεν καὶ τί παρατηρήσομεν περὶ τῶν βρωμάτων; 7 λέγει Ἰησοῦς· μὴ ψεύδεσθε καὶ ὅτι[17] μισεῖτε μὴ ποιεῖτε (for all things will be full) τῆς ἀληθείας (before heaven). Οὐδὲν γάρ ἐστιν ἀποκεκρυμμένον ὃ οὐ φανερὸν ἔσται. μακάριός ἐστιν ὁ λέων ὃν φάγεται ἄνθρωπος καὶ ὁ λέων ἔσται[18] ἄνθρωπος· καὶ οὐαὶ τῷ ἀνθρώπῳ ὃν φάγεται λέων...

> *Luke 12:2* (Jesus said) Οὐδὲν δὲ συγκεκαλυμμένον ἐστὶν[19] ὃ οὐκ ἀποκαλυφθήσεται καὶ (nothing is) κρυπτὸν ὃ οὐ γνωσθήσεται.

Vocabulary

ἀποκαλύπτω, 6. ἀπεκαλύφθην, reveal, disclose

ἀποκνέω, hesitate from

ἀπόκρυφος, -ον, hidden away; τὰ ἀπόκρυφα, hidden things

---

[9] Gen. of measure ("old in days").

[10] ἔσονται...ἔσχατοι.

[11] Cf. table 9.6.5.

[12] Nt. ptc., s.v. εἰμί.

[13] Typically ἀποκαλύπτω is followed by the dat. (to reveal something *to* somebody), but here the gen. is used.

[14] Impers. use of ἐστιν (cf. IV, 14).

[15] Nt.

[16] S.v. θάπτω.

[17] S.v. ὅστις, ἥτις, ὅτι > ὅ τι.

[18] ἔσται, here "become."

[19] Pf. periphr. (cf. IV, 18).

βρῶμα, -ματος, τό, food (sg. and pl.)

ἐλεημοσύνη, ἡ, giving alms/money to a needy person

ἔμπροσθεν (w. gen.), before, in front of; previously

ἐξετάζω, 2. ἐξετάσω, question somebody closely

θάπτω, 2. θάψω, 3. ἐτάφησα, [1]aor. inf. θάψαι, pf. pass. ptc. τεθαμμένος, [1]aor. pass. ἐτάφθην/[2]aor. pass. ἐτάφην: bury somebody; provide a funeral for (πρὸς) somebody

καλύπτω, pf. pass. ptc. κεκαλυμμένος: cover, hide, conceal; pass. be hiding

καταντάω, reach (a goal); arrive at (εἰς) a place; attain something; come to (εἰς)

κρυπτός, -ή, -όν, hidden

λέων, -οντος, ὁ, / **λέαινα, ἡ**, lion, lioness

μισέω, hate, despise, disregard

νηστεύω, to fast, observe a fast (for)

ὄψις, -εως, ἡ, appearance, countenance, face; vision, apparition; pl. eyes; sight

παλαιός, -ά, -όν, old, former

παρατηρέω, carefully observe a custom or practice

φανερός, -ά, -όν, known, visible; evident, notable; (adv.) φανερῶς, openly, publicly

φανερόω, make known, show, manifest, reveal

συγκαλύπτω, pf. pass. ptc. συγκεκαλυμμένος, to veil, cover completely (Luke 12:2)

ψεύδομαι, lie, tell a falsehood

27 λέγει Ἰησοῦς· ἐὰν μὴ νηστεύσητε τὸν κόσμον,[20] οὐ μὴ εὕρητε[21] τὴν βασιλείαν τοῦ θεοῦ· καὶ ἐὰν μὴ σαββατίσητε τὸ σάββατον, οὐκ ὄψεσθε τὸν πατέρα.

28 λέγει Ἰησοῦς· ἔστην ἐν μέσῳ τοῦ κόσμου καὶ ἐν σαρκὶ ὤφθην[22] αὐτοῖς καὶ εὗρον πάντας μεθύοντας καὶ οὐδένα εὗρον διψῶντα ἐν αὐτοῖς· καὶ πονεῖ ἡ ψυχή μου ἐπὶ[23] τοῖς υἱοῖς τῶν ἀνθρώπων ὅτι τυφλοί εἰσιν τῇ καρδίᾳ αὐτῶν καὶ οὐ βλέπουσιν.

30 + 77b λέγει Ἰησοῦς· ὅπου ἐὰν[24] ὦσιν τρεῖς (people), εἰσὶν ἄθεοι· καὶ ὅπου εἷς ἐστιν μόνος, λέγω, ἐγώ εἰμι μετ᾽ αὐτοῦ. ἔγειρον τὸν λίθον κἀκεῖ[25] εὑρήσεις με· σχίσον τὸ ξύλον κἀγὼ ἐκεῖ εἰμι.

31 λέγει Ἰησοῦς· οὐκ ἔστιν δεκτὸς προφήτης ἐν τῇ πατρίδι αὐτοῦ, οὐδὲ ἰατρὸς ποιεῖ θεραπείας εἰς[26] τοὺς γινώσκοντας αὐτόν.

---

[20] The phrase "fast from the world" (or "fast with respect to the world"), has not yet been satisfactorily explained. Perhaps it means "to abstain from the world" (BDAG 672).

[21] οὐ μή + aor. subj. (emph. fut. neg., cf. IV, 8).

[22] S.v. ὁράω.

[23] ἐπὶ, "on account of"

[24] ἐάν > ἄν.

[25] κἀκεῖ > καὶ ἐκεῖ.

[26] εἰς (w. acc.), "for."

32 λέγει Ἰησοῦς· πόλις ᾠκοδομημένη ἐπ᾽ ἄκρον ὄρους ὑψηλοῦ καὶ ἐστηριγμένη οὔτε πεσεῖν δύναται οὔτε κρυβῆναι.

Vocabulary

ἄθεος, -ον, without God

ἄκρον, τό, high point, top (of a mountain, a staff), extremity; a peel (of fruit)

δεκτός, -ή, -όν, acceptable, favorable

διψάω, be thirsty

θεραπεία, ἡ, worship of a god; pl. divine services; medical treatment, healing

ἰατρός, ὁ, physician

κρύπτω, impf. pass. ἐκρυβόμην, 3. ἔκρυψα, 6. ἐκρύβην, ²aor. pass. inf. κρυβῆναι, pf. pass. ptc. κεκρυμμένος: to cover, hide, conceal; pass. be hiding

μεθύω, be drunk, intoxicated

ξύλον, τό, wood, tree (collective, trees); cross

οἰκοδομέω, pf. pass. ᾠκοδόμημαι: build/construct; form/fashion; (fig.) build up, encourage

ὅπου, where (non-interogative)

πονέω, engage in hard work for/on behalf of (ἐπί) somebody; be troubled

σαββατίζω, 2. σαββατιῶ: keep the Sabbath; σαββατίζω τὸ σάββατον, keep the Sabbath as the Sabbath

στηρίζω, set up; establish, strengthen

σχίζω, to split, divide

τυφλός, -ή, -όν, blind

36 λέγει Ἰησοῦς· μὴ μεριμνᾶτε ἀπὸ πρωῒ ἕως ὀψέ, μήτε ἀφ᾽ ἑσπέρας ἕως πρωΐ, μήτε τῇ τροφῇ ὑμῶν τί φάγητε, μήτε τῇ στολῇ ὑμῶν τί ἐνδύσησθε. πολλῷ[27] κρείσσονές ἐστε τῶν κρίνων, ἅτινα[28] οὐ ξαίνει οὐδὲ νήθει μηδὲν ἔχοντα ἔνδυμα. τί ἐνδύεσθε καὶ ὑμεῖς; τίς ἂν προσθείη[29] ἐπὶ τὴν ἡλικίαν ὑμῶν; αὐτὸς δώσει ὑμῖν τὸ ἔνδυμα ὑμῶν.

> *Luke 12:22–23* (Jesus) εἶπεν δὲ πρὸς τοὺς μαθητὰς αὐτοῦ· διὰ τοῦτο λέγω ὑμῖν· μὴ μεριμνᾶτε τῇ ψυχῇ τί φάγητε, μηδὲ τῷ σώματι τί ἐνδύσησθε. 23 ἡ γὰρ ψυχὴ πλεῖόν ἐστιν τῆς τροφῆς καὶ τὸ σῶμα τοῦ ἐνδύματος.

37 λέγουσιν αὐτῷ οἱ μαθηταὶ αὐτοῦ· πότε ἡμῖν ἐμφανὴς ἔσει,[30] καὶ πότε σε ὀψόμεθα; λέγει· ὅταν ἐκδύσησθε καὶ μὴ αἰσχυνθῆτε...

39 λέγει Ἰησοῦς· οἱ Φαρισαῖοι καὶ οἱ γραμματεῖς ἔλαβον τὰς κλεῖδας τῆς γνώσεως καὶ ἔκρυψαν αὐτάς· οὔτε εἰσῆλθον οὔτε τοὺς εἰσερχομένους

---

[27] S.v. πολύς.

[28] S.v. ὅστις.

[29] Opt. (table 9.13.3).

[30] ἔσει > ἔσῃ.

ἀφῆκαν εἰσελθεῖν. ὑμεῖς δὲ γίνεσθε φρόνιμοι ὡς οἱ ὄφεις καὶ ἀκέραιοι ὡς αἱ περιστεραί.

Luke 11:46 ὁ δὲ (Jesus) εἶπεν· καὶ ὑμῖν τοῖς νομικοῖς οὐαί, ὅτι φορτίζετε τοὺς ἀνθρώπους φορτία[31] δυσβάστακτα, καὶ αὐτοὶ[32] ἑνὶ τῶν δακτύλων ὑμῶν οὐ προσψαύετε τοῖς φορτίοις.

Luke 11:52 (Jesus said) Οὐαὶ ὑμῖν τοῖς νομικοῖς, ὅτι ἤρατε τὴν κλεῖδα τῆς γνώσεως· αὐτοὶ οὐκ εἰσήλθατε καὶ τοὺς εἰσερχομένους[33] ἐκωλύσατε.

Vocabulary

αἰσχύνω (mid. and pass. dep. in GNT), mid. be ashamed

ἀκέραιος, -ον, innocent

ἀφίημι, impf. ἤφιον, 3. ἀφῆκα, [2]aor. 2nd sg. impv. ἄφες, 6. ἀφέθην, fut. pass. ἀφεθήσομαι, [2]aor. pl. pass. ptc. ἀφέντες: let, allow, permit; leave behind; forsake; forgive somebody (dat.); release (manumit) a slave to (ἐπί); acquit of (ἐπί) charges

γνῶσις, ἡ, knowledge, secret knowledge; personal acquaintance

δάκτυλος, ὁ, finger

δυσβάστακτος, -ον, hard to carry/bear

ἐκδύω, 6. ἐξεδύθην: strip, take off; mid. strip/undress oneself; pass. be stripped of one's clothing

ἐμφανής, -ές, visible, known

ἔνδυμα, -ματος, τό, clothing, garment

ἐνδύω, aor. inf. ἐνδῦσαι: to dress, put on (clothing); mid. put on (oneself), wear

ἑσπέρα, ἡ, evening

ἡλικία, ἡ, life span, years of age; maturity; ἐπέρχομαι εἰς ἡλικίαν, come of age; παρὰ καιρὸν ἡλικίας, past the normal age

κλείς, κλειδός, ἡ, key (cf. Luke 11:52)

κρείσσων, -ον, gen. –ονος (comp. of ἀγαθός, Att. κρείττων), stronger, better than (+ gen.), of higher rank/value; subst. τὸ κρεῖσσον, something better

κρίνον, τό, lily

κωλύω, hinder, prevent; prohibit

μεριμνάω, be anxious to do something

νήθω, spin (wool)

νομικός, -ή, -όν, pertaining to the law; subst. lawyer

ξαίνω, to card (wool)

ὄφις, -εως, ὁ, snake, serpent

ὀψέ, adv., late, late in the evening; as prep. (w. gen.), late for something

---

[31] Cogn. acc. (i.e., same root word as the verb governing it).
[32] αὐτοί intensifies the implied subject of προσψαύετε.
[33] Conative (expressing an attempted action).

περιστερά, ή, dove

πλείων (m./fm.), **πλείονα** (m./fm. acc.), **πλεῖον/πλέον** (nt.); pl. πλείονες (nom.), πλειόνων (gen.), πλείοσιν (dat.), πλείους (m. acc.): more; more (than + gen.); better/greater; ἐπὶ (τὸ) πλεῖον, all the more; ἐπὶ πλεῖον, at greater length; ἐπὶ πλείονα χρόνον, for a long time; adv. (nt. pl.), πλείονα, all the more; (superl.), πλεῖστος, -η, -ον, most; subst., πλεῖστοι, the majority

προστίθημι, aor. subj. προσθῶ, ²aor. inf. προσθεῖναι, aor. subj. προσθῶ: add to something; continue, repeat (an action)

προσψαύω, touch something (dat.)

πρωΐ (adv.), early, early in the morning

στολή, ή, robe, garment

τροφή, ή, food

φορτίζω, burden somebody with a load

φορτίον, τό (dim. of φόρτος), burden

φρόνιμος, -ον, prudent, wise; superl. φρονιμώτατος, wisest

SELECT BIBLIOGRAPHY

Ageirsson, John, April D. Deconick, and Risto Uro. *Thomasine Traditions in Antiquity: The Social and Cultural World of the Gospel of Thomas.* Leiden: Brill, 2006.

Davies, Stevan L. *Gospel of Thomas: Annotated & Explained.* Woodstock, VT: SkyLight Paths, 2002.

Foster, Paul (ed.). *The Non-Canonical Gospels.* London: T&T Clark, 2008.

Valantasis, Richard. *Gospel of Thomas.* London: Routledge, 1997.

1.5.

Gospel of Mark: Jesus' Secret and Controversial Teaching

(Mark 3:20–30, 4:10–20)

Provenance: Outside Palestine.   *Date:* 70–75 CE.

According to Mark 3:20–30, the scribes charged Jesus with being in league with demons. This charge is reminiscent of a similar charge made against Apollonios of Tyana (Philostr. *VA* 8.7.7–9 [§8.1]), an itinerant healer who was also accused of being a sorcerer or magician. The understanding of Jesus as a teacher of secret wisdom (Mark 4:10–20) is also found in the Gospel of Thomas (§1.4) and the Q Sayings Gospel.

JESUS IS CHARGED WITH BEING IN LEAGUE WITH DEMONS (MARK 3:20-30)

3:20 Καὶ (Jesus) ἔρχεται[1] εἰς οἶκον· καὶ συνέρχεται πάλιν ὁ ὄχλος, ὥστε[2] μὴ δύνασθαι αὐτοὺς[3] μηδὲ ἄρτον φαγεῖν. 21 καὶ ἀκούσαντες (what had happened) οἱ παρ' αὐτοῦ[4] ἐξῆλθον κρατῆσαι αὐτόν· ἔλεγον γὰρ ὅτι ἐξέστη. 22 Καὶ οἱ γραμματεῖς οἱ ἀπὸ Ἱεροσολύμων[5] καταβάντες ἔλεγον ὅτι Βεελζεβοὺλ ἔχει[6] καὶ ὅτι ἐν[7] τῷ ἄρχοντι τῶν δαιμονίων ἐκβάλλει τὰ δαιμόνια. 23 Καὶ προσκαλεσάμενος αὐτοὺς

---

[1] Hist. pres. (cf. IV, 11); ἔρχομαι εἰς οἶκον, "to go home."
[2] ὥστε w. inf. (cf. IV, 15).
[3] I.e., Jesus and his twelve disciples.
[4] οἱ παρ' αὐτοῦ, "those who were close to him," here, Jesus' own family (contrasting οἱ περὶ αὐτόν in 4:10).
[5] Ἱεροσολύμων > Ἱεροσόλυμα; in the NT, one always "goes up to" or "down from" Jerusalem, regardless of one's geographical location.
[6] ἔχω in this context has mng. "to be possessed (by a devil), taking Βεελζεβούλ (indecl.) as a dat.
[7] Instr., "through," "by."

ἐν παραβολαῖς (Jesus) ἔλεγεν αὐτοῖς· Πῶς δύναται σατανᾶς[8] σατανᾶν[9] ἐκβάλλειν; 24 καὶ ἐὰν βασιλεία ἐφ' ἑαυτὴν μερισθῇ, οὐ δύναται σταθῆναι[10] ἡ βασιλεία ἐκείνη· 25 καὶ ἐὰν οἰκία ἐφ' ἑαυτὴν μερισθῇ, οὐ δυνήσεται ἡ οἰκία ἐκείνη σταθῆναι. 26 καὶ εἰ ὁ σατανᾶς ἀνέστη ἐφ' ἑαυτὸν καὶ ἐμερίσθη, οὐ δύναται στῆναι ἀλλὰ τέλος ἔχει.[11] 27 ἀλλ' οὐ δύναται οὐδεὶς[12] εἰς τὴν οἰκίαν τοῦ ἰσχυροῦ[13] εἰσελθὼν τὰ σκεύη αὐτοῦ διαρπάσαι, ἐὰν μὴ[14] πρῶτον τὸν ἰσχυρὸν δήσῃ, καὶ τότε τὴν οἰκίαν αὐτοῦ διαρπάσει. 28 Ἀμὴν λέγω ὑμῖν ὅτι πάντα[15] ἀφεθήσεται[16] τοῖς υἱοῖς τῶν ἀνθρώπων[17] τὰ ἁμαρτήματα[18] καὶ αἱ βλασφημίαι ὅσα ἐὰν[19] βλασφημήσωσιν· 29 ὃς δ' ἂν βλασφημήσῃ εἰς[20] τὸ πνεῦμα τὸ ἅγιον, οὐκ ἔχει ἄφεσιν εἰς τὸν αἰῶνα, ἀλλὰ **ἔνοχός** ἐστιν αἰωνίου ἁμαρτήματος.[21] 30 (he said this) ὅτι ἔλεγον· Πνεῦμα ἀκάθαρτον (Jesus) ἔχει.

Vocabulary

ἀκάθαρτος, -ον, unclean, impure; τὰ ἀκάθαρτα, impurities, filth

ἄκανθα, ἡ, thorny plant

ἁμάρτημα, τό, sin, transgression

ἄρχων, -οντος, ὁ, prince, ruler, leader; archon (title of a city magistrate)

Βεελζεβούλ, ὁ, Beelzebul; in NT, the prince of the demons (making this charge in effect a charge of sorcery; cf. Beelzebub, 2 Kgs 1:2)

βλασφημέω, to slander, speak impiously; blaspheme

δέω, 3. ἔδησα, pf. pass. δέδεμαι, pf. pass. ptc. δεδεμένος: to bind/tie, put in chains; imprison; pass. be bound, be bound to somebody in marriage

διαρπάζω, to plunder

διωγμός, ὁ, persecution; persecution against (w. ἐπι)

εἶτα, then, next; and so, therefore

ἔνοχος (w. gen.), liable for, guilty of

ἐξίστημι, 2. ἐκστήσω/ομαι, 3. ἐξέστησα / ἐξέστην: amaze (trans.), be amazed/ astonished (intrans.); be out of one's mind

---

[8] Subject of δύναται.

[9] Obj. of inf.

[10] Cf. table 12.3.3(f).

[11] τέλος ἔχει, "to have an end," "to be finished."

[12] οὐ … οὐδεὶς, double negation strengthens negation.

[13] Art. creates generic subst. (sc. ἀνθρώπου).

[14] ἐὰν μή, "unless."

[15] πάντα…τὰ ἁμαρτήματα (disc. syn.).

[16] 3 sg. fut. pass. ind. s.v. ἀφίημι, cf. table 9.15.

[17] οἱ υἱοὶ τῶν ἀνθρώπων, i.e., "human beings."

[18] Subject of ἀφεθήσεται.

[19] ὅσα ἐάν (> ἄν), "whatever"; take w. αἱ βλασφημίαι.

[20] εἰς, "against."

[21] Here "slandering" the Holy Spirit means attributing the work of the Spirit in Jesus' healings to the work of Satan.

ἰσχυρός, -ά, -όν, strong, powerful; comp. ἰσχυρότερος, stronger

κρατέω, attain; conquer, to master, rule over (w. gen.), subdue; take possession of; take custody of (w. gen.); hold something (w. gen.)

μερίζω, Att. fut. μεριῶ, 6. ἐμερίσθην: divide; assign

προσκαλέω/έομαι (mostly mid.), 6. προσεκλήθην: summon; call to a special task; entreat; encourage

ῥίζα, ἡ, root

σκεῦος, -ους, τό, vessel, container; instrument; τὰ σκευή, equipment, possessions, ship's tackle

συνέρχομαι, assemble, gather together

After Jesus tells the parable of the sower (Mark 4:1–9), he takes his disciples aside to explain the purpose of his parables. He speaks in parables in order to hide the meaning of his teaching from the outer group. Their meaning or solution is given only to the inner group, namely Jesus' disciples (Mark 4:33–34). This use of the word παραβολή to mean "a communication that disguises meaning" is very unusual. This passage is an example of the Markan literary device known as the "messianic secret."

JESUS AS A TEACHER IS SECRET WISDOM (MARK 4:10–20)

4:10 Καὶ ὅτε (Jesus) ἐγένετο κατὰ μόνας,[22] ἠρώτων αὐτὸν οἱ[23] περὶ αὐτὸν σὺν τοῖς δώδεκα (about) τὰς παραβολάς. 11 καὶ ἔλεγεν αὐτοῖς· ὑμῖν τὸ μυστήριον δέδοται τῆς βασιλείας τοῦ θεοῦ· ἐκείνοις δὲ τοῖς ἔξω[24] ἐν παραβολαῖς τὰ πάντα γίνεται,

> 12 ἵνα[25] βλέποντες βλέπωσιν καὶ μὴ ἴδωσιν,[26]
> καὶ ἀκούοντες ἀκούωσιν καὶ μὴ συνιῶσιν,[27]
> μήποτε ἐπιστρέψωσιν καὶ (sin) ἀφεθῇ[28] αὐτοῖς. (Isa 6:9–10)

4:13 Καὶ (Jesus) λέγει αὐτοῖς· (if) οὐκ οἴδατε (the meaning of) τὴν παραβολὴν ταύτην, καὶ[29] πῶς πάσας τὰς παραβολὰς γνώσεσθε;[30] 14 ὁ σπείρων τὸν λόγον[31]

---

[22] κατὰ μόνας, "alone" (adv.).
[23] "Those around him," i.e., Jesus' followers.
[24] ἐκείνοις…τοῖς ἔξω (i.e., those beyond Jesus' inner circle).
[25] This ἵνα probably denotes purpose, indicating the belief that Jesus was fulfilling Isaiah's prophecy.
[26] Here εἶδον has the contextual meaning "to perceive."
[27] Cf. paradigm of ἵημι (table 9.15).
[28] S.v. ἀφίημι, cf. paradigm of ἵημι (table 9.15).
[29] καί ("then") introduces a question.
[30] Fut. of γινώσκω is mid.
[31] Throughout this passage trans. λόγος as "message (of faith)."

σπείρει. 15 οὗτοι δέ εἰσιν οἱ παρὰ τὴν ὁδόν· ὅπου σπείρεται ὁ λόγος καὶ ὅταν ἀκούσωσιν, εὐθὺς ἔρχεται ὁ σατανᾶς καὶ αἴρει τὸν λόγον τὸν ἐσπαρμένον[32] εἰς αὐτούς. 16 καὶ (similarly) οὗτοί[33] εἰσιν οἱ ἐπὶ τὰ πετρώδη σπειρόμενοι,[34] οἳ ὅταν ἀκούσωσιν τὸν λόγον εὐθὺς μετὰ χαρᾶς λαμβάνουσιν αὐτόν, 17 καὶ οὐκ ἔχουσιν ῥίζαν ἐν ἑαυτοῖς ἀλλὰ (only) πρόσκαιροί εἰσιν, εἶτα[35] γενομένης θλίψεως[36] ἢ διωγμοῦ διὰ τὸν λόγον εὐθὺς σκανδαλίζονται. 18 καὶ ἄλλοι εἰσὶν οἱ εἰς τὰς ἀκάνθας σπειρόμενοι· οὗτοί εἰσιν οἱ τὸν λόγον ἀκούσαντες, 19 καὶ αἱ μέριμναι τοῦ αἰῶνος καὶ ἡ ἀπάτη τοῦ πλούτου καὶ αἱ περὶ τὰ λοιπὰ ἐπιθυμίαι[37] εἰσπορευόμεναι συμπνίγουσιν τὸν λόγον καὶ ἄκαρπος (it) γίνεται. 20 καὶ ἐκεῖνοί εἰσιν οἱ ἐπὶ τὴν γῆν τὴν καλὴν σπαρέντες,[38] οἵτινες ἀκούουσιν τὸν λόγον καὶ παραδέχονται (it) καὶ καρποφοροῦσιν ἓν (seed) τριάκοντα (fold/times) καὶ ἓν (seed) ἑξήκοντα (fold/times) καὶ ἓν (seed) ἑκατόν (fold/times).

Vocabulary

ἄκαρπος, -ον, unfruitful; useless
ἀπάτη, ἡ, deception, deceitfulness
ἑκατόν, one hundred
ἑξήκοντα (indecl.), sixty
ἔξω, out, outside; (prep. w. gen.) out of, outside; ὁ ἔξω, outsider, unbeliever
ἐπιθυμία, ἡ, desire, longing; sexual desire, covetousness
ἐπιστρέφω, return; turn (in religious/moral sense), turn around/back; pass.
   (dep.), pay attention to, care about
ἐρωτάω, ask, request, beg
θλῖψις, ἡ, distress, affliction
καρποφορέω, bear fruit
μέριμνα, ἡ, worry
μυστήριον, τό, mystery, secret knowledge; pl., secret rituals
παραδέχομαι, accept, receive
πετρώδης, -ες, stony; τὰ πετρώδη, rocky ground
πλοῦτος, ὁ, wealth
πρόσκαιρος, -ον, lasting a short while, temporary
σατανᾶς, -α (gen.), ὁ, adversary, Satan (w. article), enemy of God[39]
σκανδαλίζω, cause to be caught/fall; pass. be led into sin
σπείρω, 3. ἔσπειρα, pf. pass. ptc. ἐσπαρμένος, 6. ἐσπάρην: sow (seed)
συμπνίγω, crowd out/choke out (plants)

---

[32] τὸν λόγον τὸν ἐσπαρμένον, 2nd attrib. pos.
[33] καὶ οὗτοί ... καὶ ἄλλοι ("and some ... and others," Mark 4:18).
[34] οἱ ... σπειρόμενοι.
[35] εἶτα...ἤ... ("either ... or ...").
[36] Gen. absol. (cf. IV, 9).
[37] αἱ ... ἐπιθυμίαι, with the modifer περὶ τὰ λοιπά ("for other things") in 1st attrib pos. (cf. IV, 4.1).
[38] οἱ ... σπαρέντες.
[39] Note many proper names of Hebrew origin have -ᾶ as a gen. ending.

συνίημι (fr. ἵημι), 2. συνήσω, 3. συνῆκα, ¹aor. subj. συνῶ, ptc. συνιείς, -εντος, pl. συνιέντες: understand something (gen.); subst. wise ones[40]
τριάκοντα, thirty

SELECT BIBLIOGRAPHY

Aichele, George. "Jesus' Uncanny Family Scene." *JSNT* 74 (1999), 29–49.
Busch, Austin. "Questioning and Conviction: Double-Voiced Discourse in Mark 3:22–30." *JBL* 125/3 (2006), 477–505.
Juel, Donald H. "Encountering the Sower in Mark 4:1–20." *Interpretation* (2002), 273–283.

---

[40] Do not confuse forms of συνίημι (fr. ἵημι, §9.15) with those of σύνειμι (fr. εἶμι, §9.14) or with those of σύνειμι (fr. εἰμί, §9.13).

1.6.

Shepherd of Hermas: The First Vision of Hermas

(Herm. 1:1–9)

Provenance: Written by a Christian and former slave, named Hermas (Ἑραμᾶς), who lived in Rome.

Date: 100–140 CE.

Text: Ehrman, II, 175–178.

The book known as the "Shepherd of Hermas" (Ποιμὴν τοῦ Ἑραμᾶ) was one of the most beloved Christian books in the second and third centuries CE. Indeed, it was widely considered to be canonical scripture and was often included in the Greek New Testament. The Shepherd of Hermas consists of a series of visions, precepts, and "similitudes" (parables), whose overall purpose is to exhort readers to repent of their sins. The book begins with Hermas being granted five visions, the first of which is given here.

1:1 Ὁ θρέψας με πέπρακέν με Ῥόδῃ τινὶ εἰς Ῥώμην· μετὰ πολλὰ ἔτη ταύτην ἀνεγνωρισάμην καὶ ἠρξάμην αὐτὴν ἀγαπᾶν ὡς ἀδελφήν. 2 μετὰ χρόνον τινὰ λουομένην εἰς τὸν παταμὸν τὸν Τίβεριν εἶδον (her) καὶ ἐπέδωκα αὐτῇ τὴν χεῖρα καὶ ἐξήγαγον αὐτὴν ἐκ τοῦ ποταμοῦ. ταύτης οὖν ἰδὼν κάλλος διελογιζόμην ἐν τῇ καρδίᾳ μου λέγων· μακάριος ἤμην εἰ τοιαύτην γυναῖκα εἶχον καὶ τῷ κάλλει καὶ τῷ τρόπῳ. μόνον τοῦτο ἐβουλευσάμην, ἕτερον δὲ οὐδέν.

Vocabulary
ἀδελφή, ἡ, sister, fellow believer
ἀναγνωρίζω, become reacquainted with somebody (acc.); learn to recognize
βουλεύω, resolve, decide; be a member of the Council (βουλή)
διαλογίζομαι, consider, ponder

FIG. 3. Carved face, theater, Antaleia (photo: author).

ἐκφέρω, 3. ἐξήνεγκον, 6. ἐξηνέχθην, aor. pass. subj. ἐξενέχθω: lead out, take out; produce; carry the dead for burial; declare one's opinion

ἐξάγω, lead out, bring

ἐπιδίδωμι, 6. ἐπεδόθην, pf. ptc. ἐπιδεδωκώς: give into one's hands; give somebody one's hand; surrender, give up control; give back/return; increase/grow in size

ἔτος, ἔτους, τό, year

κάλλος, -ους, τό, beauty

λούω/λόω, bathe, wash; mid. bathe oneself (the contr. impf. mid. forms, ἐλούμην and ἐλοῦτο, belong to λόω), bathe (as a baptism)

πιπράσκω, 3. πέπρακα, 6. ἐπράθησα: sell something

ποταμός, ὁ, river

Ῥώμη, ἡ, Rome

τρέφω, [1]aor. ἔθρεψα, pf. pass. ptc. τεθραμμένος: rear/raise a child

τρόπος, ὁ, way, manner; ὃν τρόπον, (just) as; καθ᾽ ὃν τρόπον, in the manner that

1:3 μετὰ χρόνον τινὰ πορευομένου μου εἰς κώμας καὶ δοξάζοντος τὰς κτίσεις τοῦ θεοῦ, ὡς μεγάλαι καὶ ἐκπρεπεῖς καὶ δυναταί εἰσιν, περιπατῶν ἀφύπνωσα. καὶ πνεῦμα με ἔλαβεν καὶ ἀπήνεγκέν με δὶ ἀνοδίας τινός, δἰ ἧς ἄνθρωπος οὐκ ἐδύνατο ὁδεῦσαι· ἦν δὲ ὁ τόπος κρημνώδης καὶ ἀπερρηγὼς ἀπὸ τῶν ὑδάτων. διαβὰς οὖν τὸν ποταμὸν ἐκεῖνον ἦλθον εἰς τὰ ὁμαλά, καὶ τιθῶ τὰ γόνατα καὶ ἠρξάμην προσεύχεσθαι τῷ κυρίῳ καὶ ἐξομολογεῖσθαί μου τὰς ἁμαρτίας. 4 προσευχομένου δέ μου ἠνοίγη ὁ οὐρανός, καὶ βλέπω τὴν γυναῖκα ἐκείνην ἣν ἐπεθύμησα ἀσπραζομένην με ἐκ τοῦ οὐρανοῦ, λέγουσαν· Ἑρμᾶ, χαῖρε.

Vocabulary

ἀνοδία, ἡ, place with no roads

ἀπερρηγώς, eroded (rare)

ἀποφέρω, [2]aor. inf. ἀπενεγκεῖν, aor. mid. inf. ἀποφέρεσθαι: carry off/away; mid. win a prize; carry away from (ἀπό) somebody to (ἐπί) somebody

ἀφυπόω, to fall asleep

γόνυ, -νατος, τό, pl. γόνατα: knee

διαβαίνω, [2]aor. ptc. διαβάς: cross over

δοξάζω, think, imagine; glorify; mid. display one's greatness; pass. supposed to be; be held in honor

δυνατός, -ή, -όν, strong, powerful; able, capable of; subst. ruler; δυνατώτερός, stronger

δύνω (also δύω), mid. δύομαι, 2. δύσομαι, [2]aor. ἔδυν: go down, set (of the sun); mid. to sink/set (of the sun)

ἐκπρεπής, -ές, remarkable, splendid

ἐξομολογέομαι, confess, acknowledge

ἐπιθυμέω, to desire

κρημνώδης, -ες, steep, precipitous
κτίσις, -εως, ἡ, creation, that which is created; creature, created thing
κώμη, ἡ, village; pl. countryside
ὁδεύω, to travel
ὁμαλός, -ή, -όν, smooth, level; τὰ ὁμαλά, level ground

1:5 Βλέψας δὲ εἰς αὐτὴν λέγω αὐτῇ· Κυρία, τί σὺ ὧδε ποιεῖς; Ἡ δὲ ἀπεκρίθη μοι· Ἀνελήμφθην ἵνα σου τὰς ἁμαρτίας ἐλέγξω πρὸς τὸν κύριον. 6 Λέγω αὐτῇ· Νῦν σύ μου ἔλεγχος εἶ; οὔ, φησίν, ἀλλὰ ἄκουσον τὰ ῥήματα ἅ σοι μέλλω λέγειν. ὁ θεὸς ὁ ἐν τοῖς οὐρανοῖς κατοικῶν καὶ κτίσας ἐκ τοῦ μὴ ὄντος τὰ ὄντα καὶ πληθύνας καὶ αὐξήσας ἕνεκεν τῆς ἁγίας ἐκκλησίας αὐτοῦ ὀργίζεταί σοι ὅτι ἥμαρτες εἰς ἐμέ. 7 Ἀποκριθεὶς αὐτῇ λέγω· Εἰς σὲ ἥμαρτον; ποίῳ τρόπῳ; ἢ πότε σοι αἰσχρὸν ῥῆμα ἐλάλησα; οὐ πάντοτέ σε ὡς θεὰν ἡγησάμην; οὐ πάντοτέ σε ἐνετράπην ὡς ἀδελφήν; τί μου καταψεύδῃ, ὦ γύναι,[1] τὰ πονηρὰ ταῦτα καὶ ἀκάθαρτα;

Vocabulary
αἰσχρός, -ά, -όν, socially or morally unacceptable, shameful, base
ἀκάθαρτος, -ον, unclean, impure; τὰ ἀκάθαρτα, impurities, filth
ἁμαρτάνω, ²aor. ἥμαρτον (but oft. ἁμαρησ- in non-ind. moods), 4. ἡμάρτηκα: to sin, commit a sin
ἀναλαμβάνω, 6. ἀνελήφθην: take up, carry; resolve; take up (a discourse); take over, carry away
αὐξάνω/αὔξω, 3. ηὔξανον: make grow/increase; pass. grow/increase in size/number/strength
ἔλεγχος, ὁ, proof, legal argument; accusation
ἐλέγχω, reprove, reproach
ἕνεκα/ἕνεκεν (w. gen.), because of, for the sake of, on account of; in honor of; for this reason; τίνος ἕνεκα, why?
ἐντρέπω, ²aor. ἐνετράπην: show deference to, respect
ἡγέομαι (w. inf.), lead the way; consider, regard; regard as necessary; subst. ptc. leader, chief; pass. be led
θεά, ἡ, goddess
καταψεύδομαι, tell lies against somebody (gen.)
κατοικέω, settle, dwell in; subst. inhabitants
κτίζω, found, create, make; build; pass. be created, constructed
κυρία, ἡ, lady
ὀργίζω, pass. become angry
πάντοτε, always (adv.)
πληθύνω, multiply, increase, grow in number

---

[1] Voc. Case.

πότε, when? (direct question); when (indirect question); ἕως πότε, how long?

τρόπος, ὁ, way, manner; ὃν τρόπον, (just) as; καθ' ὃν τρόπον, in the manner that

1:8 Γελάσασά μοι λέγει· ῾Επὶ τὴν καρδίαν σου ἀνέβη[2] ἐπιθυμία τῆς πονηρίας. ἢ οὐ δοκεῖ σοι ἀνδρὶ δικαίῳ πονηρὸν πρᾶγμα εἶναι ἐὰν ἀναβῇ αὐτοῦ ἐπὶ τὴν καρδίαν ἡ πονηρὰ ἐπιθυμία; ἁμαρτία γέ ἐστιν καὶ μεγάλη, φησίν. ὁ γὰρ δίκαιος ἀνὴρ δίκαια βουλεύεται (to do). ἐν τῷ οὖν δίκαια βουλεύεσθαι αὐτὸν κατορθοῦται ἡ δόξα αὐτοῦ ἐν τοῖς οὐρανοῖς καὶ (τὸν) εὐκατάλλακτον ἔχει τὸν κύριον ἐν παντὶ πράγματι αὐτοῦ. οἱ δὲ (to do) πονηρὰ βουλευόμενοι ἐν ταῖς καρδίαις αὐτῶν θάνατον καὶ αἰχμαλωτισμὸν ἑαυτοῖς ἐπισπῶνται, μάλιστα οἱ τὸν αἰῶνα τοῦτον περιποιούμενοι καὶ γαυριῶντες ἐν τῷ πλούτῳ αὐτῶν καὶ μὴ ἀντεχόμενοι τῶν ἀγαθῶν τῶν μελλόντων.

Vocabulary

αἰχμαλωτισμός, ὁ, captivity

ἀντέχομαι, cling to, be devoted to something (gen.)

βουλεύομαι, plan, resolve, decide; be a member of the city council (βουλή)

γαυρόω, be proud, pride oneself

γέ, even, at least, indeed (focuses attention on the previous word)

γελάω, to laugh

ἐπιθυμία, ἡ, desire for good things (longing); negative desire (lust, covetousness, craving)

ἐπισπάω, be responsible for bringing something on/making something happen; pull the foreskin over the head of the penis (in order to hide the marks of circumcision)

εὐκατάλλακτος, -ον, favorable; subst. favor

κατορθόω, set straight; pass. be established

μάλα, very; comp. **μᾶλλον,** more, all the more; instead of/rather than; by all means; μᾶλλον ἤ, more than; μᾶλλον...ἤ...; πολλῷ μᾶλλον, much more; superl. μάλιστα, most of all, above all, especially

περιποιέω, to gain possession of something, to gain for oneself

πλοῦτος, ὁ, wealth, riches

πρᾶγμα, τό, matter, event, affair; thing

1:9 μεταμελήσονται αἱ ψυχαὶ αὐτῶν, οἵτινες οὐκ ἔχουσιν ἐλπίδα, ἀλλὰ ἑαυτοὺς ἀπεγνώκασιν καὶ τὴν ζωὴν αὐτῶν. ἀλλὰ σὺ προσεύχου πρὸς τὸν θεόν, καὶ ἰάσεται τὰ ἁμαρτήματά σου καὶ ὅλου τοῦ οἴκου σου καὶ πάντων τῶν ἁγίων.

---

[2] S.v. ἀναβαίνω.

Vocabulary
ἁμάρτημα, τό, sin, transgression
ἀπογινώσκω, 4. ἀπέγνωκα: give up hope, despair
ἰάομαι, 2. ἰάσομαι, 3. ἰασάμην, 6. ἰάθην: hear/cure; find a remedy
μεταμέλομαι, to regret, be sorry
προσευχή, ἡ, prayer; (Jewish) prayer house

SELECT BIBLIOGRAPHY

Osiek, Carolyn. *Shepherd of Hermas: A Commentary.* Hermeneia. Minneapolis: Fortress, 1999.

1.7.

Gospel of Mary Magdalene: Mary's Unique Relationship with Jesus

Provenance: Unknown.

Date: Mid-second century CE.

Text: The Gospel of Mary is preserved in full in a Coptic version, which was discovered in 1896 but not published until 1955. Older Greek fragments (POxy 3525, PRyl 463) of the same text were discovered in Oxyrhynchos, Upper Egypt, in an ancient garbage dump and published in 1903.[1]

At the beginning of the extant Greek version (below), Peter addresses Mary as "sister" and invites her to tell the disciples about the secret teaching she had received from the risen savior in a vision. It seems that Peter had accepted that Mary was Jesus' favorite *among women*. However, his attitude changes when Mary implies that Jesus actually loved her more than even the *male* disciples, including Peter himself. Peter responds angrily and is called "hot-tempered." He resents the implication that he has been displaced by Mary and even accuses her of lying. Mary receives moral support from Levi, who defends her against Peter's claim that the savior would not have chosen a mere woman to communicate such a secret teaching (cf. Gos. Thom. 114, §1.4).

From a historical perspective, the Gospel of Mary probably presupposes a second-century debate between those Christians who sought *gnosis* (new spiritual truths) through private visions (cf. 2 Cor 12:1–6 [§4.9], Apoc. Pet. [§5.8]) and other

---

[1] The Coptic Gospel of Mary is part of Papyrus Berolinensis 8502; POxy 3525 = 9.5–10.14 of the Coptic version; PRyl 463 = 17.4–22, 18.5–19.3 of the Coptic version. These Greek fragments have been republished by Christopher Tuckett in *The Gospel of Mary* (Oxford: Oxford University Press, 2007), 108–115; cf. Antti Marjanen, *The Woman Jesus Loved: Mary Magdalene in the Nag Hammadi Library and Related Documents* (New York: Brill, 1996), 94–121.

FIG. 4. Carved relief of two women on limestone block, Konya (IKonya 95).

Christians, associated with the legacy of Peter, who lived according to rules of life derived from written traditions about Jesus. From this perspective, the Gospel of Mary re-enacts a debate between what may cautiously be termed "proto-gnostic" Christians and "Petrine" Christians. For their part, the "gnostic" Christians seem to have been critical of the many rules imposed by Petrine Christianity.[2] In any case, the fact that any early Christian group would attempt to validate its own Jesus tradition by claiming derivation from Mary Magdalene is remarkable indeed. In the canonical Gospels, Mary Magdalene is uniquely recorded as the witness of three key events in Jesus' life: his crucifixion, burial, and empty tomb.[3] No doubt, the tradition that Mary was a follower of Jesus and received an appearance of the risen Lord (John 20:14–18, Mark 16:9–11) accorded her special authority in some circles. The Gospel of Mary attempts to defend the theological legitimacy of ecstatic visions as legitimate sources of revelation by invoking this tradition.

GOS. MARY[1] (P^Oxy 3525)

(The lines above are missing)

1 Ταῦτα εἰπων ἐξῆλθεν. 2 οἱ δὲ λυπήθησαν δακροῦντες πολλὰ καὶ λέγοντες· Πῶς πορευώμεθα πρὸς τὰ ἔθνη κηρύσσοντες τὸ εὐαγγέλιον τῆς βασιλείας τοῦ υἱοῦ τοῦ ἀνθρώπου. 3 εἰ γὰρ μηδ᾽ ἐκείνου ἐφείσαντο πῶς ἡμῶν φείσονται; 4 τότε ἀνάστασα Μαριάμμη[4] καὶ ἀσπαζόμενη αὐτοὺς κατεφίλησε πάντας λέγουσα τοῖς ἀδελφοῖς· Μὴ δακρύετε μὴ λύπεισθε μηδὲ διστάζετε, ἡ χάρις γὰρ αὐτοῦ ἔσται μεθ᾽ ὑμῶν σκέπουσα ὑμᾶς. 5 μᾶλλον εὐχαρίστῶμεν[5] τῇ μεγαλειότητι αὐτοῦ ὅτι συνήρτηκεν ἡμᾶς καὶ ἀνθρώπους πεποίηκεν. 6 οὕτω λέγουσα Μαριάμμη μετέστρεψεν τὸν νοῦν αὐτῶν ἐπ᾽ ἀγαθόν. 7 καὶ ἤρξαν[6] συνζήτειν περὶ τῶν ἀποφθεγμάτων τοῦ σωτῆρος. 8 λέγει Πέτρος πρὸς Μαριάμμην· Ἀδελφή, οἴδαμεν ὅτι πολλὰ ἀγαπᾶσαι[7] ὑπὸ τοῦ σωτῆρος ὧς οὐκ ἄλλη γυνή. εἶπε οὖν ἡμῖν ὅσους[8] σὺ γινώσκεις λόγους τοῦ σωτῆρος οὖς ἡμεῖς οὐκ ἠκούσαμεν. 9 ὑπέλαβε Μαριάμμη λέγουσα· Ὅσα ὑμᾶς λανθάνει καὶ ἀπομνημονεύω, ἀπαγγέλω ὑμῖν, καὶ ἤρχεν αὐτοῖς τούτων τῶν λόγων ἐμοί· ποτὲ ἐν ὁράματι ἰδούσῃ τὸν κύριον καὶ εἰπούσῃ κύριε, σήμερον... *(incomplete line)*

Vocabulary
ἀπαγγέλλω, tell, inform, proclaim
ἀπομνημονεύω, remember
ἀπόφθεγμα, –ματος, τό, terse, pointed saying, apophthegm

---

[2] Marjanen, *The Woman Jesus Loved*, 121.
[3] Mark 15:40, 16:1, 9, Matt 27:56, 28:9, Luke 24:10, John 19:25, 20:1, 16.
[4] Μαριάμμη > Μαρία.
[5] Hort. subj.
[6] ἄρχω: HGr often employs mid. forms of ἄρχω to express the initiation or beginning of an action or process, but Gos. Mary employs the active voice instead (cf. Gos. Mary[1] 9, Gos. Mary[2] 8).
[7] Cf. table 9.4.
[8] ὅσους...λόγους.

ἀσπάζομαι, greet/welcome somebody; take leave of

δακρύω, weep

διστάζω, to doubt, have doubts

δοκέω, 3. ἔδοξα, pf. mid. inf. δεδόχθαι: to think, suppose, consider; seem to (w. inf.), regard to be (something); δοκεῖ + inf., it seems (to somebody) that, he purportedly; εἰ δοκεῖ (w. dat.), if it pleases (somebody); ἔδοξε/δοκεῖ, it was/is resolved (by); seem good/appropriate/best; propose/make (a request); pass. be decided; pass. inf. δεδόχθαι, be it resolved that (re a motion)

εὐχαριστέω, do a favor for somebody (dat.); give thanks

καταφιλέω, kiss, caress; kiss somebody in greeting/farewell

λανθάνω, escape notice of somebody, be unknown to somebody (acc.); adv., secretly

λυπέω, cause pain/grief; pass. be sorrowful, distressed

μάλα, very; comp. μᾶλλον, more, all the more; instead of/rather; by all means; μᾶλλον ἤ, more than; μᾶλλον...ἤ...; πολλῷ μᾶλλον, much more; superl. μάλιστα, most of all, above all, especially

μεγαλειότης, -ητος, ἡ, greatness

μεταστρέφω, change, turn (somebody's mind) to; pervert something

νοῦς, (gen.) νοός, (dat.) νοΐ/νῷ, (acc.) νοῦν, ὁ, mind, understanding; κατὰ νοῦν, in one's mind

παράκειμαι, be ready; be available, have in stock

ποτέ (encl.), once, former/formerly; sometimes; ever; at last; ὅσον ποτέ, whatever; whenever

ὅραμα, -ματος, τό, a vision

σήμερον, τό, today

σιγή, ἡ, silence, quiet

σκεπάζω, 3. ἐσκέπασα: protect, shelter

συζητέω (w. dat.), dispute, debate

συναρτάω, join together

σωτήρ, -ῆρος, ὁ, savior

ὑπολαμβάνω, reply; believe, assume, suppose; undertake to

φανερός, -ά, -όν, known, evident, notable; visible; φανερῶς (adv.), openly, publicly

φείδομαι, 3. ἐφεισάμην: refrain from; spare somebody (gen.) from something

GOS. MARY[2] (P[Ryl] 463)

And Mary said:

1 ...τὸ λοιπὸν δρόμου καιροῦ, χρόνου, αἰῶνος, (I will find) ἀνάπαυσιν ἐν σιγῇ· ταῦτα εἴπουσα ἡ Μαριάμμη ἐσιώπησεν ὡς[9] τοῦ σωτῆρος μέχρι ὧδε εἰρηκότος.[10]

---

[9] ὡς w. ptc. providing the reason for an action.
[10] S.v. λέγω in gen. absol. construction (IV, 9).

2 Ἀνδρέας λέγει· Ἄδελφοι, τι ὑμῖν δοκεῖ περὶ τῶν λαληθέντων; ἐγὼ μὲν γὰρ οὐ πιστεύω ταῦτα τὸν σωῆτρα εἰρηκέναι·[11] δοκεῖ γὰρ ἑτερογνωμόνειν τῇ ἐκείνου ἔννοια. 3 Πέτρος λέγει, Περὶ τοιούτων πρᾶγμα τῶν ἐξεταζόμενος· ὁ σωτήρ λάθρα γυναικί ἐλάλει καὶ οὐ φανερῶς ἵνα πάντες ἀκούσωμεν; (ἐστὶν αὕτη) μὴ ἀξιολογώτεραν ἡμῶν;[12] ... 4 Λευείς[13] λέγει Πέτρῳ· Πέτρε, ἀεί σοι τὸ ὀργίλον παράκειται καὶ ἄρτι οὕτως συνζητεῖς[14] τῇ γυναικὶ ὡς ἀντικείμενοι αὐτῇ. 5 εἰ ὁ σωτήρ ἀξίαν αὐτὴν ἡγήσατο, σὺ τις εἶ ἐξουθενῶν αὐτήν; 6 πάντως γὰρ ἐκεῖνος εἰδὼς[15] αὐτὴν ἀσφαλῶς ἠγάπησεν. 7 Μᾶλλον αἰσχυνθῶμεν[16] καὶ ἐνδυσάμενοι τὸν τέλειον ἄνθρωπον, ἐκεῖνο τὸ προσταχθὲν ἡμῖν ποιήσωμεν,[17] κηρύξωμεν τὸ εὐαγγέλιον, μηδὲν ὁρίζοντες, μηδὲ νομοθετοῦντες, ὡς εἶπεν ὁ σωτήρ· 8 ταῦτα εἶπων ὁ Λευεις μὲν ἀπελθὼν ἤρχεν κηρύσσειν τὸ εὐαγγέλιον κατὰ Μαριάμμην.

Vocabulary

ἀεί, ever, always; eternal, eternally, constantly; at that time

ἀνάπαυσις, ἡ, relief, rest

ἀντίκειμαι (w. dat.), be opposed to somebody; subst. adversary ἑτερογνωμονέω, be of a different opinion, not be in agreement with

ἀξιόλογος, -ον, important, worthy; comp. ἀξιολογώτερος, more important/worthy

ἐξετάζω, scrutinize, examine; question

ἄξιος, -α, -ον, worthy, deserving; proper, fitting; ἀξίως (adv.), worthily

ἀσφαλής, -ές, safe; subst. (τὸ) ἀσφαλές, safeguard; ἀσφαλῶς, safely; for certain, beyond a doubt

δρόμος, ὁ, racing, running; the course of (one's) life, course of a season (καιρός)

ἐνδύω, [1]aor. inf. ἐνδῦσαι: dress, put on (clothing); mid. clothe oneself, wear

ἔννοια, ἡ, thought

ἐξετάζω, look for, make a careful search for

ἐξουδενόω (= ἐξουδενέω), despise, treat with contempt

ἡγέομαι (w. inf.), lead the way; consider, regard it necessary, think; subst. ptc. leader, chief; pass. be led

λάθρα, secretly (adv.)

λοιπός, -ή, -όν, remaining, rest; (τὸ) λοιπόν, from now on, finally; (adv.); οἱ λοιποί/τὰ λοιπά the rest/others

νομοθετέω, enact laws, legislate

ὁρίζω, set limits; appoint, set; administer an oath; pass. be fixed/determined

---

[11] S.v. λέγω; pf. inf., table 9.1.5(d).
[12] Gen. of comp. (cf. IV, 10).
[13] Λευί, Levi (indecl.).
[14] συνζ > συζ.
[15] S.v. οἶδα.
[16] Hort. subj. (cf. IV, 12).
[17] Hort. subj.

ὀργίλος, -η, -ον, inclined to anger, quick-tempered; subst. hot temper; one of violent temper

οὕτω / οὕτως, in this way, so, in the same way; such

πάντως (adv.), certainly, doubtless; strictly

παρακαλέω, beg, urge, encourage; request, ask, appeal to; comfort

πρᾶγμα, τό, a matter, event, affair; thing

προστάσσω, pf. pass. ptc. προστεταγμένος: command, order; pass. be fixed, determined

σιωπάω, keep silent, say nothing; become quiet

τέλειος, -α, -ον, complete, perfect; mature, full-grown (of persons); superl. τελειότατος, -η, -ον, most perfect; τὰ τέλεια, mature animals

φανερός, -ά, -όν, known, visible; evident, notable; φανερῶς (adv.), openly, publicly

1.8.

Protoevangelium of James: Verifying the Virginity of Mary

(Prot. Jas. 13–16, 19–20)

Date: 75–125 CE.

Text: Ronald F. Hock, *The Infancy Gospels of James and Thomas* (Santa Rosa, CA: Polebridge Press, 1995).

This text is a proto-gospel in the sense that it narrates the events leading up to Jesus' birth, with a special interest in Mary (Μαρία/Μαριάμμη) and her purity. Other texts concerned with the purity of women include IG II² 1366 (§7.2), IMilet VI, 22 (§7.14), LSCG 154 (§7.7), and IG XII Suppl. 126 (§7.16).
Related Readings: Prot. Jas. 8, 11–12 (§1.14).

JOSEPH ACCUSES MARY

13:1 Καὶ ἐγένετο αὐτῇ ἕκτος μήν,[1] καὶ ἰδοὺ ἦλθεν Ἰωσὴφ ἀπὸ τῶν οἰκοδομῶν αὐτοῦ καὶ εἰσῆλθεν ἐν τῷ οἴκῳ καὶ εὗρεν αὐτὴν ὠγκωμένην. 2 καὶ ἔτυψεν τὸ πρόσωπον αὐτοῦ καὶ ἔρριψεν αὐτὸν χαμαὶ ἐπὶ τὸν σάκκον καὶ ἔκλαυσεν πικρῶς λέγων· Ποίῳ[2] προσώπῳ ἀτενίσω πρὸς κύριον τὸν θεόν; 3 τί ἄρα εὔξωμαι περὶ αὐτῆς ὅτι παρθένον παρέλαβον αὐτὴν ἐκ ναοῦ κυρίου τοῦ θεοῦ καὶ οὐκ ἐφύλαξα αὐτήν; 4 τίς ὁ θηρεύσας με; τίς τὸ πονηρὸν τοῦτο ἐποίησεν ἐν τῷ οἴκῳ μου; τίς ᾐχμαλώτευσε τὴν παρθένον ἀπ᾽ ἐμοῦ καὶ ἐμίανεν αὐτήν; 5 μήτι ἐν ἐμοὶ ἀνεκεφαλαιώθη ἡ ἱστορία τοῦ Ἀδάμ; ὥσπερ γὰρ Ἀδὰμ ἦν ἐν τῇ ὥρᾳ τῆς δοξολογίας αὐτοῦ καὶ ἦλθεν ὁ ὄφις καὶ εὗρεν τὴν Εὔαν μόνην καὶ ἐξηπάτησεν αὐτὴν καὶ ἐμίανεν αὐτήν, οὕτως κἀμοὶ[3] συνέβη.

---

[1] Of pregnancy.
[2] Dat., "with what sort of … ".
[3] καὶ ἐμοί.

Vocabulary

αἰχμαλοτεύω, take prisoner, lure away; pass. be taken prisoner

ἀνακεφαλαιόω, sum up, recapitulate

ἀτενίζω, 2. ἀτενίσω: stare at, look intently at (w. dat./πρός)

ἄρα, so, then

δοξολογία, ἡ, a prayer

ἕκτος, -η, -ον, sixth

ἐξαπατάω, deceive

εὔχομαι, 3. ηὐξάμην, ¹aor. mid. impv. εὖξαι: pray; vow

θηρεύω, set a trap for somebody (acc.)

ἱστορία, ἡ, story, account

μήν, ὁ, μηνός, month

μήτι, used in questions anticipating a negative answer

μιαίνω, 3. ἐμίανα, 5. μεμίαμμαι: defile, contaminate; mid. defile oneself

ναός, ὁ, temple, inner part of Jewish temple, sanctuary

ὀγκόω, pass. to swell (through pregancy); be pregnant

οἰκοδομή, ἡ, building project, construction project

παραλαμβάνω, receive, accept; take, take charge of; take over/receive somebody
 as a prisoner; inherit sacred objects; succeed to an office

παρθένος, ἡ, virgin, unmarried girl

ποῖος, -α, -ον (interrog. pron.), what, which; what sort/kind of

ῥίπτω, 3. ἔρριψα, ¹aor. impv. ῥῖψον, 6. ἐρρίφην: throw, cast away; lay/put
 something down

συλλαμβάνω, 3. συνέλαβον, inf. συλλαβεῖν, ²aor. mid. impv. συλλαβοῦ,
 6. συνελήμφθην: lay hold of, seize; comprehend; conceive a child; mid. take part
 in something with somebody

τύπτω, 3. ἔτυψα: beat, strike

φυλάσσω (Att. φυλάττω), keep; guard, protect; observe, follow; pass. be kept

χαμαί, on/to the ground

13:6 Καὶ ἀνέστη Ἰωσὴφ ἀπὸ τοῦ σάκκου καὶ ἐκάλεσεν αὐτὴν καὶ εἶπεν αὐτῇ·
Μεμελημένη θεῷ, τί τοῦτο ἐποίησας; 7 ἐπελάθου κυρίου τοῦ θεοῦ σου; τί
ἐταπείνωσας τὴν ψυχήν σου, ἡ ἀνατραφεῖσα εἰς τὰ ἅγια τῶν ἁγίων καὶ τροφὴν
λαμβάνουσα ἐκ χειρὸς ἀγγέλου; 8 Ἡ δὲ ἔκλαυσεν πικρῶς λέγουσα ὅτι καθαρά
εἰμι ἐγὼ καὶ ἄνδρα οὐ γινώσκω. 9 Καὶ εἶπεν αὐτῇ Ἰωσήφ· Πόθεν οὖν τοῦτό ἐστιν
ἐν τῇ γαστρί σου; 10 Ἡ δὲ εἶπεν· (I swear, as) Ζῆ⁴ κύριος ὁ θεός μου καθότι οὐ
γινώσκω πόθεν ἐστὶν ἐν ἐμοί.

---

⁴ Note that the root of ζῶ (-άω) is actually √ ζη (not √ ζα). The present active paradigm of ζῶ is: 1st ζῶ,
2nd ζῆς, 3rd ζῆ / pl. 1st ζῶμεν, 2nd ζῆτε, 3rd ζῶσι(ν).

Vocabulary

ἀνατρέφω, 3. ἀνέθρεψα, 6. ἀνετράφην: are for, bring up, raise

γαστήρ, -τρος, ἡ, belly, stomach; womb

ἐπιλανθάνομαι (w. gen.), 2. ἐπιλήσομαι, 3. ἐπελαθόμην, pf. pass. ptc. ἐπειλημμένος: forget; to neglect, overlook

καθαρός, -ά, -όν, pure, clean, innocent; superl. καθαρώτατος, purest

καθότι, (for an oath) "I swear that (ὅτι)"; because (= διότι)

κλαίω, pres. ptc. κλάων, 3. ἔκλαυσα: weep (for), cry

μέλω, μέλει τινι, impers., it is a care/concern to somebody (dat.); pass. be a special interest to somebody (dat.)

πικρός, -ά, -όν, bitter, harsh; fierce (animal); πικρῶς, bitterly, fiercely

πόθεν (interog. adv.), from where? how? in what way? why?

σάκκος, ὁ, sackcloth (course cloth made of goat or camel hair)

ταπεινόω, to humble, humiliate; bring low

JOSEPH'S VISION

14:1 Καὶ ἐφοβήθη ὁ Ἰωσὴφ σφόδρα καὶ ἠρέμησεν ἐξ αὐτῆς, διαλογιζόμενος (with) αὐτὴν τί ποιήσει. 2 καὶ εἶπεν Ἰωσὴφ ἐν ἑαυτῷ· Ἐὰν αὐτῆς κρύψω τὸ ἁμάρτημα,[5] εὑρεθήσομαι μαχόμενος τῷ νόμῳ κυρίου· 3 καὶ ἐὰν αὐτὴν φανερώσω τοῖς υἱοῖς Ἰσραήλ, φοβοῦμαι μήπως ἀγγελικόν ἐστιν τὸ ἐν ἑαυτῇ, καὶ εὑρεθήσομαι παραδιδοὺς ἀθῷον αἷμα εἰς κρίσμα[6] θανάτου. 4 τί οὖν (with) αὐτὴν ποιήσω; λάθρα αὐτὴν ἀπολύσω ἀπ᾽ ἐμοῦ. 5 Καὶ κατέλαβεν αὐτὸν νύξ. καὶ ἰδοὺ ἄγγελος κυρίου φαίνεται αὐτῷ κατ᾽ ὄνειρον λέγων· Μὴ φοβηθῇς τὴν παῖδα ταύτην· τὸ γὰρ ἐν αὐτῇ ὂν ἐκ πνεύματός ἐστιν ἁγίου. 6 τέξεται δέ σοι υἱὸν καὶ καλέσεις τὸ ὄνομα αὐτοῦ Ἰησοῦν· αὐτὸς γὰρ σώσει τὸν λαὸν αὐτοῦ ἐκ τῶν ἁμαρτημάτων αὐτῶν. 7 καὶ ἀνέστη Ἰωσὴφ ἀπὸ τοῦ ὕπνου καὶ ἐδόξασεν τὸν θεὸν τοῦ Ἰσραὴλ τὸν δόντα αὐτῷ τὴν χάριν ταύτην. 8 καὶ ἐφύλασσε τὴν παῖδα.

Vocabulary

ἀγγελικός, -ή, -όν, angelic, heaven-sent

ἀθῷος, -ον, innocent

ἁμάρτημα, τό, sin, transgression

διαλογίζομαι, consider, ponder

ἠρεμέω, be quiet; not speak with (ἐκ) somebody

καταλαμβάνω, obtain, attain, seize, overtake; catch up to somebody (acc.); understand; fall (of night)

---

[5]   αὐτῆς...τὸ ἁμάρτημα.

[6]   κρίσμα > κρίμα.

κρίμα, -ματος, τό (= κρίσμα), legal case; legal judgment

κρύπτω, impf. pass. ἐκρυβόμην, 3. ἔκρυψα, 6. ἐκρύβην, [2]aor. pass. inf. κρυβῆναι, pf. pass. ptc. κεκρυμμένος: cover, hide, conceal; pass. be hiding

λάθρα, secretly (adv.)

μάχομαι, quarrel, dispute; fight; fight with (ἐν/dat.), be in conflict with; οἱ μαχόμενοι, those who fight, combatants

μήπως, that perhaps, lest somehow

ὄνειρος, ὁ, a dream; κατ᾽ ὄνειρον, in a dream

παῖς, παιδός, ὁ/ἡ, child (in relation to parents); slave/servant (in relation to a master/God); ἐκ παιδός, from (one's) childhood

σφόδρα, very (much), extremely, greatly (adv.)

τίκτω, 2. τέξομαι, 3. ἔτεκον, 4. τέτοκα, pf. pass. τέτεγμαι, fm. pf. pass. ptc. τετοκυῖα, 6. ἐτέχθην: give birth (to)

ὕπνος, ὁ, sleep; καθ᾽ ὕπνον, in a dream

φαίνω, pres. pass. inf. φαίνεσθαι, 2. φανῶ/φανοῦμαι, 6. ἐφάνην, [2]aor. fm. pass. ptc. φανεῖσα, aor. pass. impv. φάνηθι: shine, give light; mid. make one's appearance; pass. appear, appear to be, be seen, become visible; attend (a meeting)

φανερόω, make known, show, manifest, reveal

φυλάσσω (Att. φυλάττω), keep; guard, protect; observe, follow; pass. be kept

MARY AND JOSEPH ACCUSED

15:1 Ἦλθεν δὲ Ἄννας ὁ γραμματεὺς πρὸς αὐτὸν καὶ εἶπεν αὐτῷ· Ἰωσήφ, διὰ τί[7] οὐκ ἐφάνης τῇ συνόδῳ ἡμῶν; 2 Καὶ εἶπεν αὐτῷ· Ὅτι ἔκαμον ἐκ τῆς ὁδοῦ καὶ ἀνεπαυσάμην τὴν μίαν[8] ἡμέραν. 3 Καὶ ἐστράφη Ἄννας καὶ εἶδεν τὴν Μαρίαν ὠγκωμένην. 4 Καὶ ἀπῄει δρομαῖος πρὸς τὸν ἀρχιερέα καὶ εἶπεν αὐτῷ· Ἰδοὺ Ἰωσήφ, ᾧ σὺ μαρτυρεῖς, ἠνόμησεν σφόδρα. 5 Καὶ εἶπεν ὁ ἀρχιερεύς· Τί τοῦτο; 6 Καὶ εἶπεν· Τὴν παρθένον ἣν Ἰωσὴφ παρέλαβεν ἐκ ναοῦ κυρίου, ἐμίανεν αὐτὴν καὶ ἔκλεψεν τοὺς γάμους[9] (with) αὐτῆς καὶ οὐκ ἐφανέρωσεν τοῖς υἱοῖς Ἰσραήλ. 7 Καὶ εἶπεν αὐτῷ ὁ ἀρχιερεύς· Ἰωσὴφ ταῦτα ἐποίησεν; 8 Καὶ εἶπεν αὐτῷ· Ἀπόστειλον ὑπηρέτας καὶ εὑρήσεις τὴν παρθένον ὠγκωμένην. 9 καὶ ἀπῆλθον οἱ ὑπηρέται καὶ εὗρον αὐτὴν καθὼς εἶπεν καὶ ἀπήγαγον αὐτὴν ἅμα τῷ Ἰωσὴφ εἰς τὸ κριτήριον.

Vocabulary

ἅμα, together with (w. dat.): adv. at the same time, when, all at once

ἀναπαύω, [1]aor. mid. ἀνεπαυσάμην, fut. mid. ἀναπαήσομαι: to cause to rest; to end, finish; mid. to rest

---

[7] διὰ τί, "why?"

[8] I.e., "first."

[9] κλέπτω τοὺς γάμους, "to secretly consummate marriage" (i.e., without the blessing of the community).

ἀνομέω, to sin, act lawlessly

ἀπάγω, 3. ἀπήγαγον: lead away by force; bring before, bring by force to (εἰς / acc. of goal) somebody/something; lead somebody somewhere

ἄπειμι (fr. εἶμι, cf. paradigm, 9.14), ptc. ἀπιόντος, impf. ἀπῆειν: leave, depart (for paradigm of εἶμι see table 9.14)

δρομαῖος, -α, -ον, running at full speed

κάμνω, ²aor. ἔκαμον: be worn out, tired

κριτήριον, τό, court

ὀγκόω, pass. to swell (through pregancy); be pregnant

παραλαμβάνω, receive, accept; take, take charge of; take over/receive somebody as a prisoner; inherit sacred objects; succeed to an office

παρθένος, ἡ, virgin, unmarried girl

στρέφω, 6. ἐστράφην (dep.): to turn, turn around; change into (εἰς) something; make revolve, turn something around; pass (dep.), turn toward; mid. turn one-self around in circles

σύνοδος, ἡ, assembly, meeting

ὑπηρέτης, -ου, ὁ, assistant, attendant; helper

15:10 Καὶ εἶπεν αὐτῇ ὁ ἀρχιερεύς· Μαρία, τί τοῦτο ἐποίησας; τί ἐταπείνωσας τὴν ψυχήν σου; 11 ἐπελάθου[10] κυρίου τοῦ θεοῦ σου, ἡ ἀνατραφεῖσα εἰς τὰ ἅγια τῶν ἁγίων καὶ λαβοῦσα τροφὴν ἐκ χειρὸς ἀγγέλων; 12 σὺ (of all people) ἡ ἀκούσασα τῶν ὕμνων αὐτῶν καὶ χορεύσασα ἐνώπιον αὐτῶν, τί τοῦτο ἐποίησας; 13 Ἡ δὲ ἔκλαυσεν πικρῶς λέγουσα· (I swear, as) Ζῇ κύριος ὁ θεὸς καθότι καθαρά εἰμι ἐνώπιον αὐτοῦ καὶ ἄνδρα οὐ γινώσκω. 14 Καὶ εἶπεν ὁ ἀρχιερεύς· Ἰωσήφ, τί τοῦτο ἐποίησας; 15 Εἶπεν δὲ Ἰωσήφ· (I swear, as) Ζῇ κύριος καθότι καθαρός εἰμὶ ἐξ αὐτῆς. 16 Καὶ εἶπεν ὁ ἀρχιερεύς· Μὴ ψευδομαρτύρει, ἀλλὰ λέγε τὰ ἀληθῆ· ἔκλεψας τοὺς γάμους σου καὶ οὐκ ἐφανέρωσας τοῖς υἱοῖς Ἰσραήλ, 17 καὶ οὐκ ἔκλινας τὴν κεφαλήν σου ὑπὸ τὴν κραταιὰν χεῖραν (of God) ὅπως εὐλογηθῇ τὸ σπέρμα σου. 18 καὶ Ἰωσὴφ ἐσίγησεν.

Vocabulary

ἀληθής (m. and fm.), -ές (nt.), true, truthful

ἀνατρέφω, 3. ἀνέθρεψα, 6. ἀνετράφην: care for, bring up, raise

γάμος, ὁ (oft. in pl. w. no different in meaning), wedding; πρὸς γάμον, in marriage

ἐνώπιον (w. gen.), before, in the presence of

ἐπιλανθάνομαι (w. gen.), 2. ἐπιλήσομαι, 3. ἐπελαθόμην, pf. pass. ptc. ἐπειλημμένος: forget; to neglect, overlook

εὐλογέω, bless; (as a Heb. euphemism) to curse

καθότι, (in an oath) "I swear that (ὅτι)," because

---

[10] S.v. ἐπιλανθάνομαι.

κλέπτω, steal

κλίνω, 3. ἔκλινα: bend down; κλίνω τὴν κεφαλήν, bow one's head; κλίνω τὰ γόνατα, fall on one's knees

κραταιός, -ά, -όν, powerful, mighty

σιγάω, be silent

σπέρμα, τό, seed, offspring, children; descendants

ταπεινόω, to humble, humiliate; bring low, be made low

τροφή, ἡ, food

ὕμνος, ὁ, hymn

χορεύω, to dance in a chorus

ψευδομαρτυρέω, give false testimony, bear false witness

THE DRINK TEST

16:1 Καὶ εἶπεν ὁ ἀρχιερεύς· Ἀπόδος τὴν παρθένον ἣν παρέλαβες ἐκ ναοῦ κυρίου. 2 Καὶ περιδάκρυτος γενόμενος ὁ Ἰωσήφ... 3 Καὶ εἶπεν ὁ ἀρχιερεύς· Ποτιῶ ὑμᾶς τὸ ὕδωρ τῆς ἐλέγξεως κυρίου, καὶ φανερώσει τὸ ἁμάρτημα ὑμῶν ἐν[11] ὀφθαλμοῖς ὑμῶν. 4 Καὶ λαβὼν ὁ ἀρχιερεὺς ἐπότισεν τὸν Ἰωσὴφ καὶ ἔπεμψεν αὐτὸν εἰς τὴν ἔρημον, καὶ ἦλθεν ὁλόκληρος. 5 καὶ ἐπότισεν καὶ τὴν παῖδα καὶ ἔπεμψεν αὐτὴν εἰς τὴν ἐρεμίαν, καὶ κατέβη ὁλόκληρος. 6 Καὶ ἐθαύμασεν πᾶς ὁ λαὸς ὅτι οὐκ ἐφάνη ἡ ἁμαρτία αὐτῶν. 7 καὶ εἶπεν ὁ ἀρχιερεύς· Εἰ κύριος ὁ θεὸς οὐκ ἐφανέρωσεν τὸ ἁμάρτημα ὑμῶν, οὐδὲ ἐγὼ κρίνω ὑμᾶς. καὶ ἀπέλυσεν αὐτούς. 8 καὶ παρέλαβεν Ἰωσὴφ τὴν Μαριὰμ καὶ ἀπῄει ἐν τῷ οἴκῳ αὐτοῦ χαίρων καὶ δοξάζων τὸν θεὸν Ἰσραήλ.

Vocabulary

ἀποδίδωμι, [2]aor. impv. ἀπόδος: give; give back, return; hand over; deliver a letter; pay; repay, reimburse, reward; ἀποδοῦναι λόγον, give account, render financial accounts; grant; to give off (smoke)

ἔλεγξις, ἡ, pleading, test

ἐρημία, ἡ, desert

θαυμάζω, (intrans.) marvel, wonder, be amazed; (trans.) marvel, wonder at, admire

ὁλόκληρος, -ον, whole, unharmed

ὀφθαλμός, ὁ, eye

περιδάκρυτος, -ον, weeping bitterly

As the story continues, Joseph finds a cave and takes Mary inside and stations his sons to guard her. Next, he tells in his own words the story of what happened as he was walking along the road.

---

[11] ἐν, "before."

A CHILD IS BORN

19:1 Καὶ εἶδον γυναῖκα καταβαίνουσαν ἀπὸ τῆς ὀρεινῆς, καὶ εἶπέν μοι· Ἄνθρωπε,[12] ποῦ πορεύῃ; 2 Καὶ εἶπον· Μαῖαν ζητῶ Ἑβραίαν. 3 Καὶ ἀποκριθεῖσα εἶπέν μοι· Ἔξ Ἰσραὴλ εἶ; 4 Καὶ εἶπον αὐτῇ· Ναί. 5 Ἡ δὲ εἶπεν· Καὶ τίς ἐστιν ἡ γεννῶσα ἐν τῷ σπηλαίῳ; 6 Καὶ εἶπον ἐγώ· Ἡ μεμνηστευμένη μοι. 7 Καὶ εἶπέ μοι· Οὐκ ἔστι σου γυνή; 8 Καὶ εἶπον αὐτῇ· Μαρία ἐστίν, ἡ ἀνατραφεῖσα ἐν ναῷ κυρίου. καὶ ἐκληρωσάμην αὐτὴν (as) γυναῖκα, 9 καὶ οὐκ ἔστιν μου γυνή, ἀλλὰ σύλλημμα ἔχει ἐκ πνεύματος ἁγίου. 10 Καὶ εἶπεν ἡ μαῖα· Τοῦτο ἀληθές; 11 Καὶ εἶπεν αὐτῇ Ἰωσήφ· Δεῦρο καὶ ἴδε. 12 Καὶ ἀπῄει ἡ μαῖα μετ᾽ αὐτοῦ. 13 καὶ ἔστησαν ἐν τῷ τόπῳ[13] τοῦ σπηλαίου. καὶ ἦν νεφέλη σκοτεινὴ ἐπισκιάζουσα τὸ σπήλαιον.

Vocabulary
ἀνατρέφω, 3. ἀνέθρεψα, 6. ἀνετράφην: care for, bring up, raise
δεῦρο (adv.), here; come here
Ἑβραῖος, -α, Hebrew-speaking
ἐπισκιάζω, to overshadow; to cover
κληρόω, obtain/appoint by lot; pass. be assigned
μαῖα, ἡ, midwife
μνηστεύω, betroth; pass. be betrothed, engaged to somebody (dat.)
ναός, ὁ, temple, inner part of Jewish temple, sanctuary
νεφέλη, ἡ, cloud
ὀρεινός, -ή, -όν, hilly, mountainous; subst. hill country
σπήλαιον, τό, cave (as a place of refuge, as a hideout)
σύλλημμα, -ματος, τό, unborn child
σκοτεινός, -ή, -όν, dark

19:14 καὶ εἶπεν ἡ μαῖα· Ἐμεγαλύνθη ἡ ψυχή μου σήμερον, ὅτι εἶδον οἱ ὀφθαλμοί μου παράδοξα σήμερον, ὅτι σωτηρία τῷ Ἰσραὴλ γεγένηται. 15 Καὶ παραχρῆμα ἡ νεφέλη ὑπεστέλλετο τοῦ σπηλαίου, καὶ ἐφάνη φῶς μέγα ἐν τῷ σπηλαίῳ ὥστε τοὺς ὀφθαλμοὺς μὴ φέρειν. 16 Καὶ πρὸς ὀλίγον[14] τὸ φῶς ἐκεῖνο ὑπεστέλλετο, ἕως ἐφάνη βρέφος· καὶ ἦλθεν καὶ ἔλαβε μαστὸν ἐκ τῆς μητρὸς αὐτοῦ Μαρίας. 17 Καὶ ἀνεβόησεν ἡ μαῖα καὶ εἶπεν· Ὡς μεγάλη μοι ἡ σήμερον ἡμέρα, ὅτι εἶδον τὸ καινὸν θέαμα τοῦτο. 18 Καὶ ἐξῆλθεν ἐκ τοῦ σπηλαίου ἡ μαῖα, καὶ ἀπήντησεν ἡ μαῖα Σαλώμη. καὶ εἶπεν αὐτῇ· Σαλώμη Σαλώμη, καίνον σοι θέαμα ἔχω ἐξηγήσασθαι· παρθένος ἐγέννησεν ἃ οὐ χωρεῖ ἡ φύσις αὐτῆς. 19 καὶ εἶπεν Σαλώμη· (I swear as) Ζῇ κύριος ὁ θεός μου, ἐὰν μὴ βαλῶ[15]

---

[12] ἄνθρωπε in voc. oft. means "sir."
[13] ἐν τῷ τόπῳ, i.e., "in front of."
[14] πρὸς ὀλίγον, "a little later."
[15] βάλλω meaning "to insert" (cf. Prot. Jas. 20:2).

τὸν δάκτυλόν μου καὶ ἐρευνήσω τὴν φύσιν αὐτῆς, οὐ μὴ πιστεύω[16] ὅτι ἡ παρθένος ἐγέννησεν.

Vocabulary

ἀναβοάω, cry out

ἀπαντάω, 3. ἀπήντησα, [1]aor. inf. ἀπαντῆσαι: meet somebody (w. dat.); attend a meeting; go (somewhere) to meet somebody (dat.)

βρέφος, ους, τό, unborn child, fetus; infant

δάκτυλος, ὁ, finger

ἐξηγέομαι, tell (in detail), report

ἐρευνάω > ἐραυνάω, examine

θέαμα, -ματος, τό, a sight, spectacle

καινός, -ή, -όν, new; strange; comp. καινότερος

μαστός, ὁ, (woman's) breast; chest

μεγαλύνω, praise, glorify, exalt

ὀλίγος, -η, -ον, little, few; pl. δι᾽ ὀλίγων, in a few (words), briefly; (πρὸς) ὀλίγον, a short while; μετ᾽ ὀλιγον, after a brief (time)

παράδοξος, -ον, strange, wonderful; τὰ παράδοξα, wonderful things

σήμερον (adv.), today

σωτηρία, ἡ, deliverance, rescue, salvation

ὑποστέλλω, withdraw; mid. draw back, disappear

φύσις, ἡ, circumstance; the nature (of something), natural condition; substance; nature; natural being, creature; female genitalia

χωρέω, go forward, make progress; (of money) be spent; hold, contain something (gen.); subst. ptc. Payment

SALOME'S FOLLY

20:1 Καὶ εἰσῆλθεν ἡ μαῖα καὶ εἶπεν· Μαρία, σχημάτισον σεαυτήν· οὐ γὰρ μικρὸς ἀγὼν πρόκειται περὶ σοῦ. 2 Καὶ ἡ Μαρία ἀκούσασα ταῦτα ἐσχημάτισεν αὐτήν. καὶ ἔβαλε Σαλώμη τὸν δάκτυλον αὐτῆς εἰς τὴν φύσιν αὐτῆς. 3 καὶ ἀνηλάλαξεν Σαλώμη καὶ εἶπεν· Οὐαὶ (to me) τῇ ἀνομίᾳ μου καὶ τῇ ἀπιστίᾳ μου, ὅτι ἐξεπείρασα θεὸν ζῶντα. 4 καὶ ἰδοὺ ἡ χείρ μου πυρὶ ἀποπίπτει ἀπ᾽ ἐμοῦ.[17] 5 Καὶ ἔκλινεν τὰ γόνατα πρὸς τὸν δεσπότην Σαλώμη λέγουσα· Ὁ θεὸς τῶν πατέρων μου, μνήσθητί[18] μου ὅτι σπέρμα εἰμὶ Ἀβραὰμ[19] καὶ Ἰσαὰκ καὶ Ἰακώβ. 6 μὴ παραδειγματίσῃς με τοῖς υἱοῖς Ἰσραήλ, ἀλλὰ ἀπόδος με τοῖς πένησιν. 7 σὺ

---

[16] οὐ μή + aor. subj. (emph. fut. neg., cf. IV, 8).

[17] ἀπό, "before."

[18] S.v. μιμνήσκομαι.

[19] Ἀβραάμ, Ἰσαάκ, Ἰακώβ (indecl.) are all gen.

γὰρ οἶδας, δέσποτα, ὅτι ἐπὶ τῷ σῷ ὀνόματι τὰς θεραπείας ἐπετέλουν καὶ τὸν μισθόν μου παρὰ σοῦ ἐλάμβανον.

Vocabulary

ἀγών, -ῶνος, ὁ, contest, game, race; struggle; legal trial, test; pl., athletic games

ἀναλαλάζω, cry out

ἀνομία, ἡ, lawless deed; lawlessness

ἀπιστία, ἡ, unbelief, incredibility

ἀποπίπτω, burn up

γόνυ, -νατος, τό, pl. γόνατα: knee

δεσπότης, master, lord, ruler; owner.

ἐκπειράζω, to test

ἐπιτελέω, to complete, perform, accomplish; celebrate a birthday

θεραπεία, ἡ, worship of a god; pl. divine services; medical treatment, healing

κλίνω, 3. ἔκλινα: bend down; κλίνω τὴν κεφαλήν, bow one's head; ἔκλινεν τὰ γόνατα, fall on one's knees

μικρός, -α, -ον, little, small, of little importance

μιμνήσκομαι (w. gen.) (also μνήσκομαι), 6. ἐμνήσθην, 2nd sg. aor. pass. impv. μνήσθητι, 4. μέμνημαι: remember somebody (gen.), recollect; make mention of (w. gen.); pass. dep. be remembered, remember

μισθός, ὁ, wages, pay; reward; physician's fee

οὐαί (w. dat.), woe/alas; concerning, by reason of (dat.)

παραδειγματίζω, make an example of somebody (acc.)

πένης, -ητος, ὁ, poor person

πρόκειμαι, to face

σχηματίζω, to position (in this context it refers to Mary positioning her body to be probed to verify her virginity) (cf. Prot. Jas. 20:2)

20:8 Καὶ ἰδοὺ ἄγγελος κυρίου ἐπέστη λέγων πρὸς αὐτήν· Σαλώμη Σαλώμη, ἐπήκουσεν ὁ πάντων δεσπότης τῆς δεήσεώς σου. 9 προσένεγκε[20] τὴν χεῖρά σου τῷ παιδίῳ καὶ βάστασον αὐτό, καὶ ἔσται σοι σωτηρία καὶ χαρά. 10 Καὶ προσῆλθε Σαλώμη τῷ παιδίῳ καὶ ἐβάστασεν αὐτὸ λέγουσα· Προσκυνήσω αὐτῷ, ὅτι οὗτος ἐγεννήθη βασιλεὺς τῷ Ἰσραήλ. 11 καὶ παραχρῆμα ἰάθη Σαλώμη καὶ ἐξῆλθεν ἐκ τοῦ σπηλαίου δεδικαιωμένη. 12 Καὶ ἰδοὺ φωνὴ λέγουσα· Σαλώμη Σαλώμα, μὴ ἀναγγείλῃς ὅσα εἶδες παράδοξα ἕως ἔλθῃ ὁ παῖς εἰς Ἱεροσάλημα.

Vocabulary

ἀναγγέλλω, tell, proclaim; report, inform

βαστάζω, pick up; carry a burden, bear a burden; remove, take away

---

[20] S.v. προσφέρω.

δέησις, -εως, ἡ, prayer

δικαιόω, declare somebody to be justified; pass. be aquitted

ἐπακούω, hear, listen to; heed

ἰάομαι, 2. ἰάσομαι, 3. ἰασάμην, 6. ἰάθην: heal/cure; find a remedy

παῖς, παιδός, ὁ/ἡ, child (in relation to parents); slave/servant (in relation to a master/God); ἐκ παιδός, from childhood

παράδοξος, -ον, strange, wonderful

παραχρῆμα, immediately, instantly; recently

προσφέρω, 3. προσήνεγκον: bring to somebody; offer something as a sacrifice; offer/reach out one's hand

SELECT BIBLIOGRAPHY

Bovon, François. *New Testament and Christian Apocrypha.* Grand Rapids, MI: Baker Academic, 2011.

Clivaz, Claire (ed.). *Infancy Gospels: Stories and Identities.* Tübingen: Mohr Siebeck, 2011.

Davies, Stevan L. *The Infancy Gospels of Jesus: Apocryphal Tales from the Childhoods of Mary and Jesus.* Woodstock, VT: SkyLight Paths, 2009.

Foskett, Mary F. *A Virgin Conceived: Mary and Classical Representations of Virginity.* Bloomington: Indiana University Press, 2002.

1.9.

Gospel of Peter: The Crucifixion of Jesus

(Gos. Pet. 2–7)

Provenance: Syria. The Gospel of Peter (Akhmim Fragment, P[Cair 10759]) was discovered, along with the Apocalypse of Peter (§5.8), in the tomb of a Christian monk in Akhmim, north of Nag Hammadi, in 1887.

Date: Early layers may date to the late first century CE, with later layers added from 125 to 150 CE.

Text: Paul Foster, *The Gospel of Peter: Introduction, Critical Edition and Commentary* (Leiden: Brill, 2010), 179–195; Bernhard: 56–78 (§§2–23).

Special Features: This is the only gospel that explicitly narrates the resurrection of Jesus (Gos. Pet. 10). It is also notable for exonerating Pontius Pilate for the crucifixion of Jesus and ascribing the responsibility to Herod Antipas (1:1–2). This gospel has many other notable features. For example, Jesus' cry of dereliction on the cross has been changed to "My power, my power, you have forsaken me" (Gos. Pet. 5:15–20; cf. Mark 15:34, Matt 27:46, Ps 21:2 [LXX = Ps 22:1 MT]). This text also includes many supernatural embellishments.

Related Readings: Gos. Pet. 8–13 (§1.15).

2:3 Εἰστήκει δὲ ἐκεῖ Ἰωσήφ, ὁ φίλος Πειλάτου καὶ τοῦ κυρίου, καὶ εἰδὼς[1] ὅτι σταυρίσκειν[2] αὐτὸν μέλλουσιν[3] ἦλθεν πρὸς τὸν Πειλᾶτον καὶ ᾔτησε τὸ σῶμα τοῦ κυρίου πρὸς ταφήν. 4 καὶ ὁ Πειλᾶτος πέμψας (a messenger) πρὸς Ἡρώδην ᾔτησεν αὐτοῦ τὸ σῶμα. 5 καὶ ὁ Ἡρώδης ἔφη· Ἀδελφὲ Πειλᾶτε, εἰ καὶ μή τις αὐτὸν

---

[1] Temp. adv. ptc. (cf. IV, 1); since the pf. of this verb functions as a pres. tense, the ptc. should be trans. using the helping word "when."

[2] σταυρίσκω = σταυρόω.

[3] μέλλω takes a complementary inf.

ᾐτήκει, ἡμεῖς αὐτὸν ἐθάπτομεν, ἐπεὶ καὶ σάββατον ἐπιφώσκει. γέγραπται γὰρ ἐν τῷ νόμῳ ἥλιον μὴ δῦναι[4] ἐπὶ πεφονευμένῳ. καὶ παρέδωκεν αὐτὸν τῷ λαῷ πρὸ μιᾶς[5] τῶν ἀζύμων, τῆς ἑορτῆς αὐτῶν.

Vocabulary

ἄζυμα, τά, Festival of Unleavened Bread (i.e., Passover)
ἐπιφώσκω, to become daylight, to dawn; draw near
ἑορτή, ἡ, festival, feast
ἥλιος, ὁ, sun; Ἥλιος, ὁ, Helios (sun god)
ταφή, ἡ, burial, burial place
φίλος, -η, -ον, beloved, pleasant; popular; subst. friend

3:6 Οἱ δὲ λαβόντες τὸν κύριον[6] ὤθουν αὐτὸν[7] τρέχοντες καὶ ἔλεγον· σύρωμεν[8] τὸν υἱὸν τοῦ θεου ἐξουσίαν αὐτοῦ ἐσχηκότες.[9] 7 καὶ πορφύραν αὐτὸν περιέβαλον καὶ ἐκάθισαν αὐτὸν ἐπὶ καθέδραν κρίσεως, λέγοντες· Δικαίως κρῖνε, βασιλεῦ τοῦ Ἰσραήλ. 8 καὶ τις αὐτῶν ἐνεγκὼν[10] στέφανον ἀκάνθινον ἔθηκεν ἐπὶ τῆς κεφαλῆς τοῦ κυρίου, 9 καὶ ἕτεροι ἑστῶτες[11] ἐνέπτυον αὐτοῦ ταῖς ὄψεσι, καὶ ἄλλοι τὰς σιαγόνας αὐτοῦ ἐράπισαν ἕτεροι καλάμῳ ἔνυσσον αὐτὸν καί τινες αὐτὸν ἐμάστιζον λέγοντες· Ταύτῃ τῇ τιμῇ τιμήσωμεν[12] τὸν υἱὸν τοῦ θεοῦ.

Vocabulary

ἀκάνθινος, -η, -ον, thorny, of thorns
ἐμπτύω, impf. ἐνέπτυον: spit on
καθέδρα, ἡ, chair, seat
καθίζω, (instrans) sit down, take one's seat; stay; (trans.) cause to sit, set
κάλαμος, ὁ, reed, stalk, staff
κρίσις, -εως, ἡ, judgment, judging; condemnation
μαστίζω, strike with a whip, scourge
νύσσω, to prick, stab
ὄψις, -εως, ἡ, appearance, countenance, face; vision, apparition
περιβάλλω, [2]aor. περιέβαλον, pf. ptc. περιβεβλημένος: lay something around, put around, clothe with something; mid. throw around oneself; to embrace, clothe oneself; pass. be clothed
πορφύρα, ἡ, purple cloth
ῥαπίζω, to strike, slap

---

[4] Impv. inf.
[5] Sc. ἡμέρας, i.e., "day one," "the first day."
[6] I.e., the body of the Lord.
[7] Perhaps on a cart.
[8] Hort. subj. (cf. IV, 12).
[9] S.v. ἔχω; causal adv. ptc. ("because") (cf. IV, 1.4).
[10] S.v. φέρω.
[11] Cf. table 9.12.
[12] Hort. subj. (IV, 12)

σιαγών, -όνος, ἡ, cheek
στέφανος, ὁ, wreath, crown; crowning
σύρω, to drag, pull
τιμάω, ¹aor. ἐτίμησα, ¹aor. ptc. τιμάς: to honor
τιμή, -ῆς, ἡ, honor, pl. honors; price/cost, value; (gen.), at a price of
τρέχω, 2. δραμοῦμαι, 3. ἔδραμον: run; exert oneself
ὠθέω, push, shove somebody

4:10 καὶ ἤνεγκον δύο κακούργους καὶ ἐσταύρωσαν ἀνὰ μέσον αὐτῶν τὸν
κύριον· αὐτὸς δὲ ἐσιώπα ὡς μηδένα πόνον ἔχων. 11 καὶ ὅτε ὤρθωσαν τὸν
σταυρόν, ἐπέγραψαν ὅτι οὗτός ἐστιν ὁ βασιλεὺς τοῦ Ἰσραήλ. 12 καὶ τεθεικότες
τὰ ἐνδύματα ἔμπροσθεν αὐτοῦ διεμερίσαντο, καὶ λαχμὸν ἔβαλον ἐπ' αὐτοῖς. 13
εἷς δέ τις τῶν κακούργων ἐκείνων ὠνείδισεν αὐτοὺς λέγων· Ἡμεῖς διὰ τὰ κακὰ ἃ
ἐποιήσαμεν οὕτω¹³ πεπόνθαμεν,¹⁴ οὕτως δὲ σωτὴρ γενόμενος τῶν ἀνθρώπων τί
ἠδίκησεν ὑμᾶς; 14 καὶ ἀγανακτήσαντες ἐπ' αὐτῷ ἐκέλευσαν ἵνα μὴ σκελοκοπηθῇ
ὅπως βασανιζόμενος ἀποθάνῃ.

Vocabulary
ἀγανακτέω, become indignant/angry at (ἐπί) somebody (regarding an assumed
    wrong)
ἀγωνιάω, be anxious
ἀδικέω, do wrong; pass. be wronged by somebody
ἀνά, each, apiece; ἀνὰ μέσον, between, within (w. gen.)
βασανίζω, to torture, torment; pass. be in torment/great pain
διαμερίζω, to divide, distribute
ἔμπροσθεν (w. gen.), before, in front of; previously
ἔνδυμα, τό, clothing; garment
ἐπιγράφω, write on/in; inscribe on
κακοῦργος, -ον, criminal, evildoer
καταλείπω / καταλιμπάνω, ²aor. κατέλιπον, ²aor. ptc. καταλι(μ)πών,
    6. κατελείφθην, aor. pass. inf. κατελείφθηναι: leave behind, abandon, forsake;
    have remaining; leave alone
κελεύω, to command, order (w. dat.)
κεράννυμι, ¹aor. ἐκέρασα: mix (oft. of water w. wine)
λαχμός, λαχμὸν βάλλειν, throw lots for (ἐπί) something
μηδείς, μηδεμία, μηδέν (w. non-ind.), no one, nothing; μηδέν (adv.), not at all, in
    no way
ὄξος, -ους, τό, vinegar
ὀνειδίζω, mock, insult, heap insults upon

---

¹³ οὕτω > οὕτως.
¹⁴ S.v. πάσχω.

ὀρθόω, set upright; pass. be erected

πάσχω, 2. πείσομαι, 3. ἔπαθον, 4. πέπονθα: suffer, endure; experience

πόνος, ὁ, hard labor, pain, affliction

σιωπάω, keep silent, say nothing, become quiet

σκελοκοπέω, break the legs of somebody

σταυρόω, crucify

χολή, ἡ, gall, bile

5:15 ἦν δὲ μεσημβρία, καὶ σκότος κατέσχεν πᾶσαν τὴν Ἰουδαίαν· καὶ ἐθορυβοῦντο καὶ ἠγωνίων μήποτε ὁ ἥλιος ἔδυ ἐπειδὴ ἔτι ἔζη· γέγραπται γὰρ αὐτοῖς[15] ἥλιον μὴ δῦναι[16] ἐπὶ πεφονευμένῳ. 16 καί τις αὐτῶν εἶπεν· Ποτίσατε αὐτὸν χολὴν μετὰ ὄξους· καὶ κεράσαντες ἐπότισαν. 17 καὶ ἐπλήρωσαν πάντα καὶ ἐτελείωσαν κατὰ τῆς κεφαλῆς αὐτῶν τὰ ἁμαρτήματα. 18 περιήρχοντα δὲ πολλοὶ μετὰ λύχνων νομίζοντες ὅτι νύξ ἐστιν ἔπεσάν τε.[17] 19 καὶ ὁ κύριος ἀνεβόησε λέγων· Ἡ δύναμίς μου, ἡ δύναμις, κατέλειψάς με[18] καὶ εἰπὼν ἀνελήφθη. 20 καὶ αὐτῆς ὥρας[19] διεράγη τὸ καταπέτασμα τοῦ ναοῦ τῆς Ἰερουσαλὴμ εἰς δύο.

Vocabulary

ἁμάρτημα, τό, sin, transgression

ἀναβοάω, cry out

ἀναλαμβάνω, 6. ἀνελήφθην: take up, carry; resolve; take up (a discourse); take over, carry away

διαρρήγνυμι/διαρήσσω, 3. διέρρηξα, 6. διεράγην: tear something, tear something to pieces; to break (shackles)

δύνω (also δύω), mid. δύομαι, 2. δύσομαι, ²aor. ἔδυν: go down, set (of the sun); sink; mid. to sink/set (of the sun)

ἐπειδή, since, because; after

ἡγεμών, -όνος, ὁ, leader; imperial governor (of a Roman province)

ἥλιος, ὁ, sun

θορυβέω, trouble/bother somebody; create a disturbance, clamor for somebody (acc.); pass. be troubled, distressed

Ἰουδαῖος, -α, ον, Jewish/Judean (adj.); Jew/Judean (noun)

καταπέτασμα, curtain; here, the curtain in the Jerusalem temple that separated the Holy of Holies (inner sanctuary) from the sanctuary

κατέχω, ²aor. κατέσχον, aor. pass. ptc. κατασχεθείς: possess, occupy, take into one's possession; hold (a ship on a certain course); hold back, bind, confine; understand that (ὅτι)

---

[15] "For them."
[16] Impv. inf.
[17] S.v. πίπτω, 3. ἔπεσον / ἔπεσα (¹aor ending on ²aor stem); in this context, "to stumble, fall down."
[18] Cf. Ps 21:2 (LXX): Ὁ θεός, ὁ θεός μου … ἵνα τί ἐγκατέλιπές με; (cf. Mark 15:34; Matt 27:46).
[19] Gen. of time (cf. IV, 5.3).

λύχνος, lamp (of metal or clay)

μεσημβρία, ή, midday, noon

μήποτε, that ... not, lest

ναός, ὁ, temple, inner part of Jewish temple, sanctuary

νομίζω, think, suppose, assume; institute a custom; pass. ptc. customary; nt. pl. ptc., customary things

περιέρχομαι, wander about (from place to place)

ποτίζω, 2. ποτιῶ, 3. ἐπότισα: give somebody a drink

σκότος, -ους, τό, darkness; sin, evil

τελειόω, fulfill, bring to full measure; pass. be accomplished (of promises, prophecies); become mature, perfect

φονεύω, to murder; to execute, put to death

6:21 καὶ τότε ἀπέσπασαν τοὺς ἥλους ἀπὸ τῶν χειρῶν τοῦ κυρίου καὶ ἔθηκαν αὐτὸν ἐπὶ τῆς γῆς· καὶ ἡ γῆ πᾶσα ἐσείσθη καὶ φόβος μέγας ἐγένετο. 22 τότε ὁ ἥλιος ἔλαμψε καὶ εὑρέθη ὥρα ἐνάτη. 23 ἐχάρησαν δὲ οἱ Ἰουδαῖοι καὶ ἔδωκαν τῷ Ἰωσὴφ τὸ σῶμα αὐτοῦ ἵνα αὐτὸ θάψῃ, ἐπειδὴ θεασάμενος ἦν[20] ὅσα ἀγαθὰ (Jesus) ἐποίησεν. 24 λαβὼν δὲ τὸν κύριον ἔλουσε καὶ ἐνείλησε (ἐν) σινδόνι καὶ εἰσήγαγεν εἰς ἴδιον τάφον καλούμενον Κῆπον Ἰωσήφ.[21]

Vocabulary

ἀποσπάω, pull out

εἴλω/εἰλέω, 3. εἴλησα: wrap in something; roll up something

εἰσάγω, lead in, bring in; introdpruce

ἔνατος, -η, -ον, ninth

ἧλος, ὁ, nail

θεάομαι, see, look at, notice, observe

κῆπος, ὁ, garden

κρύπτω, impf. pass. ἐκρυβόμην, 3. ἔκρυψα, 6. ἐκρύβην, ²aor. pass. inf. κρυβῆναι, pf. pass. ptc. κεκρυμμένος: cover, hide, conceal; pass. be hiding

λάμπω, 3. ἔλαμψα: shine, shine forth; shine upon somebody (dat.)

λούω (contract form λόω), bathe, wash

νηστεύω, to fast, observe a fast

οἷος, -α, -ον, what kind (of), such as; οἷον + inf. (impling fitness, possibility), it is possible

οὐαί (w. dat.), woe/alas; concerning, by reason of (dat.)

σείω, to shake

σινδών, -όνος, ή, linen cloth

τάφος, grave, tomb

---

[20] Periphr. cstr. (IV, 17), but oddly here w. aor. ptc. instead of the expected pf. ptc.

[21] Gen. (indecl.).

τέλος, -ους, τό, end; outcome, resolution, conclusion
φόβος, ὁ, fear, fright

7:25 τότε οἱ Ἰουδαῖοι καὶ οἱ πρεσβύτεροι καὶ οἱ ἱερεῖς γνόντες οἷον κακὸν ἑαυτοῖς ἐποίησαν, ἤρξαντο κόπτεσθαι καὶ λέγειν· Οὐαὶ ταῖς ἁμαρτίαις ἡμῶν· ἤγγισεν ἡ κρίσις καὶ τὸ τέλος Ἰερουσαλήμ.[22] 26 ἐγὼ δὲ μετὰ τῶν ἑταίρων μου ἐλυπούμην καὶ τετρωμένοι[23] κατὰ διάνοιαν ἐκρυβόμεθα. ἐζητούμεθα γὰρ ὑπ' αὐτῶν ὡς[24] (we were) κακοῦργοι καὶ ὡς τὸν ναὸν θέλοντες ἐμπρῆσαι. 27 ἐπὶ[25] δὲ τούτοις πᾶσιν ἐνηστεύομεν καὶ ἐκαθεζόμεθα πενθοῦντες καὶ κλαίοντες νυκτὸς[26] καὶ ἡμέρας ἕως τοῦ σαββάτου.

Vocabulary
διάνοια, ἡ, understanding, mind, thoughts
ἐγγίζω, approach, come near (in either a spatial or temporal sense)
ἐμπί(μ)πρημι, ¹aor. inf. ἐμπρῆσαι, set on fire, burn
ἑταῖρος, ὁ, companion, friend; ἑταίρα, ἡ, prostitute
ἱερεύς, -έως, ὁ, pl. ἱερεῖς, priest; ἐπὶ ἱρέως, during the priesthood of so-and-so
καθέζομαι, ¹aor pass. ptc. καθεσθείς, καθεσθεῖσα: sit, sit down; + ἐπί, sit by; sit as a supplicant (in a sacred service)
κακοῦργος, -ον, criminal, evildoer
κλαίω, pres. ptc. κλάων, 3. ἔκλαυσα: weep (for), cry
κόπτω, 3. ἔκοψα: to cut, beat (one's breast); strike somebody; mid. to mourn
λυπέω, cause pain or grief; pass. be sorrowful, distressed
πενθέω, be sad, grieve, mourn; πενθῶ ἐπί, mourn over
τιτρώσκω, pf. τέτρωμαι: inflict a wound, injure

SELECT BIBLIOGRAPHY

Cameron, Ron (ed.). *The Other Gospels: Non-Canonical Gospel Texts*. Philadelphia: Westminster Press, 1982.

Foster, Paul. *The Gospel of Peter: Introduction, Critical Edition and Commentary*. Leiden: Brill, 2010.

---

[22] Gen. (indecl.).
[23] S.v. τιτρώσκω.
[24] ὡς, "as if."
[25] ἐπί + dat. ("because of").
[26] Gen. of time (cf. IV, 5.3).

1.10.

Revelation: The Whore of Babylon and the Beast

(Rev 17:1–18)

Provenance: The author of the Book of Revelation is identified simply as the prophet "John." He lived on the island of Patmos, off the western coast of Asia Minor. It was here, on this island, that he received his first vision (Rev 1:9–11) and prophesied to the seven churches in Asia Minor (Rev 1:10–13).[1]

Date: This apocalypse was composed near the end of Domitian's reign (ca. 95–96 CE).

Special Features: The Greek syntax of Revelation is sometimes awkward and ungrammatical, and the text contains numerous Semitisms, suggesting that the mother tongue of its author was Aramaic. The socio-rhetorical context of Revelation is one of persecution, suffering, and injustice. The visions, which make up the bulk of this book (Rev 4:1–22:5), present alternating visions of hope and visions of conflict. In Rev 17, the prophet is taken into the wilderness to behold "the great whore … with whom the kings of the earth have committed fornication" (Rev 17:2). This "whore" is called "Babylon," a code name for the Roman Empire (cf. Rev 17:18), which, like ancient Babylon, was opposed to God. The "seven mountains" upon which the "whore of Babylon" sits (Rev 17:9) correspond to the seven hills of Rome.

This passage is part of a larger vision of despair and oppression (Rev 17:1–18:24). It is sandwiched between two visions of hope (the martyrs worshipping God [Rev 15:2–8] and worship in heaven [Rev 19:1–16]). The overall purpose of these visions was to inspire Christians to remain steadfast in the face of persecution.

---

[1] The seven churches of Asia are Ephesos, Smyrna, Pergamon, Thyatira, Sardis, Philadelphia, and Laodikea.

FIG. 5. Emperor Domitian, Ephesos (Selçuk Archaeological Museum) (photo: author).

The prophet John speaks:

17:1 Καὶ ἦλθεν εἷς ἐκ τῶν ἑπτὰ ἀγγέλων τῶν ἐχόντων τὰς ἑπτὰ φιάλας καὶ ἐλάλησεν μετ᾽ ἐμοῦ λέγων· δεῦρο, δείξω σοι τὸ κρίμα τῆς πόρνης τῆς μεγάλης τῆς καθημένης ἐπὶ ὑδάτων πολλῶν,[2] 2 μεθ᾽ ἧς ἐπόρνευσαν οἱ βασιλεῖς[3] τῆς γῆς καὶ ἐμεθύσθησαν οἱ κατοικοῦντες τὴν γῆν ἐκ τοῦ οἴνου τῆς πορνείας αὐτῆς. 3 καὶ ἀπήνεγκέν[4] με εἰς ἔρημον ἐν πνεύματι. καὶ εἶδον γυναῖκα καθημένην ἐπὶ θηρίον κόκκινον, γέμοντα ὀνόματα βλασφημίας, ἔχων[5] κεφαλὰς ἑπτὰ καὶ κέρατα δέκα. 4 καὶ ἡ γυνὴ ἦν περιβεβλημένη[6] πορφυροῦν καὶ κόκκινον καὶ κεχρυσωμένη χρυσίῳ καὶ λίθῳ τιμίῳ καὶ μαργαρίταις, ἔχουσα ποτήριον χρυσοῦν ἐν τῇ χειρὶ αὐτῆς γέμον βδελυγμάτων καὶ τὰ ἀκάθαρτα τῆς πορνείας αὐτῆς 5 καὶ ἐπὶ τὸ μέτωπον αὐτῆς ὄνομα γεγραμμένον, μυστήριον, Βαβυλὼν ἡ μεγάλη, ἡ μήτηρ τῶν πορνῶν καὶ τῶν βδελυγμάτων τῆς γῆς.

Vocabulary

ἀναφέρω, 2. ἀνοίσω, 3. ἀνήνεγκον: take up, carry away; offer up; bring back; w. ἐπί, refer to

γέμω (w. gen.), nt. pres. ptc. γέμον: be full of something

κόκκινος, -η, -ον, scarlet, red; τὸ κόκκινον, scarlet cloth

μαργαρίτης, ὁ, pearl

μέτωπον, τό, forehead

πόρνη, ἡ, prostitute, whore

πορφυροῦς, -ᾶ, -οῦν, purple; purple garment

ποτήριον, τό, cup

τίμιος, -α, -ον, precious, valuable; superl. τιμιώτερος, -α, -ον, more precious

χρυσόω, to gild, adorn with (dat.)

17:6 Καὶ εἶδον τὴν γυναῖκα μεθύουσαν ἐκ τοῦ αἵματος τῶν ἁγίων καὶ ἐκ τοῦ αἵματος τῶν μαρτύρων Ἰησοῦ. Καὶ ἐθαύμασα ἰδὼν αὐτὴν θαῦμα μέγα. 7 Καὶ εἶπέν μοι ὁ ἄγγελος· διὰ τί[7] ἐθαύμασας; ἐγὼ ἐρῶ[8] σοι τὸ μυστήριον τῆς γυναικὸς καὶ τοῦ θηρίου τοῦ βαστάζοντος αὐτὴν τοῦ ἔχοντος τὰς ἑπτὰ κεφαλὰς καὶ τὰ δέκα κέρατα. 8 τὸ θηρίον ὃ εἶδες ἦν καὶ οὐκ ἔστιν, καὶ μέλλει ἀναβαίνειν[9] ἐκ τῆς ἀβύσσου καὶ εἰς ἀπώλειαν ὑπάγει, καὶ θαυμασθήσονται οἱ κατοικοῦντες ἐπὶ τῆς γῆς, ὧν[10] οὐ γέγραπται τὸ ὄνομα[11] ἐπὶ τὸ βιβλίον τῆς ζωῆς ἀπὸ καταβολῆς

---

[2] An allusion to the Tiber River (cf. Rev 17:15)

[3] I.e., the Roman emperors.

[4] S.v. ἀναφέρω.

[5] ἔχων, m. here for nt.

[6] Plpf. periphr. (cf. IV, 17).

[7] διὰ τί, "why?"

[8] S.v. λέγω.

[9] In other words, the beast (Rome) existed in the past and then waned (becoming almost extinct), but will be revived in the future.

[10] ὧν...τὸ ὄνομα, "whose name."

[11] Nt. sg. for nt. pl.

κόσμου, βλεπόντων[12] τὸ θηρίον, ὅτι ἦν καὶ οὐκ ἔστιν καὶ παρέσται.[13] 9 Ὧδε (calls for) ὁ νοῦς ὁ ἔχων σοφίαν. Αἱ ἑπτὰ κεφαλαὶ ἑπτὰ ὄρη εἰσίν, ὅπου ἡ γυνὴ κάθηται ἐπ᾽ αὐτῶν. καὶ βασιλεῖς ἑπτά εἰσιν·[14] 10 οἱ πέντε ἔπεσαν, ὁ εἷς ἔστιν,[15] ὁ ἄλλος οὔπω ἦλθεν,[16] καὶ ὅταν ἔλθῃ ὀλίγον αὐτὸν δεῖ μεῖναι. 11 καὶ τὸ θηρίον ὃ ἦν καὶ οὐκ ἔστιν καὶ αὐτὸς ὄγδοός ἐστιν καὶ (one) ἐκ τῶν ἑπτά ἐστιν, καὶ εἰς ἀπώλειαν ὑπάγει.[17] 12 Καὶ τὰ δέκα κέρατα ἃ εἶδες δέκα βασιλεῖς εἰσιν, οἵτινες βασιλείαν οὔπω ἔλαβον, ἀλλὰ ἐξουσίαν ὡς βασιλεῖς μίαν ὥραν[18] λαμβάνουσιν μετὰ τοῦ θηρίου. 13 οὗτοι μίαν γνώμην ἔχουσιν καὶ τὴν δύναμιν καὶ ἐξουσίαν αὐτῶν τῷ θηρίῳ διδόασιν. 14 οὗτοι μετὰ τοῦ ἀρνίου πολεμήσουσιν καὶ τὸ ἀρνίον νικήσει αὐτούς, ὅτι κύριος κυρίων ἐστὶν καὶ βασιλεὺς βασιλέων καὶ οἱ μετ᾽ αὐτοῦ (are the) κλητοὶ καὶ ἐκλεκτοὶ καὶ πιστοί. 15 Καὶ λέγει μοι· τὰ ὕδατα ἃ εἶδες οὗ[19] ἡ πόρνη κάθηται λαοὶ καὶ ὄχλοι εἰσὶν καὶ ἔθνη καὶ γλῶσσαι. 16 καὶ τὰ δέκα κέρατα ἃ εἶδες καὶ τὸ θηρίον οὗτοι μισήσουσιν τὴν πόρνην καὶ ἠρημωμένην ποιήσουσιν αὐτὴν καὶ γυμνὴν καὶ τὰς σάρκας αὐτῆς φάγονται καὶ αὐτὴν κατακαύσουσιν[20] ἐν πυρί.[21] 17 ὁ γὰρ θεὸς ἔδωκεν εἰς τὰς καρδίας αὐτῶν ποιῆσαι τὴν γνώμην αὐτοῦ[22] καὶ ποιῆσαι μίαν γνώμην καὶ δοῦναι[23] τὴν βασιλείαν αὐτῶν τῷ θηρίῳ ἄχρι τελεσθήσονται οἱ λόγοι τοῦ θεοῦ. 18 καὶ ἡ γυνὴ ἣν εἶδες ἔστιν ἡ πόλις ἡ μεγάλη ἡ ἔχουσα βασιλείαν ἐπὶ τῶν βασιλέων τῆς γῆς.

Vocabulary

ἄβυσσος, ἡ, abyss (i.e., Sheol)

ἀρνίον, τό, lamb, here the Lamb[24]

ἐρημόω, pf. pass. dep. ptc. ἠρημωμένος: make uninhabitable, make desolate

θαῦμα, τό, a wonder/marvel

καταβολή, ἡ, beginning, creation

μάρτυς, -υρος, ὁ, witness; martyr

---

[12] Agreeing w. ὧν, instead of οἱ κατοικοῦντες (similar to a gen. absol. cstr., "when the …").

[13] Cf. Rev 20:2, where Satan is about to be thrown into this same bottomless pit.

[14] The "seven kings" are like the Roman emperors up to the time of the fall of Jerusalem in 70 CE. Though there were actually ten emperors during this period (Julius Caesar, Augustus, Tiberius, Caligula, Claudius, Nero, Galba, Otho, Vitellius, and Vespasian), Galba, Otho, and Vitellius each ruled less than a year, leaving seven emperors.

[15] "One is," i.e., Nero, who persecuted Christians from 64 to 68 CE.

[16] Probably a reference to Domitian, who succeeded Titus.

[17] Perhaps a reference to an eschatological Antichrist (cf. Rev 13).

[18] Acc. of duration of time ("for") (cf. IV, 5).

[19] οὗ, "where."

[20] S.v. κατακαίω.

[21] This verse seems to indicate that the ten kings (emperors) will not be united in purpose, but rather will be in conflict with one another in their quest for power, thus causing the downfall of Rome.

[22] ποιῆσαι τὴν γνώμην αὐτοῦ, "to carry out his purpose."

[23] S.v. δίδωμι.

[24] I.e., the lion-like Lamb ("slain but standing"), the resurrected Christ (Rev 5:1–7), who has twelve apostles (Rev 21:14).

νικάω, to defeat, triumph

ὄγδοος, -η, -ον, eighth

οὔπω, not yet

πολεμέω, wage war, go to war with

ὑπάγω, bring under one's power, induce somebody to do something; bring before a court of law; go away, depart

PART 2

Basic Level: The Isometric Translational Greek of the Septuagint

art 2 takes up the study of the "translation" Greek of the Septuagint, with three prose readings (§§2.1–3) and three poetic readings (§§2.4–6), as well as three additional texts online (§§2.7–9).[1] Most Septuagintal translations of the Tanakh avoid the standard literary conventions of Hellenistic Greek. Instead, they render the original Hebrew source text in a literal, or what is termed an "isometric," manner in which there is an almost word-for-word correspondence between the Hebrew parent text and the Greek translation. This "translational" Greek is characterized by linguistic interference from the source language, Hebrew.[2] On the basis of this phenomenon, one might surmise that the translators of the Septuagint understood their primary role to be that of conserving the formal syntactical and lexemic properties of the Hebrew parent text rather than rendering the Hebrew text into contemporary Hellenistic Greek. Indeed, the original Septuagintal translators may have even understood their Greek translation to be a kind of "interlinear" text that was dependent on, and meant to be read in conjunction with, its Hebrew exemplar.

The Septuagint has recently been retranslated into English, with many helpful notes, as *The New English Translation of the Septuagint*.[3] You should use this translation, rather than standard English translations of the Hebrew

---

[1] For a critical version of the Septuagint see Alfred Rahlfs and Robert Hanhart (eds.), *Septuaginta*, ed. altera (Stuttgart: Deutsche Bibelgesellschaft, 2006), which is a revision of Alread Rahlfs' original text, correcting minor errors, with reference to Vaticanus, Sinaiticus, and Alexandrinus; Dogniez, Cécile, *Bibliography of the Septuagint (1970–1993)* (Leiden: Brill, 1995).

[2] Cf. Staffan Olofsson, *The LXX Version: A Guide to the Translation Technique of the Septuagint* (Stockholm: Almqvist and Wiksell, 1999).

[3] Albert Pietersma and Benjamin G. Wright (eds.), *A New Translation of the Septuagint: A New Translation of the Greek into Contemporary English* (New York: Oxford University Press, 2007).

(Masoretic) text, to check your own translation work. Each of the vocabulary lists in Part 2 is compiled on the assumption that you have memorized the (bolded) words listed for memorization in Part 1 (only §§1.1–10).[4] But since all vocabulary for memorization is listed in the glossary (§10), there is no need to flip back to Part 1.

---

[4]   As well as all the words occurring fifty times or more in the Greek New Testament.

2.1.

Book of Genesis: The First Sin and Its Punishment

(Gen 3:1–24)

Text: Rahlfs/Hanhart, I, 4-5; ET: *NETS*, 7-8.

The Book of Genesis begins with two creation narratives, told from different perspectives. In the first narrative (Gen 1:1–2:4a), the Lord creates male and female human beings simultaneously (Gen 1:26–27). But in the second version, the Lord creates man (Adam) first, with the first woman (Eve, or "Zoe" in LXX) being created secondarily as Adam's helper in paradise (Gen 2:4b–25, §2.7). The narrative in this section follows this story, telling of Adam and Eve's disobedience and banishment from the garden of delights (Gen 3:1–24).

The style of the translational Greek of Genesis is "isometric." It is characterized by an almost word-for-word corresponence between the Hebrew exemplar and the Greek translation, resulting in linguistic interference from the source language, Hebrew. Significant instances of this interference are discussed in the footnotes.

Related Readings: This narrative inspired the Life of Adam and Eve (§3.9–10) and various Christian theological responses, including Rom 5 (§4.11), the story of Maximilla in the Acts of Andrew (§5.16), not to mention 2 Cor 11:3 and 1 Tim 2:13–15.

3:1 Ὁ δὲ ὄφις[1] ἦν φρονιμώτατος πάντων τῶν θηρίων τῶν ἐπὶ τῆς γῆς, ὧν[2] ἐποίησεν κύριος ὁ θεός, καὶ εἶπεν ὁ ὄφις τῇ γυναικί· τί (is it) ὅτι εἶπεν ὁ θεός

---

[1] The cosmologies of Babylon and Egypt shed much light on the mythological antecedents of this story. For example, in the Babylonian myth *Adapa*, a serpent-god known as Ningishzida is stationed at the gates of heaven. In the Gilgamesh story, a serpent steals the Tree of Life (which confers longevity and fertility) and intends to consume it. In Egyptian religion, the serpent was a symbol of immortality (signified by a snake forming a circle by biting its tail) and, interestingly, also a symbol of both wisdom and chaos. Indeed, it is this very "chaos" that makes the "wisdom" of the serpent so dangerous.

[2] Attr. rel. (cf. IV, 3).

Οὐ μὴ φάγητε³ ἀπὸ παντὸς ξύλου⁴ τοῦ ἐν τῷ παραδείσῳ; 2 Καὶ εἶπεν ἡ γυνὴ
τῷ ὄφει· ἀπὸ καρποῦ ξύλου τοῦ παραδείσου φαγόμεθα, 3 ἀπὸ δὲ καρποῦ τοῦ
ξύλου, ὅ ἐστιν ἐν μέσῳ τοῦ παραδείσου, εἶπεν ὁ θεός Οὐ φάγεσθε ἀπ᾽ αὐτοῦ
οὐδὲ μὴ ἄψησθε αὐτοῦ, ἵνα μὴ ἀποθάνητε. 4 καὶ εἶπεν ὁ ὄφις τῇ γυναικί· οὐ
θανάτῳ⁵ ἀποθανεῖσθε, 5 ᾔδει⁶ γὰρ ὁ θεός ὅτι ἐν ᾗ ἂν ἡμέρᾳ φάγητε ἀπ᾽ αὐτοῦ,
διανοιχθήσονται⁷ ὑμῶν οἱ ὀφθαλμοί, καὶ ἔσεσθε ὡς θεοὶ γινώσκοντες καλὸν καὶ
πονηρόν. 6 καὶ εἶδεν ἡ γυνὴ ὅτι καλὸν τὸ ξύλον εἰς βρῶσιν καὶ ὅτι (it was)
ἀρεστὸν τοῖς ὀφθαλμοῖς ἰδεῖν καὶ ὡραῖόν ἐστιν τοῦ κατανοῆσαι,⁸ καὶ λαβοῦσα
τοῦ καρποῦ αὐτοῦ ἔφαγεν, καὶ ἔδωκεν καὶ τῷ ἀνδρὶ αὐτῆς μετ᾽ αὐτῆς, καὶ
ἔφαγον.

Vocabulary

ἅπτομαι, 3. ἡψάμην, ¹aor. mid. impv. ἅψαι: touch, take hold of (w. gen.); strike,
    attack
ἀρεστός, -ή, -όν, pleasing to, acceptable to
βρῶσις, -εως, ἡ, eating/consumption; food
διανοίγω, 6. διηνοίχθην: to open; explain, interpret
θηρίον, τό, θηρσί (dat. pl.), wild animal⁹
κατανοέω, come to, arrive at; contemplate
παράδεισος, -ου, ὁ, a garden, orchard (in Eden), a place of blessedness above the
    earth, paradise
ὡραῖος, -α, -ον, beautiful; gracious

7 καὶ διηνοίχθησαν οἱ ὀφθαλμοὶ τῶν δύο, καὶ ἔγνωσαν ὅτι γυμνοὶ ἦσαν, καὶ
ἔρραψαν φύλλα συκῆς καὶ ἐποίησαν ἑαυτοῖς περιζώματα. 8 Καὶ ἤκουσαν¹⁰ τὴν
φωνὴν κυρίου τοῦ θεοῦ περιπατοῦντος ἐν τῷ παραδείσῳ τὸ δειλινόν, καὶ
ἐκρύβησαν¹¹ ὅ τε¹² Αδαμ καὶ ἡ γυνὴ αὐτοῦ ἀπὸ προσώπου κυρίου τοῦ θεοῦ
ἐν μέσῳ τοῦ ξύλου τοῦ παραδείσου. 9 Καὶ ἐκάλεσεν κύριος ὁ θεὸς τὸν Αδαμ

---

³ S.v. ἐσθίω; οὐ μή + aor. subj. (emph. fut. neg., cf. IV, 8).
⁴ ξύλου here is a collective noun (translate as pl.), cf. Gen 3:8.
⁵ Here the Greek translator renders literally the unexpected Heb. construction (in which the negative precedes a free inf.) by placing θανάτῳ ("by death") betweeen οὐ and the verb (ἀποθανεῖσθε, s.v.
   ἀποθνήσκω). θανάτῳ should be trans. as an intensifier ("surely").
⁶ S.v. οἶδα (table 9.5).
⁷ S.v. διανοίγω, with almost the same meaning as ἀνοίγω.
⁸ Art. inf. (cf. IV, 2).
⁹ To be more precise, θηρίον is the diminutive of θήρ (wild animal), whose dative plural form is θηρσί.
   The separation presupposed in this passage between domestic and wild animals also symbolically
   marks the boundary between the civilized world and the wilderness and, by extension, the boundary
   between the created world and chaos, good and evil.
¹⁰ ἀκούω can take the acc. or gen. of the thing heard. In Classical Greek, the phrase "to hear someone
   (e.g., φωνῆς, βοῆς)" takes the gen., but the LXX and NT waver between gen. and acc.
¹¹ S.v. κρύπτω.
¹² ὅ τε > ὁ τέ (= τέ ὁ) (τέ is postpos.).

καὶ εἶπεν αὐτῷ Αδαμ· ποῦ εἶ; 10 Καὶ εἶπεν αὐτῷ· τὴν φωνήν σου ἤκουσα περιπατοῦντος ἐν τῷ παραδείσῳ καὶ ἐφοβήθην, ὅτι γυμνός εἰμι, καὶ ἐκρύβην. 11 Καὶ εἶπεν αὐτῷ· τίς ἀνήγγειλέν σοι ὅτι γυμνὸς εἶ; μὴ[13] ἀπὸ τοῦ ξύλου, οὗ[14] ἐνετειλάμην[15] σοι τούτου[16] μόνου μὴ φαγεῖν ἀπ᾿ αὐτοῦ, ἔφαγες; 12 Καὶ εἶπεν ὁ Αδαμ· ἡ γυνή, ἣν ἔδωκας (to be) μετ᾿ ἐμοῦ, αὕτη μοι ἔδωκεν ἀπὸ τοῦ ξύλου, καὶ ἔφαγον. 13 Καὶ εἶπεν κύριος ὁ θεὸς τῇ γυναικί· τί τοῦτο ἐποίησας; Καὶ εἶπεν ἡ γυνή· ὁ ὄφις ἠπάτησέν με, καὶ ἔφαγον.

Vocabulary
ἀπατάω, deceive, cheat
γυμνός, -ή, -όν, naked
δειλινός, -ή, -όν, of the evening; (τὸ) δειλινόν, adv. in the evening
περίζωμα, -ματος, τό, apron, skirt
ποῦ, where?
ῥάπτω, 3. ἔρραψα: sew/alter (a garment)
συκῆ, ἡ, fig tree

3:14   Καὶ εἶπεν κύριος ὁ θεὸς τῷ ὄφει
        Ὅτι ἐποίησας τοῦτο, ἐπικατάρατος σὺ ἀπὸ πάντων τῶν κτηνῶν καὶ ἀπὸ πάντων τῶν θηρίων τῆς γῆς, ἐπὶ τῷ στήθει σου καὶ τῇ κοιλίᾳ πορεύσῃ καὶ γῆν φάγῃ πάσας τὰς ἡμέρας τῆς ζωῆς σου.

15   καὶ ἔχθραν θήσω ἀνὰ μέσον σου καὶ ἀνὰ μέσον τῆς γυναικὸς καὶ ἀνὰ μέσον τοῦ σπέρματός σου καὶ ἀνὰ μέσον τοῦ σπέρματος αὐτῆς, αὐτός[17] σου[18] τηρήσει[19] κεφαλήν, καὶ σὺ τηρήσεις αὐτοῦ πτέρναν.

16   Καὶ τῇ γυναικὶ εἶπεν· πληθύνων πληθυνῶ[20] τὰς λύπας σου καὶ τὸν στεναγμόν σου, ἐν λύπαις τέξῃ[21] τέκνα, καὶ πρὸς τὸν ἄνδρα σου ἡ ἀποστροφή[22] σου, καὶ αὐτός σου κυριεύσει.

---

[13] μή...ἔφαγες; μή indicates that the anticpated answer to this question is "no" (i.e., "surely you didn't ... did you?").

[14] Gen. (οὗ) is used owing to the pleon. ἀπ᾿ αὐτοῦ that follows.

[15] S.v. ἐντέλλω/ομαι.

[16] The antecedent of τούτου is ξύλου.

[17] Even though σπέρμα is nt., the translator has personalized σπέρμα (here αὐτός is a reference to the seed) as an individual ("he"), i.e., the offspring of the woman.

[18] σου...κεφαλήν.

[19] τηρέω in the sense of "watch carefully."

[20] πληθύνων (s.v. πληθύνω), πληθυνῶ (fut.), ptc. (πληθύνων) mirrors the Heb. syntax, intensifying the verbal idea: "*greatly* increase."

[21] S.v. τίκτω.

[22] This is an unexpected translation of the Heb. term for "sexual desire." What the translator probably means is that, even though childbirth will be painful, she will "*return*" to her husband. This interpretation makes the last clause sensible: καὶ αὐτός σου κυριεύσει. J. N. Lohr argues that the author is trying to express in poetic terms the idea that the curse on the woman and that on the man are the same: they shall both return to their places of origin ("Sexual Desire, Eve, Gen 3:16," *JBL* 130/2 [2011], 277–246).

17   Τῷ δὲ Αδαμ εἶπεν· ὅτι ἤκουσας²³ τῆς φωνῆς τῆς γυναικός σου καὶ
      ἔφαγες ἀπὸ τοῦ ξύλου, οὗ ἐνετειλάμην σοι τούτου μόνου μὴ φαγεῖν ἀπ᾽
      αὐτοῦ, ἐπικατάρατος ἡ γῆ ἐν τοῖς ἔργοις σου, ἐν λύπαις φάγῃ αὐτὴν
      πάσας τὰς ἡμέρας τῆς ζωῆς σου,

18   ἀκάνθας καὶ τριβόλους (ἡ γῆ) ἀνατελεῖ²⁴ σοι, καὶ φάγῃ τὸν χόρτον τοῦ
      ἀγροῦ.

19   ἐν ἱδρῶτι τοῦ προσώπου σου φάγῃ τὸν ἄρτον σου ἕως τοῦ
      ἀποστρέψαι²⁵ σε εἰς τὴν γῆν, ἐξ ἧς ἐλήμφθης,²⁶ ὅτι γῆ εἶ καὶ εἰς γῆν
      ἀπελεύσῃ.²⁷

Vocabulary

ἀγρός, ὁ, field, countryside

ἄκανθα, ἡ, thorny plant

ἀνά, each, apiece; ἀνὰ μέσον, between, within (w. gen.)

ἀνατέλλω, 2. ἀνατελῶ, 3. ἀνέτειλα: cause to spring/grow up

ἀπολαμβάνω, receive something; regain, recover; mid. take away/aside; receive

ἀποστρέφω, 6. ἀπεστράφην (dep.): look back at (ἐπί) somebody; look away; revoke; refrain from, turn back from doing something

ἀποστροφή, turning back, return

ἐπικατάρατος, -ον, accursed

ἔχθρα, ἡ, hatred, enmity

ἱδρώς, -ῶτος, ὁ, sweat

κοιλία, ἡ, belly, womb

κτῆνος, -ους, τό, domestic animal; mostly pl. τὰ κτήνεα, herds, cattle, livestock

λύπη, ἡ, sorrow; affliction; pl. pains, labor pains

πτέρνα, ἡ, heal

στεναγμός, ὁ, sighing, groaning

στῆθος, -ους, τό (uncontr. -εος), breast (of both sexes)

τρίβολος, ὁ, thistle

χιτών, -ῶνος, ὁ, tunic

χόρτος, ὁ, grass, χόρτος τοῦ ἀγροῦ, wild grass, hay

3:20 Καὶ ἐκάλεσεν Αδαμ τὸ ὄνομα τῆς γυναικὸς αὐτοῦ Ζωή,²⁸ ὅτι αὕτη μήτηρ
πάντων τῶν ζώντων. 21 Καὶ ἐποίησεν κύριος ὁ θεὸς τῷ Αδαμ καὶ τῇ γυναικὶ
αὐτοῦ χιτῶνας δερματίνους καὶ ἐνέδυσεν αὐτούς. 22 καὶ εἶπεν ὁ θεός· ἰδοὺ Αδαμ

---

²³ Modified by gen. τῆς φωνῆς over against acc. of Gen 3:8, 10. Here, however, the verb means "listen to" in the sense of "obey."

²⁴ Cf. ἀνατέλλω.

²⁵ Art. inf.

²⁶ S.v. λαμβάνω.

²⁷ S.v. ἀπέρχομαι.

²⁸ The woman is given the unexpected name "Zoe" (cf. Gen 4:1), not "Eve."

γέγονεν ὡς εἷς ἐξ ἡμῶν²⁹ τοῦ γινώσκειν³⁰ καλὸν καὶ πονηρόν, καὶ νῦν μήποτε ἐκτείνῃ τὴν χεῖρα (αὐτοῦ) καὶ λάβῃ τοῦ ξύλου τῆς ζωῆς καὶ φάγῃ καὶ ζήσεται εἰς τὸν αἰῶνα – ³¹ 23 καὶ ἐξαπέστειλεν αὐτὸν κύριος ὁ θεὸς ἐκ τοῦ παραδείσου τῆς τρυφῆς³² ἐργάζεσθαι τὴν γῆν, ἐξ ἧς ἐλήμφθη. 24 καὶ ἐξέβαλεν τὸν Αδαμ καὶ κατῴκισεν αὐτὸν ἀπέναντι τοῦ παραδείσου τῆς τρυφῆς καὶ ἔταξεν τὰ χερουβιμ καὶ τὴν φλογίνην ῥομφαίαν τὴν στρεφομένην φυλάσσειν τὴν ὁδὸν τοῦ ξύλου τῆς ζωῆς.

Vocabulary

ἀπέναντι, opposite

δερμάτινος, -η, -ον, leather (adj.)

ἐκτείνω, ¹aor. inf. ἐκτεῖναι, pf. ptc. ἐκτετακώς: stretch out, lay out, spread out; hold out

ἐξαποστέλλω, send somebody off/away; send on a mission, commission a senator

κατοικίζω, settle, establish; pass. be settled, dwell

ῥομφαία, ἡ, sword

τάσσω (Att. τάττω), pf. pass. ptc. τεταγμένος: to station, post somebody before; set; appoint; determine; undertake (a task), restore; pass. be ordained, pre-established that (w. acc. + inf.); τὰ τεταγμένα, instructions

τρυφή, ἡ, delight, luxury

φλόγινος, -η, -ον, flaming, fiery

Χερουβ, τό, pl. χερουβιν/ειν/ιμ: cherub, cherubim, winged creatures (like the Egyptian sphynx), half human, half lion

SELECT BIBLIOGRAPHY

Wevers, John William (ed.). *LXX: Notes on the Greek Text of Genesis*. Atlanta: Scholars Press, 1993.

---

[29] Cf. Gen 1:26 ("let us"); it is unclear whether this is a reference to a plurality of gods (as one finds elsewhere in ancient exemplars of this genre) or to a heavenly court (cf. Isa 6:8).

[30] Art. inf. (translate as gerund, "-ing").

[31] The sentence beginning καὶ νῦν μήποτε is an anacoluthon, lacking a conclusion such as "let us send him away." The next verse continues with the narrative past (καὶ ἐξαπέστειλεν).

[32] Up to this point, the Heb. term *edem* has been treated as a proper noun, Ἔδεμ ("Eden," cf. Gen 2:8, 10, 4:16). But here and in Gen 3:24 it is translated τρύφη ("delight, luxury"). Adam is banished from the "garden *of delight*," calling attention to the splendors of the garden that are no longer available to the primeval pair. As a result, man must till the very soil from which he had been formed.

2.2.

1 Kingdoms: The Anointing of David as King

(1 Kgdms 16:1–13 [1 Samuel])

Text: Rahlfs/Hanhart, I, 531-32; ET: *NETS* 260.

The Septuagintal versions of 1–2 Samuel and 1–2 Kings are known as 1–4 Kingdoms. Thus, the Septuagintal version of 1 Sam 16:1–13 is 1 Kgdms 16:1–13. Taken together, these four books present the reader with a privileged window onto the Greek transmission of these texts in antiquity: some sections preserve the so-called Old Greek version, such as found in 1 Kgdms 1–31, while other sections preserve later revisions. "Old Greek" is a technical term for the first Greek translations of the Hebrew Bible for books outside the Pentateuch. The style of the Old Greek translation is not slavishly literal but is still generally isomorphic with the Hebrew parent text.

16:1 Καὶ εἶπεν κύριος πρὸς Σαμουηλ· ἕως πότε σὺ πενθεῖς ἐπὶ Σαουλ, κἀγὼ ἐξουδένωκα αὐτὸν μὴ βασιλεύειν ἐπὶ Ισραηλ; πλῆσον[1] τὸ κέρας σου ἐλαίου, καὶ δεῦρο ἀποστείλω[2] σε πρὸς Ιεσσαι ἕως εἰς Βηθλεεμ, ὅτι ἑόρακα[3] ἐν τοῖς υἱοῖς αὐτοῦ (someone) ἐμοὶ βασιλεύειν. 2 Καὶ εἶπεν Σαμουηλ· πῶς πορευθῶ;[4] καὶ ἀκούσεται Σαουλ καὶ ἀποκτενεῖ με. Καὶ εἶπεν κύριος· δάμαλιν βοῶν λαβὲ ἐν τῇ χειρί σου καὶ ἐρεῖς[5] Θῦσαι τῷ κυρίῳ ἥκω, 3 καὶ καλέσεις τὸν Ιεσσαι εἰς τὴν θυσίαν, καὶ γνωριῶ σοι ἃ ποιήσεις, καὶ χρίσεις ὃν ἐὰν εἴπω πρὸς σέ. 4 καὶ ἐποίησεν Σαμουηλ πάντα, ἃ ἐλάλησεν αὐτῷ κύριος, καὶ ἦλθεν εἰς Βηθλεεμ. καὶ ἐξέστησαν οἱ πρεσβύτεροι τῆς πόλεως τῇ ἀπαντήσει αὐτοῦ καὶ εἶπαν · Εἰρήνη ἡ εἴσοδός σου, ὁ βλέπων;[6] 5 καὶ εἶπεν· εἰρήνη, θῦσαι τῷ κυρίῳ ἥκω, ἁγιάσθητε καὶ

---

[1] S.v. πίμπλημι.
[2] Aor. subj. for fut. ind.
[3] S.v. ὁράω.
[4] The verb πορεύομαι forms an aor. pass. dep. ἐπορεύθην and, by extension, a pass. subj.
[5] S.v. λέγω.
[6] S.v. βλέπω, ὁ βλέπων, "seer."

εὐφράνθητε μετ' ἐμοῦ σήμερον. καὶ (Σαμουηλ) ἡγίασεν τὸν Ιεσσαι καὶ τοὺς υἱοὺς αὐτοῦ καὶ ἐκάλεσεν αὐτοὺς εἰς τὴν θυσίαν. 6 καὶ ἐγενήθη[7] ἐν τῷ αὐτοὺς εἰσιέναι[8] καὶ εἶδεν τὸν Ελιαβ[9] καὶ εἶπεν· ἀλλὰ καὶ[10] ἐνώπιον κυρίου χριστὸς αὐτοῦ.[11]

Vocabulary

ἁγιάζω, make sacred, sanctify; consecrate to

ἀπάντησις, -εως, ἡ, meeting, greeting (esp. of public welcome of an official)

βασιλεύω, rule, reign; become like a king

βοῦς, βοός (gen.), **ὁ/ἡ**, ox, cow

γνωρίζω, 2. γνωριῶ: make known; gain knowledge of, recognize

δάλαμις, -εως, ἡ, young cow, heifer

εἴσειμι (fr. εἶμι), impf. εἰσῄειν, inf. εἰσιέναι: enter; come before, enter before

εἴσοδος, -ου, ἡ, entrance, entrance door, entrance hall; entering, access

εὐφραίνω, make glad; pass. rejoice, celebrate

ἥκω, pres. inf. ἥκειν, 2nd sg. pres. impv. ἧκε, 2. ἥξω: have come/arrived, be present

θύω, to sacrifice (a victim)

κέρας, -ατος, τό, horn (of an animal); container made from the horn of an animal

16:7 καὶ εἶπεν κύριος πρὸς Σαμουηλ· μὴ ἐπιβλέψῃς ἐπὶ τὴν ὄψιν αὐτοῦ μηδὲ εἰς τὴν ἕξιν μεγέθους αὐτοῦ, ὅτι ἐξουδένωκα αὐτόν, ὅτι οὐχ ὡς ἐμβλέψεται ἄνθρωπος, ὄψεται ὁ θεός, ὅτι ἄνθρωπος ὄψεται εἰς πρόσωπον, ὁ δὲ θεὸς ὄψεται εἰς καρδίαν. 8 καὶ ἐκάλεσεν Ιεσσαι τὸν Αμιναδαβ,[12] καὶ παρῆλθεν κατὰ[13] πρόσωπον Σαμουηλ, καὶ εἶπεν· οὐδὲ τοῦτον ἐξελέξατο κύριος. 9 καὶ παρήγαγεν Ιεσσαι τὸν Σαμα,[14] καὶ εἶπεν· καὶ ἐν τούτῳ[15] οὐκ ἐξελέξατο κύριος. 10 καὶ παρήγαγεν Ιεσσαι τοὺς ἑπτὰ υἱοὺς αὐτοῦ ἐνώπιον Σαμουηλ, καὶ εἶπεν Σαμουηλ· οὐκ ἐξελέξατο κύριος ἐν τούτοις. 11 καὶ εἶπεν Σαμουηλ πρὸς Ιεσσαι· ἐκλελοίπασιν[16] τὰ παιδάρια; Καὶ εἶπεν· ἔτι ὁ μικρὸς[17] ἰδοὺ ποιμαίνει ἐν τῷ ποιμνίῳ. καὶ εἶπεν Σαμουηλ πρὸς Ιεσσαι· ἀπόστειλον (a messenger) καὶ λαβὲ αὐτόν, ὅτι οὐ μὴ κατακλιθῶμεν[18] ἕως τοῦ ἐλθεῖν αὐτόν.[19] 12 καὶ ἀπέστειλεν (a messenger) καὶ εἰσήγαγεν αὐτόν, καὶ

---

[7] Semitic construction: "And it came to pass that...."

[8] Art. inf.; s.v. εἴσειμι (fr. εἶμι, cf. table 9.14); art. inf. (w. ἐν), w. αὐτούς as subj. of inf.

[9] Eliab, eldest son of Jesse and David's eldest brother.

[10] ἀλλά ("certainly/surely") + καί ("indeed").

[11] Nominal sentence (supply a form of εἰμί).

[12] Abinadab, second son of Jesse.

[13] "Before."

[14] Shammah, third son of Jesse.

[15] ἐν τούτῳ, "in this case."

[16] Cf. table 9.1.1(e).

[17] μικρός, -ά, -όν, here for superl., "smallest" (youngest).

[18] οὐ μή + aor. subj. (emph. fut. neg.).

[19] Art. inf.

οὗτος πυρράκης μετὰ κάλλους ὀφθαλμῶν καὶ ἀγαθὸς ὁράσει κυρίῳ, καὶ εἶπεν κύριος πρὸς Σαμουηλ· ἀνάστα[20] καὶ χρῖσον τὸν Δαυιδ, ὅτι οὗτος ἀγαθός ἐστιν. 13 καὶ ἔλαβεν Σαμουηλ τὸ κέρας τοῦ ἐλαίου καὶ ἔχρισεν αὐτὸν ἐν μέσῳ τῶν ἀδελφῶν αὐτοῦ, καὶ ἐφήλατο πνεῦμα κυρίου ἐπὶ Δαυιδ ἀπὸ τῆς ἡμέρας ἐκείνης καὶ ἐπάνω. καὶ ἀνέστη Σαμουηλ καὶ ἀπῆλθεν εἰς Αρμαθαιμ.

Vocabulary

Ἀρμαθαιμ, Harmathaim, a city of the tribe of Benjamin, north of Jerusalem

εἰσάγω, lead in, bring in; introduce

ἐκλέγω, [1]aor. mid. ἐξελέξαμαι: collect revenue (money): mid. choose, select

ἐκλείπω, 3. ἐξέλιπον, 4. ἐκλέλοιπα: forsake; remain, be left behind; pass away; abandon, quit

ἔλαιον, τό, olive oil

ἐμβλέπω (w. dat.), look at/upon; consider

ἕξις, -εως, ἡ, outward appearance

ἐξουδενόω (= ἐξουδενέω), despise, treat with contempt

ἐπάνω, above; on top of; onward

ἐπιβλέπω, look upon (gen.)

ἐφάλλομαι, 3. ἐφηλόμην: leap/spring upon

κατακλίνω, make somebody lay down; pass. recline at table, banquet

μέγεθος, -ους, τό, size; greatness

παιδάριον, τό, young man

παράγω, march by, introduce; (make) pass by

παρέρχομαι, 4. παρελήλυθα, [2]pf. act. inf. παρεληλυθέναι: walk past, pass by; pass away; (of time) be past, (of a fast) be over; disobey

ποιμαίνω, herd, tend flocks

ποίμνιον, τό, flock (of sheep/goats)

πυρράκης, -ου, ὁ, red/ruddy person

---

[20] ἀνάστα,[2]aor. act. impv. apoc. fr. ἀνάστηθι, cf. table 9.12.2(f).

2.3.

Book of Jeremiah: Sayings from the Book of Consolation

(Jer 38:27–34 [MT 31:27–34])

Text: Rahlfs/Hanhard, II, 722; ET: *NETS* 915.

The Septuagintal Greek text of Jeremiah is based on Hebrew texts that were substantially different from the Hebrew of the Masoretic text. Nonetheless, it is clear that the translator followed an isomorphic translation model in terms of the Hebrew parent text. Owing to the difference between the Hebrew text underlying the Septuagintal translation and the Hebrew of the Masoretic text, the numbering of chapters differs significantly. A case in point is Jer 31:27–34 of the Masoretic text, which is Jer 38:27–34 in the Septuagint.

Jer 38:27–34 is taken from the "Book of Consolation" (Jer 37–40 [MT 30–33]). This book, with its prophecy of the restoration of Israel and Judah, seems to presuppose a military invasion that left the land desolated, its population diminished, and its flocks and herds reduced. Following the invasion, the need arose to repopulate the land, replanting it with the "seed of men" and the "seed of beasts" (Jer 38:27).

Next, Jer 38:31–34 describes the "new covenant" that God would one day give his people, forgiving their sins and writing the Torah in their hearts in order that all would know him. The background to this announcement is the covenant inaugurated between the Lord and Israel at Mount Sinai (Exod 19:1–24:11). Such a new covenant was needed because the Israelites had broken the former covenant. This concept of a new covenant was later taken up both by sectarians at Qumran and by Christians. The Essenes also understood themselves to be people of a new covenant. Similarly, Christians interpreted the fulfillment of this prophecy in the emergence of the messianic movement associated with Jesus of Nazareth (Luke 22:20, 1 Cor 11:15, Heb 8:8–9:28).

38:27 Διὰ τοῦτο ἰδοὺ ἡμέραι ἔρχονται, φησὶν κύριος, καὶ σπερῶ τὸν Ισραηλ καὶ τὸν Ιουδαν σπέρμα ἀνθρώπου καὶ σπέρμα κτήνους. 28 καὶ ἔσται[1] ὥσπερ ἐγρηγόρουν[2] ἐπ᾽ αὐτοὺς καθαιρεῖν καὶ κακοῦν, οὕτως γρηγορήσω ἐπ᾽ αὐτοὺς τοῦ οἰκοδομεῖν καὶ καταφυτεύειν,[3] φησὶν κύριος. 29 ἐν ταῖς ἡμέραις ἐκείναις οὐ μὴ εἴπωσιν

> Οἱ πατέρες ἔφαγον ὄμφακα,
> καὶ οἱ ὀδόντες τῶν τέκνων ἡμωδίασαν.[4]

30 ἀλλ᾽ ἢ ἕκαστος[5] ἐν τῇ ἑαυτοῦ ἁμαρτίᾳ ἀποθανεῖται, καὶ τοῦ φαγόντος τὸν ὄμφακα αἱμωδιάσουσιν οἱ ὀδόντες αὐτοῦ.[6]

Vocabulary

αἱμωδιάω, become dumb or tingly; (of teeth) be set on edge
γρηγορέω, wake up, be alert, watchful; γρηγορέω ἐπί, to watch (over)
καθαιρέω, pull down, destroy; fig. pass. suffer the loss of (w. gen.)
κακόω, do evil, hurt/harm
καταφυτεύω, to plant
ὀδούς, -όντος, ὁ, tooth, pl. teeth
ὄμφαξ, -ακος, ἡ, sour/unripe grapes (collective)

38:31 Ἰδοὺ ἡμέραι ἔρχονται, φησὶν κύριος, καὶ διαθήσομαι τῷ οἴκῳ Ισραηλ καὶ τῷ οἴκῳ Ιουδα διαθήκην καινήν,[7] 32 οὐ κατὰ τὴν διαθήκην, ἣν διεθέμην τοῖς πατράσιν αὐτῶν ἐν ἡμέρᾳ ἐπιλαβομένου μου[8] τῆς χειρὸς αὐτῶν ἐξαγαγεῖν αὐτοὺς ἐκ γῆς Αἰγύπτου, ὅτι αὐτοὶ οὐκ ἐνέμειναν ἐν τῇ διαθήκῃ μου, καὶ ἐγὼ ἠμέλησα αὐτῶν, φησὶν κύριος, 33 ὅτι αὕτη (is) ἡ διαθήκη, ἣν διαθήσομαι τῷ οἴκῳ Ισραηλ μετὰ τὰς ἡμέρας ἐκείνας, φησὶν κύριος. Διδοὺς δώσω[9] νόμους μου εἰς τὴν διάνοιαν αὐτῶν καὶ ἐπὶ καρδίας αὐτῶν γράψω αὐτούς, καὶ ἔσομαι αὐτοῖς εἰς[10] θεόν, καὶ αὐτοὶ ἔσονταί μοι εἰς λαόν, 34 καὶ οὐ μὴ διδάξωσιν[11] ἕκαστος τὸν

---

[1] ἔσται, impers. "it shall be."
[2] Cust. impf. ("used to," cf. IV, 13.2).
[3] Two art. infinitives.
[4] The proverb quoted in Jer 38:29–30 is also quoted in Ezek 18:2. Many Jews felt that the nation was being punished for the sins of past generations and that the Lord was acting unjustly. Jeremiah, and later Ezekiel, quoted this proverb in order to deny this charge, arguing that in the future, only the one who sins will suffer for his sins (cf. Deut 24:16). Here we find the principle of individual responsibility enunciated.
[5] ἀλλ᾽ ἢ ἕκαστος, "but rather each."
[6] αὐτοῦ (functionless).
[7] This is the only reference to a διαθήκη καινή in the Tanakh.
[8] Gen. absol. w. μου as the subject of the participle.
[9] Lit. follows Heb., meaning "I will surely give."
[10] Telic εἰς expressing purpose ("as").
[11] οὐ μή + aor. subj. (emph. fut. neg.); 3 pl. apparently because of repetition of ἕκαστος

πολίτην αὐτοῦ καὶ ἕκαστος τὸν ἀδελφὸν αὐτοῦ λέγων 'Γνῶθι[12] τὸν κύριον,' ὅτι πάντες εἰδήσουσίν[13] με ἀπὸ μικροῦ[14] αὐτῶν καὶ ἕως[15] μεγάλου αὐτῶν, ὅτι ἵλεως ἔσομαι ταῖς ἀδικίαις αὐτῶν καὶ τῶν ἁμαρτιῶν αὐτῶν οὐ μὴ μνησθῶ ἔτι.

Vocabulary

ἀδικία, ἡ, wrongdoing, unjustice

Αἴγυπτος, ἡ, Egypt

ἀμελέω, disregard, neglect

διαθήκη, ἡ, treaty, covenant; last will and testament

διατίθημι, mid. establish a covenant

ἔμμενω, [1]aor. ἐνέμεινα: abide in, persevere in; abide by, stand by, be true to

ἐπιλαμβάνω, 5. ἐπείλημμαι: take hold of something; overtake, seize; pass. be imprisoned

ἐξάγω, lead out

ἵλεως, merciful, gracious, kindly (adv.)

πολίτης, ὁ, citizen, countryman

---

[12] S.v. γινώσκω (cf. table 9.6).
[13] S.v. οἶδα (cf. table 9.5).
[14] Adj. (μικρός) for superl. ("smallest," "least").
[15] ἕως, "up to."

2.4.

Book of Amos: A Lament over Israel's Sin

(Amos 5:14–27)

Provenance: The prophet Amos, of the southern kingdom of Judea, was expelled from the royal sanctuary at Bethel (north of Jerusalem) and ordered not to prophesy there again.

Text: Rahlfs/Hanhard, II, 507; ET: *NETS* 792–93.

Date: Amos lived ca. 760–750 BCE, during the peaceful reign of Jeroboam II at the height of Israel's territorial expansion and prosperity.

Text: Amos 3–6, from which the reading in this section is taken, recordse an indictment of the northern kingdom of Israel, especially of Samaria and Bethel, for sin and injustice. The Greek text of Amos is typical translation Greek.

5:14 Ἐκζητήσατε τὸ καλὸν καὶ μὴ τὸ πονηρόν, ὅπως ζήσητε,
καὶ ἔσται οὕτως μεθ᾽ ὑμῶν κύριος ὁ θεὸς ὁ παντοκράτωρ,
ὃν τρόπον εἴπατε·

15 Μεμισήκαμεν τὰ πονηρὰ καὶ ἠγαπήκαμεν τὰ καλά,
καὶ ἀποκαταστήσατε ἐν πύλαις κρίμα,
ὅπως ἐλεήσῃ κύριος ὁ θεὸς ὁ παντοκράτωρ τοὺς περιλοίπους τοῦ Ιωσηφ.

16 διὰ τοῦτο τάδε λέγει κύριος ὁ θεὸς ὁ παντοκράτωρ·
ἐν πάσαις πλατείαις κοπετός,
καὶ ἐν πάσαις ὁδοῖς ῥηθήσεται[1] Οὐαὶ οὐαί.
κληθήσεται γεωργὸς εἰς πένθος
καὶ κοπετὸν καὶ εἰς εἰδότας[2] θρῆνον,

17 καὶ ἐν πάσαις ὁδοῖς κοπετός,
διότι διελεύσομαι διὰ μέσου σου, εἶπεν κύριος.

---

[1] S.v. λέγω.
[2] S.v. οἶδα, table 9.5.

Vocabulary

ἀπερείδω, lean/rest upon, put upon

ἀποκαθίστημι, ¹aor. ἀπεκατέστησα/²aor. ἀπεκατέστην: re-establish, restore, cure

γεωργός, ὁ, farmer

διότι, for, because; therefore

εἰσπηδάω, rush in

ἐκζητέω, seek out, require

ἐλεέω, be merciful; feel pity; pass. be shown mercy

θρῆνος, ὁ, lamentation

κοπετός, ὁ, mourning, lamentation (cf. Amos 5:17)

ὅδε, ἥδε, τάδε, this

παντοκράτωρ, -ορος, ὁ, almighty

πένθος, -ους, τό, mourning, sorrow

περίλοιπος, -ον, remaining, surviving; οἱ περίλοιποι, remnant (of Joseph)

πλατεῖα, ἡ, street

πύλη, ἡ, gate

τρόπος, ὁ, way, manner; ὃν τρόπον, (just) as; καθ᾽ ὃν τρόπον, in the manner that
    (cf. Amos 5:19)

18　Οὐαὶ οἱ ἐπιθυμοῦντες τὴν ἡμέραν κυρίου,
　　ἵνα τί[3] αὕτη ὑμῖν ἡ ἡμέρα τοῦ κυρίου;
　　καὶ αὐτή ἐστιν σκότος καὶ οὐ φῶς,

19　ὃν τρόπον ὅταν[4] φύγῃ ἄνθρωπος ἐκ προσώπου τοῦ λέοντος
　　καὶ ἐμπέσῃ αὐτῷ ἡ ἄρκος,
　　καὶ εἰσπηδήσῃ εἰς τὸν οἶκον αὐτοῦ καὶ ἀπερείσηται τὰς χεῖρας αὐτοῦ
　　　ἐπὶ τὸν τοῖχον[5]
　　καὶ δάκῃ αὐτὸν ὁ ὄφις.

20　οὐχὶ[6] σκότος ἡ ἡμέρα τοῦ κυρίου καὶ οὐ φῶς;
　　καὶ γνόφος οὐκ ἔχων φέγγος αὐτῇ.

21　Μεμίσηκα, ἀπῶσμαι, ἑορτὰς ὑμῶν
　　καὶ οὐ μὴ ὀσφρανθῶ ἐν ταῖς πανηγύρεσιν ὑμῶν,

22　διότι καὶ ἐὰν ἐνέγκητέ[7] μοι ὁλοκαυτώματα καὶ θυσίας ὑμῶν, οὐ προσδέξομαι
　　　αὐτά,
　　καὶ σωτηρίου ἐπιφανείας ὑμῶν οὐκ ἐπιβλέψομαι.

23　μετάστησον ἀπ᾽ ἐμοῦ ἦχον ᾠδῶν σου,
　　καὶ ψαλμὸν ὀργάνων σου οὐκ ἀκούσομαι,

24　καὶ κυλισθήσεται ὡς ὕδωρ κρίμα καὶ δικαιοσύνη ὡς χειμάρρους ἄβατος.

---

[3] ἵνα τί, "to what end?," "why?"

[4] ὃν τρόπον ὅταν, "(it is) as if."

[5] τοῖχον > τεῖχον.

[6] οὐχὶ for a question anticipating the answer "yes" ("isn't … ?").

[7] S.v. φέρω.

25   μὴ[8] σφάγια καὶ θυσίας προσηνέγκατέ μοι ἐν τῇ ἐρήμῳ τεσσαράκοντα ἔτη, οἶκος[9] Ισραηλ;

26   καὶ ἀνελάβετε τὴν σκηνὴν τοῦ Μολοχ καὶ τὸ ἄστρον τοῦ θεοῦ ὑμῶν Ραιφαν,

        τοὺς τύπους αὐτῶν, οὓς ἐποιήσατε ἑαυτοῖς.

27   καὶ μετοικιῶ ὑμᾶς ἐπέκεινα Δαμασκοῦ,

        λέγει κύριος – ὁ θεὸς ὁ παντοκράτωρ ὄνομα αὐτῷ.[10]

Vocabulary

ἄβατος, -ον, unfordable, untrodden, inaccessible

ἀπωθέω, [1]aor. mid. ἀπωσάμην, pf. mid. ἀπῶσμαι: push away, reject

ἄρκος, ὁ/ἡ, a bear

ἀστήρ, -έρος, ὁ, star

γνόφος, ὁ, darkness, pl. storm clouds

δάκνω, [1]aor. ἔδηξα/[2]aor. ἔδακον: bite

ἐμπίπτω, [2]aor. ἐνέπεσον, aor. inf. ἐμπεσεῖν: fall into (a state/condition); intrude into/among

ἐπέκεινα (w. gen.), beyond, on the other side

ἐπιβλέπω (w. gen.), look upon

ἐπιφάνεια, ἡ, appearance, manifestation; conspicuous

ἦχος, ὁ, echo, sound

κυλίω, roll something up/down; mid. roll oneself upon something; pour down

μεθίστημι, 3. μετέστησα: remove; seduce (to apostasy); shift somebody over to (a way of life)

μετοικίζω, 2. μετοικιῶ: lead settlers to another land/into exile

Μολοχ, Moloch (Heb. Sakkuth) and Ῥαιφαν, Raephan (Heb. Kaiwan) were Assyrian deities (cf. Acts 7:42–43)

ὁλοκαύτωμα, -ματος, τό, a whole burnt offering

ὄργανον, τό, musical instrument

ὀσφραίνομαι (dep.), to smell, take delight in

πανήγυρις, -εως, ἡ, festival

σκηνή, ἡ, tent, tabernacle

σφάγιον, τό, (mostly pl.), victims, offerings, sacrifices

σωτήριον, τό, thank offering (in LXX and Philo)

τύπος, ὁ, image, form; type, archetype, figure; pl. details

χειμάρρους/ουν, -ου, ὁ, river/wadi (with abundant water in winter)

ψαλμός, ὁ, psalm, song of praise

ᾠδή, ἡ, song, ode; singing

---

[8] μή signals a question anticipating the answer "no."
[9] Nom. for voc.
[10] Dat. of poss.

2.5.

Book of Exodus: The Song of the Sea

(Exod 15:1–18)

Text: Rahlfs/Hanhart, II, 111–12; ET: *NETS* 61–62.

In Jewish prayer books, Exod 15:1–18 is known as the "Song of the Sea." In the Eastern Orthodox canon it is called the "Ode of Moses."[1] According to legend, the Song of the Sea was sung by the Israelites after they crossed the "Sea of Reeds," or the "Red Sea" (as it is known in the LXX), in safety. This poem celebrates the destruction of the Egyptian army during this crossing. The poem originally existed as a separate text but was later incorporated into the Jahwist source.

Generally speaking, the Septuagintal translation of Exodus is "expansionist" in character, in the sense that it tends to expand the underlying text. This is also true of the translation of this song, which not only expands but also amplifies the miraculous character of the narrated events.

15:1 Τότε ᾖσεν Μωυσῆς καὶ οἱ υἱοὶ Ισραηλ τὴν ᾠδὴν ταύτην τῷ θεῷ καὶ εἶπαν λέγοντες,[2]
Ἄισωμεν[3] τῷ κυρίῳ, ἐνδόξως γὰρ δεδόξασται,[4]
ἵππον καὶ ἀναβάτην ἔρριψεν εἰς θάλασσαν.

2 βοηθὸς καὶ σκεπαστὴς ἐγένετό μοι εἰς σωτηρίαν,
οὗτός (is) μου θεός, καὶ δοξάσω αὐτόν,
θεὸς τοῦ πατρός μου, καὶ ὑψώσω αὐτόν.

3 κύριος συντρίβων πολέμους,
κύριος (is) ὄνομα αὐτῷ.[5]

---

[1] Not to be confused with the "Song of Moses" in Deut 32:1–43.
[2] καὶ εἶπαν λέγοντες is pleonastic, representing the Hebrew direct speech marker.
[3] Hort. subj.
[4] ἐνδόξως...δεδόξασται, adv. + finite mid. verb, translating free inf. absol. w. the cognate finite verb (3 m. sg. qal. pf.) in the Heb. text. In your translation, leave ἐνδόξως untranslated.
[5] Dat. of poss.

Vocabulary

ᾄδω, 2. ᾄσω/ᾄσομαι, 3. ᾖσα, [1]aor. inf. ᾆσαι: sing a song

ἀναβάτης, ὁ, horseman, rider (cf. Exod 15:4)

βοηθός, ὁ, helper; protector

δοξάζω, think, imagine; glorify; mid. to display one's greatness; pass. supposed to be; be held in honor (cf. Exod 15:6)

ἔνδοξος, -ον, held in honor, of high repute; glorious; subst. glorious features; ἐνδόξως, gloriously

ἵππος, ὁ, horse; cavalry (collective noun); pl. ἵπποι, bouncers (in a men's drinking club)

πόλεμος, ὁ, war, battle

ῥίπτω, 3. ἔρριψα, [1]aor. impv. ῥῖψον, 6. ἐρρίφην: throw, cast away; lay/put something down

σκεπαστής, -οῦ, defender

συντρίβω, crush, break to pieces, annihilate (cf. Exod 15:7)

ᾠδή, ἡ, song, ode; singing

15:4   ἅρματα Φαραω[6] καὶ τὴν δύναμιν αὐτοῦ ἔρριψεν εἰς θάλασσαν,
       ἐπιλέκτους ἀναβάτας, τριστάτας,
       κατεπόντισεν ἐν ἐρυθρᾷ θαλάσσῃ.[7]

5   πόντῳ ἐκάλυψεν αὐτούς,
       κατέδυσαν εἰς βυθὸν ὡσεὶ λίθος.[8]

6   ἡ δεξιά σου, κύριε, δεδόξασται ἐν ἰσχύι,ἡ δεξιά σου χείρ, κύριε, ἔθραυσεν
       ἐχθρούς.

Vocabulary

ἅρμα, -ματος, τό, chariot

βυθός, ὁ, depth, deep

δεξιός, -ά, -όν, on the right; δεξιά, ἡ, right hand, authority

ἐπίλεκτος, ον, chosen, choice

ἐρυθρός, -ά, -όν, red

θραύω, to break, crush

καταδύω, to go down, sink into (εἰς)

καταποντίζω, throw/drown into the sea

πόντος, ὁ, open sea[9]

τριστάτης, ὁ, third-ranked officer

ὡσεί, like, as if; about, approximately

---

[6] Indecl., but here gen. ("Pharoh").

[7] ἐρυθρᾷ θαλάσσῃ ("Red Sea") for the Heb. "Sea of Reeds."

[8] LXX emphasizes the divine action. Whereas the Heb. text begins with "floods" as subject, LXX has κύριος (15:3), with πόντῳ simply the means that the Lord used.

[9] Translator reserves θάλασσα for Heb. *yam.*

15:7 καὶ τῷ πλήθει τῆς δόξης σου συνέτριψας τοὺς ὑπεναντίους,
ἀπέστειλας τὴν ὀργήν σου, καὶ κατέφαγεν αὐτοὺς ὡς καλάμην.

8 καὶ διὰ πνεύματος τοῦ θυμοῦ[10] σου διέστη τὸ ὕδωρ,
ἐπάγη[11] ὡσεὶ τεῖχος τὰ ὕδατα,
ἐπάγη τὰ κύματα ἐν μέσῳ τῆς θαλάσσης.

9 εἶπεν ὁ ἐχθρός ῾Διώξας[12] καταλήμψομαι,[13]
μεριῶ σκῦλα, ἐμπλήσω ψυχήν μου,
ἀνελῶ[14] τῇ μαχαίρῃ μου, κυριεύσει ἡ χείρ μου.᾽

10 ἀπέστειλας τὸ πνεῦμά σου,[15] ἐκάλυψεν αὐτοὺς θάλασσα,
ἔδυσαν ὡσεὶ μόλιβος ἐν ὕδατι σφοδρῷ.

Vocabulary

ἁγίασμα, -ματος, τό, sanctuary (cf. Exod 15:17)

ἀναιρέω, 2. ἀναιρήσω/ἀνελῶ, 3. ἀνεῖλον/ἀνεῖλα: destroy; execute, kill; mid., take up for oneself

διΐστημι, to separate

διώκω, pursue, chase; persecute; strive for; recite (a spell)

δύνω (also **δύω**), 1. mid. δύομαι, 2. δύσομαι, ²aor. ἔδυν: go down, set (of the sun); sink; mid. to sink/set (of the sun)

ἐμπίπλημι/ἐμπιπλάω, pres. ptc. ἐμπιπλῶν, 2. ἐμπλήσω, ¹aor. mid. impv. ἔπλησαι: fill full of (w. gen.)

ἐχθρός, -ά, -όν, enemy, hated; ὁ ἐχθρός, the enemy

καλάμη, ἡ, straw, stubble

κατεσθίω, impf. κατήσθιον, 3. κατέφαγον: eat, devour

κῦμα, -ματος, τό, wave (of the sea)

κυριεύω (w. gen.), have power over, rule over; gain mastery over; control

μάχαιρα, -ας, ἡ, sword, dagger

μερίζω, 2. μεριῶ, 6. ἐμερίσθην: to divide; to assign

μόλιβος, ὁ, lead (metal)

ὀργή, ἡ, anger, wrath

πήγνυμι, 3. ἔπηξα, ¹aor. ptc. πήξας, 6. ἐπάγην: pitch a tent; pass. become stiff, congealed

πλῆθος, -ους, τό, great number, multitude; abundance, great quantity

σκῦλον, τό, pl. τὰ σκύλα, spoils, booty

σφοδρός, -ά, -όν, mighty, strong

---

[10] MT means "by the breath (snort) of your nostrils," the term "nostrils" being a common figure of divine anger. But the translator has avoided this crude figure of speech.

[11] S.v. πήγνυμι; the subject of the verb is ὕδατα.

[12] S.v., διώκω, instr. adv. ptc. ("by") (cf. IV, 5).

[13] καταλαμβάνω.

[14] S.v. ἀναιρέω.

[15] LXX avoids the anthropomorphism of MT (God "blowing") by a neutral "you sent (ἀπέστειλας) your πνεῦμα."

τεῖχος, -ους, τό, city wall
ὑπεναντίος, -α, -ον, opposing; subst. opponent, enemy

15:11   Τίς ὅμοιός σοι ἐν θεοῖς, κύριε;
        τίς ὅμοιός σοι, δεδοξασμένος ἐν ἁγίοις,[16]
        θαυμαστὸς ἐν δόξαις, ποιῶν τέρατα;
12   ἐξέτεινας τὴν δεξιάν σου,
        κατέπιεν αὐτοὺς γῆ.
13   ὡδήγησας τῇ δικαιοσύνῃ σου τὸν λαόν σου τοῦτον, ὃν ἐλυτρώσω,
        παρεκάλεσας (them) τῇ ἰσχύι σου εἰς κατάλυμα ἅγιόν σου.
14   ἤκουσαν ἔθνη καὶ ὠργίσθησαν,
        ὠδῖνες ἔλαβον κατοικοῦντας (among the) Φυλιστιιμ.[17]
15   τότε ἔσπευσαν[18] ἡγεμόνες Εδωμ,[19]
        καὶ ἄρχοντες Μωαβιτῶν,[20] ἔλαβεν αὐτοὺς τρόμος,
        ἐτάκησαν πάντες οἱ κατοικοῦντες Χανααν.[21]

Vocabulary

ἄρχων, -οντος, ὁ, prince, ruler, leader; archon (title of a city magistrate)
ἡγεμών, -όνος, ὁ, leader; imperial governor (of a Roman province)
θαυμαστός, -ή, -όν, wonderful, marvelous
ἰσχύς, -ύος, ἡ, strength, might
κατάλυμα, -ματος, τό, lodging, inn; abode
καταπίνω, to swallow
λυτρόω, mid. to release by payment of a ransom, to redeem
ὁδηγέω, to guide, lead; to lead to (πρός/εἰς)
σπεύδω, 3. ἔσπευσα: hurry; take an interest in somebody
τέρας, -ατος, τό, portentous sign, wonder
τήκω, 3. ἐτάκησα: to melt
τρόμος, ὁ, trembling
Χανααν, Canaan (indecl.)
ὠδίν, -ῖνος, ἡ, pl. ὠδῖνες, labor pains

---

[16] LXX has ἐν ἁγίοις, where MT has a sg. noun ("holiness").
[17] Φυλιστιιμ (indecl.): the translators mistakenly use the term "Philistines" instead of the "land of the Philistines."
[18] LXX understood the corresponding Heb. term in the Late Hebrew sense of "to hasten, hurry" rather than the original meaning "to be dismayed, terrified."
[19] Edom, indecl., here gen.
[20] Moabites (gen.).
[21] Indecl., here gen.

15:16 ἐπιπέσοι²² ἐπ᾽ αὐτοὺς φόβος καὶ τρόμος,
μεγέθει βραχίονός σου ἀπολιθωθήτωσαν,²³
ἕως ἂν παρέλθῃ ὁ λαός σου, κύριε,
ἕως ἂν παρέλθῃ ὁ λαός σου οὗτος, ὃν ἐκτήσω.²⁴

17 εἰσαγαγὼν καταφύτευσον αὐτοὺς εἰς ὄρος κληρονομίας σου,
εἰς ἕτοιμον κατοικητήριόν σου, ὃ κατειργάσω, κύριε,
ἁγίασμα, κύριε, ὃ ἡτοίμασαν αἱ χεῖρές σου.

18 κύριος βασιλεύων τὸν αἰῶνα καὶ ἐπ᾽ αἰῶνα καὶ ἔτι.

Vocabulary

ἀπολιθόω, pass. become petrified, turn into stone
βασιλεύω, rule, reign; become like a king
βραχίων, -ονος, ὁ, arm; strength
εἰσάγω, lead in, bring in; introduce
ἐπιπίπτω, 4. ἐπιπέπτωκα: fall on/over; happen to
ἑτοιμάζω, prepare; pass., be ready
καταφυτεύω, to plant
κατεργάζομαι, 3. κατειργασάμην: bring about, accomplish; prepare; work out
κατοικητήριον, τό, dwelling place (neol.)
κληρονομία, ἡ, inheritance
κτάομαι, 3. ἐκτησάμην, ¹aor. mid. inf. κτήσασθαι, 4. κέκτημαι, plpf. ἐκέκτημην: get, acquire; possess; subst. ptc. οἱ κεκτήμενοι, owners
παρέρχομαι, pf. inf. παρεληλυθέναι: walk past, pass by, pass away; (of time) be past; (of a past) be over; disobey
τρόμος, ὁ, trembling
φόβος, ὁ, fear, fright

SELECT BIBLIOGRAPHY

Wevers, John William (ed.). *LXX: Notes on the Greek Text of Exodus.* Atlanta: Scholars Press, 1990.

---

²² Opt. (²aor. verbs in non-ind. moods have the same endings as the pres. tense of the same mood), cf. table 9.1.3.
²³ Cf. table 9.3.4.
²⁴ S.v. κτάομαι.

2.6.

Book of Isaiah: The Fourth Suffering Servant Song

(Isa 52:13–53:12)

Text: Rahlfs/Hanhart, II, 638–39; ET: *NETS* 865–66.

The term "Servant Songs," or "Songs of the Suffering Servant," refers to four poems written about a certain "servant of YHWH" (Isa 42:1–4, 49:1–6, 50:4–9, 52:13–53:12). In these poems, a "servant" (παῖς) is called by the Lord to lead the nations, as a result of which the servant is horribly abused, accepting the punishment due to others by sacrificing himself. In the Fourth Servant Song, this servant is said to intercede for others, bearing their punishments and afflictions. He is then posthumously vindicated by God. Whereas Jewish tradition interprets the "servant" as a metaphor of the Jewish people, early Christians interpreted the Servant Songs as messianic prophecies foretelling the coming of Jesus Christ.

Related Texts: Direct and indirect references to this song are found in the passion narratives of the canonical Gospels and in the Gospel of Peter (§§1.9, 1.15). The concept of dying vicariously for the benefit of others may have inspired the concept of the righteous martyr, who dies for the benefit of others, in 2 Macc 6:18–7:42 (§6.2), 4 Macc 1:11 (§6.3), and elsewhere (cf. 4 Macc 6:16–23, 27–28).

52:13 Ἰδοὺ συνήσει[1] ὁ παῖς μου
 καὶ ὑψωθήσεται καὶ δοξασθήσεται σφόδρα.
14 ὃν τρόπον ἐκστήσονται[2] ἐπὶ[3] σὲ πολλοί —
 οὕτως ἀδοξήσει ἀπὸ ἀνθρώπων τὸ εἶδός σου
 καὶ ἡ δόξα σου (be absent) ἀπὸ τῶν ἀνθρώπων —

---

[1] S.v. συνίημι (cf. Isa 52:15), for paradigm of ἵημι see table 9.15.
[2] S.v. ἐξίστημι.
[3] ἐπί, "at."

15   οὕτως θαυμάσονται ἔθνη πολλὰ ἐπ' αὐτῷ,
      καὶ συνέξουσιν βασιλεῖς τὸ στόμα αὐτῶν,
      ὅτι οἷς οὐκ ἀνηγγέλη[4] περὶ αὐτοῦ, ὄψονται,[5]
      καὶ οἳ οὐκ ἀκηκόασιν, συνήσουσιν.

53:1   κύριε, τίς ἐπίστευσεν τῇ ἀκοῇ ἡμῶν;
      καὶ ὁ βραχίων κυρίου τίνι ἀπεκαλύφθη;

2   ἀνέτειλεν μὲν ἐναντίον αὐτοῦ ὡς παιδίον,
      ὡς ῥίζα ἐν γῇ διψώσῃ,
      οὐκ ἔστιν εἶδος αὐτῷ οὐδὲ δόξα,
      καὶ εἴδομεν αὐτόν, καὶ οὐκ εἶχεν εἶδος (how) οὐδὲ κάλλος,

3   ἀλλὰ τὸ εἶδος αὐτοῦ ἄτιμον ἐκλεῖπον παρὰ πάντας ἀνθρώπους,
      ἄνθρωπος ἐν πληγῇ ὢν καὶ εἰδὼς φέρειν μαλακίαν,
      ὅτι ἀπέστραπται[6] τὸ πρόσωπον αὐτοῦ,
      ἠτιμάσθη καὶ οὐκ ἐλογίσθη.

Vocabulary

ἀδοξέω, be held in no esteem, be despicable

ἀκοή, ἡ, (faculty of) hearing; act of hearing; ear; account, report; obedience; pl. αἱ ἀκοαί, ears

ἀνατέλλω, 2. ἀνατελῶ, 3. ἀνέτειλα: cause to spring/grow up

ἀποστρέφω, 6. ἀπεστράφην (dep.): look back at (ἐπί) somebody; look away; revoke, refrain from, turn back from doing something

ἀτιμάζω, dishonor

ἄτιμος, -ον, dishonored, without honor

βραχίων, -ονος, ὁ, arm; strength

εἶδος, -ους, τό, form, appearance

ἐκλείπω, 3. ἐξέλιπον, 4. ἐκλέλοιπα: forsake; remain, be left; pass away (die); abandon, quit

ἐναντίος, -α, -ον (w. gen.), contrary, against, opposed; ἐναντίον (w. gen.), before; τὸ ἐναντίον, on the other hand; subst. οἱ ἐναντίοι, τὰ ἐναντία, the opposites

λογίζομαι, to count/reckon something to somebody, have regard for, esteem; reckon, estimate

μαλακία, ἡ, sickness

πληγή, ἡ, a blow, wound; sudden calamity; plague; ἔρχομαι πληγῶν, come to blows

συνέχω, keep closed; seize, torment

σφόδρα, very (much), extremely, greatly (adv.)

---

[4] S.v. ἀναγγέλλω, ²aor. pass. ἀνηγγέλην.

[5] S.v. ὁράω.

[6] S.v. ἀποστρέφω.

53:4   οὗτος τὰς ἁμαρτίας ἡμῶν φέρει
        καὶ περὶ ἡμῶν ὀδυνᾶται,
        καὶ ἡμεῖς ἐλογισάμεθα αὐτὸν εἶναι ἐν πόνῳ
        καὶ ἐν πληγῇ καὶ ἐν κακώσει.
5   αὐτὸς δὲ ἐτραυματίσθη διὰ τὰς ἀνομίας ἡμῶν
        καὶ μεμαλάκισται διὰ τὰς ἁμαρτίας ἡμῶν,
        παιδεία εἰρήνης ἡμῶν (was) ἐπ᾽ αὐτόν,
        τῷ μώλωπι αὐτοῦ ἡμεῖς ἰάθημεν.[7]
6   πάντες ὡς πρόβατα ἐπλανήθημεν,
        ἄνθρωπος τῇ ὁδῷ αὐτοῦ ἐπλανήθη,
        καὶ κύριος παρέδωκεν αὐτὸν ταῖς ἁμαρτίαις ἡμῶν.
7   καὶ αὐτὸς διὰ τὸ κεκακῶσθαι
        οὐκ ἀνοίγει τὸ στόμα,
        ὡς πρόβατον ἐπὶ σφαγὴν ἤχθη[8]
        καὶ ὡς ἀμνὸς ἐναντίον τοῦ κείροντος αὐτὸν ἄφωνος
        οὕτως οὐκ ἀνοίγει τὸ στόμα αὐτοῦ.

Vocabulary
ἀμνός, ὁ, lamb
ἄφωνος, -ον, speechless, dumb
κακόω, do evil, to hurt/harm
κάκωσις, -εως, ἡ, affliction, oppression
κείρω, shear a sheep
μαλακίζομαι, be weakly, sick
μώλωψ, -ωπος, ὁ, stripe, bruise
ὀδυνάω, suffer pain
παιδεία, ἡ, teaching, education; discipline, correction
πλανάω, lead astray; pass. wander, be led astray
πρόβατον, τό, sheep
σφαγή, ἡ, slaughter
τραυματίζω, to wound

53:8   ἐν τῇ ταπεινώσει ἡ κρίσις αὐτοῦ ἤρθη,[9]
        τὴν γενεὰν αὐτοῦ τίς διηγήσεται;
        ὅτι αἴρεται ἀπὸ τῆς γῆς ἡ ζωὴ αὐτοῦ,
        ἀπὸ[10] τῶν ἀνομιῶν τοῦ λαοῦ μου ἤχθη εἰς θάνατον.[11]

---

[7] S.v. ἰάομαι.
[8] S.v. ἄγω.
[9] S.v. αἴρω.
[10] ἀπό, "on account of."
[11] LXX translated Heb. term meaning "burial mound" as θάνατος.

9   καὶ δώσω[12] τοὺς πονηροὺς ἀντὶ τῆς ταφῆς αὐτοῦ
       καὶ (δώσω) τοὺς πλουσίους ἀντὶ τοῦ θανάτου αὐτοῦ,
       ὅτι ἀνομίαν οὐκ ἐποίησεν,
       οὐδὲ εὑρέθη δόλος ἐν τῷ στόματι αὐτοῦ.

Vocabulary

ἀντί, for, instead of, in place of
γενεά, -ᾶς, ἡ (Ion. γενεή, -ῆς), race, offspring
διηγέομαι, 3. διηγησάμην: recite, relate, tell
δόλος, ὁ, cunning, deceit, treachery
πλούσιος, -α, -ον, rich, wealthy; ὁ πλούσιος, rich man; comp. πλουσιώτερος
ταπείνωσις, -εως, ἡ, humiliation, humility

53:10   καὶ κύριος βούλεται
        καθαρίσαι αὐτὸν τῆς πληγῆς·
        ἐὰν δῶτε περὶ ἁμαρτίας,
        ἡ ψυχὴ ὑμῶν ὄψεται σπέρμα μακρόβιον,
        καὶ βούλεται κύριος ἀφελεῖν
11   ἀπὸ τοῦ πόνου τῆς ψυχῆς αὐτοῦ,
        δεῖξαι[13] αὐτῷ φῶς
        καὶ πλάσαι[14] τῇ συνέσει,
        δικαιῶσαι δίκαιον εὖ δουλεύοντα πολλοῖς,
        καὶ τὰς ἁμαρτίας αὐτῶν αὐτὸς ἀνοίσει.[15]
12   διὰ τοῦτο αὐτὸς κληρονομήσει πολλοὺς
        καὶ τῶν ἰσχυρῶν μεριεῖ σκῦλα,
        ἀνθ᾽ ὧν[16] παρεδόθη εἰς θάνατον ἡ ψυχὴ αὐτοῦ,
        καὶ ἐν τοῖς ἀνόμοις ἐλογίσθη,
        καὶ αὐτὸς ἁμαρτίας πολλῶν ἀνήνεγκεν
        καὶ διὰ τὰς ἁμαρτίας αὐτῶν παρεδόθη.

Vocabulary

ἄνομος, -ον, lawless; subst. lawless man
ἀφαιρέω, 3. ἀφεῖλον, [2]aor. inf. ἀφελεῖν, [1]aor. mid. ἀφειλάμην: take away from,
    remove; mid. take away something fr. somebody
βούλομαι, 6. ἠβουλήθην (dep.): to will, desire; mean something

---

12 Perhaps fut. ind. for subj. ("I would …"); though the servant's ταφή will be allocated ("offered"), he is
    not yet dead.
13 S.v. δείκνυμι.
14 S.v. πίμπλημι.
15 S.v. ἀναφέρω.
16 ἀνθ᾽ ὧν, "because."

δείκνυμι, 2. δείξω, 3. ἔδειξα, 4. δέδειχα, –, 6. ἐδείχθην: show, point out; reveal, explain, prove

δουλεύω, be a slave to somebody (dat.); serve somebody (dat.)

εὖ (adv.), well

μακρόβιος, -ον, long-lived

μερίζω, 2. μεριῶ, 6. ἐμερίσθην: to divide; to assign

σύνεσις, -εως, ἡ, understanding, discernment

PART 3

Intermediate Level: Jewish Recensional Greek

L ike those in Part 2, the texts in Part 3 were originally composed in Hebrew. But in contrast to the isometric translations of the former texts, the translation Greek in this section is characterized by greater assimilation of the literary conventions of Hellenistic Greek. I have termed this "recensional" Greek. These translations employ typical Greek syntactical constructions more frequently, with correspondingly less interference from the Hebrew parent text. As previously noted, the Septuagint has recently been retranslated into English, with many helpful notes, as *The New English Translation of the Septuagint.*[1] You should use this translation, rather than standard English translations of the Hebrew (Masoretic) text, when checking your own translation work.

The vocabulary lists in Part 3 have been compiled on the assumption that you have memorized the (bolded) words listed for memorization in Parts 1 and 2 (§§1.1–10, 2.1–6).[2] But all vocabulary for memorization is listed in the final glossary (§10).

---

[1] Albert Pietermas and Benjamin G. Wright (eds.), *A New Translation of the Septuagint: A New Translation of the Greek into Contemporary English* (New York: Oxford University Press, 2007).

[2] As well as the words occurring fifty times or more in the Greek New Testament.

3.1.

1 Esdras: The Last Kings of Judah and the Fall of Jerusalem

(1 Esdr 1:32–55 [2 Chr 36:1–21 MT])

1 Esdras is the name for the Septuagintal version of the Hebrew Book of Ezra. 1 Esdras actually begins with the last two chapters of 2 Chronicles, suggesting that these two texts may have previously been read as one book. As a result, the numbering of chapters in 1 Esdras (LXX) differs significantly from that in Ezra (MT). A case in point is the reading in this section from 1 Esdr 1:32–55 (LXX), which actually corresponds to 2 Chr 36:1–21 in the Masoretic text. The relation between 1 Esdras and the Hebrew-Aramaic biblical tradition is unclear. The Greek text below may actually be a translation of a text other than the Masoretic text, or it may be a loose periphrase. In any case, the Greek of 1 Esdras is generally of good quality.

1:32 Καὶ ἀναλαβόντες οἱ ἐκ τοῦ ἔθνους τὸν Ιεχονιαν[1] υἱὸν Ιωσιου[2] ἀνέδειξαν βασιλέα ἀντὶ[3] Ιωσιου τοῦ πατρὸς αὐτοῦ, ὄντα ἐτῶν εἴκοσι τριῶν. 33 καὶ ἐβασίλευσεν ἐν Ιουδα καὶ Ιερουσαλημ μῆνας τρεῖς. καὶ ἀπεκατέστησεν[4] αὐτὸν βασιλεὺς Αἰγύπτου βασιλεύειν ἐν Ιερουσαλημ 34 καὶ ἐζημίωσεν τὸ ἔθνος ἀργυρίου ταλάντοις ἑκατὸν καὶ χρυσίου ταλάντῳ ἑνί. 35 καὶ ἀνέδειξεν ὁ βασιλεὺς Αἰγύπτου βασιλέα Ιωακιμ[5] τὸν ἀδελφὸν αὐτοῦ[6] βασιλέα τῆς Ιουδαίας καὶ Ιερουσαλημ. 36 καὶ ἔδησεν Ιωακιμ τοὺς μεγιστᾶνας, Ζαριον[7] δὲ τὸν ἀδελφὸν αὐτοῦ συλλαβὼν

---

[1] Iechonias (i.e., Jehoahaz in MT, birthname "Shallum"), born 633/632 BCE. He succeeded Josiah as king of Judah at the age of twenty-three. He reigned for only three months.

[2] Iosias (Josiah), father of Iechonias.

[3] ἀντί, "in the place of."

[4] Here ἀποκαθίστημι has the special meaning "to depose (a king from ruling)."

[5] Ioakeim (Heb. Jehoiakim, birthname "Eliakim"), who ruled from 608 to 598 BCE.

[6] I.e., the brother of Iechonias.

[7] Zarios.

ἀνήγαγεν ἐξ Αἰγύπτου. 37 Ἐτῶν δὲ ἦν εἴκοσι πέντε Ιωακιμ, ὅτε ἐβασίλευσεν τῆς Ιουδαίας καὶ Ιερουσαλημ, καὶ ἐποίησεν τὸ πονηρὸν ἐνώπιον κυρίου. 38 ἐπ᾽ αὐτὸν δὲ ἀνέβη Ναβουχοδονοσορ[8] βασιλεὺς Βαβυλῶνος καὶ δήσας αὐτὸν ἐν χαλκείῳ δεσμῷ ἀπήγαγεν εἰς Βαβυλῶνα. 39 καὶ ἀπὸ τῶν ἱερῶν σκευῶν τοῦ κυρίου λαβὼν Ναβουχοδονοσορ καὶ ἀπενέγκας ἀπηρείσατο ἐν τῷ ναῷ αὐτοῦ ἐν Βαβυλῶνι. 40 τὰ δὲ ἱστορηθέντα περὶ αὐτοῦ καὶ τῆς αὐτοῦ ἀκαθαρσίας καὶ δυσσεβείας ἀναγέγραπται ἐν τῇ βίβλῳ τῶν χρόνων τῶν βασιλέων.

Vocabulary

ἀκαθαρσία, ἡ, physical/ritual/moral impurity (cf. 1 Esd 47)

ἀναγράφω, engrave/inscribe and publicly set up; record in a public register

ἀναδείχνυμι, appoint (cf. 1 Esd 1:35, 41, 44)

ἀπερείδω, to deposit

ἀργύριον, τό, silver coin (= 1 drachma); money; a fine; silver (= ἄργυρος)

ἀποκαθίστημι, 3. ἀπεκατέστησα / [2]aor. ἀπεκατέστην: re-establish, restore, cure; depose (a king)

Βαβυλών, -ῶνος, ἡ, Babylon

δεσμός, ὁ, pl. δεσμά: pl. shackles, chains, sandal straps; fig. a hindrance (that deafens or physically handicaps)

δυσσέβεια, ἡ, impiety (cf. 1 Esd 1:49)

εἴκοσι, twenty (cf. 1 Esd 1:44)

ἑκατόν, hundred

ζημιόω, fine somebody an amount (dat.); pass. suffer a loss, forfeit

ἱστορέω, visit somebody, get to know somebody; pass. be recorded

μεγιστάν, -ᾶνος, ὁ, great man, noble

τάλαντον, τό, a talent (weight ranging from 108 to 130 pounds)

χάλκεος, -έα, -εον (later χαλκεῖος, -α, -ον), Att. contr. χαλκοῦς, -ῆ, -οῦν: of bronze (adj.)

χρυσίον, τό, gold, money; anything made of gold, a gold vessel

THE REIGNS OF IOAKEIM (JECONIAH) AND SEDIKIAS (ZEDIKIAH)

1:41 Καὶ ἐβασίλευσεν ἀντ᾽ αὐτοῦ Ιωακιμ ὁ υἱὸς αὐτοῦ,[9] ὅτε γὰρ ἀνεδείχθη (king), ἦν ἐτῶν δέκα ὀκτώ, 42 βασιλεύει δὲ μῆνας τρεῖς καὶ ἡμέρας δέκα ἐν Ιερουσαλημ καὶ ἐποίησεν τὸ πονηρὸν ἔναντι κυρίου. 43 Καὶ μετ᾽ ἐνιαυτὸν ἀποστείλας Ναβουχοδονοσορ μετήγαγεν αὐτὸν εἰς Βαβυλῶνα ἅμα τοῖς ἱεροῖς σκεύεσιν τοῦ

---

[8] Nebuchadnezzar II, king of the Neo-Babylonian Empire (605–562 BCE).

[9] Ioakeim (Heb. Jeconiah), son of Ioakeim (Heb. Jehoiakim), who ruled from December 9, 598 BCE to March 15/16, 597 BCE.

κυρίου 44 καὶ ἀνέδειξε Σεδεκιαν[10] βασιλέα τῆς Ιουδαίας καὶ Ιερουσαλημ, Σεδεκιαν ὄντα ἐτῶν εἴκοσι ἑνός, βασιλεύει δὲ ἔτη ἕνδεκα. 45 καὶ ἐποίησεν τὸ πονηρὸν ἐνώπιον κυρίου καὶ οὐκ ἐνετράπη ἀπὸ τῶν ῥηθέντων[11] λόγων ὑπὸ Ιερεμιου[12] τοῦ προφήτου ἐκ στόματος τοῦ κυρίου. 46 καὶ ὁρκισθεὶς ἀπὸ τοῦ βασιλέως Ναβουχοδονοσορ τῷ ὀνόματι τοῦ κυρίου ἐπιορκήσας, ἀπέστη[13] καὶ σκληρύνας αὐτοῦ τὸν τράχηλον καὶ τὴν καρδίαν αὐτοῦ παρέβη τὰ νόμιμα κυρίου θεοῦ Ισραηλ. 47 καὶ οἱ ἡγούμενοι δὲ τοῦ λαοῦ καὶ τῶν ἱερέων πολλὰ ἠσέβησαν καὶ ἠνόμησαν ὑπὲρ πάσας τὰς ἀκαθαρσίας πάντων τῶν ἐθνῶν καὶ ἐμίαναν τὸ ἱερὸν τοῦ κυρίου τὸ ἁγιαζόμενον ἐν Ιεροσολύμοις. 48 καὶ ἀπέστειλεν ὁ θεὸς τῶν πατέρων αὐτῶν διὰ τοῦ ἀγγέλου αὐτοῦ μετακαλέσαι αὐτούς, καθὸ[14] ἐφείδετο[15] αὐτῶν καὶ τοῦ σκηνώματος αὐτοῦ. 49 αὐτοὶ δὲ ἐξεμυκτήρισαν ἐν τοῖς ἀγγέλοις αὐτοῦ, καὶ ᾗ ἡμέρᾳ ἐλάλησεν κύριος, ἦσαν ἐκπαίζοντες[16] τοὺς προφήτας αὐτοῦ ἕως τοῦ[17] θυμωθέντα αὐτὸν ἐπὶ τῷ ἔθνει αὐτοῦ διὰ τὰ δυσσεβήματα προστάξαι ἀναβιβάσαι ἐπ' αὐτοὺς τοὺς βασιλεῖς[18] τῶν Χαλδαίων.

Vocabulary

ἀναβιβάζω, mount up against (ἐπί), go up against

ἀσεβέω, act profanely/wickedly against, commit sacrilege

δυσσέβημα, -ματος, τό, impious act (neol.)

ἐκμυκτηρίζω, to hold in derision, to laugh at (ἐν)

ἐκπαίζω, laugh at somebody, scorn

ἔναντι, in the sight of, before (+ gen.)

ἔνδεκα, eleven

ἐντρέπομαι (mid. and pass. forms), reverence, feel shame (arising from)

ἐπιορκέω, break an oath

θυμόω, make angry, provoke; pass. be angry

ἱερός, -ά, -όν, sacred, holy (cf. 1 Esd 1:51)

μετάγω, carry in captivity

μετακαλέω, call back

νόμιμος, -η/ος, -ον, conforming to the law, legal; pl. τὰ νόμιμα, laws, statutes; customs

---

[10] Sedikias (Zedikiah), who ruled from 597 to 587 BCE.

[11] S.v. λέγω.

[12] Jeremiah the prophet, who was active from the thirteenth year of King Josiah (626 BCE) until 587 BCE, a period spanning the reigns of five kings of Judah.

[13] S.v. ἀφίστημι.

[14] καθό = καθώς.

[15] Conat. impf.

[16] Periph. impf. (cf. IV, 18).

[17] ἕως τοῦ…προστάξαι, art. inf. (IV, 2).

[18] τοὺς βασιλεῖς is the subject of the inf.

ὁρκίζω, make somebody swear an oath to somebody (acc.), swear by the name (τῷ ὀνόματι τοῦ) of somebody; conjure by (acc.), magically invoke by (acc.)

παραβαίνω, 3. παρέβην: transgress

σκήνωμα, -ατος, τό, tent, dwelling, tabernacle

σκληρύνω, harden

τράχηλος, ὁ, neck

Χαλδαῖος, ὁ, Chaldean

THE FALL OF JERUSALEM (597 BCE)

1:50 οὗτοι ἀπέκτειναν τοὺς νεανίσκους αὐτῶν ἐν ῥομφαίᾳ περικύκλῳ τοῦ ἁγίου αὐτῶν ἱεροῦ καὶ οὐκ ἐφείσαντο νεανίσκου καὶ παρθένου καὶ πρεσβύτου καὶ νεωτέρου, ἀλλὰ πάντας παρέδωκεν εἰς τὰς χεῖρας αὐτῶν. 51 καὶ πάντα τὰ ἱερὰ σκεύη τοῦ κυρίου τὰ μεγάλα καὶ τὰ μικρὰ καὶ τὰς κιβωτοὺς τοῦ κυρίου καὶ τὰς βασιλικὰς ἀποθήκας ἀναλαβόντες ἀπήνεγκαν εἰς Βαβυλῶνα. 52 καὶ ἐνεπύρισαν τὸν οἶκον τοῦ κυρίου καὶ ἔλυσαν τὰ τείχα Ἱεροσολύμων καὶ τοὺς πύργους αὐτῶν ἐνεπύρισαν ἐν πυρὶ 53 καὶ συνετέλεσαν πάντα τὰ ἔνδοξα αὐτῆς ἀχρεῶσαι, καὶ τοὺς ἐπιλοίπους ἀπήγαγεν μετὰ ῥομφαίας εἰς Βαβυλῶνα. 54 καὶ ἦσαν παῖδες αὐτῷ καὶ τοῖς υἱοῖς αὐτοῦ μέχρι τοῦ βασιλεῦσαι Πέρσας εἰς ἀναπλήρωσιν τοῦ ῥήματος τοῦ κυρίου ἐν στόματι Ἱερεμιου 55 Ἕως τοῦ εὐδοκῆσαι[19] τὴν γῆν τὰ σάββατα αὐτῆς, πάντα τὸν χρόνον τῆς ἐρημώσεως αὐτῆς, σαββατιεῖ εἰς συμπλήρωσιν ἐτῶν ἑβδομήκοντα.

Vocabulary

ἀναπλήρωσις, ἡ, fulfillment

ἀποθήκη, ἡ, storeroom

ἀχρειόω, to destroy

βασιλικός, -ή, -όν, royal

ἑβδομήκοντα, seventy

ἐμπυρίζω, set on fire

ἐπίλοιπος, -ον, remaining; subst. οἱ ἐπίλοιποι, survivors

ἐρήμωσις, -εως, ἡ, desolation

εὐδοκέω, take pleasure in, be pleased with; be pleased (to do something); consider something good

κιβωτός, ἡ, chest, treasure chest; sacred depository, Ark (of the Covenant); boat, ark (like a barge)

νεανίσκος, ὁ, a youth, young man; servant

νεώτερος, ὁ (comparative of νέος), young man

---

[19] Art. inf.

περικύκλῳ, round about, on every side
Πέρσης (irreg.), Persian
πρεσβυτής, ὁ, old man; ambassador
πύργος, ὁ, tower (of a city)
συμπλήρωσις, -εως, ἡ, completion (neol.)

3.2.

Book of Esther: Esther Saves the Jews

(Esth 7:1–8:8 OG)

Date: The story of Esther is set in the third year of King Ahasuerus of Persia, who is identified by the Septuagint as Artaxerxes II (Ἀρταξέρξης) Mnemon, the son of Darius II. He was the ruler of the Persian Empire from ca. 405 to 359 BCE.

Text: The Book of Esther survives in two different Greek versions, an Old Greek (OG) version (the Septuagintal version) and a second version known as the "Alpha-text" (AT), which is a somewhat freer translation, though neither OG nor AT is isomorphic.

The Book of Esther tells the story of a Jewish girl named Esther (Εσθηρ), who, following the death of her parents, was raised by her cousin Mordechai ("Mardochaios" in Greek versions). In time, she found favor in the eyes of the king, Ahasuerus (Artaxerxes), and was crowned queen of Persia. When Haman, the king's prime minister, developed a plan to kill all the Jews in the empire, Esther revealed to the king that she was Jewish and would therefore be killed if this plan was carried out. Through her intervention, the planned genocide against her people was averted.

7:1 Εἰσῆλθεν δὲ ὁ βασιλεὺς καὶ Αμαν[1] συμπιεῖν τῇ βασιλίσσῃ. 2 εἶπεν δὲ ὁ βασιλεὺς Εσθηρ[2] τῇ δευτέρᾳ ἡμέρᾳ ἐν τῷ πότῳ· τί ἐστιν,[3] Εσθηρ βασίλισσα, καὶ τί τὸ αἴτημά σου καὶ τί τὸ ἀξίωμά σου; καὶ ἔστω σοι ἕως τοῦ ἡμίσους τῆς βασιλείας μου. 3 Καὶ ἀποκριθεῖσα εἶπεν· εἰ εὗρον χάριν ἐνώπιον τοῦ βασιλέως, δοθήτω ἡ ψυχή μου τῷ αἰτήματί μου καὶ ὁ λαός μου τῷ ἀξιώματί μου,

---

[1] Haman, the prime minister of King Artaxerxes.
[2] Εσθηρ (indecl.), here dat.
[3] τί ἐστιν, "what is it?"

4 ἐπράθημεν γὰρ ἐγώ τε καὶ ὁ λαός μου εἰς ἀπώλειαν καὶ διαρπαγὴν καὶ δουλείαν – ἡμεῖς καὶ τὰ τέκνα ἡμῶν εἰς[4] παῖδας καὶ παιδίσκας – καὶ παρήκουσα, οὐ γὰρ ἄξιος ὁ διάβολος τῆς αὐλῆς τοῦ βασιλέως. 5 Εἶπεν δὲ ὁ βασιλεύς· τίς (is) οὗτος, ὅστις ἐτόλμησεν ποιῆσαι τὸ πρᾶγμα τοῦτο; 6 Εἶπεν δὲ Εσθηρ· ἄνθρωπος (who is an) ἐχθρὸς, Αμαν ὁ πονηρὸς οὗτος. Αμαν δὲ ἐταράχθη ἀπὸ[5] τοῦ βασιλέως καὶ τῆς βασιλίσσης.

Vocabulary

αἴτημα, -ματος, τό, request
ἀξίωμα, -ματος, τό, petition
ἀπώλεια, ἡ, destruction, annihilation
αὐλή, ἡ, court (of temple, palace, tabernacle)
βασίλισσα, -ης, ἡ, queen
διαρπαγή, ἡ, booty, spoils (of war)
δουλεία, ἡ, slavery
ἥμισυς, -εια, -υ, half; μέχρι τοῦ ἡμίσους, up to the middle (of one's body)
παιδίσκη, ἡ, female slave, maidservant
παρακούω, ignore, pay no attention to; disobey
πότος, ὁ, drinking, drinking party
συμπίνω, drink with/together
ταράσσω, pf. pass. ptc. τεταραγμένος: agitate physically, pervert something; fig. stir up, disturb mentally, throw into confusion; pass. be troubled, vexed; be thrown into disorder/confusion
τολμάω, dare to, be bold enough to (+ inf.); show boldness toward (ἐπί)

7:7 Ὁ δὲ βασιλεὺς ἐξανέστη ἐκ τοῦ συμποσίου (and went) εἰς τὸν κῆπον, ὁ δὲ Αμαν παρῃτεῖτο τὴν βασίλισσαν, ἑώρα[6] γὰρ ἑαυτὸν ἐν κακοῖς ὄντα. 8 ἐπέστρεψεν δὲ ὁ βασιλεὺς ἐκ τοῦ κήπου, Αμαν δὲ ἐπιπεπτώκει ἐπὶ τὴν κλίνην ἀξιῶν τὴν βασίλισσαν. εἶπεν δὲ ὁ βασιλεύς· ὥστε καὶ[7] τὴν γυναῖκα βιάζῃ ἐν τῇ οἰκίᾳ μου; Αμαν δὲ ἀκούσας διετράπη τῷ προσώπῳ. 9 εἶπεν δὲ Βουγαθαν[8] εἷς τῶν εὐνούχων πρὸς τὸν βασιλέα· ἰδοὺ καὶ ξύλον[9] ἡτοίμασεν Αμαν Μαρδοχαίῳ[10] τῷ λαλήσαντι περὶ τοῦ βασιλέως, καὶ ὤρθωται ἐν τῇ αὐλῇ Αμαν ξύλον πηχῶν πεντήκοντα (tall). Εἶπεν δὲ ὁ βασιλεύς· σταυρωθήτω ἐπ' αὐτοῦ. 10 καὶ ἐκρεμάσθη Αμαν ἐπὶ τοῦ ξύλου, ὃ ἡτοίμασεν Μαρδοχαίῳ. καὶ τότε ὁ βασιλεὺς ἐκόπασεν τοῦ θυμοῦ.

---

[4] εἰς, "as."
[5] ἀπό, "because of," "by reason of."
[6] ἑώρα, 3 sg. impf. of ὁράω (ἑώρα ἑαυτὸν "saw himself," i.e., realized).
[7] ὥστε καί, "so then."
[8] Bougathan (i.e., Harbonah), one of the seven eunuchs who served Ahasuerus (Esth 1:10).
[9] τὸ ξύλον, here a "pole, gallows" made of wood.
[10] Mardochaios (Mordecai).

Vocabulary

ἀξιόω, impf. ἠξίουν: make somebody worthy of something; deem worthy/fit, deem suitable; entreat/beseech somebody; pass. be permitted

βιάζω/ομαι, to force, use force, do something by force; lay hands upon, violate

διατρέπω, pass. be confounded

ἐξανίστημι, mid. ἐξανίσταμαι: raise up (transitive); establish; mid. arise, awake

εὐνοῦχος, ὁ, eunuch

κλίνη, ἡ, couch, bed; bier

κοπάζω, cease from

κρεμάννυμι/κρεμάζω, 1. pres. mid. κρέμαμαι, pres. mid. ptc. κρεμάμενος, 3. ἐκρέμασα, aor. mid. inf. κρέμασθαι, aor. pl. ptc. κρεμάσαντες, 6. ἐκεμάσθην: hang something from (gen.); hang (somebody as an execution); mid. hang, be suspended; pass. be hung up, suspended

παραιτέομαι, ask for, entreat, beg, request; excuse oneself (παραιτοῦμαι, "excuse me")

πεντήκοντα, fifty

πῆχυς, -εως, ὁ, cubit (measure of length from the elbow to end of the middle finger)

συμπόσιον, τό, drinking party

8:1 Καὶ ἐν αὐτῇ τῇ ἡμέρᾳ ὁ βασιλεὺς Ἀρταξέρξης ἐδωρήσατο Εσθηρ ὅσα ὑπῆρχεν Αμαν τῷ διαβόλῳ,[11] καὶ Μαρδοχαῖος προσεκλήθη ὑπὸ τοῦ βασιλέως, ὑπέδειξεν γὰρ Εσθηρ ὅτι ἐνοικείωται αὐτῇ. 2 ἔλαβεν δὲ ὁ βασιλεὺς τὸν δακτύλιον, ὃν ἀφείλατο[12] Αμαν, καὶ ἔδωκεν αὐτὸν Μαρδοχαίῳ, καὶ κατέστησεν Εσθηρ Μαρδοχαῖον ἐπὶ πάντων τῶν Αμαν. 3 Καὶ προσθεῖσα ἐλάλησεν πρὸς τὸν βασιλέα καὶ προσέπεσεν πρὸς τοὺς πόδας αὐτοῦ καὶ ἠξίου[13] ἀφελεῖν[14] τὴν Αμαν κακίαν καὶ ὅσα ἐποίησεν τοῖς Ιουδαίοις. 4 ἐξέτεινεν δὲ ὁ βασιλεὺς Εσθηρ τὴν ῥάβδον τὴν χρυσῆν, ἐξηγέρθη δὲ Εσθηρ παρεστηκέναι τῷ βασιλεῖ.

Vocabulary

ἐνοικειόω, be related to

ἐξεγείρω, awaken; raise from the dead; pass. be awakened, wake up

καθίστημι, 3. κατέστησα, 6. κατεστάθην: appoint somebody; constitute, make

κακία, ἡ, wickedness, evil

παρίστημι (also παριστάνω), pf. ptc. παρεστώς: stand before (w. dat.), approach, come near; render, present, offer, supply; show

προσπίπτω, fall upon; prostrate oneself before, fall down before

---

[11] 3rd attrib. pos. (IV, 4.3); Αμαν is dat.
[12] S.v. ἀφαιρῶ.
[13] Iterative impf. (cf. IV, 13.3).
[14] S.v. ἀφαιρῶ.

ῥάβδος, ἡ, rod, staff

ὑπάρχω, impf. ὑπῆρχον: exist, be present, to be; belong to; possess; subst. τὰ ὑπάρχοντα, possessions, property

ὑποδείκνυμι/ὑποδεικνόω, 3. ὑπέδειξα: show, reveal, indicate

χρύσεος, -α, -ον (contr. χρυσοῦς, -ῆ, -οῦν), golden

8:5 Καὶ εἶπεν Εσθηρ· εἰ δοκεῖ σοι καὶ εὗρον χάριν, πεμφθήτω[15] ἀποστραφῆναι τὰ γράμματα τὰ ἀπεσταλμένα ὑπὸ Αμαν τὰ γραφέντα ἀπολέσθαι τοὺς Ιουδαίους, οἵ εἰσιν ἐν τῇ βασιλείᾳ σου, 6 πῶς γὰρ δυνήσομαι ἰδεῖν τὴν κάκωσιν τοῦ λαοῦ μου καὶ πῶς δυνήσομαι σωθῆναι ἐν τῇ ἀπωλείᾳ τῆς πατρίδος μου; 7 Καὶ εἶπεν ὁ βασιλεὺς πρὸς Εσθηρ· εἰ πάντα τὰ ὑπάρχοντα Αμαν ἔδωκα καὶ ἐχαρισάμην σοι καὶ αὐτὸν ἐκρέμασα ἐπὶ ξύλου, ὅτι τὰς χεῖρας ἐπήνεγκε τοῖς Ιουδαίοις, τί ἔτι ἐπιζητεῖς; 8 γράψατε καὶ ὑμεῖς ἐκ τοῦ ὀνόματός μου[16] ὡς δοκεῖ ὑμῖν καὶ σφραγίσατε τῷ δακτυλίῳ μου, ὅσα γὰρ γράφεται τοῦ βασιλέως ἐπιτάξαντος[17] καὶ σφραγισθῇ τῷ δακτυλίῳ μου, οὐκ ἔστιν αὐτοῖς ἀντειπεῖν.

Vocabulary

ἀποστρέφω, 6. ἀπεστράφην (dep.): look back at (ἐπί) somebody, look away; refrain from, turn back from; revoke

γράμμα, τό, letter; pl. τὰ γράμματα, literature, learning

δακτύλιος, ὁ, signet ring (cf. 1 Esd 8:8)

δωρέομαι, give as a present to

ἐπιζητέω, seek (after), desire; request

ἐπιτάσσω (Att. ἐπιτάττω), pres. ptc. ἐπιτασσόμενος,[1] aor. inf. ἐπιτάξαι, aor. pass. ptc. ἐπιταχθείς: instruct, order somebody to do something; impose regulations; subst. ptc. regulations, things decreed

ἐπιφέρω, [1]aor ptc. ἐπενέγκας: lay upon; hover over; carry on one's person, bring on/about; bring legal action (κρίσιν) against (κατά) somebody; compel; pass. be hovering over

κάκωσις, -εως, ἡ, affliction, suffering

σφραγίζω, to seal (for a security), seal up by impressing a seal with a signet ring

χαρίζομαι, impf. ἐχαριζόμην, pf. κεχάρισμαι: freely grant, give, bestow; be pleasing, beloved; pass. be given freely

---

[15] S.v. πέμπω, cf. table 9.3.4(b).
[16] ἐκ τοῦ ὀνόματός μου, "in my name."
[17] Gen. absol. (cf. IV, 9).

3.3.

1 Maccabees: The Program of Hellenization of Antiochus Epiphanes

(1 Macc. 1:10–28)

Date: The Semitic original (probably Hebrew) of 1 Maccabees was written in the late second century BCE.

Text: The Semitic text of 1 Maccabees disappeared at an early age and was, de facto, replaced by its Greek translation. The Greek text is the product of a single translation, with no evidence of subsequent correction or revision. The text preserves many signs of the Semitic original, including such biblical phrases as "and it came to pass" and "in those days," as well as the direct transliteration of some proper names, the use of Jewish month names, and the deliberate use of some archaic terminology. Thus, even though the translator's exceptional vocabulary displays his impressive command of Hellenistic Greek, the preservation of the parataxis of the Hebrew original, as well as other features, would suggest a general disdain for Hellenistic culture.

This book tells the story of how Antiochus IV Epiphanes (175–164 BCE), the Seleucid king, attempted to suppress the observance of Torah, resulting in a Jewish revolt. The balance of the book covers the whole of the Maccabean revolt from 175 to 134 BCE, highlighting how the salvation of the Jewish people in this crisis came through the sons of Mattathias. As the narrative opens, Alexander the Great has died and his top Macedonian generals have fought over his empire, consisting of Egypt, Palestine, Syria, Asia Minor, and mainland Greece. Three dynasties survived: the Macedonian, the Ptolemaic, and the Seleucid. King Antiochus IV Epiphanes was the heir to the throne of the Seleucid Empire when his father, Antiochus III the Great, died.

1:10 Καὶ ἐξῆλθεν ἐξ αὐτῶν¹ ῥίζα ἁμαρτωλὸς Ἀντίοχος Ἐπιφανὴς² υἱὸς Ἀντιόχου³ τοῦ βασιλέως, ὃς ἦν ὅμηρα ἐν Ῥώμῃ,⁴ καὶ ἐβασίλευσεν ἐν ἔτει ἑκατοστῷ καὶ τριακοστῷ καὶ ἑβδόμῳ βασιλείας Ἑλλήνων.⁵ 11 Ἐν ταῖς ἡμέραις ἐκείναις ἐξῆλθον ἐξ Ισραηλ υἱοὶ παράνομοι καὶ ἀνέπεισαν πολλοὺς λέγοντες· πορευθῶμεν⁶ καὶ διαθώμεθα διαθήκην μετὰ τῶν ἐθνῶν τῶν κύκλῳ ἡμῶν, ὅτι ἀφ᾽ ἧς⁷ ἐχωρίσθημεν ἀπ᾽ αὐτῶν, εὗρεν ἡμᾶς κακὰ πολλά. 12 καὶ ἠγαθύνθη ὁ λόγος⁸ ἐν ὀφθαλμοῖς αὐτῶν, 13 καὶ προεθυμήθησάν τινες ἀπὸ τοῦ λαοῦ καὶ ἐπορεύθησαν πρὸς τὸν βασιλέα, καὶ ἔδωκεν αὐτοῖς ἐξουσίαν ποιῆσαι τὰ δικαιώματα τῶν ἐθνῶν.

Vocabulary

ἀγαθύνω, seem good
ἁμαρτωλός, -όν, sinful; subst. a sinner
ἀναπείθω, mislead
διαθήκη, ἡ, treaty, covenant; last will and testament
διατίθημι, mid. establish a covenant
δικαίωμα, -ματος, τό, statute; righteous act
ἕβδομος, -η, -ον, seventh
ἑκατοστός, -ή, -όν, hundredth
Ἕλλην, -ηνος, ὁ; (dat. pl.) Ἕλλησι: Greek person (here Seleucid)
ἐπιφανής, -ές, appearing, manifest (of a god); notable, distinguished
κύκλῳ, in a circle, around
ὅμηρα, τά, hostages
παράνομος, -ον, lawless, unlawful
προθυμέομαι, pass. (dep.), be eager
τριακοστός, -ή, -όν, thirtieth
χωρίζω, divide, separate; depart, go away from

1:14 καὶ ᾠκοδόμησαν γυμνάσιον ἐν Ιεροσολύμοις κατὰ τὰ νόμιμα τῶν ἐθνῶν 15 καὶ ἐποίησαν ἑαυτοῖς ἀκροβυστίας καὶ ἀπέστησαν⁹ ἀπὸ διαθήκης ἁγίας καὶ ἐζευγίσθησαν τοῖς ἔθνεσιν καὶ ἐπράθησαν¹⁰ τοῦ ποιῆσαι τὸ πονηρόν.

---

¹ I.e., the generals of Alexander the Great.
² Antiochus IV, who took up the name "Epiphanes" ("god manifest").
³ Antiochus III the Great, who took Palestine from the Ptolemies at the battle of Paneas (198 BCE).
⁴ Antiochus IV became a political hostage of Rome following the Peace of Apamea in 188 BCE. When the king, his brother Seleucus IV, was assassinated, Antiochus IV seized the throne for himself by proclaiming himself co-regent for the infant son of Seleucus IV. He had the infant murdered a few years later.
⁵ I.e., of the Seleucid era. The year 312 (autumn) BCE is the first year (year 1) of the reign of Seleucus 1 and therefore of the Seleucid era (312–137 = 175 BCE).
⁶ Hort. subj.
⁷ ἀφ᾽ ἧς (ἡμέρας).
⁸ λόγος, here "proposal."
⁹ S.v. ἀφίστημι.
¹⁰ S.v. πιπράσκω.

16 Καὶ ἡτοιμάσθη ἡ βασιλεία ἐνώπιον Ἀντιόχου, καὶ ὑπέλαβεν βασιλεῦσαι γῆς Αἰγύπτου, ὅπως βασιλεύσῃ ἐπὶ τὰς δύο βασιλείας. 17 καὶ εἰσῆλθεν εἰς Αἴγυπτον ἐν ὄχλῳ βαρεῖ, ἐν ἅρμασιν καὶ ἐλέφασιν καὶ ἐν ἱππεῦσιν καὶ ἐν στόλῳ μεγάλῳ 18 καὶ συνεστήσατο πόλεμον πρὸς Πτολεμαῖον βασιλέα Αἰγύπτου, καὶ ἐνετράπη Πτολεμαῖος ἀπὸ προσώπου αὐτοῦ καὶ ἔφυγεν,[11] καὶ ἔπεσον τραυματίαι πολλοί. 19 καὶ κατελάβοντο τὰς πόλεις τὰς ὀχυρὰς ἐν γῇ Αἰγύπτῳ, καὶ ἔλαβεν τὰ σκῦλα γῆς Αἰγύπτου.

Vocabulary

Αἴγυπτος, ἡ, Egypt

ἀκροβυστία, ἡ, foreskin; fig. state of being uncircumcised

βαρύς, -εῖα, -ύ, heavy

γυμνάσιον, τό, gymnasium, center for schooling in athletics and Greek culture (i.e., a school for educating ἔφηβοι, cf. 2 Macc 4)[12]

ἐλέφας, -αντος, ὁ, elephant

ἐντρέπω, 6. ἐνετράπην, pass., turn about

ἑτοιμάζω, prepare; pass. be ready

ζευγίζω (+ dat.), unite, join to

ἱππεύς, -έως, ὁ, horseman, cavalryman (as a collective noun)

νόμιμος, -η, -ον, conform to the law, legal; pl. τὰ νόμιμα, laws, statutes

ὀχυρός, -ά, -όν, fortified

Πτολεμαῖος, ὁ, Ptolemy (VI)

στόλος, ὁ, naval fleet

συνίστημι/συνιστάνω, 2. συστήσω, ²aor. act. inf. συστῆναι, ²aor. mid. inf. συστήσασθαι, ²aor. pass. subj. συστηθῶ: demonstrate, show; introduce/recommend somebody to somebody; be composed of (gen.); mid. establish; join (in battle)

τραυματίας, -ου, ὁ, wounded man, casualty (of war)

1:20 Καὶ ἐπέστρεψεν Ἀντίοχος μετὰ τὸ πατάξαι Αἴγυπτον ἐν τῷ ἑκατοστῷ καὶ τεσσαρακοστῷ καὶ τρίτῳ ἔτει[13] καὶ ἀνέβη[14] ἐπὶ Ισραηλ καὶ ἀνέβη εἰς Ιεροσόλυμα ἐν ὄχλῳ βαρεῖ. 21 καὶ εἰσῆλθεν εἰς τὸ ἁγίασμα ἐν ὑπερηφανίᾳ καὶ ἔλαβεν τὸ θυσιαστήριον τὸ χρυσοῦν καὶ τὴν λυχνίαν τοῦ φωτὸς καὶ πάντα τὰ σκεύη αὐτῆς 22 καὶ τὴν τράπεζαν τῆς προθέσεως καὶ τὰ σπονδεῖα καὶ τὰς φιάλας

---

[11] To avoid alarming Rome by his attack on Egypt, Antiochus allowed Ptolemy VI to continue ruling as a puppet king. Upon Antiochus's withdrawal, Ptolemy VI ruled jointly with his brother, Ptolemy VIII Euergetes.

[12] In essence, a gymnasium was an open court for wrestling and similar sports, surrounded by colonnades, which opened onto a variety of rooms (e.g., anointing room, dusting room, cold, tepid, and hot bath rooms, lecture rooms) and a running track.

[13] Cf. n. on 1:10 ("in the 143rd year" = 169 BCE).

[14] ἀναβαίνω ἐπί, here "go up against."

καὶ τὰς θυΐσκας τὰς χρυσᾶς[15] καὶ τὸ καταπέτασμα καὶ τοὺς στεφάνους καὶ τὸν κόσμον τὸν χρυσοῦν τὸν κατὰ πρόσωπον[16] τοῦ ναοῦ καὶ ἐλέπισεν πάντα, 23 καὶ ἔλαβεν τὸ ἀργύριον καὶ τὸ χρυσίον καὶ τὰ σκεύη τὰ ἐπιθυμητὰ καὶ ἔλαβεν τοὺς θησαυροὺς τοὺς ἀποκρύφους, οὓς εὗρεν, 24 καὶ λαβὼν πάντα ἀπῆλθεν εἰς τὴν γῆν αὐτοῦ.

Vocabulary

Αἴγυπτος, ἡ, Egypt

ἀργύριον, τό, silver coin (= 1 drachma); money; a fine; silver (= ἄργυρος)

ἐπιθυμητός, -ή, -όν, desirable; costly, precious

ἔτος, ἔτους, τό, year

θησαυρός, ὁ, treasury, storehouse; pl. treasures

θυΐσκη, ἡ, censer

θυσιαστήριον, τό, altar of burnt offerings (in the forecourt of the Jerusalem temple)

καταπέτασμα, -ματος, τό, veil/curtain (of the Temple)

λεπίζω, strip off

λυχνία, ἡ, lampstand

ναός, ὁ, temple, inner part of Jewish temple, sanctuary

πατάσσω, [1]aor. inf. πατάξαι: strike, slay

πρόθεσις, -εως, ἡ, plan, purpose; offering, "(the Bread of) Presence"

σπονδεῖον, τό, bowl or cup from which a drink offering/libation (σπονδή) is poured

τεσσαρακοστός, -ή, -όν, fortieth

τράπεζα, ἡ, table; offering table (for a god)

τρίτος, -η, -ον, third

ὑπερηφανία, ἡ, arrogance, pride

φιάλη, ἡ, phial, shallow bowl (from which wine was poured onto an altar while prayers were recited and then the remainder was consumed)

χρύσεος, -η, -ον (contr. χρυσοῦς, -ῆ, -οῦν), golden, gold

χρυσίον, τό, gold, money; anything made of gold, gold vessel

Poem

1:24 καὶ ἐποίησεν φονοκτονίαν
      καὶ ἐλάλησεν ὑπερηφανίαν μεγάλην.

25   καὶ ἐγένετο πένθος μέγα ἐπὶ Ισραηλ ἐν παντὶ τόπῳ αὐτῶν.

26   καὶ ἐστέναξαν ἄρχοντες καὶ πρεσβύτεροι,
      παρθένοι καὶ νεανίσκοι ἠσθένησαν,
      καὶ τὸ κάλλος τῶν γυναικῶν ἠλλοιώθη.

---

[15] Fm. acc. pl. modifying θυΐσκας.
[16] κατὰ πρόσωπον, "on the front."

27   πᾶς νυμφίος ἀνέλαβεν θρῆνον,
     καὶ καθημένη ἐν παστῷ ἐπένθει.
28   καὶ ἐσείσθη ἡ γῆ ἐπὶ[17] τοὺς κατοικοῦντας αὐτήν,[18]
     καὶ πᾶς ὁ οἶκος Ιακωβ ἐνεδύσατο[19] αἰσχύνην.

Vocabulary

αἰσχύνη, ἡ, shame, disgrace
ἀλλοιόω, change/alter (for the worse)
ἀσθενέω, be weak, sick
θρῆνος, ὁ, lamentation
κατοικέω, settle, dwell in; subst. inhabitants
νεανίσκος, ὁ, a youth, young man; servant
νυμφίος, ὁ, bridegroom
παστός, ὁ, bridal chamber (neol.)
πένθος, -ους, τό, mourning, sorrow
στενάζω, groan, sigh
φονοκτονία, ἡ, murder

---

[17] ἐπί (w. acc.), "because of."
[18] αὐτήν ("itself") refers to γῆ.
[19] S.v. ἐνδύω.

3.4.

Book of Job: The Adversary's Attack on Job

(Job 1:6–2:13)

Even though most of the Hebrew text of Job (Ιωβ) is composed in poetry, three sections, including Job 1:6–2:13, are written in Hebrew prose, even though the text is still arranged stichometrically.

The translator has avoided Hebraisms, translating the Hebrew text more freely in prose of high literary quality, as evident, for example, in the frequent use of the optative mood (e.g., Job 23:3–5, 7). The general style of this text is periphrastic rather than isometric. The translator has also substantially shortened the Hebrew text by excising obscure passages and repetitious argument. The symbol ς indicates translations added by Origen of Alexandria, in agreement with the Hebrew text but missing in the LXX (2:1), or Origen's translation of the same verse (23:9, 15a).

Complementary Reading: Luke 4:1–15 (§1.2).

At the outset of the story, we are told that Job had seven sons and three daughters. It was their custom to gather together on feast days to celebrate. On one such day, the angels gathered with God in heaven.

1:6 Καὶ ὡς[1] ἐγένετο ἡ ἡμέρα αὕτη, καὶ ἰδοὺ ἦλθον οἱ ἄγγελοι τοῦ θεοῦ παραστῆναι ἐνώπιον τοῦ κυρίου, καὶ ὁ διάβολος ἦλθεν μετ᾽ αὐτῶν. 7 Καὶ εἶπεν ὁ κύριος τῷ διαβόλῳ· πόθεν παραγέγονας; καὶ ἀποκριθεὶς ὁ διάβολος τῷ κυρίῳ εἶπεν· περιελθὼν τὴν γῆν καὶ ἐμπεριπατήσας τὴν (γῆν) ὑπ᾽ οὐρανὸν πάρειμι. 8 Καὶ εἶπεν αὐτῷ ὁ κύριος· προσέσχες τῇ διανοίᾳ σου κατὰ τοῦ παιδός μου Ιωβ, ὅτι οὐκ ἔστιν[2] κατ᾽ αὐτὸν[3] τῶν[4] ἐπὶ τῆς γῆς ἄνθρωπος ἄμεμπτος, ἀληθινός, θεοσεβής, ἀπεχόμενος ἀπὸ παντὸς πονηροῦ πράγματος;

---

[1] Temp. conj. ("when").
[2] Impers. "there is."
[3] κατά (w. acc.) denoting relation: "with respect to," "similar to," "like."
[4] τῶν functions as a demonstrative pronoun followed by a modifier (ἐπὶ τῆς γῆς).

Vocabulary

ἀληθινός, -ή, -όν, real, genuine, true, dependable

ἄμεμπτος, -ον, blameless, faultless

ἀπέχω, receive; receive a payment; mid. stay away from

ἐμπεριπατέω, walk about upon

θεοσεβής, -ές, god-fearing, pious; subst. god fearer

παραγίνομαι, be beside, present with, visit with (πρός); come to one's side/aid; arrive at/in, from (εἰς/ἐν, ἐκ) (cf. 2:11)

πάρειμι (1) (fr. εἰμί), pres. ptc. παρών, -οῦσα, -όν, impf. παρῆν, opt. παρείην: be present, be here; (impers.) come to/upon, arrive; πάρειμι + inf., be possible to (do something); subst. ptc. the present; bystander

παρίστημι (also παριστάνω), pf. ptc. παρεστώς: stand before (+ dat.); approach, come near; render, present oneself, offer, supply; show

περιέρχομαι, go about, go around, circle (from place to place)

πόθεν (interog. adv.), from where? how? in what way? why?

προσέχω, pay attention to, notice; take care of; mid. cling to something (+ dat.); προσέχω τὸν νοῦν + dat., turn one's attention/mind to

1:9 Ἀπεκρίθη δὲ ὁ διάβολος καὶ εἶπεν ἐναντίον τοῦ κυρίου· μὴ δωρεὰν σέβεται Ιωβ τὸν θεόν; 10 οὐ σὺ περιέφραξας τὰ ἔξω αὐτοῦ[5] καὶ τὰ ἔσω τῆς οἰκίας αὐτοῦ καὶ τὰ ἔξω[6] πάντων τῶν ὄντων αὐτῷ,[7] κύκλῳ; τὰ ἔργα τῶν χειρῶν αὐτοῦ εὐλόγησας καὶ τὰ κτήνη αὐτοῦ πολλὰ ἐποίησας ἐπὶ τῆς γῆς. 11 ἀλλὰ ἀπόστειλον[8] τὴν χεῖρά σου καὶ ἅψαι[9] πάντων, ὧν ἔχει· εἰ μὴν[10] εἰς (your) πρόσωπόν σε εὐλογήσει. 12 Τότε εἶπεν ὁ κύριος τῷ διαβόλῳ· ἰδοὺ πάντα ὅσα ἔστιν αὐτῷ,[11] δίδωμι ἐν τῇ χειρί σου, ἀλλὰ αὐτοῦ μὴ ἅψῃ. καὶ ἐξῆλθεν ὁ διάβολος παρὰ τοῦ κυρίου.

Vocabulary

δωρεάν (adv.), without payment, without reason/cause

ἔσω, inside, within (adv.)

κύκλῳ, in a circle, around

περιφράσσω, put a fence around

σέβω/σέβομαι: worship, reverence; mid. ptc. subst. σεβόμενοι, god fearers;[12] act. θεὸν σέβων, god fearer

---

[5] τὰ ἔξω αὐτοῦ, "the things external to him."

[6] καὶ τὰ ἔσω ... καὶ τὰ ἔξω, "*both* the things internal *and* external to him."

[7] πάντων τῶν ὄντων αὐτῷ, "of all that belongs to him."

[8] Here "stretch out."

[9] S.v. ἅπτομαι.

[10] εἰ μήν, emphatic form of μὴν ("surely").

[11] Dat. of poss.

[12] I.e., Gentiles who took part in synagogue services without becoming true προσήλυτοι

1:13 Καὶ ἦν ὡς[13] ἡ ἡμέρα αὕτη, οἱ υἱοὶ Ιωβ[14] καὶ αἱ θυγατέρες αὐτοῦ ἔπινον οἶνον ἐν τῇ οἰκίᾳ τοῦ ἀδελφοῦ αὐτῶν τοῦ πρεσβυτέρου.[15] 14 καὶ ἰδοὺ ἄγγελος ἦλθεν πρὸς Ιωβ καὶ εἶπεν αὐτῷ· τὰ ζεύγη τῶν βοῶν ἠροτρία, καὶ αἱ θήλειαι ὄνοι ἐβόσκοντο ἐχόμεναι[16] αὐτῶν, 15 καὶ ἐλθόντες οἱ αἰχμαλωτεύοντες ἠχμαλώτευσαν αὐτὰς καὶ τοὺς παῖδας ἀπέκτειναν ἐν μαχαίραις· σωθεὶς δὲ ἐγὼ μόνος ἦλθον τοῦ ἀπαγγεῖλαί σοι.

Vocabulary
ἀροτριάω, 3rd sg. impf. ἠροτρία: to plough
βόσκω, feed/tend domestic animals, graze (cattle)
ζεῦγος, -ους, τό, yoke
θῆλυς, -εια, -υ, female, she- ; subst. woman
θυγάτηρ, -τρός, ἡ, daughter; female descendant
ὄνος, ὁ/ἡ, ass, donkey
πρεσβύτερος, -α, -ον, older; ὁ πρεσβύτερος, old man, elder, official, ancestor

1:16 Ἔτι τούτου λαλοῦντος[17] ἦλθεν ἕτερος ἄγγελος καὶ εἶπεν πρὸς Ιωβ· πῦρ ἔπεσεν ἐκ τοῦ οὐρανοῦ καὶ κατέκαυσεν τὰ πρόβατα καὶ τοὺς ποιμένας κατέφαγεν[18] ὁμοίως, καὶ σωθεὶς ἐγὼ μόνος ἦλθον τοῦ ἀπαγγεῖλαί σοι. 17 ἔτι τούτου λαλοῦντος ἦλθεν ἕτερος ἄγγελος καὶ εἶπεν πρὸς Ιωβ· οἱ ἱππεῖς ἐποίησαν ἡμῖν κεφαλὰς[19] τρεῖς καὶ ἐκύκλωσαν τὰς καμήλους καὶ ἠχμαλώτευσαν αὐτὰς καὶ τοὺς παῖδας ἀπέκτειναν ἐν μαχαίραις, ἐσώθην δὲ ἐγὼ μόνος καὶ ἦλθον τοῦ ἀπαγγεῖλαί σοι. 18   Ἔτι τούτου λαλοῦντος ἄλλος ἄγγελος ἔρχεται λέγων τῷ Ιωβ· τῶν υἱῶν σου καὶ τῶν θυγατέρων σου ἐσθιόντων καὶ πινόντων[20] παρὰ τῷ ἀδελφῷ αὐτῶν τῷ πρεσβυτέρῳ 19 ἐξαίφνης πνεῦμα μέγα ἐπῆλθεν ἐκ τῆς ἐρήμου καὶ ἥψατο τῶν τεσσάρων γωνιῶν τῆς οἰκίας, καὶ ἔπεσεν ἡ οἰκία ἐπὶ τὰ παιδία σου, καὶ ἐτελεύτησαν· ἐσώθην δὲ ἐγὼ μόνος καὶ ἦλθον τοῦ ἀπαγγεῖλαί σοι.

Vocabulary
γωνία, ἡ, corner
ἐξαίφνης (adv.), suddenly
ἱππεύς, -έως, ὁ, horseman, cavalryman
κάμηλος, ὁ/ἡ, camel
κατακαίω (Att. κατακάω), impf. κατέκαιον, 2. κατακαύσω: burn completely, burn up

---

[13] Temp. conj., "when (it) was."
[14] Gen. (indecl.).
[15] **τοῦ** ἀδελφοῦ αὐτῶν **τοῦ** πρεσβυτέρου, 2nd attrib. pos. (cf. IV, 4.2).
[16] Here "keep close to," "keep beside" (w. gen.).
[17] Vv. 16, 17, and 18 all begin with gen. absol. (cf. IV, 7).
[18] S.v. κατεσθίω.
[19] κεφαλή, here "band," "troop."
[20] Gen. absol.

κυκλόω, encircle, surround
ὁμοίως (adv.), likewise, in the same way
ποιμήν, -ένος, ὁ, shepherd
τελευτάω, pres. impv. 2nd sg. τελεύτα (-α + ε = α): die, pass away (cf. 2:9ᵉ)

1:20 Οὕτως ἀναστὰς[21] Ιωβ διέρρηξεν[22] τὰ ἱμάτια αὐτοῦ καὶ ἐκείρατο τὴν κόμην τῆς κεφαλῆς αὐτοῦ καὶ πεσὼν χαμαὶ προσεκύνησεν καὶ εἶπεν· 21 αὐτὸς γυμνὸς ἐξῆλθον ἐκ κοιλίας μητρός μου, γυμνὸς καὶ ἀπελεύσομαι ἐκεῖ· ὁ κύριος ἔδωκεν, ὁ κύριος ἀφείλατο,[23] ὡς τῷ κυρίῳ ἔδοξεν, οὕτως καὶ ἐγένετο, εἴη[24] τὸ ὄνομα κυρίου εὐλογημένον. 22   Ἐν τούτοις πᾶσιν τοῖς συμβεβηκόσιν[25] αὐτῷ οὐδὲν ἥμαρτεν Ιωβ ἐναντίον τοῦ κυρίου καὶ οὐκ ἔδωκεν[26] ἀφροσύνην τῷ θεῷ.

Vocabulary
ἀφροσύνη, ἡ, foolishness
ἐπέρχομαι, come upon/against; arrive at
ἱμάτιον, τό, outer garment, cloak, robe; pl. clothes; grave clothes, funeral
  shroud
κείρω, mid. cut off one's hair
κόμη, ἡ, hair
τέσσαρες, τέσσαρα, (gen.) τεσσάρων: four
χαμαί, on/to the ground

2:1 Ἐγένετο δὲ ὡς ἡ ἡμέρα αὕτη καὶ ἦλθον οἱ ἄγγελοι τοῦ θεοῦ παραστῆναι ἔναντι κυρίου, καὶ ὁ διάβολος ἦλθεν ἐν μέσῳ αὐτῶν ※ παραστῆναι ἐναντίον τοῦ κυρίου. 2 καὶ εἶπεν ὁ κύριος τῷ διαβόλῳ· πόθεν σὺ ἔρχῃ; Τότε εἶπεν ὁ διάβολος ἐνώπιον τοῦ κυρίου· διαπορευθεὶς τὴν ὑπ᾽ οὐρανὸν (γῆν) καὶ ἐμπεριπατήσας τὴν σύμπασαν πάρειμι. 3 Εἶπεν δὲ ὁ κύριος πρὸς τὸν διάβολον· προσέσχες οὖν τῷ θεράποντί μου Ιωβ, ὅτι οὐκ ἔστιν κατ᾽ αὐτὸν[27] τῶν ἐπὶ τῆς γῆς ἄνθρωπος ἄκακος, ἀληθινός, ἄμεμπτος, θεοσεβής, ἀπεχόμενος ἀπὸ παντὸς κακοῦ; ἔτι δὲ ἔχεται[28] ἀκακίας, σὺ δὲ εἶπας τὰ ὑπάρχοντα αὐτοῦ διὰ κενῆς ἀπολέσαι.[29]

Vocabulary
ἀκακία, ἡ, innocence
ἄκακος, -ον, innocent

---

[21] S.v. ἀνίστημι.
[22] S.v. διαρρήγνυμι/διαρρήσσω.
[23] S.v. ἀφαιρέω (cf. principal parts of αἱρέω).
[24] For opt. of εἰμί see table 9.13.
[25] S.v. συμβαίνω.
[26] Here, "to ascribe."
[27] See Job 1:8.
[28] S.v. ἔχω, mid. "to hold onto," "maintain."
[29] S.v. ἀπόλλυμι, ¹aor. act. inf.

ἀπέχω, receive; receive a payment; mid. stay away from

ἀπόλλυμι, 2. ἀπολέσω, ²aor. ἀπώλεσα/²aor. ἀπωλόμην, aor. inf. ἀπολεῖν, aor. mid. inf. ἀπολέσθαι, 4. ἀπόλωλα, ²plpf. ἀπωλώλειν: destroy, kill; lose; mid. perish, be ruined; die, be lost; be destroyed

διαπορεύομαι, pass across/through, go through

ἐμπεριπατέω, walk about upon

θεράπων, -οντος, ὁ, servant

κενός, -ή, -όν, empty, void (space); τὸ κενόν, the void; no purpose; κενῶς / διὰ κενῆς / εἰς κενόν, in vain, to no purpose

παρίστημι (also παριστάνω), pf. ptc. παρεστώς: stand before (+ dat.); approach, come near; render, present oneself, offer, supply; show

προσέχω, pay attention to, notice; take care of; mid. cling to something (+ dat.); προσέχω τὸν νοῦν + dat., turn one's attention/mind to

σύμπας, σύμπασα, σύμπαν, all together (w. collective nouns); ἡ σύμπασα, the whole (world)

ὑπάρχω, impf. ὑπῆρχον: exist, be present; belong to; possess; subst. ptc. τὰ ὑπάρχοντα, possessions, property

2:4 Ὑπολαβὼν δὲ ὁ διάβολος εἶπεν τῷ κυρίῳ· δέρμα ὑπὲρ δέρματος, ὅσα ὑπάρχει ἀνθρώπῳ, ὑπὲρ τῆς ψυχῆς αὐτοῦ ἐκτείσει, 5 οὐ μὴν δὲ ἀλλὰ³⁰ ἀποστείλας τὴν χεῖρά σου ἅψαι τῶν ὀστῶν αὐτοῦ καὶ τῶν σαρκῶν αὐτοῦ, εἰ μὴν³¹ εἰς πρόσωπόν σε εὐλογήσει. 6 Εἶπεν δὲ ὁ κύριος τῷ διαβόλῳ· ἰδοὺ παραδίδωμί σοι αὐτόν, μόνον τὴν ψυχὴν αὐτοῦ διαφύλαξον. 7 Ἐξῆλθεν δὲ ὁ διάβολος ἀπὸ τοῦ κυρίου καὶ ἔπαισεν τὸν Ιωβ ἕλκει πονηρῷ ἀπὸ ποδῶν ἕως κεφαλῆς. 8 καὶ (Job) ἔλαβεν ὄστρακον, ἵνα τὸν ἰχῶρα ξύῃ, καὶ ἐκάθητο ἐπὶ τῆς κοπρίας ἔξω τῆς πόλεως.

Vocabulary

δέρμα, -ματος, τό, skin; leather, hide

διαφυλάσσω, guard carefully, preserve

ἐκτίνω, pay for (ὕπερ)

ἕλκος, -ους, τό, festering wounds, sores

ἰχώρ, -ῶρος, ὁ, discharge (fr. a wound), pus

κοπρία, ἡ, dunghill, dung heap

ξύω, scrape away

ὀστοῦν, τό (uncontr. ὀστέον), pl. ὀστᾶ, ὀστῶν (uncontr. ὀστέων), bone

ὄστρακον, τό, potsherd

παίω, to strike, wound, smite (with plague)

ὑπάρχω, impf. ὑπῆρχον: exist, be present, to be; belong to; possess; subst. τὰ ὑπάρχοντα, possessions, property

---

³⁰ οὐ μὴν δὲ ἀλλά ("nevertheless").

³¹ εἰ μήν > ἦ μήν ("surely").

2:9 Χρόνου δὲ πολλοῦ προβεβηκότος[32] εἶπεν αὐτῷ ἡ γυνὴ αὐτοῦ· μέχρι τίνος (χρόνου) καρτερήσεις λέγων 9[a] Ἰδοὺ ἀναμένω χρόνον ἔτι μικρὸν προσδεχόμενος τὴν ἐλπίδα τῆς σωτηρίας μου; 9[b] ἰδοὺ γὰρ ἠφάνισταί σου τὸ μνημόσυνον ἀπὸ τῆς γῆς, υἱοὶ καὶ θυγατέρες, ἐμῆς κοιλίας ὠδῖνες καὶ πόνοι, οὓς εἰς τὸ κενὸν ἐκοπίασα μετὰ μόχθων. 9[c] σύ τε αὐτὸς ἐν σαπρίᾳ σκωλήκων κάθησαι διανυκτερεύων αἴθριος, 9[d] κἀγὼ (am) πλανῆτις καὶ λάτρις τόπον ἐκ τόπου περιερχομένη καὶ οἰκίαν ἐξ οἰκίας προσδεχομένη τὸν ἥλιον πότε δύσεται, ἵνα ἀναπαύσωμαι τῶν μόχθων καὶ τῶν ὀδυνῶν, αἵ με νῦν συνέχουσιν. 9[e] ἀλλὰ εἰπὸν[33] τι ῥῆμα εἰς κύριον καὶ τελεύτα. 10   Ὁ δὲ ἐμβλέψας εἶπεν αὐτῇ· ὥσπερ μία τῶν ἀφρόνων γυναικῶν ἐλάλησας· εἰ τὰ ἀγαθὰ ἐδεξάμεθα ἐκ χειρὸς κυρίου, τὰ κακὰ οὐχ ὑποίσομεν;[34] ἐν πᾶσιν τούτοις τοῖς συμβεβηκόσιν[35] αὐτῷ οὐδὲν ἥμαρτεν Ιωβ τοῖς χείλεσιν ἐναντίον τοῦ θεοῦ.

Vocabulary

αἴθριος, -ον, in the open air

ἀναμένω, wait, hang on

ἀφανίζω, pf. ἠφάνισμαι: remove, get rid of; destroy, ruin; pass. vanish; be ruined, be destroyed

ἄφρων, -ονος (m./fm.), **-ον** (nt.), foolish, unlearned (contrasting φρόνιμος)

διανυκτερεύω, pass. spend the night (hapax)

δύνω, 2. δύσομαι, [2]aor. ἔδυν: go down, set (of the sun); mid. sink/set (of the sun)

ἐμβλέπω, look at (dat.), gaze on; consider

καρτερέω, be steadfast, persist

κενός, -ή, -όν, empty, without purpose; εἰς κενόν, in vain

κοπιάω, [1]aor. ἐκοπίασα: work hard, labor

λάτρις, -ιος, ἡ, hired servant

μνημόσυνον, τό, memorial, remembrance, legacy

μόχθος, ὁ, hardship

ὀδύνη, ἡ, grief

περιέρχομαι, go about

πλανῆτις, -ιδος, ἡ, wanderer

προβαίνω, pf. act. ptc. προβεβηκώς: advance, make progress; pass (of time)

σαπρία, ἡ, decayed matter, refuse

σκώληξ, -ηκος, ὁ, worm

συνέχω, to keep closed; seize, torment

ὑποφέρω, fut. ὑποίσω: bear up, endure

χεῖλος, -ους, τό; pl. τὰ χείλη: lips; edge, shore (of the sea), bank (of a river)

ὥσπερ, as, just as, even as; like

---

[32] Gen. absol.

[33] εἰπόν ([2]aor. impv. 2nd sg.), not εἶπον ([2]aor. ind.).

[34] S.v. ὑποφέρω.

[35] S.v. συμβαίνω.

2:11 Ἀκούσαντες δὲ οἱ τρεῖς φίλοι αὐτοῦ τὰ κακὰ πάντα τὰ ἐπελθόντα αὐτῷ παρεγένοντο ἕκαστος ἐκ τῆς ἰδίας χώρας πρὸς αὐτόν, Ελιφας[36] ὁ Θαιμανων βασιλεύς, Βαλδαδ[37] ὁ Σαυχαίων τύραννος, Σωφαρ[38] ὁ Μιναίων βασιλεύς, καὶ παρεγένοντο πρὸς αὐτὸν ὁμοθυμαδὸν τοῦ παρακαλέσαι καὶ ἐπισκέψασθαι αὐτόν. 12 ἰδόντες δὲ αὐτὸν πόρρωθεν οὐκ ἐπέγνωσαν (him) καὶ βοήσαντες φωνῇ μεγάλη ἔκλαυσαν[39] ῥήξαντες ἕκαστος τὴν ἑαυτοῦ στολὴν καὶ καταπασάμενοι γῆν. 13 παρεκάθισαν αὐτῷ ἑπτὰ ἡμέρας καὶ ἑπτὰ νύκτας, καὶ οὐδεὶς αὐτῶν ἐλάλησεν, ἑώρων[40] γὰρ τὴν πληγὴν (αὐτοῦ) δεινὴν οὖσαν καὶ μεγάλην σφόδρα.

Vocabulary

δεινός, -ή, -όν, terrible, fearful

ἐπιγινώσκω, recognize

ἐπισκέπτομαι, inspect something; visit

Θαιμᾶνοι, οἱ, Thaimanites

καταπάσσω, mid. to sprinkle oneself with, strew oneself with

Μιναῖοι, οἱ, Minites

ὁμοθυμαδόν, with one accord/mind

παραγίνομαι, to be beside, be present with, visit with (πρός), to come to one's side/aid; to arrive at/in/from (εἰς/ἐν/ἐκ)

παρακαθίζω, sit down beside/with

πόρρωθεν, from a distance

ῥήγνυμι/ῥήσσω, fut. ῥήξω, aor. impv. ῥῆξον, [2]aor. ptc. ῥήξας, [2]aor. pass. ptc. ῥαγείς, -εῖσα, -έν, 3rd sg. aor. pass. impv. ῥαγήτω, fut. pass. ῥαγήσομαι: tear, tear in pieces; pass. break out, burst, break in two

Σαυχαῖοι, οἱ, Sauchites

τύραννος, ὁ, tyrant, king

χώρα, ἡ, countryside, country; a place; land (as opposed to sea)

---

[36] Eliphaz.
[37] Baldad.
[38] Sophar.
[39] S.v. κλαίω.
[40] Impf. act. 3rd pl. (s.v. ὁράω).

3.5.

Book of Job: Job's Complaint Before the Lord

(Job 23:1–17)

Following Job's extended debate with his three friends, Bildad, Zophar, and Eliphaz, about the nature of suffering, Job replies to his friends' speeches. In the reading of this section, taken from the first part of his reply, Job maintains that he is innocent of wrongdoing. Nonetheless, he does not curse the Lord. In speaking to his three friends (cf. Job 4–22), Job complains:

23:1 Ὑπολαβὼν δὲ Ιωβ λέγει·

2 καὶ δὴ οἶδα ὅτι ἐκ χειρός μου¹ ἡ ἔλεγξίς ἐστιν,
   καὶ ἡ χεὶρ αὐτοῦ² βαρεῖα γέγονεν ἐπ᾽ ἐμῷ στεναγμῷ.

3 τίς δ᾽ ἄρα γνοίη³ ὅτι εὕροιμι⁴ αὐτὸν
   καὶ ἔλθοιμι⁵ εἰς τέλος;

4 εἴποιμι⁶ δὲ ἐμαυτοῦ κρίμα,
   τὸ δὲ στόμα μου ἐμπλήσαιμι⁷ ἐλέγχων,

5 γνῴην⁸ δὲ ῥήματα, ἅ μοι ἐρεῖ,⁹
   αἰσθοίμην¹⁰ δὲ τίνα μοι ἀπαγγελεῖ.

6 καὶ εἰ ἐν πολλῇ ἰσχύι ἐπελεύσεταί μοι,
   εἶτα ἐν ἀπειλῇ μοι οὐ χρήσεται,

---

¹ ἐκ χειρός μου, "out of my reach."
² I.e., the Lord's.
³ S.v. γινώσκω, cf. table 9.6.
⁴ S.v. εὑρίσκω; ²aor. has the same opt. endings as pres. tense.
⁵ S.v. ἔρχομαι.
⁶ S.v. λέγω.
⁷ S.v. ἐμπίμπλημι.
⁸ Expect γνοίην, table 9.6.
⁹ S.v. λέγω.
¹⁰ S.v. αἰσθάνομαι.

7   ἀλήθεια γὰρ καὶ ἔλεγχος παρ᾽ αὐτοῦ,[11]
      ἐξαγάγοι[12] δὲ εἰς τέλος τὸ κρίμα μου.

8   εἰς γὰρ πρῶτα[13] πορεύσομαι καὶ οὐκέτι εἰμί,[14]
      τὰ δὲ ἐπ᾽ ἐσχάτοις[15] τί οἶδα;

9   ※ἀριστερὰ ποιήσαντος αὐτοῦ[16] καὶ[17] οὐ κατέσχον,
      ※περιβαλεῖ δεξιά, καὶ οὐκ ὄψομαι.

Vocabulary

αἰσθάνομαι, impf. ἠσθόμην, [2]aor. ἠσθόμην: have the sense/perception of; perceive
    by the senses

ἀπειλή, ἡ, threat

ἀριστερός, -ά, -όν, best; euphem. for "left" (like εὐώνυμος); on the left; ἀριστερά,
    ἡ, left hand; τὰ ἀριστερά (sc. μέρη), on the left side

βαρύς, -εῖα, -ύ, heavy; fierce

δεξιός, -ά, -όν, on the right; δεξιά, ἡ, right hand, authority; τὰ δεξιά (sc. μέρη), on
    the right side

δή, really, indeed; of course, then, therefore; now, at this point; τί δή; what is
    going on?

ἔλεγξις, -εως, ἡ, refutation

ἐμαυτοῦ, – ῆς, (reflexive pron.) myself; (poss. pron.) my own

ἐξάγω, lead out, bring

ἐπέρχομαι, come upon, against; arrive at

οὐκέτι (adv.), no longer, no more

στεναγμός, ὁ, sighing, groaning

τέλος, -ους, τό, end; outcome, resolution, conclusion

χράω, pres. mid. inf. χρῆσθαι, [1]aor. mid. inf. χρήσασθαι: act. proclaim (by the
    gods in oracles), direct by an oracle (+ inf.); mid. use something/somebody,
    make use of (dat.); conduct a sacrifice; treat somebody with (+ dat. / ἐν); be
    subject to, suffer from; w. adv. treat somebody (dat.) in a particular way (e.g.,
    well/badly)

23.10   οἶδεν γὰρ ἤδη ὁδόν μου,
        διέκρινεν δέ με ὥσπερ τὸ χρυσίον.

---

[11] Nominal sentence; provide some form of the verb εἰμί.

[12] S.v. ἐξάγω.

[13] εἰς πρῶτα = πρῶτα, "first."

[14] εἰμί, here "exist."

[15] ἐπί (w. dat.), "concerning."

[16] Gen. absol.

[17] καί…καί…both of which are pleonastic (καί = Heb. *we*). By rendering the parataxis of Heb. with καί,
the translator has created confusion about how the clauses are related to one another.

11   ἐξελεύσομαι δὲ ἐν ἐντάλμασιν αὐτοῦ,
      ὁδοὺς γὰρ αὐτοῦ ἐφύλαξα καὶ οὐ μὴ ἐκκλίνω. [18]

12   ἀπὸ[19] ἐνταλμάτων αὐτοῦ καὶ[20] οὐ μὴ παρέλθω,
      ἐν δὲ κόλπῳ μου ἔκρυψα ῥήματα αὐτοῦ.

13   εἰ δὲ καὶ[21] αὐτὸς ἔκρινεν οὕτως, τίς ἐστιν ὁ ἀντειπὼν αὐτῷ;
      ὃ γὰρ αὐτὸς ἠθέλησεν, καὶ ἐποίησεν.
      (v. 14 of MT is missing in LXX)

15   διὰ τοῦτο ἐπ᾽ αὐτῷ ἐσπούδακα,
      νουθετούμενος δὲ ἐφρόντισα αὐτοῦ.

15a ※ ἐπὶ τούτῳ ἀπὸ προσώπου αὐτοῦ κατασπουδασθῶ,
      ※ κατανοήσω καὶ πτοηθήσομαι ἐξ αὐτοῦ.[22]

16   κύριος δὲ ἐμαλάκυνεν τὴν καρδίαν μου,
      ὁ δὲ παντοκράτωρ ἐσπούδασέν με.

17   οὐ γὰρ ᾔδειν ὅτι ἐπελεύσεταί μοι σκότος,
      πρὸ προσώπου δέ μου ἐκάλυψεν γνόφος.

Vocabulary

ἀντιλέγω (+ dat.), [2]aor. ptc. ἀντειπών: contradict somebody/something
γνόφος, ὁ, darkness
διακρίνω, judge, decide; pass., bring an issue to a decsion; doubt
ἐντάλματα, -ων, commands (neol.)
ἐκκλίνω, turn away, turn aside
κατασπουδάζομαι, pass. be troubled
κόλπος, ὁ, arms, breast (denoting tender physical closeness)
μαλακύνω, soften (the heart)
παντοκράτωρ, -ορος, ὁ, almighty one
πτοέω, pass. tremble, be terrified
σπουδάζω, pay serious attention to; study (books); hurry; be in a hurry to do
    something
ὥσπερ, as, just as, even as; like

---

[18] οὐ μή + aor. subj. (emph. fut. neg., cf. IV, 8).
[19] ἀπό, "by reason of."
[20] Pleon. καί.
[21] Adv. καί.
[22] V. 15a is Origen's trans. of the same verse.

3.6.

Book of Daniel: A Vision of the Resurrection of the Dead

(Dan 12:1–13)

Date: Though the stories of Daniel are set in the time of the Babylonian captivity, this book was actually written about 165 BCE. Its primary concerns are the political events of the Maccabean era and the reign of the Seleucid king Antiochus Epiphanes (cf. 1 Macc 1:10–28, §3.3). The Old Greek version of Daniel was translated about 200 BCE, while the Theodotion version, also known as the *kaige* (καίγε) text, dates ca. 50 BCE.

Text: The Book of Daniel consists of six court tales and four apocalyptic visions. The reading in this section is taken from the fourth of the apocalyptic visions, in the book's final chapter. The Theodotion version translates the Masoretic text in a literal word-for-word manner and exhibits a formal equivalence to its Hebrew source text. In contrast, the Old Greek version is more literary.

The Resurrection of the Dead, Dan 12:1–13

Old Greek	Theodotion Version
12:1 Καὶ κατὰ τὴν ὥραν ἐκείνην παρελεύσεται Μιχαηλ ὁ ἄγγελος ὁ μέγας ὁ ἑστηκὼς ἐπὶ τοὺς υἱοὺς τοῦ λαοῦ σου· ἐκείνη ἡ ἡμέρα (will be) θλίψεως, οἵα οὐκ ἐγενήθη ἀφ᾽ οὗ ἐγενήθησαν ἕως τῆς ἡμέρας ἐκείνης· καὶ ἐν ἐκείνη τῇ ἡμέρᾳ ὑψωθήσεται πᾶς ὁ λαός, ὃς ἂν εὑρεθῇ ἐγγεγραμμένος ἐν τῷ βιβλίῳ.	12:1 Καὶ ἐν τῷ καιρῷ ἐκείνῳ ἀναστήσεται Μιχαηλ ὁ ἄρχων ὁ μέγας ὁ ἑστηκὼς ἐπὶ¹ τοὺς υἱοὺς τοῦ λαοῦ σου· καὶ ἔσται καιρὸς θλίψεως, θλῖψις οἵα οὐ γέγονεν ἀφ᾽ οὗ² γεγένηται ἔθνος ἐπὶ τῆς γῆς ἕως τοῦ καιροῦ ἐκείνου· καὶ ἐν τῷ καιρῷ ἐκείνῳ σωθήσεται ὁ λαός σου, πᾶς ὁ εὑρεθεὶς γεγραμμένος ἐν τῇ βίβλῳ.
	(*continued*)

---

¹ ἐπί (w. acc.), "over."
² ἀφ᾽ οὗ (καιροῦ).

Old Greek	Theodotion Version
2 καὶ πολλοὶ τῶν καθευδόντων ἐν τῷ πλάτει τῆς γῆς ἀναστήσονται, οἱ μὲν εἰς ζωὴν αἰώνιον, οἱ δὲ εἰς ὀνειδισμόν, οἱ δὲ εἰς διασπορὰν καὶ αἰσχύνην αἰώνιον.	2 καὶ πολλοὶ τῶν καθευδόντων ἐν γῆς χώματι ἐξεγερθήσονται, οὗτοι εἰς ζωὴν αἰώνιον καὶ οὗτοι εἰς ὀνειδισμὸν καὶ εἰς αἰσχύνην αἰώνιον.
3 καὶ οἱ συνιέντες φανοῦσιν ὡς φωστῆρες τοῦ οὐρανοῦ καὶ οἱ κατισχύοντες τοὺς λόγους μου ὡσεὶ[3] τὰ ἄστρα τοῦ οὐρανοῦ εἰς τὸν αἰῶνα τοῦ αἰῶνος.[4]	3 καὶ οἱ συνιέντες ἐκλάμψουσιν ὡς ἡ λαμπρότης τοῦ στερεώματος καὶ ἀπὸ[5] τῶν δικαίων τῶν πολλῶν ὡς οἱ ἀστέρες εἰς τοὺς αἰῶνας καὶ ἔτι.
4 καὶ σύ, Δανιηλ, κάλυψον τὰ προστάγματα καὶ σφράγισαι τὸ βιβλίον ἕως καιροῦ συντελείας, ἕως ἂν ἀπομανῶσιν οἱ πολλοὶ καὶ πλησθῇ[6] ἡ γῆ ἀδικίας.	4 καὶ σύ, Δανιηλ, ἔμφραξον τοὺς λόγους καὶ σφράγισον τὸ βιβλίον ἕως καιροῦ συντελείας, ἕως διδαχθῶσιν πολλοὶ καὶ πληθυνθῇ ἡ γνῶσις.

Vocabulary

ἀδικία, ἡ, wrongdoing, injustice
αἰσχύνη, ἡ, shame, disgrace
ἀπομαίνομαι, go mad (neol.)
διασπορά, ἡ, scattering, dispersion
ἐγγράφω, record
καθεύδω, sleep; die (fig.); have sex with (πρός) somebody
κατισχύω (w. acc.), overpower, prevail over, be master of
ὀνειδισμός, ὁ, reproach, contempt
πλάτος, -ους, flat, breadth (of the land)
πρόσταγμα, -ματος, τό, ordinance, command
συντέλεια, ἡ, completion, consummation
σφραγίζω, to seal (for a security), to seal by impressing a seal with a signet ring
φωστήρ, -ῆρος, ὁ, star

ἐκλάμπω, 2. ἐκλάμψω, 3. ἐξέλαμψα: blaze up; shine, beam forth
ἐμφράσσω, 3. ἐνέφραξα: bar passage to, block up
ἐξεγείρω, awaken; raise from the dead; pass. be awakened, wake up
λαμπρός, -ά, -όν, bright, shining; superl. λαμπρότατος, -η, -ον, brightness, splendor; most excellent (w. titulature)
στερέωμα, -ματος, τό, firmament (sky)
χῶμα, -ματος, τό, sepulchral mound, mound (of earth)

The Epilogue

5 Καὶ εἶδον ἐγὼ Δανιηλ καὶ ἰδοὺ δύο ἕτεροι εἱστήκεισαν, εἷς ἔνθεν τοῦ ποταμοῦ καὶ εἷς ἔνθεν.	5 καὶ εἶδον ἐγώ, Δανιηλ, καὶ ἰδοὺ δύο ἕτεροι εἱστήκεισαν,[7] εἷς ἐντεῦθεν τοῦ χείλους τοῦ ποταμοῦ καὶ εἷς ἐντεῦθεν τοῦ χείλους τοῦ ποταμοῦ.
6 καὶ εἶπα τῷ ἑνὶ τῷ περιβεβλημένῳ τὰ βύσσινα τῷ ἐπάνω (of the river)· πότε οὖν συντέλεια ὧν εἴρηκάς[8] μοι τῶν θαυμαστῶν καὶ ὁ καθαρισμὸς τούτων;	6 καὶ εἶπεν τῷ ἀνδρὶ τῷ ἐνδεδυμένῳ τὰ βαδδιν, ὃς ἦν ἐπάνω τοῦ ὕδατος τοῦ ποταμοῦ· ἕως πότε τὸ πέρας[9] ὧν εἴρηκας τῶν θαυμασίων;

---

[3] ὡσεί > ὡς εἰ, "like," "as if."
[4] A reference to astral resurrection of departed souls (cf. afterlife theology in Isa 26:19).
[5] ἀπό, partitive use ("some").
[6] S.v. πίμπλημι.
[7] S.v. ἵστημι, cf. table 9.1.1(f); this is a stative verb. Since the perfect tense is translated as a present tense, the pluperfect should be translated as a simple past tense.
[8] S.v. λέγω.
[9] Construe τὸ πέρας w. θαυμασίων.

Old Greek	Theodotion Version
7 καὶ ἤκουσα τοῦ περιβεβλημένου τὰ βύσσινα, ὃς ἦν ἐπάνω τοῦ ὕδατος τοῦ ποταμοῦ (say)· ἕως καιροῦ συντελείας· καὶ ὕψωσε τὴν δεξιὰν καὶ τὴν ἀριστερὰν εἰς τὸν οὐρανὸν καὶ ὤμοσε[10] τὸν ζῶντα εἰς τὸν αἰῶνα θεὸν ὅτι εἰς καιρὸν καὶ καιροὺς καὶ ἥμισυ καιροῦ ἡ συντέλεια χειρῶν ἀφέσεως λαοῦ ἁγίου, καὶ συντελεσθήσεται πάντα ταῦτα.	7 καὶ ἤκουσα τοῦ ἀνδρὸς τοῦ ἐνδεδυμένου τὰ βαδδιν, ὃς ἦν ἐπάνω τοῦ ὕδατος τοῦ ποταμοῦ, καὶ ὕψωσεν τὴν δεξιὰν αὐτοῦ καὶ τὴν ἀριστερὰν αὐτοῦ εἰς τὸν οὐρανὸν καὶ ὤμοσεν ἐν τῷ ζῶντι τὸν αἰῶνα ὅτι εἰς[11] καιρὸν καιρῶν καὶ ἥμισυ καιροῦ· ἐν τῷ συντελεσθῆναι[12] διασκορπισμὸν χειρὸς λαοῦ ἡγιασμένου[13] γνώσονται πάντα ταῦτα.

Vocabulary

ἀριστερός, -ά, -όν, best; euphem. for "left" (like εὐώνυμος); on the left; ἀριστερά, ἡ, left hand; τὰ ἀριστερά (sc. μέρη), on the left side

βύσσινος, -η, -ον, of fine linen; τὰ βύσσινα, dressings of fine linen

ἔνθεν... καὶ ἔνθεν..., on this side ... on that side

ἥμισυς, -εια, -ύ, half; μέχρι τοῦ ἡμίσους, up to the middle (of one's body)

καθαρισμός, ὁ, purification

βαδδιν, fine linen (hapax)

διασκορπισμός, ὁ, scattering, dispersion

θαυμάσιος, -α, -ον, wonderful, excellent; superl. θαυμασιώτατος, -η, -ον, most admirable/excellent/wonderful; τὰ θαυμάσια, marvels, wonders

πέρας, -ατος, τό, limit, end, boundary; πέρας (adv.), finally, in conclusion, as a result

χεῖλος, -ους, τό, pl. χείλη, lips; edge, shore (sea), bank (of river)

8 καὶ ἐγὼ ἤκουσα καὶ οὐ διενοήθην παρ᾽[14] αὐτὸν τὸν καιρὸν καὶ εἶπα· κύριε, τίς ἡ λύσις τοῦ λόγου τούτου, καὶ τίνος αἱ παραβολαὶ αὗται;	8 καὶ ἐγὼ ἤκουσα καὶ οὐ συνῆκα[15] καὶ εἶπα· κύριε, τί (is) τὰ ἔσχατα τούτων;
9 καὶ εἶπέν μοι· ἀπότρεχε, Δανιηλ, ὅτι κατακεκαλυμμένα καὶ ἐσφραγισμένα τὰ προστάγματα, ἕως ἂν	9 καὶ εἶπεν· δεῦρο, Δανιηλ, ὅτι ἐμπεφραγμένοι καὶ ἐσφραγισμένοι οἱ λόγοι, ἕως καιροῦ πέρας,
10 πειρασθῶσι[16] καὶ ἁγιασθῶσι πολλοί, καὶ ἁμάρτωσιν οἱ ἁμαρτωλοί· καὶ οὐ μὴ διανοηθῶσι[17] πάντες οἱ ἁμαρτωλοί, καὶ οἱ διανοούμενοι προσέξουσιν.	10 ἐκλεγῶσιν[18] καὶ ἐκλευκανθῶσιν καὶ πυρωθῶσιν πολλοί, καὶ ἀνομήσωσιν ἄνομοι· καὶ οὐ συνήσουσιν πάντες ἄνομοι, καὶ οἱ νοήμονες συνήσουσιν.

(continued)

---

[10] S.v. ὄμνυμι.

[11] εἰς + expression of time, "for (a period of)."

[12] Art. inf.

[13] Gen. absol.

[14] παρά, "about," "concerning."

[15] S.v. συνίημι, see paradigm of ἵημι; cf. able 9.15.

[16] S.v. πειράζω.

[17] οὐ μη + aor. subj. (emph. fut. neg., cf. IV, 8).

[18] In HGr, subj. is sometimes used in place of the impv. (cf. hort. subj., cf. IV, 12).

[19] S.v. ἀφίστημι.

[20] I.e., διὰ παντὸς καιροῦ, i.e., a perpetual (sacrifice/offering).

[21] Art. inf.

[22] παραλλάξεως τοῦ ἐνδελεχισμοῦ καί...βδέλυγμα ἐρημώσεως

Old Greek	*Theodotion Version*
11 ἀφ᾽ οὗ (καιροῦ ὅτι) ἂν ἀποσταθῇ[19] ἡ θυσία διὰ παντὸς[20] καὶ ἑτοιμασθῇ δοθῆναι τὸ βδέλυγμα τῆς ἐρημώσεως (there are) ἡμέρας χιλίας διακοσίας ἐνενήκοντα.	11 καὶ ἀπὸ (that) καιροῦ παραλλάξεως τοῦ ἐνδελεχισμοῦ καὶ τοῦ δοθῆναι[21] βδέλυγμα ἐρημώσεως[22] (as) ἡμέραι χίλιαι διακόσιαι ἐνενήκοντα.
12 μακάριος ὁ ἐμμένων καὶ συνάξει εἰς ἡμέρας χιλίας τριακοσίας τριάκοντα πέντε.	12 μακάριος ὁ ὑπομένων καὶ φθάσας εἰς ἡμέρας χιλίας τριακοσίας τριάκοντα πέντε.
13 καὶ σὺ δεῦρο καὶ ἀναπαύου, ἔτι γὰρ (there are) ἡμέραι εἰς ἀναπλήρωσιν συντελείας, καὶ ἀναστήσῃ εἰς τὸν κλῆρόν σου εἰς συντέλειαν ἡμερῶν.	13 καὶ σὺ δεῦρο καὶ ἀναπαύου, ἔτι γὰρ ἡμέραι εἰς ἀναπλήρωσιν συντελείας, καὶ[23] ἀναστήσῃ[24] εἰς τὸν κλῆρόν σου εἰς συντέλειαν ἡμερῶν.

Vocabulary

ἀναπλήρσωσις, -εως, ἡ, fulfillment	ἐκλευκαίνω, become very white
ἀποτρέχω, hurry away	ἐμφράσσω, pass. ptc. ἐμπεφραγμένοι, bar
βδέλυγμα, -ματος, τό, abomination	passage to, block up
διακοσίοι, -αι, -α, two hundred	ἐνδελέχισμός, ὁ, perpetual/daily (sacrifice)
διανοέομαι, pass. dep. comprehend	ἐρήμωσις, -εως, ἡ, desolation
ἔμμένω, ¹aor. ἐνέμεινα: abide in, persevere in; abide by, stand by, be true to	**λύσις, ἡ**, a releasing; divorce; breaking (of spells); interpretation, solution (of a riddle)
ἐνενήκοντα (indecl.), ninety	νοήμων, -ον, thoughtful, intelligent
ἐρήμωσις, -εως, ἡ, desolation	παράλλαξις, -εως, ἡ, change, removal (hapax)
κατακαλύπτω, cover up, cover with	**πυρόω**, burn with fire; heat to red hot: pass. be set on fire, be purified by fire (of metals)
κλῆρος, -ου, ὁ, that which is assigned by lot, a share, portion; a legacy, inheritance, inheritable estate	**ὑπομένω**, remain, await, endure
προσέχω, pay attention to, notice; take care of; mid. cling to something (+ dat.); προσέχω τὸν νοῦν (+ dat.), turn one's attention/ mind to	
τριακόσιοι, -αι, -α, three hundred	
χιλιάς, -άδος, ἡ, thousand	

SELECT BIBLIOGRAPHY

McLay, Tim. *The Old Greek and Theodotian Versions of Daniel*. Septuagint and Cognate Studies 43. Atlanta: Scholars Press, 1996.

---

[23] Adv. Καί.
[24] Mid. voice.

3.7.

1 Enoch: The Book of the Watchers

(1 En. 1, 6:1–8:2)

Date: Late pre-Maccabean.

Text: The discovery at Qumran of an Aramaic version of 1 Enoch (4QEn, 4QEnastr, 1QGiants) has confirmed that 1 En. 1–36 was originally composed in Aramaic. The Greek text in this section is that of R. H. Charles, with the inclusion of some of the textual emendations recommended by George Nickelsburg.[1]

The Book of Enoch was considered to be scripture by the author of Jude (1 En. 1:9 is quoted in Jude 14–15; cf. Deut 33:2), by the author of the Epistle of Barnabas (Barn. 16:4), and by many of the early church fathers, including Athenagoras, Clement of Alexandria, Irenaeus, and Tertullian.[2] Even today, it has the status of a canonical text in both the Ethiopian Orthodox and Eritrean Orthodox Churches.

Comments: The two earliest apocalypses in the Jewish tradition are the Book of Watchers (third century BCE) in 1 En. 6–36 and the Book of Heavenly Luminaries (early third century BCE or before) in 1 En. 72–82. The term "Watchers" (οἱ ἐγρήγοροι) normally designates the two hundred angels who rebelled against the Lord after the Flood and thereafter remained on the earth, bound in its valleys.[3] The reading here expands on the myth found in Gen 6:1–2, narrating how these same Watchers became filled with sexual desire for the women on earth and mated with them, thereby conceiving a race of "giants" (γίγαντες, 1 En. 7:2, T. Reu. 5:7). The Watchers then imparted to the women forbidden knowledge.

---

[1] R. H. Charles, *The Book of Enoch* (Oxford: Clarendon, 1912); George W. E. Nickelsburg, *A Commentary on the Book of 1 Enoch*, ed. Klaus Baltzer, Hermeneia (Minneapolis: Fortress, 2001).

[2] Enoch was the great-grandson of Adam (Gen 5:3–18) and the great-grandfather of Noah. According to Genesis, Enoch "walked with God: and he was not; for God took him" (Gen 5:22–29), implying that he was taken up by God while still alive.

[3] Cf. Gen 6:1–2; 1 En. 1:5–7, 9, 15, 16:2; Jude 1:6.

FIG. 6. Relief of the archangel Michael, carved on recessed panel, Konya (IKonya 200).

Related Texts: The story of this mythic transgression is reinterpreted in the Testament of Reuben 5:1–7 (§6.5), which claims that no direct sexual contact actually occurred. Rather, the sexual desire (ἐπιθυμία) of the Watchers alone was sufficient to impregnate the human women.

AN ORACLE OF JUDGMENT – 1 EN. 1:3–9

1:1 Λόγος εὐλογίας Ἑνώχ, καθὼς εὐλόγησεν ἐκλεκτοὺς δικαίους οἵτινες ἔσονται (present) εἰς ἡμέραν ἀνάγκης ἐξᾶραι πάντας τοὺς ἐχθρούς, καὶ σωθήσονται δίκαιοι. 2 καὶ ἀναλαβὼν τὴν παραβολὴν[4] αὐτοῦ (Enoch) εἶπεν· Ἑνὼχ ἄνθρωπος δίκαιος ὅστις ἐκ θεοῦ ὅρασις αὐτοῦ ἀνεωγμένη,[5] καὶ ἑώρα[6] τὴν ὅρασιν τοῦ ἁγίου[7] καὶ τοῦ οὐρανοῦ ἣν ἔδειξέν μοι ἄγγελοι ἅγιοι. καὶ ἀπὸ λόγων ἐγρήγορων καὶ ἁγίων ἤκουσα ἐγὼ πάντα, καὶ ὡς ἤκουσα παρ᾽ αὐτῶν πάντα καὶ ἔγνων ἐγὼ θεωρῶν.[8] καὶ οὐκ εἰς τὴν νῦν[9] γενεὰν διενοούμην, ἀλλὰ ἐπὶ[10] πόρρω οὖσαν γενεὰν ἐγὼ λαλῶ. 3 καὶ περὶ τῶν ἐκλεκτῶν νῦν λέγω, καὶ περὶ αὐτῶν ἀνέλαβον τὴν παραβολήν μου.

Vocabulary

ἀνάγκη, ἡ, necessity, obligation; tribulation, calamity; pl. calamities

ἀναλαμβάνω, 6. ἀνελήφθην: to take up, carry; to resolve; to take up (a discourse); to take over, carry away

διανοέομαι, recollect, expound

ἐγρήγοροι, οἱ, "Watchers," rebel angels

ἐκλεκτός, -ή, -όν, chosen, elect; precious

ἔλεος, -ους, τό, mercy, compassion

ἐξαίρω, 3. ἐξῆρα: remove, drive away (do not confuse w. ἐξαιρέω)

εὐλογία, ἡ, blessing

πόρρω (adv.), far off, far away

A THEOPHANY

1:3 Καὶ ἐξελεύσεται ὁ ἅγιός μου ὁ μέγας ἐκ τῆς κατοικήσεως αὐτοῦ, καὶ ὁ θεὸς τοῦ αἰῶνος 4 ἐπὶ γῆν πατήσει ἐπὶ τὸ Σινὰ ὄρος[11] καὶ φανήσεται[12] ἐκ τῆς παρεμβολῆς

---

[4] παραβολήν, here "discourse."
[5] Based on emendation of Nickelsberg (p. 137, 2b).
[6] S.v. ὁράω, impf.
[7] "Of the Holy One."
[8] Based on the emendation of Nickelsberg (p. 137, 2g)
[9] νῦν, "present."
[10] ἐπί, "concerning."
[11] ἐπὶ γῆν…ἐπὶ τὸ Σεινὰ ὄρος.
[12] S.v. φαίνω.

αὐτοῦ καὶ φανήσεται ἐν τῇ δυνάμει τῆς ἰσχύος αὐτοῦ ἀπὸ τοῦ οὐρανοῦ τῶν οὐρανῶν. 5 καὶ φοβηθήσονται πάντες[13] καὶ πιστεύσουσιν οἱ ἐγρήγοροι καὶ ᾄσουσιν[14] ἀπόκρυφα ἐν πᾶσιν τοῖς ἄκροις τῆς γῆς καὶ λήμψεται αὐτούς[15] τρόμος καὶ φόβος μέγας μέχρι τῶν περάτων τῆς γῆς, 6 καὶ σεισθήσονται καὶ πεσοῦνται καὶ διαλυθήσονται ὄρη ὑψηλά, καὶ ταπεινωθήσονται βουνοὶ ὑψηλοὶ καὶ τακήσονται ὡς κηρὸς ἀπὸ προσώπου πυρός· 7 καὶ διασχισθήσεται ἡ γῆ σχίσμα, καὶ πάντα ὅσα ἐστὶν ἐπὶ τῆς γῆς ἀπολεῖται[16] καὶ κρίσις ἔσται κατὰ πάντων.

Vocabulary

ἄκρον, τό, high point, top (of a mountain, staff); outermost edge; end, edge (of the earth); peel (of fruit)

βουνός, ὁ, hill

διαλύω, break apart

διασχίζω, separate; pass. be separated

ἰσχύς, -ύος, ἡ, strength, might

κατοίκησις, -εως, ἡ, dwelling

κηρός, ὁ, beeswax

μέχρι(ς), (prep. w. gen.) until, to; to the extent; (conj.) until

παρεμβολή, ἡ, army; battalion

πατέω, tread/walk on (ἐπί)

πέρας, -ατος, τό, limit, end (of the earth), boundary; (adv.) πέρας, finally, in conclusion; as a result

ῥαγάς, -άδος, ἡ, fissure (in soil)

σείω, to shake

Σινᾶ, indecl., Mt. Sinai

σχίσμα, τό, crack, cleft, 1 En. 1:7; dissension, schism

τήκω, 2. τακήσομαι: melt, dissolve

1:8[a] Καὶ μετὰ τῶν δικαίων τὴν εἰρήνην ποιήσει,[17] καὶ ἐπὶ τοὺς ἐκλεκτοὺς ἔσται συντήρησις, καὶ ἐπ᾽ αὐτοὺς γενήσεται ἔλεος, 8[b] καὶ ἔσονται πάντες τοῦ θεοῦ,[18] καὶ τὴν εὐοκίαν δώσει αὐτοῖς καὶ πάντας (of them) εὐλογήσει. 8[c] καὶ πάντων ἀντιλήμψεται καὶ φανήσεται αὐτοῖς φῶς καὶ ποιήσει ἐπ᾽ αὐτοὺς εἰρήνην. 9[a] ὅτι ἔρχεται[19] σὺν ταῖς μυριάσιν αὐτοῦ καὶ τοῖς ἁγίοις αὐτοῦ ποιῆσαι κρίσιν κατὰ πάντων, καὶ ἀπολέσαι πάντας τοὺς ἀσεβεῖς, 9[b] καὶ ἐλέγξει πᾶσαν σάρκα περὶ πάντων ἔργων τῆς ἀσεβείας αὐτῶν ὧν ἠσέβησαν

---

[13] The lack of subject–verb agreement probably stems from the Heb. parent text.

[14] S.v. ᾄδω.

[15] I.e., the Watchers.

[16] S.v. ἀπόλλυμι

[17] The subject, "he," refers to τοῦ ἁγίου in 1 En. 1:2.

[18] Gen. of poss.

[19] Note the three infinitives that follow this verb.

καὶ σκληρῶν ὧν ἐλάλησαν λόγων[20] καὶ περὶ πάντων ὧν κατελάλησαν κατ᾽ αὐτοῦ ἁμαρτωλοὶ ἀσεβεῖς.[21]

Vocabulary

ἁμαρτωλός, -όν, sinful; subst. a sinner

ἀντιλαμβάνω (+ gen.), to help, support

ἀσέβεια, ἡ, impiety, iniquity

ἀσεβέω, act profanely, act wickedly (against)

ἀσεβής, -ές, irreverent, impious, ungodly

βοηθέω, to help, come to the aid of somebody (dat.), to render assistance to some-body; to defend oneself

ἐλέγχω, to reprove, reproach

ἔλεος, -ους, τό, mercy, compassion

εὐδοκία, ἡ, satisfaction, approval, good pleasure

καταλαλέω, speak against

μυριάς, -άδος, ἡ, ten thousand, a myriad; as adj. countless (mostly pl.)

σκληρός, -ά, -όν, hard, difficult

συντήρησις, ἡ, protection

THE CONSPIRACY

6:1 Καὶ ἐγένετο, οὗ ἂν ἐπληθύνθησαν οἱ υἱοὶ τῶν ἀνθρώπων, ἐν ἐκείναις ταῖς ἡμέραις ἐγεννήθησαν (αὐτοῖς) θυγατέρες ὡραῖαι καὶ καλαί. 2 καὶ ἐθεάσαντο αὐτὰς οἱ ἐγρήγοροι,[22] οἱ υἱοὶ οὐρανοῦ, καὶ ἐπεθύμησαν αὐτάς, καὶ εἶπαν πρὸς ἀλλήλους· Δεῦτε ἐκλεξώμεθα[23] ἑαυτοῖς γυναῖκας ἀπό...τῶν ἀνθρώπων καὶ γεννήσομεν ἑαυτοῖς τέκνα. 3 καὶ εἶπεν Σεμειαζᾶς[24] πρὸς αὐτούς, ὃς ἦν ἄρχων αὐτῶν· Φοβοῦμαι μὴ οὐ θελήσετε ποιῆσαι τὸ πρᾶγμα τοῦτο, καὶ ἔσομαι ἐγὼ μόνος ὀφειλέτης ἁμαρτίας μεγάλης. 4 ἀπεκρίθησαν οὖν αὐτῷ πάντες· Ὀμόσωμεν[25] ὅρκῳ πάντες καὶ ἀναθεματίσωμεν πάντες ἀλλήλους μὴ ἀποστρέψαι τὴν γνώμην ταύτην, μέχρις οὗ (χρόνου) ἂν τελέσωμεν αὐτὴν καὶ ποιήσωμεν τὸ πρᾶγμα τοῦτο. 5 τότε ὤμοσαν πάντες ὁμοῦ καὶ ἀνεθεμάτισαν ἀλλήλους ἐν αὐτῷ...[26]

(7. *Here follows the names of their twenty chiefs, with Shemihazah listed as their leader, Aretqoph, second to him, Remashel, third to him, and so forth.*)

---

[20] σκληρῶν...λόγων.

[21] ἁμαρτωλοὶ ἀσεβεῖς is the subject of the verb.

[22] Nickelsberg's restoration (174, n. 2a).

[23] Hort. subj. (cf. IV, 12).

[24] Shemihazah is chief of the Watchers.

[25] S.v. ὄμνυμι; hort. subj.

[26] I.e., by the ὅρκος.

Vocabulary
ἀναθεματίζω, bind with a curse (not turn back on an oath)
γνώμη, ἡ, intention, purpose; resolution, decision; preliminary resolution (of Council); opinion
ἐγρήγοροι, οἱ, the "Watchers," rebel angels
ἐκλέγω, ¹aor. mod. ἐξελέξαμαι: to collect revenue (money); mid. to choose, select
θυγάτηρ, -τρός, ἡ, daughter; female descendant
ὄμνυμι (later **ὀμνύω**), 2. ὀμοῦμαι, 3. ὤμοσα, aor. subj. ὀμόσω: swear/confirm an oath, swear by (ἐν or + acc.) a god
ὁμοῦ (adv.), in the same place/time, together
ὅρκος, ὁ, oath
ὀφειλέτης, ὁ, debtor, one who is under obligation, one who is guilty/liable for
τελέω, 6. ἐτελέσθην, pf. pass. ptc. τετελεσμένος: finish, complete, fulfill; to perfect; to initate (into a mystery religion), pass. be accomplished
ὡραῖος, -α, -ον, beautiful; gracious

THE DEED, ITS RESULTS, AND THE SECRETS THEY REVEALED

7:1 Καὶ ἔλαβον ἑαυτοῖς γυναῖκας· ἕκαστος αὐτῶν ἐξελέξαντο ἑαυτοῖς γυναῖκας, καὶ ἤρξαντο εἰσπορεύεσθαι πρὸς αὐτὰς καὶ μιαίνεσθαι ἐν αὐταῖς καὶ ἐδίδαξαν αὐτὰς φαρμακείας καὶ ἐπαοιδὰς[27] καὶ ῥιζοτομίας καὶ τὰς βοτάνας ἐδήλωσαν αὐταῖς. 2 Αἱ δὲ ἐν γαστρὶ λαβοῦσαι[28] ἐτέκοσαν[29] γίγαντας μεγάλους ἐκ[30] πηχῶν τρισχιλίων (in height), 3 οἵτινες κατήσθοσαν[31] τοὺς κόπους τῶν ἀνθρώπων. ὡς δὲ οὐκ ἐδυνήθησαν[32] αὐτοῖς οἱ ἄνθρωποι ἐπιχορηγεῖν, 4 οἱ γίγαντες ἐτόλμησαν (to rise up) ἐπ᾽ αὐτούς καὶ κατησθίοσαν τοὺς ἀνθρώπους. 5 καὶ ἤρξαντο ἁμαρτάνειν ἐν[33] τοῖς πετεινοῖς καὶ τοῖς θηρίοις καὶ ἑρπετοῖς καὶ τοῖς ἰχθύσιν καὶ ἀλλήλων τὰς σάρκας κατεσθίειν, καὶ τὸ αἷμα ἔπινον. 6 τότε ἡ γῆ ἐνέτυχεν κατὰ τῶν ἀνόμων.

Vocabulary
βοτάνη, ἡ, herb
γαστήρ, -τρός, ἡ, belly, stomach; womb
γίγαντες, οἱ (pl.), giants (cf. T. Reu. 5:7 [§6.5])

---

[27] ἐπαοιδή > ἐπῳδή.
[28] S.v. λαμβάνω, here "to conceive" (cf. συλλαμβάνω).
[29] S.v. τίκτω.
[30] ἐκ, "of."
[31] S.v. κατεσθίω.
[32] S.v. δύναμαι (dep.).
[33] I.e., victimize.

δηλόω, reveal; explain, make clear; pass. be announced

εἰσπορεύομαι, go in(to), enter; have sexual intercourse with

ἐντυγχάνω, 3. ἐνέτυχον, ²aor. inf. ἐντυχεῖν: bring a charge against; appeal, petition; happen to meet with/run into somebody; happen to read

ἐπιχορηγέω, provide for

ἐπῳδή, ἡ, enchantment, spell

ἑρπετόν, τό, reptile

κόπος, ὁ, labor, work; reward for labor; produce/harvest

μέταλλον, τό, mine (containing the metal of the earth)

πῆχυς, -εως, ὁ, cubit (measure of length from the elbow to the end of middle finger)

ῥιζοτομία, ἡ, gathering and cutting of roots

τολμάω, dare to, be bold enough to (+ inf.); show boldness toward (ἐπί)

τρισχίλιοι, -αι, -α, three thousand

φαρμακεία, ἡ, sorcery

8:1 Ἐδίδαξεν τοὺς ἀνθρώπους Ἀζαὴλ³⁴ μαχαίρας (how) ποιεῖν καὶ ὅπλα καὶ ἀσπίδας καὶ θώρακας, καὶ ὑπέδειξεν αὐτοῖς τὰ μέταλλα καὶ τὴν ἐργασίαν αὐτῶν καὶ (for women) ψέλια καὶ κόσμους καὶ στίβεις καὶ τὸ καλλιβλέφαρον καὶ παντοίους λίθους ἐκλεκτοὺς καὶ τὰ βαφικά. 2 καὶ ἐγένετο ἀσέβεια πολλή, καὶ ἐπόρνευσαν καὶ ἀπεπλανήθησαν καὶ ἠφανίσθησαν ἐν πάσαις ταῖς ὁδοῖς αὐτῶν.

Vocabulary

ἀποπλανάω, lead astray

ἀσπίς, -ίδος, ἡ, shield; Egyptian asp, cobra

ἀφανίζω, remove, get rid of; destroy, ruin; pass. vanish; be ruined, be destroyed

βαφικόν, τό, dye

ἐργασία, ἡ, production; business

θώραξ, -ακος, ὁ, (soldier's) breastplate, coat of mail; trunk of the body

καλλιβλέφαρον, τό, paint for the eyelids and eyelashes

μέταλλον, τό, mine (containing the metal of the earth)

ὅπλον, τό, tool, large shield; pl. τὰ ὅπλα, weapons

παντοῖος, -α, -ον, of all kinds

πορνεύω, engage in prohibited sexual activity, commit sexual immorality; fig. practice idolatry

στίβι, -ιος, τό, *stibium*, antimony, chemical used for eye painting

ὑποδείκνυμι, 3. ὑπέδειξα: show, reveal, indicate

ψέλιον, τό, bracelet

---

³⁴ Ἀζαήλ, Azazel, the tenth of the leaders of the Watchers.

3.8.

1 Enoch: The Miraculous Birth of Noah

(1 En. 106–107)

Date: Late pre-Maccabean.

Text: Chester Beatty–Michigan Papyrus (which preserves 1 En. 97:6–107:3), as edited by Campbell Bonner (ed.), *The Last Chapters of Enoch in Greek* (London: Christophers, 1937); originally written in Aramaic.

106:1 Μετὰ δὲ χρόνον ἔλαβον (for) Μαθουσάλεκ[1] τῷ υἱῷ μου γυναῖκα καὶ ἔτεκεν υἱὸν καὶ ἐκάλεσεν τὸ ὄνομα αὐτοῦ Λάμεχ·[2] ἐταπεινώθη ἡ δικαιοσύνη μέχρι τῆς ἡμέρας ἐκείνης. καὶ ὅτε εἰς ἡλικίαν (Lamech) ἐπῆλθεν, ἔλαβεν αὐτῷ γυναῖκα· 2 καὶ ἔτεκεν αὐτῷ παιδίον, καὶ ὅτε ἐγεννήθη τὸ παιδίον ἦν τὸ σῶμα (of the child) λευκότερον χιόνος[3] καὶ πυρρότερον ῥόδου, τὸ τρίχωμα πᾶν λευκὸν καὶ ὡς ἔρια λευκὰ καὶ οὖλον καὶ (he was) ἔνδοξον. καὶ ὅτε ἀνέῳξεν τοὺς ὀφθαλμούς, ἔλαμψεν ἡ οἰκία ὡσεὶ ἥλιος. 3 καὶ ἀνέστη ἐκ τῶν χειρῶν τῆς μαίας καὶ ἀνέῳξεν τὸ στόμα καὶ εὐλόγησεν τῷ κυρίῳ. 4 καὶ ἐφοβήθη Λάμεχ ἀπ᾽ αὐτοῦ καὶ ἔφυγεν[4] καὶ ἦλθεν πρὸς Μαθουσάλεκ τὸν πατέρα αὐτοῦ καὶ εἶπεν αὐτῷ·

Vocabulary
ἔριον, τό, wool
λευκός, -ή, -όν, white; comp. –τερος
οὖλος, -η, -ον, curly
πυρρός, -ά, -όν, red; comp. –τερος, redder
ῥόδον, τό, rose

---

[1] Dat.; Methuselah, son of Enoch (Gen 5:18–25).
[2] Lamech, son of Methuselah and father of Noah.
[3] Gen. of comp.
[4] S.v. φεύγω.

τρίχωμα, -ματος, τό, hair, head of hair (cf. 106:10)

χιών, -όνος, ἡ, snow

ὡσεί, like, as; about, approximately

106:5 τέκνον ἐγεννήθη μου[5] ἀλλοῖον, οὐχ ὅμοιον τοῖς ἀνθρώποις ἀλλὰ (like) τοῖς τέκνοις τῶν ἀγγέλων τοῦ οὐρανοῦ. καὶ ὁ τύπος ἀλλοιότερος, οὐχ ὁμοίοις ἡμῖν· τὰ ὄμματά ἐστιν ὡς ἀκτῖνες τοῦ ἡλίου, καὶ (is) ἔνδοξον τὸ πρόσωπον· 6 καὶ ὑπολαμβάνω ὅτι οὐκ ἔστιν ἐξ ἐμοῦ ἀλλὰ ἐξ ἀγγέλου, καὶ εὐλαβοῦμαι αὐτὸν μήποτέ τι ἔσται[6] ἐν ταῖς ἡμέραις αὐτοῦ ἐν τῇ γῇ. 7 καὶ παραιτοῦμαι, πάτερ, καὶ δέομαι, βάδισον πρὸς Ἐνὼχ τὸν πατέρα ἡμῶν καὶ ἐρώτησον ... ("the truth from him, for his dwelling is with the angels").[7]

Vocabulary

ἀκτίς, -ῖνος, ἡ, ray/beam (of sun)

ἀλλοῖος, -α, -ον, strange, of another kind, comp. ἀλλοιότερος, stranger, quite strange

βάδιζω, 3. βάδισα: go, walk, proceed; go to visit at (παρά) a place

δέομαι, [1]aor. pass. ptc. δεηθείς (dep.): miss, be in need of (+ gen.); mid. δέομαι, ask for (+ gen.), plead for something (+ gen.), beg of somebody

εὐλαβέομαι, be concerned, anxious

ὄμμα, -ματος, τό, eye

παραιτέομαι, ask for, request; demand exemption from

τύπος, ὁ, image, form; type, prototype, pattern; pl. details

106:8 ("When Methuselah heard the words of his son,") ἦλθεν πρὸς ἐμὲ (Enoch) εἰς τὰ τέρματα τῆς γῆς οὗ[8] εἶδεν τότε εἶναί με καὶ εἶπέν μοι· πάτερ μου, ἐπάκουσον τῆς φωνῆς μου καὶ ἦκε πρός με. καὶ ἤκουσα τὴν φωνὴν αὐτοῦ καὶ ἦλθον πρὸς αὐτὸν καὶ εἶπα· ἰδοὺ πάρειμι τέκνον· διὰ τί[9] ἐλήλυθας[10] πρὸς ἐμέ, τέκνον; 9 καὶ ἀπεκρίθη λέγων· δι᾽ ἀνάγκην μεγάλην ἦλθον ὧδε, πάτερ· 10 καὶ νῦν ἐγεννήθη τέκνον Λάμεχ[11] τῷ υἱῷ μου, καὶ ὁ τύπος αὐτοῦ καὶ εἰκὼν αὐτοῦ οὐχ ὅμοιος ἀθρώποις καὶ τὸ χρῶμα αὐτοῦ λευκότερον χιόνος καὶ πυρρότερον ῥόδου, καὶ τὸ τρίχωμα τῆς κεφαλῆς αὐτοῦ λευκότερον ἐρίων λευκῶν, καὶ τὰ ὄμματα αυτου᾽ (are) ἀφόμοια ταῖς τοῦ ἡλίου ἀκτίσιν, 11 καὶ ἀνέστη ἀπὸ τῶν τῆς μαίας χειρῶν καὶ ἀνοίξας τὸ στόμα εὐλόγησεν τὸν κύριον τοῦ αἰῶνος· 12 καὶ ἐφοβήθη ὁ υἱός μου Λάμεχ, καὶ ἔφυγεν πρὸς ἐμε. καὶ οὐ πιστεύει ὅτι υἱὸς αὐτοῦ ἐστιν, ἀλλὰ

---

[5] "Of me," i.e., "to me."

[6] τι ἔσται, "something happens."

[7] Two lines of the Greek text have been lost.

[8] οὗ, "where."

[9] διὰ τί, "why?"

[10] S.v. ἔρχομαι.

[11] Dat.

ὅτι (he is) ἐξ ἀγγέλων τοῦ οὐρανοῦ...."And behold, I have come to you because from the angels you have")[12] τὴν ἀκρίβειαν ἣν ἔχεις καὶ τὴν ἀλήθειαν. 13 Τότε (Enoch) ἀπεκρίθην λέγων· ἀνακαινίσει ὁ κύριος πρόσταγμα ἐπὶ τῆς γῆς, καὶ τὸν αὐτὸν τρόπον, τέκνον, τεθέαμαι[13] καὶ ἐσήμανά σοι· ἐν γὰρ τῇ γενεᾷ Ἰαρεδ[14] τοῦ πατρός μου παρέβησαν τὸν λόγον κυρίου ἀπὸ τῆς διαθήκης τοῦ οὐρανοῦ.

Vocabulary
ἀνακαινίζω, renew
ἀκρίβεια, ἡ, exact facts
ἀφόμοιον, τό, copy (of) (dat.)
διαθήκη, ἡ, treaty, covenant; last will and testament
παραβαίνω, 3. παρέβην: transgress
πυρρός, -ά, -όν, red; comp. –τερος, redder
ῥόδον, τό, rose
σημαίνω, 2. σημανῶ, 3. ἐσήμανα, aor. impv. σήμανον: give a sign/signal, indicate something (acc.) with a sign; report, make known
τέρμα, -ματος, τό, end, limit
χιών, -όνος, ἡ, snow
χρῶμα, -ματος, τό, color

106:14 καὶ ἰδοὺ ἁμαρτάνουσιν καὶ παραβαίνουσιν τὸ ἔθος, καὶ μετὰ γυναικῶν συγγίνονται καὶ μετ᾽ αὐτῶν ἁμαρτάνουσιν καὶ ἔγημαν ἐξ αὐτῶν, 17[a] καὶ τίκτουσιν, οὐχ ὁμοίους πνεύμασι ἀλλὰ σαρκίνους. 15 καὶ ἔσται[15] ὀργὴ μεγάλη ἐπὶ τῆς γῆς καὶ καταλυσμός, καὶ ἔσται ἀπώλεια μεγάλη ἐπὶ ἐνιαυτὸν ἕνα. 16 καὶ τόδε τὸ παιδίον τὸ γεννηθὲν (to you) καταλειφθήσεται, καὶ τρία αὐτοῦ τέκνα σωθήσεται, ἀποθανόντων[16] τῶν[17] ἐπὶ τῆς γῆς. 17[b] καὶ πραϋνεῖ τὴν γῆν ἀπὸ τῆς οὔσης ἐν αὐτῇ φθορᾶς. 18 καὶ νῦν λέγε Λάμεχ ὅτι Τέκνον σού ἐστιν δικαίως καὶ ὁσίως, καὶ κάλεσον αὐτοῦ τὸ ὄνομα Νῶε· αὐτὸς γὰρ ἔσται ὑμῶν κατάλειμμα ἐφ᾽ οὗ ἂν καταπαύσητε καὶ οἱ υἱοὶ αὐτοῦ ἀπὸ τῆς φθορᾶς τῆς γῆς καὶ ἀπὸ πάντων τῶν ἁμαρτωλῶν καὶ ἀπὸ ἀδικιῶν πασῶν τῶν συντελειῶν ἐπὶ τῆς γῆς....("And after this there will be stronger iniquity than that which was formerly consummated upon the earth. For I know the mysteries of the Lord that the holy ones have revealed and")[18] 19 ὑπέδειξέν μοι καὶ ἐμήνυσεν, καὶ ἐν ταῖς πλαξὶν τοῦ οὐρανοῦ ἀνέγνων[19] αὐτά.

---

[12] Greek text is lost.
[13] S.v. θεάομαι.
[14] Gen. (indecl.); Jared (Gen 5:18–20).
[15] ἔσται, impers. ("there will be").
[16] Adv. temp. ptc. ("after …").
[17] S.c. ἀνθρώπων.
[18] Two lines of Greek lost.
[19] S.v. ἀναγινώσκω.

Vocabulary

ἀπώλεια, ἡ, destruction, annihilation

γαμέω, Att. ¹aor. ἔγημα, HGr ¹aor., ἐγάμησα: marry

ἔθος, -ους, τό, custom(s)

κατάλειμμα, -ματος, τό, remnant

καταλυσμός, ὁ, flood, deluge

καταπαύω, to rest, find rest

μηνύω, 3. ἐμήνησα, ¹aor. pass. ptc. μηνυθείς: disclose a secret, reveal, report

ὁσίως, in holiness

πλάξ, πλακός, ἡ, flat stone (on which an inscription could be made), tablet (of the law)

πραΰνω, tame (wild animals)

σάρκινος, -η, -ον, fleshly

συγγίνομαι, mingle with, have sexual intercourse with

ὑποδείκνυμι/ὑποδεικνύω, 3. ὑπέδειξα: show

φθορά, ἡ, depravity, moral corruption; miscarriage

107:1 Τότε τεθέαμαι τὰ ἐγγεγραμμένα ἐπ᾽ αὐτῶν, ὅτι γενεὰ γενᾶς²⁰ κακίων ἔσται, καὶ εἶδον τόδε (will continue) μέχρις τοῦ ἀναστῆναι γενεὰν²¹ δικαιοσύνης, καὶ ἡ κακία ἀπολεῖται καὶ ἡ ἁμαρτία ἀλλάξει ἀπὸ τῆς γῆς καὶ τὰ ἀγαθὰ ἥξει ἐπὶ τῆς γῆς ἐπ᾽ αὐτούς. 2 καὶ νῦν ἀπότρεχε τέκνον καὶ σήμανον Λάμεχ τῷ υἱῷ σου ὅτι τὸ παιδίον τοῦτο τὸ γεννηθὲν τέκνον αὐτοῦ ἐστιν δικαίως καὶ οὐ ψευδῶς. 3 καὶ ὅτε ἤκουσεν Μαθουσάλεκ τοὺς λόγους Ἑνώχ²² τοῦ πατρὸς αὐτοῦ – μυστηριακῶς γὰρ (Enoch) ἐδήλσεν αὐτῳ – (Methuselah) ἐπέστρεψεν καὶ ἐδήλωσεν αὐτῷ.²³ καὶ ἐκλήθη τὸ ὄνομα αὐτοῦ Νῶε, εὐφραίνων τὴν γῆν ἀπὸ τῆς ἀπωλείας.

Vocabulary

ἀλλάσσω, 2. ἀλλάξω: change, alter; exchange one thing for another

ἀποτρέχω, hurry away

ἐγγράφω, write down, inscribe

μυστηριακῶς, mysteriously, secretly

ψευδῶς, falsely; οὐ ψευδῶς, without deception

---

²⁰ γενεὰ γενᾶς, "generation after generation."
²¹ Subject of art. inf.
²² Gen.
²³ I.e., to Lamech.

3.9.

Life of Adam and Eve: God Curses Eve

(L.A.E. 19–21, 25, 31–32)

Date: 100–300 CE.

Text: Johannes Tromp, *The Life of Adam and Eve in Greek: A Critical Edition* (Leiden: Brill, 2005).

Scholars disagree as to whether the origins of this text are Jewish or Christian or "at the crossroads of 'pagan,' Jewish and Christian cultures."[1] This text contains multiple cultural traditions and voices, sometimes in tension with themselves. The resulting figure of Eve is a construct of these diverse traditions.

Related Texts: This text narrates, in much greater detail than Gen 3 (§2.1), the first sin, with emphasis on the culpability and remorse of Eve (Εὔα); cf. 2 Cor 11:3, 1 Tim 2:13–15, Acts Andr. 5–9 (§5.16).

Related Texts: L.A.E. 1, 7–9 (§3.10)

After the snake said "Come ....follow me," Eve replied:

19:1 Ἤνοιξα δὲ (the gate) καὶ (the snake) εἰσῆλθεν ἔσω εἰς τὸν παράδεισον. καὶ διώδευσεν ἔμπροσθέν μου. καὶ περιπατήσας ὀλίγον ἐστράφη καὶ λέγει μοι· μεταμεληθεὶς οὐ δώσω σοι φαγεῖν, ἐὰν μὴ ὀμόσῃς[2] μοι ὅτι δίδεις (τὸν καρπὸν) καὶ τῷ ἀνδρί σου. 2 ἐγὼ δὲ εἶπον αὐτῷ ὅτι οὐ γινώσκω ποίῳ ὅρκῳ ὀμόσω σοι. πλὴν ὃ οἶδα λέγω σοι· μὰ τὸν θρόνον τοῦ δεσπότου καὶ τὰ χερουβὶμ καὶ τὸ ξύλου τῆς ζωῆς ὅτι δώσω (τὸν καρπὸν) καὶ τῷ ἀνδρί μου (to eat). 3 ὅτε δὲ ἔλαβεν ἀπ' ἐμοῦ τὸν ὅρκον, τότε ἦλθεν καὶ ἔθετο[3] ἐπὶ τὸν καρπὸν ὃν ἔδωκέν μοι

---

[1] Vita Daphna Arbel, *Forming Femininity in Antiquity: Eve, Gender, and Ideologies in the Greek Life of Adam and Eve* (New York: Oxford University Press, 2012), 5–6.
[2] S.v. ὄμνυμι.
[3] Cf. table 9.10.4(b).

φαγεῖν τὸν ἰὸν τῆς κακίας αὐτοῦ, τοῦτ᾽ ἐστιν τῆς ἐπιθυμίας. ἐπιθυμία γάρ ἐστιν (the origin) πάσης ἁμαρτίας. καὶ κλίνας[4] τὸν κλάδον ἐπὶ τὴν γῆν, ἔλαβον ἀπὸ τοῦ κάρπου καὶ ἔφαγον.

Vocabulary
δεσπότης, ὁ, master, lord, ruler; owner
διοδεύω, pass through
ἔμπροσθεν (+ gen.), before, in front of; previously
ἔσω, inside, within (adv.)
θρόνος, ὁ, chair, seat, throne
κακία, ἡ, wickedness, evil
κλάδος, ὁ, branch (of a tree)
μά, by (particle used in asseverations, w. acc. of the deity appealed to)
μεταμέλομαι, change one's mind
ὀλίγος, -η, -ον, little; δ᾽ ὀλίγων, in a few words, briefly; (πρὸς) ὀλίγον, a short while; μετ᾽ ὀλίγον, after a brief time
ὄμνυμι, later **ὀμνύω**, 2. ὀμοῦμαι, 3. ὤμοσα, aor. subj. ὀμόσω: swear/confirm by an oath, swear by (ἐν or + acc.) a god
ὄρκος, ὁ, an oath
πλήν, nevertheless; but only, except

20:1 Καὶ ἐν αὐτῇ τῇ ὥρᾳ ἠνεῴχθησαν οἱ ὀφθαλμοί μου, καὶ ἔγνων ὅτι γυμνὴ ἤμην τῆς δικαιοσύνης ἧς ἤμην ἐνδεδυμένη.[5] 2 καὶ ἔκλαυσα[6] λέγουσα· τί τοῦτο ἐποίησας (to me), ὅτι ἀπηλλοτριώθην ἐκ τῆς δόξης μου; 3 ἔκλαιον δὲ καὶ περὶ τοῦ ὅρκου. ἐκεῖνος[7] δὲ κατῆλθεν ἐκ τοῦ φυτοῦ καὶ ἄφαντος ἐγένετο. 4 ἐγὼ δὲ ἐζήτουν ἐν τῷ μέρει μου φύλλα ὅπως καλύψω τὴν αἰσχύνην μου, καὶ οὐχ εὗρον (any). ἅπαντα γὰρ τὰ φυτὰ τοῦ ἐμοῦ μέρους κατερρύη τὰ φύλλα, παρὲξ (those) τοῦ σύκου μόνου. 5 λαβοῦσα δὲ φύλλα ἀπ᾽ αὐτοῦ ἐποίησα ἐμαυτῇ περιζώματα.

Vocabulary
αἰσχύνη, ἡ, shame, disgrace
ἀπαλλοτριόομαι, pass. be estranged from (cf. 21:6)
ἅπας, ἅπασα, ἅπαν, alternate form of πᾶς, πᾶσα, πᾶν
ἄφαντος, -ον, invisible
καταρρέω, 3. κατερρύην: fall off
κατέρχομαι, 4. κατελήλυθα: go down; derive from, descend from; (naut.) put into port

---

[4] S.v. κλίνω.
[5] Plpf. periphr. (cf. IV, 18, s.v. ἐνδύω).
[6] S.v. κλαίω.
[7] I.e., the snake.

μέρος, -ους, τό, (pl. nom./acc.) μέρη: part, piece; one's part/role; place, region; a
   separate part (in contrast to the whole)
παρέξ, except
περίζωμα, -ματος, τό, apron, skirt
σῦκον, τό, fig
φυτόν, τό, plant, garden plant, tree

21:1 Καὶ ἐβόησα αὐτῇ τῇ ὥρᾳ λέγουσα· Ἀδάμ, Ἀδάμ, ποῦ εἶ; ἀνάστα[8] ἐλθὲ
πρός με, καὶ δείξω[9] σοι μέγα μυστήριον. 2 ὅτε δὲ ἦλθεν ὁ πατὴρ ὑμῶν[10] εἶπον
αὐτῷ λόγους (περὶ) παρανομίας οἵτινες κατήγαγον ἡμᾶς ἀπὸ μεγάλης δόξης.
3 ἅμα γὰρ ἦλθεν, ἤνοιξα τὸ στόμα μου καὶ ὁ διάβολος ἐλάλει (through me),
καὶ ἠρξάμην νουθετεῖν αὐτὸν λέγουσα· δεῦρο κύριέ μου Ἀδάμ, ἐπάκουσόν μου
καὶ φάγε ἀπὸ τοῦ καρποῦ τοῦ δένδρου οὗ εἶπεν ἡμῖν ὁ θεὸς τοῦ μὴ φαγεῖν[11]
ἀπ᾽ αὐτοῦ, καὶ ἔσει[12] ὡς θεός. 4 καὶ ἀποκριθεὶς ὁ πατὴρ ὑμῶν εἶπεν· Φοβοῦμαι
μήποτε ὀργισθῇ μοι ὁ θεός. ἐγὼ δὲ εἶπον· Μὴ φοβοῦ, ἅμα γὰρ φάγῃς ἔσει
γινώσκων καλὸν καὶ πονηρόν. 5 καὶ τότε ταχέως πείσασα[13] αὐτὸν ἔφαγεν, καὶ
ἠνεῴχθησαν[14] αὐτοῦ οἱ ὀφθαλμοί, καὶ ἔγνω τὴν γύμνωσιν αὐτοῦ. 6 καὶ λέγει
μοι· Ὦ γύναι πονηρά, τί κατειργάσω ἐν ἡμῖν; ἀπηλλοτρίωσάς με ἐκ τῆς δόξης
τοῦ θεοῦ.

Vocabulary
ἀπαλλοτριόομαι, pass. be estranged from
βοάω, cry, call out, shout
γύμνωσις, -εως, ἡ, nakedness
δένδρον, τό, tree
διάβολος, ὁ, the devil
κατάγω, 3. κατήγαγον, 6. κατήχθην: bring down; carry in procession; pass. call
   in at a port, put into shore; be brought down
κατεργάζομαι, 3. κατειργασάμην: bring about, accomplish; prepare
νουθετέω, instruct; warn, admonish
παρανομία, ἡ, transgression of the law, illegality
ταχύς, -εῖα, -ύ, swift, quick, soon; ταχέως (adv.), quickly; comp. θάσσων (Att.
   θάττων), θᾶσσον, quicker, sooner than (ἤ); superl. τάχιστος, -η, -ον, most
   quickly, as quickly as possible, as soon as

---

[8] S.v. ἀνίστημι, [2]aor. act. impv. (cf. table 12.1).
[9] S.v. δείκνυμι.
[10] Eve is now telling this story to Adam's children about their father.
[11] Art. inf.
[12] ἔσει > ἔσῃ.
[13] S.v. πείθω.
[14] S.v. ἀνοίγω.

GOD CURSES EVE (L.A.E. 25)

Then Eve said:

25:1 Στραφεὶς δὲ πρός με ὁ κύριος λέγει· ἐπειδὴ ἐπήκουσας σὺ τοῦ ὄφεως καὶ παρήκουσας τὴν ἐντολήν μου, ἔσει ἐν καμάτοις πολυτρόποις, καὶ ἐν πόνοις ἀφορήτοις. 2 τέξει[15] τέκνα ἐν πολλοῖς τρόμοις. καὶ ἐν μιᾷ ὥρᾳ ἔλθῃς τοῦ τεκεῖν[16] καὶ ἀπολέσεις[17] τὴν ζωήν σου ἐκ τῆς ἀνάγκης σου τῆς μεγάλης καὶ τῶν ὠδίνων. 3 ἐξομολογήσει δὲ καὶ εἴπεις· Κύριε, κύριε, σῶσόν με, καὶ οὐ μὴ ἐπιστρέψω[18] (again) εἰς τὴν ἁμαρτίαν τῆς σαρκός. 4 (And the Lord said) Διὰ τοῦτο ἐκ τῶν λόγων σου κρινῶ σε διὰ τὴν ἔχθραν ἣν ἔθετο ὁ ἐχθρὸς ἐν σοί· στραφεὶς δὲ πάλιν πρὸς τὸν ἄνδρα σου καὶ αὐτός σου κυριεύσει.

Vocabulary

ἀνάγκη, ἡ, necessity, obligation; tribulation; calamity; pl. calamities; ἀνάγκης, by force, through compulsion

ἀφόρητος, -ον, unendurable

κάματος, ὁ, toil; pl. labor pains

παρακούω, ignore, pay no attention to; disobey

πολυτρόπος, -ον, turning in many ways, writhing

τρόπος, ὁ, way, manner

THE DEATH OF ADAM AND EVE'S REPENTANCE (L.A.E. 31–32)

31:1 Ταῦτα δὲ (Εὕα) εἰποῦσα ἐν μέσῳ τῶν υἱῶν αὐτῆς κοιμωμένου τοῦ Ἀδάμ[19] ἐν τῇ νόσῳ αὐτοῦ (ἄλλην δὲ εἶχεν μίαν ἡμέραν[20] ἐξελθεῖν ἐκ τοῦ σώματος αὐτοῦ). 2 καὶ λέγει τῷ Ἀδάμ ἡ Εὕα· Διὰ τί ἀποθνήσκεις κἀγὼ ζῶ; ἢ πόσον χρόνον ἔχω ποιῆσαι μετὰ θάνατόν σου; ἀνάγγειλόν μοι. 3 τότε λέγει ὁ Ἀδὰμ τῇ Εὕᾳ· μὴ θέλε φροντίζειν περὶ πραγμάτων. οὐ γὰρ βραδύνεις ἀπ᾽ ἐμοῦ, ἀλλ᾽ ἴσα[21] ἀποθήσκομεν ἀμφότεροι. καὶ αὐτὴ τεθήσει εἰς τὸν τόπον τὸν ἐμόν, κἂν ἀποθάνω κατάλειψόν με καὶ μηδείς μου ἅψηται ἕως οὗ (χρονοῦ) ἄγγελος λαλήσῃ τι περὶ ἐμοῦ. 4 οὐ

---

[15] τέξει > τέξῃ, s.v. τίκτω.
[16] Art. inf.
[17] S.v. ἀπόλλυμι.
[18] οὐ μή + aor. subj. (emph. fut. neg., cf. IV, 8).
[19] Gen. absol.
[20] ἄλλην…μίαν ἡμέραν.
[21] ἴσα, "equally," "alike," nt. pl. of ἴσος, -η, -ον.

γὰρ ἐπιλήσεταί[22] μου ὁ θεός, ἀλλὰ ζητήσει τὸ ἴδιον σκεῦος ὃ ἔπλασεν. ἀνάστα μᾶλλον εὖξαι[23] τῷ θεῷ ἕως οὗ ἀποδώσω τὸ πνεῦμά μου εἰς τὰς χεῖρας τοῦ δεδωκότος[24] μοι αὐτό, διότι οὐκ οἴδαμεν πῶς ἀπαντήσωμεν τοῦ ποιήσαντος ἡμᾶς, ἢ[25] ὀργισθῇ ἡμῖν ἢ ἐπιστρέψει τοῦ ἐλεῆσαι[26] ἡμᾶς.

Vocabulary

ἀμφότεροι, -αι, -α, both, all
βραδύνω, be delayed
διότι, for, because; therefore
ἐλεάω/έω, be merciful; feel pity; pass. be shown mercy
εὔχομαι, 3. ηὐξάμην, ¹aor. mid. impv. εὖξαι: pray; vow
κοιμάομαι, ¹aor. pass. ptc. κοιμηθείς (dep.): fall asleep, sleep; subst. one who has fallen asleep; (fig.) die
νόσος, ἡ, disease, illness
πλάσσω (Att. πλάττω), 3. ἔπλασα, pf. pass. inf. πεπλάσθαι: to form, mold, fashion
πόσος, -η, -ον, how great? how much/many?
φροντίζω, consider, ponder; be concerned about, pay attention to

32:1 Τότε (Εὔα) ἀνέστη καὶ ἐξῆλθεν ἔξω. καὶ πεσοῦσα[27] ἐπὶ τὴν γῆν ἔλεγεν· 2 ἥμαρτον ὁ θεός, ἥμαρτον ὁ πατὴρ τῶν ἁπάντων, ἥμαρτόν σοι. ἥμαρτον εἰς τοὺς ἐκλεκτούς σου ἀγγέλους, ἥμαρτον εἰς τὰ χερουβίμ, ἥμαρτον εἰς τὸν ἀσάλευτόν σου θρόνον, ἥμαρτον κύριε, ἥμαρτον πολλά, ἥμαρτον ἐναντίον σου, καὶ πᾶσα ἁμαρτία δὶ ἐμὲ γέγονεν ἐν τῇ κτίσει. 3 ἔτι εὐχομένης τῆς Εὔας,[28] ἰδοὺ ἦλθεν πρὸς αὐτὴν ὁ ἄγγελος τῆς ἀνθρωπότητος, καὶ ἀνέστησεν αὐτὴν λέγων· 4 ἀνάστα, Εὔα, ἐκ τῆς μετανοίας σου. ἰδοὺ γὰρ ὁ Ἀδὰμ ὁ ἀνήρ σου ἐξῆλθεν ἀπὸ τοῦ σώματος αὐτοῦ. ἀνάστα καὶ ἰδὲ τὸ πνεῦμα αὐτοῦ ἀναφερόμενον εἰς τὸν ποιήσαντα αὐτὸν τοῦ ἀπαντῆσαι[29] αὐτῷ.

Vocabulary

ἀνθρωπότης, -ητος, ἡ, humanity
ἀσάλευτος, -ον, unshakable, steadfast
ἄφαντος, -ον, invisible

---

[22] S.v. ἐπιλανθάνομαι.
[23] S.v. εὔχομαι.
[24] S.v. δίδωμι.
[25] ἤ...ἤ... ("whether ... or ...").
[26] Art. inf.
[27] S.v. πίπτω.
[28] Gen. absol.
[29] Art. inf. expressing purpose.

γυμνός, -ή, -όν, naked
δικαιοσύνη, -ης, ἡ, justice, uprightness, righteousness; honesty
ἐκλεκτός, -ή, -όν, chosen, elect; precious
ἰός, ὁ, poison

SELECT BIBLIOGRAPHY

Anderson, Gary. *Literature on Adam and Eve: Collected Essays*. Leiden: Brill, 2000.
Anderson, Gary, and Michael Stone. *A Synopsis of the Books of Adam and Eve*, 2nd ed. Atlanta: Scholars Press, 1999.
Charlesworth, J. H. *The Old Testament Pseudepigrapha*, 2 vols. Garden City, NY: Doubleday, 1985, II, 249–295.
Eldridge, Michael D. *Dying Adam with His Multiethnic Family: Understanding the Greek Life of Adam and Eve*. Leiden: Brill, 2001.
Jonge, Marinus de. *The Life of Adam and Eve and Related Literature*. Sheffield: Sheffield Academic Press, 1997.
Knittel, Thomas. *Das griechische 'Leben Adams und Evas': Studien zu einer narrative Anthropologie im frühen Judentum*. Tübingen: Mohr Siebeck, 2002.

PART 4

Intermediate-Level Hellenistic Greek

Parts 4–8 of this reader are dedicated to the translation of "compositional Greek," which is to say, texts that were *originally composed in Greek*, in contrast to the Septuagintal texts of Parts 2 and 3. As one would expect, such texts employ a typical range of Greek syntactical constructions and vocabulary.[1] Part 4 begins with the non-literary (or so-called documentary) Greek of ancient letters. We shall begin with an introduction to the four primary types of ancient Greek letters:

1. Letters of introduction (§4.1)
2. Letters of petition (§4.2)
3. Family letters (§4.3)
4. Memoranda (§4.4)

Knowledge of the structure of different kinds of ancient letters serves as an informative point of departure for reading selections of the (much longer) letters written by the apostle Paul (§§4.5–16). For the Greek text of Paul's letters, I have used (where possible) the Chester Beatty papyrus (PChBeatty 46), or I have noted the distinctive readings of this papyrus in the footnotes. This papyrus, dating ca. 200 CE, is the earliest extant manuscript of the ten Pauline letters.[2] Each of

---

[1] The dates for these texts have been assigned on the basis of L. Michael White, *From Jesus to Christianity: How Four Generations of Visionaries & Storytellers Created the New Testament and Christian Faith* (San Francisco: HarperSanFrancisco, 2004).

[2] As published by Andrew E. Bernhard, *Other Early Christian Gospels: A Critical Edition of the Surviving Greek Manuscripts* (London: T & T Clark, 2006).

the vocabulary lists in Part 4 is compiled on the assumption that you are familiar with the (bolded) words listed in the vocabulary lists of Parts 1–3 (§§1.1–10,
2.1–6, 3.1–9).[3] All of the vocabulary for memorization can also be found in the
final glossary (§10).

---

[3]   As well, all the words occurring fifty times or more in the Greek New Testament.

4.1.

Letter of Introduction to Zenon

(PMich I, 6)

Provenance: Philadelphia, Fayum, Egypt.

This letter is part of the so-called Zenon archive, which was discovered in Philadelphia in the Fayum region of Egypt. This archive is named after Zenon (Ζήνων), who was an employee of Apollonios, the minister of finance (διοικητής) during the last fifteen years of the reign of Ptolemy II Philadelphos (283–246 BCE). In 256 BCE, Zenon moved to Philadelphia to serve as the manager of Apollonios's private estate. Since the minister of finance was the most influential figure in the Ptolemaic administrative structure, Zenon, by extension, was also a very powerful man. The reading here is a letter of introduction and recommendation addressed to Zenon by Sostratos (Σώστρατος) to introduce Aischylos (Αἴσχυλος).

Date: 24 March 257 BCE.

Text: PMich I, 6; White 11.

Structure of Letters of Introduction:

1. *Opening:* [Sender] to [Recipient (dat.)] χαίρειν ("greetings"). In letters of introduction, both the sender and recipient are usually of high social status and relative social equals, as implied by the placement of the sender's name before the recipient's name. The opening or closing may include a wish for good health (e.g., "If you are well, it would be excellent," "I pray to the gods always for you," "I pray continually for your health." "Before anything else I wish that you are well, making obeisance on your behalf to all the gods").

2. *Letter Body:* This identifies the person delivering the letter as one recommended by the sender. The sender states that the recipient can favor him by showing favor to the person hand-delivering the letter.

3. *Closing:* ἔρρωσο ("farewell) + date.

Σώστρατος Ζήνωνι χαίρειν.[1]
Οὐκ οἶμαι μέν σε ἀγνοεῖν[2] περὶ Αἰσχύλου ὅτι οὐκ ἔστιν ἡμῖν ἀλλότριος, ἀναπέπλευκεν δὲ πρὸς ὑμᾶς ἵνα συσταθῆι[3] Κλεονίκωι.[4] καλῶς ἂν οὖν ποιήσαις φιλοτιμηθεὶς ὅπως ἂν συστήσηις[5] αὐτὸν Κλεονίκωι. ἐὰν δ᾽ ἄρα μὴ καταλάβηι ἐκεῖνον[6] παρ᾽ ὑμῖν,[7] ἐπιστολὰς[8] παρὰ τῶν φίλων λαβὲ πρὸς αὐτόν.[9] τοῦτο δὲ ποιήσας εὐχαριστήσεις ἡμῖν· σπεύδω γὰρ περὶ αὐτοῦ. γράφε δὲ καὶ σὺ ἡμῖν τί ἄν σοι ποιοῦντες χαριζοίμεθα.
῎Ερρωσο. (Year) κη´[10] (in the reign of Ptolemy II Philadelphus) Περιτίου κ´.
Outside Envelope: Ζήνωνι. (Year) κη´ Περιτίου κ´. ἐμ Βουβάστωι.

Vocabulary
ἀλλότριος, -ία, -ιον, belonging to another; foreign; ὁ ἀλλότριος, stranger
ἀναπλέω, 3. ἀνέπλευσα: sail up (a river)
ἄρα, so, then
Βούβαστις/Βούβαστος, capital city of Bubastis, in the Nile delta of Upper Egypt
ἐπιστολή, ἡ, letter
εὐχαριστέω, do a favor for somebody (dat.); give thanks
καλῶς, rightly, well; καλῶς ἂν ποιήσαις/ποιήσεις, lit. "you would do well (to)";
    fig. "please" (epistolary formula expressing a polite request); hurrah for, bravo
    for (to approve the words of a speaker)
οἴομαι/οἶμαι, impf. ᾤμην: think that, suppose
Περίτιος, ὁ, Peritios (on Macedonian month names see table 9.19)
ῥώννυμι, 4. ἔρρωμαι, pf. mid. inf. ἐρρῶσθαι, pf. mid. ptc. ἐρρωμένος, pf. mid. impv.
    ἔρρωσο: be in good health/well; ἔρρωσο, "farewell"; pass. be strengthened
φιλέω, to love; kiss
φίλος, -η, -ον, beloved, pleasant; pleasing, popular; subst. friend
φιλοτιμέομαι (pass. dep.): strive after honor; be ambitious; make a sincere effort
χαρίζομαι, impf. ἐχαριζόμην, 5. κεχάρισμαι: show a favor/kindness to somebody;
    freely grant, give, bestow favor upon somebody; be pleasing/beloved; pass. be
    given freely

---

[1] S.v. χαίρω, χαῖρε, greetings (spoken address), good day (in letters).
[2] οὐκ οἶμαι μέν σε ἀγνοεῖν is a standard epistolary formula expressing confidence in the recipient's willingness to fulfill the request.
[3] συσταθῆι > συσταθῇ, s.v. συνίστημι.
[4] Kleonikos (proper name).
[5] συστήσηις > συστήσῃς.
[6] I.e., Kleonikos.
[7] παρ᾽ ὑμῖν, "with you" (i.e., in your company).
[8] I.e., letters of introduction/recommendation.
[9] I.e., Kleonikos.
[10] For alphabetic numerals see table 9.18.

SELECT BIBLIOGRAPHY

Rostovtzeff, M. *A Large Estate in Egypt in the Third Century B.C.* Madison: University of Wisconsin, 1922 (on the Zenon correspondence).

Stowers, Stanley K. *Letter Writing in Greco-Roman Antiquity.* Philadelphia: Westminster, 1986.

4.2.

Letter of Petition to the King with Respect to a Burial Association

(PEnteuxeis 20)

Provenance: Alexandrou Nesos (Alexandrou Chorion), village in the administrative unit (*nome*) of Fayum, Middle Egypt.

Date: 221 BCE.

Structure of Letters of Petition: Letters of petition (ἔντευξις) were written to request assistance from a high-status official. Like letters of introduction, these letters exhibit a tripartite structure.

1. *Opening:* The name of the high official (in dat.) appears *first*, followed by χαίρειν ("greetings") and the name of the sender (in nom. or gen.).

2. *Body:* The petitioner explains how he or she has been wronged by somebody. After making a background statement, the petitioner requests that the official rectify the situation, employing a verb of request such as δέομαι, ἀξιόω, ἱκετεύω, or παρακαλέω. Next follows an expression of appreciation for any favorable response to the request.

3. *Closing:* εὐτύχει (or διευτύχει in Roman era), meaning "farewell."

Historical Background to the Letter in This Section: In the Hellenistic and Roman periods, various kinds of voluntary associations were formed. These can be grouped into three types: (1) professional associations or guilds (e.g., bakers, §7.22; silversmiths, Acts 19:21–20:1, §5.13); (2) funerary societies; and (3) voluntary religious societies, §§7.2–5, 7.7, 7.18).

In the letter of petition here, Krateia (Κράτεια), the sister of Apollodotos ("Ἀπολλόδοτος), writes to King Ptolemy concerning a burial association to which her deceased brother belonged. Associations of this type are well attested in the Ptolemaic period.[1] Krateia complains not only that her brother was denied funerary honors by his burial association, to which he had paid the burial fee (ταφικόν), but also that the same association, having defaulted on this obligation, had refused to reimburse her for the burial fee. This burial fee was evidently deemed to be the property of the original contributor and could therefore be willed to a third party if the original contributor did not use it at the time of his death. On this basis, Krateia petitioned the king to command the local *strategos*, Diophanes, to compel the burial association to comply with its own regulations (νόμος) and to reimburse her for her brother's burial fee.

Βασιλεῖ Πτολεμαίωι[2] χαίρειν.

Κράτεια ἐκ τῆς Ἀλεξάνδρου Νήσου, ἀδικοῦμαι ὑπὸ Φιλίππου καὶ Διονυσίου.[3] τοῦ γὰρ ἐμοῦ ἀδελφοῦ Ἀπολλοδότου συνθιασιτεύοντος[4] (with) αὐτοῖς, [also with So-and-so and So-and-so] Μάρωνος, ὄντες ὃ μὲν[5] ἱερεύς, (ὄντες) ὃ δὲ ἀρχιθιασίτης. Τελευτήσαντος τοῦ Ἀπολλοδότου,[6] πρὸς τῶι (αὐτῷ) μήτε θάψαι[7] μήτε [5] ἐξακολουθῆσαι αὐτῶι (to the burial site) κατὰ[8] τὸν θιασιτικὸν νόμον, οὐδὲ τὸ γινόμενον αὐτῶι[9] ταφικὸν ἀποδεδώκασιν.[10] δέομαι οὖν σου, βασιλεῦ, εἴ σοι δοκεῖ, προστάξαι Διοφάνει[11] τῶι στρατηγῶι ἐπαναγκάσαι[12] (them) ἀποδοῦναί μοι τὸ ταφικόν. τούτου γὰρ γενομένου,[13] ἔσομαι διὰ σέ, βασιλεῦ, τοῦ δικαίου[14] τετευχυῖα.[15] Εὐτύχει.

(In a second hand):[16] Ἐπισκεψάμενος τὸν θιασιτικὸν νό(μον), ἐπανάγκασον (them) τὰ δίκαια ποιῆσαι. ἐὰν δέ τι ἀντιλέγωσιν, ἀπό(στειλον) αὐτοὺς πρὸς ἡμᾶς. Ἔτους α′[17] (in the reign of Ptolemy IV Philopater), Γορπιαίου κη′, Τῦβι ιβ′.

---

[1] Members were obliged by the terms of the association's regulations (νόμος) to contribute a burial fee (ταφικόν) and participate in the funerals of its members, with fines imposed by the association on members who failed to do so. In some cases, the association itself paid for the funeral. In other cases, it would reimburse the family or those who had assumed the costs of the member's funeral.
[2] Ptolemy IV Philopater (221–205 BCE).
[3] Philippos and Dionysios.
[4] Gen. absol.
[5] ὃ μέν...ὃ δέ ("the former ... the latter ...").
[6] Gen. absol.
[7] S.v. θάπτω.
[8] κατά, "in violation of."
[9] Dat. of poss.
[10] Cf. table 9.8.5(a).
[11] Diophanes, the local *strategos* (στραγηγός).
[12] S.v. ἐπιφέρω.
[13] Gen. absol.
[14] τὸ δίκαιον, "what is right," s.v. δίκαιος, -αία, -αιον.
[15] S.v. τυγχάνω.
[16] The second hand is probably that of the *strategos*, Diophanes, and the addressee is probably the *epistates* (head of the village police).
[17] For alphabetic numerals see table 9.18.

(Reverse side):   Ἔτους α΄, Γορπιαίου κη΄, Τῦβι ιβ΄ Κράτεια πρ(ὸς)[18] Φίλιππον καὶ Διονύσιον περὶ ταφικοῦ.

Vocabulary

ἀδικέω/έομαι, do wrong; pass. be wronged by somebody

Ἀλεξάνδρου Νῆσος, Alexandrou Nesos (village)

ἀρχιθιασίτης, ὁ, leader of a *thiasos* (θίασος)

Γορπιαῖος, Gorpiaios (on Macedonian month names see table 9.19)

ἐξακολουθέω, follow/accompany (+ dat.)

θιασιτικός, -ή, -όν, belonging to the *thiasos*

ἱερεύς, -έως, ὁ, pl. ἱερῆς (later ἱερεῖς), priest; ἐπὶ ἱρέως, during the priesthood of so-and-so

Μάρων, -ωνος, Maron (city)

στρατηγός, ὁ, military commander; Egyptian (Ptolemaic) governor of a *nome* (administrative unit)

συνθιασιτεύω, be a fellow member of a θίασος.

ταφικόν, τό, burial fee

Τυβί, Tybi, (on Egyptian month names see table 9.19)

---

[18] πρός, "versus."

4.3.

Family Letter of an Army Recruit to His Mother

(PMich VIII, 491)

Provenance: Northeast corner of the Fayum, Middle Egypt.

Date: Second century CE.

Text: PMich VIII, 491; White 104b.

Structure of Family Letters: Ancient family letters generally observe a conventional structure and are noted for their brevity and lack of emotion. The epistolary structure of the family letter is as follows:

1. *Opening:* The recipient is identified by a familial modifier (e.g., father, mother, brother, sister). The modifiers "lady" and "lord" are terms of respect for one's mother and father. The expression of greetings (χαίρειν) is often modified by πολλά or πλεῖστα ("*many* greetings").
2. *Thanksgiving:* The thanksgiving section consists of a wish for good health (ὑγιαίνειν) such as "If you are well, it would be excellent," or "I pray continually for your health." This section may also include a supplication to the gods, called an obeisance (προσκύνημα) formula. The use of an obeisance formula indicates that the sender has made supplication to a god on behalf of the recipient (gen.). A wish for good health often includes some similar sentiment.
3. *Body:* The body of the letter includes such subjects as requests for information about the recipient's welfare, requests for information about the recipient, or complaints about the recipient's failure to write.
4. *Closing:* The closing of the letter often includes greetings to or from third parties, sometimes serving as a substitute for the traditional "farewell."

The letter in this section is one of two surviving letters written by Apollinarios (Ἀπολινάριος), a young army recruit, to his mother, Taesis (Ταῆσεις). In the previous letter, he had informed his mother that he had not yet received his military assignment but would write again after he was informed of the assignment. In the follow-up letter (the reading here), Apollinarios reports to his mother that he has now arrived in Rome and has been assigned to the military fleet docked at Misenum. However, he does not yet know exactly to which century (military company) he will be assigned.

Ἀπολινάριος Ταήσει τῇ μητρί καὶ κυρίᾳ πολλὰ χαίρειν.

πρὸ μὲν πάντων εὔχομαί σε ὑγιαίνειν, κἀγὼ αὐτὸς ὑγιαίνω καὶ τὸ προσκύνημα σου ποιῶ παρὰ τοῖς ἐνθάδε θεοῖς.

Γεινώσκειν[1] σε θέλω, μῆτερ, ὅτι ἐρρωμένος[2] εἰς Ῥώμην Παχὼν μηνὶ κε[3] ἐκληρώθην εἰς Μισηνούς. οὔπω δὲ τὴν κεντυρίαν μου ἔγνων· οὐ γὰρ ἀπελήλυθειν εἰς Μισηνοὺς ὅτε σοι τὴν ἐπιστολὴν ταύτην ἔγραφον. ἐρωτῶ σε, οὖν, μῆτερ, σεαυτῇ πρόσεχε, μηδὲν δίσταζε περὶ ἐμοῦ· ἐγὼ γὰρ εἰς καλὸν τόπον[4] ἦλθον. Καλῶς δὲ ποιήσεις (something for me) γράψασά[5] μοι ἐπιστολὴν περὶ τῆς σωτηρίας σου καὶ τῶν ἀδελφῶν μου καὶ τῶν σῶν πάντων. καὶ ᾿γω[6] εἴ τινα ἐὰν[7] εὕρω (to carry the letter then) γράφω σοι· οὐ μὴ ὀκνήσω[8] σοι γράφειν.

Ἀσπάζομαι τοὺς ἀδελφούς μου πολλὰ καὶ Ἀπολινάριον[9] καὶ τὰ τέκνα αὐτοῦ καὶ Καραλᾶν[10] καὶ τὰ τέκνα αὐτοῦ. ἀσπάζομαι Πτολεμαῖον καὶ Πτολεμαΐδα[11] καὶ τὰ τέκνα αὐτῆς καὶ Ἡρακλοῦν[12] καὶ τὰ τέκνα αὐτῆς. ἀσπάζομαι τοὺς φιλοῦντάς σε πάντας κατ᾽ ὄνομα. ἐρρῶσθαι σε εὔχομαι.

Outside: Ἀπόδος εἰς Καρανίδα[13] Ταήσει ἀπὸ Ἀπολιναρίου υἱοῦ Μισηνάτου.

Vocabulary

διστάζω, worry about (περί)

ἐνθάδε, here, in this place

κεντυρία, ἡ, century (military company)

Μισηνούς, Misenum, ancient port of Campania in southern Italy

ὀκνέω, 3. ὤκνησα: hesitate

Παχών (indecl.), Pachon (on Egyptian month names see table 9.19)

προσκύνημα, -ματος, τό, act of obeisance to (παρά) a god on behalf of some-body (gen.)

ὑγιαίνω, be in good health

---

[1] γεινώσκειν > γινώσκειν, θέλω γινώσκειν, epistolary disclosure formula (signaling new information).

[2] S.v. ῥώννυμι.

[3] For alphabetic numerals see table 9.18.

[4] Here τόπος prob. refers to a "place" as a member of the fleet at Misenum rather than Rome.

[5] Instr. adv. ptc. ("by," IV, 1.6).

[6] καὶ ᾿γω > καὶ ἐγώ.

[7] ἐὰν > ἄν.

[8] οὐ μή + aor. subj. (emph. fut. neg., IV, 8).

[9] Another man named Apollinarios.

[10] Karalas.

[11] Ptolemy and Ptolemais.

[12] Heraklous.

[13] Karanis.

4.4.

Memorandum to Zenon

(PGL IV, 413)

Provenance: Philadelphia, Fayum (Zenon archive).　　　*Date:* 259–257 BCE.

Text: PGL IV, 413; White 8.

Structure of a Memorandum: A memorandum (ὑπόμνημα) is a letter (often couched in the language of petition) that serves to remind the recipient to attend to a particular business matter, whether a former or future business matter. In some cases, the memorandum is sent by a high official to a social inferior. In other cases, such as the letter in this section, a social equal makes the request, with the promise of repaying the favor with another favor in kind.

In the example here, Kydippos (Κύδιππος) sends a memorandum to Zenon (Ζήνων), whose master was Apollonios, the minister of finance (διοικητής) in the last fifteen years of the reign of Philadelphos. When this letter was written, Zenon was employed as the personal agent of Apollonios, transacting business on his behalf.

Ὑπόμνημα Ζήνωνι παρὰ Κυδίππου.

Εἰ μὲν ἦν τι τῶν ὑπογεγραμμένων[1] πράσιμον λαβεῖν ἐκ τοῦ ἐμπορίου, καθάπερ οἱ ἰατροὶ συντάσσουσιν, οὔκ ἂν[2] ἐνωχλοῦμεν[3] ὑμᾶς· νυνὶ δὲ γεγράφαμέν σοι ὧν χρείαν ἔχομεν, καθάπερ Ἀπολλώνιος ὤιετο δεῖν.[4] εἰ οὖν παράκειταί σοι, ἀπόστειλον ἡμῖν οἴνου τε ἢ Λεσβίου ἢ Χίου κεράμιον[5] ὡς ἡδίστου, καὶ μέλιτος μάλιστα μὲν χοῦν, εἰ δὲ μή (that much), ὅσον ἂν ἐνδέχηται· καὶ ταρίχου τὸ

---

[1] Plpf. periphr. (cf. IV, 18).
[2] εἰ...ἄν... + impf., contrary-to-fact statement.
[3] Kydippos uses 1st pers. pl. for 1st pers. sg. (for self-address) throughout this letter.
[4] S.v. δεῖ, pres. act. inf.
[5] κεράμιον...οἴνου.

σταμνίον σύνταξον ἡμῖν ἐπλῆσαι.⁶ τούτων γὰρ ἀμφοτέρων πλείστην χρείαν νομίζουσιν εἶναι. ἐάγ⁷ γὰρ ὑγιαίνωμεν καὶ εἰς Βυζάντιον ἀποδημήσωμεν, ἄξομεν ὑμῖν πάλιν σπουδαῖον τάριχον.

    Outside: ὑπόμνημα Κυδίππου.

Vocabulary

ἀποδημέω, travel abroad

Βυζάντιον, τό, Byzantion

ἐμπόριον, τό, market center, trading station

ἐνδέχομαι, accept, approve; be possible

ἐνοχλέω, trouble, annoy; pass. be disturbed, troubled

ἡδύς, -εῖα, -ύ, pleasant; pleasant to the taste/sweet, welcome; comp. ἡδίων (nom.), ἡδίω (acc.); superl. ἥδιστος, -η, -ον, pl. ἥδιστα, most gladly, most delicious (food); most pleasant to the taste; ἥδιστα μᾶλλον, all the more; (adv.) ἡδέως, with pleasure, gladly

καθάπερ (= καθά), just as, in the same way; in accordance with

κεράμιον, -ου, τό, earthenware jar

Λέσβιος, -α, -ον, of Lesbos, Lesbian (adj.)

μάλιστα, most of all, above all, especially

μέλι, -ιτος, τό, honey

οἶνος, ὁ, wine

οἴομαι/οἶμαι, impf. ᾤμην/ᾦμην, 3rd sg. ᾤετο/ᾦετο: think that, suppose; feel like (+ inf.)

παράκειμαι, be ready; have available, have in stock

πλεῖστος, -η, -ον, most, greatest, chief

πράσιμος, -ον, for sale/purchase

σπουδαῖος, -α, -ον, good, excellent

σταμνάριον, τό (dim. of στάμνος, wine jar), small jar

συντάσσω, arrange for something to be done, command; prescribe (a medical treatment)

τάριχος/ον, ὁ/τό, salted/pickled fish

ὑγιαίνω, be in good health

ὑπογράφω, write below

ὑπόμνημα, -ματος, τό, reminder, memorandum

Χῖος, -α, -ον, of Chios, Chian (adj.)

---

⁶   S.v. πίμπλημι.

⁷   ἐάγ > ἐάν.

χοῦς, ὁ, χοῦν (acc.) / χῶν (gen. pl.): *chous* (liquid measure = 12 κοτύλαι, or 3 quarts)

χρεία, ἡ, need, necessity; practical use

SELECT BIBLIOGRAPHY

Rostovtzeff, M. *A Large Estate in Egypt in the Third Century B.C.* Madison: University of Wisconsin, 1922 (on the Zenon correspondence).

4.5.

Galatians: Paul Defends His Apostleship

(Gal 1:1–2:10)

Provenance: According to the "south Galatian territorial hypothesis," Paul's Letter to the Galatians was addressed to Christians living in *southern* Galatian, which is to say, in the Roman administrative province of Galatia (cf. Fig. 1). These Christians were administratively "Galatians" but most were not ethnically Galatians (Celts).[1] If this theory is correct, then the "churches of Galatia" to whom this letter is addressed (Gal 1:2) are the churches located in the Galatian cities of Pisidian Antioch, Ikonion, Lystra, and Derbe. These four cities were all connected by the western part of the Augustan Highway (via Sebaste), which began in the coastal city of Attaleia and then proceeded north.[2] Indeed, if one were to set out from the port of Attaleia and travel along this highway, one would arrive at Pisidian Antioch, then Ikonion, and next Lystra, and one could travel to the city of Derbe, as narrated in Acts 13–14 (§§5.1, 5.12).

Date: ca. 55–57 CE.

Text: Comfort/ Barrett (PChBeatty 46).

Epistolary Structure: The reading in this section includes a salutation (Gal 1:1–5), the body opening (Gal 1:6–14), and the first part of the body middle (Gal 1:15–2:3). In contrast to Paul's typical style, this letter lacks a "thanksgiving" section, which is a regular feature of ancient letters. In its place, Paul has substituted an

---

[1] According to this view, the expression Γαλατικὴ χώρα (Acts 18:22–23, 19:1) would refer to the Roman province of Galatia.

[2] Cf. Acts 13–14 (§§5.1, 11), Acts Paul 3:1 (§5.15); Stephen Mitchell, *Anatolia*, 2 vols. (Oxford: Clarendon Press, 1993), I, 7, 70, 76–78 (map), 125.

ironic rebuke. Clearly Paul was not feeling very thankful to the Galatians at the time of this letter's composition!

The opening section of the letter body (Gal 1:6–14) contains four different body-opening epistolary formulas, marking the strategic importance of this section: an introductory formula expressing astonishment (Θαυμάζω ὅτι, Gal 1:6–7), a request formula asking for compliance (ὡς προειρήκαμεν καὶ ἄρτι πάλιν λέγω, Gal 1:9), a disclosure formula (γνωρίζω γὰρ ὑμῖν ὅτι, Gal 1:11), and finally the verb ἀκούω (ἠκούσατε γὰρ, 1:13, "hearing and remembrance" language), which prepares readers for the transition to the body middle of the letter (Gal 1:15ff.).

I. THE SALUTATION

The salutation is one of the most stable elements in the ancient letter. In this letter, Paul modifies the typical salutation by using it to assert his own apostolic authority. His defense of his apostleship is part of the overall purpose of this letter.

Senders and Recipients

1:1 Παῦλος ἀπόστολος οὐκ ἀπ' ἀνθρώπων οὐδὲ δι' ἀνθρώπου ἀλλὰ διὰ Ἰησοῦ Χριστοῦ καὶ θεοῦ πατρὸς τοῦ ἐγείραντος αὐτὸν ἐκ νεκρῶν, 2 καὶ οἱ σὺν ἐμοὶ πάντες ἀδελφοί, ταῖς ἐκκλησίαις τῆς Γαλατίας,

Greeting

1:3 χάρις[3] ὑμῖν καὶ εἰρήνη ἀπὸ θεοῦ πατρὸς ἡμῶν καὶ κυρίου Ἰησοῦ Χριστοῦ 4 τοῦ δόντος[4] αὐτὸν περὶ τῶν ἁμαρτιῶν ἡμῶν, ὅπως ἐξέληται ἡμᾶς ἐκ τοῦ αἰῶνος τοῦ ἐνεστῶτος[5] πονηροῦ κατὰ τὸ θέλημα τοῦ θεοῦ καὶ πατρὸς ἡμῶν, 5 ᾧ ἡ δόξα εἰς τοὺς αἰῶνας τῶν αἰώνων, ἀμήν.

Vocabulary
ἐνίστημι, [2]pf. act. ptc. ἐνεστώς, ἐνεστῶσα, ἐνεστός: be present, be impending (at the time of writing)
ἐξαιρέω, 3. ἐξεῖλον (fr. √ ἐξελ-), [2]aor. mid. ἐξειλόμην, [2]aor. ptc. ἐξελών: remove; mid. take away, destroy, bring to naught; rescue, deliver, save

---

[3] The usual word "greetings" in an ancient letter was χείρειν. Paul has modified the greeting by employing the term χάρις, which preserves the same root (√ χαρ). He then adds the Heb. greeting εἰρήνη (*shalom*) to express a fuller religious greeting.

[4] κυρίου Ἰησοῦ Χριστοῦ τοῦ δόντος αὐτὸν, the modifying phrase (τοῦ δόντος αὐτὸν ...) is in the 3rd pred. pos. (cf. IV, 4.3).

[5] S.v. ἐνίστημι.

II. LETTER BODY OPENING: PAUL'S IRONIC REBUKE

1:6 Θαυμάζω ὅτι οὕτως ταχέως μετατίθεσθε ἀπὸ τοῦ καλέσαντος ὑμᾶς ἐν χάριτι εἰς ἕτερον εὐαγγέλιον, 7 ὃ οὐκ ἔστιν ἄλλο, εἰ μή[6] τινές[7] εἰσιν οἱ ταράσσοντες ὑμᾶς καὶ θέλοντες μεταστρέψαι τὸ εὐαγγέλιον τοῦ Χριστοῦ. 8 ἀλλὰ καὶ ἐὰν ἡμεῖς ἢ ἄγγελος ἐξ οὐρανοῦ εὐαγγελίζηται παρ' ὃ[8] εὐηγγελισάμεθα ὑμῖν, ἀνάθεμα ἔστω.[9]

Vocabulary

ἀνάθεμα, -ματος, τό, votive offering; object of a curse
μεταστρέφω, to change, turn (somebody's mind) to; pervert something
μετατίθημι, put in another place, transfer; mid. change one's mind, turn away
ταράσσω, pf. pass. ptc. τεταραγμένος: agitate physically, pervert something; (fig.) stir up, disturb mentally, throw into confusion; pass. be troubled, vexed; be thrown into disorder/confusion
ταχέως (adv.), quickly

1:10 Ἄρτι γὰρ ἀνθρώπους πείθω ἢ τὸν θεόν; ἢ ζητῶ ἀνθρώποις ἀρέσκειν; εἰ[10] ἔτι ἀνθρώποις ἤρεσκον, Χριστοῦ δοῦλος οὐκ ἂν ἤμην. 11 Γνωρίζω γὰρ ὑμῖν, ἀδελφοί, τὸ εὐαγγέλιον τὸ εὐαγγελισθὲν[11] ὑπ' ἐμοῦ ὅτι οὐκ ἔστιν κατὰ[12] ἄνθρωπον· 12 οὐδὲ[13] γὰρ ἐγὼ παρὰ ἀνθρώπου παρέλαβον αὐτὸ οὔτε ἐδιδάχθην, ἀλλὰ δι' ἀποκαλύψεως Ἰησοῦ Χριστοῦ. 13 Ἠκούσατε γὰρ τὴν ἐμὴν ἀναστροφήν ποτε ἐν τῷ Ἰουδαϊσμῷ, ὅτι καθ' ὑπερβολὴν ἐδίωκον τὴν ἐκκλησίαν τοῦ θεοῦ καὶ ἐπόρθουν αὐτήν, 14 καὶ προέκοπτον[14] ἐν τῷ Ἰουδαϊσμῷ ὑπὲρ πολλοὺς συνηλικιώτας ἐν τῷ γένει μου, περισσοτέρως ζηλωτὴς ὑπάρχων τῶν πατρικῶν μου παραδόσεων.

Vocabulary

ἀναστροφή, ἡ, way of life, conduct, behavior
ἀποκάλυψις, ἡ, revelation

---

[6] εἰ μή is sts. used with the sense of ἀλλά (cf. Gal 2:16).

[7] Probably an attributive construction (cf. IV, 4): construe τίνες as a predicate and trans. εἰσιν impersonally ("there are some").

[8] παρ' ὅ, "contrary to that which."

[9] Cf. 1 Cor 12:3 "Jesus be accursed." PChBeatty 46 omits Gal 1:9: ὡς προειρήκαμεν καὶ ἄρτι πάλιν λέγω· εἴ τις ὑμᾶς εὐαγγελίζεται παρ' ὃ παρελάβετε, ἀνάθεμα ἔστω.

[10] εἰ...ἄν...provides the structure of a contrary-to-fact statement.

[11] τὸ εὐαγγέλιον τὸ εὐαγγελισθὲν ὑπὸ ἐμοῦ, modifier in 2nd attrib. position (cf. IV, 4.2). Note the prolepsis of this phrase with respect to ὅτι.

[12] κατὰ ἄνθρωπόν, "in a human way," "from a human point of view."

[13] One would expect οὐδέ...οὐδε...("neither . . nor ...") or οὔτε...οὔτε...., but here we have οὔτε...ἀλλά....

[14] Gal 1:13–14: note the three different uses of impf.: (1) ἐδίωκον: customary impf. ("used to"); (2) ἐπόρθουν: conat. impf. ("tried to"); (3) προέκοπτον (PChBeatty 46 reads ἐπροέκοπτον): prog. impf. ("was continually to") (cf. IV, 13.1–2, 4).

ἀρέσκω, strive to please, serve; impers. it is pleasing to somebody (w. dat.)
Ἰουδαϊσμός, -ου, ὁ, Judaism
ὑπερβολή, ἡ, overshooting, superiority, surpassing; surpassing quality, greatness;
  καθ᾽ ὑπερβολήν, to an extraordinary degree
παράδοσις, -εως, ἡ, tradition
πατρικός, -ή, -όν, from one's forefathers, ancestral
περισσοτέρως, especially, even more, far greater (adv.)
πορθέω, destroy
προκόπτω, advance
συνηλικιώτης, ὁ, contemporary, of the same age

III. LETTER BODY MIDDLE (GAL 1:15–4:31)

1:15 Ὅτε δὲ[15] εὐδόκησεν ὁ ἀφορίσας με ἐκ κοιλίας μητρός μου[16] 16 ἀποκαλύψαι
τὸν υἱὸν αὐτοῦ ἐν ἐμοί,[17] ἵνα εὐαγγελίζωμαι αὐτὸν ἐν τοῖς ἔθνεσιν, εὐθέως
οὐ προσανεθέμην σαρκὶ καὶ αἵματι 17 οὐδὲ ἦλθον εἰς Ἱεροσόλυμα πρὸς τοὺς
πρὸ ἐμοῦ ἀποστόλους, ἀλλὰ ἀπῆλθον εἰς Ἀραβίαν καὶ πάλιν ὑπέστρεψα εἰς
Δαμασκόν. 18 Ἔπειτα μετὰ ἔτη τρία[18] ἀνῆλθον[19] εἰς Ἱεροσόλυμα ἱστορῆσαι Κηφᾶν
καὶ ἐπέμεινα πρὸς αὐτὸν ἡμέρας δεκαπέντε, 19 ἕτερον δὲ τῶν ἀποστόλων οὐκ
εἶδον εἰ μὴ Ἰάκωβον τὸν ἀδελφὸν τοῦ κυρίου. 20 ἃ δὲ γράφω ὑμῖν, ἰδοὺ ἐνώπιον
τοῦ θεοῦ ὅτι οὐ ψεύδομαι. 21 Ἔπειτα ἦλθον εἰς τὰ κλίματα τῆς Συρίας καὶ τῆς
Κιλικίας·[20] 22 ἤμην δὲ ἀγνοούμενος[21] τῷ προσώπῳ ταῖς ἐκκλησίαις τῆς Ἰουδαίας
ταῖς ἐν Χριστῷ.[22] 23 μόνον δὲ ἀκούοντες ἦσαν[23] ὅτι ὁ διώκων ἡμᾶς ποτε νῦν
εὐαγγελίζεται τὴν πίστιν ἣν ποτε ἐπόρθει, 24 καὶ ἐδόξαζον[24] ἐν[25] ἐμοὶ τὸν θεόν.

Vocabulary
ἀποκαλύπτω, 6. ἀπεκαλύφθην: reveal, disclose
Ἀραβία, ἡ, Arabia
ἀφορίζω, separate, divide; set apart, appoint (for a purpose)

---

[15] This pivotal statement is introduced by the temporal clause ὅτε δέ, which signals a major transition in Paul's argument.

[16] Cf. Isa 49:1; PChBeatty 46 omits καὶ καλέσας διὰ τῆς χάριτος αὐτοῦ.

[17] ἐν may mean "in" (referring to an interior ecstatic experience), or it may denote a single case, i.e., "in my case" (cf. 1 Cor 9:15, 4:6, 15:22, 7:14; Rom 15:16).

[18] I.e., three years after returning from Damascus (not three years after going to Jerusalem).

[19] One always goes "up" to Jerusalem, regardless of where one is geographically located.

[20] Remember that Paul is said to be from Tarsus in Cilicia (Acts 9:11, 21:39).

[21] Impf. periphr. (cf. IV, 18).

[22] ταῖς ἐκκλησίαις τῆς Ἰουδαίας ταῖς ἐν Χριστῷ, modifier in 2nd attrib. pos. (cf. IV, 4.2).

[23] Impf. periph.

[24] (1) ἐπόρθει (Gal 1:23), conat. impf.; (2) ἐδόξαζον (Gal 1:24), incept. impf. (cf. IV, 13.4–5).

[25] ἐν denotes a single case ("in my case").

δεκαπέντε, fifteen
ἔπειτα/ἔπειτεν, then, next
ἐπιμένω, 3. ἐπέμεινα: remain, stay on
εὐδοκέω, take pleasure in, be pleased with; be pleased (to do something), consider something or somebody good
Κηφᾶς, ὁ, Cephas (Aramaic equivalent of Πέτρος, cf. Gal 2:7, 9)
Κιλικία, ἡ, province of Cilicia
κλίμα, -ματος, τό, region, district
πορθέω, to destroy
προσανατίθημι, consult with
Συρία, ἡ, Syria
ψεύδομαι, to lie

2:1 Ἔπειτα διὰ²⁶ δεκατεσσάρων ἐτῶν πάλιν ἀνέβην εἰς Ἱεροσόλυμα μετὰ Βαρναβᾶ²⁷ συμπαραλαβὼν καὶ Τίτον· 2 ἀνέβην δὲ²⁸ κατὰ²⁹ ἀποκάλυψιν· καὶ ἀνεθέμην αὐτοῖς τὸ εὐαγγέλιον ὃ κηρύσσω ἐν τοῖς ἔθνεσιν, κατ᾽ ἰδίαν³⁰ δὲ τοῖς δοκοῦσιν,³¹ μή πως³² εἰς κενὸν τρέχω ἢ ἔδραμον. 3 ἀλλ᾽ οὐδὲ Τίτος,³³ Ἕλλην ὤν,³⁴ ἠναγκάσθη περιτμηθῆναι· 4 διὰ δὲ τοὺς παρεισάκτους ψευδαδέλφους, οἵτινες παρεισῆλθον κατασκοπῆσαι τὴν ἐλευθερίαν ἡμῶν ἣν ἔχομεν ἐν Χριστῷ Ἰησοῦ, ἵνα³⁵ ἡμᾶς καταδουλώσουσιν, 5 οἷς οὐδὲ πρὸς ὥραν³⁶ εἴξαμεν τῇ ὑποταγῇ, ἵνα ἡ ἀλήθεια τοῦ εὐαγγελίου διαμείνῃ πρὸς ὑμᾶς.

Vocabulary
ἀναγκάζω, to force, compel, urge
ἀνατίθημι, 3. ἀνέθηκα, aor. mid. ἀνεθέμην, ²aor. inf. ἀναθεῖναι: refer, attribute something (acc.) to something (dat.), ascribe; set something up; dedicate (to a god); mid. confer, lay something (acc.) before somebody (dat.) for consideration
ἀποκάλυψις, ἡ, revelation

---

²⁶ διά + gen. meaning "after" is common in HGr authors (e.g., Matt 26:61; Acts 24:17); here, after Paul's second visit to Jerusalem.
²⁷ Some proper names of Heb. derivation have genitive ending in –ᾶ.
²⁸ In this context, δέ does not mean "but," rather "and moreover."
²⁹ κατά (+ acc.), "as a result of," "because of."
³⁰ κατ᾽ ἰδίαν, "in private," "privately."
³¹ τοῖς δοκοῦσιν, "to the ones who purport/suppose to be (something)" (i.e., Cephas, James, and John).
³² μή πως, an expression of apprehension that seeks to avert an undesired result ("in order that somehow ... not").
³³ PChBeatty 46 omits the words ὁ σὺν ἐμοί.
³⁴ Gal 2:3 is a notorious example of the ambiguity between the concessive ("although") and causal ("because") participle. Does Paul mean that "*although* (Titus) was Greek" or "*because* (Titus) was Greek"?
³⁵ ἵνα + fut. ind. (instead of subj.).
³⁶ πρὸς ὥραν, "for a time," denoting duration.

δεκατέσσαρες, -ων, fourteen

διαμένω, 3. διέμεινα: persist, remain, continue unchanged, survive

δοκέω, 3. ἔδοξα, pf. mid. inf. δεδόχθαι: think, suppose, consider; seem to (w. inf.), regard to be (something); δοκεῖ + inf., it seems (to somebody) that, he purportedly; εἰ δοκεῖ (w. dat.), if it pleases (somebody); ἔδοξε/δοκεῖ, it was/is resolved (by); seem good/appropriate/best; propose/make (a request); pass. be decided; pass. mid. inf. δεδόχθαι, "be it resolved that (re a motion)"

εἴκω, aor. act. inf., εἶξαι: yield to somebody; give way to (a passion/impulse)

ἐλευθερία, ἡ, freedom

καταδουλόω, enslave

κατασκοπέω, spy on, lie in wait for

παρείσακτος, -ον, adj., brought in surreptitiously

παρεισέρχομαι, intrude, slip in

περιτέμνω (Dor. περιτάμνω), pf. ptc. περιτετμηκώς, -κυῖαι, -κός, pf. pass. ptc. περιτετμημένος: cut off; circumcise

πώς (encl.), somehow, in some way

συμπαραλαμβάνω, bring/take along with

ὑποταγή, ἡ, obedience, submission, subordination

ψευδαδέλφος, ὁ, false brother

2:6 Ἀπὸ δὲ τῶν δοκούντων εἶναί τι, – [37] ὁποῖοί ποτε ἦσαν οὐδέν μοι διαφέρει· πρόσωπον ὁ θεὸς ἀνθρώπου οὐ λαμβάνει[38] – ἐμοὶ γὰρ οἱ δοκοῦντες οὐδὲν προσανέθεντο, 7 ἀλλὰ τοὐναντίον[39] ἰδόντες ὅτι πεπίστευμαι[40] τὸ εὐαγγέλιον τῆς ἀκροβυστίας καθὼς Πέτρος τῆς περιτομῆς, 8 ὁ γὰρ ἐνεργήσας Πέτρῳ εἰς[41] ἀποστολὴν τῆς περιτομῆς ἐνήργησεν καὶ ἐμοὶ εἰς τὰ ἔθνη, 9 καὶ γνόντες τὴν χάριν τὴν δοθεῖσάν μοι, Ἰάκωβος καὶ Κηφᾶς καὶ Ἰωάννης, οἱ δοκοῦντες στῦλοι εἶναι, δεξιὰς (χείρ) ἔδωκαν ἐμοὶ καὶ Βαρναβᾷ κοινωνίας, ἵνα[42] ἡμεῖς (should go) εἰς τὰ ἔθνη, αὐτοὶ δὲ εἰς τὴν περιτομήν· 10 μόνον τῶν πτωχῶν[43] ἵνα μνημονεύωμεν, ὃ καὶ ἐσπούδασα αὐτὸ τοῦτο ποιῆσαι.[44]

---

[37] Anacoluthon indicated by a long dash (–).

[38] λαμβάνω πρόσωπόν τινος, lit. "I receive the face of someone," i.e., to show partiality.

[39] τοὐναντίον > τὸ ἐναντίον.

[40] Pf. pass. of πιστεύω means "to be entrusted with something."

[41] Telic εἰς ("for").

[42] ἵνα takes the place of epex. (explanatory) inf. ("namely that").

[43] Prolepsis of τῶν πτωχῶν.

[44] This is Paul's account of how he had previously agreed at the "Jerusalem Conference" to take up a financial collection for poor Christians in Jerusalem. When Paul wrote 1 Corinthians, the collection was still in the organizing phase (1 Cor 16:1–4). By the time he wrote 2 Cor 8–9, the collection was well under way and the Corinthian Christians were in need of further encouragement. Finally, when Paul later wrote Romans, the collection was near completion and he was planning his third trip to Jerusalem in order to deliver the funds (Rom 15:25–32) before traveling to Spain. Thus, Paul probably visited Jerusalem a third time in order to deliver this collection (1 Cor 16:4).

Vocabulary

ἀκροβυστία, ἡ, foreskin; fig. state of being uncircumcised

ἀποστολή, apostleship

διαφέρω, carry through, spread through; (impers.) διαφέρει τινί, it matters to somebody, it makes a difference; pass. drift about in the sea

ἐνεργέω/έομαι, be at work (in something), be operative; activate

κοινωνία, ἡ, fellowship, partnership; sexual intercourse with (πρός)

μνημονεύω (+ gen.), remember, think of; make mention of (περί)

ὁποῖος, -α, -ον, of what sort, such as

περιτομή, -ῆς, ἡ, circumcision

προσανατίθημι, contribute/add somebody to somebody

πτωχός, -ή, -όν, poor

στῦλος, ὁ, pillar; support

4.6.

1 Thessalonians: Concerning Recently Deceased Christians

(1 Thess 4:13–5:11)

Provenance: Thessaloniki.

Letter Carrier: Timothy (or Silvanus).

Date: Paul probably wrote 1 Thessalonians while residing in Corinth ca. 50–51 CE, roughly a decade after his conversion and twenty years after the crucifixion of Jesus.

Text: Comfort/ Barrett (Papyrus 30/ POxy 1598).

Special Features: Like 1 Corinthians, 1 Thessalonians was written in response to specific questions from the congregation that Paul founded in Thessaloniki (1 Thess 4:1–5:11). The reading here is taken from the parenetic section (1 Thess 4:1–5:22) of this letter.

4:13 Οὐ θέλομεν δὲ ὑμᾶς ἀγνοεῖν,[1] ἀδελφοί, περὶ τῶν κοιμωμένων, ἵνα μὴ λυπῆσθε καθὼς καὶ οἱ λοιποὶ οἱ μὴ ἔχοντες ἐλπίδα.[2] 14 εἰ γὰρ πιστεύομεν ὅτι Ἰησοῦς ἀπέθανεν καὶ ἀνέστη, οὕτως καὶ ὁ θεὸς τοὺς κοιμηθέντας διὰ τοῦ Ἰησοῦ ἄξει σὺν αὐτῷ. 15 Τοῦτο γὰρ ὑμῖν λέγομεν ἐν λόγῳ κυρίου,[3] ὅτι ἡμεῖς οἱ ζῶντες οἱ περιλειπόμενοι εἰς[4] τὴν παρουσίαν τοῦ κυρίου οὐ μὴ φθάσωμεν[5] τοὺς κοιμηθέντας· 16 ὅτι αὐτὸς ὁ κύριος ἐν κελεύσματι, ἐν φωνῇ ἀρχαγγέλου καὶ ἐν σάλπιγγι θεοῦ, καταβήσεται ἀπ' οὐρανοῦ καὶ οἱ νεκροὶ ἐν Χριστῷ ἀναστήσονται πρῶτον, 17 ἔπειτα ἡμεῖς οἱ ζῶντες οἱ περιλειπόμενοι ἅμα σὺν αὐτοῖς ἁρπαγησόμεθα ἐν

---

[1] Οὐ θέλομεν δὲ ὑμᾶς ἀγνοεῖν is an epistolary disclosure formula.
[2] οἱ λοιποὶ οἱ μὴ ἔχοντες ἐλπίδα, note 2nd attrib. pos. of modifier (IV, 4.2).
[3] I.e., as taught by the Lord.
[4] Temp. εἰς ("until").
[5] οὐ μή + aor. subj. (emph. fut. neg., cf. IV, 8).

νεφέλαις εἰς ἀπάντησιν τοῦ κυρίου εἰς ἀέρα· καὶ οὕτως πάντοτε σὺν κυρίῳ ἐσόμεθα. 18 Ὥστε παρακαλεῖτε ἀλλήλους ἐν τοῖς λόγοις τούτοις.

Vocabulary

ἀγνοέω, not know (something), be ignorant of; pass. not be known/recognized

ἀήρ, ἀέρος, ὁ, air, atmosphere

ἅμα, together with (w. dat.); (adv.) at the same time, when; all at once

ἁρπάζω, ²aor. pass. ἡρπάγην, ²aor. ptc. ἁρπαγείς, fut. pass. ἁρπαγησόμαι: seize by force, take up (to heaven)

ἀρχάγγελος, ὁ, archangel

ἔπειτα/ἔπειτεν, then, next

κέλευσμα, -ματος, τό, command

πάντοτε, always (adv.)

παρουσία, ἡ, coming, arrival (contrasting ἀπουσία); technical term for the second "coming" of Christ; (personal) presence

περιλείπομαι, remain, survive (cf. 1 Thess 4:17)

σάλπιγξ, -ιγγος, ἡ, trumpet

5:1 Περὶ δὲ[6] τῶν χρόνων καὶ τῶν καιρῶν, ἀδελφοί, οὐ χρείαν ἔχετε (for me) ὑμῖν γράφεσθαι, 2 αὐτοὶ[7] γὰρ ἀκριβῶς οἴδατε ὅτι[8] ἡμέρα κυρίου[9] ὡς κλέπτης ἐν νυκτὶ[10] οὕτως ἔρχεται. 3 ὅταν λέγωσιν·[11] εἰρήνη καὶ ἀσφάλεια, τότ᾽ αἰφνίδιος αὐτοῖς ἐφίσταται ὄλεθρος ὥσπερ ἡ ὠδὶν τῇ ἐν γαστρὶ ἐχούσῃ,[12] καὶ οὐ μὴ ἐκφύγωσιν.[13] 4 ὑμεῖς δέ, ἀδελφοί, οὐκ ἐστὲ ἐν σκότει,[14] ἵνα[15] ἡ ἡμέρα ὑμᾶς ὡς κλέπτης καταλάβῃ· 5 πάντες γὰρ ὑμεῖς υἱοὶ φωτός[16] ἐστε καὶ υἱοὶ ἡμέρας. Οὐκ ἐσμὲν νυκτὸς οὐδὲ σκότους· 6 ἄρα οὖν μὴ καθεύδωμεν[17] ὡς οἱ λοιποὶ ἀλλὰ

---

[6] περὶ δέ (w. gen.) is an epistolary disclosure formula. It indicates that Paul is telling the Thessalonians something new (i.e., information that was not part of his original preaching to them). Paul does not actually answer the Thessalonians' question about the precise date ("when") of Christ's *parousia*. In fact, he actually deflects interest away from calendric time by focusing on "kairotic" time. This redirection of the Thessalonians' question is apparent in 1 Thess 5:2: instead of answering their "when" question, Paul answers a "how" question. He explains *how* the Thessalonian Christians should live in the days prior to Christ's *parousia*.

[7] αὐτοί intensifies the implied subject of οἴδατε.

[8] οἴδατε ὅτι, epistolary disclosure formula.

[9] ἡμέρα κυρίου, i.e., the apocalyptic *day* of judgment when the Son of Man will reveal himself (cf. 2 Thess 1:10, §4.12).

[10] Dat. of time (cf. IV, 5.2).

[11] Pres. subj. is durative in function.

[12] I.e., ἡ ὠδὶν ἐπίσταται ("as labor pains come upon") τῇ ἐν γαστρὶ ἐχούσῃ ("a [women] who has them in [her] womb"); the combination of an article with a fm. dat. ptc. (ἐχούσῃ) creates a subst.

[13] οὐ μή + aor. subj. (emph. fut. neg., cf. IV, 8).

[14] Gen. of quality (i.e., of the realm of evil and sin).

[15] ἵνα is used here to express result instead of purpose.

[16] υἱοὶ φωτός, gen. of quality; light and day are here equated with right moral behavior.

[17] Three hort. subjunctives: καθεύδωμεν, γρηγορῶμεν, νήφωμε (cf. IV, 12).

γρηγορῶμεν καὶ νήφωμεν. 7 Οἱ γὰρ καθεύδοντες νυκτὸς[18] καθεύδουσιν καὶ οἱ μεθυσκόμενοι νυκτὸς μεθύουσιν· 8 ἡμεῖς δὲ ἡμέρας[19] ὄντες[20] νήφωμεν ἐνδυσάμενοι θώρακα πίστεως[21] καὶ ἀγάπης καὶ περικεφαλαίαν[22] ἐλπίδα σωτηρίας·[23] 9 ὅτι οὐκ ἔθετο[24] ὁ θεὸς εἰς[25] ὀργὴν ἀλλὰ εἰς περιποίησιν σωτηρίας διὰ τοῦ κυρίου ἡμῶν Ἰησοῦ 10 τοῦ ἀποθανόντος ὑπὲρ ἡμῶν πάντων,[26] ἵνα[27] εἴτε γρηγορῶμεν εἴτε[28] καθεύδωμεν ἅμα σὺν αὐτῷ ζήσωμεν. 11 Διὸ παρακαλεῖτε ἀλλήλους καὶ οἰκοδομεῖτε εἰς τὸν ἕνα,[29] καθὼς καὶ ποιεῖτε.

Vocabulary

αἰφνίδιος, sudden; adv. suddenly

ἀκριβῶς, accurately, careful(ly)

ἀσφάλεια, ἡ, safety; safeguarding/security of a structure

γρηγορέω, wake up; be alert, watchful; watch over (ἐπί)

ἐκφεύγω, [2]aor. ἐξέφυγον: to escape

ἐφίστημι, pres. mid. ἐφίσταμαι, 3. ἐπέστησα/ἐπέστην, aor. ptc. ἐπιστάς, -άντος, 4. ἐφέστηκα: stand on/near, stand beside (+ παρά); approach; come upon, attack; mid. (intrans.), come upon somebody (+ dat.), overtake somebody

καθεύδω, to sleep; die; have sex with (πρός) somebody

κλέπτης, -ου, ὁ, thief

μεθύσκω, 3. ἐμέθυσα: make somebody drunk; pass. become drunk

νήφω, exercise self-control (cf. 5:8)

ὄλεθρος, -ου, ὁ, destruction

περικεφαλαία, ἡ, helmet

περιποίησις, -εως, ἡ, acquisition, obtaining (+ gen.)

χρεία, ἡ, need, necessity; practical use

---

[18] Gen. of time.

[19] Cf. υἱὸς φωτός (Gal 5:4).

[20] ὄντες is a causal adv. ptc. ("because").

[21] Epex. gen.

[22] Acc. of spec. ("as," "for").

[23] Epex. gen.

[24] Aor. mid. (ἔ-θε-το), here "to appoint."

[25] Telic εἰς ("for").

[26] διὰ τοῦ κυρίου ἡμῶν Ἰησοῦ Χριστοῦ τοῦ ἀποθανόντος ὑπὲρ ἡμῶν: i.e., ἀποθανόντος ὑπὲρ ἡμῶν is in 2nd attrib. pos. modifying κυρίου ἡμῶν Ἰησοῦ Χριστοῦ.

[27] ἵνα (as above) expressing result, not purpose.

[28] εἴτε... εἴτε... ("whether ... or ...").

[29] εἰς τὸν ἕνα, Semitism for ἀλλήλους.

4.7.

1 Corinthians: Potential in Weakness

(1 Cor 1:18–2:5)

While living in Ephesos, Paul received news from the Corinthian church in three different forms. First, Paul received an unofficial delegation from Corinth, which he refers to as "Chloe's people" (1 Cor 1:11). Second, he received an official oral report from three visitors, Stephanas, Fortunatus, and Achaïcus, who were probably church leaders (1 Cor 16:15–18). Third, Stephanas presented Paul with an official letter from the church containing many questions.

Though the pagan writer Celsus criticized the Christianity of his day for attracting "the foolish, dishonourable and stupid, and only slaves, women and little children," Origen countered by quoting Paul's words in 1 Cor 1:26. Origen points out that Paul does not say that "none were wise according to the flesh" but that "*not many* were wise according to worldly standards, *not many* were powerful, *not many* were of noble birth."[1] Building on this insight, recent scholarship has argued that among the first of Paul's converts in Corinth were a small, but influential number of Christians of high social status.[2] The emerging consensus is that the Corinthian church actually reflected a cross-section of urban society. While the majority of members came from the urban poor, a small group of influential members belonged to the upper classes.[3]

---

[1] Origen, *contra Celsus* 3.44.

[2] David G. Horrell, *The Social Ethos of the Corinthian Correspondence: Interests and Ideology from 1 Corinthians to 1 Clement* (Edinburgh: T & T Clark, 1996), 193, 195.

[3] For example, 1 Cor 11:17–34 shows that some could afford lavish amounts of food and drink, in contrast to the 'have-nots'; 1 Cor 6:1–8 reveals that some were pursuing cases of litigation, a procedure most likely to be initiated by those with wealth and status; Paul's description of their abundance in 2 Cor 8:14 is contrasted with the poverty of the Macedonian believers (2 Cor 8:2); Erastus was appointed city treasurer (*quaestor*, Rom 16:23) and was probably a person of wealth and social position; this same person seems to have been promoted to the position of *aedile* (Horrell, *Social Ethos*, 197, cf. 193).

FIG. 7. Temple of Apollo, ancient Corinth (photo: author).

The reading in this section is taken from Paul's response to the oral report to Chloe's people, which is found in 1 Cor 1–4. Chloe's people complained to Paul about internal discord in the Corinthian congregation (1:10–11). Thus the first major theme that Paul takes up in this letter concerns these social divisions (σχίσματα). The cause of these divisions seems to have had a social basis, namely rivalry, jealousy, and strife (3:3–4). Various teachers had become rallying points for divisions in the congregation (cf. 1 Cor 1:12).

Letter Carrier: Stephenanas.

Date: ca. 53–54 CE.

1:18 Ὁ λόγος γὰρ ὁ τοῦ σταυροῦ[4] τοῖς ἀπολλυμένοις[5] μωρία ἐστίν, τοῖς δὲ σῳζομένοις ἡμῖν δύναμις θεοῦ ἐστιν. 19 γέγραπται γάρ· ἀπολῶ τὴν σοφίαν τῶν σοφῶν καὶ τὴν σύνεσιν τῶν συνετῶν ἀθετήσω (Isa 29:14). 20 ποῦ σοφός; ποῦ γραμματεύς; ποῦ συνζητητὴς τοῦ αἰῶνος τούτου; οὐχὶ[6] ἐμώρανεν ὁ θεὸς τὴν σοφίαν τοῦ κόσμου; 21 ἐπειδὴ γὰρ ἐν τῇ σοφίᾳ τοῦ θεοῦ οὐκ ἔγνω ὁ κόσμος διὰ τῆς σοφίας τὸν θεόν, εὐδόκησεν ὁ θεὸς διὰ τῆς μωρίας τοῦ κηρύγματος σῶσαι τοὺς πιστεύοντας· 22 ἐπειδὴ καὶ Ἰουδαῖοι σημεῖα αἰτοῦσιν καὶ Ἕλληνες σοφίαν ζητοῦσιν, 23 ἡμεῖς δὲ κηρύσσομεν Χριστὸν ἐσταυρωμένον,[7] Ἰουδαίοις μὲν σκάνδαλον, ἔθνεσιν δὲ μωρίαν, 24 αὐτοῖς δὲ τοῖς κλητοῖς, Ἰουδαίοις τε[8] καὶ Ἕλλησιν, Χριστὸς (is) θεοῦ δύναμις καὶ θεοῦ σοφία· 25 ὅτι τὸ μωρὸν τοῦ θεοῦ σοφώτερον[9] τῶν[10] ἀνθρώπων.[11]

Vocabulary
ἀθετέω, reject, ignore, set aside
αἰτέω/έομαι, ask, beg; make a request
ἐπειδή, since, because; after
εὐδοκέω, be pleased (to do something); consider something or somebody good
καταργέω, deactivate, render ineffective, make powerless (contrasting ἐνεργῶ); release from, estrange from
κήρυγμα, τό preaching (cf. 2:4)
κλητός, -ή, -όν, called (adj.)
μωραίνω, [1]aor. ἐμώρανα: show that something is foolish
μωρία, -ας, ἡ, foolishness

---

[4] ὁ λόγος ... ὁ τοῦ σταυροῦ, modifier in 2nd attrib. pos. (cf. IV, 4.2).
[5] Mid. subst. ptc., τοῖς ... ἀπολλυμένοις. The double λλ occurs only in the pres. tense of this verb. Since this is an athematic verb in the present tense, no connecting vowel is used.
[6] οὐχί introduces a question anticipating the answer "yes."
[7] Fifth principal part of σταυρόω is ἐσταύρωμαι.
[8] τε is postpositive.
[9] The suffixes -τερος and –τερον turn an adjective into comparative (which takes the gen.).
[10] Gen. of comp. ("than").
[11] PChBeatty 46 omits ἐστὶν καὶ τὸ ἀσθενὲς τοῦ θεοῦ ἰσχυρότερον τῶν ἀνθρώπων.

ποῦ, where?
σημεῖον, τό, sign, token; a marking (on approved sacrificial animals); pl. stripes
σκάνδαλον, -ου, τό, obstacle, that which causes one to stumble
σύνεσις, -εως, ἡ, understanding, discernment
συνετός, -ή, -όν, intelligent, discerning
συνζητητής, -ου, ἡ, debater

1:26 Βλέπετε [12] γὰρ τὴν κλῆσιν[13] ὑμῶν, ἀδελφοί, ὅτι οὐ πολλοὶ σοφοὶ κατὰ σάρκα,[14] οὐ πολλοὶ δυνατοί, οὐ πολλοὶ εὐγενεῖς· 27 ἀλλὰ τὰ μωρὰ[15] τοῦ κόσμου ἐξελέξατο[16] ὁ θεός, ἵνα καταισχύνῃ τοὺς σοφούς, 28 καὶ τὰ ἀσθενῆ[17] τοῦ κόσμου ἐξελέξατο[18] ὁ θεός, ἵνα καταισχύνῃ τὰ ἰσχυρά, καὶ τὰ ἀγενῆ τοῦ κόσμου καὶ τὰ ἐξουθενημένα ἐξελέξατο ὁ θεός, τὰ μὴ ὄντα,[19] ἵνα καταργήσῃ τὰ ὄντα, 29 ὅπως μὴ καυχήσηται πᾶσα σὰρξ ἐνώπιον τοῦ θεοῦ. 30 ἐξ αὐτοῦ[20] δὲ ὑμεῖς[21] ἐστε ἐν Χριστῷ Ἰησοῦ, ὃς ἐγενήθη σοφία ἡμῖν ἀπὸ θεοῦ, δικαιοσύνη[22] τε καὶ ἁγιασμὸς καὶ ἀπολύτρωσις, 31 ἵνα, καθὼς γέγραπται· ὁ καυχώμενος ἐν κυρίῳ καυχάσθω (Jer 9:22–23).

Vocabulary
ἀγενής, -ές, insignificant, inferior
ἁγιασμός, -οῦ, ὁ, dedication, sanctification
ἀπολύτρωσις, ἡ, setting free, deliverance, redemption, manumission
ἀσθενής, -ές, weak, helpless
εὐγενής, -ές, of noble birth, high social status
καταισχύνω, humiliate, shame, disgrace
καυχάομαι, boast; take pride in
κλῆσις, ἡ, calling, vocation
μωρός, -ά, -όν, foolish, stupid; subst. foolish thing

---

[12] βλέπετε, here "regard, consider."
[13] κλῆσις here refers to the *act* of calling, not to the state of being called.
[14] κατὰ σάρκα, "humanly speaking," "in human estimation."
[15] The use of the nt. for human beings emphasizes the attribute.
[16] S.v. ἐκλέγω.
[17] Follows the same paradigm as ἀληθής.
[18] S.v. ἐκλέγω, ἐκ- becomes ἐξ- before an augment (ε).
[19] τὰ μὴ ὄντα, "things regarded as nothing," "lowly things."
[20] "From this," (i.e., God's act of choosing) (cf. 1 Cor 1:24, 3:23).
[21] Emphatic.
[22] The following three nouns are examples of metonymy (i.e., the use of an abstract term for a term that is more concrete). Paul employs metonymy elsewhere, describing Christ as a "curse" (Gal 3:13, §4.15) and as "sin" (Rom 8:3), and he names the Jews and Gentiles using the abstract terms "circumcision" and "uncircumcision."

2:1 Κἀγὼ ἐλθὼν²³ πρὸς ὑμᾶς, ἀδελφοί, ἦλθον οὐ καθ᾽ ὑπεροχὴν λόγου ἢ σοφίας καταγγέλλων ὑμῖν τὸ μυστήριον τοῦ θεοῦ. 2 οὐ γὰρ ἔκρινά τι εἰδέναι²⁴ ἐν ὑμῖν εἰ μὴ Ἰησοῦν Χριστὸν καὶ τοῦτον ἐσταυρωμένον. 3 κἀγὼ ἐν ἀσθενείᾳ καὶ ἐν φόβῳ καὶ ἐν τρόμῳ πολλῷ ἐγενόμην πρός²⁵ ὑμᾶς,²⁶ 4 καὶ ὁ λόγος μου καὶ τὸ κήρυγμά μου (were) οὐκ ἐν πειθοῖς σοφίας λόγοις²⁷ ἀλλ᾽ ἐν ἀποδείξει πνεύματος καὶ δυνάμεως, 5 ἵνα ἡ πίστις ὑμῶν μὴ ᾖ ἐν σοφίᾳ ἀνθρώπων ἀλλ᾽ ἐν δυνάμει θεοῦ.²⁸

Vocabulary

ἀπόδειξις, -εως, ἡ, proof, demonstration

ἀσθένεια, ἡ, weakness, illness

καταγγέλλω, announce, preach

μυστήριον, τό, a secret, mystery

πειθός, -ή, -όν, persuasive, skillful

ὑπεροχή, ἡ, pre-eminence; state of superiority, καθ᾽ ὑπεροχὴν, with superior (+ gen.)

---

²³ When an adv. aor. ptc. is formed from the same verb as the finite verb in the sentence (as it is here), it should be translated as simultaneous action ("when ...").

²⁴ Cf. table 9.5.

²⁵ πρός, "with."

²⁶ This is probably a reference to Paul's illness at the time of his founding visit.

²⁷ πειθοῖς...λόγοις (disc. syn.).

²⁸ Paul seems to be referring to apparent miracles and ecstatic phenomena.

4.8.

1 Corinthians: On Slavery and Freedom, Marriage and Celibacy

(1 Cor 7:17–31)

As previously noted, while living in Ephesos, Paul also received an *official* oral report from Stephanas, Fortunatus, and Achaïcus (1 Cor 16:15–18). They also presented Paul with an official letter from the Corinthian church. This letter contained many questions. Paul attempted to answer these questions in 1 Cor 7:1–16:2. This new section of the letter begins with the phrase "now concerning" (περὶ δὲ + gen.) (1 Cor 7:1). This is a small-scale epistolary formula, indicating that Paul is replying to one of these written questions. The formula "now concerning ..." occurs six times in the last ten chapters of 1Corinthians. In each case, Paul is responding to written questions of the Corinthians. Thus 1 Cor 7:1–40 begins with the words "Now concerning the matters *about which you wrote....*" The first of these questions concerns marriage and celibacy (1 Cor 7:1–40). The reading in this section begins with Paul's discussion of marriage (7:1–24), which includes a discussion of the manumission of slaves (7:21–24). Paul then turns his attention to the subject of the unmarried ("now concerning virgins," 7:25–38).

Related Texts: On early Christian understandings of female celibacy, see Acts of Paul (§§5.9, 5.15), Acts of Andrew (§5.16), and Acts of Thomas (§5.10); on redemption/manumission, see manumission inscriptions (§§7.8, 7.19).

7:17 Εἰ μὴ¹ ἑκάστῳ ὡς ἐμέρισεν ὁ κύριος, ἕκαστον² ὡς κέκληκεν ὁ θεός, οὕτως περιπατείτω. καὶ οὕτως ἐν ταῖς ἐκκλησίαις πάσαις διατάσσομαι. 18 περιτετμημένος τις ἐκλήθη, μὴ ἐπισπάσθω· ἐν ἀκροβυστίᾳ κέκληταί τις, μὴ περιτεμνέσθω. 19 ἡ

---

¹ εἰ μή is sometimes used where one would expect ἀλλά (e.g., Gal 1:7, 19, 2:16; Rom 14:14; Mark 6:5; Luke 4:25–27; Rev 21:27).

² Prolep. of ἕκαστον.

περιτομὴ οὐδέν ἐστιν καὶ ἡ ἀκροβυστία οὐδέν ἐστιν, ἀλλὰ³ τήρησις ἐντολῶν θεοῦ. 20 ἕκαστος ἐν τῇ κλήσει ᾗ ἐκλήθη, ἐν ταύτῃ μενέτω.⁴ 21 δοῦλος⁵ ἐκλήθης, μή σοι μελέτω· ἀλλ' εἰ καὶ⁶ δύνασαι ἐλεύθερος γενέσθαι, μᾶλλον⁷ χρῆσαι. 22 ὁ γὰρ ἐν κυρίῳ κληθεὶς δοῦλος⁸ ἀπελεύθερος κυρίου ἐστίν, ὁμοίως ὁ ἐλεύθερος⁹ κληθεὶς δοῦλός Χριστοῦ ἐστιν. 23 τιμῆς ἠγοράσθητε· μὴ γίνεσθε δοῦλοι ἀνθρώπων. 24 ἕκαστος ἐν ᾧ¹⁰ ἐκλήθη, ἀδελφοί, ἐν τούτῳ¹¹ μενέτω παρὰ¹² θεῷ.

Vocabulary

ἀγοράζω (+ gen.), buy (with), ransom (with)

ἀκροβυστία, ἡ, foreskin; fig. state of being uncircumcised

ἀπελεύθερος, ὁ, freedman (i.e., an emancipated slave)

διατάσσομαι, instruct, give instructions

ἐλεύθερος, -έρα, -ον, free; subst. freeman, freewoman

ἐπισπάω, be responsible for bringing something on/making something happen; pull the foreskin over the head of the penis (in order to hide the marks of circumcision)

κλῆσις, ἡ, a calling, vocation

περιτέμνω (Dor. περιτάμνω), pf. ptc. περιτετμηκώς, -κυῖαι, -κός, pf. pass. ptc. περιτετμημένος: cut off; circumcise

περιτομή, -ῆς, ἡ, circumcision

τήρησις, ἡ, observance, keeping (a law)

τιμή, -ῆς, ἡ, honor, pl. honors; price/cost, value; (gen.), at a price of

7:25 Περὶ δὲ¹³ τῶν παρθένων ἐπιταγὴν κυρίου οὐκ ἔχω, γνώμην δὲ δίδωμι ὡς¹⁴ ἠλεημένος ὑπὸ κυρίου πιστὸς¹⁵ εἶναι. 26 Νομίζω οὖν τοῦτο¹⁶ καλὸν ὑπάρχειν διὰ

---

³ "But (what counts is).…"

⁴ Before his conversion, Paul was involved in the tent-making industry. According to Acts 20:34, Paul was involved in a "guild" of tent makers (cf. 1 Thess 2:9; 2 Thess 3:8). When he arrived in Corinth for the first time, he *maintained* this way of life, working as a tent maker within a guild of craftsmen. This is why Paul states, "We labor, working with our own hands" (1 Cor 4: 12).

⁵ "You, as slave.…"

⁶ εἰ καί ("even though/if").

⁷ μᾶλλον can convey the sense of "instead"/"rather" or "by all means," two translations that produce very different meanings in this verse.

⁸ ὁ…δοῦλος.

⁹ The article ὁ turns the adj. ἐλεύθερος into a noun.

¹⁰ Supply "condition"/"state."

¹¹ ἐν ᾧ…ἐν τούτῳ, "in which (situation) … in that (situation).…"

¹² παρά, "with."

¹³ περὶ δέ (+ gen.) is an epistolary disclosure formula signaling that Paul is responding to a question in the letter he received from the Corinthians.

¹⁴ ὡς + ptc. here supplies the reason for an action ("as one who …").

¹⁵ The adj. πιστός refers to Paul.

¹⁶ Points forward to ὅτι.

τὴν ἐνεστῶσαν[17] ἀνάγκην,[18] ὅτι καλὸν ἀνθρώπῳ τὸ οὕτως εἶναι.[19] 27 δέδεσαι[20] γυναικί, μὴ ζήτει λύσιν· λέλυσαι ἀπὸ γυναικός, μὴ ζήτει γυναῖκα. 28 ἐὰν δὲ καὶ γαμήσῃς, οὐχ ἥμαρτες,[21] καὶ ἐὰν γήμῃ ἡ παρθένος, οὐχ ἥμαρτεν· θλῖψιν δὲ τῇ σαρκὶ[22] ἕξουσιν οἱ τοιοῦτοι, ἐγὼ δὲ ὑμῶν φείδομαι (this). 29 Τοῦτο δέ φημι, ἀδελφοί, ὁ καιρὸς συνεσταλμένος ἐστίν·[23] τὸ λοιπόν, ἵνα καὶ οἱ ἔχοντες[24] γυναῖκας ὡς μὴ[25] ἔχοντες ὦσιν, 30 καὶ οἱ κλαίοντες ὡς μὴ κλαίοντες, καὶ οἱ χαίροντες ὡς μὴ χαίροντες, οἱ ἀγοράζοντες ὡς μὴ κατέχοντες, 31 καὶ οἱ χρώμενοι τὸν κόσμον ὡς μὴ καταχρώμενοι· παράγει γὰρ τὸ σχῆμα τοῦ κόσμου τούτου.

Vocabulary

γνώμη, ή, intention, purpose; resolution, decision; preliminary resolution (of a city council); opinion

ἐλεέω, be merciful; feel pity; pass. be shown mercy

ἐνίστημι, pf. act. ptc. ἐνεστώς, ἐστῶσα, ἐστός: be present, be impending (at the time of writing)

ἐπιταγή, ή, command, order

καταχράομαι, make full use of something (dat.), have full ownership of something

λύσις, ή, a releasing; divorce; breaking (of spells); interpretation; solution (of a riddle)

συστέλλω, mid. inf. συστέλλεσθαι, [1]aor. act. συνέστειλα, pf. pass. ptc. συνεσταλμένος: fold up/furl a sail; humiliate; mid. be discouraged; pass. (of time), grow shorter

---

[17] For pf. act. ptc. of ἵστημι (cf. table 9.12.5).

[18] ἀνάγκη is an apocalyptic term, i.e., the *parousia*.

[19] The syntax of this sentence is unclear: prob. "(I think this [τοῦτο] …), ὅτι (that) τὸ οὕτως εἶναι (art. inf., either "to remain as one is" or "to remain as I am") (is) καλόν (predicate of art. inf.).

[20] S.v. δέω (1).

[21] Proleptic aor., "you will not have sinned."

[22] τῇ σαρκί, "in (the outward side of) life," "in this earthly life."

[23] Pf. periphr. (cf. IV, 18).

[24] οἱ ἔχοντες, οἱ κλαίοντες, οἱ χαίροντες, οἱ ἀγοράζοντες, οἱ χρώμενοι: subst. use of participles (i.e., article turns ptc. into a noun).

[25] Paul repeats the formula ὡς μή ("as not") five times, by which he emphasizes that the Christian calling revokes one's prior way of life as an "*as not.*" Paul uses the words "as not" rather than "as if." In other words, he is not saying that one should pretend "as if" the world is somehow different than it really is, nor is he saying that one can ignore the facts of one's material existence without penalty. Indeed, for the most part, slaves *remain* slaves and masters *remain* masters. People still have husbands and wives; they still weep and rejoice; they still buy things and make use of them. These facts of daily life in the world remain operative. Nonetheless, the "as not" of the Christian calling means that one's life does not *receive its final significance* in these things. Instead, the way in which one lives out one's calling redefines one's relations to the world and the significance of the world for one's life. To treat one's relations to the world "as not" means that the conditions of one's life (e.g., married or unmarried, circumcised or uncircumcised, slave or free) no longer determine one's character and manner of living in the world.

σχῆμα, -ματος, τό, bodily form, shape; looks, outward appearance; a way of life; the character or property of a thing; style

ὑπάρχω, impf. ὑπῆρχον: exist, be present, to be; belong to; possess; subst. τὰ ὑπάρχοντα, possessions, property

φείδομαι, spare somebody from something, refrain from

SELECT BIBLIOGRAPHY

Instone-Brewer, David. "1 Corinthians 7 in the Light of the Graeco-Roman Marriage and Divorce Papyri." Tyndale Bulletin 52/1 (2001), 101–115.

4.9.

2 Corinthians: Paul's Ecstatic Journey to the Third Heaven

(2 Cor 12:1–10)

Date: ca. 55–58 CE.

Text: Comfort/ Barrett (PChBeatty 46).

Special Features: 2 Corinthians is composed of at least four separate letters:

- 2 Cor 1–7 (excluding 2 Cor 6:14–7:1), a letter of reconcilation after Paul's painful visit;[1]
- 2 Cor 8–9, a letter of encouragement regarding the collection for Jerusalem;[2]
- 2 Cor 10–13, a polemical letter against the "superative apostles"[3] and Paul's own self-defense in terms of "weakness"; and
- 2 Cor 6:14–7:1.[4]

In the decade following the death of Paul, his letters to various churches were collected and assembled into a kind of corpus. When these letters were recopied, it

---

[1] Following his visit to Corinth, Timothy returned to Ephesos with news of the failure of 1 Corinthians and of growing opposition to Paul (cf. 1 Cor 16:11; cf. 2 Cor 2:5, 10). This prompted Paul to make an unplanned visit to Corinth directly from Ephesos. This second visit was so disastrous for Paul that he later refers to it as his "painful" visit (2 Cor 2:1–2). At this time, opposition to Paul in Corinth was at its peak. One member of the congregation actually verbally attacked Paul (2 Cor 2:5–11, 7:12).

[2] On the "Jerusalem Collection" see Gal 2:10, n. 45 (§4.5).

[3] Other apostles had arrived in Corinth who claimed to be "preeminent" or "superlative apostles" (2 Cor 11:5). These superlative apostles identified themselves as apostles of Christ and servants of righteousness. Paul refers to them as "false apostles" (2 Cor 11:13) and servants of Satan (2 Cor 11:14–15).

[4] Most scholars consider 2 Cor 6:14–7:1 to be an interpolation, on the following basis: (1) it constitutes a drastic change of subject matter; (2) its deletion produces a smoother reading; (3) it appears to be a self-contained unit that reads like a short homily; and (4) there is evidence that 2 Corinthians as a whole is a product of editorial compilation.

is likely that the formulaic introductory and concluding sections of some of them were deleted. They were then combined with other letters addressed to the same church. Thus 2 Cor 10:1–12:13 probably preserves the body of a letter that was originally longer, including its original saluation and thanksgiving.[5]

The reading in this section is take from 10:1–12:13. In the reading, Paul describes his mystical ascent into "Paradise," which was located in the "third heaven," though even Paul himself cannot decide whether this voyage took place in his body or out of his body (cf. Gal 1:15–16, 1 Cor 15:8).[6]

12:1 Καυχᾶσθαι δεῖ, οὐ συμφέρον[7] μέν,[8] ἐλεύσομαι δὲ εἰς[9] ὀπτασίας καὶ ἀποκαλύψεις κυρίου.[10] 2 οἶδα ἄνθρωπον[11] ἐν Χριστῷ πρὸ[12] ἐτῶν δεκατεσσάρων, εἴτε[13] ἐν σώματι οὐκ οἶδα, εἴτε ἐκτὸς τοῦ σώματος οὐκ οἶδα – ὁ θεὸς οἶδεν – ἁρπαγέντα τὸν τοιοῦτον ἕως τρίτου οὐρανοῦ.[14] 3 καὶ οἶδα τὸν τοιοῦτον ἄνθρωπον, εἴτε ἐν σώματι εἴτε χωρὶς τοῦ σώματος οὐκ οἶδα – ὁ θεὸς οἶδεν – 4 ὅτι ἡρπάγη εἰς τὸν παράδεισον καὶ ἤκουσεν ἄρρητα ῥήματα ἃ οὐκ ἐξὸν[15] ἀνθρώπῳ λαλῆσαι.

Vocabulary

ἀποκάλυψις, ἡ, revelation

ἁρπάζω, 6. ἡρπάγην, [2]aor. pass. ptc. ἁρπαγείς, fut. pass. ἁρπαγησόμαι: snatch away, seize by force, take up (to heaven)

ἄρρητος, -ον, ineffable, inexpressible

ἀσθένεια, ἡ, weakness, illness

καυχάομαι, boast, take pride in

ὀπτασία, -ας, ἡ, ecstatic vision

---

[5] This hypothesis is based on many factors. For example, the tone and purpose of 2 Cor 10–13 change dramatically in comparison with the chapters that precede it. Paul's tone becomes angry, and his style abrupt and hurried. Moreover, Paul's criticism of the so-called superlative apostles (the theme that predominates in 2 Cor 10–13) is hardly mentioned in 2 Cor 1–9 (cf. 2:17, 3:1, 5:12).

[6] Paul's longest discussion employing the language of bodily transformation is found in 2 Cor 3:18–4:6. Sharing in the divine nature is a common motif in Jewish apocalypticism; cf. Alan F. Segal, "Paul and the Beginning of Jewish Mysticiam," in *Death, Ecstasy and Other Worldly Journeys*, 95–122, esp. 112, ed. J. J. Collins and Michael Fishbane (Albany: State University of New York Press, 1995).

[7] The verb ἐστιν must be supplied (which is why the sentence is negated by οὐ and not μή).

[8] μέν...δέ....

[9] εἰς = πρός ("to").

[10] Obj. gen. (cf. IV, 16).

[11] Paul is speaking of himself.

[12] πρό, "before"/"ago," construe w. ἁρπαγέντα; the position of πρό is a HGr idiom.

[13] εἴτε...εἴτε... ("whether ... or ...").

[14] Here we have the concept of three levels of heaven, arranged hierarchically. The highest of these is identified with Paradise (cf. 2 En. 7, L.A.E. 37:5). The number of heavens in Jewish apocalyptic writings varies greatly. For example, 3 Baruch has five heavens.

[15] S.v. ἔξεστιν, ἐξόν, nt. ptc.; the verb, ἐστιν, must be supplied, which is why it is negated by οὐ.

συμφέρω, help, be advantageous; bring together, collect; (impers.) it is useful/ good/best; subst. nt. ptc. (τὸ) συμφέρον, what is useful/best/beneficial; the welfare

χωρίς/χωρὶς ἤ (+ gen.), except for, apart from

12:5 ὑπὲρ τοῦ τοιούτου καυχήσομαι, ὑπὲρ δὲ ἐμαυτοῦ οὐδὲν καυχήσομαι εἰ μὴ ἐν ταῖς ἀσθενείαις. 6 Ἐὰν γὰρ θέλω καυχήσομαι, οὐκ ἔσομαι ἄφρων, ἀλήθειαν γὰρ ἐρῶ·[16] φείδομαι δέ, μή[17] τις εἰς ἐμὲ λογίσηται ὑπὲρ ὃ βλέπει με (to be) ἢ ἀκούει τι ἐξ ἐμοῦ 7 καὶ[18] τῇ[19] ὑπερβολῇ τῶν ἀποκαλύψεων.[20] ἵνα μὴ ὑπεραίρωμαι, ἐδόθη μοι σκόλοψ τῇ σαρκί, ἄγγελος σατανᾶ,[21] ἵνα με κολαφίζῃ, ἵνα μὴ ὑπεραίρωμαι. 8 ὑπὲρ τούτου τρὶς τὸν κύριον παρεκάλεσα ἵνα ἀποστῇ[22] ἀπ' ἐμοῦ. 9 καὶ εἴρηκέν[23] μοι· ἀρκεῖ σοι ἡ χάρις μου, ἡ γὰρ δύναμις ἐν ἀσθενείᾳ τελεῖται. Ἥδιστα[24] οὖν μᾶλλον καυχήσομαι ἐν ταῖς ἀσθενείαις μου, ἵνα ἐπισκηνώσῃ ἐπ' ἐμὲ ἡ δύναμις τοῦ Χριστοῦ. 10 διὸ εὐδοκῶ ἐν ἀσθενείαις, ἐν ὕβρεσιν, ἐν ἀνάγκαις, ἐν διωγμοῖς καὶ στενοχωρίαις, ὑπὲρ Χριστοῦ· ὅταν γὰρ ἀσθενῶ, τότε δυνατός εἰμι.

Vocabulary

ἀρκέω (+ dat.), be enough for; be satisfied with, be self-sufficient for

ἄφρων, -ονος (m./fm.), **-ον** (nt.), foolish, unlearned (contrasting φρόνιμος)

ἐπισκηνόω, come to rest upon

ἡδύς, -εῖα (fm.), **-ύ** (nt.), pleasant; pleasant to the taste, sweet; superl. ἥδιστος, -η, -ον, ἥδιστα, most gladly, most delicious (food); most pleasant to the taste; ἡδέως (adv.), with pleasure, gladly; ἥδιστα μᾶλλον, all the more

κολαφίζω, to torment

παρακαλέω, beg, request; urge, encourage; console, comfort; appeal to

σκόλοψ, -λοπος, ὁ, something pointed that causes an injury (e.g. a thorn, stake)[25]

τελέω, 6. ἐτελέσθην, pf. pass. ptc. τετελεσμένος: finish, complete, fulfill; perfect; initate (into a mystery religion); pass. be accomplished

τρίς, three times

στενοχωρία, -ας, ἡ, difficulty, distress

ὕβρις, -εως, ἡ, damage; act of insolence, insolence; pl. insults

ὑπεραίρομαι, become too elated

---

[16] S.v. λέγω.
[17] μή has the sense of "lest" (i.e., "in order that [something might] not [happen]").
[18] Adverbial καί ("even").
[19] Dat. of respect.
[20] As mentioned earlier in 2 Cor 12:1–4 (cf. Gal 1:16).
[21] σατανᾶ is in the gen. case (ὁ σατανᾶς, τοῦ σατανα).
[22] S.v. ἀφίστημι.
[23] Pf. tense indicates that God has said something and it still stands (i.e., the reply was final).
[24] S.v. ἡδύς.
[25] Here, a vivid metaphor for intense pain.

SELECT BIBLIOGRAPHY

Callan, Terence. "Prophecy and Ecstacy in Greco-Roman Religion and in 1 Corinthians." NovT 27 (1985), 125–140.

Tabor, James D. *Things Unutterable: Paul's Ascent to Paradise in Its Greco-Roman, Judaic, and Early Christian Contexts*. Lanham, MD, Univeristy of America Press, 1986.

4.10.

Philippians: Paul Breaks with His Past

(Phil 3:1b–16)

Philippi (Φίλιπποι) was a Roman colony that, like Thessaloniki, was located on the great via Egnatia ('Εγνατία ὁδός). Paul wrote his letter while under "praetorian guard" (ὅλῳ τῷ πραιτρωρίῳ, Phil 1:13, cf. 4:22). Though the meaning of this statement is contested, the almost casual exchange of information implied by this letter suggests that Paul was imprisoned in a location that was in close proximity to Philippi.

Letter Carrier: Epaphroditos.

Date: 55–56 CE.

Like 2 Corinthians, Paul's letter to the Philippians seems to be a compilation of several letters. Indeed, there is evidence that Paul did in fact write more than one letter to the church in Philippi, for in Polycarp's *Letter to the Phpippians* its author writes, "Paul ... wrote you *letters*," indicating that Paul wrote more than one letter to the Philippian church. In chronological order, these letters are referred to as Letter 1 and Letter 2. Letter 1 consists of Phil 1:1–3:1a + 4:2–7, 10–23. It is a letter of thanks, sent after Epaphroditos recovered from his sickness. Letter 2, consisting of Phil 3:1b–4:1 + 4:8–9, is a later letter, which was sent by Paul after he was released from prison.[1]

---

[1] L. Michael White, *From Jesus to Christianity: How Four Generations of Visionaries & Storytellers Created the New Testament and Christian Faith* (San Francisco: HarperSanFrancisco, 2004), 191.

3:1b Τὰ αὐτὰ γράφειν ὑμῖν ἐμοὶ μὲν² (is) οὐκ ὀκνηρόν, ὑμῖν δὲ (is) ἀσφαλές. 2 βλέπετε³ τοὺς κύνας, βλέπετε τοὺς κακοὺς ἐργάτας, βλέπετε τὴν κατατομήν. 3 ἡμεῖς γάρ ἐσμεν ἡ περιτομή, οἱ ἐν πνεύματι θεοῦ λατρεύοντες⁴ καὶ καυχώμενοι ἐν Χριστῷ Ἰησοῦ καὶ οὐκ ἐν σαρκὶ πεποιθότες,⁵ 4 καίπερ ἐγὼ ἔχων (grounds for) πεποίθησιν καὶ ἐν σαρκί. Εἴ τις δοκεῖ ἄλλος⁶ πεποιθέναι ἐν σαρκί, ἐγὼ μᾶλλον· 5 περιτομῇ⁷ ὀκταήμερος,⁸ ἐκ γένους Ἰσραήλ,⁹ φυλῆς Βενιαμίν,¹⁰ Ἑβραῖος ἐξ Ἑβραίων, κατὰ νόμον Φαρισαῖος, 6 κατὰ ζῆλος διώκων¹¹ ἐκκλησίαν, κατὰ δικαιοσύνην τὴν ἐν νόμῳ¹² γενόμενος ἄμεμπτος.¹³

Vocabulary

Ἑβραῖος, ὁ, Hebrew person
ἐργάτης, ὁ, worker, worker in a trade
ζῆλος, ὁ, but also **ζῆλος, -ους, τό**: jealousy; zeal
καίπερ, although (+ ptc.)
κατατομή, ἡ, a cut, incision
καυχάομαι, to boast, take pride in
κύων, ὁ, κυνός (gen.), κύνα (acc.), dog
ὀκνηρός, -ά, -όν, troublesome
ὀκταήμερος, -ον, on the eighth day
πεποίθησις, ἡ, confidence, self-confidence
περιτομή, -ῆς, ἡ, circumcision
φυλή, ἡ, the tribe

---

² μέν...δέ....
³ βλέπετε in the impv. means "look out for," "beware of."
⁴ οἱ...λατεύοντες.
⁵ The pf. form of πείθω has its own meaning, distinct from the pres. form, namely "to have confidence/trust in" (+ dat.); verbal stem has changed from πειθ- to ποιθ- .
⁶ τις...ἄλλος, "any other (person)."
⁷ Dat. of respect.
⁸ I.e., in conformity to Torah, in contrast to proselytes, who were circumcised later in life.
⁹ Ἰσραήλ (indecl.), here gen.
¹⁰ The tribe of Benjamin was held in high regard within Judaism. It was descended from Rachael, Jacob's favorite wife. This tribe remained loyal to David and, after the Exile, formed a new nation with Judah.
¹¹ Pres. ptc. w. iterative force.
¹² κατὰ δικαιοσύνην τὴν ἐν νόμῳ, modifier in 3ʳᵈ attrib. pos. (cf. IV, 4.3). HGr normally omits the definite article after prep. (here κατὰ); ἐν νόμῳ, "in the sphere of Torah."
¹³ On the basis of this passage, Krister Stendahl has argued that Paul's conscience was robust and untroubled both before and after his conversion. It was not Paul's plagued conscience that he left behind at his conversion but rather his "glorious achievements as a righteous Jew" (cf. 2 Cor 1:12; 5:11; 1 Cor 4:4; Gal 1:13–14). It was Paul's *accomplishments* that seemed worthless to him (*Paul Among Jews and Gentiles, and Other Essays* [Philadelphia: Fortress, 1976], 80). Paul acknowledges his physical handicaps and sufferings, not his sin (cf. 2 Cor 12:7, 10; Gal 4:13). Stendahl blames Augustine and Luther for imposing their own introspective consciences onto Paul (*Paul Among Jews and Gentiles*, 83–87). The troubled "I" of Rom 7:7–25 is rhetorical, designating all non-Christians, not evidence for Paul's guilt-ridden conscience (Werner Kümmel, *Römer 7 und das Bild des Menschen im Neuen Testament* [Munich: C. Kaiser, 1974], 74–138).

3:7 Ἅτινα ἦν μοι κέρδη, ταῦτα ἥγημαι[14] διὰ τὸν Χριστὸν ζημίαν. 8 ἀλλὰ μενοῦνγε καὶ ἡγοῦμαι πάντα ζημίαν εἶναι διὰ τὸ ὑπερέχον[15] τῆς γνώσεως Χριστοῦ Ἰησοῦ τοῦ κυρίου μου, δι᾽ ὃν τὰ πάντα ἐζημιώθην, καὶ ἡγοῦμαι (them) σκύβαλα, ἵνα Χριστὸν κερδήσω 9 καὶ εὑρεθῶ ἐν αὐτῷ, μὴ ἔχων ἐμὴν δικαιοσύνην τὴν[16] ἐκ νόμου ἀλλὰ τὴν[17] διὰ πίστεως Χριστοῦ,[18] τὴν ἐκ θεοῦ δικαιοσύνην ἐπὶ[19] τῇ πίστει, 10 τοῦ γνῶναι[20] αὐτὸν καὶ τὴν δύναμιν τῆς ἀναστάσεως αὐτοῦ καὶ τὴν κοινωνίαν τῶν παθημάτων αὐτοῦ, συμμορφιζόμενος τῷ θανάτῳ αὐτοῦ, 11 εἴ πως καταντήσω εἰς τὴν ἐξανάστασιν[21] τὴν ἐκ νεκρῶν.[22]

Vocabulary

ἀνάστασις, -εως, ἡ, resurrection (of the dead); the erection (of a building)
ἐξανάστασις, -εως, ἡ, resurrection from (ἐκ)
ζημία, ἡ, loss, damage; fine, financial penalty
ζημιόω, fine somebody (dat.); pass. suffer a loss, forfeit
κερδαίνω, 3. ἐκέρδησα/ἐκέρδανα: gain, profit; spare oneself, avoid
κέρδος, -δους, τό, pl. κέρδη, gain, profit
κοινωνία, ἡ, fellowship, partnership; sexual intercourse with (πρός)
μενοῦνγε, indeed
παθημά, τό, suffering

---

[14] ἥγημαι is athematic (i.e., ἥγη-μαι).

[15] Nt. ptc. employed as an abstr. noun.

[16] Modifier is in the 3rd attrib. pos.: ἐμὴν δικαιοσύνη **τὴν** ἐκ νόμου (cf. IV, 4.3).

[17] τὴν (δικαιοσύνα) διὰ πίστεως Χριστοῦ.

[18] The interpretation of the gen. case of Χριστοῦ in the phrase διὰ πίστεως Χριστοῦ has been a matter of great debate. This same phrase also occurs twice in Gal 2:16 (διὰ πίστεως Ἰησοῦ Χριστοῦ, ἐκ πίστεως Χριστοῦ). In all three cases, one must determine whether this gen. case is an objective gen. or a subjective gen. This matter is complicated by the fact that the noun πίστις can mean both "faith/believing" and "being faithful." The distinction between the objective and subjective gen. can be explained as follows. If the term that precedes the gen. term (here Χριστοῦ) is imagined as a verbal action ("believing"), which *acts upon* the gen. term (Χριστοῦ), then the gen. term is an *objective* gen. cstr., and the phrase would mean "through believing/faith that is directed towards Christ" (as the object of faith). If, however, the term that precedes the gen. term (Χριστοῦ) implies a verbal action that is *initiated by* the following gen. term, then the gen. is a subjective gen. In this case, the expression διὰ πίστεως Χριστοῦ would mean "through the faithfulness *of Christ*" or "through Christ's faithfulness." The subjective gen. interpretation was the preferred interpretation prior to Martin Luther. More recently, Richard Hays has defended the subjective gen. interpretation ("through the faithfulness of Christ") based on the overall plot or narrative of Galatians, namely that Jesus was obedient (i.e., faithful) to God, as demonstrated by his willingness to die on the cross (*The Faith of Christ: The Narrative Substructure of Galatians 3:1–4:11*, 2nd ed. [Grand Rapids, MI: Wm. B. Eerdmans, 2002]). In other words, Christ saved humanity through his *faithfulness* to God. Hays widened his examination to include the entire literary context of Romans. According to his reading, "obedience of (Christ's) faithfulness" (ὑπαρκοὴν πίστεως, Rom 1:5) is a close parallel to the concept of "Christ's faithfulness" in Philippians and Galatians, which in each case concerns Jesus' *own* obedience to his Father's will.

[19] ἐπί (w. dat.), "based on."

[20] Art. inf. expressing purpose (cf. IV, 2).

[21] ἐξανάστασιν = ἀνάστασιν.

[22] On the theme of personal transformation see 2 Cor 12:1–10 (§4.9).

σκύβαλον, τό, dung, excrement

συμμορφίζομαι (+ dat.), take on the likeness of (+ gen.)

ὑπερέχω, be of more value, better than; excel; ptc. subst. great value; rise above; transcend

3:12 Οὐχ ὅτι ἤδη ἔλαβον ἢ ἤδη τετελείωμαι, διώκω (it) δὲ εἰ καὶ καταλάβω (it), ἐφ᾽ ᾧ²³ καὶ κατελήμφθην ὑπὸ Χριστοῦ Ἰησοῦ. 13 ἀδελφοί, ἐγὼ ἐμαυτὸν οὐ λογίζομαι κατειληφέναι (it)· ἓν δέ (I do), τὰ²⁴ μὲν²⁵ ὀπίσω ἐπιλανθανόμενος τοῖς δὲ ἔμπροσθεν ἐπεκτεινόμενος,²⁶ 14 κατὰ²⁷ σκοπὸν διώκω εἰς τὸ βραβεῖον τῆς²⁸ ἄνω κλήσεως τοῦ θεοῦ. 15 Ὅσοι οὖν τέλειοι, τοῦτο φρονῶμεν·²⁹ καὶ εἴ τι ἑτέρως³⁰ φρονεῖτε, καὶ τοῦτο ὁ θεὸς ὑμῖν ἀποκαλύψει· 16 πλὴν εἰς ὃ (ever stage) ἐφθάσαμεν, τῷ αὐτῷ στοιχεῖν.³¹

Vocabulary

ἄνω, above; upward

βραβεῖον, τό, prize (awarded by an adjudicator [βραβεύς])

ἔμπροσθεν (+ gen.), before, in front of

ἐπεκτείνομαι (+ dat.), reach for, stretch forward

κλῆσις, ή, calling, vocation

πλήν, nevertheless; but only, except

στοιχέω, walk; fig. conduct oneself

σκοπός, ό, aim, goal

φρονέω, think, have in mind, set one's mind on, be concerned about

---

²³ ἐφ᾽ ᾧ, "for which."
²⁴ τά and τοῖς (dat. of τά) are both nt. and function as nouns.
²⁵ μέν and δέ (both postpos.) coordinate two closely related clauses.
²⁶ The verb ἐπεκτείνομαι takes the dat.
²⁷ κατά, "toward."
²⁸ Epex. gen., "which is," "namely."
²⁹ Hort. subj. (cf. IV, 12).
³⁰ ἑτέρως, adv. of ἕτερος.
³¹ Imperatival inf.

4.11.

Romans: Paul's Typological Interpretation of Adam

(Rom 5:6–21)

Date: ca. 58 CE.

Paul wrote Romans while living in Corinth. He hoped to visit the congregation in Rome on his way to Spain, where he planned to commence a new mission. In connection with this trip, he sought financial support and assistance from the church in Rome (Rom 1:10–15; 15:22–24). This letter was hand-delivered by Phoebe, a διάκονος in the church located in the port of Cenchreae near Corinth. By Paul's own admission, she was "patron of many" (προστάτις πολλῶν), including himself (Rom 16:1–2). Phoebe traveled ahead to Rome in order to prepare the way for Paul's arrival.

The bulk of this letter consists of Paul's carefully reasoned and balanced account of his gospel (Rom 1:16–15:13). This seems to be Paul`s way of introducing himself to a church to which he was not personally known. His forms of argumentation exhibit some degree of literary elegance, including such figures of speech as assonance (Rom 1:29, 31), climax (5:3–5; 8:29–30; 10:14–15), paronomasia (12:3; 14:23), parallelism (2:6–10, 21–23; 8:33–35; 12:6–8; 13:7), typology (5:6–21; cf. 1 Cor 10:1–15 [§4.13]), as well as allegory (Gal 4:21–31 [§4.16]).

The reading in this section is taken from Rom 5:1–8:39, which describes the life promised to those who are righteous by faith. Paul makes use of typology to establish a relation between the biblical past (Adam's sin) and the present (Christ's righteousness). The climax is found in Rom 5:19 (echoing 5:12). Paul does not actually speak of "original sin" in this passage (as St. Augustine would later) but rather of humanity's estrangement from God through Adam.

5:6 Ἔτι γὰρ Χριστὸς[1] ὄντων[2] ἡμῶν ἀσθενῶν ἔτι[3] κατὰ καιρὸν[4] ὑπὲρ ἀσεβῶν ἀπέθανεν. 7 μόλις γὰρ ὑπὲρ δικαίου τις ἀποθανεῖται· ὑπὲρ γὰρ τοῦ ἀγαθοῦ τάχα τις καὶ τολμᾷ ἀποθανεῖν· 8 συνίστησιν[5] δὲ τὴν ἑαυτοῦ ἀγάπην εἰς ἡμᾶς ὁ θεός, ὅτι ἔτι ἁμαρτωλῶν ὄντων ἡμῶν Χριστὸς ὑπὲρ ἡμῶν ἀπέθανεν. 9 πολλῷ οὖν μᾶλλον[6] δικαιωθέντες νῦν ἐν τῷ αἵματι αὐτοῦ σωθησόμεθα δι' αὐτοῦ ἀπὸ τῆς ὀργῆς. 10 εἰ γὰρ ἐχθροὶ ὄντες κατηλλάγημεν τῷ θεῷ διὰ τοῦ θανάτου τοῦ υἱοῦ αὐτοῦ, πολλῷ μᾶλλον καταλλαγέντες σωθησόμεθα ἐν τῇ ζωῇ αὐτοῦ· 11 οὐ μόνον (this) δέ, ἀλλὰ καὶ καυχώμενοι[7] ἐν τῷ θεῷ διὰ τοῦ κυρίου ἡμῶν Ἰησοῦ Χριστοῦ δι' οὗ νῦν τὴν καταλλαγὴν ἐλάβομεν. 12 Διὰ τοῦτο[8] ὥσπερ δι' ἑνὸς ἀνθρώπου ἡ ἁμαρτία εἰς τὸν κόσμον εἰσῆλθεν, καὶ διὰ τῆς ἁμαρτίας ὁ θάνατος (εἰσῆλθεν), καὶ οὕτως εἰς πάντας ἀνθρώπους ὁ θάνατος διῆλθεν, ἐφ' ᾧ[9] πάντες ἥμαρτον· 13 ἄχρι γὰρ (the coming of) νόμου ἁμαρτία ἦν ἐν κόσμῳ, ἁμαρτία δὲ οὐκ ἐλλογεῖται μὴ ὄντος[10] νόμου,[11] 14 ἀλλὰ ἐβασίλευσεν ὁ θάνατος ἀπὸ Ἀδὰμ μέχρι Μωϋσέως καὶ[12] ἐπὶ τοὺς μὴ ἁμαρτήσαντας[13] ἐπὶ[14] τῷ ὁμοιώματι τῆς παραβάσεως Ἀδάμ[15] ὅς ἐστιν τύπος τοῦ μέλλοντος.[16]

Vocabulary
ἀσεβέω, act profanely/wickedly (against), commit sacrilege
ἐλλογέω, charge with a financial obligation; take into account
καταλλάσσω, 6. κατηλλάγην, aor. pass. ptc. καταλλαγείς: reconcile; pass. become reconciled
καυχάομαι, boast, take pride in
ὁμοίωμα, -ματος, τό, likeness, form, appearance
μόλις, with difficulty; only rarely, not readily, hardly
ὁμοίωμα, τό, likeness, form, appearance

---

[1] Prolep. of Χριστός, but the term belongs to the principal clause (subject of ἀπέθανεν).
[2] Gen. absol. (repeated in Rom 5:8).
[3] ἔτι, "even "
[4] κατά with expression of time means "at" or "during."
[5] Cf. paradigm of ἵστημι, table 9.10.
[6] S.v. μάλα (cf. Rom 5:10, 15, 17).
[7] Pres. ptc. here seems to stand for the pres. ind. ("we take pride in").
[8] διὰ τοῦτο should be understood as the conclusion to Rom 5:1–11 (not just 5:11). Paul is attributing death to two causes, Adam's sin and the sin of human beings, who were affected by him.
[9] ἐφ' ᾧ = ἐπὶ τούτῳ ὅτι, "for this (reason) that."
[10] Gen. absol.
[11] I.e., even though humans committed evil in this period, they did not (and could not) transgress the law, "until the law was added" (Gal 3:19, cf. Rom 5:20).
[12] καί, adv.
[13] Since the [2]aor. of ἁμαρτάνω is ἥμαρτον, one would have expected the [2]aor. ptc., ἁμαρτόντας, but instead Paul uses the [1]aor. ptc., ἁμαρτήσαντος (cf. Rom 5:16).
[14] ἐπί, "in."
[15] Ἀδάμ (indecl.), gen.
[16] Ptc. of μέλλω.

παράβασις, -εως, ἡ, disobedience, formal violation of a boundary or precept
πολλῷ μᾶλλον, much more
τάχα, quickly; perhaps
ὑπακοή, ἡ, obedience; answer

5:15 Ἀλλ' οὐχ ὡς[17] τὸ παράπτωμα, οὕτως καὶ (is) τὸ χάρισμα· εἰ γὰρ τῷ[18] τοῦ ἑνὸς παραπτώματι οἱ πολλοὶ ἀπέθανον, πολλῷ μᾶλλον ἡ χάρις τοῦ θεοῦ καὶ ἡ δωρεὰ ἐν[19] χάριτι τῇ τοῦ ἑνὸς ἀνθρώπου Ἰησοῦ Χριστοῦ[20] εἰς τοὺς πολλοὺς ἐπερίσσευσεν. 16 καὶ (is) οὐχ ὡς (that which came) δι' ἑνὸς ἁμαρτήσαντος τὸ δώρημα· τὸ μὲν[21] γὰρ κρίμα ἐξ ἑνὸς (παραπτώματος) (led) εἰς κατάκριμα, τὸ δὲ χάρισμα (following) ἐκ πολλῶν παραπτωμάτων (leading) εἰς δικαίωμα. 17 εἰ γὰρ τῷ τοῦ ἑνὸς παραπτώματι ὁ θάνατος ἐβασίλευσεν[22] διὰ τοῦ ἑνός, πολλῷ μᾶλλον οἱ[23] τὴν περισσείαν τῆς χάριτος καὶ τῆς δωρεᾶς τῆς δικαιοσύνης λαμβάνοντες ἐν ζωῇ βασιλεύσουσιν διὰ τοῦ ἑνὸς Ἰησοῦ Χριστοῦ.

Vocabulary
δωρέα, -ας, ἡ, gift
δώρημα, τό, gift
καταλλαγή, ἡ, reconciliation (of a broken relationship)
παράπτωμα, τό, offense, wrongdoing
περισσεία, ἡ, abundance, overflow
περισσεύω, be present in abundance; increase, overflow
χάρισμα, τό, gift, something freely given

5:18 Ἄρα οὖν[24] ὡς δι' ἑνὸς παραπτώματος εἰς[25] πάντας ἀνθρώπους (led) εἰς κατάκριμα, οὕτως καὶ δι' ἑνὸς δικαιώματος εἰς πάντας ἀνθρώπους (led) εἰς δικαίωσιν ζωῆς·[26] 19 ὥσπερ γὰρ διὰ τῆς παρακοῆς τοῦ ἑνὸς ἀνθρώπου ἁμαρτωλοὶ κατεστάθησαν[27] οἱ πολλοί, οὕτως καὶ διὰ τῆς ὑπακοῆς τοῦ ἑνὸς δίκαιοι κατασταθήσονται οἱ πολλοί. 20 νόμος[28] δὲ παρεισῆλθεν, ἵνα[29] πλεονάσῃ τὸ

---

[17] οὐχ ὡς...οὕτως καί, "not like ... so indeed...."
[18] τῷ τοῦ ἑνὸς **παραπτώματι.**
[19] ἐν, instr. ("by").
[20] Modifier (τοῦ ἑνὸς ἀνθρώπου Ἰησοῦ Χριστοῦ) in 3rd pred. pos. (cf. IV, 4.3). HGr normally omits the definite article (here τῇ) after a prep.
[21] τὸ μέν...τὸ δέ....
[22] Incept. impf. ("began to...", cf. IV, 13.5).
[23] οἱ...λαμβάνοντες.
[24] ἄρα οὖν...οὕτως καὶ... ("so then ... so also ...").
[25] Telic εἰς, "for."
[26] Epex. gen., "which is life."
[27] S.v. καθίστημι.
[28] νόμος, i.e., the Torah.
[29] There is disagreement as to whether ἵνα expresses purpose ("in order that"), which is the expected meaning of ἵνα, or result ("so that").

παράπτωμα· οὗ[30] δὲ ἐπλεόνασεν ἡ ἁμαρτία, ὑπερεπερίσσευσεν ἡ χάρις, 21 ἵνα[31] ὥσπερ ἐβασίλευσεν ἡ ἁμαρτία ἐν[32] τῷ θανάτῳ, οὕτως καὶ ἡ χάρις βασιλεύσῃ διὰ δικαιοσύνης εἰς[33] ζωὴν αἰώνιον διὰ Ἰησοῦ Χριστοῦ τοῦ κυρίου ἡμῶν.

Vocabulary

δικαίωμα, -ματος, τό, statute; righteous act

δικαίωσις, ἡ, acquittal, vindication

καθίστημι, 3. κατέστησα, 6. κατεστάθην, [1]aor. pass. ptc. καθεσθείς: appoint somebody; constitute, make

κατάκριμα, τό, condemnation, punishment

παρακοή, ἡ, disobedience

παρεισέρχομαι, be introduced

πλεονάζω, [1]aor. ἐπλεόνασα: (trans.) increase, cause to grow, multiply, (intrans.) become more/abundant

ὑπερπερισσεύω, be present in abundance

---

[30] οὗ, adv. of place, "where."
[31] Epex. ἵνα ("that").
[32] ἐν, instr. ("by means of").
[33] Telic εἰς, "for."

PART 5

High-Intermediate-Level Hellenistic Greek

L ike Part 4, Part 5 consists of texts that were *originally composed in Greek* (in contrast to the Septuagint). These texts exhibit the high literary aspirations of their authors. They employ a broad range of Greek syntactical constructions and vocabulary. The vocabulary lists in Part 5 do not repeat the bolded words in the vocabulary lists Parts 1–4 (§§1.1–10, 2.1–6, 3.1–9, 4.1–11). All bolded vocabulary is also compiled in the final glossary (§10).

5.1.

Acts: The People of Lystra Mistake Paul and Barnabas for Hermes and Zeus

(Acts 14:1–20)

Provenance: Probably outside of Palestine.   *Date:* 80–110 CE.

The Book of Acts is the second part of a two-part work written by the author of the Gospel of Luke. The reading in this section continues the story, begun in Acts 13 (§5.12), of Paul's journey on the "Augustan Highway" (via Sebaste). As previously explained (§4.5), this highway connected the cities of Pisidian Antioch, Ikonion, and Lystra, among others. The churches in these cities are probably the so-called churches of Galatia to which Paul addressed his letter by the same name.[1]

14:1 Ἐγένετο[2] δὲ ἐν Ἰκονίῳ κατὰ τὸ αὐτὸ[3] εἰσελθεῖν αὐτοὺς εἰς τὴν συναγωγὴν τῶν Ἰουδαίων καὶ λαλῆσαι οὕτως ὥστε[4] πιστεῦσαι Ἰουδαίων τε[5] καὶ Ἑλλήνων πολὺ πλῆθος. 2 οἱ δὲ ἀπειθήσαντες Ἰουδαῖοι ἐπήγειραν καὶ ἐκάκωσαν τὰς ψυχὰς τῶν ἐθνῶν κατὰ τῶν ἀδελφῶν. 3 ἱκανὸν μὲν οὖν[6] χρόνον διέτριψαν παρρησιαζόμενοι ἐπὶ[7] τῷ κυρίῳ τῷ μαρτυροῦντι ἐπὶ τῷ λόγῳ τῆς χάριτος αὐτοῦ, διδόντι σημεῖα καὶ τέρατα γίνεσθαι διὰ τῶν χειρῶν αὐτῶν. 4 ἐσχίσθη δὲ τὸ πλῆθος τῆς πόλεως, καὶ οἱ μὲν[8] ἦσαν σὺν τοῖς Ἰουδαίοις, οἱ δὲ σὺν

---

[1] See S. Mitchell, *Anatolia*, 2 vols. (Oxford: Clarendon Press, 1993), I, 7, 70, 76–78 (map), 125 (photo); II, 6.

[2] ἐγένετο + inf. + acc., "it came about … that they (αὐτούς).… "

[3] κατὰ τὸ αὐτό = "in the same way" (i.e., as they did before in Antioch).

[4] οὕτως ὥστε, "in such a way that" + inf.

[5] τε postpos.

[6] μὲν οὖν, "so then" (postpos.)

[7] ἐπί + dat. supplying ground for action ("relying on").

[8] οἱ μέν…οἱ δέ.…

FIG. 8. Relief of sacrificial ox head wearing a garland, Ephesos (photo: author).

τοῖς ἀποστόλοις. 5 ὡς[9] δὲ ἐγένετο ὁρμὴ τῶν[10] ἐθνῶν τε καὶ Ἰουδαίων σὺν τοῖς ἄρχουσιν αὐτῶν ὑβρίσαι καὶ λιθοβολῆσαι αὐτούς, 6 συνιδόντες κατέφυγον εἰς τὰς πόλεις τῆς Λυκαονίας (namely) Λύστραν καὶ Δέρβην καὶ τὴν περίχωρον, 7 κἀκεῖ[11] εὐαγγελιζόμενοι ἦσαν.[12]

Vocabulary

ἀπειθέω, 3. ἠπείθησα, [1]aor. ptc. ἀπειθήσας: disobey, be disobedient

Δέρβη, ἡ, city of Derbe (cf. Acts 14:20)

διατρίβω, spend time

ἐπεγείρω, awaken; excite, stir up, rise up against, assault; pass. wake up

ἱκανός, -ή, -όν, sufficient, considerable; many, a number of; (adv.) ἱκανῶς, sufficiently, adequately

Ἰκόνιον, τό, Ikonion (Lat. Iconium)

καταφεύγω, [1]aor. κατέφυγα/[2]aor. κατέφυγον: flee; take refuge

λιθοβολέω, stone to death

Λυκαονία, Lycaonia (a province in the interior of Asia Minor)

Λύστρα, ἡ/τά, anomalously declined, Λύστροις (dat.), Λύστραν (acc.): Lystra, city and Roman colony in Lykaonia (north of modern Hatunsaray, Turkey)

ὁρμή, ἡ, impulse

παρρησιάζομαι, speak openly/freely

συνοράω, become aware of, perceive

ὑβρίζω, insult, mistreat

14:8 Καί τις ἀνὴρ ἀδύνατος ἐν Λύστροις τοῖς ποσὶν[13] ἐκάθητο, χωλὸς ἐκ κοιλίας μητρὸς αὐτοῦ ὃς οὐδέποτε περιεπάτησεν. 9 οὗτος ἤκουσεν τοῦ Παύλου λαλοῦντος· ὃς[14] ἀτενίσας αὐτῷ καὶ ἰδὼν ὅτι ἔχει πίστιν τοῦ σωθῆναι, 10 εἶπεν μεγάλῃ φωνῇ· ἀνάστηθι[15] ἐπὶ τοὺς πόδας σου ὀρθός. καὶ ἥλατο καὶ περιεπάτει. 11 οἵ τε ὄχλοι ἰδόντες ὃ ἐποίησεν Παῦλος ἐπῆραν τὴν φωνὴν αὐτῶν Λυκαονιστὶ λέγοντες· οἱ θεοὶ ὁμοιωθέντες ἀνθρώποις κατέβησαν πρὸς ἡμᾶς, 12 ἐκάλουν[16] τε τὸν Βαρναβᾶν Δία, τὸν δὲ Παῦλον Ἑρμῆν, ἐπειδὴ αὐτὸς ἦν ὁ ἡγούμενος[17] τοῦ λόγου. 13 ὅ τε[18] ἱερεὺς τοῦ Διὸς τοῦ ὄντος[19] πρὸ τῆς

---

[9] ὡς of time ("when").

[10] τῶν, "on the part of."

[11] κἀκεῖ > καὶ ἐκεῖ.

[12] Impf. periph. (cf. IV, 18).

[13] ἀδύνατος … τοῖς ποσίν (s.v. πούς, dat. of respect).

[14] ὅς, dem. pron. ("this man, he") (cf. Acts 14:16); take with εἶπεν.

[15] Cf. table 9.12.2(f).

[16] Incept. impf. (cf. IV, 13.5).

[17] ὁ ἡγούμενος τοῦ λόγου, "the chief speaker."

[18] ὅ τε = ὁ τέ (τέ is enclitic).

[19] Διὸς τοῦ ὄντος, "of Zeus who(se temple) was" (i.e., the temple of Zeus at the entrance of the city). The epigraphical evidence from this region demonstrates that Zeus was often associated with Hermes. For example, a bust of Zeus holding an eagle (the bird of Zeus) and accompanied by his personal messenger,

πόλεως ταύρους καὶ στέμματα ἐπὶ τοὺς πυλῶνας ἐνέγκας σὺν τοῖς ὄχλοις ἤθελεν θύειν.

Vocabulary

ἀδύνατος, -ον, impossible; weak, crippled

ἄλλομαι, 3. ἡλάμην: to leap (up)

ἐπαίρω, 3. ἐπῆρα, ¹aor ptc. ἐπάρας: lift up something, hoist

Ἑρμῆς, -οῦ, ὁ, Hermes, the messenger of the gods; Mercury (the planet)

Ζεύς, ὁ, Διός (gen.), Διί (dat.), Δία (acc.), Ζεῦ (voc.), Zeus

ἱερεύς, -έως, ὁ, priest; ἐπὶ ἱερέως, during the priesthood of so-and-so

Λυκαονιστί, adv. in the Lycaonian (language)

ξένος, -η, -ον, strange, foreign; subst. a stranger, foreigner; guest

ὁμοιόω, make like, become like (w. dat.)

ὀρθός, -ή, -όν, upright, erect; straight, true, correct; ὀρθῶς, correctly, rightly, strictly; normally, in good order; duly

οὐδέποτε, never

πυλών, -ῶνος, ὁ, city gate; gateway, door

στέμμα, garland (hung around the neck of victims for sacrifice)

ταῦρος, ὁ, bull

χωλός, -ή, -όν, lame, unable to walk

14:14 Ἀκούσαντες δὲ οἱ ἀπόστολοι Βαρναβᾶς καὶ Παῦλος διαρρήξαντες τὰ ἱμάτια αὐτῶν ἐξεπήδησαν εἰς τὸν ὄχλον κράζοντες 15 καὶ λέγοντες· ἄνδρες, τί ταῦτα ποιεῖτε; καὶ ἡμεῖς ὁμοιοπαθεῖς ἐσμεν ὑμῖν ἄνθρωποι εὐαγγελιζόμενοι ὑμᾶς ἀπὸ τούτων τῶν ματαίων ἐπιστρέφειν ἐπὶ θεὸν ζῶντα, ὃς ἐποίησεν τὸν οὐρανὸν καὶ τὴν γῆν καὶ τὴν θάλασσαν καὶ πάντα τὰ ἐν αὐτοῖς (Exod 20:11)· 16 ὃς ἐν ταῖς παρῳχημέναις γενεαῖς εἴασεν πάντα τὰ ἔθνη πορεύεσθαι ταῖς ὁδοῖς αὐτῶν·

Vocabulary

ἐάω, pres. mid. inf. ἐᾶσθαι, impf. εἴων, 2. ἐάσω, 3. εἴασα: allow, permit; leave, let go; mid. be left to oneself

ἐκπηδάω, rush out

μάταιος, -α, -ον, empty, useless, powerless; foolish

Hermes, has recently been unearthed, bearing the inscription "Neikomas, son of Alexander, (fulfilled) a vow to Zeus Ampelites (i.e., protector of vines)" (Louis Robert, "Documents d'Asie Mineure," *BCH* 107 [1983], 497–599, esp. 539–342 [fig. 17]; L. Robert, *Opera minora selecta: Epigraphie et antiquités grecque.s* Amsterdam: A. M. Hakkert, 1969], II, 1357–1160). The concentration of the evidence in the area around Lystra confirms that this narrative is rooted in the local culture of this particular region. It is also noteworthy that in Gal 4:14, Paul writes that he had been received as though he were the "messenger" (i.e., Hermes) of god/God, a phrase that seems to recall this incident. The crowd's identification of Barnabas and Paul as the gods Zeus and Hermes respectively and the plan of the priest of Zeus to offer a sacrifice to them demonstrate that the townspeople understood Paul's act of healing as a divine benefaction.

ὁμοιοπαθής, -ές, of the same nature

παροίχομαι, be past

14:17 καίτοι οὐκ ἀμάρτυρον αὐτὸν ἀφῆκεν ἀγαθουργῶν, οὐρανόθεν ὑμῖν ὑετοὺς διδοὺς καὶ καιροὺς καρποφόρους, ἐμπιπλῶν τροφῆς καὶ εὐφροσύνης τὰς καρδίας ὑμῶν. 18 καὶ ταῦτα λέγοντες μόλις κατέπαυσαν τοὺς ὄχλους τοῦ μὴ θύειν[20] αὐτοῖς. 19 Ἐπῆλθαν δὲ ἀπὸ Ἀντιοχείας καὶ Ἰκονίου Ἰουδαῖοι καὶ πείσαντες[21] τοὺς ὄχλους καὶ λιθάσαντες τὸν Παῦλον ἔσυρον ἔξω τῆς πόλεως νομίζοντες αὐτὸν τεθνηκέναι. 20 κυκλωσάντων δὲ τῶν μαθητῶν[22] αὐτὸν ἀναστὰς εἰσῆλθεν εἰς τὴν πόλιν. Καὶ τῇ ἐπαύριον ἐξῆλθεν σὺν τῷ Βαρναβᾷ εἰς Δέρβην.

Vocabulary

Ἀντιόχεια, ἡ, Antioch, either Syrian Antioch (on the Orontes River) or Pisidian Antioch

ἐπαύριον (adv.), the next day

καίτοι, although, and yet

ἀγαθουργέω, show kindness

ἀμάρτυρος, -ον, without witness

εὐφροσύνη, ἡ, joy, cheerfulness

θνήσκω, 3. ἔθανον, ptc. θανών, pf. inf. θνηκέναι: die, be dead; subst. the deceased

καρποφόρος, -ον, fruitful

καταπαύω, restrain, dissuade

λιθάζω, [1]aor. ptc. λίθασας: stone somebody (as a means of execution)

οὐρανόθεν, from heaven

σύρω, drag, pull

ὑετός, ὁ, rain

---

[20] Art. inf. (cf. IV, 2).
[21] S.v. πείθω.
[22] Gen. absol. (cf. IV, 9).

5.2.

Acts: Paul Preaches to the Epicurean and Stoic Philosophers

(Acts 17:16–34)

17:16 Ἐν δὲ ταῖς Ἀθήναις ἐκδεχομένου αὐτοὺς[1] τοῦ Παύλου[2] παρωξύνετο[3] τὸ πνεῦμα αὐτοῦ ἐν αὐτῷ θεωροῦντος κατείδωλον οὖσαν τὴν πόλιν. 17 διελέγετο μὲν οὖν ἐν τῇ συναγωγῇ τοῖς Ἰουδαίοις καὶ τοῖς σεβομένοις καὶ ἐν τῇ ἀγορᾷ κατὰ[4] πᾶσαν ἡμέραν πρὸς τοὺς παρατυγχάνοντας. 18 τινὲς δὲ καὶ τῶν Ἐπικουρείων καὶ Στοϊκῶν φιλοσόφων συνέβαλλον αὐτῷ, καί τινες ἔλεγον· τί ἂν θέλοι[5] ὁ σπερμολόγος οὗτος λέγειν; οἱ δέ·[6] ξένων δαιμονίων δοκεῖ καταγγελεὺς εἶναι, ὅτι τὸν Ἰησοῦν καὶ τὴν ἀνάστασιν[7] εὐηγγελίζετο.

Vocabulary

ἀγορά, ἡ, marketplace (of a city); **Ἀθῆναι, -ῶν, αἱ,** Athens

δαιμόνιον, τό, god; semi-divine go/spirit; demon, evil spirit

διαλέγω, aor. pass. ptc. (dep.) διαλεχθείς: examine, check; mid. debate with (w. dat.), converse with, discourse, instruct, lecture

ἐκδέχομαι, expect, look forward to, wait for somebody (acc.)

Ἐπικούρειος, ὁ, Epicurean philosopher (i.e., a follower of Epicurus)

καταγγελεύς, ὁ, proclaimer

κατείδωλος, -ον, full of cult images

ξένος, -η, -ον, strange, foreign; subst. a stranger, foreigner; guest

παρατυγχάνω, [2]aor. ptc. παρατυχών: be somewhere by chance, be present

---

[1] αὐτούς, i.e., Silas and Timothy, who were traveling from Berea (Acts 17:10–15).

[2] Παύλου functions in gen. absol. constructions with both ἐκδεχομένου and θεωροῦντος.

[3] Iter. impf.

[4] Distributive κατά ("every").

[5] Cf. table 9.1.3.

[6] οἱ δέ, "and others (said)."

[7] ἀνάστασιν, here misunderstood polytheistically as a Greek goddess named "Anastasis" or "Resurrection" (Ἀνάστασις), standing alongside Jesus.

παροξύνω, become enraged, exasperated

σέβω/ομαι, to worship, reverence; mid. ptc. subst. σεβόμενοι, god-fearers (i.e., Gentiles who took part in synagogue services without becoming fully-entitled members of the Jewish religious community [προσήλυτοι])

Σοϊκός, ὁ, Stoic philosopher

σπερμολόγος, ὁ, dabbler[8]

συμβάλλω (w. dat.), impf. συνέβαλλον: converse with, engage in an argument; communicate (a proposal/motion)

φιλοσόφος, ὁ, philosopher; adj. φιλοσόφος, -ον; superl. φιλοσοφώτατος, most philosophical

17:19 ἐπιλαβόμενοί τε αὐτοῦ ἐπὶ τὸν Ἄρειον πάγον ἤγαγον λέγοντες· Δυνάμεθα γνῶναι τίς[9] ἡ καινὴ αὕτη ἡ ὑπὸ σοῦ λαλουμένη διδαχή;[10] 20 ξενίζοντα γάρ τινα εἰσφέρεις εἰς τὰς ἀκοὰς ἡμῶν· βουλόμεθα οὖν γνῶναι τίνα θέλει ταῦτα εἶναι.[11] 21 (Ἀθηναῖοι δὲ πάντες καὶ οἱ ἐπιδημοῦντες ξένοι εἰς οὐδὲν ἕτερον ἠυκαίρουν ἢ λέγειν τι ἢ ἀκούειν τι καινότερον.)[12]

Vocabulary

Ἀθηναῖος, -α, -ον, Athenian (adj.); subst. ὁ Ἀθηναῖος, the Athenian

ἀκοή, ἡ, (faculty of) hearing; act of hearing; ear; account, report; obedience; pl. αἱ ἀκοαί, ears; chamber where the voice of Aklepios is heard

Ἄρειος πάγος, Areopagus[13]

εἰσφέρω, bring in/to (εἰς); introduce; enter into (πρός) the presence of a high official; mid. contribute/pay, provide

ἐπιδημέω, come to stay in a city, reside temporarily in a place (i.e., resident aliens); live at home; stay at home

ἐπιλαμβάνω, 5. ἐπείλημμαι: take hold of something, overtake, seize; pass. be imprisoned

εὐρκαιρέω, have leisure/time

καινός, -ή, -όν, new, strange; comp. καινότερος

---

[8] This term was originally used to describe birds that pick up grain and scrap collectors who search the marketplace for junk. It later came to be applied to anyone who snapped up ideas of others without understanding them and then spread the ideas about as his own.

[9] τίς, fm. ("what"), agreeing with διδαχή.

[10] ἡ καινὴ αὕτη ἡ...διδαχή, modifier in 2nd attri. pos.

[11] τίνα θέλει ταῦτα εἶναι, lit. "what these things want to be" (i.e., what these things mean).

[12] Comp. for superl.

[13] The meaning of this term is unclear (cf. Acts 17:22). The supreme Athenian Council was named the "Areopagus" (or "Mars Hill") because this was the original place where the Council used to meet. However, a reference to the Council in Acts 17:19 seems doubtful because the public was excluded from its meetings. Moreover, the Council did not deal with questions of religious doctrine. Of course, this term also designates the rocky summit in front of the Athenian Acropolis. However, there would be insufficient room on this summit to accommodate the large crowd presupposed by Acts 17.

ξενίζω, entertain as a guest; to surprise, startle; nt. pl. ptc., strange things/
notions

17:22 Σταθεὶς[14] δὲ ὁ Παῦλος ἐν μέσῳ τοῦ Ἀρείου πάγου ἔφη· Ἄνδρες Ἀθηναῖοι,
κατὰ πάντα ὡς δεισιδαιμονεστέρους ὑμᾶς θεωρῶ. 23 διερχόμενος γὰρ καὶ
ἀναθεωρῶν τὰ σεβάσματα ὑμῶν εὗρον καὶ βωμὸν ἐν ᾧ ἐπεγέγραπτο· Ἀγνώστῳ
θεῷ.[15] ὃ οὖν ἀγνοοῦντες εὐσεβεῖτε, τοῦτο ἐγὼ καταγγέλλω ὑμῖν. 24 ὁ θεὸς ὁ
ποιήσας τὸν κόσμον καὶ πάντα τὰ ἐν αὐτῷ, οὗτος οὐρανοῦ καὶ γῆς ὑπάρχων
κύριος οὐκ ἐν χειροποιήτοις ναοῖς κατοικεῖ 25 οὐδὲ ὑπὸ χειρῶν ἀνθρωπίνων
θεραπεύεται προσδεόμενός[16] τινος, αὐτὸς διδοὺς πᾶσι ζωὴν καὶ πνοὴν καὶ τὰ
πάντα· 26 ἐποίησέν τε ἐξ ἑνὸς[17] πᾶν ἔθνος ἀνθρώπων κατοικεῖν[18] ἐπὶ παντὸς
προσώπου τῆς γῆς, ὁρίσας προστεταγμένους[19] καιρούς[20] καὶ τὰς ὁροθεσίας
τῆς κατοικίας αὐτῶν, 27 ζητεῖν τὸν θεόν, εἰ ἄρα γε ψηλαφήσειαν[21] αὐτὸν καὶ
εὕροιεν,[22] καί γε οὐ μακρὰν ἀπὸ ἑνὸς ἑκάστου ἡμῶν ὑπάρχοντα.

Vocabulary
ἄγνωστος, -ον, unknown
ἀναθεωρέω, examine/observe carefully
ἀνθρώπινος, -η, -ον, belonging/suited to humans, common to humanity,
human
βωμός, ὁ, altar
δεισιδαίμων, -ον, religious/devout; comp. δεισιδαιμονέστερος, exceptionally
religious
ἐπιγράφω, write on/in; inscribe on
εὐσεβέω, worship/reverence (gods)
κατοικία, ἡ, dwelling place; territory (for habitation)
μακράν, adv., far (away)
ὁρίζω, set limits; appoint, set; administer an oath; pass. be fixed/determined; be
limited
ὁροθεσία, ἡ, fixed boundaries

---

[14] Cf. table 9.12.7 ("took his stand").
[15] The most relevant piece of archaeological evidence for this cult is a mutilated inscription from Pergamon (cf. P. W. van der Horst, "The Altar of the 'Unknown God' in Athens [17:23] and the Cult of 'Unknown Gods' in the Hellenistic and Roman Periods," *ANRW* (Berlin: W. de Gruyter, 1984), II, 18.2, 1426–1456).
[16] Causal adv. ptc. ("because," cf. IV, 1.4).
[17] "From one (person)" (i.e., from Adam).
[18] κατοκεῖν (inf.) depends on ἐποίησεν and is followed by inf. of purpose (ζητεῖν, 17:27).
[19] S.v. προστάσσω.
[20] καιροί, either "seasons" of the year or "epochs" of history.
[21] Cf. table 1.3(b).
[22] Aor., cf. table 1.3 (a); ²aor verbs in non-indicative moods have the same endings as the present tense of the same mood.

προσδέομαι, have need of something (gen.)

προστάσσω, pf. pass. ptc. προστεταγμένος: command, order (w. dat.); pass. be fixed, determined

σέβασμα, τό, object of worship/religious devotion

χειροποίητος, -ον, made by hand

ψηλαφάω, feel around for, grope for

17:28 ἐν αὐτῷ γὰρ ζῶμεν καὶ κινούμεθα καὶ ἐσμέν, ὡς καί τινες τῶν καθ'[23] ὑμᾶς ποιητῶν εἰρήκασιν· Τοῦ[24] γὰρ καὶ γένος ἐσμέν.[25] 29 γένος οὖν ὑπάρχοντες τοῦ θεοῦ οὐκ ὀφείλομεν νομίζειν[26] χρυσῷ ἢ ἀργύρῳ ἢ λίθῳ, χαράγματι τέχνης καὶ ἐνθυμήσεως ἀνθρώπου, τὸ θεῖον εἶναι ὅμοιον.[27] 30 τοὺς μὲν οὖν χρόνους τῆς ἀγνοίας ὑπεριδὼν ὁ θεός, τὰ νῦν[28] παραγγέλλει τοῖς ἀνθρώποις (that) πάντας[29] πανταχοῦ μετανοεῖν,[30] 31 καθότι ἔστησεν ἡμέραν ἐν ᾗ μέλλει κρίνειν τὴν οἰκουμένην ἐν δικαιοσύνῃ, ἐν[31] ἀνδρὶ ᾧ[32] ὥρισεν, πίστιν[33] παρασχὼν πᾶσιν ἀναστήσας[34] αὐτὸν ἐκ νεκρῶν. 32 Ἀκούσαντες δὲ ἀνάστασιν νεκρῶν οἱ μὲν[35] ἐχλεύαζον, οἱ δὲ εἶπαν· Ἀκουσόμεθά σου περὶ τούτου καὶ πάλιν. 33 οὕτως ὁ Παῦλος ἐξῆλθεν ἐκ μέσου αὐτῶν. 34 τινὲς δὲ ἄνδρες κολληθέντες αὐτῷ ἐπίστευσαν, ἐν οἷς καὶ Διονύσιος[36] ὁ Ἀρεοπαγίτης καὶ γυνὴ ὀνόματι Δάμαρις[37] καὶ ἕτεροι σὺν αὐτοῖς.

Vocabulary

Ἀρεοπαγίτης, -ου, ὁ, Areopagite (member of the Council of the Areopagus)

ἐνθύμησις, ἡ, thought, idea

θεῖος, -α, -ον, divine; τὸ θεῖον, deity, the Divinity, divine substance; τὰ θεῖα, acts of the gods; (adv.) θείως, divinely

καθότι, to swear (an oath) that; because (= διότι)

κινέω, move; stir up; pass. be moved/resolved (of an inward personal disposition)

κολλάω, join with, associate with

---

[23] κατά is sometimes possesive ("your").

[24] τοῦ, "of/from him."

[25] Quoting a verse of poetry from the poet Aratus (*Phaenomena* 1.5).

[26] νομίζειν...τὸ θεῖον εἶναι ὅμοιον.

[27] ὅμοιος, -α, -ον often takes the dative (χρυσῷ ἢ ἀργύρῳ ...).

[28] τὰ νῦν, "now."

[29] πάντας (acc.), subject of inf.

[30] Imperatival inf.

[31] ἐν, instr. ("by").

[32] ᾧ for ὅν, attr. rel. to case of the antecedent, ἀνδρί.

[33] πίστις, "assurance."

[34] Adv. ptc. of means ("by").

[35] οἱ μέν...οἱ δέ....

[36] Διονύσιος, Dionysios (cf. Acts 17:34).

[37] Damaris (fm.).

ὀφείλω/έω, 2. ὀφειλήσω, 3. ὠφείλησα: owe somebody something, be indebted to somebody; be obligated to, should/must (w. inf.); ἁμαρτίαν ὀφείλω (w. dat.), incur sin against

παντᾱχοῦ, everywhere

παραγγέλλω, command/instruct somebody (dat.); subst. ptc. instructions, things announced

παρέχω, 3. παρέσχον, ²aor. ptc. παρασχών: to provide/give; +inf., to allow/grant to somebody (dat.) to do something

ποιητής, ὁ, poet

τέχνη, ἡ, trade, skill, craftsmanship

ὑπεροράω, overlook

χάραγμα, τό, work of sculpture

χλεύαζω, jeer, mock

5.3.

Acts: Burning the Handbooks of Magicians

(Acts 19:11–20)

The story opens with Paul living in Ephesos:

19:11 Δυνάμεις[1] τε[2] οὐ τὰς τυχούσας[3] ὁ θεὸς ἐποίει[4] διὰ τῶν χειρῶν Παύλου, 12 ὥστε[5] καὶ ἐπὶ τοὺς ἀσθενοῦντας ἀποφέρεσθαι[6] ἀπὸ τοῦ χρωτὸς αὐτοῦ[7] σουδάρια ἢ σιμικίνθια καὶ (τοὺς ἀσθενοῦντας) ἀπαλλάσσεσθαι ἀπ' αὐτῶν τὰς νόσους, τά τε πνεύματα τὰ πονηρὰ ἐκπορεύεσθαι. 13 Ἐπεχείρησαν δέ τινες καὶ τῶν περιερχομένων Ἰουδαίων ἐξορκιστῶν ὀνομάζειν ἐπὶ τοὺς ἔχοντας τὰ πνεύματα τὰ πονηρὰ τὸ ὄνομα τοῦ κυρίου Ἰησοῦ λέγοντες· Ὁρκίζω ὑμᾶς τὸν Ἰησοῦν ὃν Παῦλος κηρύσσει.

Vocabulary

ἀπαλλάσσω, 6. dep. ἀπηλλάγην, [2]aor. pass. ptc. ἀπαλλαγείς, fut. pass. ἀπαλλαγήσομαι: make something go away; pass. be released/separated from (ἀπό), be cured of

ἐκπορεύομαι, go away, come out (of gods/evil spirits)

ἐξορκιστής, ὁ, exorcist

ἐπιχειρέω, endeavor, try

νόσος, ἡ, disease, illness

ὀνομάζω, to name/call something (by a certain name); utter a name (acc.) (for magical purposes) on (ἐπί) somebody

---

[1] Here "works of power."
[2] Postpos.
[3] (τὰς) Δυνάμεις...οὐ τὰς τυχούσας (s.v. τυγχάνω).
[4] Iter. impf. (cf. IV, 13.3).
[5] ὥστε followed by three infinitives (cf. IV, 15).
[6] Subj. of the inf. is σουδάρια ἢ σιμικίνθια.
[7] I.e., Paul's.

ὁρκίζω, make somebody swear an oath to somebody (acc.), swear by the name (τῷ ὀνόματι τοῦ) of somebody; to solemnly command/bind somebody by magically invoking somebody (acc.)

περιέρχομαι, be itinerant; make a circuit

σιμικίνθιον, τό (Lat. loanw. *semi-cinctium*), apron

σπουδάριον, τό (Lat. loanw. *sudarium*), handkerchief

τυγχάνω, pres. fm. ptc. τυχοῦσα, ²aor. ἔτυχον, ²aor. 3rd sg. subj. τήχῃ, inf. τυχεῖν, pf. ptc. τετ(ε)υχώς: gain, experience; happen, turn out (as a result); happen to be; gain/receive something (gen.), attain to (ἐπί); obtain one's request (w. gen.); ἔτυχεν δέ, "and it came to pass that (w. acc.)"; adj. ptc. ordinary, everyday

χρώς, -ωτός, ὁ, skin; ἀπὸ τοῦ χρωτὸς αὐτοῦ, from (contact with) his skin

19:14 Ἦσαν[8] δέ τινος Σκευᾶ Ἰουδαίου ἀρχιερέως ἑπτὰ υἱοὶ[9] τοῦτο ποιοῦντες. 15 ἀποκριθὲν δὲ τὸ πνεῦμα τὸ πονηρὸν εἶπεν αὐτοῖς· τὸν μὲν[10] Ἰησοῦν γινώσκω καὶ τὸν Παῦλον ἐπίσταμαι, ὑμεῖς δὲ τίνες ἐστέ; 16 καὶ ἐφαλόμενος[11] ὁ ἄνθρωπος ἐπ᾽ αὐτοὺς ἐν ᾧ ἦν τὸ πνεῦμα τὸ πονηρόν, κατακυριεύσας ἀμφοτέρων ἴσχυσεν κατ᾽ αὐτῶν ὥστε[12] γυμνοὺς καὶ τετραυματισμένους ἐκφυγεῖν ἐκ τοῦ οἴκου ἐκείνου. 17 τοῦτο δὲ ἐγένετο γνωστὸν πᾶσιν Ἰουδαίοις τε καὶ Ἕλλησιν τοῖς κατοικοῦσιν τὴν Ἔφεσον καὶ ἐπέπεσεν φόβος ἐπὶ πάντας αὐτοὺς καὶ ἐμεγαλύνετο τὸ ὄνομα τοῦ κυρίου Ἰησοῦ.

Vocabulary

ἀρχιερεύς, -έως, ὁ, high priest

γνωστός, -η, -ον, known; subst. knowledge

ἐπίσταμαι, know, understand

ἐφάλλομαι, leap upon (ἐπί) somebody

Ἔφεσος, ἡ, Ephesos

ἰσχύω, be able/strong; defeat, overcome; prevail against (κατά); be valid, be in force; + inf., be able to, have the power to; subst., something strong; dissolution, breaking up

κατακυριεύω, subdue, overpower

μεγαλύνω, praise, glorify, exalt

πρᾶξις, -εως, ἡ, way of acting/conducting; action/deed; (magical) ritual

Σκευᾶ, -ᾶς, ὁ, Skeva, who was the high priest

τραυματίζω, to wound

---

[8] ἦσαν...ποιοῦντες, impf. perphr. (cf. IV, 18).

[9] ἑπτὰ υἱοί, subject of sentence.

[10] μέν...δέ....

[11] ἐφαλόμενος...ἐπ᾽ αὐτούς.

[12] ὥστε + inf.

18 Πολλοί τε τῶν πεπιστευκότων ἤρχοντο ἐξομολογούμενοι καὶ ἀναγγέλλοντες τὰς πράξεις αὐτῶν. 19 ἱκανοὶ δὲ τῶν τὰ περίεργα πραξάντων συνενέγκαντες[13] τὰς βίβλους κατέκαιον ἐνώπιον πάντων, καὶ συνεψήφισαν τὰς τιμὰς αὐτῶν καὶ εὗρον (it was) ἀργυρίου μυριάδας πέντε. 20 Οὕτως κατὰ κράτος τοῦ κυρίου ὁ λόγος ηὔξανεν καὶ ἴσχυεν.

Vocabulary

αὐξάνω/αὔξω, 3. ηὔχανον: to make grow/increase; pass. to grow/increase in size/ numbers/strength

κατακαίω (Att. κατακάω), impf. κατέκαιον, 2. κατακαύσω: burn completely, burn up

κράτος, -ους, τό, power; κατὰ κράτος, powerfully, mightily

περίεργος, -ον, belonging to magic; τὰ περίεργα πράσσειν, practice magic[14]

πράσσω (Att. πράττω), 3. ἔπραξα, [1]aor. ptc. πράξας, [1]aor pass. ptc. πραχθείς: do something; commit an act; achieve, accomplish, be busy with; τὰ περίεργα πράσσειν, practice magic; charge somebody money for something; pass. take place, happen

συμφέρω, to help, be advantageous; bring together, collect; (impers.) it is useful/ good/best; subst. (nt. ptc.) (τὸ) συμφέρον, what is useful/best/beneficial; the welfare

συμψυφίζω, add up, calculate the value (τιμή) of something

---

[13] S.v. συμφέρω.
[14] Cf. reference to ἔργα μαγικά in Acts Thom. 89:6 (§5.10).

5.4.

A Magical Handbook

(PGM XIII, 230–334)

Provenance: Egypt.

Date: Fourth century CE.

Text: PGM XIII, 230–334 (pp. 99–104); translated by Hans Dieter Betz (ed.), *The Greek Magical Papyri in Translation including the Demotic Spells*, 2nd ed. (Chicago: University of Chicago Press, 1992), 179–182.

The Greek magical papyri are a body of papyri from Greco-Roman Egypt, dating from the second century BCE to the fifth century CE. These papyri include a plethora of magical spells, remedies, hymns, and rituals. These texts are syncretistic, comprising a mixture of Egyptian, Greek Babylonian, Jewish, and Christian elements, with the Greek god Apollo Helios being invoked most frequently.

The text in this section is an excerpt from a magical handbook entitled the "Eight Books of Moses."[1] This text begins with a lengthy description of initiation ritual (not printed here). The handbook then continues with a lengthy collection of magical spells for various occasions. Each spell is introduced with a clause indicating the particular purpose of the spell (e.g., "If you want to do such-and-such" or "If you want to make such-and-such happen …").

Throughout this handbook, one is repeatedly instructed to "say the Name" (or "write the Name").[2] This instruction concerns the utterance of the full

---

[1] PGM XIII, 1–334; Betz, *Greek Magical Papyri*, 172–182.
[2] E.g., *ll.* 237–238, 242–246, 253, 259, 261, 264, 269, 277, 282, 288, 296, 303, 308, 317, 323

FIG. 9. Relief of man holding a bird, Konya (IKonya 86).

name of the primary deity, which is revealed in the course of a rite previously described: "When the god comes in, look down and write the things he says and the Name which he gives you for himself" (*l.* 211). As in the case of PGM IV, 1496–1595 (§7.3), the use of capital letters indicates magical words that were probably untranslatable even by the intended users of this manual.

Related Readings: PGM IV, 1496–1595, XXXVI, 320–332 (§7.3).

LINES 230–236

Ὑποτάξω δέ σοι, τέκνον, καὶ τὰς χρείας τῆς ἱερᾶς βίβλου, ἃς πάντες οἱ σοφισταὶ ἐτέλησαν ἀπὸ ταύτης ἱερᾶς καὶ μακάριδος βίβλου. ὡς ἐξώρκισά σε, τέκνον, ἐν τῷ ἱερῷ τῷ ἐν Ἱερωσολύμῳ, πλησθείς³ τῆς θεοσοφίας ἀνεύρετον ποίησον τὴν βίβλον.

ἔστιν οὖν (ἡ) πρώτη (of these uses) ἡ θαυμάσιος ἀμαυρά (spell)· λαβὼν ᾠὸν ἱέρακος τὸ ἥμισυ αὐτοῦ χρύσωσον, τὸ δὲ ἄλλο ἥμισυ χρῖσον κινναβάρει. τοῦτο φορῶν ἀθεώρητος ἔσῃ ἐπιλέγων τὸ ὄνομα.

Vocabulary

ἀθεώρητος, -ον, invisible (cf. *l.* 330)

ἀμαυρά, ἡ, invisibility

ἀνεύρετος, -ον, undiscovered, not found; ἀνεύρετον ποίησον, lit. "make undiscovered," i.e., dispose of, hide μάκαρ, -άριδος (m./fm.), blessed (cf. *l.* 341)

βίβλος/βύβλος, ὁ, Egyptian papyrus; a scroll of papyrus (book)

ἐπιλέγω, 3. ἔπειπον: utter a spell, pronounce a magical word

ἥμισυς, -εια, -υ, τό, (the) half; μέχρι τοῦ ἡμίσους, up to the middle (of one's body)

θαυμάσιος, -α, -ον, wonderful, excellent; superl. θαυμασιώτατος, -η, -ον, most admirable/excellent/wonderful; τὰ θαυμάσια, marvels, wonders

θεοσοφία, ἡ, divine wisdom

ἱέραξ, -ακος, ὁ, falcon

κιννάβαρι, -εως, τό, cinnabar (vermilion), a red pigment made from mercuric sulfide

σοφιστής, ὁ, master, expert

ὑποτάσσω, make subject; append; pass. be subjected to

χρυσόω, make golden, gild

ᾠόν, τό, egg

---

³ πλησθείς, m. sg. agreeing with σέ.

LINES 236-245

Ἐπὶ[4] δὲ ἀγωγῆς·[5] (facing) πρὸς τὸν ἥλιον εἰπὲ γ΄[6] τὸ ὄνομα· (This spell) ἄγει γυναῖκα ἀνδρὶ καὶ ἄνδρα γυναικὶ (in a way) ὥστε θαυμάσαι.

ἐάν τινα θέλῃς μὴ ῥικνῶσαι (ἢ) πρὸς ἄνδρα γυναῖκα ἢ ἄνδρα πρὸς γυναῖκα· λαβὼν ἀφόδευμα κυνὸς βάλε κατὰ τοῦ στροφέως τῆς θύρας αὐτῶν εἰπὼν τὸ ὄνομα γ΄, λέγων· Διακόπτω τὸν δεῖνα ἀπὸ τοῦ δεῖνος.[7]

ἐάν δαιμονιζομένῳ εἴπῃς τὸ ὄνομα προσάγων τῇ ῥινὶ αὐτοῦ[8] θεῖον καὶ ἄσφαλτον, εὐθέως (the demon) λαλήσει, καὶ ἀπελεύσεται. ἐάν εἴπῃς (τὸ ὄνομα) ἐπὶ ἐρυσιπέλατος, χρίσας αὐτὸν κορκοδείλου ἀφοδεύματι, εὐθέως ἀπαλλαγήσεται (the disease).

Vocabulary

ἀγωγή, ἡ, policy; love spell

ἀπαλλάσσω (Att. ἀπαλλάττω), 6. ἀπηλλάγην, [2]aor. pass. ptc. ἀπαλλαγείς, fut. pass. ἀπαλλαγήσομαι: make something go away; pass. be released/separated from (ἀπό); be cured of

ἄσφαλτος, ἡ, bitumen, asphalt

ἀφόδευμα, -ματος, τό, excrement

δαιμονίζομαι, be possessed by a demon/hostile spirit

δεῖνα, ὁ/ἡ, τοῦ δεῖνος, τῷ δεῖνι, τὸν δεῖνα: so-and-so

διακόπτω, sever

ἐρυσιπέλας, -ατος, τό, erysipelas (red skin);[9] here "somebody suffering from erysipelas"

θεῖον, τό, sulfur (used to fumigate/purify)

θύρα, ἡ, door, doorway (of a house); entrance (of cave/tomb); ἐπὶ θύραις, lit. "at the doors" (i.e., impending)

κορκόδειλος (> κροκόδιλος), crocodile

ῥικνόω, have sexual intercourse

ῥίς, ἡ, ῥινός, nose

προάγω, draw near to, approach; bring up to; lead forward

στροφίς, ὁ (= στρόφιγξ, -ιγγος), socket at the top and bottom of a door hinge

---

[4] ἐπί (w. gen.) expresses purpose ("for").

[5] See other love spells of attraction mentioned in Acts Andr. 5.65 (§5.16), SIG[3] 985, *l.* 20 (§7.3), PGM IV, 1496–1595 (§7.3).

[6] For alphabetic numbers see table 9.18 (cf. *ll.* 242, 246, 264, 292, 327).

[7] This formula cues the reader to fill in the appropriate proper names, in this case the name of the person who is to be "severed" from another person (cf. *ll.* 269, 308, 324).

[8] I.e., of the demoniac.

[9] A type of skin infection (cellulitis) with such symptoms as blisters, fever, shaking. and chills.

LINES 245–253

Ἐάν εἴπῃς ἐπὶ (ἢ) σπάσματος ἢ συντρίμματος τὸ ὄνομα γ΄, καταχρίσας (on it)
   γῆν μετὰ ὄξους, ἀπαλλάξεις.
ἐὰν ἐπείπῃς (τὸ ὄνομα) ἐπὶ παντὸς πετεινοῦ εἰς τὸ ὠτίον,[10] τελευτήσει.
ἐὰν ἴδῃς ἀσπίδα καὶ θέλῃς αὐτὴν στῆσαι,[11] λέγε στρεφόμενος[12] ὅτι Στῆθι. λέγεται
   τὰ ὀνόματα,[13] καὶ (ἡ ἀσπίς) στήσεται.
θυμοκάτοχον· πρὸς (the presence of) βασιλέα ἢ μεγιστᾶνα εἴσαγε, τὰς χεῖρας
ἐντὸς (your garment) ἔχων λέγε τὸ ὄνομα τὸ δίσκου, βαλὼν ἅμμα τοῦ παλλίου
σου ἢ τοῦ ἐπικαρσίου, καὶ θαυμάσεις.

ἐὰν (θέλῃς) πρὸς λύσιν φαρμάκων· εἰς ἱερατικὸν κόλλημα γράψας τὸ ὄνομα
φόρει (it).

Vocabulary
ἅμμα, -ματος, τό, knot; βάλλω ἅμμα, tie a knot in something (gen.)
δίσκος, ὁ, disk; sun disk (i.e., sun); discus event
ἐπικάρσιον, τό, shawl (if this magician were a Jew, perhaps a *talith*)
ἐπιλέγω, 3. ἔπειπον, to utter a spell/magical word
θυμοκάτοχον, τό, spell for restraining anger
ἱερατικός, -ή, -όν, hieratic (name of a kind of papyrus)
καταχρίω, to rub down, coat, smear
κόλλημα, -ματος, τό, sheet of papyrus gummed together to form a roll
μεγιστάν, -ᾶνος, ἡ, magistrate
ὄξος, -ους, τό, vinegar
πάλλιος, *pallium* (cloak worn by people who claimed to be philosophers)
σπάσμα, -ματος, τό, muscle sprain
συντρίμμα, -ματος, τό, fracture
φάρμακον, τό, drug, medicine; magic potion; spell cast using a magic potion

LINES 253–261

(To bring about)   Ἡλίου[14] δεῖξις. λέγε πρὸς ἀνατολάς· Ἐγώ εἰμι ὁ ἐπὶ τῶν δύο
χερουβείν,[15] ἀνὰ μέσον τῶν δύο φύσεων, οὐρανοῦ καὶ γῆς, ἡλίου τε καὶ σελήνης,

---

[10] τὸ ὠτίον, dim. of τὸ οὖς.
[11] I.e., to fix it in its place, make it stand still.
[12] Mid. voice.
[13] The use of the pl. (τὰ ὀνόματα) here indicates that parts of this list of spells did not originally belong
   to the preceding rite.
[14] Here, the god "Helios" (cf. *ll.* 258, 334–335, 339).
[15] This spell clearly has a Jewish background, for the magician identifies himself with Yahweh, who "sits
   upon the cherubim" (1 Sam 4:4, 2 Sam 6:2).

φωτὸς καὶ σκότους, νυκτὸς καὶ ἡμέρας, ποταμῶν καὶ θαλάσσης· φάνηθι μοι, ὁ ἀρχάγγελος τῶν (ἀνθρώπων) ὑπὸ[16] τὸν κόσμον, αὐθέντα Ἥλιε, ὁ ὑπ᾽ αὐτὸν τὸν ἕνα[17] καὶ μόνον τεταγμένος· προστάσσει σοι ὁ Ἀεὶ καὶ Μόνος. λέγε τὸ ὄνομα.

ἐὰν δὲ (Helios) σκυθρωπὸς φανῇ, λέγε· Δός[18] (μοι) ἡμέραν, δὸς ὥραν, δὸς μῆνα, δὸς ἐνιαυτόν, κύριε τῆς ζωῆς. λέγε τὸ ὄνομα.

Vocabulary

ἀνά, each, apiece; ἀνὰ μέσον, between, within (w. gen.)

ἀνατολή, ἡ (poet. ἀντολίη), east; κατὰ ἀνατολάς, eastward; εἰς τὴν ἀνατολήν, πρὸς ἀνατολάς, toward the east

αὐθέντης, ὁ, ruler

δεῖξις, -εως, ἡ, calling up a god (gen.), making a god (gen.) appear

ποταμός, ὁ, river

σελήνη, ἡ, moon

σκυθρωπός, -όν, angry in appearance

τάσσω (Att. τάττω), pf. pass. τέτακμαι, pf. pass. ptc. τεταγμένος: to station, post somebody before; to set, appoint; determine; undertake (a task), restore; pass. be ordained that (w. acc. + inf.); τὰ ταταγμένα, instructions

φύσις, ἡ, circumstance; nature (of something), natural condition; substance; natural being, creature; female genitalia

LINES 261–269

Ἐὰν θέλῃς ὄφιν ἀποκτεῖναι, λέγε· Στῆθι, ὅτι σὺ εἶ ὁ Ἀφυφις, καὶ λαβὼν βάϊν χλωρὰν καὶ τῆς καρδίας[19] (of it) κρατήσας σχίσον εἰς δύο ἐπιλέγων τὸ ὄνομα (over it) ζ΄(times), καὶ εὐθέως (the snake) σχισθήσεται ἢ ῥαγήσεται.[20]

πρόγνωσις· ἥδε τῇ προειρημένῃ πράξει γίνεται, (that is) τῇ (πράξει) διὰ τοῦ νίτρου,[21] καὶ ὡς θεῷ (ὁ θεός) διαλαλήσει σοι· σοῦ γὰρ παρόντος[22] πολλάκις ἐποίησα τὴν πρᾶξιν.

---

[16] "Under," "subject to."

[17] The "One," i.e., the supreme God.

[18] It is unclear whether this is a request to "specify" a suitable time for a magical rite or "add" to the length of one's life.

[19] I.e., the center of the triangular end of the branch.

[20] S.v. ῥήγνυμι.

[21] Since this ritual is not mentioned in this text, this must be a reference to a ritual in a closely related document.

[22] Gen. absol. (s.v. πάρειμι).

ἀβλεψίας· δὲ (λέγε) οὕτως· Δευρό μοι, τὸ πρωτοφαὲς σκότος, καὶ κρύψον με προστάγματι τοῦ ὄντος ἐν οὐρανῷ αὐτογενέτορος, τὸν δεῖνα. λέγε τὸ ὄνομα.

Vocabulary
ἀβλεψία, ἡ, invisibility
αὐτογενέτωρ, -ορος, ὁ, self-generating
Ἀφυφις, Aphyphis (?)
βάϊς, ἡ, palm branch
διαλαλέω, talk with somebody (dat.)
κρατέω, attain something; conquer, master, rule over (w. gen.), subdue; take possession of (w. gen.); take custody of; hold something (w. gen.)
νίτρον, τό, natron (used as mouthwash, antiseptic, to preserve fish and meat, for mummification)
πολλάκις, often, repeatedly
πρόγνωσις, -εως, ἡ, foreknowledge, ability to know beforehand
προλέγω, 3. προεῖπον, 4. προείρηκα: warn in advance; say beforehand/above
πρωτοφαής, -ές, appearing first

LINES 269–282

Ἄλλως (say this)·[23] Σὲ μόνον ἐπικαλοῦμαι, τὸν μόνον ἐν κόσμῳ διαταξαντα θεοῖς καὶ ἀνθρώποις, τὸν ἑαυτὸν ἀλλάξαντα μορφαῖς ἁγίαις καὶ ἐκ μὴ ὄντων εἶναι[24] ποιήσαντα καὶ ἐξ ὄντων μὴ εἶναι, Θαῦθ ἅγιος, οὗ οὐδεὶς ὑποφέρει θεῶν[25] τὴν ἀληθινὴν ὄψιν ἰδεῖν τοῦ προσώπου.[26] ποίησόν με γενέσθαι ἐν ὄμμασι πάντων κτισμάτων λύκον, κύνα, λέοντα, πῦρ, δένδρον, γῦπα, τεῖχος, ὕδωρ, (ἢ ὃ ἂν θέλεις), ὅτι δυνατός εἶ. λέγε τὸ ὄνομα.

ἔγερσις σώματος νεκροῦ Ὁρκίζω σε, πνεῦμα ἐν ἀέρι φοιτώμενον, εἴσελθε, ἐμπνευμάτωσον, δυνάμωσον, διέγειρον τῇ δυνάμει τοῦ αἰωνίου θεοῦ τόδε τὸ σῶμα, καὶ περιπατείτω ἐπὶ τόνδε τὸν τόπον, ὅτι ἐγώ εἰμι ὁ ποιῶν τῇ δυνάμει τοῦ Θαῦθ, ἁγίου θεου. λέγε τὸ ὄνομα.

Vocabulary
γύψ, -υπός, ὁ, vulture
διατάσσω, appoint, order somebody (w. dat.)
διέγειρω, wake up, stir up

---

[23] "Otherwise" (cf. *l.* 335).
[24] εἶναι (existence)...μὴ εἶναι (non-existence).
[25] οὐδεὶς...θεῶν.
[26] τὴν ἀληθινὴν ὄψιν ἰδεῖν τοῦ προσώπου > ἰδεῖν τὴν ἀληθινὴν ὄψιν τοῦ προσώπου.

δυναμόω, put power (magically) into something
ἔγερσις, -εως, ἡ, resurrection
ἐμπνευματόω, inspire
Θαῦθ, god Thoth
κτίσμα, τό, creature
λέων, -οντος, ὁ / λέαινα, ἡ, lion, lioness
λύκος, ὁ, wolf
μορφή, ἡ, form, outward appearance
φοιτάω, come into, go about

LINES 282–288

Ἐάν θέλῃς (mounted) ἐπάνω κορκοδείλου διαβαίνειν (the Nile River), καθίσας (ἐπάνω κορκοδείλου) λέγε· Ἄκουέ μου, ὁ[27] ἐν τῷ ὑγρῷ τὴν διατριβὴν ποιούμενος· ἐγώ εἰμι ὁ ἐν οὐρανῷ σχολὴν ἔχων φοιτώμενός τε ἐν ὕδατι καὶ ἐν πυρὶ καὶ ἐν ἀέρι καὶ γῇ. ἀπόδος χαριστήριον τῆς ἡμέρας ἐκείνης, ὅτε σε ἐποίησα καὶ ᾐτήσω με τὴν αἰτησίαν. διαπεράσεις (με) εἰς τὸ πέραν, ὅτι ἐγώ τις. λέγε τὸ ὄνομα.

Vocabulary
αἰτέω/έομαι, ask, beg, make a request
αἰτησία, ἡ (= αἴτησις), ἡ, request
διαπεράω, take somebody over/across
διατριβή, ἡ, place of habitation
ἐπάνω, above, over; on top of; onward
κορκόδειλος (> κροκόδιλος), crocodile
πέραν, on the other side, across; τὸ πέραν, the opposite side
σχολή, ἡ, leisure, ease
ὑγρός, -ά, -όν, wet, moist; subst. liquid, the wet/water
φοιτάω, come in, go about
χαριστήριον, τό, favor

LINES 288–297

(Spell for) Δεσμόλυτον· λέγε· Κλῦθί μοι, ὁ Χριστός, ἐν βασάνοις, βοήθησον (με) ἐν ἀνάγκαις, (ὁ) ἐλεήμων ἐν ὥραις βιαίοις, πολὺ δυνάμενος (to do) ἐν κόσμῳ, ὁ κτίσας τὴν ἀνάγκην καὶ τιμωρίαν καὶ τὴν βάσανον. (λέγε) ιβʹ (times) ἡμ(έρας)[28] συρίσας τρὶς ὀκτάκις. λέγε τοῦ Ἡλίου τὸ ὄνομα ὅλον (beginning) ἀπὸ τοῦ

---

[27] ὁ...ποιούμενος.
[28] Gen. of time (cf. IV, 5.3).

ΑΧΕΒΥΚΡΩΜ.[29] (λέγε·) Λυθήτω πᾶς δεσμός, (λυθήτω) πᾶσα βία, ῥαγήτω[30] πᾶς σίδηρος, (ῥαγήτω) πᾶν σχοινίον ἢ πᾶς ἱμάς, πᾶν ἄμμα, πᾶσα ἄλυσις ἀνοιχθήτω, καὶ μηδείς με καταβιάσαιτο, ὅτι ἐγώ εἰμι. λέγε τὸ ὄνομα.

Vocabulary
ἄλυσις, -εως, ἡ, chain
βάσανος, ἡ, torture, torment
βίαιος, -α, -ον, violent
βοηθέω, help, come to the aid of somebody (dat.), render assistance to somebody; defend oneself
δεσμόλυτον, τό, release from chains
δεσμός, ὁ, pl. δεσμά: shackles/chains (of prison), sandal straps; (fig.) a hindrance that deafens or physically handicaps
ἱμάς, -άντος, ὁ, strap
καταβιάζω, subdue by force
κλύω, aor. impv. κλῦθι: hear, attend to
ὀκτάκις, eight times (cf. *l.* 334)
σίδηρος, ὁ, iron, anything made of iron
συρίζω, make a hissing sound (like a snake)
σχοινίον, τό, rope
τιμωρία, ἡ, retribution, vengeance
τρίς (adv.), three times

LINES 298–303

(Spell) πῦρ σβέσαι·[31] Ἄκουε, πῦρ, ἔργον ἔργων εὑρήματος θεοῦ, δόξα τοῦ ἐντίμου φωστῆρος, σβέσθητι, χιονίσθητι· αὐτὸς γάρ ἐστιν ὁ Αἰὼν ὁ ἐπιβαλόμενος πῦρ ὡς [300] ἀμίαντον· ἀποσκεδασθήτω μου πᾶσα φλόξ, πᾶσα δύναμις οὐσίας, προστάγματι Αὐτοῦ ἀεὶ ὄντος. οὐ μή μου θίγῃς, πῦρ, οὐ μή μου λυμάνῃς σάρκα (μου),[32] ὅτι ἐγώ εἰμι. λέγε τὸ ὄνομα.

Vocabulary
Αἰών, ὁ, the god Aion, whose name signifies eternity (cf. *l.* 329)
ἀμίαντος, ὁ, asbestos
ἀποσκευδάζω, get rid of; pass. be expelled

---

[29] Referring to the full name given (cf. *ll.* 590–92): ΑΧΕΒΥΚΡΩΜ, whose is the glory, ΑΑΑ ΕΕΕ ΟΟΟ ΙΙΙ ΑΑΑ ΟΟΟ ΣΑΒΑΟΘ ΑΡΒΑΘΙΑΟ ΖΑΓΟΥΡΗ, the god, ΑΡΑΘ ΑΔΟΝΑΙ ΒΑΣΥΜΜ ΙΑΟ.
[30] S.v. ῥήγνυμι.
[31] S.v. σβέννυμι.
[32] μου...σάρκα.

ἔντιμος, -ον, honored
ἐπιβάλλω, lay on; put on something; board a ship
εὕρημα, -ματος, τό, invention
θιγγάνω, ²aor. ἔθιγον: touch (w. gen.), take hold of; pass. be touched
λυμαίνω, ¹aor. ἐλύμηνα: harm, injure
οὐσία, ἡ, being, essence; substance
πρόσταγμα, -ματος, τό, command
σβέννυμι, 3. ἔσβεσα, aor. inf. σβέσαι, aor. pass. impv. σβέσθητι: extinguish, put out
   (a fire); pass. be extinguished
φλόξ, (gen.) φλογός, ἡ, flame; πῦρ φλογός, flaming fire
φωστήρ, -ῆρος, ὁ, star
χιονίζω, snow upon; pass. become snow

LINES 303–318

(Spell for) πῦρ μεῖναι· Ἐξορκίζω σε, πῦρ, δαίμων ἔρωτος ἁγίου, τὸν ἀόρατον καὶ πολυμερῆ, τὸν ἕνα καὶ πανταχῇ, ἐνμεῖναι ἐν τῷ λύχνῳ τούτῳ ἐπὶ τόνδε τὸν χρόνον λαμπρυνόμενον καὶ μὴ μαραινόμενον, τῷ προστάγματι τοῦ δεῖνος. λέγε τὸ ὄνομα.

(Spell for) ὀνειροπομπόν· ποίησον ἱπποπόταμον ἐκ κηροῦ πυρροῦ κοῖλον καὶ ἔνθες[33] εἰς τὴν κοιλίαν αὐτοῦ τοῦ ἱπποποτάμου καὶ[34] χρυσὸν καὶ ἄργυρον καὶ τὸ καλούμενον (τὸ) βαλλαθὰ[35] τὸ τῶν Ἰουδαίων καὶ στόλισον αὐτὸν λίνῳ καθαρῷ καὶ θὲς ἐπὶ θυρίδος καθαρᾶς καὶ λαβὼν χάρτην ἱερατικὸν γράψον εἰς αὐτὸν ζμυρνομέλανι καὶ αἵματι κυνοκεφάλου, ἃ (dreams) βούλει[36] πέμψαι (to somebody), καὶ εἰλήσας εἰς ἐνλύχνιον καὶ ἐνλυχνιάσας λύχνον καθαρὸν καινὸν (with it), ἐπίθες ἐπὶ τὸν λύχνον τὸν πόδα ἱπποποταμίου καὶ λέγε τὸ ὄνομα, καὶ πέμπει [the specified dreams].

Vocabulary
ἀόρατος, -ον, unseen, invisible
βουλή, ἡ, plan, decision; τίθημι βουλήν, reach a decision, decide; City Council
   (βουλή) (which was subordinate to the ἐκκλησία [Assembly]); will (of God)
δαίμων, -ονος, ὁ, lesser god, "demon," semi-divine being
ἐνλυχνιάζω, to light (a lamp)
ἐνλύχνιον, τό, wick
ἐνμένω (> ἐννένω), dwell in, inhabit

---

[33] Cf. table 9.12.2(d).
[34] καί... καί... ("both ... and ...").
[35] "Ballatha," unknown term.
[36] βούλει > βούλη

ἐντίθημι, put in

ἐξορκίζω (= ἐξορκόω), make somebody swear/taken an oath; conjure by
    (κατά) a god

ἔρως, -ωτος, ὁ, love;   Ἔρως, god of love

ζμυρνόμελαν, -ανος, mixture of ink and myrrh used in magic

θυρίς, -ίδος, ἡ, window

ἱερατικός, -ή, -όν, hieratic (name of a kind of papyrus)

ἱπποπόταμος, ὁ, hippopotamus (cf. ll. 311, 317)

κοιλόω, hollow out

κηρός, ὁ, beeswax

κυνοκέφαλος, ὁ, baboon

λαμπρύνω, make bright; pass. shine

λίνον, τό, linen cloth, linen garments

μαραίνω, quench; pass. die out (of a flame); waste/wither away

ὀνειροπομπόν, τό, the sending of dreams (to somebody) (cf. l. 339)

πανταχῇ, everywhere

πολυμερής, -ές, consisting of many parts, manifold

στολίζω, to dress, adorn, decorate

χάρτης, -ου, ὁ, roll of papyrus

χρυσός, ὁ, gold, gold coin

LINES 318–326

φίλτρον πότιμον· λαβὼν (τοὺς) σφηκαλέοντας τοὺς (caught) ἐν τῇ ἀράχνῃ,
λειώσας (them, sprinkle the powder) ἐπὶ ποτόν (καὶ) δὸς (to the appropriate person) πεῖν.[37] (Spell) ἐὰν θέλῃς γυναῖκάς (σου) μὴ σχεθῆναι[38] ὑπὸ ἄλλου ἀνδρός·
λαβὼν γῆν πλάσον (a molded figure in the shape of a) κορκόδειλον προσμείξας
αὐτῷ μέλαν καὶ ζμύρναν καὶ θὲς εἰς σόριον μολιβοῦν καὶ ἐπίγραφε (it) τὸ μέγα
ὄνομα καὶ τὸ (ὄνομα) τῆς γυναικὸς (σου) καὶ (ἐπίγραφε) ὅτι· Μὴ συγγενέσθω ἡ
δεῖνα ἑτέρῳ ἀνδρὶ πλὴν ἐμοῦ, τοῦ δεῖνος. ἔστι δὲ τὸ ὄνομα τὸ ἐπιγραφόμενον
εἰς τοὺς πόδας τοῦ ζῳδίου· ΒΙΒΙΟΥ ΟΥΗΡ ΑΨΑΒΑΡΑ ΚΑΣΟΝΝΑΚΑ ΝΕΣΕΒΑΧ
ΣΦΗ ΧΦΟΥΡΙΣ.

Vocabulary

ἀράχνη, ἡ, spider's web

ζμύρνη/σμύρνα, ἡ, myrrh (gum from an Arabian tree used for embalming the
    dead, as incense, and as a salve)

ζῴδιον, τό, molded figure

---

[37] The expected benefit of this procedure is clear if φίλτρον means "love potion."

[38] σχεθῆναι, s.v. ἔχω, aor. pass. inf. "to be (sexually) had."

κορκόδειλος (> κροκόδιλος), crocodile
λειόω (= λεαίνω), pound in a mortar, grind up
μέλαν, -ανος, τό, ink
μολιβοῦς, -ης, -οῦν (adj.), leaden, made of lead
πότιμος, -ον, drinkable, for drinking
ποτόν, τό, drink
προσμείγνυμι, mix in
σόριον, τό, small coffin
συγγίνομαι, pf. συγγεγένημαι, associate with (w. dat.); mingle with, have sexual
    intercourse with; be a companion
σφηκαλέων, -οντος, ό, lion wasp
φίλτρον, τό, love potion

LINES 327–333

(Spell for) ἄνοιξις (doors) διὰ τοῦ ὀνόματος· Ἄνοιγε, ἄνοιγε, τὰ δ᾽ μέρη[39] τοῦ κόσμου, ὅτι ὁ κύριος τῆς οἰκουμένης ἐκπορεύεται. χαίρουσιν ἀρχάγγελοι δεκανῶν, ἀγγέλων· Αὐτὸς γὰρ ὁ Αἰὼν Αἰῶνος, ὁ μόνος καὶ ὑπερέχων, ἀθεώρητος διαπορεύεται τὸν τόπον. ἀνοίγου,[40] θύρα, ἄκουε, μοχλέ, εἰς δύο γενοῦ, κλειδών. διὰ τὸ ὄνομα ΑΙΑ ΑΙΝΡΥΧΑΘ, ἀνάβαλε, γῆ, δεσπότῃ, πάντα, ὅσα ἔχεις ἐν σεαυτῇ· Αὐτὸς γάρ ἐστιν ὁ λαιλαφέτης καὶ χανοῦχος, πυρὸς κρατύντωρ. ἄνοιξον· λέγει σοι. λέγει ΑΧΕΒΥΧΡΩΜ ὀκτάκις· (It is) Ἡλίου ὄνομα.

Vocabulary
ἀθεώρητος, -ον, invisible
ἀναβάλλω, cast up, throw up
ἄνοιξις, -εως, ἡ, opening (of gates and doors)
δεκανοί, οἱ, *decans*, the thirty-six divinities that preside over ten degrees of the
    Zodiac
διαπορεύομαι, pass/go through
θύρα, ἡ, door, doorway (of a house); entrance (of cave/tomb); ἐπὶ θύραις, lit. "at
    the doors" (i.e., impending)
κλειδόω, lock up
κρατύντωρ, -ορος, ὁ, ruler, master
λαιλαφέτης, ἡ, sender of storms
μοχλός, ὁ, bar (placed across a door to lock it)
ὑπερέχω, be of more value, better than; excel; ptc. subst. great value; rise above;
    transcend

---

[39] I.e., four quarters.
[40] Cf. table 9.3.4(a).

χανοῦχος, ὁ, controller of the abyss

LINES 333–343

Ἄλλως ὁ λόγος[41] πρὸς τὸν Ἥλιον· Ἐγώ εἰμι ὁ ἐπὶ τῶν δύο χερουβείν, ἀνὰ μέσον τοῦ κόσμου, (between) οὐρανοῦ καὶ γῆς, φωτὸς καὶ σκότους, νυκτὸς καὶ ἡμέρας, ποταμῶν καὶ θαλάσσης, φάνηθί μοι, ἀρχάγγελε τοῦ θεοῦ, ὁ ὑπ᾽ αὐτὸν τὸν ἕνα καὶ μόνον τεταγμένος.

τούτῳ δὲ τῷ λόγῳ ποίει πρὸς τὸν Ἥλιον χαριτήσια, (including) ἀγωγάς, ὀνειροπομπά, ὀνειραιτητά, Ἡλίου δεῖξιν, ἐπιτευκτικά, νικητικά, καὶ (indeed) πάντα ἁπλῶς. ἀπέχεις τὴν ἱεράν,[42] ὦ τέκνον, καὶ μακάριδα Μονάδα βίβλον, ἣν οὐδεὶς (until now) ἴσχυσε μεθερμηνεῦσαι ἢ πρᾶξαι. ἔρρωσο,[43] τέκνον.

Vocabulary
ἀνεύρετος, -ον, undiscovered, not found; ἀνεύρετον ποίησον, lit. "make undiscov-
    ered," i.e., dispose of, hide
ἀπέχω, receive; receive a payment; mid. stay away from
ἁπλῶς, sincerely, with integrity; absolutely; generally
ἐπιτευκτικόν, τό, spell for securing success
μεθερμηνεύω, translate
ὀνειροπομπόν, τό, the sending of dreams (to somebody) (cf. *l.* 339)
μάκαρ, -άριδος (m./fm.), blessed (cf. *l.* 341)
Μονάδα > μοναδικόν, s.v. μοναδικός, -ή, -όν, unique; here "Unique" is the name of
    the magical handbook
νικητικόν, τό, spell for securing victory
ὀνειραιτητόν, τό, spell for obtaining revelations in dreams
χαριτήσιον, τό, spell for winning favor

---

[41] λόγος, "spell" (cf. *l.* 339).
[42] ἱεράν…καὶ μακάριδα…βίβλον.
[43] S.v. ῥώννυμι.

5.5.

Book of Acts: Shipwrecked on the Island of Malta

(Acts 27:1–28:1)

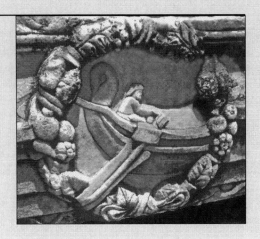

As the story begins, Paul is under house arrest in Caesarea Maritima, during which time he appeared before King Herod Agrippa I, governor of Judea, and Porcius Festus, procurator of Palestine.

PAUL SETS SAIL FOR ROME – ACTS 27:1–28:1

27:1 Ὡς δὲ ἐκρίθη τοῦ ἀποπλεῖν[1] ἡμᾶς[2] εἰς τὴν Ἰταλίαν, (Agrippa and Porcius) παρεδίδουν[3] τόν τε Παῦλον καί τινας ἑτέρους δεσμώτας ἑκατοντάρχῃ ὀνόματι Ἰουλίῳ[4] σπείρης Σεβαστῆς. 2 ἐπιβάντες δὲ πλοίῳ Ἀδραμυττηνῷ μέλλοντι πλεῖν εἰς[5] τοὺς κατὰ[6] τὴν Ἀσίαν τόπους, ἀνήχθημεν ὄντος[7] σὺν ἡμῖν Ἀριστάρχου[8] Μακεδόνος Θεσσαλονικέως.

Vocabulary
Ἀδραμυττηνός, -ή, -όν, of Adramyttium (adj. pertaining to the ancient city of Adramyttium, Mysia, northwest Asia Minor (cf. Fig. 3)
ἀποπλέω, sail away

---

[1] Art. inf. (cf. IV, 2).
[2] This story is told primarily in 1st pers. pl. (cf. Acts 27:1–8, 15–16, 18, 20, 26, 29, 37).
[3] παρεδίδουν > παρεδίδοσαν, 3rd pl. impers.
[4] Julius (cf. Acts 27:3).
[5] εἰς τοὺς...τόπους.
[6] κατὰ τὴν Ἀσίαν, "along (the coast of) Asia."
[7] ὄντος... Ἀριστάχου..., gen. absol.
[8] Aristarchus (cf. Acts 19:29).

FIG. 10. Relief of a man holding the tiller of a small boat, ancient Corinth (photo: author).

Ἀσία, ἡ, Roman province of Asia
δεσμώτης, ὁ, prisoner
ἑκατοντάρχης, ὁ, centurion
ἐπιβαίνω, set foot on, walk on; get upon, mount upon; embark in a ship (dat.)
Θεσσαλονικεύς, -έως, ὁ, Thessalonian
κρίνω, judge, reach a decision, decide; pass. be decided
Μακεδών, -όνος, ὁ, Macedonian person
παραδίδωμι, hand over to another, transmit
πλέω, inf. πλεῖν, 3. ἔπλευσα: sail, travel by ship
Σεβαστός, -ή, -όν, Augustan (adj.); Σεβαστός, for Lat. Augustus
σπεῖρα, ἡ, cohort of soldiers (one-tenth part of a legion, normally 600 men)

27:3 τῇ τε ἑτέρᾳ (ἡμέρᾳ)[9] κατήχθημεν εἰς Σιδῶνα, φιλανθρώπως τε ὁ Ἰούλιος τῷ Παύλῳ χρησάμενος ἐπέτρεψεν πρὸς (his) τοὺς φίλους (Παύλῳ) πορευθέντι ἐπιμελείας τυχεῖν. 4 κἀκεῖθεν[10] ἀναχθέντες ὑπεπλεύσαμεν τὴν Κύπρον διὰ τὸ τοὺς ἀνέμους εἶναι[11] ἐναντίους, 5 τό τε πέλαγος τὸ κατὰ[12] τὴν Κιλικίαν καὶ Παμφυλίαν διαπλεύσαντες κατήλθομεν εἰς Μύρα τῆς Λυκίας.

Vocabulary
διαπλέω, 3. διέπλευσα: sail through/across
ἐπιμέλεια, ἡ, care, attention; responsibility
ἐπιτρέπω, allow somebody (dat.) to do something (inf.), permit; tolerate, put up with; pass. be entrusted as a legal guarantor
κατέρχομαι, 4. κατελήλυθα: go down; derive from, descend from; put into port
Κιλικία, ἡ, province of Cilicia
Κύπρος, ἡ, Cyprus
Λυκία, ἡ, Lykia
Μύρα, coastal city of Lykia, Asia Minor
Παμφιλία, ἡ, Pampylia, Roman province in the south of Asia Minor
πέλαγος, ὁ, open sea
Σιδών, -ῶνος, ἡ, Sidon
τυγχάνω, pres. fm. ptc. τυχοῦσα, [2]aor. ἔτυχον, [2]aor. 3rd sg. subj. τήχῃ, inf. τυχεῖν, pf. ptc. τετ(ε)υχώς: to gain, experience; happen, turn out (as a result); happen to be; gain/receive something (gen.), attain to (ἐπί); obtain one's request (w. gen.); ἔτυχεν δέ, "and it came to pass that (w. acc.)"; adj. ptc. ordinary, everyday
ὑποπλέω, 3. ὑπέλευσα: sail under the protective shelter of (acc.)

---

[9] τῇ ἑτέρᾳ ἡμέρᾳ, means "on the day after tomorrow," "on the third day."
[10] κἀκεῖθεν > καὶ ἐκεῖθεν.
[11] Causal art. inf. ("because," cf. IV, 1.4).
[12] κατά, "along the coast of" (cf. Acts 27:2).

φιλάνθρωπος, -ον, humane; τὰ φιλάνθρωπα, humane concessions (technical term for privileges given to ethnic communities); adv. φιλανθρώπως, humanely, kindly

φίλος, -η, -ον, beloved, pleasant; pleasing, popular; subst. friend

27:6 Κἀκεῖ[13] εὑρὼν ὁ ἑκατοντάρχης πλοῖον Ἀλεξανδρῖνον πλέον[14] εἰς τὴν Ἰταλίαν ἐνεβίβασεν ἡμᾶς εἰς αὐτό. 7 ἐν ἱκαναῖς δὲ ἡμέραις βραδυπλοοῦντες καὶ μόλις γενόμενοι κατὰ[15] τὴν Κνίδον, μὴ προσεῶντος[16] ἡμᾶς τοῦ ἀνέμου ὑπεπλεύσαμεν τὴν Κρήτην κατὰ[17] Σαλμώνην, 8 μόλις τε παραλεγόμενοι αὐτὴν ἤλθομεν εἰς τόπον τινὰ καλούμενον Καλοὺς λιμένας ᾧ ἐγγὺς[18] πόλις ἦν Λασαία.

Vocabulary

Ἀλεξανδρῖνος, -η, -ον, Alexandrian (i.e., from the Egyptian city of Alexandria)
βραδυπλοέω, sail slowly, make little headway
ἐμβιβάζω, put (somebody/something) on board a ship
Ἰταλία, ἡ, Italy
Καλοὶ λιμένες, Fair Havens, a bay on the south coast of Crete, a major bunkering spot for ships in the southern Mediterranean
Κνίδος, ἡ, Knidus, peninsular city on the coast of Karia
Κρήτη, ἡ, Crete
Λασαία, ἡ, Lasea, city on the south coast of Crete
νῆσος, ἡ, island
παραλέγομαι (w. acc.), sail past
προσεάω, allow to proceed
Σαλαμώνη, ἡ, Salmone, a promontory on the northeast corner of Crete
ὑποπλέω, 3. ὑπέλευσα: sail under the protective shelter of (acc.)

27:9 Ἱκανοῦ δὲ χρόνου διαγενομένου[19] καὶ ὄντος[20] ἤδη ἐπισφαλοῦς τοῦ πλοὸς διὰ τὸ καὶ τὴν νηστείαν ἤδη παρεληλυθέναι[21] παρήνει[22] ὁ Παῦλος 10 λέγων αὐτοῖς· ἄνδρες, θεωρῶ ὅτι[23] μετὰ ὕβρεως καὶ πολλῆς ζημίας οὐ μόνον τοῦ φορτίου καὶ τοῦ

---

[13] κἀκεῖ > καὶ ἐκεῖ.
[14] Ptc. of πλέω.
[15] κατά, "off (the coast of)."
[16] Gen. absol. (cf. IV, 9).
[17] "Off of."
[18] In later Hellenistic writers ἐγγύς frequently takes dative case.
[19] Gen. absol.
[20] Gen. absol.
[21] Art. inf. cstr; the Day of Atonement fell on 10 Tishri, which corresponds to late September or early October. Sailing was deemed to be unsafe after 15 September and ceased altogether after 11 November.
[22] Either conat. or incept. impf. (s.v. παραινέω) (cf. IV, 14.4–5).
[23] θεωρῶ ὅτι + acc. + inf. (μέλλειν ἔσεσθαι).

πλοίου ἀλλὰ καὶ τῶν ψυχῶν ἡμῶν μέλλειν ἔσεσθαι[24] (accompanied) τὸν πλοῦν. 11 ὁ δὲ ἑκατοντάρχης τῷ κυβερνήτῃ καὶ τῷ ναυκλήρῳ μᾶλλον[25] ἐπείθετο[26] ἢ τοῖς ὑπὸ Παύλου λεγομένοις. 12 ἀνευθέτου δὲ τοῦ λιμένος ὑπάρχοντος[27] πρὸς παραχειμασίαν οἱ πλείονες ἔθεντο βουλὴν ἀναχθῆναι ἐκεῖθεν, εἴ πως δύναιντο[28] καταντήσαντες εἰς Φοίνικα παραχειμάσαι (there) λιμένα[29] τῆς Κρήτης βλέποντα κατὰ[30] λίβα καὶ κατὰ χῶρον.

Vocabulary
ἀνεύθετος, -ον, unsuitable
βουλή, ἡ, plan, decision; τίθημι βουλήν, reach a decision, decide; City Council (βουλή) (which was subordinate to the ἐκκλησία [Assembly]); will (of God)
διαγίνομαι, pass, elapse (of time)
ἐπισφαλής, -ές, unsafe, dangerous
κυβερνήτης, ὁ, shipmaster (who is responsible for the crew), captain
λιμήν, -μένος, ὁ, harbor
λίψ, λιβός, ὁ, southwest
ναύκληρος, ὁ, owner of a ship or one who charters a ship
νηστεία, ἡ, day of fasting, esp. the Day of Atonement
παραινέω, urge somebody (dat.)
παραχειμάζω, to winter (in a place)
παραχειμσία, ἡ, wintering, harboring during the winter
πλόος, (contr.) πλοῦς, ὁ, πλοός (gen.), πλοῦν (acc.), sailing, voyage; voyage (of life)
Φοῖνιξ, -ικος, ὁ, Phoinix, a seaport on the south coast of Crete
φορτίον, τό, a load, cargo; burden
χῶρος, ὁ, northwest

THE STORM AT SEA

27:13 Ὑποπνεύσαντος[31] δὲ νότου δόξαντες[32] τῆς προθέσεως κεκρατηκέναι, ἄραντες[33] (anchor) ἆσσον παρελέγοντο τὴν Κρήτην. 14 μετ' οὐ πολὺ (time) δὲ ἔβαλεν

---

[24] Fut. inf.
[25] μᾶλλον ... ἤ, "more ... [verb] ... than."
[26] S.v. πείθω.
[27] Gen. absol. (causal) (cf. IV, 9).
[28] Table 9.2.3(b).
[29] εἰς Φοίνικα...λιμένα τῆς Κρήτης.
[30] βλέπω κατά, "to face."
[31] Gen. absol. (inceptive aor.).
[32] S.v. δοκέω.
[33] S.v. αἴρω.

κατ᾽[34] αὐτῆς[35] ἄνεμος τυφωνικὸς ὁ καλούμενος εὐρακύλων· 15 συναρπασθέντος[36] (by it) δὲ τοῦ πλοίου καὶ μὴ δυναμένου ἀντοφθαλμεῖν τῷ ἀνέμῳ ἐπιδόντες ἐφερόμεθα[37] (by it).

Vocabulary
ἄνεμος, ὁ, wind
ἀντοφθαλμέω (w. dat.), to face (the wind), hold one's own against
ἆσσον, nearer
εὐφρακύλων, -ωνος, ὁ, Euraquilo, the "North-Easter"
νότος, ὁ, south wind
παραλέγομαι (w. acc.), sail past
συναρπάζω, seize and carry off, be caught up by
τυφωνικός, -ή, -όν, like a hurricane
ὑποπνέω, blow gently

27:16 Νησίον[38] δέ τι ὑποδραμόντες καλούμενον Καῦδα ἰσχύσαμεν μόλις περικρατεῖς γενέσθαι τῆς σκάφης, 17 ἣν ἄραντες, βοηθείαις ἐχρῶντο ὑποζωννύντες τὸ πλοῖον, φοβούμενοί τε μὴ εἰς τὴν Σύρτιν ἐκπέσωσιν, χαλάσαντες τὸ σκεῦος,[39] οὕτως ἐφέροντο (by the current). 18 σφοδρῶς δὲ χειμαζομένων[40] ἡμῶν τῇ ἑξῆς (ἡμέρᾳ) ἐκβολὴν (of cargo) ἐποιοῦντο[41] 19 καὶ τῇ τρίτῃ (ἡμέρᾳ) αὐτόχειρες τὴν σκευὴν τοῦ πλοίου ἔρριψαν. 20 μήτε[42] δὲ ἡλίου μήτε ἄστρων ἐπιφαινόντων[43] ἐπὶ πλείονας[44] ἡμέρας, χειμῶνός τε οὐκ ὀλίγου ἐπικειμένου[45] (us), λοιπὸν περιῃρεῖτο ἐλπὶς πᾶσα τοῦ σῴζεσθαι[46] ἡμᾶς.

Vocabulary
ἄστρον, τό, constellation of stars
αὐτόχειρ, -ος, with one's own hand(s)
βοήθεια, ἡ, help; reinforcing cables (nautical)[47]
ἐκβολή, ἡ, throwing overboard

---

[34] "Down from" (i.e., from the landward side).
[35] I.e., Crete.
[36] Two gen. absol. constructions.
[37] "Were being carried" (i.e., drifted).
[38] νησίον, τό, dim. of νῆσος.
[39] σκεῦος, here a "kedge" or "driving anchor," i.e., a light anchor, dropped at a distance from the boat used to haul (kedge) a boat into position.
[40] Gen. absol.
[41] Incept. impf. (cf. IV, 13.5).
[42] μήτε…μήτε… ("neither … nor …").
[43] Gen. absol. (cf. IV, 9).
[44] Comp. for positive, "many."
[45] Gen. absol.
[46] Art. inf. (cf. IV, 2).
[47] The nautical term βοηθείαι refers to heavy cables that were passed under the ship's keel during bad weather to reinforce the hull (Casson, *Ships and Seamanship*, 91).

ἐκπίπτω, impf. pass. ἐξεπεμπόμην, 3. ἐξέπεσον: fall off; lose, forfeit; run off course, run aground; be issued/published (of a decree); resolve that (w. inf.); pass. come forth from

ἑξῆς (adv.), next, following; τὰ ἑξῆς, the following things; that which follows, the consequences

ἐπιφαίνω, ²aor. pass. ptc. ἐπιφανείς: show, appear; divinely manifest (of gods in visions and dreams)

ἰσχύω, be able/strong; defeat, overcome; prevail against (κατά); be valid, be in force; + inf., be able to, have the power to; subst., something strong; dissolution, breaking up

Καῦδα, Cauda (Clauda), small island off the south coast of Crete

νῆσος, ἡ, island; νησίον, τό, dim., small island

περιαιρέω, aor. inf. περιελεῖν, ptc. περιελών, impf. 3rd sg. περιῃρεῖτο: take away, remove; cut away (of anchors)

περικρατής, -ές, in control; γενέσθαι περικρατής, gain control

σκάφη, ἡ (Lat. loanw. *scapha*), skiff (ship's boat for towing)

Σύρτις, -εως, ἡ, Sytris, two treacherous sandbanks in the Gulf of Sytris off the Libyan coast, greatly feared by mariners

σφοδρῶς, violently

ὑποζώννυμι, undergird, brace

ὑποτρέχω, run under the protection/shelter of something

χαλάω, lower, let down

χειμάζομαι, be tossed/battered by a storm

χειμών, -ῶνος, ὁ, storm; winter

27:21 Πολλῆς τε ἀσιτίας ὑπαρχούσης[48] τότε σταθεὶς ὁ Παῦλος ἐν μέσῳ αὐτῶν εἶπεν· ἔδει[49] (ὑμᾶς) μέν, ὦ ἄνδρες, πειθαρχήσαντάς μοι μὴ ἀνάγεσθαι ἀπὸ τῆς Κρήτης κερδῆσαί τε τὴν ὕβριν ταύτην καὶ τὴν ζημίαν. 22 καὶ τὰ νῦν[50] παραινῶ ὑμᾶς εὐθυμεῖν· ἀποβολὴ γὰρ ψυχῆς οὐδεμία[51] ἔσται ἐξ ὑμῶν πλὴν τοῦ πλοίου. 23 παρέστη[52] γάρ μοι ταύτῃ (past) τῇ νυκτὶ τοῦ θεοῦ, οὗ εἰμι ἐγὼ ᾧ καὶ λατρεύω, ἄγγελος λέγων· 24 μὴ φοβοῦ, Παῦλε, Καίσαρί σε δεῖ παραστῆναι, καὶ ἰδοὺ κεχάρισταί σοι ὁ θεὸς πάντας τοὺς πλέοντας μετὰ σοῦ. 25 διὸ εὐθυμεῖτε, ἄνδρες· πιστεύω γὰρ τῷ θεῷ ὅτι οὕτως ἔσται καθ' ὃν τρόπον λελάληταί μοι. 26 εἰς νῆσον δέ τινα δεῖ ἡμᾶς ἐκπεσεῖν.

---

[48] Gen. absol.

[49] S.v. δεῖ (impf.), "(You) should have" + ptc.

[50] τὰ νῦν, "now."

[51] οὐδεμία functions as a negative adj. modifying ἀποβολή.

[52] The subject of the verb is ἄγγελος...τοῦ θεοῦ (disc. syn.).

Vocabulary

ἀποβολή, ἡ, loss

ἀσιτία, ἡ, going without food (here, probably owing to seasickness)

ἐκπίπτω, impf. pass. ἐξεπεμπόμην, 3. ἐξέπεσον: fall off; lose, forfeit; run off course, run aground; be issued/published (of a decree); resolve that (w. inf.); pass. come forth from

εὐθυμέω, cheer up, keep one's courage

Καῖσαρ, -αρος, ὁ, Caesar, emperor

παραινέω, urge somebody (w. dat.)

παρίστημι (also παριστάω), pf. ptc. παρεστώς: stand before (w. dat.); approach, come near; render, present, offer, supply; show

πειθαρχέω, obey somebody (dat.), follow somebody's (dat.) advice (dat.)

χαρίζομαι, impf. ἐχαριζόμην, 5. κεχάρισμαι: show a favor/kindness to somebody; freely grant, give, bestow favor upon somebody; be pleasing/beloved; pass. be given freely

27:27 Ὡς δὲ τεσσαρεσκαιδεκάτη νὺξ ἐγένετο διαφερομένων[53] ἡμῶν ἐν τῷ Ἀδρίᾳ (Sea), κατὰ μέσον τῆς νυκτὸς ὑπενόουν[54] οἱ ναῦται προσάγειν τινὰ αὐτοῖς χώραν.[55] 28 καὶ βολίσαντες εὗρον ὀργυιὰς εἴκοσι, βραχὺ δὲ διαστήσαντες καὶ πάλιν βολίσαντες εὗρον ὀργυιὰς δεκαπέντε· 29 φοβούμενοί τε μή που κατὰ[56] τραχεῖς τόπους ἐκπέσωμεν, ἐκ πρύμνης ῥίψαντες ἀγκύρας τέσσαρας ηὔχοντο ἡμέραν γενέσθαι. 30 Τῶν δὲ ναυτῶν ζητούντων[57] φυγεῖν ἐκ τοῦ πλοίου καὶ χαλασάντων τὴν σκάφην εἰς τὴν θάλασσαν προφάσει ὡς ἐκ πρῴρης ἀγκύρας μελλόντων[58] ἐκτείνειν, 31 εἶπεν ὁ Παῦλος τῷ ἑκατοντάρχῃ καὶ τοῖς στρατιώταις· ἐὰν μὴ οὗτοι μείνωσιν ἐν τῷ πλοίῳ, ὑμεῖς σωθῆναι οὐ δύνασθε. 32 τότε ἀπέκοψαν οἱ στρατιῶται τὰ σχοινία τῆς σκάφης καὶ εἴασαν αὐτὴν ἐκπεσεῖν.

Vocabulary

Ἀδρίας, -ου, ὁ, Adriatic Sea (between Crete and Sicily)

ἄγκυρα, ἡ, anchor

ἀποκόπτω, cut off/away; castrate

βολίζω, lit. "to heave the lead," take soundings (with a lead weight to determine the depth of the water)

βραχύς, -εῖα, -ύ, farther

διΐστημι, go farther

---

[53] Gen. absol.

[54] Incept. impf.

[55] τινὰ … χώραν (dis. syn.), χώρα in this context means "land," as opposed to sea.

[56] κατὰ w. acc., "onto," "against."

[57] Gen. absol.

[58] Gen. absol., taken with τῶν…ναυτῶν.

ἐάω, pres. mid. inf. ἐᾶσθαι, impf. εἴων, 2. ἐάσω, 3. εἴασα: allow, permit; leave, let
   go; mid. be left to oneself
ναύτης, ὁ, sailor
ὀργυιά, ἡ, fathom[59]
πού (enclit.), somewhere; perhaps, "I suppose"
προσάγω, bring to; put in; bring forward (committee business); intrans. come
   near, approach, draw near
πρόφασις, -εως, ἡ, motive, pretext, excuse; προφάσει ὡς, as a pretext, under the
   pretext
πρύμνα, stern (of a ship)
πρῷρα, ἡ, prow of a ship (opp. of πρύμνα)[60]
σκάφη, ἡ (Lat. loanw. *scapha*), skiff (ship's boat for towing)
σχοινίον, τό, rope
τεσσαρεσκαιδέκατος, -άτη, -ατον, fourteenth
στρατιώτης, ὁ, soldier
τραχύς, -εῖα, -ύ, rough, rocky
ὑπονοέω, surmise, suspect

27:33 Ἄχρι δὲ οὗ (χρόνου) ἡμέρα ἤμελλεν γίνεσθαι,[61] παρεκάλει ὁ Παῦλος
ἅπαντας μεταλαβεῖν τροφῆς λέγων· τεσσαρεσκαιδεκάτην[62] σήμερον (being) ἡμέραν
προσδοκῶντες ἄσιτοι διατελεῖτε μηθὲν προσλαβόμενοι. 34 διὸ παρακαλῶ ὑμᾶς
μεταλαβεῖν τροφῆς· τοῦτο γὰρ πρὸς[63] τῆς ὑμετέρας σωτηρίας ὑπάρχει, οὐδενὸς[64]
γὰρ ὑμῶν θρὶξ ἀπὸ τῆς κεφαλῆς ἀπολεῖται. 35 εἴπας δὲ ταῦτα καὶ λαβὼν
ἄρτον εὐχαρίστησεν τῷ θεῷ ἐνώπιον πάντων καὶ κλάσας ἤρξατο ἐσθίειν. 36
εὔθυμοι δὲ γενόμενοι πάντες καὶ αὐτοὶ προσελάβοντο τροφῆς.[65] 37 ἤμεθα δὲ αἱ
πᾶσαι ψυχαὶ ἐν τῷ πλοίῳ[66] διακόσιαι ἑβδομήκοντα ἕξ. 38 κορεσθέντες δὲ τροφῆς
ἐκούφιζον[67] τὸ πλοῖον ἐκβαλλόμενοι τὸν σῖτον εἰς τὴν θάλασσαν.

Vocabulary
ἄσιτος, -ον, without eating/good
διακόσιοι, -ίαι, -ία, two hundred
διατελέω, continue to do something
ἑβδομήκοντα, seventy

---

[59] 1 fathom = distance between an average person's outstretched hands (ca. 1.85 meters).
[60] I.e., the forwardmost part of a ship's bow that cuts through the water.
[61] I.e., "to dawn."
[62] τεσσαρεσκαιδεκάτην...ἡμέραν (cf. Acts 27:27).
[63] πρός (w. gen.), "for."
[64] κεφαλῆς...οὐδενός.
[65] Partitive gen. ("some of ...").
[66] ἐν τῷ πλοίῳ, "on board."
[67] Incept. impf. (cf. IV, 13.5).

εὔθυμος, -ον, cheerful
θρίξ, τριχός (gen.), ἡ, hair
κλάω, 6. ἐκλάσθην: break, break off; pass. be damaged
κορέννυμι (w. gen.), 6. ἐκορέσθην: pass. be satiated, have enough of
κουφίζω, to lighten
μεταλαμβάνω, take/eat (some food)
προσδοκάω (Ion. –έω), wait in suspense; anticipate
προλαμβάνω, take something on one's own; anticipate
σῖτος, ὁ, wheat
ὑμέτερος, -α, -ον, your

SHIPWRECKED ON THE ISLAND OF MALTA

27:39 Ὅτε δὲ ἡμέρα ἐγένετο, τὴν γῆν οὐκ ἐπεγίνωσκον, κόλπον δέ τινα κατενόουν ἔχοντα αἰγιαλὸν εἰς ὃν ἐβουλεύοντο εἰ δύναιντο[68] ἐξῶσαι τὸ πλοῖον. 40 καὶ τὰς ἀγκύρας περιελόντες εἴων[69] (them) εἰς τὴν θάλασσαν, ἅμα ἀνέντες τὰς ζευκτηρίας τῶν πηδαλίων καὶ ἐπάραντες[70] τὸν ἀρτέμωνα τῇ πνεούσῃ (αὔρᾳ) κατεῖχον εἰς τὸν αἰγιαλόν. 41 περιπεσόντες δὲ εἰς τόπον διθάλασσον ἐπέκειλαν τὴν ναῦν καὶ ἡ μὲν[71] πρῷρα ἐρείσασα ἔμεινεν ἀσάλευτος, ἡ δὲ πρύμνα ἐλύετο[72] ὑπὸ τῆς βίας τῶν κυμάτων.

Vocabulary
αἰγιαλός, ὁ, beach
ἄγκυρα, ἡ, anchor
ἀνίημι, [2]aor. ἀνῆκα: loosen, unfasten
ἀρτέμων, -ωνος, ὁ, bowspritsail[73]
ἀσάλευτος, -ον, immovable
αὔρα, ἡ, breeze
βία, ἡ, strength, force
διθάλλασος, -ον, with the sea on both sides, where two seas meet
ἐξωθέω, run a boat ashore, to beach
ἐπικέλλω, run a ship aground

---

[68] Cf. table 9.2.3(b).
[69] S.v. ἐάω.
[70] S.v. ἐπαίρω.
[71] μέν...δέ..., "indeed ... but ...," "while ... yet ..."
[72] Incep. impf.
[73] The "bowspritsail" is so named because it is attached to the "bowsprit," the pole that extends forward from a boat's prow.

ἐρείδω, become jammed
ζευκτηρία, ἡ, pl. pennants[74]
κόλπος, ὁ, bay
ναῦς, ἡ, ναός (gen., Att. νεώς), ναῦν (acc.), ship
περιαιρέω, 3. περιεῖλον: slip anchor, cast off an anchor
περιπίπτω, strike (ground)
πηδάλιον, τό, steering oar
πρύμνα, stern (of a ship)
πρῷρα, ἡ, prow of a ship

27:42 Τῶν δὲ στρατιωτῶν βουλὴ ἐγένετο ἵνα[75] τοὺς δεσμώτας ἀποκτείνωσιν, μή τις (of them) ἐκκολυμβήσας διαφύγῃ. 43 ὁ δὲ ἑκατοντάρχης βουλόμενος διασῶσαι τὸν Παῦλον ἐκώλυσεν αὐτοὺς τοῦ (their) βουλήματος, ἐκέλευσέν τε τοὺς δυναμένους κολυμβᾶν ἀπορίψαντας πρώτους ἐπὶ τὴν γῆν ἐξιέναι 44 καὶ τοὺς λοιποὺς (should follow) οὓς μὲν[76] ἐπὶ σανίσιν, οὓς δὲ ἐπί τινων (parts) τῶν ἀπὸ τοῦ πλοίου. καὶ οὕτως ἐγένετο πάντας διασωθῆναι ἐπὶ τὴν γῆν. 28:1 καὶ διασωθέντες τότε ἐπέγνωμεν ὅτι Μελίτη ἡ νῆσος καλεῖται.

Vocabulary
ἀπορίπτω, jump overboard
βούλημα, τό, intention
διασῴζω, bring safely through, convey to safety
διαφεύγω, escape
ἐκκολυμβάω, swim away
ἔξειμι (fr. εἶμι), inf. ἐξιέναι, ptc. ἐξιών, -οῦσα, -όν: go out, leave, depart from a place
κολυμβάω, swim
Μελίτη, ἡ, Melite (mod. Malta), an island south of Sicily
σανίς, -ίδος, ἡ, plank

SELECT BIBLIOGRAPHY

Casson, Lionel. *Ships and Seamanship in the Ancient World*. Baltimore: Johns Hopkins University Press, 1971.

---

[74] Owing to the weight of the two "steering oars" (πηδάλιοι), so-called pennants (ζευκτηρίαι), or rudder ropes, fitted with tackles, were used to lift the oars when a ship was at anchor to prevent the oars from moving and banging together. Pennants were also used to connect the two steering oars to each other, allowing the helmsman to use both oars at the same time (Casson, *Ships and Seamanship*, 228, n. 16).
[75] Explanatory ἵνα ("that").
[76] οἱ μέν...οἱ δέ, "some ... others...."

5.6.

Epistle of Barnabas: A Typological Interpretation of the Levitical Scapegoat

(Barn. 7:1–11)

Provenance: Syria or Alexandria.

Date: 100–120 CE.

Text: Ehrman, I, 340–409.

Typological interpretation was widely practiced in Alexandria, as well as by Paul himself (§§4.11, 4.13). The Epistle of Barnabas also engages in typological interpretation, drawing a direct connection between the Levitical "scapegoat" and the death of Christ. Its author describes the corporate sin of the people as a curse, the force of which was removed by its transfer to the scapegoat, Christ.

It is worthy of note that the account of the Levitical scapegoat in Barn. 7 passes on three points of information about the scapegoat ritual that are absent from Lev 16:20–28 but are corroborated in the Mishnah: the mistreatment of the goat (*Yoma* 6.4), the scarlet thread around the scapegoat's horns (*Yoma* 6.6), and the emphasis on the equality of the two goats (*Yoma* 6.1). Barnabas also passes on the Mishnaic tradition that the purification goat (i.e., "inside" goat; Lev 16:5, 7–11, 15) was eaten by the priests (*Menahoth* 11.7).

CULTURAL BACKGROUND

Life in the ancient Mediterranean world was governed by many taboos and sacred laws that were connected with issues of purity and ritual pollution (μίασμα).

FIG. 11. Panel relief on sarcophagus (Istanbul Archaeological Museum) (photo: author).

In some cases, contact with such defilement was unavoidable, as in the case of familial burial, disease, childbirth, and menstruation. But ritual pollution could also result from the willful transgression of sacred laws. Such ritual pollution would contaminate society as a curse unless an apotropaic (ἀποτρόπαιος) victim or "scapegoat" was provided, upon which it could be discharged.[1] To address this need, a great variety of apotropaic victims were employed in the ancient world, including the Levitical scapegoat (Lev 16), the Gedarene demoniac of the Synoptic Gospels, and many others.[2]

Related Texts: The typological use of the scapegoat bears a strong resemblance to Paul's apotropaic language in Gal 3:1–14 (§4.15).

7:1 Οὐκοῦν νοεῖτε, τέκνα εὐφροσύνης, ὅτι πάντα ὁ καλὸς κύριος προεφανέρωσεν ἡμῖν, ἵνα γνῶμεν, ᾧ κατὰ πάντα εὐχαριστοῦντες ὀφείλομεν αἰνεῖν. 2 εἰ οὖν ὁ υἱὸς τοῦ θεοῦ, ὢν κύριος καὶ μέλλων κρίνειν ζῶντας καὶ νεκρούς, ἔπαθεν, ἵνα ἡ πληγὴ αὐτοῦ ζωοποιήσῃ ἡμᾶς, πιστεύσωμεν[3] ὅτι ὁ υἱὸς τοῦ θεοῦ οὐκ ἠδήνατο[4] παθεῖν εἰ μὴ δι᾽ ἡμᾶς. 3 ἀλλὰ καὶ σταυρωθεὶς ἐποτίζετο ὄξει καὶ χολῇ. ἀκούσατε, πῶς περὶ τούτου πεφανέρωκαν οἱ ἱερεῖς τοῦ ναοῦ. γεγραμμένης ἐντολῆς·[5] Ὃς ἂν μὴ νηστεύσῃ τὴν νηστείαν, θανάτῳ ἐξολεθρευθήσεται (Lev 23:29), ἐνετείλατο κύριος, ἐπεὶ καὶ αὐτὸς ὑπὲρ τῶν ἡμετέρων ἁμαρτιῶν ἔμελλεν τὸ σκεῦος τοῦ πνεύματος προσφέρειν θυσίαν,[6] ἵνα καὶ ὁ τύπος ὁ γενόμενος ἐπὶ[7] Ἰσαὰκ τοῦ προσενεχθέντος[8] ἐπὶ τὸ θυσιαστήριον τελεσθῇ.

Vocabulary
αἰνέω, to praise
ἄπλυτος, -ον, unwashed
ἔντερον, τό, entrails
ἐξολεθρεύω, utterly destroy, put to death
εὐφροσύνη, ἡ, joy, cheerfulness
ζωοποιέω, give life to, make alive
ἡμέτερος, -α, -ον, our
θυσία, ἡ, sacrifice
θυσιαστήριον, τό, altar of burnt offerings (in the forecourt of the Jerusalem temple)

---

[1] Robert Parker, *Miasmus: Pollution and Purification in Early Greek Religion* (Oxford: Clarendon, 1983), 191; cf. Ἀποτρόπαιος, "one who averts evil" (Philostr. *VA* 8.7.9[415] [§8.1]).

[2] Mark 5:1–14/Matt 8:28–34/Luke 8:26–39; cf. B. H. McLean, *The Cursed Christ: Mediterranean Expulsion Rituals and Pauline Soteriology* (Sheffield: JSOT Press, 1996), 65–104.

[3] Hort. subj. (cf. IV, 12).

[4] S.v. δύναμαι, impf. ἠδηνάμην.

[5] Gen. absol. (cf. IV, 9).

[6] Acc. of spec.

[7] "In (Isaac)."

[8] S.v. προσφέρω; ἐπὶ Ἰσαὰκ τοῦ προσενεχθέντος = ἐπὶ **τοῦ** Ἰσαὰκ **τοῦ** προσενεχθέντος.

ἱερεύς, -έως, ὁ, priest
νηστεία, ἡ, day of fasting, esp. the Day of Atonement
νοέω (w. acc.), aor. pass. ptc. νοηθείς: perceive, understand (that); mid. bear in mind, think; pass. be thought of, be perceived
ὄξος, -ους, τό, vinegar (cf. Barn. 7:4)
οὐκοῦν, therefore (cf. Barn. 7:10)
ὀφείλω (and –έω), 2. ὀφειλήσω, 3. ὠφείλησα: owe somebody something, be indebted to; must (w. inf.); ἁμαρτίαν ὀφείλω (w. dat.), incur sin against
προφανερόω, reveal beforehand
φοβερός, -ά, -όν, terrible, horrifying, dreadful
χολή, ἡ, gall, bile

7:4 τί οὖν (God) λέγει ἐν τῷ προφήτῃ; Καὶ φαγέτωσαν ἐκ τοῦ τράγου τοῦ προσφερομένου τῇ νηστείᾳ ὑπὲρ πασῶν τῶν ἁμαρτιῶν. προσέχετε ἀκριβῶς· Καὶ φαγέτωσαν οἱ ἱερεῖς μόνοι πάντες τὸ ἔντερον ἄπλυτον μετὰ ὄξους.⁹ 5 πρὸς τί;¹⁰ ἐπειδὴ ἐμὲ ὑπὲρ ἁμαρτιῶν μέλλοντα¹¹ τοῦ λαοῦ μου τοῦ καινοῦ¹² προσφέρειν τὴν σάρκα μου μέλλετε ποτίζειν (me) χολὴν μετὰ ὄξους, φάγετε ὑμεῖς μόνοι, τοῦ λαοῦ νηστεύοντος¹³ καὶ κοπτομένου¹⁴ ἐπὶ σάκκου καὶ σποδοῦ, ἵνα δείξῃ ὅτι δεῖ αὐτὸν παθεῖν ὑπ᾽ αὐτῶν. 6 ἃ ἐνετείλατο, προσέχετε· Λάβετε δύο τράγους καλοὺς καὶ ὁμοίους καὶ προσενέγκατε (them), καὶ λαβέτω ὁ ἱερεὺς τὸν ἕνα εἰς ὁλοκαύτωμα ὑπὲρ ἁμαρτιῶν (Lev 16:7, 9).

Vocabulary
κόπτω, 3. ἔκοψα: to cut, beat (one's breast); strike somebody, fight; mid. mourn
ὁλοκαύτωμα, τό, whole burnt offering
ὄξος, -ους, τό, vinegar
σάκκος, ὁ, sackcloth
σποδός, ἡ, ashes
τράγος, ὁ, goat
χολή, ἡ, gall, bile

7:7 (With) τὸν δὲ ἕνα τί ποιήσουσιν; Ἐπικατάρατος, φησίν, ὁ εἷς (Lev 16:8).¹⁵ προσέχετε, πῶς ὁ τύπος τοῦ Ἰησοῦ φανεροῦται. 8 Καὶ ἐμπτύσατε πάντες¹⁶ καὶ

---

⁹ Quoting an unknown source (cf. Lev 16).
¹⁰ πρὸς τί, "what is this?", "why?"
¹¹ ἐμέ...μέλλοντα, "when I am about to" + inf. (προσφέρειν).
¹² ὑπὲρ ἁμαρτιῶν...**τοῦ** λαοῦ μου **τοῦ** καινου.
¹³ Gen. absol.
¹⁴ Gen. absol.
¹⁵ Tertullian likewise referred to the Levitical scapegoat as "cursed." He interprets *both* the "scapegoat" and the "purification" goat as types of Christ (*Adversus Marcionem* 7.7).
¹⁶ πάντες + verb, "you all...."

κατακεντήσατε καὶ περίθετε[17] τὸ ἔριον τὸ κόκκινον περὶ τὴν κεφαλὴν αὐτοῦ, καὶ οὕτως εἰς ἔρημον βληθήτω[18] (Lev 16:10, 20–22). καὶ ὅταν γένηται οὕτως, ἄγει ὁ βαστάζων τὸν τράγον εἰς τὴν ἔρημον καὶ ἀφαιρεῖ τὸ ἔριον καὶ ἐπιτίθησιν αὐτὸ ἐπὶ φρύγανον τὸ λεγόμενον ῥαχήλ, οὗ καὶ τοὺς βλαστοὺς εἰώθαμεν[19] τρώγειν ἐν τῇ χώρᾳ εὑρίσκοντες. οὕτω μόνης τῆς ῥαχῆς οἱ καρποὶ γλυκεῖς εἰσίν. 9 τί οὖν τοῦτό ἐστιν;[20] προσέχετε· Τὸν μὲν ἕνα ἐπὶ τὸ θυσιαστήριον, τὸν δὲ ἕνα ἐπικατάρατον, καὶ ὅτι τὸν ἐπικατάρατον ἐστεφανωμένον. ἐπειδὴ ὄψονται αὐτὸν τότε τῇ ἡμέρᾳ τὸν ποδήρη ἔχοντα τὸν κόκκινον περὶ τὴν σάρκα καὶ ἐροῦσιν·[21] Οὐχ οὗτός ἐστιν, ὅν ποτε ἡμεῖς ἐσταυρώσαμεν ἐξουθενήσαντες[22] καὶ κατακεντήσαντες καὶ ἐμπτύσαντες; ἀληθῶς οὗτος ἦν, ὁ τότε λέγων ἑαυτὸν υἱὸν θεοῦ εἶναι.

Vocabulary

βλαστός, ὁ, bud, sprout

γλυκύς, -εῖα, -ύ, sweet; comp. γλυκερός, -ή, -ον

εἴωθα (pf. of obsol. pres. ἔθω; pf. w. pres. meaning): be accustomed to

ἐμπτύω, to spit (cf. Barn. 7:9)

ἐπιτίθημι, [2]aor. ptc. ἐπιθείς: lay/put something (acc.) on (ἐπί) somebody/something (acc.); give something (acc.) to somebody (dat.)

κατακεντέω, stab, goad (cf. Barn. 7:9)

κόκκινος, -η, -ον, scarlet, red; τὸ κόκκινον, scarlet cloth

ῥαχήλ, ἡ, blackberry

περιτίθημι, put around, wrap around

ποδήρης, -ες, long robe

στεφανόω, to crown; to honor; pass. be crowned with; be honored by (ὑπό) somebody for (some virtue [acc.]) with a crown (dat.)

τρώγω, eat

φρύγανον, τό, bush

7:10 πῶς γὰρ ὅμοιος ἐκείνῳ; εἰς τοῦτο ὁμοίους τοὺς τράγους, καλούς, ἴσους, ἵνα ὅταν ἴδωσιν αὐτὸν τότε ἐρχόμενον, ἐκπλαγῶσιν[23] ἐπὶ[24] τῇ ὁμοιότητι τοῦ τράγου. οὐκοῦν ἴδε τὸν τύπον τοῦ μέλλοντος πάσχειν Ἰησοῦ. 11 τί δέ, ὅτι[25] τὸ ἔριον εἰς μέσον τῶν ἀκανθῶν τιθέασιν; τύπος ἐστὶν τοῦ Ἰησοῦ τῇ ἐκκλησίᾳ κείμενος,

---

[17] S.v., περιτίθημι, cf. table 9.12.2(d).

[18] S.v. βάλλω.

[19] S.v. εἴωθα.

[20] τί οὖν τοῦτό ἐστιν; ("what therefore does this mean?").

[21] S.v. λέγω.

[22] ἐξουθενέω, s.v. ἐξουδενόω.

[23] S.v. ἐκπλήσσω.

[24] ἐπί, "at."

[25] τί δέ ὅτι, "but why (is it) that … ?"

ὅτι ὃς ἐὰν θέλῃ τὸ ἔριον ἆραι[26] τὸ κόκκινον,[27] δεῖ αὐτὸν πολλὰ παθεῖν διὰ τὸ εἶναι[28] φοβερὰν τὴν ἄκανθαν, καὶ θλιβέντα κυριεῦσαι αὐτοῦ. οὕτω, (Jesus) φησίν, οἱ θέλοντές με ἰδεῖν καὶ ἅψασθαί[29] μου τῆς βασιλείας ὀφείλουσιν θλιβέντες καὶ παθόντες λαβεῖν με.

Vocabulary

ἐκπλήσσω, impf. ἐξεπλησσόμην, 6. ἐξεπλάγην, aor. pass. ptc. πλαγείς: amaze; pass., be amazed

θλίβω, pf. pass. ptc. τεθλιμμένος: push; oppress, afflict; pass. be oppressed, experience pain

κεῖμαι, 2. κείσομαι: stand/be standing; recline; lie sick; lie buried; be appointed, established; subst. (τά) κείμενα, something established/existing

ὁμοιότης, -ητος, ἡ, state of being similar to something (gen.), likeness

φοβερός, -ά, -όν, terrible, horrifying, dreadful

---

[26] S.v. αἴρω.
[27] τὸ ἔριον...τὸ κόκκινον (disc. syn. [Y² hyp.]).
[28] Art. inf. expressing cause (IV, 2).
[29] S.v. ἅπτω.

5.7.

Martyrdom of Polycarp: The Glorification of Martyrdom

(Mart. Pol. 2, 15–18)

Polycarp (69–155 CE) was the bishop of Smyrna (mod. İzmir, Turkey). He was martyred for refusing to "swear by the fortune of Caesar," which is to say, for refusing to pay homage to the emperor's divine spirit. The following account of his martyrdom was written by Christians in Smyrna. This text exemplifies that glorification of martyrdom, which is evident in the second century CE. Martyrdom was promoted as the ideal means by which to secure an eternal reward in the heavenly kingdom.

Date: 249–251 CE, during the Decian persecution.

Text: Ehrman, II, 309–45.

2:1 Μακάρια μὲν οὖν καὶ γενναῖα (are) τὰ μαρτύρια πάντα τὰ κατὰ τὸ θέλημα τοῦ θεοῦ γεγονότα. δεῖ[1] γὰρ εὐλαβεστέρους ἡμᾶς ὑπάρχοντας τῷ θεῷ τὴν κατὰ πάντων ἐξουσία ἀνατιθέναι. 2 τὸ γὰρ γενναῖον αὐτῶν καὶ ὑπομονητικὸν καὶ φιλοδέσποτον τίς οὐκ ἂν θαυμάσειεν;[2]

Vocabulary

γενναῖος, -α, -ον, high-born; noble; subst., τὸ γενναῖον, nobility

ἐπιδείκνυμι/ἐπιδεικνύω, pres. mid. inf. ἐπιδείκνυσθαι, 3. ἐπέδειξα, [1]aor mid. ἐπεδειξάμην: to show, point out; discuss; prove that (ὅτι)

εὐλαβής, -ές, prudent; reverent, pious; comp. εὐλαβέστερος; adv. εὐλαβῶς, cautiously, piously keeping clean from

μαρτυρία, ἡ, evidence; martyrdom

μαρτύριον, τό, testimony, proof; martyrdom

---

[1] δεῖ…ὑμᾶς…ἀνατιθέναι.

[2] Cf. table 1.3(b).

ὑπομένω, remain, await, endure
ὑπομονητικός, -ή, -όν, showing endurance; subst., τὸ ὑπομονητικόν, endurance
φιλοδέσποτος, -ον, loving one's master; nt. subst. τὸ φιλοδέσποτον, love of one's
master

2:2 οἱ μάστιξιν[3] μὲν[4] καταξανθέντες,[5] ὥστε[6] μέχρι[7] τῶν ἔσω φλεβῶν καὶ ἀρτηριῶν
τὴν τῆς σαρκὸς οἰκονομίαν θεωρεῖσθαι, ὑπέμειναν,[8] ὡς[9] καὶ τοὺς περιεστῶτας
ἐλεεῖν καὶ ὀδύρεσθαι· τοὺς δὲ[10] καὶ εἰς τοσοῦτον γενναιότητος ἐλθεῖν,[11] ὥστε μήτε
γρύξαι μήτε στενάξαι τινὰ αὐτῶν, ἐπιδεικνυμένους ἅπασιν ἡμῖν, ὅτι ἐκείνῃ τῇ
ὥρᾳ βασανιζόμενοι[12] τῆς σαρκὸς ἀπεδήμουν οἱ μάρτυρες τοῦ Χριστοῦ, μᾶλλον
δέ, ὅτι παρεστὼς ὁ κύριος ὡμίλει αὐτοῖς.

Vocabulary
ἀποδημέω, travel abroad
ἀρτηρία, ἡ, artery
γενναιότης, -τητος, ὁ, nobility
γρύζω, complain, mutter
ἐλεέω, be merciful; feel pity; pass. be shown mercy
καταξαίνω, be torn to shreds
μάστιξ, -ιγος, ἡ (mostly pl.), lashes (of a whip)
ὀδύρομαι, wail, lament
οἰκονομία, ἡ, management of a household; economy; administration of an office;
    arrangement, structure (of parts), "anatomy"
ὁμιλέω, speak to (of Christ talking to martyrs)
περιίστημι, pf. stand around; subst. ptc. bystander
τοσοῦτος, -αύτη, -οῦτον, so much/great/large, etc.; pl. so many
ὑπομένω, remain, await; endure, stand one's ground, hold out; bear an ordeal,
    put up with
φλέψ, ἡ, φλεβός, vein

2:3 καὶ προσέχοντες τῇ τοῦ Χριστοῦ χάριτι τῶν κοσμικῶν κατεφρόνουν
βασάνων,[13] διὰ μιᾶς ὥρας τὴν αἰώνιον ζωὴν ἐξαγοραζόμενοι. καὶ τὸ πῦρ ἦν

---

[3] Dat. of means.
[4] μέν (postpos.) is coordinated with ὥστε and οἱ functions like a dem. pron. (οὗτοι) or pron. (αὐτοί).
[5] Concessive adv. ptc. (cf. IV, 1.5).
[6] ὥστε ("so that") w. inf. (cf. IV, 15).
[7] "As far as," "down to."
[8] Main verb of the sentence.
[9] Like ὥστε, ὡς ("while") can take the inf.
[10] τοὺς δέ (fr. οἱ δέ, "but they"); here acc. as subj. of inf.
[11] ἐλθεῖν...εἰς, "to come to (such nobility)," i.e., to "show, display (such nobility)."
[12] Temp. adv. ptc. ("while," cf. IV, 1.1).
[13] τῶν κοσμικῶν...βασάνων (dis. syn. [Y¹ hyp.]).

αὐτοῖς ψυχρὸν τὸ τῶν ἀπανθρώπων βασανιστῶν·[14] πρὸ ὀφθαλμῶν (αὐτῶν) γὰρ εἶχον φυγεῖν[15] τὸ αἰώνιον καὶ μηδέποτε σβεννύμενον, καὶ τοῖς τῆς καρδίας ὀφθαλμοῖς[16] ἀνέβλεπον τὰ τηρούμενα τοῖς ὑπομείνασιν ἀγαθά,[17] ἃ οὔτε οὖς ἤκουσεν[18] οὔτε ὀφθαλμὸς εἶδεν οὔτε ἐπὶ καρδίαν ἀνθρώπου ἀνέβη, ἐκείνοις δὲ ὑπεδείκνυτο ὑπὸ τοῦ κυρίου, οἵπερ μηκέτι ἄνθρωποι ἀλλ᾽ ἤδη ἄγγελοι ἦσαν.

Vocabulary
ἀναβλέπω, look up/above at (w. acc.); regain sight
ἀπάνθρωπος, -ον, inhuman
βασανιστής, ὁ, guard in a prison (frequently under orders to torture prisoners)
βάσανος, ἡ, torture, torment
εἴπερ, since; if really/indeed
ἐξαγοράζω, purchase something, to ransom
καταφρονέω, despise, treat with contempt
κοσμικός, -ή, -όν, earthly, worldly
ὅσπερ, ὅνπερ (acc.) / ἥπερ (fm.) / ὅπερ (nt.) / ἅπερ (nt. pl.): the very man/woman/thing(s); which indeed/exactly; ὅνπερ τρόπον, in the same way
σβέννυμι, 3. ἔσβεσα, aor. inf. σβέσαι: extinguish, put out (a fire); pass. be extinguished
ψυχρός, -ή, -όν, cold

2:4 ὁμοίως δὲ καὶ οἱ εἰς τὰ θηρία κατακριθέντες ὑπέμειναν δεινὰς κολάσεις, κήρυκας[19] μὲν ὑποστρωννύμενοι καὶ ἄλλαις ποικίλων βασάνων ἰδέαις κολαζόμενοι, ἵνα, εἰ δυνηθείη,[20] διὰ τῆς ἐπιμόνου κολάσεως εἰς ἄρνησιν αὐτοὺς τρέψῃ.

Vocabulary
ἄρνησις, ἡ, denial
ἐπίμονος, -ον, continuous
ἰδέα, ἡ, idea, kind, form
κατακρίνω, condemn; sentence somebody to do something
κῆρυξ, -υκος, ὁ, herald, public messenger; trumpet shell (seashell with sharp edges used in torture)
κολαφίζω, to slap
κόλασις, ἡ, punishment, torture

---

[14] τὸ πῦρ...τὸ τῶν ἀπανθρώπων βασανιστῶν (dis. syn. [Y² hyp.]).
[15] Gerundive inf., "escaping" (s.v. φεύγω).
[16] "With the eyes of the(ir) heart(s)."
[17] τὰ...ἀγαθά.
[18] ἀκούω + gen. When a gen. form follows the verb ἀκούω in Classical Greek, it often indicates the person or source of the sound, whereas the acc. case denotes the object or thing which is heard. However, in Hellenistic Greek these distinctions often became blurred.
[19] S.v. κῆρυξ.
[20] Aor. pass. opt., cf. table 9.3.3(b) ("if possible").

ποικίλος, -η, -ον, various, various kinds
τρέπω, 3. ἔτρεψα, aor. pass. inf. τραπῆναι: incline/turn somebody toward (εἰς); mid. turn/take oneself to (εἰς)
ὑποστρώννυμι, stretch/spread out on something

POLYCARP'S MARTYRDOM (15–18)

This section follows Polycarp's prayer, which ends with an "Amen."

15:1 Ἀναπέμψαντος δὲ αὐτοῦ[21] τὸ ἀμὴν καὶ πληρώσαντος τὴν εὐχήν, οἱ τοῦ πυρὸς ἄνθρωποι[22] ἐξῆψαν τὸ πῦρ. μεγάλης δὲ ἐκλαμψάσης φλογός,[23] θαῦμα εἴδομεν, οἷς ἰδεῖν ἐδόθη· οἳ καὶ[24] ἐτηρήθημεν εἰς τὸ ἀναγγεῖλαι[25] τοῖς λοιποῖς τὰ γενόμενα.

Vocabulary
ἀναπέμπω, send up
ἐκλάμπω, 2. ἐκλάμψω, 3. ἐξέλαμψα: blaze up; shine, beam forth
ἐξάπτω, 3. ἐξῆψα: light a fire
εὐχή, ἡ, prayer; vow, oath; εὐχῆς ἕνεκεν, in fulfillment of a vow
θαῦμα, τό, a wonder, amazing event
φλόξ, ἡ, φλογός, flame

15:2 τὸ γὰρ πῦρ καμάρας εἶδος ποιῆσαν, ὥσπερ ὀθόνη πλοίου ὑπὸ πνεύματος πληρουμένη, κύκλῳ περιετείχισεν τὸ σῶμα τοῦ μάρτυρος· καὶ ἦν μέσον[26] οὐχ ὡς σὰρξ καιομένη, ἀλλ' ὡς ἄρτος ὀπτώμενος ἢ ὡς χρυσὸς καὶ ἄργυρος ἐν καμίνῳ πυρούμενος. καὶ γὰρ εὐωδίας τοσαύτης ἀντελαβόμεθα ὡς λιβανωτοῦ πνέοντος ἢ ἄλλου τινὸς τῶν τιμίων ἀρωμάτων.

Vocabulary
ἄργυρος, ὁ, silver
ἄρωμα, -ματος, τό, spice; spices and aromatic oils (esp. used for embalming the dead)
εἶδος, -ους, τό, form, appearance
εὐωδία, ἡ, aroma, fragrance, perfume
καίω (Att. κάω), ἔκαυσα: light something, kindle a fire, to burn

---

[21] Gen. absol. (αὐτοῦ refers to Polycarp, cf. IV, 9).
[22] οἱ τοῦ πυρὸς ἄνθρωποι, i.e., men in charge of the fire.
[23] Gen. absol.; μεγάλης...φλογός.
[24] οἳ καί (see οἱ μέν above) functions like the pronoun αὐτοί, intensifying the implied subject of the verb ("we ourselves").
[25] Art. inf. w. εἰς (cf. IV, 2.1).
[26] Adv. nt. form (s.v. μέσος), "in the midst."

καμάρα, ἡ, arch
καμίνος, ἡ, furnace, oven
λιβανωτός, ὁ, frankincense
ὀθόνη, ἡ, sail
ὀπτάω, to bake
περιτειχίζω, surround with a wall
πνέω, 3. ἔπνευσα: to blow (of wind); subst. (ptc.), wind
πυρόω, burn with fire; heat to red hot: pass. be set on fire, be purified by fire (of metals)
τίμιος, -α, -ον, precious, valuable; superl. τιμιώτερος, -α, -ον, more precious
χρυσός, ὁ, gold, gold coin

16:1 Πέρας γοῦν ἰδόντες οἱ ἄνομοι μὴ δυνάμενον αὐτοῦ τὸ σῶμα ὑπὸ τοῦ πυρὸς δαπανηθῆναι, ἐκέλευσαν προσελθόντα αὐτῷ κομφέκτορα παραβῦσαι ξιφίδιον. καὶ τοῦτο (αὐτοῦ) ποιήσαντος, ἐξῆλθεν περιστερὰ καὶ πλῆθος αἵματος, ὥστε[27] κατασβέσαι τὸ πῦρ καὶ θαυμάσαι πάντα τὸν ὄχλον, εἰ τοσαύτη τις διαφορὰ μεταξὺ τῶν τε[28] ἀπίστων καὶ τῶν ἐκλεκτῶν·

Vocabulary
ἄπιστος, -ον, unbelieving, faithless; unbelievable; subst. unbelievers
γοῦν, thus, then; at any rate
δαπανάω, destroy, here "consume"
κατασβέννιμι, quench (a fire)
κομφέκτωρ, -τορα, ὁ, executioner (Lat. loanw.)
ξιφίδιον, τό, dagger
παραβύω, stab with (acc.)
πέρας, -ατος, τό, limit, end (of the earth), boundary; (adv.) πέρας, finally, in conclusion; as a result

16:2 ὧν εἷς[29] καὶ οὗτος[30] γεγόνει[31] ὁ θαυμασιώτατος μάρτυς Πολύκαρπος, ἐν τοῖς καθ᾽ ἡμᾶς[32] χρόνοις διδάσκαλος ἀποστολικὸς καὶ προφητικὸς γενόμενος, ἐπίσκοπός τε τῆς ἐν Σμύρνῃ καθολικῆς ἐκκλησίας. πᾶν γὰρ ῥῆμα, ὃ ἀφῆκεν ἐκ τοῦ στόματος αὐτοῦ, καὶ ἐτελειώθη καὶ τελειωθήσεται.

Vocabulary
ἀποστολικός, -ή, -όν, apostolic

---

[27] ὥστε w. inf. (cf. IV, 15).
[28] τε (postpos.)…καί….
[29] ὧν εἷς, "one of whom."
[30] οὗτος…ὁ θαυμασιώτατος Πολύκαρπος.
[31] Here γίνομαι functions as a substitute for εἰμί.
[32] καθ᾽ ἡμᾶς ("our").

ἐπίσκοπος, ὁ, bishop
καθολικός, -ή, -όν, universal
προφητικός, -ή, -όν, prophetic
Σμύρνα, -ης, Smyrna (mod. İzmir)

17:1 Ὁ δὲ ἀντίζηλος καὶ βάσκανος καὶ πονηρός, ὁ ἀντικείμενος τῷ γένει τῶν δικαίων, ἰδὼν τό τε μέγεθος αὐτοῦ τῆς μαρτυρίας καὶ τὴν ἀπ' ἀρχῆς ἀνεπίληπτον πολιτείαν, ἐστεφανωμένον τε τὸν τῆς ἀφθαρσίας στέφανον καὶ βραβεῖον ἀναντίρρητον ἀπενηνεγμένον,[33] ἐπετήδευσεν, ὡς μηδὲ τὸ σωμάτιον αὐτοῦ ὑφ' ἡμῶν ληφθῆναι, καίπερ πολλῶν ἐπιθυμούντων[34] τοῦτο ποιῆσαι καὶ κοινωνῆσαι τῷ ἁγίῳ αὐτοῦ σαρκίῳ.

Vocabulary
ἀναντίρρητος, -ον, undeniable, incontestable
ἀνεπίληπτος, -ον, irreproachable
ἀντίζηλος, ὁ, jealous one
ἀντίκειμαι, oppose somebody; subst. adversary (here, the "devil")
ἀποφέρω, ²aor. inf. ἀπενεγκεῖν, aor. mid. inf. ἀποφέρεσθαι: carry off/away; mid. win a prize; carry away from (ἀπό) somebody to (ἐπί) somebody
ἀφθαρσία, ἡ, immortality
βάσκανος, ὁ, envious one
βραβεῖον, τό, prize awarded by an adjudicator (βραβεύς)
γένος, -ους, τό, family; race; nation, people; offspring, descendants; sort, kind
ἐπιτηδεύω, take care that (ὡς = ὅτι)
κοινωνέω, have a share of something (w. gen.)
πολιτεία, ἡ, citizenship; way of life, conduct
σαρκίον, τό, piece of flesh (dim.)
στεφανόω, crown; honor; pass. be crowned with; be honored by (ὑπό) somebody for (some virtue [acc.]) with a crown (dat.)
σωμάτιον, τό, poor body (dim. of σῶμα)

17:2 (The adversary) ὑπέβαλεν γοῦν Νικήτην[35] τὸν τοῦ Ἡρώδου[36] πατέρα, ἀδελφὸν δὲ Ἄλκης,[37] ἐντυχεῖν τῷ ἄρχοντι, ὥστε[38] μὴ δοῦναι αὐτοῦ τὸ σῶμα, Μή, φησίν, ἀφέντες τὸν ἐσταυρωμένον[39] τοῦτο ἄρξωνται σέβεσθαι.[40] καὶ ταῦτα εἶπον ὑποβαλλόντων

---

[33] S.v. ἀποφέρω.
[34] Gen. absol.
[35] Niketes.
[36] Herod, an irenarch (εἰήναρχος) in Smyrna.
[37] Alce, a woman of Smyrna.
[38] ὥστε w. inf. (cf. IV, 15).
[39] I.e., Jesus Christ.
[40] ἄρξωνται σέβεσθαι...τοῦτο.

καὶ ἐνισχυόντων τῶν Ἰουδαίων,[41] οἳ καὶ ἐτήρησαν, μελλόντων ἡμῶν[42] ἐκ τοῦ πυρὸς αὐτὸν λαμβάνειν, ἀγνοοῦντες, ὅτι οὔτε[43] τὸν Χριστόν[44] ποτε καταλιπεῖν δυνησόμεθα, τὸν[45] ὑπὲρ τῆς τοῦ παντὸς κόσμου τῶν σωζομένων σωτηρίας[46] παθόντα, (though) ἄμωμον ὑπὲρ ἁμαρτωλῶν, οὔτε ἕτερόν τινα σέβεσθαι.

Vocabulary
ἄμωμος, -ον, faultless, above reproach
ἐνισχύω, urge insistently
ἐντυγχάνω, 3. ἐνέτυχον, [2]aor. inf. ἐντυχεῖν: bring a charge against; appeal, petition; happen to meet with/run into somebody
πάσχω, 1. πείσομαι, [2]aor. ἔπαθον, ptc. παθών, 4. πέπονθα: suffer, endure, undergo; experience
σβέννυμι, aor. inf. σβέσαι, aor. pass. impv. σβέσθητι: extinguish, put out (a fire); pass. be extinguished
ὑποβάλλω, suggest

17:3 τοῦτον μὲν[47] γὰρ υἱὸν ὄντα τοῦ θεοῦ προσκυνοῦμεν, τοὺς δὲ μάρτυρας ὡς μαθητὰς καὶ μιμητὰς τοῦ κυρίου ἀγαπῶμεν ἀξίως ἕνεκα εὐνοίας ἀνυπερβλήτου τῆς[48] εἰς τὸν ἴδιον βασιλέα καὶ διδάσκαλον· ὧν[49] γένοιτο[50] (possible for) καὶ ἡμᾶς κοινωνούς τε καὶ συμμαθητὰς γενέσθαι.

Vocabulary
ἀνυπέρβλητος, -ον, unsurpassable
ἀξίως, worthily
εὔνοια, ἡ, affection, enthusiasm; goodwill
κοινωνός, ὁ, companion, partner
μιμητής, -οῦ, ὁ, imitator
συμμαθητής, fellow disciple

18:1 Ἰδὼν οὖν ὁ κεντυρίων τὴν τῶν Ἰουδαίων γενομένην φιλονεικίαν, θεὶς[51] αὐτὸν[52] ἐν μέσῳ, ὡς (was the) ἔθος αὐτοῖς, ἔκαυσεν[53] (his body). 2 οὕτως τε ἡμεῖς

---

[41] Gen. absol.
[42] Gen. absol. ("when …").
[43] οὔτε… οὔτε… ("neither … nor …")
[44] Prolep. of τὸν Χριστόν.
[45] τὸν Χριστόν…τὸν… παθόντα, modifier in 2nd attrib. pos. (cf. IV, 4.2).
[46] ὑπὲρ τῆς…σωτηρίας.
[47] μὲν…δέ….
[48] εὐνοίας…τῆς (modifying phrase).
[49] ὧν, "with whom."
[50] Opt., "may it happen," "may it be."
[51] S.v. τίθημι.
[52] I.e., (the body of) Polycarp.
[53] S.v. κλαίω.

ὕστερον ἀνελόμενοι[54] τὰ[55] τιμιώτερα λίθων πολυτελῶν καὶ δοκιμώτερα ὑπὲρ χρυσίον ὀστᾶ αὐτοῦ ἀπεθέμεθα, ὅπου καὶ ἀκόλουθον ἦν.

Vocabulary

ἀκόλουθος, -ον, suitable
ἀποτίθημι, [2]aor. mid. ἀπεθέμην: mid. lay something down, put something away
δόκιμος, -ον, genuine, fine; comp. δοκιμώτερα, finer
ἔνθα (adv.), there; where
κεντυρίων, -ωνος, ὁ, centurion (Lat. loanw., cf. ἑκατοντάρχη)
πολυτελής, -ές, expensive
ὕστερος, -α, -ον, coming after; last; ὕστερον (adv.), later, after, finally
φιλονεικία, ἡ, contentiousness

18:3 ἔνθα ὡς[56] δυνατὸν ἡμῖν συναγομένοις ἐν ἀγαλλιάσει καὶ χαρᾷ παρέξει[57] ὁ κύριος ἐπιτελεῖν τὴν τοῦ μαρτυρίου αὐτοῦ ἡμέραν γενέθλιον, εἴς τε τὴν τῶν προηθληκότων[58] μνήμην καὶ (εἰς τὴν) τῶν μελλόντων ἄσκησίν τε καὶ ἑτοιμασίαν.

Vocabulary

ἀγαλλίασις, -εως, ἡ, exultation, gladness
ἄσκησίς, ἡ, practice (of athletics, here applied to martyrs)
γενέθλιος, -ον, belonging to one's birth; ἡμέρα γενέθλιον, birthday celebration
ἔνθα (adv.), here; where
ἑτοιμασία, ἡ, preparation
μνήμη, ἡ, memory of something (gen.), commemoration
παρέχω, 3. παρέσχον, ptc. παρασχών, [2]aor. mid. impv. παράσχου: provide/give; + inf., allow/grant to somebody (dat.), do something
προέρχομαι, go forward, approach; come/go before; come/go forth; go (read) forward

---

[54] S.v. ἀναιρέω.
[55] τὰ...ὀστᾶ.
[56] ὡς...παρέξει ὁ κύριος.
[57] παρέξει (Att.) > παρέξῃ.
[58] Cf. table 9.1.6(d).

5.8.

Apocalypse of Peter: *A Tour of Hell*

(Apoc. Pet. 21–34)

Provenance: Syria-Palestine.

Date: 135–140 CE.

Text: Thomas J. Kraus, Tobias Nicklas, *Das Petrusevangelium und die Petrusapokalypse: Die griechsichen Fragment emit deutscher und englisher Übersetzung* (Berlin: Walter de Gruyter, 2004); ET: Bart D. Ehrman, *The New Testament and Other Early Christian Writings: A Reader* (New York: Oxford University Press, 1998), 407–12.

The Apocalypse of Peter was discovered, along with the Gospel of Peter, in 1887 in the tomb of a Christian monk in Akhmim, north of Nag Hammadi, Upper Egypt. This pseudonymous text was counted among the books of canonical scripture in some places, appearing in the canonical lists of both the Muratorian Canon and Codex Claramontanus, as well as in patristic allusions. The Apocalypse of Peter belongs to the genre of tour apocalypses.[1] However, this text is unique for being the only tour apocalypse in which a deity or savior (here Jesus) takes a sage (here the apostle Peter) on a *descent* to tour the abode of hell before ascending for the typical apocalyptic tour of heaven.[2] Thus, this text can also be situated within the Christian tradition of Christ's descent into hell.[3] For its detail, the author drew on

---

[1] Martha Himmelfarb, *Tours of Hell: An Apocalyptic Form in Jewish and Christian Literature* (Philadelphia, University of Pennsylvania Press, 1983), 170, cf. 169.

[2] The two earliest apocalypses in the Jewish tradition are the Book of Watchers (third century BCE) and the Book of Heavenly Luminaries (early third century BCE or before) in 1 En. 6–36 and 72–82 respectively.

[3] Cf. Acts 2:27, 31; 1 Pet 3:19, 20, 4:6, 8–10; and later in the Apostles' Creed (κατελθόντα εἰς τὰ κατώτατα) and Athanasian Creed. A. Dieterich has argued that this tour apocalypse is a Christianized version of the pagan Orphic-Pythagorean Hades and the conjuring of ghosts to learn of the future (ἡ νέκυια)

FIG. 12. Head, Smyrna (photo: author).

Jewish and Christian traditions, with an interest in punishment after death (e.g. 3 Baruch, Testament of Abraham, 1 En. 14, 17–36), adding fiery punishments and geographical details.

After describing the terrifying events that will accompany Christ's second coming, the Apocalypse of Peter narrates the apostle Peter's tour of hell, depicted as an anti-utopian abode of bodily torment. Hell is a place where the condemned sit in filth and in a variety of bodily discharges such as blood, sweat, pus, and excrement. The taxonomy of transgressions in this text maps out, in an unsystematic way, the categories of sin, specifying an appropriate post mortem punishment for each category. In each case, the punishment is made to fit the crime.[4]

Special Features: Note the use of *iota*-adscripts (cf. IV, 16).

Related Texts: Narrations of sages being taken on heavenly tours is a common feature of Jewish apocalyptic texts (e.g., 1 En. 17–36, 72–82, 3 Baruch, T. Levi, 2 Cor 11:30–12:1 [§4.9]).

While Jesus takes Peter on a tour of hell, Peter declares:

21 Εἶδον δὲ καὶ ἕτερον τόπον καταντικρὺς ἐκείνου[5] (and it was) αὐχμηρόν, καὶ ἦν τόπος κολάσεως καὶ οἱ καλαζόμενοι ἐκεῖ καὶ οἱ κολάζοντες ἄγγελοι σκοτεινὸν εἶχον αὐτῶν τὸ ἔνδυμα[6] κατὰ τὸν ἀέρα τοῦ τόπου. 22 καί τινες ἦσαν ἐκεῖ ἐκ τῆς γλώσσης κρεμάμενοι· οὗτοι δὲ ἦσαν οἱ βλασφημοῦντες τὴν ὁδὸν τῆς δικαιοσύνης, καὶ ὑπέκειτο αὐτοῖς πῦρ φλεγόμενον καὶ κολάζον αὐτούς.

Vocabulary
αὐχμηρός, -ά, -όν, dry, parched
καταντικρύ(ς), directly opposite (w. gen.)
κολάζω, punish, punish for (ἐπί), chastise
κόλασις, ἡ, punishment, torture
κρεμάννυμι/κραμάζω, pres. mid. κρέμαμαι, pres. mid. ptc. κρεμάμενος, 3. ἐκρέμασα, aor. mid. inf. κρέμασθαι, aor. pl. ptc. κρεμάσαντες, 6. ἐκρεμάσθην: hang up something, hang something from (gen.); hang somebody in execution; mid. hang, be suspended; pass. be hung up, suspended
σκοτεινός, -ή, -όν, dark

---

going back to archaic Greece (*Nekyia: Beiträge zur Erklärung der neuentdeckten Petrusapokalypse,* 2nd ed. [Leipzig: Teubner, 1913]); cf. Orphic tendencies of the Pythagorean tradition, which emphasized Orpheus's ἡ κατάβασις εἰς Ἅιδου, and Aeneas's visit to the underworld (Virgil, *Aeneid,* VI).

[4] D. Fiensy, "*Lex talionis* in the Apocalypse of Peter," *HTR* 76 (1983), 255–258, esp. 256; Lautaro R. Lanzillotta, "Does the Punishment Reward the Righteous? The Justice Pattern Underlying the Apocalypse of Peter," in *The Apocalypse of Peter,* 127–157, ed. Bremmer and Czachesz; Alan E. Bertstein, *The Formation of Hell: Death and Retribution in the Ancient and Early Christian worlds* (London: UCL Press, 1993).

[5] I.e., heaven.

[6] σκοτεινόν...τὸ ἔνδυμα.

ὑποκείμαι, lie under, below; be subject to somebody/something
φλέγω, to burn; pass. be on fire

23 καὶ λίμνη τις ἦν μεγάλη πεπληρωμένη βοβόρου φλεγομένου, ἐν ὧι ἦσαν
ἄνθρωποί τινες ἀποστρέφοντες τὴν δικαιοσύνην, καὶ ἐπέκειντο[7] αὐτοῖς ἄγγελοι
βασανισταί. 24 ἦσαν δὲ καὶ ἄλλοι, γυναῖκες τῶν πλοκάμων ἐξηρτημέναι ἀνωτέρω
τοῦ βορβόρου ἐκείνου τοῦ ἀναπαφλάζοντος. αὗται δὲ ἦσαν αἱ πρὸς μοιχείαν
κοσμηθεῖσαι. οἱ δὲ συμμιγέντες αὐτῶν τῷ μιάσματι τῆς μοιχείας [were hanging]
ἐκ τῶν ποδῶν,[8] καὶ τὰς κεφαλὰς εἶχον ἐν τῶι βορβόρωι...[and]...ἔλεγον· οὐκ
ἐπιστεύομεν ἐλεύσεσθαι[9] εἰς τοῦτον τὸν τόπον.

Vocabulary
ἀναπαφλάζω, to boil/bubble up
ἀνώτερος, -έρα, -ον, above (w. gen.)
βασανιστης, ὁ, guard who tortures prisoners, tormenting jailor
βόβορος, ὁ, filth (in the netherworld)
ἐξαρτάω, hang
ἐπίκειμαι (w. dat.), set over, set/lay upon; adorn with; confront
κοσμέω, arrange, put in order; adorn, dress
λίμνη, ἡ, lake
μίασμα, -ματος, τό, defilement, pollution
μοιχεία, ἡ, adultery
πλόκαμος, ὁ, braid of hair
συμμείγνυμι, pf. pass. ptc. συμμεμιγμένος: mix together, mingle with; mid. associate with; be joined sexually with (gen.)

25 Καὶ τοὺς φονεῖς ἔβλεπον καὶ τοὺς συνειδότας αὐτοῖς βεβλημένους[10] ἔν τινι
τόπωι τεθλιμμένωι καὶ πεπληρωμένωι ἑρπετῶν πονηρῶν καὶ πλησσομένους ὑπὸ
τῶν θηρίων ἐκείνων καὶ οὕτω στρεφομένους ἐκεῖ ἐν τῆι κολάσει ἐκείνηι. ἐπέκειντο
δὲ αὐτοῖς σκώληκες ὥσπερ νεφέλαι σκότους. αἱ δε ψυχαὶ τῶν πεφονευμένων
ἑστῶσαι[11] καὶ ἐφορῶσαι τὴν κόλασιν ἐκείνων τῶν φονέων ἔλεγον· ὁ θεός,[12] δικαία
σου ἡ κρίσις.

---

[7] Athematic verb (no connecting vowel).
[8] The term "feet" is a euphemism for "testicles"; cf. Saul Lieberman, "On Sins and Their Punishment," in
   his *Texts and Studies* (New York: Ktav, 1974), 33, 41–43, 47; Himmelfarb, *Tours of Hell*, 82–92. Hanging
   by the testicles is also a punishment for adultery in the hell of Lucian's *True Story* 2.25–26, 31 (trans.
   Bryan P. Reardon, *Collected Ancient Greek Novels* [Berkeley: University of California Press, 2008]);
   Richard Bauckham, *The Fate of the Dead: Studies on the Jewish and Christian Apocalypses* (Leiden:
   Brill, 1998), 216.
[9] S.v. ἔρχομαι.
[10] S.v. βάλλω.
[11] S.v. ἵστημι, pf. fm. ptc.
[12] Nom. for voc.

Vocabulary

ἑρπετόν, τό, reptile

θλίβω, pf. pass. ptc. τεθλιμμένος: push; oppress, afflict; pass. be oppressed, experience pain

σκώληξ, -ηκος, ὁ, worm

σύνοιδα (pf.), be aware of information, consent to

φονεύς, -εως, ὁ, φονέα (acc.), φονέας (acc. pl.), murderer

φονεύω, to murder, kill

φορέω, wear (clothing/armor); bear, suffer; here, "bear/endure somebody's torment by looking or gazing upon those being tormented"

26 πλησίον δὲ τοῦ τόπου ἐκείνου εἶδον ἕτερον τόπον τεθλιμμένον, ἐν ὧι ὁ ἰχὼρ καὶ ἡ δυσωδία τῶν κολαζομένων κατέρρεε, καὶ (something) ὥσπερ λίμνη ἐγίνετο ἐκεῖ, κἀκεῖ ἐκάθηντο[13] γυναῖκες ἔχουσαι τὸν ἰχῶρα μέχρι τῶν τραχήλων, καὶ ἀντικρὺς αὐτῶν πολλοὶ παῖδες...ἄωροι ἐτίκτοντο καθήμενοι ἔκλαιον. καὶ προήρχοντο ἐξ αὐτῶν πυρὸς καὶ τὰς γυναῖκας ἔπλησσον κατὰ τῶν ὀφθαλμῶν. αὗται δὲ ἦσαν αἱ [women who conceived out of wedlock] καὶ ἐκτρώσασαι.

Vocabulary

ἀντικρύς (w. gen.), opposite

ἄωρος, -ον, (aborted) prematurely

δυσωδία, ἡ, foul smell, stench

ἐκτρώσκω, cause an abortion

ἰχώρ, -ῶρος, ὁ, discharge (from a wound), pus

καταρρέω, impf. κατέρρεον: to stream/run down

πλησίον (w. gen.), near, nearby

πλήσσω, [2]aor. pass. ptc. πληγείς, pf. pass. inf. πεπλᾶσθαι: to wound, strike; sting (of bees), bite

προέρχομαι, go forward, approach; go (read) forward; come/go before; come/go forth

τράχηλος, ὁ, neck

27 Καὶ ἕτεροι ἄνδρες καὶ γυναῖκες φλεγόμενοι ἦσαν[14] μέχρι τοῦ ἡμίσους αὐτῶν καὶ βεβλημένοι ἐν τόπωι σκοτεινῶι καὶ μαστιζόμενοι ὑπὸ πνευμάτων πονηρῶν καὶ ἐσθιόμενοι (their) τὰ σπλάγχνα ὑπὸ σκωλήκων ἀκοιμήτων. οὗτοι δὲ ἦσαν οἱ διώξαντες τοὺς δικαίους καὶ παραδόντες αὐτούς, 28 καὶ πλησίον ἐκείνων πάλιν γυναῖκες καὶ ἄνδρες μασώμενοι αὐτῶν τὰ χείλη καὶ κολαζόμενοι καὶ πεπυρωμένον σίδηρον κατὰ τῶν ὀφθαλμῶν λαμβάνοντες. οὗτοι δὲ ἦσαν οἱ βλασφημήσαντες καὶ κακῶς εἰπόντες τὴν ὁδὸν τῆς δικαιοσύνης. 29 καὶ καταντικρὺ τούτων ἄλλοι

---

[13] S.v. κάθημαι, impf.

[14] Impf. periphr. (cf. IV, 17)

πάλιν ἄνδρες καὶ γυναῖκες τὰς γλώσσας αὐτῶν μασώμενοι καὶ πῦρ φλεγόμενον
ἔχοντες ἐν τῶι στόματι. οὗτοι δὲ ἦσαν οἱ ψευδομάρτυρες.

Vocabulary
ἀκοίμητος, -ον, never-resting
ἥμισυς, -εια, -υ, half; μέχρι τοῦ ἡμίσους, up to the middle (of one's body)
κακῶς (adv.), wrongly, wickedly
καταντικρύ, directly opposite (w. gen.)
μασάομαι, to bite, gnaw
μαστίζω, strike with a whip, to scourge
σίδηρος, ὁ, iron, anything made of iron
σκώληξ, -ηκος, ὁ, worm
σπλάγχα, τά, inward parts, entrails (esp. heart, lungs, liver, kidneys); fig.
    affection, love
χεῖλος, -ους, τό; pl. τὰ χείλη: lips; edge, shore (of the sea), bank (of a river)
ψευδόμαρτυς, -υρος, ὁ, false witness

30 Καὶ ἐν ἑτέρωι τινὶ τόπωι χάλικες ἦσαν ὀξύτεροι (than) ξιφῶν καὶ παντὸς
ὀβελίσκου πεπυρωμένοι, καὶ γυναῖκες καὶ ἄνδρες ῥάκη ῥυπαρὰ ἐνδεδυμένοι
ἐκυλίοντο ἐπ᾽ αὐτῶν[15] κολαζόμενοι.[16] οὗτοι δὲ ἦσαν οἱ πλουτοῦντες καὶ τῶι
πλούτωι αὐτῶν πεποιθότες καὶ μὴ ἐλεήσαντες ὀρφανοὺς καὶ χήρας, ἀλλ᾽
ἀμελήσαντες τῆς ἐντολῆς τοῦ θεοῦ. 31 ἐν δὲ ἑτέραι λίμνηι μεγάληι πεπληρωμένηι
πύου καὶ αἵματος καὶ βορβόρου ἀναζέοντος ἱστήκεισαν[17] ἄνδρες καὶ γυναῖκες
μέχρι γονάτων. οὗτοι δὲ ἦσαν οἱ δανίζοντες καὶ ἀπαιτοῦντες τόκους τόκων.

Vocabulary
ἀμελέω, disregard, neglect
ἀναζέω, to boil
ἀπαιτέω, demand payment of a loan
βόβορος, ὁ, filth
δανίζω, lend money
ἐλεέω, be merciful; feel pity; pass. be shown mercy
κυλίω, roll something up/down; mid., roll oneself upon something; pour down
ξίφος, -εος, τό, sword
ὀβελίσκος, ὁ, skewer, spit
ὀξύς, -εῖα, -ύ, sharp; swift, quick (of spirit/mind); comp. ὀξύτερος
ὀρφανός, -ή, -όν, orphaned; subst. orphan
πλουτέω, be rich
πύον, τό, pus

---

[15] I.e., the sharp stones.
[16] Cf. Job 8:17, 41:30 (LXX).
[17] S.v. ἵστημι, cf. table 1.1(f).

ῥάκος, -ους, τό, tattered garment, rag
ῥυπαρός, -ά, -ον, filthy, dirty
τόκος, ὁ, childbirth; offspring; interest (on money owed)
χάλιξ, -ικος, ὁ, sharp stones
χήρα, ἡ, widow

32 Ἄλλοι ἄνδρες καὶ γυναῖκες ἀπὸ κρημνοῦ μεγάλου καταστρεφόμενοι ἤρχοντο κάτω καὶ πάλιν ἠλαύοντο ὑπὸ τῶν ἐπικειμένων ἀναβῆναι ἄνω ἐπὶ τοῦ κηρμνοῦ καὶ κατεσρέφοντο ἐκεῖθεν κάτω καὶ ἡσυχίαν οὐκ εἶχον ἀπὸ ταύτης τῆς κολάσεως. οὗτοι δὲ ἦσαν οἱ μιάναντες τὰ σώματα ἑαυτῶν ὡς γυναῖκες ἀναστρεφόμενοι, αἱ δὲ μετ' αὐτῶν γυναῖκες αὗται ἦσαν αἱ συγκοιμηθεῖσαι ἀλλήλαις ὡς ἂν ἀνὴρ πρὸς γυναῖκα.

Vocabulary
ἀναστρέφω, 6. ἀνεστράφην, fut. pass. ἀναστραφήσομαι: overturn something; pass. behave, conduct oneself; associate with
ἐκεῖθεν, from there
ἐλαύνω, to drive, compel
ἡσυχία, ἡ, quietness, silence; decorum; rest
καταστρέφω, cast down
κρημνός, ὁ, cliff, precipice
συγκοιμάομαι (w. dat.), lie/sleep with somebody

33 καὶ παρὰ τῶι κρημνῶι ἐκείνωι τόπος ἦν πυρὸς πλείστου γέμων. κἀκεῖ ἱστήκεισαν ἄνδρες οἵτινες ταῖς ἰδίαις χερσὶ ξόανα ἑαυτοῖς ἐποίησαν ἀντὶ[18] θεοῦ. καὶ παρ' ἐκείνοις ἄνδρες ἕτεροι καὶ γυναῖκες ῥάβδους πυρὸς ἔχοντες καὶ ἀλλήλους τύπτοντες καὶ μηδέποτε παυόμενοι τῆς τοιαύτης κολάσεως, 34 καὶ ἕτεροι πάλιν ἐγγὺς ἐκείνων γυναῖκες καὶ ἄνδρες φλεγόμενοι καὶ στρεφόμενοι καὶ τηγανιζόμενοι. οὗτοι δὲ ἦσαν οἱ ἀφέντες τὴν ὁδὸν τοῦ θεοῦ.

Vocabulary
γέμω (w. gen.), nt. pres. ptc. γέμον: be full of something
ἐγγύς (adv.), near, close to; on the verge of
ξόανον, τό, wooden cult image
μηδέποτε, never
πλείστος, -η, -ον, most, greatest, chief
ῥάβδος, ἡ, rod, staff
τηγανίζω, fry, roast
τύπτω, ἔτυψα: beat, strike

---

[18] ἀντί, "instead of."

SELECT BIBLIOGRAPHY

Bremmer, Jan N., and István Czachesz (eds). *The Apocalypse of Peter*. Leuven: Peeters, 2003.

Buchholz, Dennis D. *Your Eyes Will Be Opened: A Study of Greek (Ethiopic) Apocalypse of Peter*. Atlanta: Scholars Press, 1988.

Collins, Adela Yarbro. *Cosmology and Eschatology in Jewish and Christian Apocalypticism*. Leiden: Brill, 1996.

Czachesz, Istvan. "Grotesque Body in the Apocalypse of Peter." In *The Apocalypse of Peter*, 108–126. Ed. J. N. Bremmer and I. Czachesz. Leuven: Peeters, 2003.

Stroumsa, Guy. "Mystical Descents." In *Death, Ecstasy and Other Worldly Journeys*, 137–152. Ed. J. J. Collins and Michael Fishbane. Albany: State University of New York Press, 1995.

5.9.

Acts of Paul: The Story of Thekla

(Acts Paul 30–34, 37–42)

Provenance: Southwest Asia Minor, perhaps in Ikonion (Iconium) or Antioch.
Date: 180–200 CE.

Genre: Hagiographic romance.[1]

Text: R. A. Lypsius and M. Bonnet, *Acta Apostolorum Apocrypha post Constantinum Tischendorf*, 2 vols. (Leipzig: Mendelssohn, 1891–1903; reprinted Hildesheim, 1972); ET: Bart D. Ehrman, *The New Testament and Other Early Christian Writings: A Reader* (New York: Oxford University Press, 1998), 177–82; ET: *NTA*, II, 361064; cf. Klauck 47–49.

Related Texts: Acts of Paul: The Mission of Paul (Acts Paul 1–8 [§5.15]); Acts of Thomas (Acts Thom. 9:82–83, 87–88, 96–98, [§5.10]); Acts of Andrew (Acts Andr. 5–9 [§5.16]).

The Acts of Paul was widely disseminated and read in early Christian antiquity. It appears in the canonical list of Codex Claramontanus and is quoted by Tertullian (*De baptismo*, 17:5). This text was also widely circulated by the Eastern Orthodox Church, which commemorates Thekla's life on 24 September. Her cult was probably centered in Ikonion.

In this writing, Paul is portrayed both as a preacher to women of sexual asceticism and, curiously, as a man with whom many women became infatuated, including Thekla (Θέκλα) herself, an elite woman living in Ikonion. She became enraptured with Paul after hearing him preach "the word of God concerning

---

[1] Alison Goddard Elliot, *Roads to Paradise: Reading the Lives of the Early Saints* (Hanover, NH: University Press of New England, 1987), 42–76.

FIG. 13. Lion charging a man, Smyrna (İzmir Archaeological Museum) (photo: author).

sexual abstinence." In contrast to 1 Cor 7:17–31 (§4.8), in which Paul expresses some ambivalence about marriage, this text (as well as the Acts of Thomas [§5.10] and the Acts of Andrew [§5.16]) praises the virtue of female virginity with great extravagance. This narrator also provides a vivid description of Paul's physical appearance (Acts Paul 3, §5.15), which functions rhetorically to establish the author of this text as an authority on Paul's life and teaching.[2]

In the preceding narrative, an "influential citizen of (Syrian) Antioch" named Alexander became enamored of Thekla. Having failed to gain access to her by bribing Paul, he "embraced her in the street" (Acts Paul 26). By repulsing him publically – tearing his cloak and pulling off his crown – she made him a laughing-stock in the streets. In revenge, Alexander led Thekla to the governor to fight with wild beasts. In the days preceding Thekla's ordeal, Queen Tryphaina (Τρύφαινα), whose daughter Falconilla (Φαλκονίλλη) had recently died, took Thekla under her care (Acts Paul 27–29). Tryphaina became so fond of Thekla that she referred to her as her "second" child (Acts Paul 29).

30:1 Καὶ ὅτε ὄρθρος ἐγένετο, ἦλθεν Ἀλέξανδρος παραλαβεῖν αὐτήν,[3] αὐτὸς γὰρ ἐδίδου[4] τὰ κυνήγια, λέγων· Ὁ ἡγεμὼν κάθηται[5] καὶ ὁ ὄχλος θορυβεῖ ἡμᾶς· δός[6] ἀπαγάγω (Thekla) τὴν θηριομαχίαν. 2 Ἡ δὲ Τρύφαινα ἀνέκραξεν ὥστε φυγεῖν αὐτὸν λέγουσα· Φαλκονίλλης[7] μου δεύτερον πένθος ἐπὶ τὴν οἰκίαν γίνεται, καὶ οὐδεὶς ὁ βοηθῶν (μοῦ)· οὔτε[8] (my) τέκνον (will come to my aid), ἀπέθανεν γάρ, οὔτε συγγενής, χήρα γάρ εἰμι. 3 ὁ θεὸς[9] Θέκλης τοῦ τέκνου μου, βοήθησον Θέκλῃ.

Vocabulary

ἀνακράζω, cry out, shout

βοηθέω, to help, come to the aid of somebody (dat.), render assistance to some-body; defend oneself

δεύτερος, -α, -ον, second; secondary

θηριομαχία, ἡ, fight with wild beasts (as a spectator event) (Lat. *venatio*)

κυνήγια, ἡ, public games with wild animals

ὄρθρος, ὁ, dawn

συγγενής, -ές, related to (gen.); subst. a relative

---

[2] Jan N. Bremmer, "Magic, Martyrdom and Women's Liberation in the Acts of Paul and Thecla," in *The Apocryphal Acts of Paul and Thecla*, 36–59, esp. 38, ed. Jan N. Bremmer (Kampen: Kok Pharos, 1996).

[3] αὐτήν, i.e., Thekla.

[4] δίδωμι here "provide," "arrange for."

[5] Here "sit," in the sense of sitting as a judge at a sporting event.

[6] δός, "grant that."

[7] Tryphaina considered Thekla to be her second Falconilla.

[8] οὔτε… οὔτε…("neither … nor …").

[9] Nom. for voc.

χήρα, ή, widow

31:1 Καὶ πέμπει ὁ ἡγεμὼν στρατιώτας ἵνα ἀχθῇ[10] Θέκλα. 2 ἡ δὲ Τρύφαινα οὐκ ἀπέστη[11] (Thekla),[12] ἀλλὰ αὐτὴ λαβομένη τῆς χειρὸς αὐτῆς ἀνήγαγεν λέγουσα· Τὴν μὲν θυγατέρα μου Φαλκονίλλαν ἀπήγαγον εἰς τὸ μνημεῖον· σὲ δέ, Θέκλα, εἰς θηριομαχίαν ἀπάγω. 3 καὶ ἔκλαυσεν Θέκλα πικρῶς καὶ ἐστέναξεν πρὸς κύριον, λέγουσα· Κύριε ὁ θεός, ᾧ ἐγὼ πιστεύω, ἐφ᾽ ὃν ἐγὼ κατέφυγα, ὁ ῥυσάμενός με ἐκ πυρός,[13] ἀπόδος μισθὸν Τρυφαίνῃ τῇ εἰς τὴν δούλην σου συμπαθησάσῃ, καὶ ὅτι με ἀγνὴν ἐτήρησεν.

Vocabulary
ἁγνός, -ή, -όν, pure, chaste (of women)
δούλη, ή, female slave
ἐρύω, mid. ἐρύομαι/ῥύομαι, 2. ῥύσομαι, 3. ἐρρυσάμην: mid. rescue, save, deliver
καταφεύγω, ¹aor. κατέφυγα/²aor. κατέφυγον: flee; take refuge
μισθός, ό, wages, pay; physician's fee
μνημεῖον, τό, tomb, sepulchre,
στρατιώτης, ό, soldier
συμπαθέω, show sympathy for, have compassion for

32:1 Θόρυβος οὖν ἐγένετό τε καὶ πάταγος τῶν θηρίων καὶ βοὴ τοῦ δήμου καὶ τῶν γυναικῶν ὁμοῦ καθεσθεισῶν,[14] τῶν μὲν[15] λεγόντων·[16] Τὴν ἱερόσυλον εἰσάγεγε· τῶν δὲ λεγουσῶν· Ἄρθήτω[17] ἡ πόλις ἐπὶ τῇ ἀνομίᾳ ταύτῃ· 2 αἶρε πάσας ἡμᾶς, ἀνθύπατε· πικρὸν θέαμα, κακὴ κρίσις.

Vocabulary
ἀνθύπατος, ό, proconsul
βοή, ή, shouting (of a crowd); outcry
δῆμος, ό, people, crowd; the People (i.e., the full citizen body of a Greek *polis*, as represented by the ἐκκλησία)
ἱερόσυλος, -ον, sacrilegious; subst. temple robber, sacrilegious person
θέαμα, -ματος, τό, spectacle, sight
θόρυβος, ό, uproar, public disturbance
πάταγος, ό, roar

---

[10] S.v. ἄγω.
[11] S.v. ἀφίστημι.
[12] S.v. ἀφίστημι.
[13] Previously, in Acts Paul 22, the governor tried to execute Thekla by burning her on a pyre, but God sent a cloud to extinguish the fire with a shower of rain and hail.
[14] S.v. καθέζομαι.
[15] τῶν μέν... τῶν δέ...(take with λεγόντων as part of a gen. absol.).
[16] Gen. absol.
[17] S.v. αἴρω.

33:1 Ἡ δὲ Θέκλα (from) χειρὸς Τρυφαίνης ληφθεῖσα ἐξεδύθη καὶ ἔλαβεν διαζώστραν καὶ ἐβλήθη[18] εἰς τὸ στάδιον. 2 καὶ λέοντες καὶ ἄρκοι ἐβλήθησαν ἐπ' αὐτήν. 3 καὶ πικρὰ λέαινα προσδραμοῦσα εἰς τοὺς πόδας αὐτῆς ἀνεκλίθη· ὁ δὲ ὄχλος τῶν γυναικῶν ἐβόησεν μέγα. καὶ ἔδραμεν ἐπ' αὐτὴν ἄρκος. 4 ἡ δὲ λέαινα δραμοῦσα ὑπήντησεν καὶ διέρρηξεν[19] τὴν ἄρκον. καὶ πάλιν λέων δεδιδαγμένος[20] (to fight) ἐπ' ἀνθρώπους, ὃς ἦν Ἀλεξάνδρου[21] ἔδραμεν ἐπ' αὐτήν· καὶ ἡ λέαινα συμπλέξασα τῷ λέοντι συνανηρέθη. 5 μειζόνως δε ἐπένθησαν αἱ γυναῖκες, ἐπειδὴ καὶ ἡ βοηθὸς αὐτῇ λέαινα ἀπέθανεν.

Vocabulary

ἁγνός, -ή, -όν, pure, chaste (of women); holy

ἀνακλίνω, 3. ἀνεκλίθην: lay something down; pass. lie down, recline at a meal

ἄρκος, ὁ/ἡ, a bear

βοηθός, ὁ, helper; protector

διαζώστρα, ἡ (= διάζομα), belt, cord, or cincture worn about the waist

ἐκδύω, 6. ἐξεδύθην: strip, take off; mid. strip/undress oneself; pass. be stripped (of one's clothing)

λέων, -οντος, ὁ, / λέαινα, ἡ, lion, lioness

μειζόνως, yet more, all the more (adv.)

προστρέχω, 3. προσέδραμον: run up to somebody

ὑπαντάω, meet somebody

στάδιον, τό, stadium, arena

συμπλέκω, come together with (w. dat.)

συναναιρέω, 6. συνανηρέθην: destroy; pass. be killed along with

34:1 Τότε εἰσβάλλουσιν πολλὰ θηρία, ἑστώσης[22] αὐτῆς καὶ ἐκτετακυίας[23] τὰς χεῖρας καὶ προσευχομένης. 2 ὡς δὲ ἐτέλεσεν τὴν προσευχήν, ἐστράφη καὶ εἶδεν ὄρυγμα μέγα πλῆρες ὕδατος, καὶ εἶπεν· Νῦν καιρὸς λούσασθαί με. 3 καὶ ἔβαλεν ἑαυτὴν λέγουσα· Ἐν τῷ ὀνόματι Ἰησοῦ Χριστοῦ ὑστέρᾳ ἡμέρᾳ βαπτίζομαι.[24] 4 Καὶ ἰδοῦσαι αἱ γυναῖκες καὶ πᾶς ὁ ὄχλος ἔκλαυσαν λέγοντες· Μὴ βάλῃς ἑαυτὴν εἰς τὸ ὕδωρ, ὥστε καὶ τὸν ἡγεμόνα δακρῦσαι, ὅτι τοιοῦτον κάλλος φῶκαι ἔμελλον ἐσθίειν. 5 ἡ μὲν[25] οὖν ἔβαλεν ἑαυτὴν εἰς τὸ ὕδωρ ἐν τῷ ὀνόματι Ἰησοῦ

---

[18] S.v. βάλλω, here "to be let loose/released."

[19] S.v. διαρρήγνυμι/ διαρήσσω.

[20] S.v. διδάσκω, pass. "to be trained."

[21] Gen. of poss.

[22] Cf. table 12.5; three genitive absolute constructions, with αὐτῆς functioning as subject of all three participles: ἑστωσης αὐτῆς…ἐκτετακυίας (s.v. ἐκτείνω)…προσευχομένης.

[23] S.v. ἐκτείνω.

[24] βαπτίζομαι, probably middle ("baptize oneself") rather than passive ("am baptized").

[25] ἡ μέν…αἱ δέ…(cf. ὁ μέν…ὁ δέ …).

Χριστοῦ· αἱ δὲ φῶκαι πυρὸς ἀστραπῆς φέγγος ἰδοῦσαι νεκραὶ ἐπέπλευσαν.²⁶ 6 καὶ ἦν περὶ αὐτὴν νεφέλη πυρός, ὥστε²⁷ μήτε²⁸ τὰ θηρία ἅπτεσθει αὐτῆς, μήτε θεωρεῖσθαι αὐτὴν γυμνήν.

Vocabulary

ἀστραπή, ἡ, lightning

βάλλω, 3. ἔβαλον, 4. βέβληκα: throw; put/place; mid. lay down (as a foundation/ beginning)

εἰσβάλλω, put/send in

ἐπιπλέω, float on the water

λούω/λόω, bathe, wash; mid. bathe oneself (the contr. impf. mid. forms, ἐλούμην and ἐλοῦτο, belong to λόω), bathe (as a baptism)

ὄρυγμα, τό, pit

προσευχή, ἡ, prayer

τοιοῦτος, -αύτη, -οῦτον, of such a kind, such as this; τὰ τοιαῦτα, similar/related things **ὕστερος, -α, -ον**, coming after, last

φέγγος, -ους, τό, light, radiance

φῶκη, ἡ, seal (*phoca monarchus*)

37:1 Καὶ ἐκάλεσεν ὁ ἡγεμὼν τὴν Θέκλαν ἐκ μέσου τῶν θηρίων καὶ εἶπεν αὐτῇ· Τίς εἶ σύ; καὶ τίνα τὰ περὶ σέ, ὅτι²⁹ οὐδὲ ἓν τῶν θηρίων ἥψατό σου; 2 ἡ δὲ εἶπεν· Ἐγὼ μέν εἰμι θεοῦ τοῦ ζῶοντος δούλη· (With respect to) τὰ δὲ περὶ ἐμέ, εἰς ὃν εὐδόκησεν ὁ θεὸς υἱὸν αὐτοῦ ἐπίστευσα·³⁰ δι' ὃν οὐδὲ ἓν τῶν θηρίων ἥψατό μου. 3 οὗτος γὰρ μόνος σωτηρίας ὅρος καὶ ζωῆς ἀθανάτου ὑπόστασίς ἐστιν· (τοῖς) χειμαζομένοις γὰρ (θεὸς) γίνεται καταφυγή, (τοῖς) θλιβομένοις (γίνεται) ἄνεσις, (τοῖς) ἀπηλπισμένοις (γίνεται) σκέπη, καὶ ἀπαξαπλῶς ὃς ἐὰν μὴ πιστεύσῃ εἰς αὐτόν, οὐ ζήσεται ἀλλὰ ἀποθανεῖται εἰς τοὺς αἰῶνας.

Vocabulary

ἀθάνατος, -ον, immortal

ἄνεσις, -εως, ἡ, rest, relaxation, relief

ἀπαξαπλῶς, in brief

ἀπελπίζω, to despair; pass. be despairing

---

²⁶ On the use of aquatic displays in the Roman Empire see K. Coleman, "Launching into History: Aquatic Displays in the Early Empire," Journal of Roman Studies 83 (1993), 48–74; on Greco-Roman ideas about seals see Marcel Detienne and Jean-Pierre Vernant, *Cunning Intelligence in Greek Culture and Society*, trans. Janet Lloyd (Chicago: University of Chicago Press, 1991 [1978]), 246–250; POxy 61.4096, frag. 1.

²⁷ ὥστε w. inf. (cf. IV, 15).

²⁸ μήτε… μήτε… ("neither … nor …").

²⁹ τίνα τὰ περὶ σέ ὅτι, lit. "what things (are there) concerning you that" (i.e., what is it about you that …).

³⁰ ἐπίστευσα, causal adv. ptc. ("because").

καταφηγή, ή, place of refuge
ὅρος, ὁ, boundary, landmark; standard, measure
σκέπη, ή, protection, shelter, shade
ὑπόστασις, -εως, ή, basis; frame of mind
χειμάζομαι, be tossed/battered by a storm

38:1 Καὶ ταῦτα ἀκούσας ὁ ἡγεμὼν ἐκέλευσεν ἐνεχθῆναι[31] ἱμάτια καὶ εἶπεν· Ἔνδυσαι[32] τὰ ἱμάτια. 2   Ἡ δὲ εἶπεν· Ὁ ἐνδύσας με (when I was) γυμνὴν ἐν τοῖς θηρίοις, οὗτος ἐν ἡμέρᾳ κρίσεως ἐνδύσει με σωτηρίαν. 3 καὶ λαβοῦσα τὰ ἱμάτια ἐνεδύσατο. καὶ ἐξέπεμψεν εὐθέως ὁ ἡγεμὼν ἄκτον λέγων· Θέκλαν τὴν τοῦ θεοῦ δούλην τὴν θεοσέβη ἀπολύω ὑμῖν. 4 Αἱ δὲ γυναῖκες πᾶσαι ἔκραξαν φωνῇ μεγάλῃ καὶ ὡς ἐξ ἑνὸς στόματος ἔδωκαν αἶνον τῷ θεῷ λέγουσαι· Εἷς θεὸς ὁ θέκλαν σώσας, 5 ὥστε ἀπὸ (their one) τῆς φωνῆς σεισθῆναι πᾶσαν τὴν πόλιν. 39:1 Καὶ τὴν Τρύφαιναν[33] εὐαγγελισθεῖσαν ἀπαντῆσαι μετὰ ὄχλου καὶ περιπλακῆναι τῇ Θέκλῃ καὶ εἰπεῖν· νῦν πιστεύω ὅτι νεκροὶ ἐγείρονται· Νῦν πιστεύω ὅτι τὸ τέκνον μου ζῇ· δεῦρο ἔσω, καὶ τὰ ἐμὰ πάντα σοὶ καταγράψω. 2 ἡ μὲν Θέκλα εἰσῆλθεν μετ' αὐτῆς καὶ ἀνεπαύσατο εἰς τὸν οἶκον αὐτῆς ἡμέρας ὀκτώ, κατηχήσασα αὐτὴν τὸν λόγον τοῦ θεοῦ, ὥστε πιστεῦσαι καὶ τῶν παιδισκῶν τὰς πλείονας, καὶ μεγάλην εἶναι χαρὰν ἐν τῷ οἴκῳ.

Vocabulary
αἶνος, ὁ, praise
ἄκτον, edict (Latin loanw. *acta*)
ἐκπέμπω, send out; issue an edict (ἄκτον)
καταγράφω, legally transfer by deed
κατηχέω, 3. κατήχησα: teach, instruct
κράζω (= κραυγάζω), to scream, screech
παιδίσκη, ή, female slave, maidservant
περιπλέκω, pf. inf. περιπλακῆναι, 6. περιεπλάκην: embrace; pass. be embraced
σείω, shake

40:1 Ἡ δὲ Θέκλα Παῦλον ἐπεπόθει[34] καὶ ἐζήτει αὐτὸν περιπέμπουσα (messengers) πανταχοῦ· καὶ ἐμηνύθη αὐτῇ ἐν Μύροις εἶναι αὐτόν. 2 καὶ λαβοῦσα νεανίσκους καὶ παιδίσκας, ἀναζωσαμένη καὶ ῥάψασα[35] τὸν χιτῶνα εἰς ἐπενδύτην σχήματι ἀνδρικῷ ἀπῆλθεν ἐν Μύροις, καὶ εὗρεν Παῦλον λαλοῦντα τὸν λόγον

---

[31] S.v. φέρω.
[32] Imperatival inf.; the infinitive often occurs in place of the 3rd pers. impv. (esp. in official and legal language such as degrees).
[33] Subject of the two infinitives that follow.
[34] S.v. πείθω.
[35] S.v. ῥάπτω.

τοῦ θεοῦ καὶ ἐπέστη[36] αὐτῷ. 3 ὁ δὲ ἐθαμβήθη βλέπων αὐτὴν καὶ τὸν ὄχλον τὸν μετ᾽ αὐτῆς, λογισάμενος μὴ[37] τις αὐτῇ πειρασμὸς πάρεστιν ἕτερος.[38] 4 ἡ δὲ συνιδοῦσα (what Paul was thinking) εἶπεν αὐτῷ· Ἔλαβον τὸν λουτρόν, Παῦλε· ὁ γὰρ σοὶ συνεργήσας εἰς τὸ εὐαγγέλιον κἀμοὶ[39] συνήργησεν εἰς τὸ λούσασθαι.

Vocabulary

ἀναζώννυμι/-ύω, aor. mid. ἀναζωσάμην: gird up long robes

ἀνδρικός, -ή, -όν, masculine, manly

ἐπενδύτης, -ου, ὁ, coat

ἐπιποθέω, long for somebody (acc.), earnestly desire

ἐφίστημι, pres. mid. ἐφίσταμαι, 3. ἐπέστησα/ἐπέστην, aor. ptc. ἐπιστάς, -άντος, 4. ἐφέστηκα: stand on/near, stand beside (w. παρά); approach; come upon, attack; mid. (intrans.), come upon somebody (w. dat.), overtake somebody

θαμβέω, astound; pass. be amazed

λουτρόν, τό, bath, washing (here, of baptism)

μηνύω, 3. ἐμήνησα, [1]aor. pass. ptc. μηνυθείς: disclose a secret, report

Μύρα, -ων, τά, Myra, on the south coast of Lykia, Asia Minor

πανταχοῦ, everywhere

πειρασμός, ὁ, trial, test; temptation

περιπέμπω, to send somebody from one place to another

συνεργέω, work together with somebody (to attain something or bring about something), assist

συνοράω, become aware of

χιτών, -ῶνος, ὁ, tunic

41:1 Καὶ λαβόμενος Παῦλος τῆς χειρός αὐτῆς ἀπήγαγεν αὐτὴν εἰς τὸν οἶκον Ἑρμείου[40] καὶ πάντα ἀκούει παρ᾽ αὐτῆς, ὥστε ἐπὶ πολὺ[41] θαυμάσαι τὸν Παῦλον, καὶ τοὺς ἀκούοντας[42] στηριχθῆναι καὶ προσεύξασθαι ὑπὲρ τῆς Τρυφαίνης. 2 καὶ ἀναστᾶσα Θέκλα εἶπεν τῷ Παύλῳ· Πορεύομαι εἰς Ἰκόνιον. 3 Ὁ δὲ Παῦλος εἶπεν· Ὕπαγε καὶ δίδασκε τὸν λόγον τοῦ θεοῦ. 4 ἡ μὲν οὖν Τρύφαινα πολὺν ἱματισμὸν καὶ χρυσὸν ἔπεμψεν αὐτῇ, ὥστε (Θέκλαν) καταλιπεῖν (πάντα) τῷ Παύλῳ εἰς διακονίαν τῶν πτωχῶν.

Vocabulary

διακονία, ἡ, service; aid, support, distribution

Ἰκόνιον, τό, Ikonion (Lat. Iconium)

---

[36] S.v. ἐφίστημι.
[37] μή as conj. following verbs of fearing, etc., "that … not," "lest" (usually followed by pres. subj.).
[38] τις…πειρασμός…ἕτερος.
[39] κἀμοί, s.v. κἀγώ.
[40] Hermias.
[41] ἐπὶ πολυ, adv., "more than once," "often."
[42] τοὺς ἀκούοντας is the subject of the two following infinitives.

ἱματιασμός, ὁ, clothing
στηρίζω, set up, establish, strengthen

42:1 Αὐτὴ δὲ ἀπῆλθεν εἰς Ἰκόνιον. καὶ εἰσέρχεται εἰς τὸν Ὀνησιφόρου[43] οἶκον, καὶ ἔπεσεν εἰς τὸ ἔδαφος ὅπου Παῦλος καθεζόμενος ἐδίδασκεν τὰ λόγια τοῦ θεοῦ, 2 καὶ ἔκλαιεν λέγουσα· Ὁ θεός μου καὶ τοῦ οἴκου τούτου, ὅπου μοι τὸ φῶς ἔλαψμεν, (καὶ) Χριστὲ Ἰησοῦ ὁ υἱὸς τοῦ θεοῦ, ὁ ἐμοὶ βοηθὸς ἐν φυλακῇ, βοηθὸς ἐπὶ ἡγεμόνων, βοηθὸς ἐν πυρί, βοηθὸς ἐν θηρίοις, αὺς εἶ θεός, καὶ σοὶ ἡ δόξα εἰς τοὺς αἰῶνας, ἀμήν.

Vocabulary
ἔδαφος, -ους, τό, ground
λάμπω, 3. ἔλαμψα: shine forth; shine upon somebody (dat.)
λόγιον, τό, a saying, oracle; omen
φυλακή, ἡ, prison

SELECT BIBLIOGRAPHY

Bremmer, Jan N. *The Apocryphal Acts of Paul and Thekla.* Kampen: Kok Pharos, 1996.
Brown, Peter. *The Body and Society: Men, Women, and Sexual Renunciation in Early Christianity.* New York: Columbia University Press, 1988.
Burrus, Virginia. "Chastity as Autonomy: Women in the Stories of the Apocryphal Acts." In *The Apocryphal Acts of Apostles*, 101–117. Ed. Dennis R. Macdonald. Semeia 38. 1986.
Lipsett, B. Diane. *Desiring Conversion: Hermas, Thecla, Aseneth.* Oxford: Oxford University Press, 2011.
Streete, Gail P. C. *Redeemed Bodies: Women Martyrs in Early Christianity.* Louisville: Westminster John Knox Press, 2009, 73–102.

---

[43] Cf. Onesiphoros (cf. 2:1, 4:1).

5.10.

Acts of Thomas: The Story of Mygdonia

(Acts Thom. 9:82–83, 87–88, 96–98)

Provenance: Eastern Syria. *Date:* 220–240 CE.

Text: Lypsius/Bonnet, II², 197–211; ET: *NTA*, II, 486–93; cf. Klauck, 141–179.

The Acts of Thomas was originally composed in Syriac. It should be understood in the context of Eastern Christianity rather than second-century Gnosticism. The so-called School of St. Thomas was not especially gnostic and shared many central values and themes with "orthodox" Christianity. According to Bentley Layton, this text would have been read along with the *Odes of Solomon* and Tatian's *Harmony* (*Diatessaron*).[1] Other expressions of "Thomas Christianity" include the Gospel of Thomas (§1.4), the Book of Thomas, and the Acts of Thomas (cf. §5.10).[2]

The reading in this section concerns sexual asceticism and the glorification of virginity, as illustrated by the life of a noblewoman named Mygdonia. Her renunciation of married life for the sake of the gospel is reminiscent of the lives of both Thekla (§5.9) and Maximilla (§5.16).

At the outset of the Acts of Thomas, the twelve apostles have divided up the world, with "India" (i.e., the Persian Empire) allotted to the apostle Thomas. He

---

[1] Bentley Layton, *Nag Hammadi Codex II, 2–7, together with XIII, 2*, Brit. Lib. Or. 4926(1), and P. Oxy. 1, 654, 655,* vol. 1 (Leiden: Brill, 1989), 361.

[2] G. J. Riley, "Thomas Tradition and the Acts of Thomas," in *SBL 1991 Seminar Papers* (Atlanta: Scholars Press, 1991), 533–542, ed. E. H. Lovering, as summarized by Philip Sellew in "Thomas Christianity: Scholars in Quest of a Community," in *Apocryphal Acts of Thomas,* 11–35, esp. 27–35, ed. Jan N. Bremmer (Leuven: Peeters, 2001),

FIG. 14. Funerary relief (Neapolis Archaeological Museum) (photo: author).

then sets out to travel to India on the back of a donkey. The present reading tells the story of Mygdonia as a high-status woman and the wife of Charisios, a close relation to King Misdaios.

As the story opens, Mygdonia is being carried in a palanquin through the town by her slaves. She is probably quite young, since she has been married less than a year and has no children. When she returns home, after meeting the apostle Thomas, she is confronted by her husband for having left the house unattended and thus exposed the family to shame. The conflict between Charisios and Mygdonia builds to a climax over the course of the narrative.

82:1 Ἔτυχεν δὲ[3] γυναῖκά τινα, Χαρισίου[4] τοῦ ἔγγιστα[5] τοῦ βασιλέως, ᾗ ὄνομα Μυγδονία, ἐλθεῖν[6] ἐπὶ τὸ θεάσασθαι[7] καὶ ἰδεῖν ὄνομα νέον καὶ θεὸν νέον καταγγελλόμενον καὶ νέον ἀπόστολον[8] ἐπιδημήσαντα τῇ αὐτῶν χώρᾳ· ἐφέρετο δὲ ὑπὸ τῶν ἰδίων δούλων· καὶ διὰ τὸν πολὺν ὄχλον καὶ τὴν στενοχορίαν οὐκ ἠδύναντο αὐτὴν εἰσαγαγεῖν πρὸς αὐτόν. 2 ἔπεμψεν δὲ (a message) πρὸς τὸν ἴδιον ἄνδρα[9] ἵνα πέμψῃ αὐτῇ πλείονας τοὺς (δούλους) αὐτῇ ἐξυπηρετουμένους· ἦλθον δὲ καὶ προσῆλθον αὐτῇ θλίβοντες καὶ δέροντες τοὺς ἀνθρώπους.

Vocabulary
δέρω, flay the skin, whip
ἐξυπηρετέω, provide special assistance
στενοχορία, ἡ, narrowness (of space)
τυγχάνω, pres. fm. ptc. τυχοῦσα, ²aor. ἔτυχον, ²aor. 3rd sg. subj. τήχῃ, inf. τυχεῖν, pf. ptc. τετ(ε)υχώς: to gain, experience; happen, turn out (as a result); happen to be; gain/receive something (gen.), attain to (ἐπί); obtain one's request (w. gen.); ἔτυχεν δέ, "and it came to pass that (w. acc.)"; adj. ptc. ordinary, everyday

82:3 Ἰδὼν δὲ ὁ ἀπόστολος (Thomas) εἶπεν αὐτοῖς· Τίνος ἕνεκεν καταστρέφετε τοὺς ἐρχομένους ἀκοῦσαι τὸν λόγον, οἳ καὶ προθυμίαν ἔχουσιν (for it); ὑμεῖς δὲ βούλεσθε παρ᾽ ἐμοὶ μὲν εἶναι, πόρρω τυγχάνοντες· καθὼς εἴρηται[10] ἐπὶ τοῦ ὄχλου τοῦ ἐρχομένου πρὸς τὸν κύριον, ὅτι Ὀφθαλμοὺς μὲν ἔχοντες οὐ βλέπετε, καὶ ὦτα ἔχοντες οὐκ ἀκουέτω. [11] Καὶ ἔλεγεν πρὸς τοὺς ὄχλους· Ὁ ἔχων ὦτα

---

[3] ἔτυχεν δέ (s.v. τυγχάνω), "And it came to pass that ..." (w. acc. + inf.).
[4] Gen. of poss. (Charisios is the husband of Mygdonia).
[5] Superl., s.v. ἐγγύς ("akin to"), hence "closest relation/relative."
[6] ἔτυχεν...ἐλθεῖν.
[7] The accusative articular infinitive following ἐπί is not very common but here seems to be used instead of εἰς or πρός to express a purpose or goal.
[8] I.e., Thomas.
[9] I.e., to Charisios.
[10] S.v. λέγω.
[11] Combining Mark 8:18 with Mark 4:9 (passim).

ἀκούειν ἀκουετω. Καὶ· Δεῦτε πρός με πάντες οἱ κοπιῶντες καὶ πεφορτισμένοι, κἀγὼ ἀναπαύσω ὑμᾶς.

Vocabulary

καταστρέφω, trample on, subdue

νέος, -α, -ον, new; ὁ νεός, boy/ young man

οὖς, τό, (gen.) **ὠτός**, (dat.) ὠτί; pl. τὰ ὦτα

πόρρω (adv.), far away, far off

προθυμία, ἡ, willingness, eagerness

φορτίζω, to load/burden

83:1 Ἀπιδὼν δὲ πρὸς τοὺς βαστάζοντας αὐτὴν εἶπεν αὐτοῖς· Οὗτος ὁ μακαρισμὸς καὶ ἡ παραίνεσις ὁ ἐκείνοις[12] ἐπαγγελθεὶς ὑμῖν περὶ ὑμῶν εἴρηται, οἵτινες αὐτοῖς ἐστιν τοῖς ἐπιφορτισμένοις νῦν. 2 ὑμεῖς ἐστε οἱ τὰ δυσβάστακτα φορτία βαστάζοντες καὶ (now) αὐτῆς κελεύσει, παραφερόμενοι· 3 καὶ ἀνθρώποις ὑμῖν οὖσιν ὥσπερ τοῖς ἀλόγοις ζῴοις ἐπιτιθέασιν ὑμῖν φόρτους, τοῦτο νομίζοντες οἱ τὴν ἐξουσίαν καθ᾽ ὑμῶν ἔχοντες (namely) ὅτι οὐκ ἐστὲ ἄνθρωποι οἷοι καὶ αὐτοί εἰσιν, εἴτε δοῦλοι εἴτε ἐλεύθεροι·

Vocabulary

ἄλογος, -ον, irrational

ἀφοράω, look at (πρός)

δυσβάστακτος, -ον, intolerable

ἐπαγγέλλω, [1]aor. mid. ἐπηγγειλάμην, [1]aor. ptc. ἐπαγγειλάμενος: promise

ἐπιφορτίζω, load heavily

ζῷον, τό, animal, living creature

κέλευσις, ἡ, directive, order

μακαρισμός, ὁ, pronouncement of blessing, beatitude

παραίνεσις, -εως, ἡ, exhortation

παραφέρω, carry forward; pass. be driven forward

τοιοῦτος, -αύτη, -οῦτον, of such a kind, such as this; τὰ τοιαῦτα, similar/related things

φόρτος, ὁ, freight, heavy load, burden

83:4 οὔτε[13] γὰρ τοὺς πλουσίους ἡ κτῆσις ὀφειλήσει τι, οὔτε τοὺς πένητας ἡ πενία ῥύσεται[14] ἀπὸ τῆς δίκης· 5 οὔτε εἰλήφαμεν ἐντολὴν ἣν οὐ δυνάμεθα ποιῆσαι· οὔτε φορτία δυσβάστακτα ἡμῖν ἐπέθηκεν ἃ οὐ δυνάμεθα βαστάσαι· 6 οὔτε (ἐπέθηκεν) οἰκοδομὴν τοιαύτην ἣν οἱ ἄνθρωποι κτίζουσιν· οὔτε λίθους λατομῆσαι καὶ

---

[12] I.e., to those originally addressed by Jesus in the earlier quotations.

[13] οὔτε...οὔτε....

[14] S.v. ἐρύω.

οἴκους κατασκευάσαι ὡς οἱ τεχνῖται ὑμῶν διὰ τῆς ἰδίας ἐπιστήμης ποιοῦσιν. 7 ταύτην δὲ τὴν ἐντολὴν εἰλήφαμεν παρὰ τοῦ κυρίου ἵνα ὃ οὐκ ἀρέσκει ἡμῖν ὑπὸ ἄλλου (person) γινόμενον τοῦτο[15] ἄλλῳ τινὶ μὴ ποιούμεν.

Vocabulary

δίκη, ἡ, judgment, punishment
δυσβάστακτος, -ον, intolerable
ἐπιστήμη, ἡ, knowledge
ἐρύω, mid. ἐρύομαι/ῥύομαι, 2. ῥύσομαι, 3. ἐρρυσάμην: mid. rescue, save, deliver
κατασκευάζω, construct, build; prepare
κτῆσις, -εως, ἡ, property, possessions
κτίζω, found, create, make; build; pass. be created, constructed
λατομέω, quarry stone
οἰκοδομή (= δομή), building
ὀφείλω (and –έω), 2. ὀφειλήσω, 3. ὠφείλησα: owe somebody something, be indebted to; must (w. inf.); ἁμαρτίαν ὀφείλω (w. dat.), incur sin against
πένης, -ητος, ὁ, poor person
πενία, ἡ, poverty
πλούσιος, -α, -ον, rich, wealthy; ὁ πλούσιος, rich man
τεχνίτης, -ου, ὁ, craftsman, artisan, skilled worker; musician
φορτίον, τό, a load, cargo; burden

87:1 Ταῦτα εἰπόντος τοῦ ἀποστόλου παντὸς τοῦ ὄχλου ἀκούοντος[16] ἀλλήλους συνεπάτουν θλίβοντες (them down)· 2 ἡ δὲ γυνὴ Χαρισίου τοῦ συγγενοῦς[17] τοῦ βασιλέως ἐκπηδήσασα ἐκ τοῦ δίφρου καὶ ἑαυτὴν ῥίψασα ἐπὶ τῆς γῆς ἔμπροσθεν τοῦ ἀποστόλου καὶ τῶν ποδῶν αὐτοῦ ἁπτομένη καὶ δεομένη ἔλεγεν· 3 Μαθητὰ τοῦ θεοῦ τοῦ ζῶντος, εἰσῆλθες εἰς χώραν ἔρημον· ἐν ἐρημίᾳ γὰρ οἰκοῦμεν, ἐοικότες[18] ζῴοις ἀλόγοις ἐν τῇ ἀναστροφῇ ἡμῶν·

Vocabulary

ἐκπηδάω, leap up
δέω (2), ¹aor. pass. ptc. δεηθείς (dep.): miss, be in need of (w. gen.); mid. δέομαι, ask for (w. gen.), plead for something (w. gen.), beg of somebody
δίφρος, ὁ, palanquin, litter[19]
ἔοικα (pf. w. pres. sense), pf. inf. ἐοικέναι, ptc. ἐοικώς: be like, resemble (w. dat.)

---

[15] Resumptive dem. pron.
[16] Two gen. absol. constructions.
[17] Modifier of Χαρισίου in 3rd pred. pos. (cf. IV, 4.3).
[18] Causal adv. ptc. ("because").
[19] I.e., an enclosed couch, carried by poles on the shoulders of four or more bearers.

θλίβω, pf. pass. ptc. τεθλιμμένος: push; oppress, afflict; pass. be oppressed, experience pain συμπατέω, impf. συνέπατον, trample under foot

87:4 Νῦν δὲ διὰ τῶν σῶν χειρῶν σωθησόμεθα· δέομαι οὖν σου, φρόντισόν μου καὶ εὖξαι[20] ὑπὲρ ἐμοῦ, ἵνα ἡ εὐσπλαγχνία τοῦ ὑπὸ σοῦ καταγγελλομένου θεοῦ γένηται ἐπ' ἐμέ, κἀγὼ γένωμαι αὐτοῦ οἰκητήριον, καὶ καταλλαγῶ ἐν τῇ εὐχῇ καὶ τῇ ἐλπίδι καὶ τῇ πίστει αὐτοῦ, καὶ δέξωμαι κἀγὼ σφραγῖδα, καὶ γένωναι ναὸς ἅγιος, καὶ κατοικήσῃ ἐν ἐμοὶ αὐτός.

Vocabulary
εὐσπλαγχνία, ἡ, compassion
οἰκητήριον, τό, dwelling place
σφραγίς, -ῖδος, ἡ, (wax) seal
φροντίζω, consider, ponder; be concerned about somebody (gen.), pay attention to something (gen.)

88:1 Καὶ ὁ ἀπόστολος (Thomas) εἶπεν· Εὔχομαι καὶ δέομαι ὑπὲρ ὑμῶν πάντων ἀδελφοὶ τῶν εἰς τὸν κύριον πιστευόντων καὶ (ὑπὲρ) ὑμῶν τῶν ἀδελφιδῶν τῶν εἰς τὸν Χριστὸν ἐλπιζουσῶν ἵνα εἰς πάντας κατασκηνώσῃ ὁ λόγος τοῦ θεοῦ καὶ ἐν αὐτοῖς ἐνσκηνώσῃ· ἡμεῖς γὰρ αὐτῶν ἐξουσίαν[21] οὐκ ἔχομεν. 2 Καὶ ἤρξατο λέγειν πρὸς τὴν γυναῖκα Μυγδονία· Ἀνάστα[22] ἀπὸ τῆς γῆς καὶ ἀναπόλησον σεαυτήν· οὐδὲν γάρ σε ὠφελήσει ὁ ἐπίθετος κόσμος οὗτος, οὐδὲ τὸ κάλλος τοῦ σώματός σου, οὐδὲ τὰ ἀμφιάσματά σου· 3 ἀλλ' οὔτε ἡ φήμη τοῦ περὶ σὲ ἀξιώματος, οὔτε ἡ ἐξουσία τοῦ κόσμου τούτου, οὔτε ἡ κοινωνία ἡ ῥυπαρὰ ἡ πρὸς τὸν ἄνδρα σου αὕτη[23] ὀνήσει σε στερηθεῖσαν[24] ἀπὸ τῆς κοινωνίας[25] τῆς ἀληθινῆς·

Vocabulary
ἀδελφιδός, ὁ / ἀδελφιδῆ, ἡ, beloved one; fm. sister
ἀμφίασμα, τό, garment
ἀναπολέω, govern again, repeat
ἀξίωμα, -ματος, τό, honor, rank
ἐνσκηνόω, dwell in
ἐπίθετος, -ον, additional, acquired
κατασκηνόω, rest on
ὀνίνημι, 2. ὀνήσω: profit, benefit somebody (acc.)

---

[20] S.v. εὔχομαι.
[21] αὐτῶν ἐξουσίαν, i.e., "authority over you."
[22] Even though the 2nd pers. ²aor. act. impv. form of ἵστημι is στῆθι, the comp. form, ἀνίστημι, has two possible impv. forms: ἀνάστηθι and ἀνάστα.
[23] ἡ κοινωνία...αὕτη = αὕτη ἡ κοινωνία.
[24] Cond. adv. ptc. ("if," cf. IV, 1.8).
[25] This second use of the term κοινωνία is figurative.

ῥυπαρός, -ά, -όν, filthy, dirty
στερέω, deprive, rob of something; pass. be deprived of something
ὠφελέω, gain, profit, achieve (something); help, benefit

88:4 ἡ γὰρ φαντασία τους καλλωπισμοῦ καταργεῖται, καὶ τὸ σῶμα γηράσκει καὶ ἀλλάσσεται, καὶ τὰ ἐνδύματα παλαιοῦτα, καὶ ἡ ἐξουσία καὶ ἡ δεσποτεία παρέρχεται μετ' αὐτῶν καὶ ὑπόδικον εἶναι, ἐν ᾧ ἤδη πολλοὶ ἐπολιτεύσαντο. παρέρχεται δὲ καὶ ἡ κοινωνία τῆς παιδοποιίας ὡς δὴ κατάγνωσις οὖσα. 5 Ἰησοῦς μόνος μένει ἀεὶ καὶ οἱ εἰς αὐτὸν ἐλπίζοντες. 6 Ταῦτα εἰπὼν λέγει πρὸς τὴν γυναῖκα· Ἄπελθε μετ' εἰρήνης, καὶ ὁ κύριος τῶν ἰδίων μυστηρίων ἀξίαν σε ποιήσει. 7 Ἡ δὲ εἶπεν· Φοβοῦμαι ἀπελθεῖν, μή με ἄρα καταλείψας ἀπέλθῃς εἰς ἄλλο ἔθνος. 8 Ὁ δὲ ἀπόστολος εἶπεν αὐτῇ· Κἂν ἐγὼ πορευθῶ, οὐ καταλείψω σε μόνην, ἀλλὰ Ἰησοῦς διὰ τὴν εὐσπλαγχνία αὐτοῦ (will be) μετὰ σοῦ. 9 Ἡ δὲ πεσοῦσα προσεκύνησεν αὐτὸν καὶ ἀπῆλθεν εἰς τὸν οἶκον αὐτῆς.

Vocabulary
ἀλλάσσω, 2. ἀλλάξω, 6. ἠλλάγην: change, alter; exchange one thing for another
ἀπάντησις, -εως, ἡ, meeting, greeting (esp. of the public welcome of an official)
γηράσκω, grow old
δεσποτεία, ἡ, power of a master over slaves
εὐσπλαγχνία, ἡ, compassion
καλλωπισμός, ὁ, ornamentation
κατάγνωσις, ἡ, object of contempt/moral condemnation
καταργέω, deactivate, render ineffective, make powerless (contrasting ἐνεργῶ); release from, estrange from
κοινωνία, ἡ, fellowship, partnership; sexual intercourse with (πρός)
παιδοποιία, ἡ, procreation of children
παλαιόω, wear out
ὑπόδικος, -ον, liable to forfeit
φαντασία, ἡ, fantasy; appearance, presentation

89:1 Χαρίσιος δὲ ὁ συγγενὴς Μισδαίου[26] τοῦ βασιλέως λουσάμενος ἀνῆλθεν καὶ ἀνεκλίθη δειπνῆσαι. 2 ἐξήταζεν δὲ (his wife's female slaves) περὶ τῆς ἰδίας γαμετῆς ποῦ ἐστιν· οὐ γὰρ ἐληλύθει εἰς ἀπάντησις αὐτοῦ ἀπὸ τοῦ ἰδίου κοιτῶνος ὡς ἔθος εἶχεν·[27] 3 αἱ δὲ θεραπαινίδαι αὐτῆς εἶπον αὐτῷ· Ἀνωμάλως ἔχει. 4 Ὁ δὲ εἰσπηδήσας εἰσῆλθεν εἰς τὸν κοιτῶνα καὶ εὗρεν αὐτὴν κατακειμένην εἰς τὴν κοίτην καὶ ἐσκεπασμένην· 5 καὶ ἀνακαλύψας αὐτὴν κατεφίλησεν αὐτὴν λέγων· Τίνος ἕνεκεν σήμερον περίλυπος εἶ; Ἡ δὲ εἶπεν· Ἀνωμάλως ἔχω. 6 Ὁ δὲ λέγει πρὸς αὐτήν· Διὰ τί γὰρ σχῆμα οὐκ ἐποίησας τῆς σῆς ἐλευθερίας καὶ ἔμεινας

---

[26] Misdaios.
[27] The verb ἔχω sometimes functions like εἰμί.

ἐν τῷ οἴκῳ σου, ἀλλ' (instead) ἀπελθοῦσα κατήκουσας λόγων ματαίων καὶ ἔργα μαγικὰ[28] ἐθεάσω; 7 ἀλλὰ ἀνάστα, συνδείπνησόν μοι. ἄνευ γὰρ σοῦ οὐ δύναμαι δειπνῆσαι. Ἡ δὲ εἶπεν πρὸς αὐτόν· Σήμερον παραιτοῦμαι· πάνυ γὰρ πεφόβημαι.

Vocabulary

ἀνακαλύπτω, unveil

ἀνακλίνω, 6. ἀνεκλίθην: lay down; pass. lie down, recline at a meal

ἄνευ, without (w. gen.)

ἀνωμάλως ἔχω, feel unwell

γαμετή, ἡ, wife

δειπνέω, dine

εἰσπηδάω, burst in, rush in

ἐξετάζω, question somebody closely

θεραπαινιδίς (fm. of θεράπων), female slave/servant

κατάκειμαι, lie down in/on (dat. / εἰς)

κατακούω, listen to (w. gen.)

κοιτών, -ῶνος, ὁ, bed chamber

μαγικός, -ή, -όν, magical; pl. subst. works of sorcery

μάταιος, -α, -ον, empty, useless, powerless

πάνυ, very, very much

παραιτέομαι, ask for, entreat, beg, request; excuse oneself (παραιτοῦμαι, "excuse me")

περίλυπος, -ον, very sad

πολιτεύω/ομαι, mid. inf. πολιτεύεσθαι: conduct one's life in a particular way; live under a certain set of laws; deal with in one's private affairs

σκεπάζω, cover; pass. be veiled

συνδειπνέω, dine with somebody, dine together

90:1 Ταῦτα ἀκούσας ὁ Χαρίσιος παρὰ τῆς Μυγδονίας οὐκ ἠβουλήθη ἐξελθεῖν ἐπὶ τὸ δεῖπνον, ἀλλὰ παρεκελεύσατο τοῖς οἰκείοις αὐτοῦ ἵνα προσαγάγωσιν αὐτὴν συνδειπνῆσαι αὐτῷ· 2 εἰσαγαγόντων[29] (αὐτῶν) οὖν ἠξίουν[30] αὐτὴν συνδειπνῆσαι αὐτῷ· Ἡ δὲ παρῃτεῖτο. 3 μὴ βουληθείσης οὖν αὐτῆς[31] μόνος ἐδείπνησεν λέγων αὐτῇ· Διὰ σὲ παρῃτησάμην δειπνῆσαι παρὰ τῷ βασιλεῖ Μισδαίῳ,[32] καὶ σὺ οὐκ ἠβουλήθης συνδειπνῆσαι μοι; 4 Ἡ δὲ ἔφη· Διὰ τὸ ἀνωμάλως με ἔχειν. Ἀναστὰς οὖν ὁ Χαρίσιος κατὰ τὸ εἰωθὸς ἐβούλετο συγκαθεύδειν αὐτῇ· ἡ δὲ ἔφη· Οὐκ εἶπόν σοι τὴν σήμερον παραιτήσασθαι;

---

[28] Cf. Acts Thom. 96:3, Acts 19:19.

[29] Gen. absol.

[30] Iter. impf. (cf. IV, 13.3).

[31] Gen. absol.

[32] Misdaios.

Vocabulary

ἀνωμάλως ἔχω, feel unwell

δεῖπνον, τό, meal, dinner

εἴωθα (pf. of obsol. pres. ἔθω; pf. w. pres. meaning), ²pf. ptc. εἰωθώς, -υῖα, -ός: be
     accustomed to; nt. ptc. subst., τὸ εἰωθός, custom

οἰκεῖος, -α, -ον, of a household; belonging to the same kin/family; proper to a
     thing, suitable; individual; οἱ οἰκεῖοι, family members

παρακελεύομαι, exhort, encourage

συγκαθεύδω, have sex with

96:1 Ἀκούσας (Charisios) δὲ ὅτι οὐ βούλεται ἐξελθεῖν ἀπὸ τοῦ κοιτῶνος (αὐτῆς),
εἰσελθὼν εἶπεν αὐτῇ· Τίνος ἕνεκεν οὐ βούλει[33] συνδειπνῆσαί μοι, τάχα δὲ οὐδὲ
συγκαθευδῆσαι κατὰ τὸ εἰωθός; 2 καὶ περὶ τούτου μείζονα τὴν ὑποψίαν ἔχω·
ἤκουσα γὰρ ὅτι ὁ μάγος ἐκεῖνος[34] καὶ (ὁ) πλάνος τοῦτο διδάσκει, ἵνα μή τις
συνοικήσῃ γυναικὶ ἰδίᾳ, καὶ ὃ ἡ φύσις ἀπαιτεῖν οἶδεν καὶ ἡ θεότης ἐνομοθέτησεν
αὐτὸς ἀνατρέπει. 3 Ταῦτα εἰπόντος τοῦ Χαρισίου[35] ἡ Μυγδονία ἡσύχαζεν. λέγει
πάλιν πρὸς αὐτήν· Κυρία μου καὶ σύμβιέ μου Μυγδονία μὴ πλανῶ[36] λόγοις
ἀπατηλοῖς καὶ ματαίοις, μηδὲ τοῖς ἔργοις τῆς μαγείας οἷς[37] ἤκουσα τοῦτον
διαπραττόμεν εἰς ὄνομα πατρὸς υἱοῦ καὶ ἁγίου πνεύματος·

Vocabulary

ἀνατρέπω, overturn, reverse

ἀπαιτέω, demand something

ἀπατηλός, -ή, -όν, deceptive, illusory

διαπράσσω (Att. διαπράττω), accomplish something

ἡσυχάζω, keep quiet; find rest

θεότης, -ητος, ἡ, divinity

μαγεία, ἡ, magic, sorcery

μάγος, ὁ, magician

νομοθέτω, ordain by law

πλάνος, -ον, deceiving; subst. deceiver

σύμβιος, -ον, living together; ὁ / ἡ, husband, wife

συνοικέω, cohabit with (one's spouse)

ὑποψία, ἡ, suspicion

---

[33] βούλει (Att.) > βούλῃ.
[34] I.e., Thomas.
[35] Gen. absol.
[36] Cf. table 9.4.4(c).
[37] οὕς → οἷς (attr. rel.).

96:4 οὐ γὰρ ἠκούσθη ποτὲ ἐν τῷ κόσμῳ τούτῳ ὅτι νεκρόν τις ἤγειρεν· ὡς δὲ ἀκούω τὰ περὶ τούτου φημιζόμενα ὅτι νεκροὺς ἐγείρει. 5 καὶ ὅτι οὐδὲ ἐσθίει οὔτε πίνει, μὴ οὖν νομίσῃς ὅτι διὰ δικαιοσύνην οὔτε ἐσθίει οὔτε πίνει· τοῦτο δὲ ποιεῖ διὰ τὸ μηδὲν κεκτῆσθαι[38] αὐτόν· 6 τί γὰρ ἂν ποιήσειεν[39] ὃς οὐδὲ τὸν ἡμερήσιον ἄρτον ἔχει; καὶ ἓν ἔνδυμα ἔχει διὰ τὸ πένητα εἶναι αὐτόν· 7 (As for) τὸ δὲ μὴ λαμβάνειν παρά τινός τί, (it does it) συγγινώσκων[40] ἑαυτὸν θεραπεύειν.

Vocabulary

ἡμερήσιος, -α, -ον, for a day
συγγινώσκω, be conscious of something, be aware
φημίζω, spread a report

97:1 Ταῦτα δὲ τοῦ Χαρισίου εἰπόντος[41] ἡ Μυγδονία ὥσπερ πέτρα τις ἡσύχαζεν· ηὔχετο δὲ (that) πότε (night) διαφαύσει, ἵνα ἀπέλθῃ πρὸς τὸν ἀπόστολον τοῦ Χριστοῦ· 2 (Charisios) ἀναχωρεῖ δὲ ἀπ᾽ αὐτῆς, καὶ ἀπέρχεται ἐπὶ τὸ δεῖπνον ἀθυμῶν· ἐμερίμνα γὰρ κατὰ τὸ ἔθος συγκαθευδῆσαι αὐτῇ. 3 ἐξελθόντος[42] δὲ ἐκείνου (Mygdonia) κλίνασα τὰ γόνατα ηὔχετο λέγουσα· Κύριε θεὲ δέσποτα, πατὴρ ἐλεήμων, σωτὴρ Χριστέ, σὺ δός μοι δύναμιν ἵνα νικήσω τὴν ἀναίδειαν Χαρισίου, καὶ παράσχου μοι φυλάξαι τὴν ἁγιωσύνην εἰς ἣν σὺ χαίρεις, ἵνα κἀγὼ δι᾽ αὐτῆς εὕρω ζωὴν αἰώνιον. 4 Ταῦτα δὲ εὐξαμένης[43] αὐτῆς ἔθηκεν ἑαυτὴν ἐπὶ τὴν κλίνην σκεπασθεῖσα.

Vocabulary

ἁγιωσύνη, ἡ, holiness, sanctity
ἀθυμόω, be disheartened, saddened
ἀναίδεια, ἡ, shamelessness
ἀναχωρέω, withdraw from (ἀπό)
διαφαύω, come to an end
πέτρα, -ας, ἡ, rock
σκεπάζω, to veil

98:1 Ὁ δὲ Χαρίσιος δειπνήσας ἐπέστη[44] αὐτῇ· αὐτὴ δὲ ἐβόα[45] λέγουσα· Οὐκ ἔχεις λοιπὸν χώραν πρὸς ἐμέ· ὁ γὰρ κύριός μου Ἰησοῦς κρείττων[46] σού[47] ἐστιν, ὁ σὺν

---

[38] Art. inf. (s.v. κτάομαι).
[39] Cf. table 9.1.3(b).
[40] Causal adv. ptc. ("because," cf. IV, 1.4).
[41] Gen. absol.
[42] Gen. absol.
[43] Gen. absol.
[44] S.v. ἐφίστημι.
[45] Incept. impf. (cf. IV, 13.5).
[46] κρείττων (Att.) > κρείσσων.
[47] Gen. of comp. (cf. IV, 10).

ἐμοὶ ὢν καὶ ἐν ἐμοὶ ἀναπαυόμενος. 2 Ὁ δὲ γελάσας εἶπεν· Καλῶς χλευάζεις ταῦτα λέγουσα περὶ ἐκείνου τοῦ φαρμακέως, καὶ καλῶς αὐτοῦ καταγελᾷς λέγοντος ὅτι Ζωὴν οὐκ ἔχετε παρὰ τῷ θεῷ ἐὰν μὴ ἁγνίσητε αὐτούς. 3 Ταῦτα εἰπόντος[48] αὐτοῦ ἐπεχείρει πρὸς αὐτὴν καθευδῆσαι·[49]: ἡ δὲ μὴ ὑπομένουσα ἀλλὰ πικρῶς κραυγάζουσα[50] ἔλεγε· Ἐπικαλοῦμαί σε κύριε Ἰησοῦ, μὴ ἐγκαταλίπῃς με· πρὸς σὲ γὰρ τὴν καταφυγὴν ἐποιησάμην· ὡς γὰρ ἀνέμαθον ὅτι σὺ εἶ ὁ ἐπιζητῶν τοὺς ἐν ἀγνοίᾳ ἐπειλημμένους[51] καὶ (ὁ) ῥυόμενος τοὺς ἐν τῇ πλάνῃ κατεχομένους·

Vocabulary

ἁγνίζω, clease with water, purify

ἀναμανθάνω, learn, perceive

ἐγκαταλείπω, [1]aor. ἐγκατέλιψα/[2]aor. ἐγκατέλιπον: forsake, abandon, desert

ἐπιζητέω, seek after, desire

ἐπικαλέω, call upon; mid. to call in as a helper; pass. be called

ἐπιλαμβάνω, 5. ἐπείλημμαι: take hold of something, to overtake, seize; pass. be imprisoned

ἐπιχειρέω, make an attempt, try

ἐφίστημι, pres. mid. ἐφίσταμαι, 3. ἐπέστησα/ἐπέστην, aor. ptc. ἐπιστάς, -άντος, 4. ἐφέστηκα: stand on/near, stand beside (w. παρά); approach; come upon, attack; mid. (intrans.), come upon somebody (w. dat.), overtake somebody

καλῶς, rightly, well καλῶς ἂν ποιήσαις/ποιήσεις, lit. "you would do well [to]"; fig. "please" (epistolary formula expressing a polite request); "hurrah for," "bravo for" (to approve the words of a speaker)

καταγελάω, laugh scornfully at somebody (gen.), mock

κράζω (= κραυγάζω), to scream, to screech

φαρμακεύς, ὁ, sorcerer

χλευάζω, jest, scoff

98:4 νυνὶ δὲ ἐγὼ σοῦ δέομαι οὗ τὴν φήμην ἤκουσα καὶ ἐπίστευσα, σὺ ἐλθὲ εἰς τὴν βοήθειάν μου, καὶ ῥῦσαί με ἀπὸ τῆς ἀναισχυντίας Χαρισίου, ὥστε μὴ κατεξουσιάσῃ μου ἡ τούτου μιαρότης. 5 καὶ τύψασα ἑαυτῆς τὰς χεῖρας ἔφυγεν ἀπ᾽ αὐτοῦ γυμνή· 6 καὶ ἐξιοῦσα κατέσπασεν τὸ βῆλον τοῦ κοιτῶνος, καὶ τοῦτο περιβαλομένη ἀπῄει[52] πρὸς τὴν ἑαυτῆς τροφόν, κἀκεῖ παρ᾽ αὐτῇ ὕπνωσεν.

Vocabulary

ἀναισχυντία, ἡ, shamelessness

βῆλον, τό, covering, curtain (Lat. loanw. *velum*)

---

[48] Gen. absol.

[49] ἡ = ἐκείνη.

[50] κραυγάζω = κράζω.

[51] S.v. ἐπιλαμβάνω.

[52] S.v. ἄπειμι (fr. εἶμι, cf. table 9.14).

ἔξειμι (fr. εἶμι), inf. ἐξιέναι, ptc. ἐξιών, -οῦσα, -όν: go out, leave, depart from a place (for paradigm of εἶμι cf. table 9.14)

κατασπάω, pull down

κατεξουσιάζω, exercise authority over

μιαρότης, -ητος, ἡ, foulness

νυνί, strengthened form of νῦν, now, at this time

τροφός, ἡ, nurse (i.e., the woman who raised her as a child)

τύπτω, ἔτυψα: beat, strike

ὑπνόω, sleep

SELECT BIBLIOGRAPHY

Attridge, Harold W. (trans.). *The Acts of Thomas*. Ed. Julian V. Hills. Salem, OR: Polebridge Press, 2010.

Bremmer, Jan N. (ed.). *The Apocryphal Acts of Thomas*. Leuven: Peeters, 2001.

Burrus, Virginia. "Chastity as Autonomy: Women in the Stories of the Apocryphal Acts." In *The Apocryphal Acts of Apostles*, 101–117. Ed. Dennis R. Macdonald. Semeia 38. 1986.

Elliott, J. K. *The Apocryphal New Testament*. Oxford: Clarendon Press, 1999, 16–20.

Festugière, A. J. *Les Actes apocryphes de Jean et de Thomas: traduction française et notes critiques*. Geneva: P. Cramer, 1983.

Klijn, A. F. J. *The Acts of Thomas: Introduction, Text, and Commentary*, 2nd ed. Leiden: Brill, 2003 (Syriac edition).

PART 6

Advanced-Level Hellenistic Greek: Jewish Literary Greek

Part 6 presents a number of texts that reflect what could be termed Jewish *literary* Greek, such as is found in the writings of Philo of Alexandria (§6.4), 2 Maccabees (§6.1, §6.2), and 4 Maccabees (§6.3). Such Jewish compositional Greek is highly literary, making full use of the expressive range of the Hellenistic Greek language. Included in this part is the metrical Jewish tractate of Ezekiel the Tragedian (§6.6), which is remarkable for having been composed in iambic trimeter, in the poetic style of ancient Greek tragedy. The imprint of Hellenization is also evident in the Jewish Testament of Reuben (§§6.5, 6.7), which reflects ideas found in contemporaneous Stoic philosophical speculation.

The vocabulary lists in Part 6 do not repeat the vocabulary for memorization in Parts 1–5 (§§1.1–10, 2.1–6, 3.1–9, 4.1–11, 5.1–10). However, all such vocabulary is compiled in the glossary (§10).

6.1.

2 Maccabees: Jason's Hellenistic Reforms in Jerusalem

(2 Macc 4:7–17)

Following the murder of his brother, Seleucus IV (175 BCE), Antiochus IV Epiphanes (175–164 BCE) seized control of the Seleucid Empire and reorganized its imperial administration along Roman lines. Despite this reorganization, the central institutions of the Antiochene polity remained Greek (Hellenistic), including the centrality of gymnasia and the ephebic system (cf. 1 Macc 1:1–28, §3.3).[1] It is this aspect of the political situation that the author of 2 Maccabees focused on.

Before Antiochus Epiphanes took the throne, Onias III (Ονιος) had served as high priest. But Onias was aligned with the pro-Ptolemaic (Egyptian) party in Jerusalem, whereas his brother, Jason (Ἰάσων), was aligned with the pro-Seleucid party. Jason took advantage of this political rivalry by successfully negotiating a deal with the Seleucid king Antiochus IV in 175 BCE to purchase the office of high priest and thereby supplant Onias (2 Macc 4:7). As the reading in this section illustrates, Jason's actions polarized Jewish factional interests to such an extent that violent conflict erupted. For the author of 2 Maccabees, this conflict was primarily a religious issue – hence his portrayal of Jason as an impious fraud, who set in motion a Deuteronomic cycle of apostasy, punishment, and deliverance (2 Macc 4:16).

2 Maccabees is composed in highly literate Greek, without any Hebrew precursor. The majority of the text (2 Macc 3:1–15:36) is an abridged version of a five-volume work composed by Jason of Cyrene.

---

[1] Jonathan A. Goldstein, *II Maccabees* (New York: Doubleday, 1983), 227.

4:7 Μεταλλάξαντος δὲ τὸν βίον Σελεύκου[2] καὶ παραλαβόντος τὴν βασιλείαν Ἀντιόχου[3] τοῦ προσαγορευθέντος Ἐπιφανοῦς ὑπενόθευσεν Ἰάσων ὁ ἀδελφὸς Ονιου τὴν ἀρχιερωσύνην 8 ἐπαγγειλάμενος[4] τῷ βασιλεῖ δι᾽ ἐντεύξεως ἀργυρίου τάλαντα ἑξήκοντα πρὸς[5] τοῖς τριακοσίοις καὶ προσόδου τινὸς ἄλλης τάλαντα ὀγδοήκοντα. 9 πρὸς δὲ τούτοις ὑπισχνεῖτο[6] καὶ ἕτερα διαγράφειν πεντήκοντα[7] πρὸς τοῖς ἑκατόν, ἐὰν ἐπιχωρηθῇ διὰ τῆς ἐξουσίας αὐτοῦ γυμνάσιον καὶ ἐφηβεῖον αὐτῷ συστήσασθαι[8] καὶ τοὺς ἐν Ἱεροσολύμοις Ἀντιοχεῖς ἀναγράψαι.

Vocabulary

ἀναγράφω, engrave and set up publicly

Ἀντιοχεῖς, citizens of Antioch[9]

ἀρχιερωσύνη, high priesthood

διαγράφω, to pay

ἔντευξις, -εως, ἡ, petition

ἐπιφανής, -ές, appearing, manifest (of gods, and used as title by Antiochus IV Epiphanes); notable, distinguished

ἐπιχωρέω, permit/grant somebody to do something

ἐφηβεῖον, τό, *ephebeion*, an institution for training ephebes (adolescents)

μεταλλάσσω, [1]aor ptc. μεταλλάξας: to change/alter, die; μεταλλάξαντος τὸν βίον, euphem. "having passed away"

ὀγδοήκοντα, eighty

πεντήκοντα, fifty

προσαγορεύω, to call

πρόσοδος, ἡ, access, approach; revenue, public revenue

τάλαντον, τό, a talent (measure of weight ranging from 108 to 130 pounds)

τριακόσιοι, -αι, -α, three hundred

ὑπισχνέομαι, to promise to do something (w. inf.)

ὑπονοθεύω, procure by corruption, gain by stealth

4:10 ἐπινεύσαντος[10] δὲ τοῦ βασιλέως καὶ τῆς ἀρχῆς κρατήσας[11] εὐθέως πρὸς τὸν Ἑλληνικὸν χαρακτῆρα τοὺς ὁμοφύλους (αὐτοῦ) μετέστησε.[12] 11 Καὶ τὰ κείμενα τοῖς

---

[2] Seleucus IV; gen. absol.

[3] Antiochus IV Epiphanes; gen. absol.

[4] Instr. adv. ptc. ("by," cf. IV, 1.6).

[5] πρός (w. dat.) with numbers means "plus," "in addition" (cf. 2 Macc 4:9).

[6] Impf. here conveys the idea of conniving.

[7] ἕτερα...πεντήκοντα.

[8] S.v. συνίστημι.

[9] This was similar to becoming a Roman citizen. Leading cities formed citizen bodies, whose members were registered as citizens of the Seleucid Republic.

[10] Gen. absol.

[11] Gen. absol. with Jason as the implied subject.

[12] S.v. μεθίστημι.

Ἰουδαίοις φιλάνθρωπα[13] βασιλικὰ[14] (secured) διὰ Ἰωάννου[15] τοῦ πατρὸς Εὐπολέμου τοῦ ποιησαμένου[16] τὴν πρεσβείαν ὑπὲρ φιλίας καὶ συμμαχίας πρὸς τοὺς Ῥωμαίους παρώσας καὶ τὰς μὲν νομίμους[17] καταλύων[18] πολιτείας παρανόμους ἐθισμοὺς ἐκαίνιζεν.[19]12 ἀσμένως γὰρ ὑπ᾽ αὐτὴν[20] τὴν ἀκρόπολιν γυμνάσιον καθίδρυσεν καὶ τοὺς κρατίστους τῶν ἐφήβων ὑποτάσσων[21] ὑπὸ πέτασον ἤγαγεν.[22]

Vocabulary

ἀκρόπολις, -εως, ἡ, citadel, castle

ἀσμένως, gladly, readily

ἐθισμός, ὁ, custom

Ἑλληνικός, -ή, -όν, Hellenic, Greek (adj.); τὰ Ἑλληνικά, Greek customs

ἐπινεύω, lit. to nod, grant/promise something (acc.) to somebody (dat.)

ἔφηβος, ὁ, ephebe/adolescent enrolled in an institution for educating young men for citizenship and military service

καινίζω, innovate; introduce something strange

καθιδρύω, consecrate, dedicate; found/establish something

καταλύω, destroy, abolish; eradicate

κράτιστος, -η, -ον, most excellent, noblest; most excellent; "his Excellency" (official title given to senators and magistrates)

νόμιμος, -η, -ον, conform to the law, legal; pl. τὰ νόμιμα, laws, statutes

ὁμόφυλος, ὁ, compatriot

παρωθέω, aor. ptc. παρώσας: set aside

πέτασος, *petasos*, a broad-brimmed hat, often worn in combinatioin with a cape, by ephebes as a sign of their membership in the *ephebeion*

πρεσβεία, ἡ, embassy, mission

Ῥωμαῖος, -α, -ον, of the Romans, Roman; subst. Roman person

συμμαχία, ἡ, military alliance, confederacy (the treaty with the Romans is parenthetic; it is used to identify Eupolemus)

ὑποτάσσω, make subject; append; pass. be subjected to

φιλία, ἡ, friendship

χαρακτήρ, -ῆρος, ὁ, outward appearance; distinctive features

---

[13] τὰ...φιλάνθρωπα is the subject of the ptc. παρώσας.

[14] Modifies φιλάνθρωπα (2nd pred. pos.).

[15] John, father of Eupolemus; διὰ Ἰωάννου...πρὸς τοὺς Ῥωμαίους is a subordinate clause.

[16] Gen. absol. (aor. ptc.) introduces first subordinate idea: τοῦ ποιησαμένου...τὴν πρεσβείαν.

[17] τὰς...νομίμους...πολιτείας.

[18] Participle introduces the second subordinate idea.

[19] Main verb of sentence.

[20] αὐτήν, "itself" is emphatic, but ironically this is precisely where one would expect a gymnasium to be located.

[21] Instr. adv. ptc. ("by," cf. IV, 1.6).

[22] Here "bring up," "educate."

4:13 Ἦν δ᾽ οὕτως ἀκμή τις[23] Ἑλληνισμοῦ καὶ πρόσβασις ἀλλοφυλισμοῦ διὰ τὴν[24] τοῦ ἀσεβοῦς καὶ οὐκ (a true) ἀρχιερέως Ἰάσωνος ὑπερβάλλουσαν ἀναγνείαν 14 ὥστε[25] μηκέτι[26] περὶ τὰς τοῦ θυσιαστηρίου λειτουργίας προθύμους εἶναι τοὺς ἱερεῖς, ἀλλὰ τοῦ μὲν νεὼ[27] καταφρονοῦντες καὶ τῶν θυσιῶν ἀμελοῦντες ἔσπευδον μετέχειν τῆς ἐν παλαίστρη παρανόμου χορηγίας μετὰ τὴν τοῦ δίσκου πρόσκλησιν, 15 καὶ τὰς μὲν πατρῴους τιμὰς ἐν οὐδενὶ τιθέμενοι,[28] τὰς δὲ Ἑλληνικὰς δόξας καλλίστας ἡγούμενοι.

Vocabulary

ἀκμή, ἡ, highest point, culminating point
ἀλλοφυλισμός, the adoption of foreign ways (neol.)
ἀναγνεία, ἡ, abominable wickedness (rare)
ἀρχιερωσύνη, high priesthood
δίσκος, ὁ, disk; sun disk (i.e., sun); discus event
Ἑλληνισμός, ὁ, imitation of the Greeks, Hellenism
θυσία, ἡ, sacrifice
κάλλιστος, -ον, -ον (superl. of καλός), best
λειτουργία, ἡ, public service, public liturgical service; priestly ministry
μετέχω, partake of (gen.), participate in
παλαίστρα, ἡ, place for exercise, wrestling school
πατρῴος, -α, -ον, of one's father(s), hereditary
πρόθυμος, -ον, ready, eager; προθύμως, zealously, earnestly
πρόσβασις, εως, ἡ, opportunity
πρόσκλησις, ἡ, summons, here "sounding of the gong"
τιμή, -ῆς, ἡ, honor, pl. honors; price/cost, value; (gen.) at a price of
ὑπερβάλλω, exceed, surpass
χορηγία, ἡ, public spectacle

4:16 ὧν καὶ χάριν περιέσχεν αὐτοὺς χαλεπὴ περίστασις, καὶ ὧν[29] ἐζήλουν τὰς ἀγωγὰς καὶ καθ᾽ ἅπαν[30] ἤθελον ἐξομοιοῦσθαι, τούτους πολεμίους[31] καὶ τιμωρητὰς ἔσχον, 17 ἀσεβεῖν γὰρ εἰς τοὺς θείους νόμους οὐ ῥάδιον, ἀλλὰ ταῦτα ὁ ἀκόλουθος καιρὸς[32] δηλώσει.

---

[23] τις here follows the word it modifies (i.e., τις ἀκμή); it functions as an emphatic particle.
[24] διὰ τὴν...ἀναγνεία.
[25] ὥστε + inf. (cf. IV, 15).
[26] μηκέτι...προθύμους.
[27] νεώ, gen. of νεώς, Att. of ναός, νεῴ (dat.), νεών (acc.); this term is the usual rendition of היכל (the inner shrine of the Jewish temple).
[28] S.v. τίθημι, here "to make something as (ἐν)."
[29] Gen. of poss. ("whose, of whom") + τὰς ἀγωγάς.
[30] καθ᾽ ἅπαν, "completely."
[31] Acc. of spec. ("as").
[32] Here in the sense of "event(s)."

Vocabulary

ἀκόλουθος, -ον, following, later; (adv.) ἀκολούθως, following, next; according to
ἐξομοιόομαι, imitate

ζηλόω, strive; be filled with envy or jealousy

περιέχω, ²aor. ptc. περίσχων, ²aor. pass. inf. περισχέσθαι: include; encompass,
surround; come upon, befall

περίστασις, -εως, ἡ, crisis, disaster

πολεμίος, -α, -ον, hostile; subst. enemy; superl. πολεμιώτατος, most
bitter enemy

ῥᾴδιος, -α, -ον, easy; ῥᾴδιον, a light matter

τιμωρητής, ὁ, oppressor

χαλεπός, -ή, -όν, difficult; cruel, harsh; χαλεπῶς, with difficulty, with great
discomfort

χάριν (w. gen.), because of, by reason of (generally situated after the noun it modifies); ὧν χάριν, for which

6.2.

2 Maccabees: The Martyrdom of Eleazar

(2 Macc 6:1–23)

Date: First century BCE.

This reading recounts the culmination of a series of ill-judged religious reforms that were initiated by Antiochus IV Epiphanes in Jerusalem. Antiochus probably viewed the existing Jewish cult as politically subversive and, having witnessed the recent success of the Roman authorities in suppressing the Bacchanalia in Rome, adopted what he considered to be a reasonable religious policy. However, his religious reforms actually alienated a significant portion of the population. Moreover, the brutal manner in which the reforms were implemented prepared the way for the violent political upheaval that followed.

The text in this section describes Antiochus's imposition of Hellenism (2 Macc 6:1–11), the author's evaluation (2 Macc 6:12–17), and finally the well-known story of the martyrdom of Eleazar (Ἐλεάζαρος) (2 Macc 6:18–31). According to the author's narration of the events leading up to the Maccabean revolt, it was the martyrdom of observant Jews such as Eleazar that became the pivotal political moment.

Related Texts: The concept of righteous martyr who dies for the benefit of others is also found in 4 Macc 1:11 (§6.3) and 4 Macc 6:16–23, 27–28. This concept may have been inspired by Isa 52:13–53:12 (§2.6).

6:1 Μετ᾽ οὐ πολὺν δὲ χρόνον ἐξαπέστειλεν ὁ βασιλεὺς (Antiochus Epiphanes) γέροντα Ἀθηναῖον ἀναγκάζειν τοὺς Ιουδαίους μεταβαίνειν ἀπὸ τῶν πατρίων νόμων καὶ τοῖς τοῦ θεοῦ νόμοις μὴ πολιτεύεσθαι – 2 μολῦναι δὲ καὶ τὸν ἐν

Ἱεροσολύμοις νεὼ[1] καὶ προσονομάσαι (it) Διὸς Ὀλυμπίου καὶ τὸν (temple) ἐν Γαριζιν, καθὼς ἐντύγχανον οἱ τὸν τόπον οἰκοῦντες, Διὸς[2] Ξενίου.

Vocabulary

ἀναγκάζω, force, compel, urge

ἀρχαῖος, -α, -ον, old, ancient; τὰ ἀρχαῖα, things of old

Γαριζιν, Mount Gerazin, site of the Samaritan temple

γέρων, -οντος, ὁ, old man, elder, senator (often an expert on religious matters)

ἐξαποστέλλω, send on a mission, commission a senator

Ζεύς, ὁ, Διός (gen.), Διί (dat.), Δία (acc.), Ζεῦ (voc.), Zeus

μεταβαίνω, switch from (ἀπό) something to something else

μολύνω, pollute, defile

Ὀλύμπιος, -α, -ον (adj.), Olympian, dwelling on Olympus (epithet of various gods, including Demeter and Zeus)

πάτριος, -α, -ον (= πατρικός), derived from one's fathers, hereditary; customary; subst. τὸ πάτριον, tradition; τὰ πάτρια, ancestral customs

προσονομάζω, call by name (w. acc.)

6: 3 Χαλεπὴ δὲ καὶ τοῖς ὅλοις[3] ἦν δυσχερὴς (was) ἡ ἐπίτασις τῆς κακίας. 4 τὸ μὲν γὰρ ἱερὸν ἀσωτίας καὶ κώμων ὑπὸ τῶν ἐθνῶν ἐπεπληροῦτο[4] ῥαθυμούντων μεθ᾽ ἑταιρῶν καὶ ἐν τοῖς ἱεροῖς περιβόλοις γυναιξὶ πλησιαζόντων, ἔτι δὲ τὰ μὴ καθήκοντα ἔνδον εἰσφερόντων.

Vocabulary

ἀσωτία, ἡ, debauchery

δυσχερής, -ης, -ές, grievous, serious

ἔνδον, inside, within

ἐπιπληρόω, fill up with

ἐπίτασις, ἡ, increase (in intensity/force), outburst

ἑταῖρος, ὁ, companion, friend; ἑταίρα, ἡ, prostitute

καθήκω, be appropriate, suitable, proper; nt. ptc. (τὸ) καθῆκον, what is appropriate

κακία, ἡ, wickedness, evil

κῶμος, ὁ, carousing, wild partying

ξένιος, -α, -ον, hospitable; epithet of Zeus, "the protector of the rights of hospitality"

---

[1] S.v. νεώς, Att. > ναός (LXX), but νεώς (nom.) in 2 Macc. This is the usual rendition of לכיה ("inner shrine of the temple"). νεώς has two acc. forms, νεών, and later form, νεώ.

[2] S.v. Ζεύς.

[3] τοῖς ὅλοις ("altogether," "utterly") … δυσχερής.

[4] The basic sentence is followed by three clauses (genitive absolutes) describing the behavior of the Gentiles.

περίβολος, ὁ, outer enclosure wall of a temple

πλησιάζω, have sexual intercourse with (dat.)

ῥᾳθυμέω, be idle, hang around with

χαλεπός, -ή, -όν, difficult; cruel, harsh; χαλεπῶς, with difficulty, with great discomfort

6:5 τὸ δὲ θυσιαστήριον τοῖς ἀποδιεσταλμένοις ἀπό⁵ τῶν νόμων ἀθεμίτοις ἐπεπλήρωτο. 6 ἦν⁶ δ᾽ οὔτε⁷ σαββατίζειν οὔτε πατρῴους ἑορτὰς διαφυλάττειν οὔτε ἁπλῶς Ἰουδαῖον ὁμολογεῖν εἶναι, 7 (the Judeans) ἤγοντο⁸ δὲ⁹ μετὰ πικρᾶς ἀνάγκης εἰς τὴν κατὰ μῆνα¹⁰ τοῦ βασιλέως γενέθλιον ἡμέραν¹¹ ἐπὶ σπλαγχνισμόν, γενομένης¹² δὲ Διονυσίων ἑορτῆς ἠναγκάζοντο¹³ κισσοὺς ἔχοντες πομπεύειν τῷ Διονύσῳ.

Vocabulary

ἀθέμιτος, -ον, against the law

ἀποδιαστέλλω, divide; pass. be forbidden

διαφυλάσσω (Att. διαφυλάττω), keep/observe (a feast/festival)

Διονυσία, τά, Festival of Dionysos

Διόνυσος, ὁ, god Dionysos

κισσός, ὁ, ivy leaves¹⁴

πομπεύω, walk in a procession

σπλαγχνισμός, ὁ, lit. the eating of internal organs of a sacrificial victim (neol.); a sacrifice

6:8 Ψήφισμα δὲ ἐξέπεσεν¹⁵ εἰς τὰς ἀστυγείτονας Ἑλληνίδας πόλεις Πτολεμαίου¹⁶ ὑποθεμένου¹⁷ τὴν αὐτὴν ἀγωγὴν κατὰ¹⁸ τῶν Ιουδαίων ἄγειν καὶ (to require

---

⁵ ἀπό, "by."

⁶ Here εἶναι carries the sense of "to be possible," hence ἦν... εἶναι ("it was possible").

⁷ Vv. 6–7, οὔτε...οὔτε...οὔτε ἁπλῶς...δε...δέ....

⁸ ἄγω (main verb), mid. "to observe (a feast)," "to partake (of a sacrifice)" (iter. impf.).

⁹ Greek often uses δέ as a developmental marker, temporally, in narrative. Here the impf. that follows signals continuous action with all the preceding action.

¹⁰ κατὰ μῆνα, "monthly."

¹¹ εἰς τὴν...ἡμέραν, referring to the time when something occurs ("on the day").

¹² Gen. absol.

¹³ ἠναγκάζοντο...πομπεύειν (iter. impf., cf. IV, 13.3).

¹⁴ I.e., they were expected to become bacchantes by "wearing" ivy leaves on feast days of Dionysos. Ivy leaves were deemed to be sacred to Dionysos.

¹⁵ The three infinitives that follow (ἄγειν, σπλαγχνίζειν, μεταβαίνειν) are all dependent upon the verb ἐξέπεσεν.

¹⁶ Ptolemy, cf. 2 Macc 4:45, where Menelaus bribes a man named "Ptolemy, son of Dorymenes," to win over the king.

¹⁷ Gen. absol.

¹⁸ κατά, "toward," "with respect to."

them) σπλαγχνίζειν, 9 τοὺς δὲ μὴ προαιρουμένους[19] μεταβαίνειν ἐπὶ τὰ Ἑλληνικὰ κατασφάζειν. παρῆν[20] οὖν ὁρᾶν τὴν ἐνεστῶσαν ταλαιπωρίαν.

Vocabulary
ἀστυγείτων, -ον, neighboring
Ἑλληνίς, -ίδος, ἡ, Greek (in language and culture)
κατασφάζω, slaughter, murder
προαιρέομαι, decide beforehand, choose beforehand
σπλαγχνίζω (= σπλαγχνεύω), eat the entrails of a sacrificial victim[21]
ταλαιπωρία, distress, misery
ὑποτίθημι, aor. mid. ptc. ὑποθέμενος: suggest, advise
ψήφισμα, -ματος, τό, decree

6:10 δύο γὰρ γυναῖκες ἀνήχθησαν περιτετμηκυῖαι[22] τὰ τέκνα, τούτων δὲ ἐκ τῶν μαστῶν κρεμάσαντες[23] τὰ βρέφη καὶ δημοσίᾳ περιαγαγόντες αὐτὰς τὴν πόλιν κατὰ τοῦ τείχους ἐκρήμνισαν. 11 ἕτεροι δὲ πλησίον συνδραμόντες[24] εἰς τὰ σπήλαια λεληθότως[25] ἄγειν τὴν ἑβδομάδα μηνυθέντες τῷ Φιλίππῳ[26] συνεφλογίσθησαν διὰ τὸ εὐλαβῶς ἔχειν[27] βοηθῆσαι ἑαυτοῖς κατὰ τὴν δόξαν τῆς σεμνοτάτης ἡμέρας.[28]

Vocabulary
βρέφος, -ους, τό, infant
ἑβδομάς, -μάδος, ἡ, (number) 7; τὴν ἑβδομάδα, on the seventh (day), i.e., on the Sabbath
εὐλαβής, -ές, prudent; reverent, pious; comp. εὐλαβέστερος; adv. εὐλαβῶς, cautiously, piously keeping clean from
κρημνίζω, hurl down (neol.)
μαστός, ὁ, woman's breast; man's breast
μηνύω, 3. ἐμήνησα, ¹aor. pass. ptc. μηνυθείς: disclose a secret, report
περιάγω, aor. ptc.: περιαγαγόντες: go about; lead around/about

---

[19] τούς...μὴ προαιρουμενους → μεταβαίνειν ἐπί (to).
[20] S.v. πάρειμι.
[21] The entrails of a sacrificial victim (stomach and intestines) were deemed to be the most desirable part of a sacrifice. These were boiled (stewed) and usually distributed on the basis of social status, or prior arrangement, for consumption.
[22] Ptc. (s.v. περιτέμνω) picks up on what the women did, functioning adverbially and modifying pass. of ἀνάγω ("for having").
[23] The two adverbial aorist participles (κρεμάσαντες, περιαγαγόντες) are loosely related to the main verb ἐκρήμνισαν. Aorist particles often pick out antecedant actions in a narrative sequence of actions.
[24] This verse expresses two antecedent actions, as indicated by the aorist participles, συνδραμόντες and μηνυθέντες.
[25] S.v. λανθάνω.
[26] Philip, the governor of Jerusalem, appointed by Antiochus Epiphanes elsewhere. He is described as "more barbarous" than Antiochus himself (2 Macc 5:22).
[27] διὰ τὸ...ἔχειν (ἔχω with states of being often has the same meaning as εἰμί).
[28] I.e., because it was the Sabbath.

σεμνός, -ή, -όν, solemn, reverent; honorable, above reproach; σεμνῶς, reverently; superl. σεμνότατος, -η, -ον, most solemn/holy

σπήλαιον, τό, cave

συμφλογίζω, set on fire together

συντρέχω, aor. ptc. συνδραμόντες: run together; assemble together

6:12 Παρακαλῶ οὖν τοὺς ἐντυγχάνοντας τῇδε τῇ βίβλῳ μὴ συστέλλεσθαι διὰ τὰς συμφοράς, λογίζεσθαι²⁹ δὲ τὰς τιμωρίας μὴ πρὸς ὄλεθρον ἀλλὰ πρὸς παιδείαν τοῦ γένους ἡμῶν εἶναι, 13 καὶ γὰρ τὸ μὴ πολὺν χρόνον ἐᾶσθαι τοὺς δυσσεβοῦντας,³⁰ ἀλλ᾽ εὐθέως περιπίπτειν ἐπιτίμοις, μεγάλης εὐεργεσίας σημεῖόν ἐστιν.

Vocabulary

δυσσεβέω, act impiously; subst. "impious ones"

ἐντυγχάνω, 3. ἐνέτυχον, ²aor. inf. ἐντυχεῖν: bring a charge against; appeal, petition; happen to meet with/run into somebody; happen to read

ἐπιτίμιον, τό, contractual penalty, assessment of damages

εὐεργεσία, ἡ, benefaction

παιδεία, ἡ, teaching, education; discipline, correction

περιπίπτω, incur (punishment)

συμφορά, ἡ, misfortune, calamity

συστέλλω, mid. inf. συστέλλεσθαι, ¹aor. συνέστειλα, pf. pass. ptc. συνεσταλμένος: humiliate; (naut.) fold up, furl a sail; mid. be discouraged; pass. (of time), grow shorter

τιμωρία, ἡ, retribution, vengeance

6:14 Οὐ³¹ γὰρ καθάπερ καὶ ἐπὶ³² τῶν ἄλλων ἐθνῶν ἀναμένει μακροθυμῶν ὁ δεσπότης μέχρι τοῦ³³ καταντήσαντας αὐτοὺς πρὸς ἐκπλήρωσιν ἁμαρτιῶν κολάσαι, οὕτως καὶ ἐφ᾽ ἡμῶν³⁴ ἔκρινεν εἶναι, 15 ἵνα μὴ πρὸς τέλος ἀφικομένων ἡμῶν τῶν ἁμαρτιῶν ὕστερον ἡμᾶς ἐκδικᾷ. 16 διόπερ οὐδέποτε μὲν τὸν ἔλεον ἀφ᾽ ἡμῶν ἀφίστησιν, παιδεύων δὲ μετὰ συμφορᾶς οὐκ ἐγκαταλείπει τὸν ἑαυτοῦ λαόν. 17 πλὴν ἕως³⁵ ὑπομνήσεως ταῦθ᾽³⁶ ἡμῖν εἰρήσθω,³⁷ δι᾽ ὀλίγων δ᾽ ἐλευστέον ἐπὶ τὴν διήγησιν.

---

²⁹ λογίζεσθαι…εἶναι.

³⁰ Subject of inf.

³¹ The main clause is οὐ γὰρ…οὕτως καὶ ἐφ᾽ ἡμῶν ἔκρινεν εἶναι ("for he decided not to be so also in our case").

³² ἐπί, "in the case of."

³³ τό…κολάσαι, art. inf.

³⁴ ἐφ᾽ ἡμῶν, "with us," "in our case."

³⁵ ἕως, expressing purpose ("for").

³⁶ ταῦθ᾽ > ταῦτα.

³⁷ S.v. λέγω; endings of the pf. pass. impv. are sg. –σο (2), -σθω (3); pl. –σθε (2), -σθων (3).

Vocabulary

ἀναμένω, wait for/until

ἀφικνέομαι, 3. ἀφικόμην: arrive at (εἰς), come to; reach (a certain condition)

διήγησις, -εως, ἡ, narrative, story, account

διόπερ, therefore (emphatic for διό)

ἐγκαταλείπω, ¹aor. ἐγκατέλιψα/²aor. ἐγκατέλιπον: forsake, abandon, desert

ἐκδικέω, avenge, punish

ἐκπλήρωσις, ἡ, full measure, completion

ἐλευστέον (fr. ἔρχομαι),verbal adj. (nt. sg. form), functionally equivalent to δεῖ + inf. of ἔρχομαι, "one must go on"

καθάπερ (= καθά), just as, in the same way, in accordance with

μακροθυμέω, be long-suffering, patient

παιδεύω, teach, instruct; correct, discipline

ὑπομνήσις, -εως, ἡ, reminder

THE STORY OF ELEAZAR, THE SCRIBE

6:18 Ἐλεάζαρός τις³⁸ τῶν πρωτευόντων γραμματέων, ἀνὴρ ἤδη προβεβηκὼς τὴν ἡλικίαν³⁹ καὶ τὴν πρόσοψιν⁴⁰ τοῦ προσώπου κάλλιστος, ἀναχανὼν ἠναγκάζετο φαγεῖν ὕειον κρέας. 19 ὁ ⁴¹δὲ τὸν μετ᾽ εὐκλείας θάνατον μᾶλλον ἢ τὸν μετὰ μύσους βίον ἀναδεξάμενος, αὐθαιρέτως ἐπὶ τὸ τύμπανον προσῆγεν, 20 προπτύσας (the flesh) δὲ καθ᾽ ὃν ἔδει τρόπον προσέρχεσθαι (τὸ τύμπανον) τοὺς ὑπομένοντας ἀμύνασθαι⁴² ὧν οὐ θέμις γεύσασθαι (even) διὰ τὴν πρὸς τὸ ζῆν⁴³ φιλοστοργίαν.

Vocabulary

ἀμύνω, defend; mid. defend oneself against; keep from, ward off from

ἀναδέχομαι, accept, receive, undertake

ἀναχαίνω (= ἀναχάσκω), ²aor. act. ptc., ἀναχανών: open the mouth

αὐθαίρετος, -ον, voluntary; αὐθαιρέτως, by free choice, voluntarily

εὔκλεια, ἡ, good repute, honor

θέμις, ὁ, θέμιστος, that which is lawful

κρέας, ὁ, κρέως, meat/flesh

μύσος, -εος, τό, defilement

πρωτεύω, be pre-eminent, be first among

προβαίνω, pf. ptc. προβεβηκώς: advance, make progress; pass (of time)

---

³⁸ τις in the sense of εἷς (εἷς τῶν, "one of").

³⁹ Acc. of spec. of character/quality ("with respect to …").

⁴⁰ Acc. of spec.

⁴¹ ὁ…ἀναδεξάμενος.

⁴² ἀμύνασθαι…γεύσασθαι.

⁴³ ζῆν, pres. act. inf.

προπτύω, spit out (neol.)

πρόσοψις, -εως, ἡ, appearance

τύμπανον, here probably the "rack" as an instrument of torture

ὕειος, -α, -ον, of pigs, swine

ὑπομένω, remain, await; endure, stand one's ground, hold out; bear an ordeal, put up with

φιλοστοργία, ἡ, tender love, strong affection

6:21 Οἱ[44] δὲ πρός[45] τῷ παρανόμῳ σπλαγχνισμῷ τεταγμένοι διὰ τὴν[46] ἐκ τῶν παλαιῶν χρόνων πρὸς τὸν ἄνδρα γνῶσιν ἀπολαβόντες αὐτὸν κατ' ἰδίαν[47] παρεκάλουν ἐνέγκαντα[48] κρέα, οἷς καθῆκον αὐτῷ χρᾶσθαι, δι' αὐτοῦ παρασκευασθέντα, ὑποκριθῆναι δὲ ὡς ἐσθίοντα τὰ ὑπὸ τοῦ βασιλέως προστεταγμένα τῶν ἀπὸ τῆς θυσίας κρεῶν, 22 ἵνα τοῦτο πράξας ἀπολυθῇ τοῦ θανάτου καὶ διὰ τὴν[49] ἀρχαίαν πρὸς αὐτοὺς φιλίαν τύχῃ[50] φιλανθρωπίας.

Vocabulary

ἀπολαμβάνω, receive something; regain, recover; mid. take away/aside; receive

ἀρχαῖος, -α, -ον, old, ancient; τὰ ἀρχαῖα, things of old

παρασκευάζω, provide, prepare for somebody/something (dat.)

σπλαγχνισμός, ὁ (rare). probably "performing sacrifices"

ὑποκρίνομαι, aor. pass. inf. ὑποκριθῆναι: play a part; pretend, deceive

φιλανθρωπία, ἡ, clemency

6:23 ὁ δὲ λογισμὸν ἀστεῖον ἀναλαβὼν καὶ ἄξιον τῆς[51] ἡλικίας καὶ τῆς τοῦ γήρως ὑπεροχῆς καὶ τῆς[52] ἐπικτήτου καὶ ἐπιφανοῦς πολιᾶς καὶ τῆς[53] ἐκ παιδὸς καλλίστης ἀναστροφῆς, μᾶλλον δὲ[54] τῆς[55] ἁγίας καὶ θεοκτίστου νομοθεσίας ἀκολούθως ἀπεφήνατο ταχέως λέγων (them) προπέμπειν (him) εἰς τὸν Ἅδην.

Vocabulary

Ἅδης, -ου, ο, (uncontr. Ἀΐδης, Ἀΐδαο), Hades, She'ol, the Netherworld

ἀναστροφή, ἡ, way of life, conduct, behavior

---

[44] οἱ…τεταγμένοι.

[45] πρός (w. dat.) is often used in papyri to indicate an appointment to an office.

[46] διὰ τὴν…γνῶσιν.

[47] κατ' ἰδίαν, "on his own," "privately."

[48] S.v. φέρω.

[49] διὰ τήν…φιλίαν.

[50] S.v. τυγχάνω.

[51] τῆς…ὑπεροχῆς.

[52] τῆς…πολιᾶς.

[53] τῆς…ἀναστοφῆς.

[54] μᾶλλον δέ, "and moreover."

[55] τῆς…νομοθεσίας; construe w. ἀκολούθως.

ἀποφαίνομαι, 3. ἀπέφηνα: make known; mid. declare oneself

ἀστεῖος, -α, -ον, pleasing, beautiful; refined, honorable

γῆρας, τό, gen. -ραος and -ρως, old age

ἐπίκτητος, -ον, acquired (rare)

θεόκτιστος, -ον, established by God

λογισμός, ὁ, deliberation, reasoning, resolve; reasoning (as a faculty of the mind)

νομοθεσία, ἡ, code of laws

πολιά, ἡ, grayness of hair

προπέμπω, send somebody on one's way

ὑπεροχή, ἡ, pre-eminence, dignity; state of superiority

6.3.

4 Maccabees: The Supremacy of Devout Reason

(4 Macc 1:1–17)

Date: First century CE.

4 Maccabees is composed in fluent Greek. The author has been nurtured by Greek classical literature. He consciously employs Attic where he can, including the middle voice.[1] It begins in a rhetorically affected Greek style on the subject of the supremacy of reason over passion. The author's primary thesis is that reason rules the emotions, a common theme in contemporary philosophy.

In his argument, the author draws upon the Platonic notion of the four cardinal virtues – temperance, fortitude, justice, and prudence – which are connected with reason. These virtues were subsequently widely popularized by Stoicism. The author was able to affirm the specific claims of Judaism by qualifying the faculty of "reason" as *devout* reason (εὐσεβὴς λογισμός) and by defining reason in relation to education in the Torah. In so doing, he was able to resist the assimilating powers of Greek intellectual discourse.

THE AUTHOR'S CLARIFICATION OF HIS TASK

1:1 Φιλοσοφώτατον λόγον ἐπιδείκνυσθαι μέλλων,[2] (namely) εἰ αὐτοδέσποτός[3] ἐστιν τῶν παθῶν ὁ εὐσεβὴς λογισμός, συμβουλεύσαιμ[4] ἄν ὑμῖν ὀρθῶς ὅπως

---

[1] In contrast, in mainstream HGr and non-literary Greek such as inscriptions and papyri, the force of the middle voice was diminished, having become "lexicalized" in the Hellenistic period: authors normally employed one verb to express action and chose a different verb to express involvement or reflexivity, rather than employ the middle voice.

[2] μέλλω w. fut. means "about to." Here it expresses intent as causal adv. ptc., with 1st pers. sg. suject (determined by the sentence's finite verb, συμβουλεύσαμι), "since I intend to …".

[3] αὐτοδέσποτός...τῶν παθῶν.

[4] Construe w. ὅπως w. subj.

προσέχητε⁵ προθύμως τῇ φιλοσοφίᾳ. 2 καὶ γὰρ (is) ἀναγκαῖος εἰς ἐπιστήμην παντὶ⁶ ὁ λόγος καὶ ἄλλως⁷ τῆς μεγίστης ἀρετῆς, λέγω δὴ φρονήσεως, περιέχει ἔπαινον.⁸

Vocabulary
ἀναγκαῖος, -α, -ον, necessary, indispensable, essential; (ἐστιν) ἀναγκαῖον (w. inf.), it is necessary to, one must
ἀνδρεία, ἡ, courage
ἀρετή, ἡ, virtue
αὐτοδέσποτος, ὁ, absolute master (neol.)
ἐπαινέω, commend somebody, praise; approve (statutes)
ἔπαινος, ὁ, praise, commendation of something
ἐπιδείκνυμι/ἐπιδεικνύω, pres. mid. inf. ἐπιδείκνυσθαι, 3. ἐπέδειξα, ¹aor mid. ἐπεδειξάμην: show, point out, discuss; prove that (ὅτι)
λογισμός, ὁ, deliberation, reasoning; reasoning (as a faculty of the mind)
μέγιστος, -η, -ον (superl. of μέγας, μεγάλη, μέγα): best; topmost, foremost; mighty
πάθος, -ους (uncontr. -εος), **τό**, misfortune, calamity; emotions, passions; pain; pl. τὰ πάθη, feelings
περιέχω, ²aor. ptc. περίσχων, ²aor. pass. inf. περισχέσθαι: include; encompass, surround; come upon, befall
πρόθυμος, -ον, ready, eager; (adv.) πρόθυμως, zealously, earnestly
συμβουλεύω, advise, counsel
φιλοσοφία, ἡ, philosophy
φρόνησις, -εως, ἡ, practical wisdom, insight

1:3 εἰ ἄρα⁹ τῶν σωφροσύνης κωλυτικῶν παθῶν ὁ λογισμὸς φαίνεται ἐπικρατεῖν, γαστριμαργίας τε καὶ ἐπιθυμίας, 4 ἀλλὰ¹⁰ (then) καὶ τῶν¹¹ τῆς δικαιοσύνης ἐμποδιστικῶν παθῶν (reason) κυριεύειν ἀναφαίνεται, οἷον κακοηθείας, καὶ (over) τῶν τῆς ἀνδρείας ἐμποδιστικῶν παθῶν, θυμοῦ τε καὶ φόβου καὶ πόνου.

Vocabulary
ἀναφαίνομαι (impers.), be apparent that (w. inf.)
ἀνδρεία, ἡ, courage

---

⁵ προσέχω τὸν νοῦν + dat. ("turn your attention/mind to") is a very common idiom, even in translation Greek; here τὸν νοῦν is omitted.
⁶ παντί, "for everyone."
⁷ καὶ ἄλλως, "and moreover."
⁸ ἔπαινον...τῆς μεγίστης ἀρετῆς.
⁹ Protasis: εἰ ἄρα ("if then"); the apodosis begins with ἀλλα (which is odd).
¹⁰ ἀλλά, pleon.
¹¹ τῶν...παθῶν ← κυριεύειν ← ἀναφαίνεται.

γαστριμαργία, ἡ, gluttony
ἐμποδιστικός, -ή, -όν, hampering, impeding, hindering (rare)
ἐπικρατέω, have power/mastery over (w. gen.)
κακοήθεια, ἡ, malice
κωλυτικός, -ή, -όν, hindering
οἷος, -α, -ον, what kind (of), such as; οἷόν + inf. (impling fitness, possibility), it
    is possible
σωφροσύνη, ἡ, prudence, discretion; self-control, esp. sexual self-restraint
φόβος, ὁ, fear, fright

1:5 πῶς οὖν (is it that), ἴσως εἴποιεν[12] ἄν τινες, εἰ τῶν παθῶν ὁ λογισμὸς κρατεῖ,
λήθης καὶ ἀγνοίας οὐ δεσπόζει; (is) γελοῖον[13] ἐπιχειροῦντες λέγειν (this way).
6 οὐ γὰρ τῶν αὐτοῦ παθῶν ὁ λογισμὸς κρατεῖ, ἀλλὰ τῶν τῆς δικαιοσύνης
καὶ ἀνδρείας καὶ σωφροσύνης ἐναντίων, καὶ (κρατεῖ) τούτων οὐχ ὥστε αὐτὰ
καταλῦσαι, ἀλλ᾽ ὥστε αὐτοῖς μὴ εἶξαι.

Vocabulary
γελοῖος, -α, -ον, ridiculous, absurd
δεσπόζω, to control (w. gen.)
εἴκω, [1]aor. act. inf., εἶξαι: yield to somebody; give way to (a passion or impulse)
ἐπιχειρέω, make an attempt to (w. inf.)
ἴσος, -η, -ον, same, equal, equivalent; nt. pl., on an equality; adv. ἴσως, equally
λήθη, ἡ, forgetfulness

1:7 Πολλαχόθεν μὲν οὖν καὶ ἀλλαχόθεν ἔχοιμ᾽[14] ἄν ὑμῖν ἐπιδεῖξαι ὅτι αὐτοκράτωρ
ἐστὶν τῶν παθῶν ὁ λογισμός, 8 πολὺ δὲ πλέον[15] τοῦτο ἀποδείξαιμι ἀπὸ τῆς
ἀνδραγαθίας τῶν ὑπὲρ ἀρετῆς ἀποθανόντων, Ἐλεαζάρου τε καὶ τῶν ἑπτὰ
ἀδελφῶν καὶ τῆς τούτων μητρός. 9 ἅπαντες γὰρ οὗτοι τοὺς ἕως θανάτου
πόνους ὑπεριδόντες[16] ἐπεδείξαντο ὅτι περικρατεῖ τῶν παθῶν ὁ λογισμός. 10 (for
their) τῶν μὲν οὖν ἀρετῶν ἔπεστί μοι ἐπαινεῖν τοὺς[17] κατὰ τοῦτον τὸν καιρὸν[18]
ὑπὲρ τῆς καλοκἀγαθίας ἀποθανόντας μετὰ τῆς μητρὸς ἄνδρας, τῶν δὲ τιμῶν
μακαρίσαιμ᾽ ἄν.

Vocabulary
ἀλλαχόθεν (rare), from other places
ἀνδραγαθία, ἡ, bravery

---

[12] I.e., "ask."
[13] Loosely qualifying λέγειν.
[14] Opt. of ἔχω + ἄν w. inf. expresses possibility ("I could … do something").
[15] S.v. πλείων.
[16] Instr. adv. ptc. ("by," cf. IV, 1.6).
[17] τούς…ἄνδρας.
[18] "At this time/season," perhaps referring to the anniversary of their deaths.

ἀρετή, ἡ, virtue, excellence

αὐτοκράτωρ, ὁ, absolute master of somebody; emperor

ἐπαινέω, commend, praise; approve (statutes)

ἔπειμι (fr. εἰμί), be upon; ἔπεστί μοι, "it is right that I should," "it is incumbent upon me to do something"

καλοκἀγαθία (καλος + ἀγαθος), nobility of character

μακαρίζω, 2. μακαριῶ: to call/consider blessed; pronounce blessed for (w. gen.)

περικρατέω, control something (gen.)

πολλαχόθεν (rare), in many ways

τιμή, -ῆς, ἡ, honor, pl. honors; price/cost, value; (gen.) at a price of

ὑπεροράω, ²aor. ptc. ὑπεριδών: overlook, disregard

1:11 θαυμασθέντες[19] γὰρ οὐ μόνον ὑπὸ πάντων ἀνθρώπων ἐπὶ τῇ ἀνδρείᾳ καὶ ὑπομονῇ, ἀλλὰ καὶ ὑπὸ τῶν αἰκισαμένων (αὐτῶν), αἴτιοι κατέστησαν[20] τοῦ καταλυθῆναι[21] τὴν[22] κατὰ (our) τοῦ ἔθνους τυραννίδα, νικήσαντες τὸν τύραννον τῇ ὑπομονῇ ὥστε[23] καθαρισθῆναι δι' αὐτῶν τὴν πατρίδα. 12 ἀλλὰ καὶ περὶ τούτου νῦν αὐτίκα δὴ λέγειν ἐξέσται ἀρξαμένῳ τῆς ὑποθέσεως, ὅπερ[24] εἴωθα ποιεῖν, καὶ οὕτως εἰς τὸν[25] περὶ αὐτῶν τρέψομαι λόγον δόξαν διδοὺς τῷ πανσόφῳ θεῷ.

Vocabulary

αἰκίζομαι, torture; subst. torturer

αἴτιος, -ία, -ιον, responsible for, guilty of; subst. the accused, the one who is the cause

αὐτίκα (adv.), at once

ἔθω, be accustomed to (pres. only in ptc.), εἴωθα (pf. oft. used in place of pres.), be in the habit of doing something (w. inf.)

νικάω, to defeat; win a court case

ὅσπερ, ὅνπερ (acc.) / **ἥπερ** (fm.) / **ὅπερ** (nt.) // **ἅπερ** (nt. pl.): the very man/woman/thing; which indeed/exactly; ὅνπερ τρόπον, in the same way

πάνσοφος, -ον, all-wise

τυραννίς, -ίδος, ἡ, tyranny, despotic conduct

ὑπόθεσις, -εως, ἡ, general theory, doctrine

ὑπομονή, ἡ, endurance, perseverance

---

[19] θαυμάζω, pass., "to be admired by (ὑπό) somebody for (ἐπί) something."
[20] S.v. καθίστημι.
[21] Art. inf. (cf. IV, 2).
[22] τὴν...τυραννίδα (subject of τοῦ καταλυθῆναι).
[23] ὥστε + inf. (cf. IV, 15).
[24] ὅπερ > ὅσπερ.
[25] εἰς τὸν περὶ αὐτῶν...λόγον (disc. syn.).

SUPREMACY OF REASON

1:13 Ζητοῦμεν δὴ τοίνυν εἰ αὐτοκράτωρ ἐστὶν τῶν παθῶν ὁ λογισμός. 14 διακρίνομεν τί ποτέ ἐστιν λογισμὸς καὶ τί πάθος, καὶ πόσαι παθῶν ἰδέαι (there are), καὶ εἰ πάντων[26] ἐπικρατεῖ τούτων ὁ λογισμός. 15 λογισμὸς μὲν δὴ τοίνυν ἐστὶν νοῦς μετὰ ὀρθοῦ λόγου προτιμῶν τὸν σοφίας βίον. 16 σοφία δὴ τοίνυν ἐστὶν γνῶσις θείων καὶ ἀνθρωπίνων πραγμάτων καὶ τῶν τούτων αἰτιῶν. 17 αὕτη[27] δὴ τοίνυν ἐστὶν ἡ τοῦ νόμου παιδεία, δι᾽ ἧς τὰ θεῖα σεμνῶς καὶ τὰ ἀνθρώπινα συμφερόντως μανθάνομεν.

Vocabulary
αἴτιον, τό, cause, reason
βίος, ὁ, life, mode of life
διακρίνω, judge, decide; pass., bring an issue to a decision; doubt
προτιμάω, inf. προτιμᾶν: prefer
συμφερόντως, profitably (rare)
τοίνυν, indeed, then; therefore; δὴ τοίνυν, "I suggest/submit (that)"

---

[26] πάντων...τούτων.
[27] The antecedent of αὕτη is γνῶσις.

6.4.

Philo of Alexandria, *Allegories of the Sacred Laws*

(Alleg. Interp. 1.1.31–42)

Philo (20 BCE–50 CE) belonged to the large Jewish community in Alexandria, Egypt. He is well known for his scriptural interpretation, and especially for his use of allegory. A case in point is his allegorical interpretation of Gen 2:7, which is the reading in this section. His thought was strongly influenced by Middle Platonism, as well as Pythagorean and Stoic philosophy.

Related Texts: Gen 2 (§2.7), L.A.E. (§3.9–10); on Eve, Acts Andr. 5–9 (§5.16); on Adam, Rom 5:6–21 (§4.11).

This reading begins with Philo's quotation of Gen 2:7.

1.1.31 Καὶ ἔπλασεν ὁ θεὸς τὸν ἄνθρωπον χοῦν λαβὼν ἀπὸ τῆς γῆς, καὶ ἐνεφύσησεν εἰς τὸ πρόσωπον αὐτοῦ πνοὴν ζωῆς, καὶ ἐγένετο ὁ ἄνθρωπος εἰς[1] ψυχὴν ζῶσαν (Gen 2:7). (There are) διττὰ[2] ἀνθρώπων γένη· ὁ μὲν[3] γάρ ἐστιν οὐράνιος ἄνθρωπος, ὁ δὲ γήϊνος. ὁ μὲν οὖν οὐράνιος ἅτε κατ᾽ εἰκόνα θεοῦ γεγονὼς (is) φθαρτῆς καὶ συνόλως γεώδους οὐσίας ἀμέτοχος,[4] ὁ δὲ γήϊνος ἐκ σποράδος ὕλης, ἣν χοῦν (Moses) κέκληκεν, ἐπάγη· διὸ τὸν μὲν οὐράνιόν (ἄνθρωπον) (Moses) φησιν οὐ πεπλάσθαι, κατ᾽ εἰκόνα δὲ τετυπῶσθαι θεοῦ, τὸν δὲ γήϊνον (ἄνθρωπον) πλάσμα, ἀλλ᾽ οὐ γέννημα, εἶναι τοῦ τεχνίτου.[5]

Vocabulary
ἀμέτοχος, -ον (w. gen.), not partaking of, free from (w. gen.)
ἅτε, just as, as if

---

[1] εἰς (w. acc.) expressing manner ("as").
[2] διττά...γένη.
[3] ὁ μέν...ὁ δέ....
[4] συνόλως...ἀμέτοχος.
[5] τεχνίτης refers here to the "Lord."

γέννημα, τό, child, offspring
γεώδης, -ες, earthlike
γηγενής, -ές, earthly
γήϊνος, -η, -ον, earthly
δισσός, -ή, -όν (Att. διττός, -ή, -όν), double, twofold
ἐμφυσάω, 3. ἐνεφύσησα: blow in, breathe into
οὐράνιος, -ον, heavenly, from heaven; meteorological
οὐσία, ἡ, being, essence; substance
πήγνυμι, 6. ἐπάγην: make solid
πλάσμα, τό, anything formed; a body, a molded thing
σπορά, -άδος, ὁ/ἡ, (mostly pl.), scattered
συνόλως, altogether, totally
τυπόω, stamp a shape into something
ὕλη, ἡ, matter
φθαρτός, -ή, -όν, perishable
χοῦς, τό, χοός (gen.), dust, clay

1.1.32 ἄνθρωπον δὲ τὸν ἐκ γῆς λογιστέον εἶναι νοῦν εἰσκρινόμενον σώματι, οὔπω δ᾽ (fully) εἰσκεκριμένον (σώματι). ὁ δὲ νοῦς οὗτος γεώδης ἐστὶ τῷ ὄντι[6] καὶ φθαρτός, εἰ μὴ ὁ θεὸς ἐμπεύσειεν αὐτῷ δύναμιν ἀληθινῆς ζωῆς· τότε γὰρ γίνεται, οὐκέτι πλάττεται[7] εἰς ψυχήν, οὐκ ἀργὸν καὶ ἀδιατύπωτον (ψυχήν), ἀλλ᾽ εἰς[8] νοερὰν καὶ ζῶσαν ὄντως· Εἰς ψυχὴν γάρ (Moses) φησι, ζῶσαν ἐγένετο ὁ ἄνθρωπος.

Vocabulary
ἀδιατύπωτος, -ον, imperfectly formed
ἀργός, -όν, pointless, inefficient
γεώδης, -ες, earthlike
εἰσκρίνω, admit; pass., be mixed with
ἐμπνέω, 3. ἐνέπνευσα, [1]aor. ptc. ἔμπνευσας, aor. pass. ptc. ἐμπνευσθείς: blow/breath uponλογιστέον (verbal adjective governing accusative-infinitive construction), "one must reckon/take into account"
νοερός, -ή, -όν, intellectual
νοῦς ὁ, νοός, (gen.), νοΐ/νῷ (dat.), νοῦ (gen.), νοῦν (acc.), mind, understanding; κατὰ νοῦν, in one's mind
ὄντως, actually, really

---

[6] τῷ ὄντι, "in reality."
[7] πλάττεται (Att.) > πλάσσεται.
[8] εἰς (w. acc.), expressing manner ("as").

FOUR QUESTIONS

1.1.33 Ζητήσαι[9] δ᾽ ἄν τις, διὰ τί ἠξίωσεν ὁ θεὸς ὅλως τὸν γηγενῆ καὶ φιλοσώματον νοῦν πνεύματος θείου, ἀλλ᾽ οὐχὶ τὸν (νουν) κατὰ τὴν ἰδέαν γεγονότα καὶ τὴν εἰκόνα ἑαυτοῦ· δεύτερον δέ, τί ἐστι[10] τὸ ἐνεφύσησε. τρίτον, διὰ τί εἰς τὸ πρόσωπον ἐμπνεῖται· τέταρτον, διὰ τί πνεύματος ὄνομα εἶδ ὥς, ὅταν (Moses) λέγῃ· Καὶ πνεῦμα θεοῦ ἐπεφέρετο ἐπάνω τοῦ ὕδατος (Gen 1:2), πνοῆς νῦν ἀλλ᾽ οὐχὶ πνεύματος μέμνηται.[11]

Vocabulary
γηγενής, -ές, earthly
φιλοσώματος, -ον, body-loving

RESPONSE TO THE FIRST QUESTION

1.1.34 Πρὸς μὲν οὖν τὸ πρῶτον (question) λεκτέον ἓν μέν, ὅτι φιλόδωρος ὢν ὁ θεὸς χαρίζεται τὰ ἀγαθὰ πᾶσι καὶ τοῖς μὴ τελείοις, προσκαλούμενος αὐτοὺς εἰς μετουσίαν καὶ ζῆλον ἀρετῆς, ἅμα καὶ τὸν περιττὸν[12] πλοῦτον ἐπιδεικνύμενος αὐτοῦ, ὅτι ἐξαρκεῖ καὶ τοῖς μὴ λίαν ὠφεληθησομένοις. τοῦτο δὲ καὶ ἐπὶ τῶν ἄλλων (ways) ἐμφαντικώτατα παρίστησιν. ὅταν γὰρ ὕῃ μὲν κατὰ θαλάττης,[13] πηγὰς δὲ ἐν τοῖς ἐρημοτάτοις[14] ἀνομβρῇ, τὴν δὲ λεπτόγεων (ground) καὶ τραχεῖαν καὶ ἄγονον γῆν ἄρδῃ ποταμοὺς ἀναχέων[15] ταῖς πλημμύραις, τί ἕτερον[16] παρίστησιν ἢ τὴν ὑπερβολὴν τοῦ τε πλούτου καὶ τῆς ἀγαθότητος ἑαυτοῦ; ἥδ᾽ ἐστὶν αἰτία δι᾽ ἣν ἄγονον οὐδεμίαν ψυχὴν ἐδημιούργησεν ἀγαθοῦ, κἂν[17] ἡ χρῆσις[18] ἀδύνατος ἐνίοις (people) ᾖ αὐτοῦ.

Vocabulary
ἀγαθότης, -ητος, ἡ, goodness
ἄγονος, -ον, unfruitful, barren
αἰτία, τό, cause; accusation, legal charge
ἀναχέω, pour out/over
ἀνομβρέω, cause to gush out (with water)

---

[9] Cf. table 9.1.5(c).
[10] τί ἐστι, "what does … mean?"
[11] S.v. μιμνήσκομαι.
[12] περιττός (Att.) > περισσός.
[13] θαλάττης (Att.) > θαλάσσης.
[14] ἐρημοτάτοις (s.v. ἔρημος, -ον), superl., "in the most deserted places."
[15] Instr. adv. ptc. ("by," cf. IV, 1.6).
[16] τί ἕτερον, "what else?"
[17] κἂν > καὶ ἄν, "even if."
[18] ἡ χρῆσις…αὐτοῦ ("of it").

ἄρδω, to water
δημιουργέω, create
ἐμφαντικός, -ή, -όν, expressive; superl., ἐμφαντιώτατος, -η, -ον, most clearly
ἔνιοι, -αι, -α, some
ἐξαρκέω, be sufficient
λεκτέον (verbal adj. expressing necessity), (it) must be said
λεπτόγεως, -εων, infertile
λίαν, very, exceedingly
μετουσία, ἡ, participation, partnership
περισσός, -ή, -όν (Att. περιττός), abundant, profuse
πηγή, ἡ, running water; a spring source, fountain; source
πλήμμυρα, ἡ, flood, overflowing
ὕω, to rain
φιλόδωρος, -ον, generous, bountiful
χρῆσις, -εως, ἡ, use, employment of something

SECOND RESPONSE TO THE FIRST QUESTION

1.1.35 Ἕτερον δὲ λεκτέον (is) ἐκεῖνο·[19] (God) βούλεται τὰ θέσει δίκαια[20] εἰσαγαγεῖν. ὁ μὲν οὖν μὴ ἐμπνευσθεὶς τὴν ἀληθινὴν ζωήν, ἀλλ᾽ ἄπειρος ὢν ἀρετῆς, κολαζόμενος ἐφ᾽ οἷς ἡμάρτανεν εἶπεν ἂν[21] ὡς ἀδίκως κολάζεται, ἀπειρίᾳ γὰρ τοῦ ἀγαθοῦ σφάλλεσθαι περὶ αὐτό,[22] (τὸ) αἴτιον δὲ εἶναι τὸν μηδεμίαν[23] ἐμπνεύσαντα ἔννοιαν αὐτοῦ (into him)· τάχα δὲ μηδὲ ἁμαρτάνειν φήσει τὸ παράπαν, εἴ γε τὰ ἀκούσια καὶ (acts committed) κατὰ ἄγνοιαν οὐδὲ ἀδικημάτων ἔχειν[24] (as) λόγον φασί τινες.[25]

Vocabulary
ἀδίκημα, -ματος, τό, wrongdoing
ἄδικος, -ον, unjust, adv. ἀδίκως, unjustly
ἀκούσιος, -ιον, involuntary, nt. subst. involuntary act
ἄπειρος, -ον, boundless, limitless; inexperienced
θέσις, -εως, ἡ, ordinance, dat. "by ordinance"
λεκτέον (verbal adj. expressing necessity), (it) must be said

---

[19] ἐκεῖνο = τοῦτο.
[20] S.v. δίκαιος, -α, -ον, τὰ δίκαια, "legal standards."
[21] ἄν, here creating a hypothetical situation.
[22] Agreeing with ἀγαθοῦ.
[23] Agreeing with τὴν ἀληθινὴν ζωήν.
[24] Here ἔχειν = εἶναι.
[25] λόγον φασί τινες, "as some people say."

παράπαν, τό, altogether, at all

σφάλλω, 6. ἐσφάλην: make fall; pass. stumble/fall over something (acc.), transgress

RESPONSE TO THE SECOND QUESTION

1.1.36 Τό (term) γε μὴν ἐνεφύσησεν ἴσον ἐστὶ τῷ ἐνέπνευσεν ἢ ἐψύχωσε τὰ ἄψυχα· μὴ γὰρ τοσαύτης ἀτοπίας ἀναπλησθείημεν,[26] ὥστε νομίσαι θεὸν στόματος ἢ μυκτήρων ὀργάνοις χρῆσθαι πρὸς τὸ ἐμφυσῆσαι· ἄποιος γὰρ ὁ θεός, οὐ μόνον οὐκ ἀνθρωπόμορφος.

Vocabulary
ἀναπίμπλημι, fill up
ἀνθρωπόμορφος, -η, -ον, of human form
ἄποιος, -α, -ον, without quality or attribute
ἀτοπία, ἡ, absurdity, folly
ἄψυχος, ον, lifeless, soulless
ἴσος, -η, -ον, same, equal, equivalent; nt. pl., on an equality; adv. ἴσως, equally
ὀργάνον, τό, tool, bodily organ, device; musical instrument
μυκτήρ, nostril
ψυχόω, give a soul to, to "be-soul"

1.1.37 ἐμφαίνει δέ τι καὶ φυσικώτερον ἡ προφορά. τρία (things) γὰρ εἶναι δεῖ, τὸ ἐμπνέον, τὸ δεχόμενον, τὸ ἐμπνεόμενον· τὸ μὲν οὖν ἐμπνέον ἐστὶν ὁ θεός, τὸ δὲ δεχόμενον ὁ νοῦς, τὸ δὲ ἐμπνεόμενον τὸ πνεῦμα. τί οὖν ἐκ τούτων συνάγεται;[27] ἕνωσις γίνεται τῶν τριῶν, τείναντος τοῦ θεοῦ[28] τὴν ἀφ᾿ ἑαυτοῦ δύναμιν διὰ τοῦ μέσου πνεύματος ἄχρι (it reaches) τοῦ ὑποκειμένου – (καὶ) τίνος ἕνεκα[29] ἢ (τίνος) ὅπως[30] ἔννοιαν αὐτοῦ λάβωμεν;

Vocabulary
ἐμφαίνω, indicate
ἕνωσις, -εως, ἡ, union
προφορά, ἡ, expression
τείνω, 3. ἔτεινα: stretch, reach out, extend; apply
ὑποκείμαι, lie under, below; be subject to somebody/something
φυσικός, -ή, -όν, natural, inborn; (adv.) φυσικῶς, naturally, physically; comp. φυσικώτερος, more natural

---

[26] Cf. table 9.3.3(b).
[27] S.v., συνάγω, here "to infer."
[28] Gen. absol.
[29] τίνος ἕνεκα, "for what purpose."
[30] ὅπως + τίνος, "in order for what?"

1.1.38 ἐπεὶ πῶς ἂν ἐνόησεν ἡ ψυχὴ θεόν, εἰ μὴ (θεὸς) ἐνέπνευσε καὶ ἥψατο αὐτῆς κατὰ δύναμιν; οὐ γὰρ ἀπετόλμησε τοσοῦτον ἀναδραμεῖν ὁ ἀνθρώπινος νοῦς, ὡς ἀντιλαβέσθαι θεοῦ φύσεως, εἰ μὴ αὐτὸς ὁ θεὸς ἀνέσπασεν αὐτὸν πρὸς ἑαυτόν, ὡς (much as) ἐνῆν (for) ἀνθρώπινον νοῦν ἀνασπασθῆναι, καὶ (θεὸς) ἐτύπωσε (it) κατὰ τὰς ἐφικτὰς νοηθῆναι δυνάμεις.

Vocabulary

ἀνασπάω, ἀνέσπασα: pull up, draw up
ἀνατρέχω, ²aor. inf. ἀναδραμεῖν: soar up
ἀποτολμάω, dare, venture to
ἔνειμι (fr. εἰμί), 3rd impf. ἐνῆν: be possible, be in one's power
ἐφικτός, -ή, -όν, accessible, attainable

RESPONSE TO THE THIRD QUESTION

1.1.39 Εἰς δὲ τὸ πρόσωπον ἐμπνεῖ καὶ (is to be understood) φυσικῶς καὶ ἠθικῶς· φυσικῶς μέν, ὅτι ἐν προσώπῳ τὰς αἰσθήσεις (θεὸς) ἐδημιούργει· τοῦτο (face) γὰρ μάλιστα τοῦ σώματος (is) τὸ μέρος (that) ἐψύχωται καὶ ἐμπέπνευσται· ἠθικῶς δὲ οὕτως· ὥσπερ σώματος ἡγεμονικόν ἐστι τὸ πρόσωπον, οὕτως ψυχῆς ἡγεμονικόν ἐστιν ὁ νοῦς· τούτῳ μόνῳ ἐμπνεῖ ὁ θεός, τοῖς δ᾽ ἄλλοις μέρεσιν οὐκ ἀξιοῖ, ταῖς τε αἰσθήσεσι καὶ τῷ λόγῳ[31] καὶ τῷ γονίμῳ· δεύτερα γὰρ (these) ἐστι τῇ δυνάμει. 40 ὑπὸ τίνος οὖν καὶ ταῦτα ἐνεπνεύσθη; ὑπὸ τοῦ νοῦ δηλονότι· οὗ γὰρ[32] μετέσχεν ὁ νοῦς παρὰ θεοῦ, τούτου (ὁ νοῦς) μεταδίδωσι τῷ ἀλόγῳ μέρει τῆς ψυχῆς, ὥστε τὸν μὲν νοῦν ἐψυχῶσθαι ὑπὸ θεοῦ, τὸ δὲ ἄλογον (μέρος) ὑπὸ τοῦ νοῦ· ὡσανεὶ γὰρ θεός ἐστι τοῦ ἀλόγου ὁ νοῦς, παρὸ[33] καὶ Μωυσῆν (God) οὐκ ὤκνησεν εἰπεῖν (is) θεὸν τοῦ Φαραώ (Exod 7:1).

Vocabulary

αἴθησις, ή, perception, sensation; pl. (physical) senses
γόνιμος, (-η), -ον, reproductive; subst. reproductive organs
δηλονότι, it is plain that, clearly, of course
ἡγεμονικός, -ή, -όν, authoritative, dominant
ἠθικός, -ή, -όν, ethical; (adv.) ἠθικῶς, ethically
μεταδίδωμι, give a share, impart
ὡσανεί, so to speak

1.1.41 τῶν γὰρ γινομένων[34] τὰ μὲν[35] καὶ ὑπὸ (the power) θεοῦ γίνεται καὶ δι᾽ (agency) αὐτοῦ, τὰ δὲ ὑπὸ (the power) θεοῦ μέν, οὐ δι᾽ (agency) αὐτοῦ δέ· τὰ

---

[31] τῷ λόγῳ, "(organs) for speech."
[32] οὗ γὰρ, "for (that) of which."
[33] παρό = παρ᾽ ὅ, "for which reason."
[34] τῶν γὰρ γινομένων, "of the things that have come into being."
[35] τὰ μὲν... τὰ δε....

μὲν οὖν ἄριστα καὶ ὑπὸ θεοῦ γέγονε καὶ δι' αὐτοῦ· προελθὼν γοῦν (Moses) ἐρεῖ ὅτι Ἐφύτευσεν ὁ θεὸς παράδεισον (Gen 2:8). τούτων καὶ ὁ νοῦς ἐστι· τὸ δὲ ἄλογον (part) ὑπὸ θεοῦ μὲν γέγονεν, οὐ διὰ θεοῦ δέ, ἀλλὰ (rather) διὰ τοῦ λογικοῦ (part) τοῦ ἄρχοντός τε καὶ βασιλεύοντος ἐν ψυχῇ.

Vocabulary

ἄριστος, -η, -ον, best; finest
λογικός, -ή, -όν, rational; τὰ λογικά, rational beings
προλέγω, 3. προεῖπον, 4. προείρηκα: warn in advance; say beforehand/above
φυτεύω, to plant something

RESPONSE TO THE FOURTH QUESTION

1.1.42 Πνοὴν δέ, ἀλλ' οὐ πνεῦμα, (Moses) εἴρηκεν, ὡς[36] διαφορᾶς οὔσης (between these terms)· τὸ μὲν γὰρ πνεῦμα νενόηται κατὰ τὴν ἰσχὺν καὶ εὐτονίαν καὶ δύναμιν, ἡ δὲ πνοὴ ὡς ἂν αὔρά τίς ἐστι καὶ ἀναθυμίασις ἠρεμαία καὶ πραεῖα. ὁ[37] μὲν οὖν κατὰ τὴν εἰκόνα γεγονὼς καὶ τὴν ἰδέαν νοῦς πνεύματος ἂν λέγοιτο[38] κεκοινωνηκέναι – ῥώμην γὰρ ἔχει ὁ λογισμὸς αὐτοῦ – ὁ (νοῦς γεγονὼς) δὲ ἐκ τῆς ὕλης (κεκοινωνηκέναι) τῆς κούφης καὶ ἐλαφροτέρας αὔρας ὡς ἂν ἀποφορᾶς τινος, ὁποῖαι γίνονται ἀπὸ τῶν ἀρωμάτων· (ἀρωμάτων) φυλαττομένων[39] γὰρ οὐδὲν ἧττον[40] καὶ μὴ ἐκθυμιωμένων εὐωδία τις γίνεται.[41]

Vocabulary

ἀναθυμίασις, -εως, ἡ, vapor
ἀποφορά, ἡ, exhalation
αὔρα, ἡ, morning air, breeze
ἐκθυμιόω, burn as incense
ἐλαφρός, -ή, -όν, light (in weight); comp. – τερος, lighter
εὐτονία, ἡ, vigor
ἠρεμαῖος, -α, -ον, gentle
ἧσσων, -ον (Att. ἥττων, -ον), lesser, inferior, weaker; (adv.) nt. less
κοῦφος, -η, -ον, light (in weight), airy
λογισμός, ὁ, deliberation, reasoning, resolve; reasoning (as a faculty of the mind);
    λογισμοί, financial accounts
ῥώμη, ἡ, strength, robustness

---

[36] ὡς + ptc. (here in gen. absol.) supplies the reason for or cause of an action.

[37] ὁ...νοῦς.

[38] Cf. table 9.9.9(a).

[39] φυλαττομένων (Att.) > φυλασσομένων, gen. absol.

[40] ἧττον (Att.) > ἧσσον.

[41] εὐωδία τις γίνεται...οὐδὲν ἧττον (from them).

6.5.

Testament of Reuben:
The Evil of Women

(T. Reu. 1:1–6, 3:9–6:4)

Date: ca. 250 BCE (with some later Christian interpolations).

Text: Marinus de Jonge, *Testamenta XII Patriarcharum* (Leiden: Brill, 1964).

The Testament of Reuben was originally composed in Greek, although it was later translated into Aramaic and Hebrew, as well as other languages. This is the first of the books of the Testament of the Twelve Patriarchs, a pseudepigraphical work that narrates the dying commands of each of the twelve sons of Jacob. The style of these commands is modeled after Jacob's own testament, as recounted in Gen 49.

The primary theme of the Testament of Reuben is the admonishment of sexual immorality or unlawful sexual practice (πορνεία), which is exemplified by Reuben's own sinfulness when he had sexual intercourse with Bilhah, his father's concubine (T. Reu. 3). The brief narration of this event in Gen 35:22 has been expanded in the Testament of Reuben on the basis of the story of David and Bathsheba: we are told that Reuben spied on Bilhah as she bathed in secret and then, when she became drunk, he raped her while she remained unconscious. In contrast to Reuben's behavior, Joseph's resistance to Potiphar's wife is set up as a model for all righteous men to follow (Gen 39:7–14).

Overall, this testament seems to illustrate the growing anxiety concerning women in the Hellenistic age, portraying them as the cause of the downfall, first, of the fallen angels, or "Watchers," and, second, of men in general. The story of the mythic sexual transgression of the Watchers (as recorded in Gen 6:1–2 and expanded in 1 En. 1, 6–8, §3.7) is reinterpreted in T. Reu. 5:1–7, which claims that no direct sexual contact occurred between them. Rather the Watchers' sexual desire (ἐπιθυμία) alone was sufficient to impregnate the women, causing them to give birth to giants.

Related Texts: T. Reu. 2:1:3:8 (§6.7); 1 En. 1, 6–8 (§3.7).

1:1 Ἀντίγραφον διαθήκης Ῥουβήμ[1] ὅσα ἐνετείλατο τοῖς υἱοῖς αὐτοῦ, πρὶν ἀποθανεῖν αὐτόν, ἐν ἑκατοστῷ εἰκοστῷ πέμπτῳ ἔτει τῆς ζωῆς αὐτοῦ. 2 μετὰ ἔτη δύο τῆς τελευτῆς Ἰωσήφ, ἀρρωστοῦντι[2] συνήχθησαν ἐπισκέψασθαι αὐτὸν οἱ υἱοὶ καὶ υἱοὶ τῶν υἱῶν αὐτοῦ. 3 καὶ (Reuben) εἶπεν αὐτοῖς· Τεκνία μου, ἐγὼ ἀποθνήσκω καὶ πορεύομαι ὁδὸν πατέρων μου.

Vocabulary
ἀντίγραφον, τό, copy (of a text)
ἀρρωστέω, be very sick
εἰκοστός, -ή, -όν, twentieth
πέμπτος, -η, -ον, fifth
πρὶν / πρὶν ἤ, before, until; formerly
τελευτή, ἡ, death

1:4 Καὶ ἰδὼν ἐκεῖ Ἰούδαν καὶ Γὰδ καὶ Ἀσήρ, τοὺς ἀδελφοὺς αὐτοῦ, εἶπεν αὐτοῖς· Ἀναστήσατέ με, ἀδελφοί, ὅπως εἴπω τοῖς ἀδελφοῖς μου καὶ τοῖς τέκνοις μου, ὅσα ἔχω ἐν τῇ καρδίᾳ μου κρυπτά· ἐκλιπὼν γὰρ ἐγώ εἰμι ἀπὸ τοῦ νῦν. 5 καὶ ἀναστὰς κατεφίλησεν αὐτοὺς καὶ κλαύσας εἶπεν· Ἀκούσατε, ἀδελφοί μου, ἐνωτίσασθε Ῥουφήμ[3] τοῦ πατρὸς ὑμῶν ὅσα ἐντέλλομαι ὑμῖν. 6 καὶ ἰδοὺ ἐπιμαρτύρομαι ὑμῖν τὸ θεὸν τοῦ οὐρανοῦ σήμερον, τοῦ μὴ πορευθῆναι[4] ἐν ἀγνοίᾳ νεότητος, καὶ πορνείᾳ, ἐν ᾗ ἐξεχύθην ἐγὼ καὶ ἐμίανα τὴν κοίτην τοῦ πατρός μου Ἰακώβ.

Vocabulary
ἄγνοια, ἡ, ignorance
ἐκχέω, 3. ἐξέχεα, 6. ἐξεχύθην: pour out; pass. be poured out, abandon oneself
ἐνωτίζομαι, listen to
ἐπιμαρτυρέω, bear witness to something; mid. call upon somebody (acc.) to witness to somebody (dat.)
κοίτη, ἡ, bed, marriage bed
νεότης, -ητος, ἡ, youth, state of youthfulness
πορνεία, ἡ, unlawful sexual practice, sexual promiscuity/immorality
ὑπακούω, obey (w. dat.), be subject to

3:9 Καὶ νῦν, τέκνα, τὴν ἀλήθεια ἀγαπήσατε καὶ αὕτη φυλάξει ὑμᾶς. Διδάσκω ὑμᾶς, ἀκούσατε Ῥουβήμ τοῦ πατρὸς ὑμῶν. 10 μὴ προσέχετε ἐν ὄψει

---

[1] Ῥουβήμ and Ἰωσήφ are both indecl., but here gen.
[2] Dat. of time, "when he (Reuben) …" (cf. IV, 5.2).
[3] Indecl. (gen.).
[4] Art. inf. expressing purpose (cf. IV, 2).

γυναικός, μηδὲ ἰδιάζετε μετὰ θηλείας ὑπάνδρου, μηδὲ περιεργάζεσθε πρᾶξιν γυναικῶν. 11 εἰ[5] μὴ γὰρ εἶδον ἐγὼ Βάλλαν λουομένην ἐν σκεπεινῷ τόπῳ, οὐκ ἐνέπιπτον[6] εἰς τὴν ἀνομίαν τὴν μεγάλην. 12 συλλαβοῦσα γὰρ ἡ διάνοιά μου τὴν γυναικείαν γύμνωσιν, οὐκ εἴασέ με ὑπνῶσαι, ἕως οὗ (χρόνου) ἔπραξα τὸ βδέλυγμα.

Vocabulary
Βάλλα, Bilhah, the concubine of Jacob (Gen 30:4–8)[7]
βδέλυγμα, -ματος, τό, abomination
γυναικεῖος, -α, -ον, of a woman, matters pertaining to women; nt. pl. τὰ γυναικεῖα, menstruation
ἰδιάζω, to be alone
περιεργάζομαι, meddle in
πρᾶξις, -εως, ἡ, way of acting/conducting; action/deed; (magical) rite
σκεπεινός, -ή, -όν, sheltered
συλλαμβάνω, 3. συνέλαβον, [2]aor act. inf. συλλαβεῖν, [2]aor. mid. impv. συλλαβοῦ, 6. συνελήμφθην: lay hold of, seize; comprehend; conceive a child; mid. take part in something with somebody
ὑπάνδρος, -ον, to be under the authority of a man; subst., ἡ   ὑπάνδρος, married woman

3:13 Ἀπιόντος[8] γὰρ Ἰακὼβ τοῦ πατρὸς ἡμῶν πρὸς Ἰσαὰκ τὸν πατέρα αὐτοῦ, ὄντων ἡμῶν[9] ἐν Γαδέρ,[10] πλησίον Ἐφραθὰ οἴκου Βηθλεέμ, Βάλλα ἦν μεθύουσα καὶ κοιμωμένη[11] ἀκάλυφος κατέκειτο ἐν τῷ κοιτῶνι. 14 κἀγὼ εἰσελθὼν καὶ ἰδὼν τὴν γύμνωσιν αὐτῆς, ἔπραξα τὴν ἀσέβειαν, καὶ καταλειπὼν αὐτὴν κοιμωμένην, ἐξῆλθον. 15 καὶ εὐθέως ἄγγελος τοῦ θεοῦ ἀπεκάλυψε τῷ πατρί μου Ἰακὼβ περὶ τῆς ἀσεβείας μου· καὶ ἐλθὼν ἐπένθει ἐπ᾽ ἐμοί, μηκέτι ἁψάμενος αὐτῆς.

Vocabulary
ἀκάλυφος (= ἀκάλυπτος), uncovered
κατάκειμαι, lie down in/on (dat. / εἰς)
κοιτών, -ῶνος, ὁ, bed chamber
πράσσω (Att. πράττω), 3. ἔπραξα, [1]aor. ptc. πράξας, [1]aor pass. ptc. πραχθείς: do, commit an act; achieve, accomplish; be busy with; charge somebody money for something; pass. take place, happen

---

[5] Contrary-to-fact cond. statement.
[6] S.v. ἐμπίπτω.
[7] Cf. Gen 35:22; this story has been expanded on the basis of the story of David and Bathsheba.
[8] S.v. ἄπειμι (fr. εἶμι, cf. table 9.14), gen. absol.
[9] Gen. absol.
[10] Gader, near Ephratah.
[11] Impf. perphr. (cf. IV, 17).

REUBEN CONTINUES HIS EXHORTATION

4:1 Μὴ οὖν προσέχετε κάλλος γυναικῶν, μηδὲ ἐννοεῖσθε τὰς πράξεις αὐτῶν· ἀλλὰ πορεύεσθε ἐν ἁπλότητι καρδίας, ἐν φόβῳ κυρίου, καὶ μοχθῶντες ἐν ἔργοις, καὶ ἀποπλανώμενοι ἐν γράμμασι, καὶ ἐν τοῖς ποιμνίοις ὑμῶν, ἕως ὁ κύριος δώῃ ὑμῖν σύζυγον, ἣν αὐτὸς θέλει, ἵνα μὴ πάθητε, ὡς κἀγώ. 2 ἄχρι τελευτῆς τοῦ πατρὸς ἡμῶν οὐκ εἶχον παρρησίαν ἀτενίσαι εἰς πρόσωπον Ἰακώβ,[12] ἢ λαλῆσαί τινι τῶν ἀδελφῶν, διὰ τοὺς ὀνειδισμούς. 3 καὶ ἕως νῦν ἡ συνείδησίς μου συνέχει με περὶ τῆς ἁμαρτίας μου. 4 καίγε παρεκάλεσέ με ὁ πατήρ μου, ὅτι ηὔξατο περὶ ἐμοῦ πρὸς κύριον, ἵνα παρέλθῃ ἀπ᾽ ἐμοῦ ἡ ὀργὴ κυρίου, (which is actually) καθὼς ἔδειξέ μοι κύριος. ἀπὸ τότε οὖν παρεφυλαξάμην, καὶ οὐχ ἥμαρτον. 5 διὰ τοῦτο, τέκνα μου, φυλάξασθε πάντα, ὅσα ἐντέλλομαι ὑμῖν, καὶ οὐ μὴ ἁμαρτήσητε.

Vocabulary
ἁπλότης, -ητος, ἡ, simplicity, sincerity
ἀποπλανάω, lead astray; pass. wander about
γράμμα, τό, letter, pl. τὰ γράμματα, literature, learning
ἐννοέω, reflect on, occupy one's mind with
εὔχομαι, 3. ηὐξάμην, ¹aor. mid. impv. εὖξαι: pray; vow
καίγε, and yet (cf. T. Reu. 5:3)
μοχθέω, work hard, labor
παραφυλάσσω, keep watch, be on guard
παρρησία, ἡ, boldness, confidence
πρᾶξις, -εως, ἡ, way of acting/conducting; action/deed; (magical) ritual
σύζυγος, ὁ, companion, mate
συνείδησις, ἡ, conscience
τελευτή, ἡ, death

4:6 Ὄλεθρος γὰρ ψυχῆς ἐστίν ἡ πορνεία, χωρίζουσα (it) θεοῦ, καὶ προσεγγίζουσα τοῖς εἰδώλοις, ὅτι αὕτη ἐστὶ πλανῶσα τὸν νοῦν καὶ τὴν διάνοια, καὶ κατάγει νεανίσκους εἰς Ἅδην, οὐκ ἐν καιρῷ αὐτῶν. 7 καὶ γὰρ πολλοὺς ἀπώλεσεν ἡ πορνεία· ὅτι κἂν[13] ᾖ τις γέρων, ἢ εὐγενής, ὄνειδος αὐτὸν (ἡ πορνεία) ποιεῖ καὶ γέλωτα παρὰ τῷ Βελίαρ[14] καὶ τοῖς υἱοῖς τῶν ἀνθρώπων.

Vocabulary
Ἅδης, -ου, ὁ (uncontr. Ἀΐδης, Ἀΐδαο), Hades, She'ol, the Netherworld
γέλως, -ωτος, ὁ, object of laughter
γέρων, -οντος, ὁ, old man, elder; senator (often experts on religious matters)
εἴδωλον, τό, statue/image of a deity, idol

---

[12] Indecl. (gen.).
[13] κἂν > καὶ ἐάν.
[14] Cf. T. Reu. 2:2.

εὐγενής, -ές, of noble birth, high social status
νεανίσκος, ὁ, a youth, young man; servant
ὄνειδος, -ους, τό, object of reproach
προσεγγίζω, bring somebody near

4:8 Ἐπειδὴ γὰρ ἐφύλαξεν ἑαυτὸν Ἰωσὴφ ἀπὸ πάσης γυναικός, καὶ τὰς ἐννοίας
ἐκαθάρισεν ἀπὸ πάσης προνείας, εὗρεν χάριν ἐνώπιον κυρίου καὶ ἀνθρώπων.
9 καὶ γὰρ πολλὰ ἐποίησεν αὐτῷ ἡ Αἰγυπτία,[15] καὶ μάγους παρεκάλεσε, καὶ
φάρμακα[16] αὐτῷ προσήνεγκε·[17] καὶ οὐκ ἐδέξατο τὸ διαβούλιον τῆς ψυχῆς αὐτοῦ
ἐπιθυμίαν πονηράν. 10 διὰ τοῦτο ὁ θεὸς τῶν πατέρων μου ἐρρύσατο αὐτὸν ἀπὸ
παντὸς ὁρατοῦ καὶ κεκρυμμένου[18] θανάτου. 11 ἐὰν γὰρ μὴ κατισχύσῃ ἡ πορνεία
τὴν ἔννοιαν, οὐδὲ Βελίαρ κατισχύσει ὑμῶν.

Vocabulary
Αἰγύπτιος, -ία, -ιον, Egyptian (adj.); subst. ὁ Αἰγύπτιος, Egyptian man; Αἰγυπτία,
    ἡ, Egyptian woman
διαβούλιον, τό, counsel, deliberation
ἐρύω, mid. ἐρύομαι/ῥύομαι, 2. ῥύσομαι, 3. ἐρρυσάμην: mid. rescue, save, deliver
κατισχύω, overpower; prevail over (acc.), become master of
μάγος, ὁ, magician
ὁρατός, -ή, -όν, visible
φάρμακον, τό, drug, medicine; magic potion; spell cast using a magic potion

5:1 Πονηραί εἰσιν αἱ γυναῖκες, τέκνα μου, ὅτι μὴ ἔχουσαι ἐξουσίαν ἢ δύναμιν ἐπὶ
τὸν ἄνθρωπον, δολιεύονται ἐν σχήμασι, πῶς αὐτὸν πρὸς αὐτὰς ἐπισπάσονται·
2 καὶ ὃν διὰ δυνάμεως οὐχ ἰσχύει καταγωνίσασθαι, τοῦτον δι' ἀπάτης
καταγωνίζεται. 3 ὅτι καίγε περὶ αὐτῶν εἶπέ μοι ὁ ἄγγελος τοῦ θεοῦ, καὶ
ἐδίδαξέ με, ὅτι αἱ γυναῖκες ἡττῶνται τῷ πνεύματι τῆς πορνείας ὑπὲρ[19] τὸν
ἄνθρωπον, καὶ ἐν (their) καρδίᾳ μηχανῶνται κατὰ τῶν ἀνθρώπων, καὶ διὰ τῆς
κοσμήσεως πλανῶσιν αὐτῶν πρῶτον τὰς διανοίας, καὶ διὰ τοῦ βλέμματος τὸν
ἰὸν ἐνσπείρουσιν, καὶ τότε τῷ ἔργῳ αἰχμαλωτίζουσιν·[20] 4 οὐ γὰρ δύναται γυνὴ
ἄνθρωπον βιάσασθαι.

---

[15] When Pharaoh appointed Joseph as his chancellor, he gave him a beautiful Egyptian woman as
his wife.
[16] Cf. PGM IV, 1496–1595 (§7.3), love spell of attraction; cf. also SIG³ 985, *l.* 18 (§7.3); spell, PGM XIII,
230–334 (§5.4).
[17] S.v. προσφέρω.
[18] S.v. κρύπτω.
[19] ὑπέρ, "more than."
[20] S.v. αἰχμαλωτίζω = αἰχμαλοτεύω.

Vocabulary
ἀπάτη, ἡ, deception, deceitfulness
βιάζω, to force, use force, do something by force; lay hands on, violate (a law); pass. be forced
βλέμμα, -ατος, τό, a look, glance
δολιεύομαι, use trickery, deal treacherously
ἐνσπείρω, sow in
ἐπισπάω, draw to oneself, attract somebody to oneself
ἡσσάομαι (Att. ἡττάομαι), 6. ἡσσήθην: overcome; pass. give way to, give into (w. dat.), succumb to
ἰσχύω, be able; defeat, overcome; be strong
καίγε, and yet (cf. T. Reu. 5:3)
καταγωνίζομαι, overcome, prevail against
κοσμήσις, -εως, ἡ, adornment (of a women)
μηχανάομαι, plot against, contrive against a person

5:5 Φεύγετε οὖν τὴν πορνείαν, τέκνα μου, καὶ προστάσσετε ταῖς γυναιξὶν ὑμῶν καὶ ταῖς θυγατράσιν, ἵνα μὴ κοσμῶνται τὰς κεφαλὰς καὶ τὰς ὄψεις αὐτων,[21] ὅτι πᾶσα γυνὴ δολιευομένη ἐν τούτοις εἰς κόλασιν τοῦ αἰῶνος τετήρηται. 6 Οὕτως γὰρ ἔθελξαν τοὺς Ἐγρηγόρους πρὸ τοῦ καταλυσμοῦ· κἀκεῖνοι συνεχῶς ὁρῶντες αὐτάς,[22] ἐγένοντο ἐν ἐπιθυμίᾳ ἀλλήλων, καὶ συνέλαβον τῇ διανοίᾳ τὴν πρᾶξιν καὶ μετεσχηματίζοντα εἰς ἀνθρώπους, καὶ ἐν τῇ συνουσίᾳ τῶν ἀνδρῶν αὐτῶν συνεφαίνοντο αὐταῖς. 7 κἀκεῖνοι[23] ἐπιθυμοῦσαι τῇ διανοίᾳ τὰς φαντασίας αὐτῶν, ἔτεκον γίγαντας. ἐφαίνοντο γὰρ αὐταῖς οἱ Ἐγρήγορες ἕως τοῦ οὐρανοῦ φθάνοντες.

Vocabulary
γίγαντες, οἱ (pl.), giants (cf. 1 En. 7:2)
δολιεύομαι, use trickery, deal treacherously
Ἐγρηγόροι, Watchers (i.e., fallen angels, cf. Gen 6:1–2)[24]
θέλγω, 3. ἔθελξα, [1]aor. inf. θέλξαι: to bewitch, enchant
κοσμέω, put in order, arrange; adorn, dress
μετασχηματίζω, change form; pass. be changed into
συνεχῶς, continually
συνουσία, ἡ, being with/together with; sexual intercourse
συνφαίνομαι, appear along with/together with

---

[21] Cf. Rev 17:4 (§1.10), Apoc. Pet. 24 (§5.8), 1 Pet 3:1–3, 1 Tim 2:9–15.
[22] I.e., the women.
[23] κἀκεῖνοι > κἀκεῖναι.
[24] For an explanation of this term, see 1 En. 1:2 (§3.7).

φαντασία, ἡ, fantasy (technical Stoic term for the impression in the soul of what is received through the senses); appearance, presentation

6:1 Φυλάσσεσθε οὖν ἀπὸ τῆς πορνείας· καὶ εἰ θέλετε καθαρεύειν τῇ διανοίᾳ, φυλάσσετε τὰς αἰσθήσεις ἀπὸ πάσης θηλείας. 2 κἀκείναις[25] δὲ ἐντείλασθε μὴ συνδυάζειν ἀνθρώποις, ἵνα καὶ αὐταὶ καθαρεύωσι τῇ διανοίᾳ. 3 αἱ γὰρ συνεχεῖς συντυχίαι, κἂν μὴ πραχθῇ[26] τὸ ἀσέβημα, αὐταῖς μέν ἐστι νόσος ἀνίατος, ἡμῖν δὲ ὄνειδος τοῦ Βελίαρ αἰώνιον· 4 ὅτι ἡ πορνεία οὔτε σύνεσιν οὔτε εὐσέβειαν ἔχει ἐν ἑαυτῇ καὶ πᾶς ζῆλος κατοικεῖ ἐν τῇ ἐπιθυμίᾳ αὐτῆς.

Vocabulary
αἴθησις, ἡ, perception; pl. (physical) senses
ἀνίατος, -ον, incurable
ἀσέβημα, -ματος, τό, profane act
εὐσέβεια, ἡ, reverence toward the gods, piety
καθαρεύω, be pure, clean; be free from
νόσος, ἡ, disease, illness
ὄνειδος, -ους, τό, disgrace, object of reproach
συνδυάζω, associate with, join oneself with
συνεχής, -ές, successive, recurrent
συντυχία, ἡ, chance meeting

SELECT BIBLIOGRAPHY

Hollander, H. W., and M. de Jonge. *The Testament of the Twelve Patriarchs: A Commentary.* Leiden: Brill, 1985.

Kee, Howard C. "The Ethical Dimension of the Teaching of the XII as a Clue to the Provenance." NTS 24 (1978), 259–270.

---

[25] I.e., the women.
[26] S.v. πράσσω.

6.6.

Ezekiel the Tragedian

(Ezek. Trag. 68–119)

Provenance: Alexandria, Egypt   *Date:* Second century BCE.

Ezekiel the Tragedian, also known as Ezekiel the Dramatist, wrote in the second century BCE in Alexandria, Egypt. Though only fragments of this text have survived, its extensive quotation in the writings of Eusebius, Clement of Alexandria, and Pseudo-Eustathios has made its reconstruction possible.[1]

Over the course of its five parts, this poem retells the story of the Exodus in the style of Greek tragedy, which heightens the dramatic and tragic elements. The text is written in the poetic iambic trimeter of Greek tragic drama. A metron is the basic unit of a line of verse.[2] An iambic metron is defined as $x \; ^- \; ^\smile \; ^-$, where:

x	represents an anceps (a doubtful syllable whose quantity can be either long or short)
$^-$	represents a long syllable
$^\smile$	represents a short syllable

An iambic trimeter is composed of three iambic metra, with each metron consisting of two "feet":

---

[1] For a collated, edited edition see Jacobson, *The Exagoge of Ezekiel.*
[2] For a more detailed explanation of the rules of Greek prosody see: M. L. West, *Introduction to Greek Metre* (Oxford: Clarendon Press, 1987); Paul Maas, *Greek Metre*, trans. Hugh Lloyd-Jones (Oxford: Clarendon, 1962); D. S. Raven, Greek Metre: An Introduction (London: Faber and Faber, 1962).

	1	2	3	4	5	6	(feet)
	x^-	$\breve{} ^-$	$x\,\vert^-$	$\breve{}\,\vert^-$	x^-	$\breve{} x$	

In order to determine the meter of an epigram, the quantity of each syllable must be determined as to whether it is long or short. A syllable may count as short for prosodic purposes, despite the fact that it is long by nature, and vice versa.[3] A caesura (a break between two words in the middle of a metron), indicated by a vertical bar (|), occurs after the first syllable of the third or fourth foot. No word can end after a long anceps, except at a caesura in the middle of a line.

Moses	Ἔδοξ᾽ [4] ὄρους κατ᾽ [5] ἄκρα Σιναίου[6] θρόνον
	μέγαν τιν᾽ [7] εἶναι (reaching) μέχρι᾽ ϛ[8] οὐρανοῦ πτύχας,
70	ἐν τῷ (θρόνῳ) καθῆσθαι φῶτα γενναῖόν τινα
	διάδημ᾽ ἔχοντα καὶ μέγα σκῆπτρον χερί[9]
	εὐωνύμῳ μάλιστα. δεξιᾷ (χειρί) δέ μοι
	ἔνευσε, κἀγὼ πρόσθεν ἐστάθην[10] θρόνου.[11]
	σκῆπτρον δέ μοι πάρδωκε καὶ εἰς θρόνον μέγαν
75	εἶπεν (μοι) καθῆσαι· βασιλικὸν[12] δ᾽ ἔδωκέ μοι
	διάδημα καὶ αὐτὸς ἐκ θρόνων χωρίζεται.

---

[3] A "metron" is the basic unit of a line of verse. The determination of vowel quantity can be summarized by the following rules: *Rule 1 (epic correption)*: Syllables containing η, ω, or double vowels (diphthongs) are long by nature. A vowel that is long by nature is short *by position*, if in hiatus (a final vowel of a word is said to be in hiatus if it is followed by a word beginning with a vowel and is unelided). *Rule 2*: The quantity of the vowels α, ι, and υ may be either long or short and must be determined by the requirements of the meter. *Rule 3*: Syllables containing ε and ο are short by nature; but any vowel that is short by nature becomes long by position when followed by two or more consonants or by a double consonant (e.g., ζ, ξ, ψ). For example, the vowels ε and ο in ἔρχονται are short by nature but count as long for the purpose of scansion because they are each followed by double consonants. Similarly, when a short vowel–consonant combination occurs at the end of a word, followed by a word beginning with a consonant, the short vowel becomes long by position (e.g., πένθος τῆς). *Rule 4 (Attic correption)*: This is a major exception to Rule 3. A naturally short vowel that is followed by two consonants can remain short if the consonants are a combination of a mute (π, τ, κ, φ, θ, χ, β, δ, γ) followed by a liquid consonant (λ, μ, ν, ρ). This phenomenon is known as "Attic correption." For example, the vowel α in πατρός can be treated as either long or short because it is followed by a mute–liquid combination (-τρ). Similarly, a final short vowel followed by a word beginning with a mute–liquid combination can be treated as either long or short (e.g., ποτε βρέφος). However, when the mute and liquid belong to different words (e.g., ἐκ λόγων) or belong to different parts of a compound word (e.g., ἐκλέγω), the vowel must be long.

[4] ἔδοξ᾽ > ἔδοξα.

[5] κατά (w. acc.), "upon."

[6] ὄρους...Σιναίου.

[7] τιν᾽ > τινα.

[8] μέχρι᾽ ϛ > μέχρι εἰς.

[9] χερί > χειρί.

[10] Cf. table 9.11.4(c).

[11] πρόσθεν...θρόνου.

[12] βασιλικὸν...διάδημα.

Vocabulary

ἄκρος, -α, -ον, end, extremity; subst. top
γενναῖος, -α, -ον, high-born; noble; subst., τὸ γενναῖον, nobility
διάδημα, τό, crown
εὐώνυμος, -α, -ον, honored; euphem. for "left" (cf. ἀριστερός)
νεύω, nod, beckon with the hand
πρόσθεν, (τό), before, in front of; earlier, formerly
πτύξ, ἡ, pl. πτύχες (nom.), πτύχας (acc.), layer, fold (of a garment)
Σίναιον ὄρος, Mount Sinai
σκῆπτρον, τό, scepter (of a king)
φώς, φωτός, ὁ, man

77   ἐγὼ δ' ἐσεῖδον γῆν ἅπασαν ἔγκυκλον
      καὶ (saw) ἔνερθε γαίας καὶ ἐξύπερθεν οὐρανοῦ,
      καὶ μοί τι πλῆθος ἀστέρων πρὸς[13] γούνατα
80   ἔπιπτ',[14] ἐγὼ δὲ πάντας ἠριθμησάμην,
      κἀμοῦ[15] παρῆγεν ὡς παρεμβολὴ βροτῶν.
      εἶτ' ἐμφοβηθεὶς ἐξανίσταμ' ἐξ ὕπνου.

Vocabulary

ἀριθμέω, [1]aor. mid. ἠριθμησάμην: count, number
ἀστήρ, -έρος, ὁ, star
βροτός, ὁ, man (poet.)
γαῖα, ἡ, earth (poet.)
γόνυ, -νατος, τό (Ep. and Ion. γούνατος; nt. pl. γούνατα); pl. γόνατα: knee
ἔγκυκλος, -ον, around
εἰσοράω/ἐσοράω, pres. ptc. εἰσορῶν, εἰσορῶντος: look upon (w. admiration), gaze
   toward (πρός)
ἔνερθε(ν), beneath
ἐξανίστημι, mid. ἐξανίσταμαι: raise up; establish; arise, get up, awake
ἐξύπερθεν (= ὕπερθεν), above
ἐμφοβέω, terrify; pass. be alarmed
παράγω, march by
παρεμβολή, ἡ, army; battalion
ὕπνος, ὁ, sleep

---

[13] πρός (w. acc.), "before."
[14] ἔπιπτ' > ἔπιπτον.
[15] κἀμου > καὶ ἐμου (ablative gen. signifying movement away from).

Raguel   Ὦ ξένε, καλόν σοι τοῦτ᾽ ἐσήμηνεν θεός·
           ζώην[16] δ᾽, ὅταν σοι ταῦτα συμβαίνῃ ποτέ.
85   ἆρά γε μέγαν[17] τιν᾽ ἐξαναστήσεις θρόνου
           καὶ αὐτὸς βραβεύσεις καὶ καθηγήσῃ βροτῶν;
           τὸ δ᾽ εἰσθεᾶσθαι[18] γῆν ὅλην τ᾽ οἰκουμένην
           καὶ τὰ ὑπένερθε καὶ ὑπὲρ οὐρανὸν θεοῦ·
           ὄψει τά τ᾽ [19] ὄντα τά τε πρὸ τοῦ τά θ᾽ [20] ὕστερον.

Vocabulary

ἄρα, interrogative particle expecting negative response
βραβεύω, act as judge
εἰσθεάομαι, gaze upon
καθηγέομαι, lead, command (w. gen.)
σημαίνω, 2. σημανῶ, 3. ἐσήμηνα, aor. impv. σήμανον: give a sign/signal, indicate
   something (acc.) with a sign; report, make known
ὑπένερθε(ν), below

Moses

90   Ἔα· τί μοι σημεῖον ἐκ βάτου τόδε,
           τεράστιόν τε καὶ βροτοῖς ἀπιστία;
           ἄφνω βάτος μὲν καίεται πολλῷ πυρί,
           αὐτοῦ δὲ χλωρὸν πᾶν[21] μένει τὸ βλαστάνον.
           τί δή; προελθὼν ὄψομαι τεράστιον
95   μέγιστον· οὐ γὰρ πίστιν ἀνθρώποις φέρει.

Vocabulary

ἀπιστία, ἡ, unbelief, incredibility
ἄφνω, suddenly
βάτος, ἡ, bramble bush, prickly shrub
βλαστάνω, to sprout, shoot forth; nt. subst. ptc., foliage
ἔα (exclamation), ha!, oh!
καίω (Att. κάω), 3. ἔκαυσα: light something, kindle a fire, burn
τεράστιος, -ον, astonishing (of portents)
χλωρός, -ά, -όν, greenish-yellow; subst. a green plant

---

[16] ζώην (s.v. ζάω), 1ˢᵗ pers. sg. pres. act. opt. (-α + -οίμην), cf. table 9.2.3(a).
[17] μέγαν...θρόνου.
[18] Art. inf.
[19] τ᾽ > τε (postpos.).
[20] θ᾽ > τε.
[21] πᾶν...τὸ βλαστάνον.

God   Ἐπίσχες, ὦ φέριστε, μὴ προσεγγίσῃς,
Μωσῆ, πρὶν ἢ τῶν σῶν ποδῶν λῦσαι δέσιν·
ἁγία γὰρ ἧς σὺ γῆς[22] ἐφέστηκας[23] πέλει,
ὁ δ᾽ ἐκ βάτου σοι θεῖος[24] ἐκλάμπει λόγος.

100   θάρσησον, ὦ παῖ, καὶ λόγων ἄκου ἐμῶν·[25]
ἰδεῖν γὰρ ὄψιν τὴν ἐμὴν ἀμήχανον
θνητὸν γεγῶτα, τῶν λόγων[26] δ᾽ ἔξεστί σοι
ἐμῶν ἀκούειν, τῶν ἑκάτ᾽ [27] ἐλήλυθα.

Vocabulary

ἀμήχανος, -ον, unmanageable; impossible

δέσις, ἡ (= ὑπόδημα), sandal

ἐπέχω, [2]aor. act. impv. ἐπίσχες: hold firmly to; stay, halt; stay on (for a period of time); to offer, extend

ἐφίστημι, pres. mid. ἐφίσταμα, 3. ἐπέστησα/ἐπέστην, aor. ptc. ἐπιστάς, -άντος, 4. ἐφέστηκα: stand on; stand near, stand beside (w. παρά); approach somebody (w. dat.); come upon, attack; mid. (intrans.), come upon somebody (w. dat.), overtake somebody

θαρσέω (Att. θαρρέω), be of good courage

θνητός, -ή, -όν, mortal; subst. a mortal; stillbirth; τὰ θνητά, things affecting mortals

πέλω, become, have become

πρίν / πρὶν ἤ, before, until

προσεγγίζω, to approach, come near

φέριστος, bravest; mostly voc. φέριστε, Oh brave one

104   ἐγὼ θεὸς σῶν, ὧν λέγεις, γεννητόρων,
Ἀβραάμ τε καὶ Ἰσαὰκ καὶ Ἰακώβου τρίτου.
μνησθεὶς δ᾽ ἐκείνων καὶ ἔτ᾽ ἐμῶν δωρημάτων
πάρειμι σῶσαι λαὸν Ἑβραίων ἐμόν,
ἰδὼν κάκωσιν καὶ πόνον δούλων ἐμῶν.
ἀλλ᾽ ἕρπε καὶ σήμαινε τοῖς ἐμοῖς λόγοις

110   πρῶτον μὲν αὐτοῖς πᾶσιν Ἑβραίοις ὁμοῦ,
ἔπειτα βασιλεῖ τὰ ὑπ᾽ ἐμοῦ ταταγμένα,[28]
ὅπως σὺ λαὸν τὸν ἐμὸν ἐξάγοις χθονός.

---

[22] γῆς...πέλει... ἁγία.
[23] S.v. ἐφίστημι.
[24] θεῖος...λόγος.
[25] λόγων...ἐμῶν (dis. syn. [Y[2] hyp.]).
[26] τῶν λόγων...ἐμῶν.
[27] ἑκάτ᾽ > ἑκάτων.
[28] S.v. τάσσω.

Vocabulary

γεννήτωρ, ὁ > γενέτωρ > γενέτης, ὁ, ancestor, patriarch

ἐξάγω, lead out, bring

ἕρπω, go/come

κάκωσις, -εως, ill-treatment, suffering

μιμνήσκομαι (w. gen.) (also μνήσκομαι), 3. ἐμνήσθην, 4. μέμνημαι, 6. ἐμνήσθην: remember somebody, recollect; make mention of (w. gen.); pass. (dep.) remembered/be remembered

χθών, -ονός, ἡ (poet.), land, country

Moses	Οὐκ εὔλογος πέφυκα, γλῶσσα δ᾽ ἐστί μοι
	δύσφραστος, ἰσχνόφωνος, ὥστε μὴ λόγους
115	ἐμοὺς γενέσθαι βασιλέως ἐναντίον.[29]
God	Ἀάρωνα πέμψω σὸν κασίγνητον ταχύ,
117	ᾧ πάντα λέξεις τὰξ[30] ἐμοῦ λελεγμένα,
	καὶ αὐτὸς λαλήσει βασιλέως ἐναντίον,
	σὺ μὲν πρὸς ἡμᾶς, ὁ δὲ λαβὼν[31] σέθεν[32] πάρα.

Vocabulary

Ααρων, Aaron

δύσφραστος, -ον, speaking with difficulty

εὔλογος, -ον, reasonable; suitable; eloquent

ἰσχνόφωνος, -ον, weak-voiced, having a speech impediment

κασίγνητος, ὁ, brother; κασιγνήτη, ἡ, sister

φύω, 4. πέφυκα: bring forward, produce/form; create, put forth

SELECT BIBLIOGRAPHY

Jacobson, Howard. *The Exagoge of Ezekiel.* Cambridge: Cambridge University Press, 1983.

Lanfranchi, Pierluigi. *L'exagoge d'Ezéchiel le tragique.* Leiden: Brill, 2006.

Robertson, R. G. "Ezekiel the Tragedian." In *The Old Testament Pseudepigrapha*, II, 803ff. Ed. J. H. Charlesworth. Garden City, NY: Doubleday, 1985.

Strugnell, John. "Notes on the Text and Metre of Ezekiel the Tragedian's *Exagôgê*." HTR 60 (1967), 449–457.

---

[29] βασιλέως ἐναντίον = ἐναντίον βασιλέως.

[30] τὰξ > ταχύ.

[31] I.e., Aaron.

[32] σέθεν (s.v. σύ), variant of σου; σέθεν πάρα = πάρα σέθεν.

PART 7

Inscriptions

E pigraphic monuments are especially valuable in reconstructing the social and religious background of Hellenistic Judaism and early Christianity. They are primary witnesses to society's laws and institutions, its social structures, public cults, and private associations, its thoughts and values, and, of course, its language.[1] Part 7 surveys a representative sample of some of the primary types of Greek inscriptions, including decrees (§§7.1, 7.12), honorary decrees (§7.13), sacred laws (§§7.2–4, 7.14–17), foundation inscriptions (§§7.5–6, 7.18), healing testimonials (§§7.9, 7.21), manumission inscriptions (§§7.8, 7.19), oracles (§§7.10, 7.23), building inscriptions (§7.20), and metrical funerary inscriptions (§§7.11, 7.24).

Epigraphical texts can be challenging to translate owing to their particular grammatical constructions, specific functions, and dialectical features. Indeed, included in Part 7 are seven inscriptions that reflect the lingering influence in the Hellenistic period of some of the Greek dialects: for example, texts influenced by Doric (§§7.7), Lesbian (§7.16), Ionic/Attic (§7.17), Northwest Greek (§7.18), Phokean (§7.8). and Argolic (§7.9).[2] The assumption that Hellenistic Greek was uniformly a "common language" (ἡ κοινὴ διάλεκτος) is false: dialectical Greek, or what is more properly termed "epichoric" Greek, did not suddenly vanish at

---

[1] B. H. McLean, *An Introduction to the Study of Greek Epigraphy of the Hellenistic and Roman Periods from Alexander the Great Down to the Reign of Constantine (323 BCE–337 CE)* (Ann Arbor: University of Michigan Press, 2002).

[2] Doric was spoken in many parts of the Peloponnese (except Arcadia and Elis), on the islands of Crete, Kos, Melos, Thera, and Rhodes, and in parts of Sicily and southern Italy. The Aeolic group of dialects were spoken in Aeolia, as well as in Lesbos as the Lesbian dialect. Ionic was spoken in Ionia (Magnesia on the Meander) and in most of the islands of the Aegean, including Delos (central Ionic).

the onset of the so-called Hellenistic age but continued to exercise an influence on Hellenistic Greek for several centuries. For this reason, dialectical Greek texts should not be excluded from a Hellenistic Greek reader such as this on purely chronological grounds. Indeed, from a practical standpoint, the serious student of the social and religious background of early Christianity and Hellenistic Judaism cannot afford to ignore dialectical texts simply because they do not conform to his or her notion of "pure" Hellenistic Greek.

The Northwest dialect was spoken in Lokris (Opous), as well as in Phokis as the Phokean dialect (Delphi). The Argolic dialect (West Greek) was spoken in Epidauros.

7.1.

Gospel of the Savior, Caesar Augustus, Son of God

(IPriene 105)

Provenance: Priene, Ionia (cf. Fig. 2).   *Date:* 9 CE.

Text: IPriene 105, OGI 458, SEG IV, 490, XV, 815, MAMA VI, 174–175; R. K. Sherk, *Roman Documents from the Greek East* (Baltimore: Johns Hopkins Press, 1969), no. 65; V. Ehrenberg and A. H. M. Jones (eds.), *Documents Illustrating the Reigns of Augustus and Tiberius* (Oxford: Oxford University Press, 1949), no. 98; PHI (McCabe 5).

The beginning of this inscription (*ll.* 1–30) records a letter from the proconsul of Asia, Paulus Fabius Maximus (Παῦλλος Φάβιος Μάξιμος), to the Asian provincial assembly (Ἀσίας Ἕλλησιν). According to the letter of Fabius Maximus, the birthday of Caesar Augustus (23 September 63 BCE) represents a new beginning for all of humanity.[1] He then proceeds to commemorate the many benefactions that have been realized through the reign of Augustus. He declares that Augustus is a savior (σωτήρ) sent by divine providence and that he has brought peace to the world. The proclamation of the life and benefactions of Augustus is termed the "gospel" (εὐαγγέλια, *ll.* 37, 40). On this basis, Fabius Maximus argues that it would be appropriate to adopt the birthday (γενέθλιος ἡμέρα) of Augustus as the first day of the civil calendar of the Province of Asia, according to which all future events and provincial appointments would be dated.

In response to this letter, the provincial assembly passed two decrees (*ll.* 30–76, 77–84). The first of these (cited here) gives fulsome praise to Augustus, their "god" and "savior," for his many benefactions ("salvation").

---

[1] Augustus reigned as emperor from 27 BCE to 14 CE. Gaius Octavius was adopted (post mortem) by Julius Caesar and was then renamed Gaius Iulius Caesar Octavianus. He became the first emperor (*imperator*) of the Roman Empire. The title of "Augustus" was conferred upon him when he became emperor in 27 BCE.

THE CULT OF THE EMPERORS

Augustus's father, Julius Caesar, provides the point of departure for understanding the phenomenon of the deification of emperors such as Augustus. For example, an inscription from Ephesos (49 BCE) describes Julius Caesar, while he was still living, as the "descendant of (the gods) Ares and Aphrodite, the god who has appeared visibly (θεὸν ἐπιφανῆ) and the universal savior of the life of human beings" (SIG³ 760). After his death, Julius Caesar was formally enrolled among the gods of the state by the Senate. This act constituted the beginning of the cult of the emperors.

Octavian (Augustus) was Caesar's adopted son. The deification of Julius Caesar provided the rationale for calling Augustus *divi filius*, a title that could be translated into Greek only as υἱὸς τοῦ θεοῦ ("son of god"): if Julius Caesar was a god, then Augustus must be the "son of (a) god." Though Augustus himself stopped short of proclaiming *himself* a god (for the apotheosis of an emperor required the approval of the Roman Senate), he did allow others to address him as the "son of deified (*divi filius*) Caesar." Indeed, in the Eastern empire, even a reigning emperor could be called a god (θεός). Thus in numerous Egyptian texts the relationship between Octavius and Julius Caesar is described as θεὸς ἐκ θεοῦ ("god from god").[2]

Note: For an explanation of the process of passing Greek decrees, see §7.12–13 (and table 9.22).

FIRST DECREE OF THE ASIAN PROVINCIAL ASSEMBLY (LINES 30–40)

30 Ἔδοξεν τοῖς ἐπὶ τῆς Ἀσίας Ἕλλησιν, γνώμῃ τοῦ ἀρχιερέως Ἀπολλωνίου[3] τοῦ Μηνοφίλου Ἀζανίτου·

1. Preamble

The preamble is a clause that provides an explanation, sometimes very brief, of the background of the decree, setting forth the reasons the decree should be given serious attention. The preamble often begins with ἐπειδή ("whereas"/"inasmuch as") or ἐπεί ("since").

---

[2] POxy 1453, *l.* 11; OGI 655, *l.* 2.
[3] Apollonios, son of Menophilos, (native) of (the city of) Aizanoi (mod. Çavdarhisar).

Ἐπειδὴ ἡ⁴ θείως διατάξασα τὸν βίον ἡμῶν πρόνοια σπουδὴν εἰσενενκαμένη⁵ καὶ φιλοτιμίαν τὸ⁶ τελεότατον⁷ τῶι βίωι διεκόσμησεν ἀγαθὸν εἰσενενκαμένη (us) τὸν Σεβαστόν, ὃν εἰς⁸ εὐεργεσίαν ἀνθρώπων⁹ (she) ἐπλήρωσεν ἀρετῆς, ὥσπερ (ἡ πρόνοια) ἡμεῖν¹⁰ καὶ τοῖς (who come) μεθ' ἡμᾶς σωτῆρα¹¹ χαρισαμένη τὸν¹² παύσαντα μὲν πόλεμον, κοσμήσοντα¹³ δὲ εἰρήνην, (ἐπειδὴ) ἐπιφανεὶς¹⁴ δὲ ὁ Καῖσαρ (Augustus) τὰς ἐλπίδας τῶν προλαβόντων εὐανγέλια¹⁵ πάντων¹⁶ ὑπερέθηκεν, οὐ μόνον¹⁷ τοὺς¹⁸ πρὸ αὐτοῦ γεγονότας εὐεργέτας ὑπερβαλόμενος, ἀλλ' οὐδ' ἐν τοῖς ἐσομένοις¹⁹ ἐλπίδα²⁰ ὑπολιπὼν ὑπερβολῆς (him), 40 (with the result that) ἦρξεν δὲ τῶι κόσμωι τῶν δι' αὐτὸν εὐανγελίων ἡ γενέθλιος ἡμέρα τοῦ (our) θεοῦ.²¹

Vocabulary

ἀρχιερεύς, -έως, ὁ, high priest

διακοσμέω, adorn somebody/something (dat.) with something (acc.)

διατάσσω, direct, appoint; put in order

ἐπιφαίνω, ²aor. pass. ptc. ἐπιφανείς: show, appear; divinely manifest (a standard term for expressing the manifestation of a deity)

εὐεργεσία, ἡ, benefaction

Ἀσία, ἡ, Asia (Minor)

προλαμβάνω, take something on one's own; anticipate

πρόνοια, ἡ, Providence

---

⁴ ἡ…πρόνοια.

⁵ ἐνενκαμένη > ἐνεγκαμένη, instr. adv. ptc. ("by," cf. IV, 1.6) (s.v. φέρω, 3. ἤνεγκα, √ ἐνεγκ-).

⁶ τὸ τελεότατον τῶι βίωι…ἀγαθόν (disc. syn.).

⁷ τελεότατον > τελειότατον.

⁸ Telic εἰς ("for").

⁹ Here, "humanity."

¹⁰ ἡμεῖν > ἡμῖν.

¹¹ On the certainty of this restoration see Paul Wendland, "ΣΩΤΗΡ," *ZNTW* 5 (1904), 335–353; cf. IG III, 719, *ll*. 3–5, which describes Augustus as "benefactor and savior of the entire world."

¹² Introduces a modifier of σωτῆρα (3rd attrib. pos.).

¹³ Fut. ptc.

¹⁴ Temp. adv. ptc. (cf. IV, 1.1–2).

¹⁵ εὐανγέλια > εὐαγγέλια (s.v. εὐαγγέλιον). In Attic this term is always used in the pl. (cf. 40); cf. A. Dieterich, "*Euaggelistes*," *ZNTW* 1 (1900), 336–338; O. Michel, "Evangelium," *RAC* 6 (1966), 1107–1160, esp. 1110.

¹⁶ προλαβόντων … πάντων.

¹⁷ οὐ μόνον…οὐδ(έ) ("not only … nor …").

¹⁸ τοὺς…εὐεργέτας.

¹⁹ I.e., who will come after him.

²⁰ ἐλπίδα … ὑπερβολῆς (disc. syn.). The theme of Augustus's unsurpassable benefactions may have led to the declaration in Acts 4:12 that salvation cannot be associated with any other benefactor who has appeared in human form except Jesus Christ. For a detailed comparison of the Augustus legend and NT themes see W. Deonna, "La Légende d'Octave-Auguste: Dieu, Sauveur et Maitre du Monde," *RHR* 83 (1921), 32–58, 163–195; *RHR* 84 (1921), 77–107.

²¹ I.e., Caesar Augustus.

Σεβαστός, -ή, -όν, Augustan (adj.); Σεβαστός for Lat. Augustus
σπουδή, ἡ, diligence, concern, attention; haste, hurry; ἐν σπουδῇ, in concern
ὑπερβάλλω, exceed, surpass
ὑπερτίθημι, surpass, exceed
ὑπολείπω, leave (behind)
φιλοτιμία, ἡ, love of honor, generosity

(LINES 40–49)

(Ἐπειδὴ δὲ) τῆς δὲ Ἀσίας ἐψηφισμένης²² ἐν Σμύρνῃ ἐπὶ ἀνθυπάτου Λευκίου²³ Οὐολκακίου Τύλλου, γραμματεύοντος Παπίωνος Διοσιεριτοῦ²⁴ (that) τῶι²⁵ μεγίστας²⁶ γ'²⁷ εἰς²⁸ τὸν θεὸν καθευρόντι τιμὰς εἶναι στέφανον,²⁹ (ἐπειδὴ δὲ) Παῦλλος Φάβιος Μάξιμος ὁ ἀνθύπατος τῆς ἐπαρχήας³⁰ εὐεργέτης ἀπὸ τῆς ἐκείνου³¹ δεξιᾶς καὶ γνώμης ἀπεσταλμένος – ξὺν³² τοῖς ἄλλοις (benefactions) – οἷς εὐεργέτησεν τὴν ἐπαρχήαν, ὧν εὐεργεσιῶν τὰ μεγέθη λόγος³³ εἰπεῖν οὐδεὶς ἂν ἐφίκοιτο, καὶ (so) τὸ (way) μέχρι νῦν ἀγνοηθὲν ὑπὸ τῶν Ἑλλήνων εἰς τὴν τοῦ Σεβαστοῦ τιμὴν εὕρετο,³⁴ (namely) τὸ ἀπὸ τῆς ἐκείνου γενέσεως ἄρχειν³⁵ (reckoning) τῷ βίῳ τὸν (calendric) χρόνον·

Vocabulary
ἀνθύπατος, ὁ, proconsul
γένεσις, -εως, τό, generation, offspring, birth; beginning, origin
γνώμη, ἡ, intention, purpose; resolution, decision; preliminary resolution (of a city council); opinion
γραμματεύω, serve as secretary/clerk (of Assembly/Council)
ἐπαρχία, ἡ, province (Lat. *provincia*)
εὐεργετέω, confer benefits
εὐεργέτης, ὁ, benefactor
ἐφικνέομαι, ²aor. ἐφικόμην: reach (to); attain (to)

---

²² Gen. absol.
²³ Lucius Volcacius Tullus.
²⁴ Papion, son of Diosierites.
²⁵ τῶι...καθευρόντι.
²⁶ μεγίστας...τιμάς.
²⁷ γ' < γέ.
²⁸ Telic εἰς ("for").
²⁹ εἶναι στέφανον is grammatically dependent on ἐψηφισμένης.
³⁰ ἐπαρχήας > ἐπαρχίας.
³¹ I.e., Caesar Augustus.
³² ξύν > σύν ("besides").
³³ λόγος...οὐδείς (subject of the finite verb) + inf.
³⁴ The implied subject is Paulus Fabius Maximus.
³⁵ Art. inf. (cf. IV, 2).

καθευρίσκω (cf. εὑρίσκω), think up something

μέγιστος, -η, -ον (superl. of μέγας, μεγάλη, μέγα): best; topmost, foremost; mighty

Σμύρνα, -ης, ἡ, Smyrna (mod. İzmir)

ψηφίζω, freq. mid. ψηφίζομαι (for citation of formal motion), aor. mid. inf. ἐψηφίσθαι, aor. mid. inf. ἐψήφισθαι: approve a motion, to decree; aor. mid. inf. "be it resolved that"

2. CITATION OF FORMAL MOTION (LINES 49–60)

Διὸ τύχῃ ἀγαθῇ[36] καὶ ἐπὶ σωτηρίᾳ δεδόχθαι[37] τοῖς ἐπὶ τῆς Ἀσίας Ἕλλησι, ἄρχειν τὴν νέαν νουμηνίαν πάσαις ταῖς πόλεσιν τῇ (ἡμέρᾳ) πρὸ ἐννέα καλανδῶν Ὀκτωβρίων, ἥτις ἐστὶν γενέθλιος ἡμέρα τοῦ Σεβαστοῦ. ὅπως[38] δὲ ἀεὶ ἡ (first) ἡμέρα (of the year) στοιχῇ καθ᾽[39] ἑκάστην πόλιν, συνχρηματίζειν τῇ Ῥωμαϊκῇ καὶ τὴν Ἑλληνικὴν ἡμέραν. ἄγεσθαι[40] δὲ τὸν πρῶτον μῆνα Καίσαρα,[41] καθὰ[42] καὶ (was) προεψήφισται, ἀρχόμενον ἀπὸ πρὸ ἐννέα μὲν καλανδῶν Ὀκτωβρίων, (that is from) γενεθλίου δὲ ἡμέρας Καίσαρος, τὸν δὲ ἐψηφισμένον στέφανον τῷ τὰς μεγίστας[43] εὑρόντι τιμὰς ὑπὲρ Καίσαρος δεδόσθαι Μαξίμωι τῶι ἀνθυπάτωι, ὃν καὶ ἀεὶ ἀναγορεύεσθαι ἐν τῷ γυμνικῷ ἀγῶνι τῶι ἐν Περγάμωι (in honor) τῶν Ῥωμαίων Σεβαστῶν, ὅτι στεφανοῖ ἡ Ἀσία Παῦλον Φάβιον Μάξιμον (for his) εὐσεβέστατα παρευρόντα τὰς εἰς Καίσαρα τιμάς.

Vocabulary

ἀναγορεύω, publicly proclaim

ἄρχω, begin, mark the beginning of something (gen.) for somebody (dat.), rule

γυμνικός, -ή, -όν, gymnastic, athletic (adj.)

ἐννέα, nine (indecl.)

εὐσεβής, -ές, discharging sacred duties; pious, devout; superl. εὐσεβέστατα, most pious

---

[36] The formula ἀγαθῆι τύχηι ("for good fortune") seems to indicate that the prescribed religious observances had been performed before the decree was passed.

[37] Coming after the preamble and enactment formulae, the exact wording of the preliminary resolution (which was voted upon by the Council and Assembly) is cited. The formal motion often begins with a middle infinitival form of ψήφιζω or δοκέω: ἐψήφισθαι/δεδόχθαι ("be it resolved that ...") and an infinitival construction.

[38] The second part of the preamble may begin with ὅπως ἄν (οὖν) ("in order that [therefore])."

[39] Distributive use of κατά ("in each").

[40] Imperatival inf. ("let ... observed be").

[41] "Caesar," the name of a month (which had thirty-one days).

[42] καθά > καθάπερ.

[43] τὰς μεγίστας...τιμάς (disc. syn.).

Καῖσαρ, -αρος, ὁ, Emperor, Caesar; Caesar (a name of a month in the Province of Asia)

καλάνδαι, -ῶν, calends[44] (Lat. loanw. *calendae*)

μήν, μηνός, ὁ, month

νέος, -α, -ον, new, young; ὁ νεός, young man; ἡ νέα νουμηνία, New Year

νουμηνία, ἡ, new moon; first day of the lunar month; ἡ νέα νουμηνία, New Year

Ὀκτώβριος, -α, -ον, belonging to October

παρευρίσκω, propose

Πέργαμος, ἡ, Pergamon (Mysia)

προψηφίζομαι, mid. be previously decreed

Ῥωμαϊκός, -ή, -όν, Roman/Latin

στεφανόω, crown; honor; pass. be crowned with; be honored by (ὑπό) somebody for (some virtue [acc.]) with a crown (dat.)

στοιχέω, correspond to, coincide

συνχρηματίζειν > συγχρηματίζειν, s.v. συγχρηματίζω, correspond with (dat.)

τύχη, ἡ, luck; ἀγαθῇ τύχῃ, for good fortune; Τύχη Ἀγαθή, Agathe Tyche (goddess)

SELECT BIBLIOGRAPHY

Danker, F. W. *Benefactor: Epigraphic Study of a Graeco-Roman and New Testament Semantic Field.* MO, Clayton Publ. House, 1982, no. 33, cf. 38–39.

Harrison, J. R. *Paul's Language of Grace in Its Graeco-Roman Context.* Tübingen: Mohr Siebeck, 2003, 226–234.

Horsley, R.A. "The Gospel of the Saviour's Birth." In *Christmas Unwrapped: Consumerism, Christ and Culture,* 113–138. Edited by R. A. Horsley and J. Tracy. Harrisburg, PA: Trinity Press International, 2001.

Judge, E. A. *The First Christians in the Roman World: Augustan and New Testament Essays.* Ed. J. R. Harrison. Tübingen: Mohr Siebeck, 2008, 52–58.

Price, S. R. F. *Rituals and Power: The Roman Imperial Cult in Asia Minor.* New York: Cambridge University Press, 1984.

---

[44] Each Roman month was divided into three parts with respect to three particular dates: the "calends" (καλάνδαι, -ῶν, Lat. *calendae*) was the first day of each month; "nones" was the ninth day before the ides (εἰδοί/ ἰδοί, Lat. *idus*); and the "ides" was the middle day of each month. Days were not numbered from the "calends," but rather were counted backward from the *next* nones, ides, or calends, as the case may be. The days were counted inclusively (i.e., including the final day itself). Thus to calculate τῇ πρὸ ἐννέα καλανδῶν ("the ninth [day] before the calends of October") one must count backward nine days from 1 October (counting 1 October), which is to say, 23 September (which was the birthday of Augustus).

7.2.

Sacred Laws of a Silver Miners' Association Dedicated to the Lunar God

(IG II² 1366)

Provenance: Laurion, southern Attica (cf. Fig. 2).   *Date:* First century CE.

Text: IG II² 1366, CMRDM I, 9–10, no. 13 (pl. X), *NewDocs* III, 20–31, no. 6; GRA §53.

Voluntary associations of the Hellenistic and Roman periods can be grouped into three types: (1) professional associations or guilds (e.g., bakers [§7.22], silversmiths [§5.13]); (2) funerary societies (e.g., §4.2); and (3) voluntary religious societies or cults (§§7.2–5, 7.18). Voluntary religious associations prescribed sacred laws concerning many aspects of their communal cultic life and membership, including laws concerning the nature, time, and cost of sacrifices, the duties of membership, and the appointment of functionaries. These laws were often publicly displayed on a stele (a stone pillar or monument) at the entrance of temple precincts.

The inscription in this section concerns a Lykian slave named Xanthos. He probably worked in the silver mines for his Roman master, Gaius Orbius, in eastern Achaia. While Xanthos was sleeping, the god of his homeland, Men Tyrannos, directed him to found a religious association dedicated in Laurion. This event and the sacred laws of this association were then inscribed on a stone stele.

The attestation of the cult of the moon god, Men Tyrannos, in Achaia is striking given the fact that Men was a Phrygian god, whose cult was concentrated in Pisidian Antioch and around Maionia (east of Sardis) in northeastern Lydia. The importation of slaves from Phrygia to work in the silver mines around Laurion resulted in the introduction of many Eastern cults as well, including that of Men Tyrannos. Men Tyrannos was popular among miners by virtue of his chthonic character and owing to his association with water springs (which were

---

FIG. 15. Sacred laws of Men Tyrannos, Laurion, Attica (IG II² 1366).

used for the washing of mined ore and the extraction of precious metals). Hence, it is probable that Xanthos, the founder of this religious association, was also imported from Phrygia to labor in some aspect of the Laurion mining industry. He subsequently founded an association and shrine on the hill overlooking the harbor so that he and his fellow Phrygian slaves might worship the god of their homeland. The cult of Men Tyrannos was characterized by (1) a total submission of humans to Men (as is implied by the epithets "Tyrannos" and "Kyrios"); (2) fear of unwittingly offending Men; (3) Men as punisher of wrongdoers; (4) the notion that one could be in bondage to Men because of one's misdeeds and thus in need of a ransom (λύτρον).[1]

LINES 1–6

ξάνθος[2] Λύκιος Γαίου Ὀρβίου[3] καθειδρύσατο ἱερὸν[4] τοῦ Μηνὸς Τυράννου, αἱρετίσαντος[5] τοῦ θεοῦ, ἐπ᾽ ἀγαθῇ τύχῃ. καὶ μηθένα[6] ἀκάθαρτον προσάγειν·[7] καθαριζέστω δὲ ἀπὸ σκόρδων καὶ χοιρέων καὶ γυναικός.[8] λουσαμένους δὲ κατακέφαλα αὐθημερὸν εἰσπορεύεσθαι· καὶ (a woman) ἐκ τῶν γυναικέων διὰ ἑπτὰ ἡμερῶν[9] λουσαμένην κατακέφαλα εἰσπορεύεσθαι αὐθήμερον.

Vocabulary
αἱρετίζω, choose somebody (acc.)
αὐθημερόν, on the same day
κατακέφαλα, from head to foot
Λύκιος, ethnic (ethnic),[10] in this case of Λυκία, in southwestern Anatolia
Μὴν Τύραννος, the god Men Tyrannos (cf. *ll*. 15, 21)
σκόρδον, τό, garlic
τύχη, ἡ, luck; ἀγαθῇ τύχῃ, "for good fortune"; Τύχη Ἀγαθή, Agathe Tyche (goddess)
χοίρειος, ὁ, swine

---

[1] Cf. *CMRDM*, I, nos. 57, 61, 90.
[2] Xanthos, a Lykian slave.
[3] Gaius Orbius, the master of Xanthos. Gaius Orbius's *duo nomina* indicates that he was a Roman citizen. The mention of Xanthos's master is striking because it was omitted in the first version of this inscription (IG II² 1365). This omission may explain why the inscription was reinscribed.
[4] This ἱερόν is a private sanctuary dedicated to Men Tyrannos. Xanthos was to have taken over an abandoned heroon, previously built on the same site. The fact that Xanthos was a slave, with presumably limited financial resources, makes it all the more likely that he took over an existing structure.
[5] Gen. absol.
[6] μηθένα > μηδένα, cf. *ll*. 7, 13.
[7] Imperatival infinitives in *ll*. 4, 6–7, 9, 14 (infinitive often occurs in place of the 3rd pers. impv., esp. in official and legal language).
[8] I.e., from sexual intercourse (συνουσία) with a woman.
[9] Gen. of time, cf. *ll*. 6, 7.
[10] "Ethnic" is a technical term indicating the place, region, or nation of origin. Ethnics often occur in an adjectival form.

LINES 6–14

καὶ (likewise) ἀπὸ (contact with) νεκροῦ[11] διὰ ἡμερῶν δέκα καὶ ἀπὸ φθορᾶς ἡμερῶν τετταράκοντα, καὶ μηθένα θυσιάζειν[12] ἄνευ τοῦ καθειδρυσαμένου (being present) τὸ ἱερόν· ἐὰν δέ τις βιάσηται (these provisions), ἀπρόσδεκτος ἡ θυσία (αὐτοῦ) παρὰ τοῦ θεοῦ· παρέχειν δὲ τῶι θεῶι τὸ καθῆκον, (namely) δεξιὸν σκέλος καὶ δορὰν καὶ κεφαλὴν καὶ πόδας καὶ στηθύνιον καὶ ἔλαιον ἐπὶ βωμὸν καὶ λύχνον καὶ σχίζας καὶ σπονδήν, καὶ εὐείλατος γένοιτο ὁ θεὸς τοῖς θεραπεύουσιν ἁπλῆ τῆ ψυχῆ· ἐὰν (the founder) δέ τινα ἀνθρώπινα (ailment) πάσχη[13] ἢ ἀσθενήση ἢ ἀποδημήση που, μηθένα ἀνθρώπων ἐξουσίαν ἔχειν, ἐὰν μὴ ὧι ἂν αὐτὸς παραδῶι·

Vocabulary
ἁπλή, ἡ, simplicity
ἀπρόσδεκτος, -ον, unacceptable
δέκα, ten
δορά, ἡ, hide
εὐίλατος, -ον (var. εὐείλατος), very merciful
θυσιάζω, offer a sacrifice (τὸ ἱερόν)
καθῆκω, be appropriate, suitable, proper; nt. ptc. (τὸ) καθῆκον, what is
    appropriate
καθιδρύω, consecrate, dedicate; found/establish something
λύχνος, ὁ, lamp (of metal or clay)
σκέλος, -εος, τό, leg (fr. the hip downward)
σπονδή, ἡ, drink offering, libation; donation of wine
στηθύνιον, τό, chest
σχίζα, -ης, ἡ, wood, kindling
φθορά, ἡ, depravity, moral corruption; miscarriage

LINES 14–20

ὃς ἂν δὲ πολυπραγμονήση τὰ τοῦ θεοῦ[14] ἢ περιεργάσηται, ἁμαρτίαν ὀφειλέτω Μηνὶ Τυράννωι, ἣν οὐ μὴ δύνηται[15] ἐξειλάσασθαι· ὁ δὲ θυσιάζων τῆ ἑβδόμη (day of the month) τὰ καθήκοντα πάντα ποιείτω τῶι θεῶι· λαμβανέτω δὲ τῆς θυσίας ἧς ἂν φέρη σκέλος καὶ ὦμον, τὰ δὲ λοιπὰ κατακοπτέτω (ἐν τῶι) ἱερῶι· εἰ δέ τις προσφέρει θυσίαν τῶι θεῶι, ἐγ[16] νουμηνίας μέχρι πεντεκαιδεκάτης (day)·

---

[11] I.e., a corpse.
[12] Imperatival inf.
[13] The implied subject of the verbs πάσχη, ἀσθενήση, and ἀποδημήση is the founder ξάνθος.
[14] τὰ τοῦ θεοῦ, the god's possessions.
[15] οὐ μή + aor. subj. (emph. fut. neg.).
[16] ἐγ > ἐν.

Vocabulary
δορά, ἡ, animal hide
ἐξιλάσκομαι, expiate
θυσιάζω, offer sacrifice
κατακόπτω, cut up in pieces
νουμηνία, ἡ, new moon; first day of the lunar month; ἡ νέα νουμηνία
πεντεκαιδεκάτος, -η, -ον, fifteenth
περιεργάζομαι, meddle in
πολυπραμονέω, interfere with
ὦμος, ὁ, shoulder with upper arm

LINES 20–26

ἐὰν δέ τις τράπεζαν πληρῶι τῶι θεῶι, λαμβανέτω τὸ ἥμισυ (its contents). τοὺς δὲ βουλομένους ἔρανον συνάγειν Μηνὶ Τυράννωι ἐπ' ἀγαθῆι τύχηι·[17] ὁμοίως δὲ παρέξουσιν οἱ ἐρανισταὶ τὰ καθήκοντα τῶι θεῶι, δεξιὸν σκέλος καὶ δορὰν καὶ κοτύλην ἐλαίου καὶ χοῦν οἴνου καὶ ναστὸν χοινικιαῖον καὶ ἐφίερα τρία καὶ κολλύβων χοίνικες δύο καὶ ἀκρόδρυα, (καὶ) ἐὰν κατακλιθῶσιν οἱ ἐρανισταί, καὶ (they shall also provide) στέφανον καὶ λημνίσκον·[18] καὶ εὐείλατος γένοιτο ὁ θεὸς τοῖς ἁπλῶς προσπορευομένοις.

Vocabulary
ἀκρόδρυα, τά, hard-shelled
ἁπλῶς, sincerely, with integrity; absolutely; generally; οὔτε ἁπλῶς, not at all, nor so much as
ἐρανισταί, οἱ, club member (cf. *l.* 25)
ἔρανος, ὁ, club, association
εὐίλατος, -ον (var. εὐείλατος), very merciful
ἐφίερα, τά, sacred cakes
κόλλυβοι, οἱ, small cakes
κοτύλη, ἡ, *kotyle*, pl. *kotylai* (liquid measure = 6 κύαθοι / half a pint)
λημνίσκος, ὁ, woolen fillet/ribbon by which a hat, wreath, or garland is fastened to the head
ναστός,-ή, -όν, well-kneaded; subst. cake
χοινικιαῖος, -α, -ον, made from one *choenix* measure of flour (cf. *l.* 24)
χοῖνιξ, *choenix* (measure of flour); person's daily allowance
χοῦς,[19] ὁ, χοῦν (acc.), χῶν (gen. pl.): *chous* (liquid measure = 12 κοτύλαι, or 3 quarts)

---

[17] This implies that numerous religious associations with different demographic characteristics may have met in the same sanctuary.

[18] The reference to a wreath and woolen fillet suggests that the statue of Men Tyrannos was crowned and adorned as a way of signifying his participation in the banquet (*NewDocs* III, 21).

[19] Contr. of χοός.

7.3.

Sacred Laws of a Religious Association Dedicated to Zeus Savior and Two Magical Spells

(SIG³ 985 / PGM IV, 1496–1595, XXXVI, 320–332)

Provenance: Philadelphia, Lydia, Asia Minor (cf. Fig. 2) *Date:* First century BCE.

Text: SIG³ 985; Stephen Barton, G. H. R. Horsley, "A Hellenistic Cult Group and the New Testament Churches," *JAC* 24 (1981), 7–41.

In the first part of this inscription (*ll.* 1–11), the founder of this religious association is identified as Dionysios. The god Zeus had communicated to him, through a dream, the sacred laws that his association should observe. Dionysios then opened up an οἶκος (his private house doubling as a sanctuary)[1] for cultic fellowship dedicated to Zeus and his consort, Agdistis, to like-minded men and women, slaves and free, living in the neighborhood. Subsequently, through some sort of "modernization," Agdistis was superseded by a pantheon of Greco-Roman gods, for whom new cultic images and altars had recently been set up.

At the beginning of Part 2 (*ll.* 12–49), Dionysios is instructed that all members must take an oath before participating in the cultic membership. This section also specifies religious laws and various moral offenses, including a variety of sexual misdemeanors. The reader of this inscription is told that the gods love those who are obedient (*ll.* 46–48). During the meeting, those who had a good conscience were required to place a hand on the stele to demonstrate that they were following the commandments, with the founder being the first to touch the stele and swear by it. In Part 3 (*ll.* 50–60), further laws are stipulated with respect to the original household goddess, Agdistis, who (we are told) inspires a good attitude in men and women. Good thoughts, as well as correct actions, are required of all members of this association. The inscription concludes with Dionysios's prayer to Zeus Savior requesting his favor (*ll.* 60–65).

Special Feature: Frequent use of the *iota*-adscript (cf. IV, 16).

---

[1] The term οἶκος (cf. *ll.* 5–6) probably designates the actual house of Dionysios. But subsequently (cf. *ll.* 15, 23, 32, 52) it designates the voluntary association itself. The main verb of this sentence (periphr. cstr.) can be found in *l.* 11.

PART 1: THE FOUNDER (LINES 1–11)

Ἀγαθῆι Τύχηι· ἀνεγράφησαν ἐφ᾽ ὑγιείαι καὶ κοινῆι σωτηρίαι καὶ δόξηι[2] τῆι
ἀρίστηι[3] τὰ δοθέντα παραγγέλματα Διονυσίωι[4] καθ᾽ ὕπνον πρόσοδον διδόντ᾽
εἰς τὸν ἑαυτοῦ οἶκον ἀνδράσι καὶ γυναιξὶν ἐλευθέροις καὶ οἰκέταις. Διὸς[5] γὰρ ἐν
τούτωι (οἴκῳ) τοῦ Εὐμενοῦς[6] καὶ Ἑστίας τῆς παρέδρου αὐτοῦ καὶ τῶν ἄλλων
θεῶν Σωτήρων[7] καὶ Εὐδαιμονίας καὶ Πλούτου καὶ Ἀρετῆς καὶ Ὑγιείας, 10 καὶ
Τύχης Ἀγαθῆς καὶ Ἀγαθοῦ Δαίμονος καὶ Μνήμης καὶ Χαρίτων καὶ Νίκης εἰσὶν
ἱδρυμένοι[8] βωμοί.

Vocabulary

Ἀγαθός Δαίμων, Agathos Daimon (god)

ἀναγράφω, engrave and publicly set up; record in a public register

Ἀρετή, Arete (goddess)

ἄριστος, -η, -ον, best; finest

ἐλεύθερος, -έρα, -ον, free; subst. freeman/freewoman

Ἑστίας, Hestia (goddess)

Εὐδαιμονία, Eudaimonia (goddess)

Εὐμενής, kindly disposed, benevolent (epithet of Zeus)

ἱδρύω, 2. ἱδρύσομαι, 3. ἵδρυσα / ἱδρυσάμην, 5. ἵδρυμαι: found, dedicate; set up
    something (altar, statue); mid. establish (a temple); dedicate

κοινός, -ή, -όν, common, shared; public; κοινῇ σωτηρίᾳ, for common safety

νίκη, ἡ, victory; Νίκη, goddess Nike

οἰκέτης, ὁ, household slave

παράγγελμα, τό, commandment

παρέδρος, -ον, sitting beside, coadjutor (of Zeus)

Μνήμη, Mneme (goddess)

Πλούτων, -ωνος, Pluto, god of the underworld

τύχη, ἡ, luck; ἀγαθῇ τύχῃ, "for good fortune"; Τύχη Ἀγαθή, Agathe Tyche
    (goddess)

ὑγίεια, ἡ, health;   Ὑγίεια, goddess Hygeia, daughter of Asklepios

ξάριτες, the Graces

---

[2] δόξα, here "reputation."

[3] δόξῃι τῆι ἀρίστηι, modifier in 3rd attrib. pos.

[4] Dionysios, the founder of this religious association.

[5] S.v. Ζεύς.

[6] Διὸς…τοῦ Εὐμενοῦς (dis. syn. [Y² hyp.]).

[7] "Savior gods."

[8] εἰσὶν ἱδρυμένοι, primary verb (pf. periph., cf. IV, 18).

PART 2: THE SACRED LAWS (LINES 11–25)

Τούτωι⁹ δέδωκεν ὁ Ζεὺς παραγγέλματα τούς τε ἁγνισμοὺς καὶ τοὺς καθαρμοὺς καὶ τὰ μυστήρια ἐπιτελεῖν κατά τε τὰ πάτρια καὶ ὡς νῦν γέγραπται· πορευόμενοι εἰς τὸν οἶκον τοῦτον ἄνδρες καὶ γυναῖκες ἐλεύθεροι καὶ οἰκέται τοὺς θεοὺς πάντας ὀρκούσθωσαν δόλον μηθένα μήτε ἀνδρὶ μήτε γυναικὶ εἰδότες,¹⁰ μὴ φάρμακον πονηρὸν πρὸς ἀνθρώπους, μὴ ἐπωιδὰς¹¹ πονηρὰς μήτε γινώσκειν¹² μήτε ἐπιτελεῖν, μὴ φίλτρον,¹³ μὴ φθορεῖον, μὴ ἀτοκεῖον, μὴ ἄλλο τι παιδοφόνον, μήτε αὐτοὺς ἐπιτελεῖν μήτε ἑτέρωι συμβουλεύειν μηδὲ συνιστορεῖν, ἀποστεροῦντες δὲ μηδὲν εὐνοεῖν τῶι οἴκωι τῶιδε, καὶ ἐάν τις τούτων τι ποιῆι ἢ ἐπιβουλεύῃ, (members) μήτε ἐπιτρέψειν¹⁴ μήτε παρασιωπήσειν, ἀλλ᾽ ἐμφανιεῖν καὶ ἀμυνεῖσθαι.

Vocabulary

ἁγνισμοί, οἱ, purifications (i.e., rituals to avoid defilement)

ἀμύνω, defend; mid. defend oneself against, keep from, ward off from

ἀποστερέω, refrain from doing something (inf.)

ἀτοκεῖον, τό, contraceptive drug¹⁵

ἐμφανίζω, explain; inform, make a report; present evidence, show plainly

ἐπιβουλεύω, to plot, plan

ἐπιτρέπω, allow somebody (dat.) to do something (inf.); permit somebody to do something; tolerate, put up with; pass. be entrusted as a legal guarantor

ἐπῳδή, ἡ, enchantment, spell

εὐνοέω, to be well-intentioned

καθαρμός, ὁ, cleansing, ritual to remove defilement (once it has been contracted)

ὀκόω, make somebody swear an oath to a god (acc.); pass. be bound by an oath to a god (acc.)

παιδοφόνος, -ον, fatal to children; subst. drug that is fatal to children

παρασιωπάω, keep silence

πάτριος, -α, -ον (= πατρικός), derived from one's fathers, hereditary; customary; subst. τὸ πάτριον, tradition; τὰ πάτρια, ancestral customs

συμβουλεύω, recommend

συνιστορέω, conspire with somebody

φάρμακον, τό, drug, medicine; magic potion; spell cast using a magic potion

---

⁹ I.e., to Dionysios (cf. *l.* 60).

¹⁰ "Knowing of " δόλον (acc) + (directed) "at"/"toward" (dat.) somebody.

¹¹ ἐπωιδάς > ἐπῳδάς.

¹² γινώσκω, "to know of " something.

¹³ Cf. other love spells of attraction mentioned in Acts Andr. 5.65 (§5.16), PGM IV, 1496–1595 (presented later), PGM XIII, 238–240 (§5.4).

¹⁴ Imperatival inf.

¹⁵ Cf. contraceptive spell (PGM XXXVI, 320–332), presented later.

φθορεῖον, τό, abortifacient (drug for inducing an abortion)
φίλτρον, τό, love potion

(LINES 25–36)

Ἄνδρα παρὰ[16] τὴν ἑαυτοῦ (wife) γυναῖκα ἀλλοτρίαν ἢ ἐλευθέραν ἢ δούλην ἄνδρα
ἔχουσαν μὴ φθερεῖν μηδὲ παῖδα μηδὲ παρθένον μηδὲ ἑτέρωι συμβουλεύσειν (its),
ἀλλ᾽ ἂν τινι συνιστορήσηι (with another), τὸν τοιοῦτον φανερὸν ποιήσειν,[17] καὶ τὸν
ἄνδρα καὶ τὴν γυναῖκα καὶ μὴ ἀποκρύψειν μηδὲ παρασιωπήσειν· γυνὴ καὶ ἀνήρ, ὃς
ἂν ποιῆι τι τῶν προγεγραμμένων, εἰς τὸν οἶκον τοῦτον μὴ εἰσπορευέσθω· θεοὶ γὰρ
ἐν αὐτῶι ἵδρυνται (are) μεγάλοι καὶ ταῦτα ἐπισκοποῦσιν καὶ τοὺς παραβαίνοντας τὰ
παραγγέλματα οὐκ ἀνέξονται· γυναῖκα ἐλευθέραν ἁγνὴν εἶναι[18] καὶ μὴ γινώσκειν[19]
ἄλλου ἀνδρὸς πλὴν τοῦ ἰδίου εὐνὴν ἢ (have) συνουσίαν (with him)·

Vocabulary
ἀλλότριος, -ία, -ιον, belonging to another; foreign; ὁ ἀλλότριος, stranger
ἀνέχω, hold/lift up, hold up, detain, delay something; mid. tolerate, endure
ἀποκρύπτω, conceal something
ἐπισκοπέω, watch over, inspect, observe
εὐνή, ἡ, bed, bedding
Μεγάλοι Θεοί, the Great Gods
παρασιωπάω, keep silence
προγράφω, write above; set forth as a public notice, advertise; exhibit in a public
    place; register/record (names)
συνουσία, ἡ, being with/together with; sexual intercourse
φθείρω, fut. pass. φθαρήσομαι: sexually seduce; pass. be dissolved

(LINES 36–50)

ἐὰν δὲ γνῶι, τὴν τοιαύτην μὴ εἶναι ἁγνήν, ἀλλὰ μεμιασμένην[20] καὶ μύσους ἐμφυλίου
πλήρη καὶ σέβεσθαι ἀναξίαν τὸν θεὸν τοῦτον οὗ ταῦτα τὰ ἱερὰ ἵδρυται, μηδὲ
θυσίαις παρατυγχάνειν μηδὲ τοῖς ἁγνισμοῖς καὶ καθαρμοῖς προσκόπτειν[21] μηδὲ
ὁρᾶν ἐπιτελούμενα τὰ μυστήρια· ἐὰν δὲ ποιῆι τι τούτων, ἀφ᾽ οὗ (time) τὰ
παραγγέλματα εἰς τήνδε τὴν ἀναγραφὴν ἥκουσιν, κακὰς ἀρὰς παρὰ τῶν θεῶν
ἕξει (for) τὰ παραγγέλματα ταῦτα παρορῶσα· ὁ θεὸς γὰρ ταῦτα οὔτε βούλεται

---

[16] παρά, "apart from, besides."
[17] Imperatival inf.; ποιέω φανερόν, "to expose (somebody)."
[18] Imperatival inf.
[19] γινώσκειν...εὐνήν.
[20] S.v. μιαίνω.
[21] The meaning of this verb in this context is unclear.

γίνεσθαι μηθαμῶς, οὔτε θέλει, ἀλλὰ κατακολουθεῖν. οἱ θεοὶ τοῖς μὲν ἀκολουθοῦσιν (the laws) ἔσονται ἵλεως καὶ δώσουσιν αὐτοῖς ἀεὶ πάντα τἀγαθά, ὅσα θεοὶ ἀνθρώποις, οὓς φιλοῦσιν, διδόασιν· ἐὰν δέ τινες παραβαίνωσιν, τοὺς τοιούτους μισήσουσι καὶ μεγάλας[22] αὐτοῖς τιμωρίας περιθήσουσιν.

Vocabulary
ἀναγραφή, ἡ, inscription; inventory
ἀρά, ἡ, curse, imprecation
ἀνάξιος, -ία, -ιον, unworthy
ἐμφύλιος, among the people, endemic
ἵλεως, merciful, gracious, kindly (adv.)
κατακολουθέω (w. dat.), obey commandments
μηθαμῶς, not at all
μισέω, to hate, despise
μύσος, -εος, τό, pollution, defilement
περιτίθημι, put around, wrap around
παροράω, disregard
τιμωρία, ἡ, retribution, vengeance

PART 3: AGDISTIS, THE ORIGINAL GODDESS OF THE HOUSE (LINES 50–60)

Τὰ παραγγέλματα ταῦτα ἐτέθησαν παρὰ Ἄγγδιστιν τὴν ἁγιωτάτην[23] φύλακα καὶ οἰκοδέσποιναν τοῦδε τοῦ οἴκου, ἥτις ἀγαθὰς διανοίας[24] ποιείτω ἀνδράσι καὶ γυναιξὶν ἐλευθέροις καὶ δούλοις, ἵνα κατακολουθῶσιν τοῖς ὧδε γεγραμμένοις, καὶ ἐν ταῖς θυσίαις ταῖς τε ἐμμήνοις καὶ ταῖς κατὰ ἐνιαυτὸν ἁπτέσθωσαν,[25] ὅσοι πιστεύουσιν ἑαυτοῖς ἄνδρες τε καὶ γυναῖκες τῆς γραφῆς ταύτης, ἐν ἧι τὰ τοῦ θεοῦ παραγγέλματά εἰσιν γεγραμμένα ἵνα φανεροὶ γίνωνται οἱ κατακολουθοῦντες τοῖς παραγγέλμασιν καὶ οἱ μὴ κατακολουθοῦντες.

Vocabulary
Ἄγγδιστις, Agdistis, divine patroness of the *oikos*
γραφή, ἡ, writing, written/engraved text, scripture
ἔμμηνος, -ον, monthly
οἰκοδέσπποινα, mistress of a family (rare)
φύλαξ, -ακος, ἡ, guard, guardian, protector

---

[22] μεγάλας...τιμωρίας (dis. syn. [Y¹ hyp.]).
[23] Superl. of ἅγιος, -α, -ον.
[24] Note the tendency to look at the inner person as well as the outer body, which is typical of cults of the Hellenstic age.
[25] ἁπτέσθωσαν...τῆς γραφῆς ταύτης.

A PRAYER TO ZEUS (LINES 60–64)

Ζεῦ Σωτήρ, τὴν ἀφὴν τοῦ Διονυσίου ἵλεως καὶ εὐμενῶς προσδέχου καὶ (be)
προσηνὴς αὐτῶι καὶ τῶι γένει. πάρεχε ἀγαθὰς ἀμοιβάς, ὑγίειαν, σωτηρίαν,
εἰρήνην, ἀσφάλειαν ἐπὶ γῆς καὶ ἐπὶ θαλάσσης ἀσφάλειαν [........] μένοις ὁμοίως
[– – – –]

Vocabulary
ἀμοιβή, ἡ, repayment, recompense
ἀφή, ἡ, touch
εὐμενῶς (adv.), with goodwill, favorably
ἵλεως (adv.), merciful, gracious, kindly
προσηνής, -ές, well-disposed

A LOVE SPELL OF ATTRACTION OVER MYRRH (PGM IV, 1496–1595)

The sacred laws of Zeus Savior (SIG³ 985) include a prohibition of the use of
love potions (φίλτροι).[26] The spell given here provides a concrete example of such
a love potion. The use of capital letters in this text (*ll.* 1536–1540, 1555–1557,
1662–1690) indicates magical words. Though such words were deemed to be
powerful, they were probably semiologically meaningless to the intended readers
of this spell (cf. Mark 7:34, §1.12).[27]

LINES 1496–1504

Ἀγωγὴ ἐπὶ ζμύρνας[28] ἐπιθυομένης· ἐπιθύων ἐπὶ ἀνθράκων δίωκε τὸν λόγον.[29]
λόγος· Σὺ εἶ ἡ Ζμύρνα, ἡ πικρά, ἡ χαλεπή, ἡ καταλλάσσουσα τοὺς μαχομένους,
ἡ φρύγουσα καὶ ἀναγκάζουσα φιλεῖν τοὺς μὴ προσποιουμένους τὸν Ἔρωτα.

Vocabulary
ἔρως, -ωτος, ὁ, love;   Ἔρως, god of love
ζμύρνα / σμύρνα, ἡ, myrrh; Ζμύρνα, the deity Myrrh
μάχομαι, quarrel, dispute; fight; μάχομαι ἐν, fight with (ἐν/dat.), be in conflict
    with; οἱ μαχόμενοι, those who fight, combatants
προσποιέομαι, acknowledge
σαρκοφάγος, -ον, flesh-eating; subst. sarcophagus (coffin); flesh eater
φιλέω, to love; kiss
φρύγω, to roast

---

[26] Cf. Acts Andr. 5.65 (§5.16).
[27] On *nomina barbara* see *NewDocs* I, no. 8.
[28] ζμύρνας > σμύρνας.
[29] λόγος, here "spell," "formula."

LINES 1505–1510

Πάντες σε λέγουσιν[30] Ζμύρναν, ἐγὼ δὲ λέγω σε σαρκοφάγον καὶ φλογικὴν τῆς καρδίας. οὐ πέμπω σε μαρκὰν εἰς τὴν Ἀραβίαν, οὐ πέμπω σε εἰς Βαβυλών, ἀλλὰ πέμπω σε πρὸς τὴν δεῖνα τῆς δεῖνα,[31] ἵνα μοι διακονήσῃς πρὸς αὐτήν, ἵνα μοι ἄξῃς[32] αὐτήν.

Vocabulary
Βαβυλών, -ῶνος, ἡ, Babylon
δεῖνα, ὁ/ἡ, τοῦ δεῖνος, τῷ δεῖνι, τὸν δεῖνα: so-and-so
διακονέω (w. dat./gen.), serve, render assistance to
μακράν (adv.), far (away)
φλογικός, -ήν, -όν, apt to scorch; subst. one who inflames (the heart)

LINES 1510–1522

Εἰ κάθηται, μὴ καθήσθω, εἰ λαλεῖ πρός τινα, μὴ λαλείτω, εἰ ἐμβλέπει τινί, μὴ ἐμβλεπέτω, εἰ προσέρχεταί τινι, μὴ προσερχέσθω, εἰ περιπατεῖ, μὴ περιπατείτω, εἰ πίνει, μὴ πινέτω, εἰ ἐσθίει, μὴ ἐσθιέτω, εἰ καταφιλεῖ τινα, μὴ καταφιλείτω, εἰ τέρπεταί τινι ἡδονῇ, μὴ τερπέσθω, εἰ κοιμᾶται, μὴ κοιμάσθω, ἀλλ᾽ ἐμὲ μόνον, τὸν δεῖνα, κατὰ νοῦν ἐχέτω, ἐμοῦ μόνου ἐπιθυμείτω, ἐμὲ μόνον στεργέτω, τὰ ἐμὰ θελήματα πάντα ποιείτω.

Vocabulary
ἡδονή, ἡ, enjoyment, pleasure
στέργω, feel affection for somebody, show affection to
τέρπω, enjoy

LINES 1522–1545

Μὴ εἰσέλθῃς αὐτῆς διὰ τῶν ὀμμάτων, μὴ διὰ τῶν πλευρῶν, μὴ διὰ τῶν ὀνύχων μηδὲ ὀμφαλοῦ μηδὲ διὰ τῶν μελῶν, ἀλλὰ διὰ τῆς ψυχῆς, καὶ ἔμμεινον αὐτῆς[33] ἐν τῇ καρδίᾳ καὶ καῦσον[34] αὐτῆς τὰ σπλάγχνα, τὸ στῆθος, τὸ ἧπαρ, τὸ πνεῦμα, τὰ ὀστᾶ, τοὺς μυελούς, ἕως ἔλθῃ πρὸς ἐμέ, τὸν δεῖνα, φιλοῦσά με καὶ ποιήσῃ πάντα τὰ θελήματά μου, ὅτι ἐξορκίζω σε, Ζμύρνα, κατὰ τῶν τριῶν ὀνομάτων[35]

---

[30] "Call," cf. *l.* 1504.
[31] τὴν δεῖνα τῆς δεῖνα (i.e., so-and-so, mother of so-and-so); in other words, this is where the reciter of the spell is cued to fill in the name of the woman who is the object of the spell (cf. *ll.* 1520, 1532, 1543, 1547, 1579–1580, 1591–1592).
[32] S.v. ἄγω, here "to attract."
[33] αὐτῆς...τῇ καρδίᾳ.
[34] S.v. καίω.
[35] See Bonner, "Liturgical Fragments on Gnostic Amulets"; Bonner, "The Transparency of Divine Attributes."

ΑΝΟΧΩ, ΑΒΡΑΣΑξ, ΤΡΩ καὶ (κατὰ) τῶν ἐπακολουθοτέρων καὶ τῶν ἰσχυροτέρων (ὀνομάτων) ΚΟΡΜΕΙΩΘ, ΙΑΟ, ΣΑΒΑΟΘ, ΑΔΩΝΑΙ, ἵνα μοι τὰς ἐντολὰς ἐπιτελέσῃ, Ζμύρνα· ὡς ᾽γώ σε κατακαίω καὶ δυνατὴ εἶ, οὕτω[36] ἧς φιλῶ, τῆς δεῖνα, κατάκαυσον τὸν ἔγκέφαλον, ἔκκαυσον καὶ ἔκστρεψον αὐτῆς τὰ σπλάγχνα, ἔκσταξον αὐτῆς τὸ αἷμα, ὡς ἔλθῃ πρός ἐμέ, τὸν δεῖνα τῆς δεῖνα.

Vocabulary
ἔγκέφαλος, ὁ, brain
ἐκκαίω, inflame
ἐκστάζω, drain out
ἐκστρέφω, turn inside out
ἐξορκίζω (= ἐξορκόω), make somebody swear/take an oath; conjure by (κατά) a god
ἐπακολουθός, -όν, coercive; (comp.) more coercive
ἧπαρ, -ατος, τό, liver
κατακαίω (Att. κατακάω), impf. κατέκαιον, 2. κατακαύσω: burn completely, burn up
μέλος, -ους, τό, bodily frame (usually pl.); melody, music
μυελός, ὁ, marrow
ὀμφαλός, ὁ, navel
ὄνυξ, -υχος, ὁ, fingernail
πλευρά, -ᾶς, ἡ, ribs, side (of a person)
στέργω, feel affection for somebody, show affection to somebody

LINES 1546–1595

Ὁρκίζω σε κατὰ[37] τοῦ ΜΑΡΠΑΡΚΟΥΡΙΘ, ΝΑΣΑΑΡΙ, ΝΑΙΕΜΑΡΕ ΠΑΙΠΑΡΙ ΝΕΚΟΥΡΙ. βάλλω σε εἰς τὸ πῦρ τὸ καιόμενον καὶ ὁρκίζω σε κατὰ τοῦ παντοκράτορος θεοῦ ζῶντες ἀεί· Ὁρκίσας σε νῦν ὁρκίζω σε ΑΔΩΝΑΙ, ΒΑΡΒΑΡ, ΙΑΩ, ΖΑΓΟΥΡΗ, ΑΡΣΑΜΩΣΙ, ΑΛΑΟΥΣ, καὶ ΣΑΛΑΩΣ· ὁρκίζω σε τὸν στηρίζοντα ἄνθρωπον εἰς ζωήν· ἄκουε, ἄκουε, ὁ μέγας θεός, ΑΔΩΝΑΙΕ, ΕΘΥΙΑ, αὐτογενέτωρ, ἀείζων θεέ, ΕΙΩΗ ΙΑΩ ΑΙΩ ΑΙΩ ΦΝΕΩΣ ΣΦΙΝΤΗΣ ΑΡΒΑΘΙΑΩ ΙΑΩ ΙΑΗ ΙΩΑ ΑΙ, ὁ ὢν ᾽ΟΥΕΡ ΓΟΝΘΙΑΩΡ ῬΑΡΑΗΛ ΑΒΡΑ ΒΡΑΧΑ ΣΟΡΟΟΡΜΕΡΦΕΡΓΑΡ ΜΑΡΒΑΦΡΙΟΥῪΡΥΓξ ΙΑΟ ΣΑΒΑΩΘ ΜΑΣΚΕΛΛΙ ΜΑΣΚΕΛΛΩ (the formula) ΑΜΟΝΣΩΕ· ΑΝΟΧ· ΡΙΓΧ· ΦΝΟΥΚΕΝΤΑΒΑΩΘ· ΣΟΥΣΑΕ ΦΙΝΦΕΣΗΧ ΜΑΦΙΡΑΡ ΑΝΟΥΡΙΝ ΙΒΑΝΑΩΘ ΑΡΟΥΗΡ ΧΝΟΥΦ ΑΝΟΧ ΒΑΘΙ ΟΥΧ ΙΑΡΒΑΣ ΒΑΒΑΥΒΑΡ ΕΛΩΑΙ· ἄγε μοι *τὴν δεῖνα τῆς δεῖνα* πρός ἐμέ, τὸν δεῖνα τῆς δεῖνα, ἐν τῇ σήμερον ἡμέρα[38] ἐν τῇ νυκτὶ ταύτῃ, ἐν τῇ ἄρτι ὥρα, ΜΟΥΛΩΘΦΩΥΘ ΦΟΦΙΘ ΦΘΩΙΘ ΦΘΩΥΘ ΠΕΝΙΩΝ· ἐπικαλοῦμαι καὶ σέ, τὸν πῦρ κρατοῦντα, ΦΘΑΝ ΑΝΟΧ·

---
[36] οὕτω > οὕτως.
[37] κατά, "by."
[38] ἐν τῇ σήμερον ἡμέρᾳ, "on this very day."

Εἰσάκουσόν μου, ὁ εἷς, μονογενής, ΜΑΝΕΒΙΑ ΒΑΙΒΑΙ ΧΥΡΙΡΩΟΥ ΘΑΝΔΕΙΝ, ΑΔΩΝΑΙ ῈΡΟΥ ΝΟΥΝΙ ΜΙΩΩΝΧ· ΧΟΥΤΙΑΙ ΜΑΡΜΑΡΑΥΩΘ· Ἄξον τὴν δεῖνα τῆς δεῖνα πρὸς ἐμέ, τὸν δεῖνα τῆς δεῖνα, ἄρτι, ἄρτι, ἄρτι, ἤδη, ἤδη, ταχύ, ταχύ. Λέγε δὲ καὶ τὸν κατὰ πάντων (occasions) λόγον.

Vocabulary
αὐτογενέτωρ, -ορος, ὁ, self-generating
ἀείζων, -ονος, everlasting
εἰσακούω (w. gen.), hear, obey
μονογενής, -ές, only, unique
ὁρκίζω: make somebody swear an oath to somebody (acc.), swear by the name (τῷ ὀνόματι τοῦ) of somebody; conjure by (acc.), magically invoke by (acc.)
ταχύς, -εῖα, -ύ, swift, quick, soon

A CONTRACEPTIVE SPELL (PGM XXXVI, 320–332)

The sacred laws of Zeus Savior (SIG[3] 985) also include a prohibition of contraceptive potions (ἀτοκεῖον). The spell in this section provides an example of a contraceptive spell.

LINES 320–326

Ἀσύνλημπτον, τὸ μόνον (such spell) ἐν κόσμῳ. λαβὼν ὀρόβους, ὅσους ἐὰν[39] θέλῃς πρὸς τὰ (number of) βούλει ἔτη,[40] ἵνα μένῃς ἀσύνλημπτος, βρέξον αὐτὰ[41] εἰς τὰ καταμήνια τῆς γυναικὸς οὔσης ἐν ἀφέδρῳ, βρεξάτω αὐτὰ εἰς τὴν φύσιν[42] ἑαυτῆς. καὶ λαβὼν βάτραχον ζῶντα βάλε εἰς τὸ στόμα αὐτοῦ τοὺς ὀρόβους ἵνα καταπίῃ αὐτούς, καὶ ἀπόλυσον τὸν βάτραχον ζῶντα, ὅθεν αὐτὸν ἔλαβας.

Vocabulary
ἀσύνλημπτος, -ον, τό, sterile, infertile (i.e., contraceptive spell)
ἄφεδρος, ἡ, menstrual flow;[43] ἐν ἀφέδρῳ, in menstruation, menstruating
βάτραχος, ὁ, frog
βρέχω, to rain; soak (in a liquid)
καταμήνιος, -ον, monthly; pl. subst. τὰ καταμήνια, menstrual flow (menses) of women
καταπίνω, swallow something

---

[39] ἐάν > ἄν.
[40] πρὸς τὰ βούλει ἔτη, i.e., πρὸς (for) τα... ἔτη ("for ... the years ...").
[41] I.e., the seeds.
[42] φύσις here "(female) genitals."
[43] Cf. Lev 15:18, 19.

ὅθεν (adv. of place), from where, from which; for which reason

ὄροβος, ὁ, bitter vetch (*Vicia ervilia*); pl. bitter vetch seeds

LINES 326–332

καὶ λαβὼν σπέρμα ὑοσκυέμου βρέξον αὐτὸ γάλακτος ἱππίου, καὶ λαβὼν ἀπομύξῃς ἀπὸ βοὸς μετὰ κριθῶν βάλε (these) εἰς (a piece of) δέρμα ἐλάφιον καὶ ἔξωθεν δῆσον δέρματι βουρδῶνος καὶ περίαψον ἀποκρουστικῆς οὔσης τῆς σελήνης[44] (which is) ἐν θηλυκῷ ζωδίῳ ἐν ἡμέρᾳ Κρόνου ἢ Ἑρμοῦ. μῖξον[45] δὲ καὶ ταῖς κριθεῖς καὶ ῥύπον ἀπὸ ὠτίου μούλας.

Vocabulary

ἀποκρουστικός, -ή, -όν, waning (of the moon)

ἀπομύξη (= ἀπομυξία), nose mucus

βουρδών, -ῶνος, ὁ, mule

γάλα, τό, γάλακτος, milk

δέω, 3. ἔδησα: bind/tie, put in chains; imprison

ἐλάφιον, fawn (dim. of ἔλαφος, deer)

ἔξωθεν, on the outside

ζώδιον, τό, sign of the Zodiac

θηλυκός, -ή, -όν, female, woman-like, feminine (gram. gender)

ἵππιος, -α, -ον, of a horse (m.), of a mare (fm.)

κριθή, ἡ, pl. barley grains

Κρόνος, Chronos (god); the planet Saturn

μ(ε)ίγνημι, 3. ἔμ(ε)ιξα, [1]aor. impv. μῖξον,[1]aor. pass. ἐμ(ε)ίχθην, more oft. [2]aor. pass. ἐμ(ε)ίγην: to mix; bring together; pass. be brought into contact with, be intermingled

μοῦλος (m.) / μοῦλα (fm.), mule

περιάπτω, fasten, put around oneself

ῥύπος, ὁ, earwax

ὑοσκύεμος, ὁ, henbane, *Hyoscyamus niger*

SELECT BIBLIOGRAPHY

Betz, Hans Dieter (ed). *The Greek Magical Papyri in Translation Including the Demotic Spells*, 2nd ed, vol. 1: *Texts*. Chicago: University of Chicago Press, 1992.

Bonner, C. "Liturgical Fragments on Gnostic Amulets." HTR 25 (1932), 362–367.

Bonner, C. "The Transparency of Divine Attributes." HTR 37 (1944), 338–339.

---

[44] Temporal gen. absol. ("when," "during," cf. IV, 1.1).

[45] S.v. μ(ε)ίγνημι.

7.4.

Sacred Laws of an Athenian Men's Drinking Club

(IG II² 1368)

The best-known men's drinking club in ancient Greece was that of the Iobakchoi in Athens. The name ἰόβακχος is derived from the Dionysian invocation, ἰώ, combined with the alternate name for Dionysos, Bakchos.[1] The inscription in this section was discovered in the banqueting hall (ἐστιατόρειον) of this club, which was located between the Pnyx and the Areopagos, just west of the Acropolis. This same building also contained an altar decorated with Dionysian frescos.

Date: 175–176 CE.

Text: IG II² 1368, SIG³ 1109, LSCG 51; GRA 51; cf. Marcus N. Tod, *Sidelights on Greek History* (Oxford: Basil Blackwell, 1932), 71–93.

The inscription is engraved in two columns on a stone pillar. The variety of functionaries attested in this Dionysian association is extensive, numbering ten in total: these include a priest (ἱερεύς), deputy priest (ἀνθιερεύς), chief *bakchos* (ἀρχίβακχος), president (προστάτης), cowherd (βουκολικός), treasurer (ταμίας), secretary (γραμματεύς), *eukosmos* (εὔκοσμος), bouncers (ἵπποι), and sacred servants (ἱεροὶ παῖδες).[2] This inscription also alludes to a sacred drama, which is

---

[1] Cf. Eur. *Bacchae*, 576–85; Dionysos, later known as Bakchos, was perhaps the best loved of all the Greek gods, even though he was not numbered among the original twelve gods of the Olympian pantheon. Nevertheless, his cult was ubiquitous in the Hellenistic world, partly owing to its remarkable ability to assimilate local religious beliefs and practices. Dionysos was first and foremost the god of wine and the grapevine was sacred to him. By the Hellenistic period, he was even credited as the founder of viticulture.

[2] On this terminology see B. H. McLean, "The Agrippinilla Inscription: Religious Associations and Early Church Formation," in *Origins and Method: Towards a New Understanding of Judaism and Christianity*, 239–70, esp. 244, ed. B. H. McLean (Sheffield: University Press, 1993).

FIG. 16. Larnax with relief depicting funeral banquet, Çatmakaya, Turkey (IKonya 190).

to say, the enactment of a religious myth (cf. *ll.* 65–66, 123–126). The symbol V denotes denarius currency (cf. *ll.* 38, 40, 55, 90) and the symbol δρ. denotes the "light drachma" (cf. *ll.* 80, 82, 99, 110).[3] For the interpretation of numbers see the table of alphabetic numerals (table 9.18).

Related Texts: Other Dionysian religions include IMagn-Mai 215 (§7.10), IMilet VI, 22 (§7.14), IG IX/1² 670 (§7.15), and MAMA VI, 239 (§7.20).

LINES 1–10

Ἀγαθῇ τύχῃ· ἐπὶ ἄρχοντος Ἀρ(ρίου) Ἐπαφροδείτου,[4] μηνὸς Ἐλαφηβολιῶνος η′ ἐσταμένου,[5] ἀγορὰν συνήγαγεν πρώτως ὁ ἀποδειχθεὶς ἱερεὺς ὑπὸ Αὐρ(ηλίου) Νεικομάχου[6] τοῦ ἀνθιερασαμένου ἔτη ιζ′ καὶ ἱερασαμένου ἔτη κγ′ καὶ παραχωρήσαντος ζῶντος εἰς κόσμον καὶ δόξαν τοῦ Βακχείου τῷ κρατίστῳ Κλα(υδίῳ) Ἡρώδῃ,[7] ὑφ᾽ οὗ (as) ἀνθιερεὺς ἀποδειχθείς·

Vocabulary

ἀγορά, ἡ, marketplace (of a city); meeting, assembly; ἀγορὰν ἄγω/συνάγω, convene a meeting

ἀνθιεράομαι, serve as vice-priest

ἀνθιερεύς, ὁ, vice-priest (cf. *ll.* 27, 85, 104, 109, 122)

ἀποδείκυνμι, nominate somebody; reserve for somebody; demonstrate; mark out an area (of asylum, market, etc.)

Βακχεῖον, τό, a Bacchic society

Ἐλαφηβολιών, Elaphebolion (cf. *l.* 120; see table 19)

ἱερατεύω, ¹aor mid. ἱερασάμενος: serve as priest/priestess (cf. *ll.* 11, 116)

κρατίστος, -η, -ον, most excellent, noblest; his excellency (official title given to senators and magistrates)

παραχωρέω, resign

---

[3] The light drachma was instituted in the time of Hadrian (117–138 CE); when the denarius superseded the old Attic drachma, the name "drachma" was retained to signify the old obol (= 1/6 dr.), here called λεπτόν (νόμισμα).

[4] Ar(rios) or A(u)r(elios) Epaphroditos; the archonship of Ar. Epaphroditos can be dated to 175/176 CE. Most decrees are dated by specifying the name of the eponymous magistrate presiding at the time. The eponymous magistrate in Athens was the (chief) "Archon" (ὁ ἄρχων), which is to say, the head of the board of magistrates known as the "Archons" (ἄρχοντες). The chief Archon was the formal head of state, with all civic decrees being dated with his name. The dating formula begins with ἐπί followed by the term ἄρχων and the name of the Archon in the genitive case: ἐπὶ ἄρχοντος τοῦ δεῖνος ("[In the year] when *so-and-so* was Archon"). In Athens, the name of the prytanizing tribe, the ordinal sequence of the prytany and the day of the month were also specified: e.g., ἐπὶ τῆς (the tribe of) Αἰγεῖδος πρώτης πρυτανείας ("in the first day *prytaneis* of the tribe of Aigeis").

[5] ἐσταμένου > ἱσταμένου (on this formula see IV, 6); on alphabetic numerals see table 9.18.

[6] The previous priest, Aurelius Nikomachos, had the right to nominate his successor.

[7] Claudius Herodes (Atticus), 101–179 CE, distinguished Athenian orator and philanthropist (cf. *l.* 25).

LINES 10-17

(The vice-priest) ἀνέγνω δόγματα (drawn up by the former) τῶν ἱερασαμένων Χρυσίππου καὶ Διονυσίου,[8] καὶ ἐπαινέσαντος[9] τοῦ ἱερέως καὶ τοῦ ἀρχιβάχχου καὶ τοῦ προστάτου (and they all) ἐξεβόησαν· τούτοις (δόγμασι) ἀεὶ χρώμεθα,[10] καλῶς ὁ ἱερεύς, ἀνάκτησαι τὰ δόγματα· σοὶ πρέπει (to do so), εὐστάθειαν τῷ Βακχείῳ καὶ εὐκοσμίαν, (inscribe) ἐν στήλῃ τὰ δόγματα, ἐπερώτα.

Vocabulary
ἀνακτάομαι, reinstate, revive
ἀρχιβάχχου > ἀρχιβάκχου, s.v. ἀρχιβάκχος, chief *bakchos*[11] (cf. *l.* 67)
δόγμα, -ματος, τό, statute
ἐκβοάω, call out, shout out
εὐκοσμία, ἡ, good order (cf. *l.* 65)
εὐστάθεια, ἡ, good health
καλῶς, rightly, well καλῶς ἂν ποιήσαις/ποιήσεις, lit. "you would do well [to]"; fig. "please" (epistolary formula expressing a polite request); "hurrah for," "bravo for" (approve the words of a speaker)
πρέπω, be fitting (here impers.)
προστάτης, president
στήλη, ἡ, stele, stone slab (upon which an inscription is engraved)
ταμίας, ὁ, treasurer

LINES 17-31

Ὁ ἱερεὺς εἶπεν· ἐπεὶ καὶ ἐμοὶ καὶ τοῖς συνιερεῦσί μου καὶ ὑμεῖν[12] πᾶσιν (it) ἀρέσκει, ὡς ἀξιοῦτε ἐπερωτήσομεν. καὶ ἐπηρώτησεν ὁ πρόεδρος Ῥοῦφος Ἀφροδεισίου·[13] ὅτῳ[14] δοκεῖ κύρια εἶναι τὰ ἀνεγνωσμένα δόγματα καὶ ἐν στήλῃ (ought) ἀναγραφῆναι, ἀράτω[15] τὴν χεῖρα. πάντες ἐπῆραν (their hands). ἐξεβόησαν· πολλοῖς ἔτεσι (we wish) τὸν κράτιστον ἱερέα Ἡρώδην. Νῦν εὐτυχεῖς. Νῦν (we are) πάντων πρῶτοι τῶν Βακχείων,[16] καλῶς ὁ ἀνθιερεύς, ἡ στήλη γενέστω.[17] ὁ ἀνθιερεὺς εἶπε· ἔσται

---

[8] Chrysippos and Dionysios, who were priests prior to Nikomachos.
[9] Gen. absol.
[10] Hort. subj.
[11] Since Dionysos was known as the "bull god" and his devotees were called "cowherds," their leader is called the "chief *bakchos*" (cf. *ll.* 68, 93, 117, 123, 140).
[12] ὑμεῖν > ὑμῖν.
[13] Rufus, son of Aphrodisios.
[14] ὅτῳ, Att. (m. dat., s.v. ὅστις).
[15] S.v. αἴρω.
[16] πάντων...τῶν Βακχείων.
[17] γενέστω > γενέσθω.

ἡ στήλη[18] (set) ἐπὶ τοῦ κείονος, καὶ (the statutes) ἀναγραφήσονται· εὐτονήσουσι γὰρ οἱ προεστῶτες τοῦ μηδὲν αὐτῶν[19] λυθῆναι.[20]

Vocabulary

ἐπαίρω, 3. ἐπῆρα, ¹aor ptc. ἐπάρας: lift up something, hoist

εὐτονίζω, be empowered (cf. *l.* 49)

εὐτυχέω, be prosperous, have good fortune; εὐτύχει freq. employed at the close of letters to express "farewell"

κείονος > κίωνονος, s.v. κίων, ἡ, column

κύριος, -α, -ον, valid/good (re law and statutes); ἀγορά κυρία, regular meeting/ assembly

πρόεδρος, ὁ, chair of the meeting

προΐστημι, be a leader; subst. οἱ προεστωτες, presiding officers

συνιερεύς, -έως, ὁ, fellow priest

A RECORD OF THE RATIFIED STATUTES LINES 31–46

Μηδενὶ ἐξέστω ἰόβακχον εἶναι, ἐὰν μὴ πρῶτον ἀπογράψηται παρὰ τῷ ἱερεῖ τὴν νενομισμένην ἀπογραφὴν καὶ δοκιμασθῇ ὑπὸ τῶν ἰοβάκχων ψήφῳ, εἰ ἄξιος φαίνοιτο καὶ ἐπιτήδειος τῷ Βακχείῳ· Ἔστω δὲ τὸ ἰσηλύσιον τῷ (applicant) μὴ ἀπὸ πατρός[21] δηνάρια ν΄ καὶ σπονδή·[22] ὁμοίως καὶ οἱ (applicants) ἀπὸ πατρός[23] ἀπογραφέσθωσαν, ἐπὶ δηνάρια κε΄ διδόντες,[24] (which is) ἡμιφόριον μέχρις ὅτου[25] (time) πρὸς γυναῖκας ὦσιν·[26] συνίτωσαν δὲ οἱ ἰόβακχοι τάς τε ἐνάτας (day of each month) καὶ τὰς ἀμφιετηρίδας καὶ Βακχεῖα, καὶ εἴ τις πρόσκαιρος ἑορτὴ τοῦ θεοῦ, ἕκαστος (member shall) ἢ λέγων ἢ ποιῶν ἢ φιλοτειμούμενος[27] (for this Bacchic society), καταβάλλων μηνιαίαν τὴν[28] ὁρισθεῖσαν εἰς τὸν οἶνον φοράν·

---

[18] This inscription itself, with its frame and pediment, is actually inscribed *on* a marble column (even though it is carved to resemble a stele).

[19] I.e., the statutes.

[20] Art. inf. expressing purpose; s.v. λύω, (pass. here "to be violated").

[21] I.e., whose father was not a member.

[22] New members were required to donate a quantity of wine for communal consumption (cf. *ll.* 57–58, 113–114, 127–129). These donations are piously termed "libations" (σπονδαί). Additional donations of wine were required on a monthly basis, as well as on important occasions in a member's life. Moreover, certain functionaries (e.g., priest, chief *bakchos*, and treasurer) were also required to provide extra donations of wine on festival occasions. In the case of daily consumption and ritual libations (pour out to the gods), the wine was diluted with water. But on Dionysian festivals (such as Choes), wine was not mixed with water.

[23] I.e., those applicants whose fathers were members.

[24] δίδωμι ἐπί, "to pay in addition."

[25] ὅτου, Att. gen., s.v. ὅστις.

[26] I.e., until puberty.

[27] φιλοτειμούμενος > φιλοτιμούμενος.

[28] τὴν…φοράν.

Vocabulary

ἀμφιετηρίς -ίδος, ἡ, annual festival (cf. *ll.* 70, 112, 152)

ἀπογραφή, notice (of intention), application

ἀπογράφω, register; file a report

Βακχεῖα, Bacchic days

δοκιμάζω, approve for (membership)

ἐπιτήδειος, -α, -ον, suitable for (w. dat.)

ἰόβακχος, ὁ, Iobakchos, a member of this Bakcheion

ἰσηλύσιον > τὸ εἰσηλύσιον, entrance fee (cf. *ll.* 61, 103)

καταβάλλω, lead/bring down; contribute something to

ἡμιφόριον, τό, half-subscription (i.e., half the usual rate)

μηνιαῖος, -α, -ον, monthly

πρόσκαιρος, -ον, occasional

σπονδή, ἡ, drink offering, libation; donation of wine

φιλοτιμέομαι (pass. dep.): strive after honor, be ambitious; make a sincere effort

φορά, ἡ, payment, (membership) dues; tribute; rapid motion

LINES 47–58

ἐὰν (someone) δὲ μὴ πληροῖ (these obligations), εἰργέσθω τῆς στιβάδος, καὶ εὐτονείτωσαν (to enforce this) οἱ τῷ ψηφίσματι ἐνγεγραμμένοι, χωρὶς ἢ (in the cases of persons who are) ἀποδημίας ἢ πένθους ἢ νόσου ἢ (εἰ) σφόδρα ἀνανκαῖός τις ἦν ὁ προσδεχθησόμενος ἰς²⁹ τὴν στιβάδα, κρεινάντων³⁰ τῶν ἱερέων (this situation)· ἐὰν δὲ ἰοβάκχου ἀδελφὸς ἰσέρχηται ψήφῳ δοκιμασθείς, διδότω δηνάρια ν´· ἐὰν δὲ ἱερὸς παῖς³¹ ἐξωτικὸς καθεσθεὶς ἀναλώσῃ τὰ (fee) πρὸς τοὺς θεοὺς καὶ τὸ Βακχεῖον, (and) ἔστω μετὰ τοῦ πατρὸς ἰόβακχος ἐπί³² μιᾷ σπονδῇ τοῦ πατρός·

Vocabulary

ἀναλόω / ἀναλίσκω, use up; spend, pay a fee; pass. be used, consumed

ἀποδημία, ἡ, being out of town, abroad

ἐνγ- > ἐγγ-, s.v. ἐγγράφω, to record; pass. be recorded/named (cf. *l.* 61)

ἐξωτικός, -η, -ον, uninitiated

ἔργω / εἴργω, shut out; pass. be shut out of (gen.)

εὐτονέω, be empowered (to do something)

στιβάς, -άδος, ἡ, (lit.) straw couch; ³³ (fig.) gathering (cf. *ll.* 51, 63, 70, 112, 114, 152)

---

²⁹ ἰς, Att. > εἰς (cf. *ll.* 70, 82); cf. ἰσέρχηται (*l.* 54); ἰσέρχεσθαι (*l.* 72).

³⁰ κρεινάντων > κρινάντων, s.v. κρίνω; gen. absol. ("with ...").

³¹ ἱερὸς παῖς, i.e., an acolyte (i.e., one who participates in the sacred services).

³² ἐπί, "on the basis of."

³³ Such straw couches were used at the feasts. The name *stibas* was subsequently applied to the gathering of the Iobakchoi at such feasts.

χωρίς / χωρίς ἤ (w. gen.), except, apart from; without
ψήφισμα, -ματος, τό, decree

LINES 58–83

τῷ δὲ (everyone) ἀπογραψαμένῳ καὶ ψηφοφορηθέντι διδότω ὁ ἱερεὺς ἐπιστολὴν (verifying) ὅτι ἐστὶν ἰόβακχος, (but only) ἐὰν (the member) πρῶτον δοῖ³⁴ τῷ ἱερεῖ τὸ ἰσηλύσιον, ἐγγραφομένου τῇ ἐπιστολῇ τὰ χωρήσαντα εἰς τόδε τι·³⁵ οὐδενὶ δὲ ἐξέσται ἐν τῇ στιβάδι οὔτε ἆσαι³⁶ οὔτε θορυβῆσαι οὔτε κροτῆσαι, μετὰ δὲ πάσης εὐκοσμίας καὶ ἡσυχίας τοὺς μερισμοὺς λέγειν³⁷ καὶ ποιεῖν, προστάσσοντος³⁸ τοῦ ἱερέως ἢ τοῦ ἀρχιβάκχου· μηδενὶ³⁹ ἐξέστω τῶν ἰοβάκχων τῶν μὴ συντελεσάντων (the contributions) εἴς τε (meetings on) τὰς ἐνάτας (of the month) καὶ ἀμφιετηρίδας εἰσέρχεσθαι ἰς τὴν στιβάδα μέχρις ἂν ἐπικριθῇ αὐτῷ ὑπὸ τῶν ἱερέων ἢ⁴⁰ ἀποδοῦναι αὐτὸν ἢ (be allowed) ἰσέρχεσθαι (anyway)· μάχης δὲ ἐάν τις ἄρξηται ἢ εὑρεθῇ τις ἀκοσμῶν ἢ ἐπ' ἀλλοτρίαν κλισίαν ἐρχόμενος ἢ ὑβρίζων ἢ λοιδορῶν τινα, ὁ μὲν λοιδορηθεὶς ἢ ὑβρισθεὶς παραστανέτω⁴¹ δύο (witnesses) ἐκ τῶν ἰοβάκχων ἐνόρκους, (testifying) ὅτι ἤκουσαν ὑβριζόμενον ἢ λοιδορούμενον, καὶ ὁ ὑβρίσας ἢ λοιδορήσας ἀποτιννύτω τῷ κοινῷ λεπτοῦ δρ(αχμὰς)⁴² κε΄, ἢ ὁ αἴτιος γενόμενος τῆς μάχης ἀποτιννύτω τὰς αὐτὰς δρ(αχμὰς) κε΄, ἢ μὴ συνίτωσαν ἰς τοὺς ἰοβάκχους μέχρις ἂν ἀποδῶσιν·

Vocabulary

ἀκοσμέω, be disorderly; pl. subst. disorderly people
ἀποτιννύω, to pay (cf. *l.* 81)
δραχμή, ἡ, drachma (abbrev. δρ.), light drachma
ἐνγ- > ἐγγ-, s.v. ἐγγράφω, pass. be written/indicated (in a letter)
ἐνόρκος, -ον, having sworn, bound by oath
ἐπικρίνω, approve (cf. *l.* 139)
ἐπιστολή, ἡ, letter
κλισία, ἡ, seat
κοινός, -ή, -όν, common, shared; public; κοινῇ σωτηρίᾳ, for common security/ safety; subst. κοινόν, τό, treasury; religious association; τὰ κοινά, common funds, public money; κοινῇ (adv.), in common, as a group, in public

---

³⁴ δοῖ > δῷ, cf. table 9.12.1(a).
³⁵ εἰς τόδε τι, "for what purpose."
³⁶ S.v. ἄδω.
³⁷ Note the two imperatival infinitives.
³⁸ Gen. absol.
³⁹ μηδενὶ...**τῶν** ἰοβάκχων **τῶν** μὴ συντελεσάντων.
⁴⁰ ἤ...ἤ... ("whether ... or ...").
⁴¹ Fr. παριστάω, s.v. παρίστημι.
⁴² This term refers here (and in *ll.* 82, 99, 110) to the so-called light drachma (cf. n. 3).

κροτέω, applaud

λεπτός, -ή, -όν, light (in weight); light (diet); thin; fine, delicate, subtle; superl. λεπτότητος; τὸ λεπτόν δρ., "light drachma" (= 1 obol)

λοιδορέω, rebuke, abuse somebody

μάχη, ἡ, fight/fighting, quarrel, dispute; battle

μερισμός, ὁ, part in a theatrical (sacred) play

σύνειμι (fr. εἶμι), ptc. συνιών, συνιοῦσα, συνιόν, 3rd pl. pres. impv. συνίτωσαν: meet together (on), assemble

συντελέω, ¹aor. pass. ptc. συντελεσθείς: bring to an end, finish, carry out, accomplish; arrange, agree upon; pay (toward common expenses); pass. be brought to perfection

LINES 84–99

Ἐὰν δέ τις ἄχρι πληγῶν ἔλθῃ, ἀπογραφέστω ὁ πληγείς[43] πρὸς τὸν ἱερέα ἢ τὸν ἀνθιερέα, ὁ (ἱερεύς) δὲ ἐπάνανκες ἀγορὰν ἀγέτω, καὶ ψήφῳ οἱ ἰόβακχοι κρεινέτωσαν[44] προηγουμένου[45] τοῦ ἱερέως, καὶ (the offender) προστειμάσθω πρὸς χρόνον[46] μὴ εἰσελθεῖν (the Bacchic society) – ὅσον (time) ἂν δόξῃ – καὶ (by paying) ἀργυρίου μέχρι δηνάρια κε· ἔστω δὲ τὰ αὐτὰ ἐπιτείμια[47] καὶ τῷ δαρέντι καὶ μὴ ἐπεξελθόντι[48] παρὰ τῷ ἱερεῖ ἢ τῷ ἀρχιβάκχῳ, ἀλλὰ (instead) δημοσίᾳ ἐνκαλέσαντι.[49] (τὰ) ἐπιτείμια δὲ ἔστω τὰ αὐτὰ τῷ εὐκόσμῳ μὴ ἐκβαλόντι[50] τοὺς μαχομένους. εἰ δέ τις τῶν ἰοβάκχων εἰδὼς ἐπὶ τούτου (purpose) ἀγορὰν ὀφείλουσαν[51] ἀχθῆναι μὴ ἀπαντήσῃ, ἀποτεισάτω τῷ κοινῷ λεπτοῦ δρ(αχμὰς) ν'·

Vocabulary

ἀποτίνω, 2. ἀποτείσω, 3. ἀπέτεισα, ¹aor. inf. ἀποτεῖσαι, ¹aor. impv. ἀποτεισάτω: pay a fine, pay what is due; mid. exert oneself, strive

δέρω, ¹aor. pass. ptc. δερθείς: beat somebody

δημόσιον, -α, -ον, public; nt. subt. τὸ δημόσιον, the state; ἡ δημοσία, public court; (adv.) δημοσίᾳ, publicly

ἐγκαλέω, bring a charge against somebody (dat.); pass. be charged with (w. gen.)

---

[43] S.v. πλήσσω.
[44] κρεινέτωσαν > κρινέτωσαν, s.v. κρίνω (cf. *l.* 53).
[45] Gen. absol.
[46] πρὸς χρόνον, "for a time."
[47] ἐπιτείμια > ἐπιτίμια (cf. *l.* 94).
[48] Cond. adv. ptc. ("if," cf. IV, 1.8).
[49] ἐνκαλέσαντι > ἐγκαλέσαντι (cf. 1 Cor 6:1–8).
[50] Cond. adv. ptc. ("if").
[51] Modifying ἀγοράν.

ἐπάνανκες > ἐπάναγκες (adv.), without fail

ἐπεξέρχομαι, report a crime to (παρά) somebody

ἐνκαλέσαντιν > ἐγκαλέσαντιν, s.v. ἐγκαλέω, charge something against somebody; take a fellow member to court (within a larger spectrum, this verb belongs to other forms of agonistic behavior such as attempts to assume somebody's place at a banquet and physical insults).

ἐπιτίμιον, τό, assessment of damages, penalty; punishment

εὐκόσμος, ὁ, *eukosmos* (the officer in charge of good order) (cf. *l.* 136)

κοινός, -ή, -όν, common, shared; public; κοινῇ σωτηρίᾳ, for common safety; subst. τὸ κοινόν, treasury; religious association; τὰ κοινά, common funds, public money; κοινῇ (adv.), in common, as a group; in public

μάχομαι, to quarrel, dispute; fight; μάχομαι ἐν, fight with (ἐν/dat.), be in conflict with; οἱ μαχόμενοι, those who fight, combatants

προηγέομαι, preside

προστειμάσθω > προστιμάσθω, s.v. προστιμάω, penalize (cf. *l.* 145)

ψῆφος, ἡ, vote

LINES 99–117

ἐὰν δε ἀπειθῆι πρασσόμενος (this), ἐξέστω τῶι ταμίαι κωλῦσαι αὐτὸν τῆς εἰσόδου τῆς εἰς τὸ Βακχεῖον μέχρις ἂν ἀποδοῖ·[52] ἐὰν δέ τις τῶν εἰσερχομένων τὸ ἰσηλύσιον μὴ διδοῖ τῶι ἱερεῖ ἢ τῶι ἀνθιερεῖ, εἰργέσθω τῆς ἑστιάσεως μέχρις ἂν ἀποδοῖ, καὶ πρασσέσθω (payment) ὅτωι ἂν τρόπωι ὁ ἱερεὺς κελεύσηι. μηδεὶς δ᾽ ἔπος φωνείτω μὴ ἐπιτρέψαντος[53] τοῦ ἱερέως ἢ τοῦ ἀνθιερέως ἢ ὑπεύθυνος (to pay) ἔστω τῶι κοινῶι λεπτοῦ δρ(αχμῶν) λ'· ὁ ἱερεὺς δὲ ἐπιτελείτω τὰς ἐθίμους λιτουργίας[54] στιβάδος καὶ ἀμφιετηρίδος εὐπρεπῶς καὶ τιθέτω[55] τὴν[56] τῶν καταγωγίων σπονδὴν στιβάδι μίαν καὶ (recite) (τὰ) θεολογίαν, ἣν ἤρξατο ἐκ φιλοτειμίας[57] ποιεῖν ὁ ἱερασάμενος Νεικόμαχος·[58]

Vocabulary

ἐθίμος, -ον, usual, customary (cf. *l.* 153)

ἔπος, ὁ, a word; speech

ἑστίασις, ἡ, banquet

εὐπρεπῶς, in a fitting manner

θεολογία, τά, discourse about the god (Dionysos), sermon

καταγώγια, τά, Katagogia (the Festival of Return): a festival celebrating the epiphany of Dionysos, celebrated on the tenth day of the month of Elaphebolion,

---

[52] ἀποδοῖ > ἀποδῷ (cf. *l.* 105), cf. διδοῖ (*l.* 104).

[53] Cond. gen. absol. ("unless").

[54] λιτουργία > λειτουργία.

[55] τιθέτω...στιβάδι (disc. syn.).

[56] τὴν...σπονδὴν...μίαν.

[57] φιλοτειμίας > φιλοτιμία.

[58] Nichomachos, a former priest.

when the absence and subsequent return of Dionysos were celebrated symbolically in the cycle of sowing and reaping

λειτουργία, ἡ, public service, public liturgical service, priestly ministry
ταμίας, ὁ, treasurer
ὑπεύθυνος, -ον (w. gen.), liable to/for (cf. *l.* 144)
φωνέω, speak, give (a speech)

LINES 117–141

ὁ δὲ ἀρχίβακχος θυέτω τὴν θυσίαν τῷ θεῷ καὶ τὴν σπονδὴν τιθέτω κατὰ δεκάτην (day) τοῦ Ἐλαφηβολιῶνος μηνός· μερῶν (of the sacrificial victims) δὲ γεινομένων αἱρέτω ἱερεύς, ἀνθιερεύς, ἀρχίβακχος, ταμίας, (those playing the roles of):

βουκολικός
Διόνυσος
Κόρη
Παλαίμων
Ἀφροδείτη
Πρωτεύρυθμος

Vocabulary
δέκατος, -η, -ον, tenth
γείνομαι, bring into life, bring forth (cf. *l.* 160)

The following is a list of the dramatic parts in the sacred play (cf. *l.* 66):

- βουκολικός, ὁ, "cowherd," specifying one who plays a part in the Dionysian drama
- Κόρη (Kore/Persephone, daughter of Demeter)
- Παλαίμων (Palaimon)
- Ἀφροδείτη (Aphrodite, goddess of fruitfulness)
- Πρωτεύρυθμος (Proteurythmos)

τὰ δὲ ὀνόματα[59] αὐτῶν συγκληρούσθω πᾶσι· ὃς δ᾽ ἂν τῶν ἰοβάκχων λάχη[60] κλῆρον ἢ τειμὴν[61] ἢ τάξιν, τιθέτω τοῖς ἰοβάκχοις σπονδὴν ἀξίαν τῆς τάξεως, (such as)

---

[59] "Names," i.e., their dramatic roles.
[60] S.v. λαγχάνω.
[61] τειμήν > τιμήν (cf. *l.* 154).

γάμων[62]
γενήσεως
Χοῶν
ἐφηβείας
(a grant of) πολειτείας,[63]
(being honored as) ῥαβδοφορίας
(member of) βουλείας
(being chosen as) ἀθλοθεσίας
Πανέλληνος
γερουσίας
θεσμοθεσίας

Vocabulary
ἀθλοθεσία, ἡ, office of president of the games
βουλεία, ἡ, office of council member
γάμος, ὁ (oft. in pl. with no difference in meaning), wedding
γένεσις, -εως, τό, generation, offspring, birth; beginning, origin
γερουσία, ἡ, Council of Elders
ἐφηβεία, ἡ, coming-of-age celebration
θεσμοθεσία, ἡ, office of Themothetes (legislator)
κλῆρος, ου, ὁ, that which is assigned by lot, a share, portion; inheritance, inheritable estate
λαγχάνω, [2]aor. ἔλαχον, subj. λάχην, ptc. λαχών: receive (an inheritance/honor), obtain an office; choose by lot
Πανέλληνος, Panhellene, councilor of the League of All Hellenes
ῥαβδοφορίας, ὁ, rod bearer, an official responsible for policing order
τάξις, -εως, ἡ, arrangement; official appointment; position, order
Χόες, οἱ, Pitcher Festival: festival of ritual wine drinking, celebrated in connection with the transition of a boy from infancy to childhood[64]
(or any) ἀρχῆς ἡσδηποτεοῦν, (such as) συνθυσίας, εἰρηναρχίας, ἱερονείκου, καὶ εἴ τις ἐπὶ τὸ κρεῖσσον ἰόβακχος ὢν τύχοιτο· εὔκοσμος δὲ κληρούσθω ἢ

---

[62] γάμος oft. used in pl. with no difference in meaning.
[63] πολειτείας > πολιτείας.
[64] Chloes was celebrated on the second day of the Anthesteria, when a wine-drinking contest was held. Participation was limited to male Athenians more than three years of age and to people on the fringe of society such as slaves and prostitutes. Special pitchers (χοές) were designed for this ceremony, with a capacity of about 3¼ liters. Young boys were issued miniature pitchers. The prize to the winner was a skin full of wine. At the end of the day, the contestants removed their garlands, wound them around their pitchers, and presented them to the priestess of the sanctuary of Dionysos (ἐν Λίμναις). The remainder of the wine was poured out as an offering to Dionysos.

καθιστάσθω ὑπὸ τοῦ ἱερέως, ἐπιφέρων τῷ ἀκοσμοῦντι ἢ θορυβοῦντι τὸν θύρσον τοῦ θεοῦ· ᾧ δὲ ἂν παρατεθῇ ὁ θύρσος, (and) ἐπικρείναντος⁶⁵ τοῦ ἱερέως ἢ τοῦ ἀρχιβάκχου, ἐξερχέσθω τοῦ ἑστιατορείου·

Vocabulary

εἰρηναρχία > εἰρηναρχεῖον, office of Eirenarch (εἰρηνάρχης)
ἑστιατόρειον > ἑστιατόριον, τό (> ἑστιατήριον), banqueting hall
ἧσδηποτεοῦν > ἧς δή ποτε οὖν, whatsoever
θύρσος, ὁ, thyrsus, a staff wreathed in ivy and vine leaves with a pinecone on top
ἱερονείκου > ἱερονίκης, s.v. ἱερονίκη, ἡ, sacred victor (in the games)
παρατίθημι, place beside somebody (dat.)
συνκληρούσθω > συγκληρούσθω, s.v. συγκληρόω, be apportioned together by lot
συνθυσία, ἡ, office of fellow sacrificer (συνθηύτης)

LINES 141–163

ἐὰν δὲ ἀπειθῇ, αἱρέτωσαν αὐτὸν ἔξω τοῦ πυλῶνος οἱ κατασταθησόμενοι⁶⁶ ὑπὸ τῶν ἱερέων ἵπποι,⁶⁷ καὶ ἔστω ὑπεύθυνος τοῖς περὶ τῶν μαχομένων προστείμοις·⁶⁸ ταμίαν δὲ αἱρείσθωσαν οἱ ἰόβακχοι ψήφῳ εἰς διετίαν, καὶ παραλαμβανέτω πρὸς ἀναγραφὴν τὰ τοῦ Βακχείου πάντα, καὶ παραδώσει ὁμοίως τῷ μετ᾽ αὐτὸν ἐσομένῳ⁶⁹ ταμίᾳ· παρεχέτω δὲ οἴκοθεν τὸ θερμόλυχνον τάς⁷⁰ τε (meetings) ἐνάτας (day of the month) καὶ ἀμφιετηρίδα καὶ στιβάδα, καὶ ὅσαι ἔθιμοι τοῦ θεοῦ ἡμέραι καὶ τὰς⁷¹ ἀπὸ κλήρων ἢ τειμῶν ἢ τάξεων (celebrating) ἡμέρας· αἱρείσθω δὲ γραμματέα, ἐὰν βούληται, τῷ ἰδίῳ κινδύνῳ, συνκεχωρήσθω δὲ αὐτῷ ἡ ταμιευτικὴ σπονδὴ καὶ ἔστω ἀνείσφορος τὴν διετίαν· ἐὰν δέ τις τελευτήσῃ ἰόβακχος, γεινέσθω⁷² στέφανος αὐτῷ μέχρί (a cost of) δηνάρια εʹ, καὶ τοῖς ἐπιταφήσασι τιθέσθω οἴνου κεράμιον ἕν, ὁ δὲ μὴ ἐπιταφήσας εἰργέσθω τοῦ οἴνου.

Vocabulary

αἱρέω, pres. inf. αἱρεῖν, ¹aor. ἥρησα / εἷλον (√ ἑλ-), ²aor. mid. εἱλάμην/όμην: take by the hand; take away, remove; entrap, take captive; mid. take for oneself, choose; pass. be chosen
ἀνείσφορος, -ον, exempt from membership fees

---

⁶⁵ ἐπικρείναντος > ἐπικρίναντος, gen. absol. (cf. *l.* 71).
⁶⁶ S.v. καθίστημι.
⁶⁷ οἱ...ἵπποι, "bouncers" (lit. "horses"), prob. related to Silenus and Satyrs, who are often represented as half horse.
⁶⁸ προστείμοις > προστίμοις.
⁶⁹ S.v. εἰμί, 2. ἔσομαι, cf. table 9.13.1(c).
⁷⁰ Acc. of time (cf. IV, 5.1).
⁷¹ τάς...ἡμέρας.
⁷² γεινέσθω > γενέσθω.

διετία, ἡ (= διετηρίς), for two years; εἰς διετίαν, for a term of two years (cf. *l.* 159)

ἐθίμος, -ον, usual, customary (cf. *l.* 153)

ἐπιταφέω, attend a funeral (cf. *l.* 163)

θερμόλυχνον, τό, lamp oil

κεράμιον, τό, earthenware jar

κίνδινος, ὁ, risk

οἴκοθεν, lit. from one's house; fig. at one's own expense

πυλών, -ῶνος, ὁ, city gate; gateway, door

συνχορέω > συγχορέω (w. acc.), pass. give something up

ταμιευτικός, -ή, -όν, belonging to the treasurer (cf. *l.* 159)

7.5.

Founding a Voluntary Religious Association: The God Sarapis Arrives on the Island of Delos

(IG XI/4, 1299)

Delos, situated in the center of the Cyclades, is one of the smallest islands in that group. But despite its size, Delos's renown as the birthplace of Apollo and Artemis led to the founding of more than fifteen temple cults there. Alongside these cults were numerous voluntary associations, comprising people of many nationalities, including freemen, freedmen, and slaves. The epigraphical evidence from Delos documents more than twenty-four voluntary associations that existed more or less concurrently.[1] Thus this island is a microcosm of the religious and social pluralism of Greco-Roman antiquity.

The situation on Delos demonstrates the possible diversity of voluntary associations in a single locale. This diversity can be described from many perspectives, including social, religious, linguistic, national, and cultural. A case in point is the Egyptian voluntary association dedicated to the god Sarapis, which gathered in a sanctuary known today (by archaeologists) as "Sarapeion A." This association began as an Egyptian cult but later attracted followers of many nationalities. Sarapeion A, the oldest of these (ca. 220 BCE), served as the center of a private cult of Sarapis for the Egyptian residents. It consisted of a small temple, two meeting halls, a portico, and a courtyard. The inscription in this section was discovered in the temple courtyard of Sarapeion A. It tells the story of the introduction of the cult of Sarapis to Delos. At its height, Delos actually boasted three Sarapeia (temples) of Sarapis.

Date: ca. late third to early second century BCE.

---

[1] B. H. McLean, "The Place of Cult in Voluntary Associations and Christian Churches on Delos," in *Voluntary Associations in the Graeco-Roman World*, 186–225, ed. Steven Wilson and John S. Kloppenborg (London: Routledge Press, 1996).

Text: IG XI/4, 1299; SIG³ 663; Helmut Engelmann, *The Delian Aretalogy of Sarapis,* trans. Ewald Osers (Leiden: Brill, 1964 [1975]).

The primary purpose of foundation inscriptions, such as this one, is to explain the circumstances whereby a religious cult came to be founded in a particular place. This typically entails naming its (human) founder, narrating the circumstances by which the god commanded him to establish the cult (thereby vesting him with divine authority), and the authorization of his successors. The inscription here can be divided into two sections, a prose aretalogy (*ll.* 1–28) and a metrical hymn (*ll.* 29–94). Only the prose section is given.

    In this inscription, we are told that an Egyptian priest, named Apollonios I, immigrated from Memphis (Egypt) to Delos bearing a small statue of Sarapis. Upon his arrival, he rented accommodations and conducted the worship of Sarapis in his own home. Apollonios I was succeeded by his son Demetrios and later by his grandson Apollonios II, who relates the story of how Sarapis appeared to him one night in a dream and announced his desire to have a permanent sanctuary built in his honor. The god gave detailed instructions on how and where the sanctuary was to be built. The resulting sanctuary (Sarapeion A) was completed within six months. But upon its completion, evil men organized opposition to the cult, which culminated in a legal trial. As the story goes, when the moment came for the prosecution to present its case, Sarapis struck the opponents dumb, and the trial came to an abrupt end.

PART 1. THE FOUNDATION OF THE CULT OF SARAPIS ON DELOS (LINES 1–11)

Ὁ ἱερεὺς Ἀπολλώνιος ἀνέγραψεν (this stele) κατὰ πρόσταγμα τοῦ θεοῦ·[2] ὁ γὰρ πάππος ἡμῶν Ἀπολλώνιος, ὢν Αἰγύπτιος ἐκ τῶν ἱερέων,[3] τὸν θεὸν ἔχων[4] παρεγένετο ἐξ Αἰγύπτου[5] θεραπεύων[6] (Sarapis) τε διετέλει καθὼς πάτριον ἦν ζῶσαί τε δοκεῖ ἔτη ἐνενήκοντα καὶ ἑπτά.[7] διαδεξαμένου[8] δὲ τοῦ πατρός

---

[2] τοῦ θεοῦ, i.e., of Sarapis. Apollonius seems reluctant to utter the actual name of his god (cf. *ll.* 4, 10–11, 13, 21, 24, 26, 28).

[3] I.e., of a sacerdotal/priestly class.

[4] τὸν θεὸν ἔχων, i.e., having a statue of the god (Sarapis) with him.

[5] ἐξ Αἰγύπτου, Apollonios came from Memphis, Egypt (cf. *ll.* 37–38).

[6] The inscription mentions offerings of incense (*ll.* 40, 63), praising of miracles (*l.* 49), and a ritual meal (*l.* 65).

[7] Apollonios I lived from ca. 312 to 215 BCE. His son, Demetrios, was priest from 215 to 210 BCE, at which time Apollonios II assumed priestly office (ca. 210–205 BCE).

[8] Gen. absol. with two gen. participles.

μου Δημητρίου ἀκολούθως τε (likewise) θεραπεύοντος τοὺς θεούς,[9] δία δὲ τὴν εὐσέβειαν ἐστεφανώθη ὑπὸ τοῦ θεοῦ[10] εἰκόνι χαλκεῖ ἣ ἀνάκειται ἐν τῶι ναῶι τοῦ θεοῦ·[11] ἔτη δὲ ἐβίωσεν ἑξήκοντα καὶ ἕν.

Vocabulary

ἀκόλουθος, -ον, following, later; ἀκολούθως (adv.), following, next, according to

ἀνάκειμαι, be set up (in a place)

βιόω, live (for a period of time), pass one's life

διαδέχομαι, succeed somebody in office

διατελέω, continue to do something

πάππος, ὁ, grandfather

πάτριος, -α, -ον (= πατρικός), derived from one's fathers, hereditary; πάτριον, customary; subst. τὸ πάτριν, tradition

προστάγμα, -ματος, τό, command

χάλκεος, -έα, -εον (later form, χαλείος, -α, -ον; Att. contr. χαλκοῦς, -ῆ, -οῦν), (of) bronze

PART 2. THE BUILDING OF THE TEMPLE (LINES 12–23)

Παραλαβόντος δέ μου[12] τὰ ἱερὰ[13] καὶ προσκαθημένου ταῖς θεραπείαις ἐπιμελῶς, ὁ θεός (Sarapis) μοι ἐχρημάτισεν κατὰ τὸν ὕπνον ὅτι Σαραπιεῖον[14] δεῖ αὐτῶι ἀναδειχθῆναι ἴδιον καὶ μὴ εἶναι ἐν μισθωτοῖς (rooms) καθὼς πρότερον,[15] εὑρήσειν[16] τε τόπον (Sarapis) αὐτὸς οὗ δεῖ ἑδρασθῆναι (the Sarapeion) σημανεῖν τε τὸν τόπον, ὃ καὶ ἐγένετο. ὁ γὰρ τόπος[17] οὗτος ἦν κόπρου μεστὸς ὃς προεγέγραπτο πωλούμενος ἐν βιβλιδίωι ἐν τεῖ[18] διόδωι τῆς ἀγορᾶς·[19] τοῦ δὲ

---

[9] τοὺς θεούς, presumably the statues of Sarapis, Isis, Anubis, and Harpocrates, which are the deities most often mentioned in Delian inscriptions of Sarapis.

[10] In contrast to Greek associations, the god Sarapis decided that he himself would honor the devout priest. In line 43, we are told that the statue is erected according to instructions received in a dream. Demetrios had been hoping for this distinction, but neither he nor his community could fulfill this wish. Just as Apollonios II could not embark on the construction of a temple without a specific divine directive (*ll*. 14–15), Sarapis must give the command for the erection of the statue of himself.

[11] Previously, this statue had been set up in a rented room, which served as a temporary sanctuary (*l*. 15).

[12] Two participles in gen. absol. cstr.

[13] τὰ ἱερά, "sacred rites," cf. IG X/2, 255, *l*. 22 (§7.18), IMilet VI, 22, *l*. 1 (§7.14).

[14] ἴδιον...Σαραπιεῖον.

[15] The god had previously been worshipped in a rented room from the time that Apollonios I came to Delos (cf. *ll*. 39, 51–52).

[16] Here fut. inf. in indirect discourse = fut. ind.

[17] The plot of land (τόπος) for the Sarapeion was in a residential area of the Inopus valley.

[18] τεῖ, Att. > τῆι > τῆ.

[19] The placard was displayed at the passageway through which one entered the agora from the portico adjoining it from the south (cf. *ll*. 56–57).

θεοῦ βουλομένου[20] (this plot) συνετελέσθη ἡ ὠνὴ κατεσκευάσθη τε τὸ ἱρὸν[21] συντόμως ἐν μησὶν ἕξ.

Vocabulary

ἀναδείκνυμι, dedicate, consecrate

βιβλίδιον, τό, placard

δίοδος, ἡ, pathway

ἑδράζω, establish, situate

ἐπιμελής, -ές, careful, attentive; ἐπιμελῶς, diligently

κόπρος, ὁ, excrement, dung

μεστός, -ή, -όν, filled with, full of (gen.); subst. something that is full/filled

μισθωτός, -ή, -όν, hired, rented

προγράφω, write above; set forth as a public notice, advertise; exhibit in a public place; register/record (names)

προσκάθημαι (w. dat.), pres. mid. ptc. προσκαθήμενος: attend to

πρότερος, -α, -ον, former, earlier, past; πρότερον (ἤ) (adv.), before; previously

πωλέω, sell, offer for sale; pass. be for sale; subst. ptc. vendor

Σαραπιεῖον, τό, Sarapeion, temple of Sarapis

συντόμως, quickly

χρηματίζω (w. dat.), deliberate on (committee business); give ear to (an oracle), make known a divine injunction/warning; issue instructions to somebody; pass. be warned

ὠνή, ἡ, contract for purchase, price

PART 3. THE LAWSUIT (LINES 23–28)

Ἀνθρώπων δέ τινων ἐπισυνστάντων[22] ἡμῖν τε καὶ (our) τῶι θεῶι καὶ ἐπενεγκάντων κρίσιν κατὰ τοῦ ἱεροῦ καὶ ἐμοῦ (εἰς) δημοσίαν, τί χρὴ παθεῖν ἢ ἀποτεῖσαι,[23] ἐπηνγείλατο[24] δ᾽ ἐμοὶ ὁ θεὸς κατὰ τὸν ὕπνον ὅτι νικήσομεν. τοῦ δ᾽ ἀγῶνος συντελεσθέντος[25] καὶ νικησάντων ἡμῶν ἀξίως τοῦ θεοῦ, ἐπαινοῦμεν τοὺς θεοὺς ἀξίαν χάριν[26] ἀποδιδόντες.

---

[20] Causal gen. absol. ("because," cf. IV, 1.4).

[21] ἱρόν, Ion. > ἱερόν.

[22] Gen. absol. with two gen. participles.

[23] τί χρὴ παθεῖν ἢ ἀποτεῖσαι is an Attic legal formula meaning "with a penalty of a corporal punishment or a fine."

[24] ἐπηνγείλαμην > ἐπηγγείλαμην.

[25] Two gen. absol. constructions.

[26] χάριν, "thanks."

Vocabulary
ἀποτίνω, 2. ἀποτείσω, 3. ἀπέτεισα, ¹aor. inf. ἀποτεῖσαι, impv. ἀποτεισάτω: pay a
  fine, pay what is due; mid. exert oneself, strive
ἐπισυνίστημι, conspire against somebody (w. dat.)
χρή (impers.), impf. ἐχρῆν: it is necessary (w. acc. + inf.)

SELECT BIBLIOGRAPHY

Platt, Verity. *Facing the Gods: Epiphany and Representation in Graeco-Roman Art,
  Literature and Religion*. Cambridge: Cambridge University Press, 2011, 124–169.

7.6.

The Sacred Laws of the Civic Mysteries of Andania

(IG V/1, 1390)

Provenance: Andania in Messenia (southwestern Peloponnese).

Date: 92/91 BCE.

The venerable Greek traveler and geographer Pausanias (second century CE) regarded the mysteries of Andania as almost as venerable as the famed Eleusinian Mysteries (Paus. *Periegesis* IV). The principal goddess of these mysteries was Hagna.

The inscription in this section records the sacred laws of the Eleusinian Mysteries, enacted at the time of the reinstatement of these mysteries in 92/91 BCE, when Mnasistratos held the office of Hierophant (cf. *ll.* 12, 28, 85, 92, 97). The text is subdivided into many sections. (The headings of each section have been underlined for clarity.)

Text: IG V/1, 1390, GDI 4689, DGE 74; LSCG 65; SIG³ 736; Nadine Deshours, *Les mystères d'Andania: Étude d'épigraphie et d'histoire religieuses* (Paris: Ausonius, 2006); J. and L. Robert, *BE* (1941), 61, (1960), 198.

Dialect: Doric; ποτί > πρός, κα > ἄν, εἶμεν > εἶναι, -ἔι > -η.

LINES 1–5

Ὅρκος ἱερῶν καὶ ἱερᾶν· ὁ γραμματεὺς τῶν συνέδρων τοὺς γενηθέντας ἱεροὺς ὁρκιξάτω παραχρῆμα, ἄμ[1] μή τις ἀρρωσστῆι, ἱερῶν καιομένων, αἷμα καὶ οἶνον

---

[1] ἄμ > ἀνά (before labials).

σπένδοντες, τὸν ὅρκον τὸν ὑπογεγραμμένον· Ὀμνύω τοὺς θεούς, οἷς τὰ μυστήρια ἐπιτελεῖται, ἐπιμέλειαν ἕξειν,[2] ὅπως γίνηται τὰ κατὰ τὰν τελετὰν θεοπρεπῶς καὶ ἀπὸ παντὸς τοῦ δικαίου,[3] καὶ μήτε αὐτὸς μηθὲν ἄσχημον μηδὲ ἄδικον ποιήσειν ἐπὶ καταλύσει[4] τῶν μυστηρίων μηδὲ ἄλλωι ἐπιτρέψειν[5] (to do so), ἀλλὰ κατακολουθήσειν τοῖς γεγραμμένοις, ἐξορσκίσειν δὲ καὶ τὰς ἱερὰς καὶ τὸν ἱερῆ κατὰ τὸ διάγραμμα· εὐορκοῦντι μέν μοι εἴη ἃ τοῖς εὐσεβέοις, ἐφιορσκοῦντι δὲ τἀναντία[6] ·

Vocabulary

ἀρρωστέω, be very sick

ἄσχημος, unseemly

διάγραμμα, τό, instructions, ordinances (containing specific directions or schedules rather than general legislation)

εὐορκέω, swear truly, be faithful to one's oath

ἐξορκίζω (= ἐξορκόω), make somebody swear/take an oath; conjure by · (κατά) a god

ἐφιορκέω > ἐπιορκέω, swear falsely

θεοπρεπῶς, solemnly

ἱερός / ἱερά, male and female officers (not priests or initiates) in charge of organizing and directing the mysteries (cf. *ll.* 5, 7, 10, 12, 19–20, 23, 26, 31, 34)

κατάλυσις, ἡ, disruption

παραχρῆμα, immediately, instantly; recently

σπένδω, pour a drink offering (σπονδή)

τελετή, initiation rite

ὑπογράφω, write below

LINES 5-8

ἂν δέ τις μὴ θέλει ὀμνύειν, ζαμιούτω[7] δραχμαῖς χιλίαις καὶ (then) ἄλλον ἀντὶ τούτου κλαρωσάτω[8] ἐκ τᾶς αὐτᾶς φυλᾶς·[9] τὰς δὲ ἱερὰς ὀρκιζέτω ὁ ἱερεὺς καὶ

---

[2] S.v. ἔχω (fut. act. inf.).

[3] ἀπὸ παντὸς τοῦ δικαίου, "of all that is prescribed."

[4] Cf. *l.* 44.

[5] Cf. *ll.* 38–39.

[6] τἀναντια > τὰ ἐναντία.

[7] ζαμιούτω > ζημιούτω.

[8] κλαρωσάτω > κληρωσάτω.

[9] αὐτᾶς φυλᾶς > αὐτῆς φυλῆς.

οἱ ἱεροὶ ἐν τῶι ἱερῶι τοῦ (Ἀπόλλωνος) Καρνείου¹⁰ τᾶι πρότερον ἁμέραι¹¹ τῶν μυστηρίων τὸν αὐτὸν ὅρκον, καὶ ποτεξορσκιζόντω·

Vocabulary

Ἀπόλλων, -ωνος, ὁ, Apollo
δραχμή, ἡ, drachma (abbrev. δρ.)
ζημιόω, fine somebody (dat.)
ποτεξορκίζω > προσεξορκίζω, swear yet again
χίλιοι, -αι, -α, thousand

LINES 8–11

Πεποίημαι¹² δὲ καὶ ποτὶ τὸν ἄνδρα τὰν συμβίωσιν ὁσίως καὶ δικαίως· τὰν δὲ μὴ θέλουσαν ὀμνύειν ζαμιούντω οἱ ἱεροὶ δραχμαῖς χιλίαις καὶ μὴ ἐπιτρεπόντω ἐπιτελεῖν τὰ κατὰ τὰς θυσίας μηδὲ μετέχειν τῶν μυστηρίων, αἱ δὲ ὀμόσασαι¹³ ἐπιτελούντω (it)· οἱ δὲ γεγενημένοι ἱεροὶ καὶ ἱεραὶ ἐν τῶι πέμπτωι καὶ πεντηκοστῶι ἔτει¹⁴ ὀμοσάντω τὸν αὐτὸν ὅρκον ἐν τῶι ἑνδεκάτωι μηνὶ πρὸ τῶν μυστηρίων.

Vocabulary

ἑνδέκατος, -η, -ον, eleventh
μετέχω, partake of (gen.), participate in (cf. *ll.* 44, 85)
πεντηκοστός, -ή, -όν, fiftieth
συμβίωσις, ἡ, living with

LINES 11–13

Παραδόσιος· τὰν δὲ κάμπτραν καὶ τὰ βιβλία, ἃ δέδωκε Μνασίστρατος,¹⁵ παραδιδόντω οἱ ἱεροὶ τοῖς ἐπικατασταθέντοις, παραδιδόντω δὲ καὶ τὰ λοιπὰ ὅσα ἂν κατασκευασθῆι χάριν τῶν μυστηρίων.

---

¹⁰ Temple of Karneios: "Karneios" is the title of Apollo in the Peloponnesos (cf. *ll.* 34, 69). The title of the priestess, συνιέρεα τοῦ Καρνείου (*l.* 97) indicates that at the time of the domination of Sparta, these mysteries were united with the cult of Karneios and that the priestess of the mysteries was also the priestess of Apollo Karneios.

¹¹ τᾶι...ἁμέραι > τῆι...ἁμέρηι.

¹² S.v. πείθω.

¹³ S.v. ὄμνυμι.

¹⁴ I.e., the fifty-fifth year since the creation of the province of Achaia in 146 BCE. In this year, the oath was taken before the ceremonies, followed by an election, all in accordance with the reforms of Mnasistratos.

¹⁵ Mnasistratos.

Vocabulary
ἐπικαθίστημι, appoint
κάμπτρα, ἡ, chest
παραδίδωμι, hand over to another, transmit
παραδόσιος, ὁ, endowments

LINES 13–15

Στεφάνων· στεφάνους δὲ ἐχόντω οἱ μὲν ἱεροὶ καὶ αἱ ἱεραὶ πῖλον λευκόν, τῶν
δὲ τελουμένων οἱ πρωτομύσται (shall wear) στλεγγίδα· ὅταν δὲ οἱ ἱεροὶ
παραγγείλωντι, τὰμ[16] μὲν στλεγγίδα ἀποθέσθωσαν, [15] στεφανούσθωσαν δὲ
πάντες δάφναι.

Vocabulary
ἀποτίθημι, put/stow away
δάφνη, ἡ, bay leaf (laurel)
πῖλον, felt (Phrygian) cap (cf. *l.* 23)
πρωτομύστης, ὁ, new initiate (cf. *ll.* 50, 68)
στλεγγίς, ἡ, tiara overlaid with metal

LINES 15–19

(Περὶ) εἱματισμοῦ· [17] οἱ τελούμενοι τὰ μυστήρια ἀνυπόδετοι ἔστωσαν καὶ ἐχόντω
τὸν εἱματισμὸν λευκόν, αἱ δὲ γυναῖκες μὴ διαφανῆ μηδὲ τὰ σαμεῖα[18] ἐν (border
of their) τοῖς εἱματίοις[19] πλατύτερα ἡμισδακτυλίου, καὶ αἱ μὲν ἰδιώτιες ἐχόντω
χιτῶνα λίνεον καὶ εἱμάτιον μὴ πλείονος ἄξια[20] δραχμᾶν ἑκατόν, αἱ δὲ παῖδες
καλάσηριν ἢ σινδονίταν καὶ εἱμάτιον μὴ πλείονος ἄξια μνᾶς, αἱ δὲ δοῦλαι
καλάσηριν ἢ σινδονίταν καὶ εἱμάτιον μὴ πλείονος ἄξια δραχμᾶν πεντήκοντα·

Vocabulary
ἀνυπόδετος, -ον, barefoot
διαφανής, -ές, shear, transparent
ἡμιδακτύλιον, τό, half-finger's breadth
ἰδιῶτις, pl. -τιες, uninstructed
εἱματισμός, ὁ, clothing

---

[16] τάμ > τήν.
[17] εἱματισμου > ἱματισμου (cf. *ll.* 16, 24–25, 27).
[18] σαμεῖα > σημεῖα.
[19] εἱματίοις > ἱματίοις (cf. *ll.* 17–19).
[20] πλείονος ἄξια, "worth more (than)" (cf. *ll.* 18–19, 38, 82).

καλάσηρις, ἡ, long Persian garment with a fringe or tassels at bottom (cf. *ll.* 18–19,
  20–21)
λίνεος, -α, -ον, linen
μνᾶ, ἡ, μνᾶς (gen.), μνῆν, pl. μναῖ, μνέων (gen. pl. > NW μνᾶν): mina (see
  table 9.21)
πλατύς, -εῖα, -ύ, wide
σινδονίτης, ὁ, fine linen garment

LINES 19–26

αἱ δὲ ἱεραὶ αἱ μὲν γυναῖκες καλάσηριν ἢ ὑπόδυμα μὴ ἔχον σκιὰς καὶ εἱμάτιον
μὴ πλέονος ἄξια δύο μνᾶν, αἱ δὲ παῖδες καλάσηριν ἢ εἱμάτιον μὴ πλείονος
ἄξια δραχμᾶν ἑκατόν· ἐν δὲ τᾶι πομπᾶι[21] αἱ μὲν ἱεραὶ γυναῖκες ὑποδύταν
καὶ εἱμάτιον γυναικεῖον οὖλον, σαμεῖα ἔχον μὴ πλατύτερα ἡμιδακτυλίου, αἱ
δὲ παῖδες καλάσηριν καὶ εἱμάτιον μὴ διαφανές· μὴ ἐχέτω δὲ (women) μηδεμία
χρυσία μηδὲ φῦκος μηδὲ ψιμίθιον μηδὲ ἀνάδεμα μηδὲ τὰς τρίχας ἀνπεπλεγμένας
μηδὲ ὑποδήματα εἰ μὴ πίλινα ἢ δερμάτινα ἱερόθυτα· δίφρους δὲ ἐχόντω αἱ
ἱεραὶ εὐσυΐνους στρογγύλους καὶ ἐπ’ αὐτῶν ποτικεφάλαια ἢ σπῖραν λευκά, μὴ
ἔχοντα μήτε σκιὰν μήτε πορφύραν· ὅσα δὲ δεῖ διασκευάζεσθαι εἰς θεῶν διάθεσιν,
ἐχόντω τὸν εἱματισμὸν καθ’ ὃ ἂν οἱ ἱεροὶ διατάξωντι· ἂν δέ τις ἄλλως ἔχει τὸν
εἱματισμὸν παρὰ τὸ διάγραμμα ἢ ἄλλο τι τῶν κεκωλυμένων, μὴ ἐπιτρεπέτω ὁ
γυναικονόμος καὶ ἐξουσίαν ἐχέτω λυμαίνεσθαι (their garments), καὶ ἔστω ἱερὰ
τῶν θεῶν.

Vocabulary
ἀνάδημα, (woman's) hair band
ἀναπλέκομαι, to braid/plait hair
γυναικονόμος, supervisor of women at gymnasium
διάθεσις, ἡ, placing in order, arrangement
διασκευάζω, prepare
διαφανής, -ές, shear, transparent
δίφος, ὁ, couch
εὐσυΐνος > οὐσυΐνος, -η, -ον, of wickerwork, wicker
ἡμιδακτύλιον, τό, half-finger's breadth
ἱερόθυτος, -ον, made from (the skins) of sacrificial animals
λυμαίνομαι, tear/ruin (garments)
οὖλος, -η, -ον, wooly, of thick wool, of ewe's wool
πομπή, ἡ, solemn procession

---

[21] τᾶι πομπᾶι > τῆι πομπῆι (cf. *ll.* 28, 33, 68).

πορφύρα, ἡ, purpose dye; purple cloth; purple stripe
προσκεφάλαιον (NW ποτικεφάλαιον), pillow, head cushion
σκιά, -ᾶς, ἡ, colored border (on a garment)
στρόβιλος, -η, -ον, twisted, interlaced
ὑπόδημα, τό, pl. -ματα, sandal, shoe
ὑπόδυμα, -ματος, τό, undergarment for a *khiton* (cf. *ll.* 20–21)
φῦκος, -εος, τό, orchil (violet colored) used by Greek women for rouge
ψιμίθιον, τό, white lead used as face makeup

LINES 26–28

Ὅρκος γυναικονόμου· οἱ δὲ ἱεροὶ ὅταν καὶ αὐτοὶ ὁμόσωντι, ὁρκιζόντω τὸν γυναικονόμον ἐπὶ[22] τῶν αὐτῶν ἱερῶν, εἶ μὰν ἕξειν ἐπιμέλειαν περί τε τοῦ εἱματισμοῦ καὶ τῶν λοιπῶν τῶν ἐπιτεταγμένων μοι ἐν τῶι διαγράμματι.

LINES 28–34

Πομπᾶς· ἐν δὲ τᾶι πομπᾶι ἁγείστω Μνασίστρατος, ἔπειτεν ὁ ἱερεὺς τῶν θεῶν οἷς τὰ μυστήρια γίνεται μετὰ τᾶς ἱερέας,[23] ἔπειτα ἀγωνοθέτας, ἱεροθύται, οἱ αὐληταί· μετὰ δὲ ταῦτα αἱ παρθένοι αἱ ἱεραὶ καθὼς ἂν λάχωντι, ἄγουσαι τὰ ἅρματα ἐπικειμένας[24] κίστας ἐχούσας ἱερὰ μυστικά· εἶτεν ἁ θοιναρμόστρια ἁ εἰς Δάματρος[25] καὶ αἱ ὑποθοιναρμόστριαι αἱ ἐμβεβακυῖαι, εἶτεν ἁ ἱέρεια τᾶς Δάματρος τᾶς ἐφ᾽ ἱπποδρόμωι, εἶτεν ἁ τᾶς (sanctuary) ἐν Αἰγίλᾳ· ἔπειτεν αἱ ἱεραὶ κατὰ μίαν καθὼς κα λάχωντι, ἔπειτεν οἱ ἱεροὶ καθὼς κα οἱ δέκα διατάξωντι· ὁ δὲ γυναικονόμος κλαρούτω τάς τε ἱερὰς καὶ παρθένους καὶ ἐπιμέλειαν ἐχέτω ὅπως πομπεύωντι, καθὼς κα λάχωντι· ἀγέσθω δὲ ἐν τᾶι πομπᾶι καὶ τὰ θύματα, καὶ θυσάντω τᾶι μὲν Δάματρι σῦν ἐπίτοκα, Ἑρμᾶι[26] κριόν, Μεγάλοις θεοῖς[27] δάμαλιν σῦν, Ἀπόλλωνι Καρνείωι κάπρον, Ἅγναι οἶν.

Vocabulary
Ἅγναι > Ἅγνηι > Ἅγνῃ, Hagna (goddess) (cf. *ll.* 69, 84)
Αἰγίλα, Aigila
αὐλητης, ὁ, flute player
γυναικονόμος, supervisor of women at gymnasium

---

[22] ἐπί, "in the presence of."
[23] One priest and one priestess, subordinate only to the Hierophant, Mnasistratos (cf. *ll.* 96–97).
[24] Gen. absol.
[25] Δάματρος > Δήμητρος (cf. *l.* 31).
[26] Ἑρμᾶι > Ἑρμῆι (cf. *l.* 69).
[27] Μεγάλοι θεοί, "Great Gods," namely Hagna, Demeter, and Kore (cf. *ll.* 34, 68–69, 91).

δάμαλις, -εως, ἡ, young cow, heifer (cf. *l.* 69); but here "young," modifying σῦν

Δημήτηρ, -τερος/-τρος, ἡ (Dor. Δαμάτηρ): Demeter

εἶτεν, then, next (cf. *l.* 31)

ἐμβαίνω, 4. ἐμβέβηκα, pf. ptc. ἐμβεβηκώς: embark (in a boat); plunge into water; to march/process

ἐμβάλλω, throw in/against

ἐπίτοκος, -ον, pregnant (cf. *l.* 68)

θοιναρμόστρια, ἡ, mistress of the banquet (cultic title)[28]

θῦμα, -ματος, τό, sacrificial victim, sacrifice

ἱέρεια, ἡ, priestess

ἱεροθύται > ἱεροθύτηι > ἱεροθύτη, s.v. ἱεροθύτης, sacrificing priest

ἱπποδρόμος, hippodrome

κάπρος, ὁ, wild boar (cf. *l.* 69)

κίστη, ἡ, basket

κριός, ὁ, ram (cf. *ll.* 67, 69)

ὄϊς, ὁ/ἡ, οἶν (acc.), sheep (= πρόβατον) (cf. *l.* 69)

πομπεύω, walk in a solemn procession

σῦς, συός (gen.), ὁ/ἡ, hog/sow (cf. *l.* 69)

ὑποθοιναρμόστρια, assistant to mistress of the banquet

LINES 34–37

(Περὶ) σκανᾶν·[29] σκανᾶν δὲ μὴ ἐπιτρεπόντω οἱ ἱεροὶ μηθένα ἔχειν ἐν τετραγώνωι μείζω ποδῶν τριάκοντα, μηδὲ περιτιθέμεν ταῖς σκαναῖς μήτε δέρρεις μήτε αὐλείας, μηδὲ ἐν ὧι ἄν τόπωι περιστεμματώσωντι οἱ ἱεροὶ μηθένα τῶν μὴ ὄντων ἱερῶν ἔχειν σκανάν· μηδὲ παρερπέτω μηθεὶς ἀμύητος εἰς τὸν τόπον ὅν κα περιστεμματώσωντι· χωραξάντω δὲ καὶ ὑδράνας· ἀναγραψάντω δὲ καὶ ἀφ᾽ ὧν δεῖ καθαρίζειν (oneself) καὶ ἃ μὴ δεῖ ἔχοντας εἰσπορεύεσθαι.

Vocabulary

ἀμύητος, -ον, uninitiated

αὐλαία, ἡ, curtain, curtain partitions

δέρρις, -εως, ἡ, leather covering

παρέρπω, Dor. > πάρειμι (fr. εἶμι), enter

περιστεμματόω = περιστέφω, put round in a circle (cf. *l.* 36)

τετράγωνος, -ον, square, here square (feet)

ὑδράνα, ἡ, vase for water for ritual purification

χωράζω, set up; build (cf. *l.* 91)

---

[28] The mistress and her assistant presided at the banquet of the initiates.

[29] σκανᾶν > σκηνῶν.

LINES 37–39

Ἄ μὴ δεῖ ἔχειν ἐν ταῖς σκαναῖς· μηθεὶς κλίνας ἐχέτω ἐν τᾶι σκανᾶι (αὐτοῦ) μηδὲ ἀργυρώματα πλείονος ἄξια δραχμᾶν τριακοσιᾶν. εἰ δὲ μή, μὴ ἐπιτρεπόντω (it) οἱ ἱεροί, καὶ τὰ πλειονάζοντα ἱερὰ ἔστω τῶν θεῶν.

Vocabulary
ἀργυρώμα, τό, pl. silver jewelry
πλειονάζω, to be worth more (than)

LINES 39–41

Ἀκοσμούντων· ὅταν δὲ αἱ θυσίαι καὶ τὰ μυστήρια συντελεῖται, εὐφαμεῖν πάντας καὶ ἀκούειν τῶν παραγγελλομένων· τὸν δὲ ἀπειθοῦντα ἢ ἀπρεπῶς ἀναστρεφόμενον εἰς τὸ θεῖον μαστιγούντω οἱ ἱεροὶ καὶ ἀποκωλυόντω τῶν μυστηρίων.

Vocabulary
ἀπρεπῶς, disreputably, indecently (cf. *l.* 43)
εὐφημέω, keep a religious silence

LINES 41–44

(Περὶ) ῥαβδοφόρων· ῥαβδοφόροι δὲ ἔστωσαν ἐκ τῶν ἱερῶν εἴκοσι, καὶ πειθαρχούντω τοῖς ἐπιτελοῦντοις τὰ μυστήρια, καὶ ἐπιμέλειαν ἐχόντω, ὅπως εὐσχημόνως καὶ εὐτάκτως ὑπὸ τῶν παραγεγενημένων πάντα γίνηται, καθὼς ἂν παραγγέλλωντι οἱ ἐπὶ τούτων τεταγμένοι· τοὺς δὲ ἀπειθοῦντας ἢ ἀπρεπῶς ἀναστρεφομένους μαστιγούντω· ἂν δέ τις τῶν ῥαβδοφόρων μὴ ποιεῖ καθὼς γέγραπται ἢ ἄλλο τι ἀδικοῖ ἢ ποιοῖ ἐπὶ καταλύσει τῶν μυστηρίων, κριθεὶς ἐπὶ τῶν ἱερῶν ἂν κατακριθεῖ[30] μὴ μετεχέτω τῶν μυστηρίων.

Vocabulary
εὐσχημόνως, in a dignified manner
εὐτάκτως, in an orderly manner
μαστιγόω, to whip, flog (cf. *ll.* 76, 79, 102, 105, 110, 156)
πειθαρχέω, be obedient (to) (cf. *l.* 58)
ῥαβδοφόροι, οἱ, rod bearers (cf. *ll.* 43, 147, 165)

---

[30] κατακριθεῖ > κατακριθῆι > κατακριθῇ.

LINES 45–64

Περὶ τῶν διαφόρων· τὰ δὲ πίπτοντα διάφορα ἐκ τῶν μυστηρίων ἐγλεγόντω[31] οἱ κατασταθέντες ὑπὸ τοῦ δάμου[32] πέντε, εἰσφερόντω δὲ οἱ ἄρχοντες ἀνάνκαι[33] πάντες, μὴ δὶς τοὺς αὐτούς, τίμαμα ἔχοντα ἕκαστον (archon) μὴ ἔλασσον ταλάντου (of silver), καὶ (τὸ) (payment) τῶν κατασταθέντων παραγραψάτω ἁ γερουσία τὸ τίμαμα, ὡσαύτως δὲ καὶ τὸ (payment) τῶν εἰσενεγκάντων·[34]

Vocabulary
δίς, twice
ἐκδίδωμι, surrender; pay for something
ἐλάσσων, -ονος (m./fm.), **ἔλασσον** (nt.), smaller, less
παραγράφω, to record (a payment)
συνέδρος, ὁ, member of the council (συνέδριον)
τίμαμα > τίμημα, payment (cf. *l.* 47)
ὡσαύτως, in like manner

LINES 64–74

(Περὶ) θυμάτων παροχᾶς· οἱ ἱεροὶ μετὰ τὸ κατασταθῆμεν προκαρύξαντες ἐγδόντω[35] τὰν παροχὰν τῶν θυμάτων ὧν δεῖ θύεσθαι καὶ παρίστασθαι ἐν τοῖς μυστηρίοις καὶ τὰ εἰς τοὺς καθαρμούς, ἐγδιδόντες ἄν τε δοκεῖ συνφέρον εἶμεν[36] ἐπὶ τὸ αὐτὸ πάντα τὰ θύματα, ἄν τε κατὰ μέρος, τῶι τὸ ἐλάχιστον ὑφισταμένωι λάμψεσθαι διάφορον· ἔστι δὲ ἃ δεῖ παρέχειν πρὸ τοῦ ἄρχεσθαι τῶν μυστηρίων· ἄρνας δύο λευκούς, ἐπὶ τοῦ καθαρμοῦ κριὸν εὔχρουν, καὶ ὅταν ἐν τῶι θεάτρωι καθαίρει, χοιρίσκους τρεῖς, ὑπὲρ τοὺς πρωτομύστας ἄρνας ἑκατόν, ἐν δὲ τᾶι πομπᾶι Δάματρι σῦν ἐπίτοκα, τοῖς δὲ Μεγάλοις θεοῖς δάμαλιν διετῆ σῦν, Ἑρμᾶνι κριόν, Ἀπόλλωνι Καρνείωι κάπρον, Ἄγναι οἶν·[37]

Vocabulary
ἄρνας, ἀρνός (gen.); pl. ἄρνας (acc.): sheep (cf. *l.* 68)
διαφόρον, τό, money; pl. revenues
διετής, -ές, two years old
ἐλάχιστος, -ον, the lowest/least (price)
εὔθετος, -ον, fit, suitable, qualified (cf. *ll.* 148, 154–155)

---

[31] ἐγλεγόντω > ἐκλεγόντω (cf. *l.* 47).
[32] δάμου > δήμου.
[33] ἀνάνκαι > ἀνάγκηι > ἀνάγκη.
[34] *Ll.* 48–63 omitted.
[35] ἐγδόντω > ἐκδόντω (cf. *l.* 66).
[36] εἶμεν > εἶναι (cf. *l.* 80).
[37] *Ll.* 69ᵇ–73 omitted.

εὔχροος, -ον, healthy (animal)

καθαίρω, ¹aor. ἐκάθηρα: wash, clean; purge, perform a purification ritual

κιθαριστής, ὁ, kithara player

λειτουργέω, provide service (during sacrifices) (cf. *ll.* 97–98)

παρίστημι, set before, present

παροχή, ἡ, supply (of something)

προκηρύσσω, make a public declaration

πρωτομύστης, ὁ, one who has just been initiated

ὑφίστημι, to offer

χοιρίσκος, piglet

LINES 73–74

(Περὶ) τεχνιτᾶν³⁸ εἰς τὰς χορείας· οἱ ἱεροὶ προγραφόντω κατ' ἐνιαυτὸν τοὺς λειτουργήσοντας ἔν τε ταῖς θυσίαις καὶ μυστηρίοις αὐλητὰς καὶ κιθαριστάς, ὅσους κα εὑρίσκωντι εὐθέτους ὑπάρχοντας, καὶ οἱ προγραφέντες λειτουργούντω τοῖς θεοῖς.

Vocabulary

προγράφω, write above; set forth as a public notice, advertise; exhibit in a public place; register/record (names) (cf. *ll.* 145, 152, 160)

χορεία, ἡ, choral dance with music (cf. *l.* 98)

LINES 75–78

(Περὶ) ἀδικημάτων· ἂν δέ τις ἐν ταῖς ἁμέραις ἐν αἷς αἵ τε θυσίαι καὶ τὰ μυστήρια γίνονται, ἁλῶι³⁹ εἴτε κεκλεβὼς⁴⁰ εἴτε ἄλλο τι ἀδίκημα πεποιηκώς, ἀγέσθω ἐπὶ τοὺς ἱερούς, καὶ ὁ μὲν ἐλεύθερος ἂν κατακριθῆι ἀποτινέτω διπλοῦν, ὁ δὲ δοῦλος μαστιγούσθω καὶ ἀποτεισάτω διπλοῦν (the value of) τὸ κλέμμα, τῶν δὲ ἄλλων ἀδικημάτων ἐπιτίμιον δραχμὰς εἴκοσι· ἂν δὲ μὴ ἐκτίνει παραχρῆμα, παραδότω ὁ κύριος τὸν οἰκέταν τῶι ἀδικηθέντι εἰς ἀπεργασίαν, εἰ δὲ μή, ὑπόδικος ἔστω ποτὶ διπλοῦν.

Vocabulary

ἀδίκημα, -ματος, τό, wrongdoing, offense (cf. *ll.* 111, 113)

ἀπεργασία, ἡ, εἰς ἀπεργασίαν, settle/work off (a debt)

---

³⁸ τεχνιτᾶν > τεχνιτῶν.

³⁹ S.v. ἁλίσκομαι.

⁴⁰ S.v. κλέπτω.

ἀποτίνω, 2. ἀποτείσω, 3. ἀπέτεισα, ¹aor. inf. ἀποτεῖσαι, impv. ἀποτεισάτω: pay a
   fine, pay what is due; mid. exert oneself, strive
διπλόος, -η, -ον, double, twofold
ἐκτίνω, pay in full
κλέμμα, τό, theft, stolen item
ὑπόδικος, liable (for the amount of a debt), accountable to (cf. *l.* 82)

LINES 78–80

Περὶ τῶν κοπτόντων ἐν τῶι ἱερῶι· μηθεὶς κοπτέτω (any other person) ἐκ τοῦ
ἱεροῦ τόπου· ἂν δέ τις ἁλῶι (doing so), (if a slave) ὁ μὲν δοῦλος μαστιγούσθω
ὑπὸ τῶν ἱερῶν, (if a freeman) ὁ δὲ ἐλεύθερος ἀποτεισάτω ὅσον κα οἱ ἱεροὶ
ἐπικρίνωντι· ὁ δὲ ἐπιτυχὼν ἀγέτω αὐτοὺς ἐπὶ τοὺς ἱεροὺς καὶ λαμβανέτω τὸ
ἥμισυ.

Vocabulary
ἁλίσκομαι (defective pass., act. supplied by αἱρέω), subj. ἁλῶ, -ῶς (2nd), -ῷ (3rd):
   be caught doing something
ἐπικρίνω, decide (on the amount of a fine) (cf. *l.* 82)
ἐπιτυγχάνω, to chance to catch/meet somebody

LINES 80–84

Φύγιμον εἶμεν τοῖς δούλοις· τοῖς δούλοις φύγιμον ἔστω τὸ ἱερόν, καθὼς ἂν
οἱ ἱεροὶ ἀποδείξωντι τὸν τόπον, καὶ μηθεὶς ὑποδεχέσθω τοὺς δραπέτας μηδὲ
σιτοδοτείτω μηδὲ ἔργα παρεχέτω· ὁ δὲ ποιῶν παρὰ τὰ γεγραμμένα ὑπόδικος
ἔστω τῶι κυρίωι τᾶς τοῦ σώματος⁴¹ ἀξίας διπλασίας καὶ ἐπιτιμίου δραχμᾶν
πεντακοσιᾶν, ὁ δὲ ἱερεὺς ἐπικρινέτω (the fate) περὶ τῶν δραπετικῶν, ὅσοι κα
εἶσαν⁴² ἐκ τᾶς ἁμετέρας⁴³ πόλεος,⁴⁴ καὶ ὅσους κα κατακρίνει, παραδότω (them)
τοῖς κυρίοις·⁴⁵

Vocabulary
διπλασίος, -α, -ον, double
δραπέτης, ὁ, runaway slave

---

41 σῶμα, i.e., "slave."
42 Opt. εἰμί (cf. paradigm, table 9.13.3).
43 ἁμετέρας > ἡμετέρας.
44 πόλεος > πόλεως (cf. *l.* 99).
45 *L.* 84ᵃ omitted.

δραπετικός, ὁ, runaway slave

ὀνομάζω, name/call something (by a certain name); utter a name (acc.) (for magical purposes) on (ἐπι) somebody

πεντακόσιοι, -αι, -α, five hundred

σιτοδοτέω, provide somebody with food

ὑποδέχομαι, entertain as a guest; submit to; provide hospitality for (a god);
    undertake, promise

φύγιμον, τό, place of asylum

LINES 84–90

<u>Περὶ τᾶς κράνας</u>· τᾶς δὲ κράνας τᾶς ὠνομασμένας διὰ τῶν ἀρχαίων ἐγγράφων
Ἁγνᾶς[46] καὶ τοῦ γεγενημένου ποτὶ[47] τᾶι κράναι ἀγάλματος τὰν ἐπιμέλειαν ἐχέτω
Μνασίστρατος ἕως ἂν ζῆι,[48] καὶ μετεχέτω μετὰ τῶν ἱερῶν τᾶν τε θυσιᾶν καὶ τῶν
μυστηρίων, καὶ ὅσα κα οἱ θύοντες ποτὶ τᾶι κράναι τραπεζῶντι καὶ τῶν θυμάτων
τὰ δέρματα λαμβανέτω Μνασίστρατος· τῶν δὲ διαφόρων ὅσα κα οἱ θύοντες
ποτὶ τᾶι κράναι προτιθῆντι ἢ εἰς τὸν θησαυρόν, ὅταν κατασκευασθῆι (ποτὶ
τᾶι κράναι), ἐμβάλωντι (ποτὶ τᾶι κράναι), λαμβανέτω Μνασίστρατος τὸ τρίτον
μέρος·[49] τὰ δὲ (remaining) δύο μέρη καὶ ἄν τι ἀνάθεμα ὑπὸ τῶν θυσιαζόντων
ἀνατιθῆται, ἱερὰ ἔστω τῶν θεῶν·[50]

Vocabulary
ἄγαλμα, -ματος, τό, statue dedicated to a god
ἔγγραφος, -ον, written; τὰ ἔγγραφα, documents
θυμιάζω, offer sacrifice
κράνα > κρήνη, well (cf. *ll.* 86, 87, 90, 92)
λίθινος, -α, -ον, made of stone
προτίθημι, hand over, deliver something
τραπέζόω, offer to a god

LINES 90–95

(Περὶ) θησαυρῶν κατασκευᾶς· οἱ ἱεροὶ οἱ κατεσταμένοι ἐν τῶι πέμπτωι
καὶ πεντηκοστῶι ἔτει ἐπιμέλειαν ἐχόντω μετὰ τοῦ ἀρχιτέκτονος ὅπως

---

[46] Gen. of poss.
[47] ποτί > πρός ("near"), cf. *ll.* 86–87, 91.
[48] ζῆι > ζῆι > ζῆ.
[49] τὸ τρίτον μέρος...τὰ δύο μέρη, "one third of a share ... two shares."
[50] *Ll.* 88[b]–89 omitted.

κατασκευασθῆντι θησαυροὶ λίθινοι δύο κλαιστοί, καὶ χωραξάντω τὸν μὲν ἕνα
εἰς τὸν ναὸν τῶν Μεγάλων θεῶν, τὸν δ' ἄλλον ποτὶ τᾶι κράναι ἐν ὧι ἂν τόπωι
δοκεῖ αὐτοῖς ἀσφαλῶς ἕξειν· καὶ ἐπιθέντω κλαῖδας, καὶ τοῦ μὲν παρὰ τᾶι κράναι
ἐχέτω τὰν ἀτέραν[51] κλαῖδα Μνασίστρατος, (ἐχέτωσαν) τὰν δὲ ἄλλαν (κλαῖδα)
οἱ ἱεροί.[52]

Vocabulary
ἀρχιτέχτων, -ονος, ὁ, master builder (cf. *l.* 115)
κλαῖδας > κλεῖδας, s.v. κλείς, ἡ, κλειδός (gen.), key
κλαιστοί > κλειστοί, s.v. κλειστός, -ή, -όν, that can be locked
χωράζω, set up; build

LINES 95–98

(Περὶ) ἱεροῦ δείπνου· οἱ ἱεροὶ ἀπὸ τῶν θυμάτων τῶν ἀγομένων ἐν τᾶι πομπᾶι
ἀφελόντες[53] ἀφ' ἑκάστου τὰ νόμιμα (apportionment) τοῖς θεοῖς τὰ λοιπὰ κρέα
καταχρησάσθωσαν εἰς τὸ ἱερὸν δεῖπνον μετὰ τᾶν ἱερᾶν καὶ παρθένων καὶ
παραλαβόντω τόν τε ἱερῆ καὶ τὰν ἱέρειαν καὶ συνιέρειαν τοῦ (Ἀπόλλωνος)
Καρνείου καὶ Μνασίστρατον καὶ τὰν γυναῖκά (αὐτοῦ) τε καὶ τὰς γενεὰς αὐτοῦ
καὶ τῶν τεχνιτᾶν τοὺς λειτουργήσαντας ἐν ταῖς χορείαις καὶ τᾶν ὑπηρεσιᾶν
τοὺς (domestic) λειτουργοῦντας αὐτοῖς·[54]

Vocabulary
συνιέρεια, associate priestess

LINES 98–101

(Περὶ) ἀγορᾶς· οἱ ἱεροὶ τόπον ἀποδειξάντω ἐν ὧι πριαθήσεται πάντα· ὁ δὲ
ἀγορανόμος ὁ ἐπὶ πόλεος [100] ἐπιμέλειαν ἐχέτω, ὅπως οἱ πωλοῦντες (τὰ) ἄδολα
καὶ καθαρὰ (articles) πωλοῦντι καὶ χρῶνται σταθμοῖς καὶ μέτροις συμφώνοις
ποτὶ τὰ δαμόσια[55] (standards), καὶ μὴ τασσέτω μήτε πόσου δεῖ πωλεῖν, μηδὲ
καιρὸν (for selling) τασσέτω μηδὲ πρασσέτω μηθεὶς τοὺς πωλοῦντας τοῦ τόπου
μηθέν·

---

[51] τὰν ἀτέραν > τὴν ἑτέραν.
[52] *Ll.* 93[b]–95[a] omitted.
[53] S.v. ἀφαιρέω.
[54] *L.* 98[b] omitted.
[55] δαμόσια > δημόσια.

Vocabulary
ἀγορανόμος, ὁ, clerk of the market (responsible for regulating the buying and
  selling of goods)
ἄδολος, -ον, genuine
πριάμαι, buy, purchase
στραθμὰ καὶ μέτρα, weights and measures
σύμφωνος, -ον, harmonious, in agreement

LINES 103–105

(Περὶ) ὕδατος· ἐχέτω δὲ ἐπιμέλειαν ὁ ἀγορανόμος καὶ περὶ τοῦ ὕδατος, ὅπως
κατὰ τὸν τᾶς παναγύριος χρόνον μηθεὶς κακοποιῆι (the water) μήτε (κακοποιῆι)
τὸ βήλημα μήτε τοὺς ὀχετοὺς μήτε ἄν τι ἄλλο κατασκευασθῆι ἐν τῶι ἱερῶι χάριν
τοῦ ὕδατος, καὶ ὅπως, καθὼς ἂν μερισθῆι, ῥῆι τὸ ὕδωρ καὶ μηθεὶς ἀποκωλύει
τοὺς χρωμένους·[56]

Vocabulary
ἀποκωλύω, hinder, prevent
βήλημα, -ματος, τό, water control system
κακοποιέω, harm, here "to poison" and "damage"
ὀχετός, ὁ, water conduits/channel
ῥέω, ¹aor. impv. 3rd pl. ῥευσάτωσαν: to flow, stream, waft
τᾶς παναγύριος > τῆς πανήγυρεως, s.v. πανήγυρις, -εως, ἡ, festal assembly in
  honor of the civic god (cf. *l.* 112)

LINES 106–111

(Περὶ) ἀλείμματος καὶ λουτροῦ· ὁ ἀγορανόμος ἐπιμέλειαν ἐχέτω, ὅπως οἱ θέλοντες
βαλανεύειν[57] ἐν τῶι ἱερῶι μὴ πλεῖον[58] πράσσωντι τοὺς λουομένους δύο χαλκῶν
καὶ παρέχωντι πῦρ καὶ μάκραν εὔκρατον καὶ τοῖς κατακλυζομένοις ὕδωρ
εὔκρατον,[59] καὶ ὅπως ὁ ἐγδεξάμενος[60] τῶν ξύλων τὰν παροχὰν εἰς τὸ ἀλειπτήριον

---

[56] *Ll.* 105ᵇ–106ᵃ omitted.
[57] I.e., the βαλανεύς.
[58] πλεῖον…δύο χαλκῶν.
[59] Cf. PEnteuxeis 82 (221 BCE), which reads: "I had stepped out (of the baths) to soap myself, he being bath-
   attendant in the women's rotunda and having brought in the jugs of hot water, emptied one over me and
   scalded my belly and my left thigh down to the knee, so that my life was in danger " (Roger S. Bagnall and Peter
   Derow, *Greek Historical Documents: The Hellenistic Period* [Chico, CA: Scholars Press, 1981], 195–196).
[60] ἐγδεξάμενος > ἐκδεξάμενος.

παρέχει ξύλα ξηρὰ (with which to heat the oil) καὶ ἱκανὰ τοῖς ἀλειφομένοις κατ᾽ ἀμέραν ἀπὸ τετάρτας ὥρας ἕως ἑβδόμας· δοῦλος δὲ μηθεὶς ἀλειφέσθω· οἱ δὲ ἱεροὶ ἐγδιδόντω τὰν παροχὰν τῶν ξύλων τῶν εἰς τὸ ἀλειπτήριον· ἂν δέ τις τῶν ἐγδεξαμένων (ξύλα) ἢ τῶν βαλανέων μὴ ποιεῖ καθὼς γέγραπται, (if a slave) τὸν μὲν δοῦλον μαστιγούτω ὁ ἀγορανόμος, (if a freeman) τὸν δὲ ἐλεύθερον ζαμιούτω καθ᾽ ἕκαστον ἀδίκημα εἴκοσι δραχμαῖς, καὶ τὸ κρίμα ἔστω ἐπὶ[61] τῶν ἱερῶν.

Vocabulary

ἄλειμα, -ματος, τό, anointing oil

ἀλειπτήριον, τό, anointing room (cf. *ll.* 110)

ἀλείφω, anoint with oil; be rubbed down with oil (cf. *l.* 109)

βαλανεύς, ὁ, bath attendant (responsible for heating the bathwater)

βαλανεύω, heat bathwater

εὔκρατος, temperate (water) (cf. *ll.* 108)

κατακλύζω, wash somebody down (in a bath)

λουτρόν, τό, bathwater

μάκρα, ἡ, bathtub

ξηρός, -ά, -όν, dry; paralyzed

χαλκός, bronze; anything made of metal; χαλκός, chalkos (copper coin; 8 chalkos = 1 obol)

LINES 112–194 OMITTED

---

[61] ἐπί, "at the discretion of."

Circumcising the High Priestess of Demeter

(LSCG 154)

Provenance: Inscribed in the Asklepieion located on the island of Kos in the Dodecanese (cf. Fig. 2).

Date: ca. 270–260 BCE.

Text: R. Herzog, *Heilige Gesetze von Kos*, Abhandlungen der preussischen Akademie der Wissenschaften zu Berlin (Berlin, 1928), no. 8; LSCG 154.

The text here is the second part of an inscription that was carved in two columns (A and B) and three sections. The first section is a decree concerning the publication of these regulations (A 1–20). The second section records the regulations themselves. These concern the purification of the priestesses of the cult of Demeter of Olympia (A, *ll.* 21–35) and of the cult of Demeter of Isthmia (A, *ll.* 36–45). In the event that a priestess becomes ritually unclean, various purifications are prescribed, including the requirement that the priestess in question be circumcised (A, *ll.* 28, 43). The third section records a discussion of particular cultic issues (B, *ll.* 1–45, not included here).

The dialect of the inscription is Doric. In contrast to Attic and Ionic (H-dialects), the Doric dialect retained the proto-Greek long ᾱ.[1] The 3rd declension gen. pl. ending is -ιος (e.g., πόλιος > πόλεως); κα is used in place of Attic ἄν. Note also the use of the *iota*-adscript throughout (e.g., αἶ > ᾆ, ὁποίαι > ὁποίᾳ, συμβᾶι > συμβᾷ > συμβῇ, cf. IV, 16).[2]

---

[1] Smythe §30; Buck, §242ff.
[2] Cf. IV, 16.

A

LINES 21–27
(Η ΙΕΡΕΙΑ) ΔΑΜΑΤΡΟΣ ΟΛΥΜΠΙΑΣ ΤΑΣ ΕΜ ΠΟΛΙ

Ἁγνεύεσθαι[3] τὰν[4] ἱερείαν τῶνδε· μυσαρῶι μὴ συμμείγνυσθαι μηδενὶ μηδαμῶς μηδὲ παρ' ἥρῶνα ἔσθεν[5] μηδὲ ἐπιβαίνειν ἐφ' ἡρῶιον μηδὲ ἐς[6] οἰκίαν ἐσέρπεν[7] ἐν αἷ[8] κα γυνὰ τέκηι[9] ἢ ἐκτρῶι ἀμερᾶν[10] τριῶν ἀφ' ἇς[11] κα ἀμέρας[12] τέκηι ἢ ἐκτρῶι, μηδὲ ἐς[13] οἰκίαν ἐσέρπεν ἐν ὁποίαι κα ἄνθρωπος ἀποθάνῃ ἀμερᾶν τριῶν ἀφ' ἇς (day) κα ἀμέρας ὁ νεκρὸς ἐξενιιχθῆι,[14] μηδὲ τῶν θνασιδίων μηδενὸς ἅπτεσθαι, μηδὲ τῶν σφιγκτῶν μηδενὸς ἔσθεν·

Vocabulary

ἀγνεύω (w. gen.), keep pure from; mid. keep oneself pure from

Δημήτηρ, -τερος/-τρος, ἡ (Dor. Δαμάτηρ): Demeter, goddess of grain and the harvest

εἰσέρπω, go into, enter

ἔκτρωσις, -εως, ἡ, miscarriage (cf. *l.* 38)

ἥρων, -ονος, ὁ, meal dedicated to a hero,

ἡρῶον, τό, (uncontr. ἡρῶιον), grave or shrine of a hero (ἥρως)

θνασιδίων > θηησείδιον, carcass of an animal (cf. *l.* 41)

ἱέρεια, ἡ, priestess

κα, Dor. > Att. ἄν (cf. *ll.* 25, 29)

μηδαμῶς, by no means, not at all

Ὀλύμπιος, -α, -ον, Olympia (adj.)

σφιγκτός, -ή, -όν, strangled (cf. *l.* 41)

LINES 27–35

τούτων τῶν μυσαρῶν αἴ τι[15] κα[16] τᾶι ἱερεία συμβᾶι[17] ποιεῖν ὥστε παραμαρτεῖν ὅτι μέγ[18] κα μυσαρὸν ἔσθηι, (her) περιταμέσθω[19] χοίρωι θηλείαι καὶ ἀπὸ χρυσίου

---

[3] Imperatival inf. here and below.
[4] τάν > τήν (Dor. retention of proto-Greek long ᾱ) (cf. *l.* 37).
[5] ἔσθεν Dor. inf. > Att. ἔσθειν (s.v. ἔσθω, poet. form of ἐσθίω, cf. *ll.* 27, 42).
[6] ἐς > εἰς.
[7] Dor. inf. for Att. –ειν, s.v. εἰσέρπω.
[8] ἇι > ἧι > ἧ (retention of proto-Greek long ᾱ).
[9] S.v. τίκτω.
[10] ἀμερᾶν > ἀμερῶν, Dor. 1st decl. gen. pl. –ᾶν > –ῶν.
[11] ἇς > ἧς (cf. *l.* 39).
[12] ἀμέρας > ἀμέρης.
[13] ἐς > εἰς (cf. *l.* 31).
[14] ἐξενίχθηι > ἐξενέχθηι, s.v. ἐκφέρω (cf. *l.* 40).
[15] τί...τούτων τῶμ μυσαρῶν (cf. *l.* 42).
[16] αἴ...κα (cf. *l.* 42).
[17] συμβᾶι > συμβῆι + inf. (cf. *ll.* 30, 42).
[18] Assim. (ν before κ becomes γ).
[19] περιταμέσθω > περιτεμέσθω.

καὶ προσπερμείας καθαράσθω καὶ περιρανάσθω· αἰ δέ τί κα τῶν ἄλλων συμβᾶι,
ἀπὸ χρυσίου (cup) προσπερμείας περιρανάσθω καὶ καθαρὰ ἔστω. τὰ δὲ τέλεια
ἃ κα ἀναλωθῆι ἐς τὰν τελετὰν τᾶς ἱερείας, ἀποδιδωτι ἁ πόλις ἅπαντα χωρὶς
ἢ ἃ γέγραπται τὰν ἱέρειαν παρέχεν· ἁ δὲ ἱέρεια ξενίζει τὸν μόναρχον καὶ τὸς[20]
ἱεροποιὸς καὶ κάρυκας·[21] τὰν δὲ ἐπὶ τᾶι τελετᾶι[22] θυσίαν θύει ἁ ἱέρεια ἁ ἱερωσύνα
ταῦτα ἔστω τριακάδος [– – – –] πεντηκοστύος Πολλωνδᾶν· τὰν ἱέρειαν τελέζει
ἁ πόλις.

Vocabulary
αἰ, Dor. for Att. εἰ (cf. *l*. 29)
ἀναλόω / ἀναλίσκω, use up; spend, pay a fee; pass. be used, consumed
ἱεροποιός, ὁ, magistrate who oversees the temples and sacred rites
ἱερωσύνη, ἡ, priesthood
μόναρχος, ὁ, monarch, the chief magistrate of Kos
μυσαρός, -ά, -όν, foul, dirty; subst. polluted thing
παραμαρτάνω, 3. παρήμαρτον: transgress a law (cf. *ll*. 42)
πεντηκοστύς, -ύος, fifty, group of fifty
περιρραίνω, purify (cf. *ll*. 44–45)
προσπερμεία, ἡ, (ritual of) sprinkling with grain[23] (cf. *ll*. 30, 44–45)
τελετή, ἡ, initiation rite (into the mysteries)
τριακάς, -άδος, thirty, group of thirty
χοῖρος, ὁ, young pig; genital organs of a woman (*pudenda*)

LINES 36–45
(Η ΙΕΡΕΙΑ) ΔΑΜΑΤΡΟΣ ΤΑΣ ΕΝ ΙΣΘΜΩΙ

Ἁγνεύεσθαι δὲ τὰν ἱέρειαν τῶνδε· μυσαρῶι μὴ συμμείγνυσθαι μηδενὶ μηδὲ
ἐπιβαίνειν ἐφ᾽ ἡρῶιον μηδὲ ἐς οἰκίαν ἐσέρπεν ἐν ἇι κα γυνὰ τέκηι ἢ ἐκτρῶι
ἁμερᾶν τριῶν ἀφ᾽ ἇς κα ἁμέρας τέκηι ἢ ἐκτρῶι, μηδὲ ἐς οἰκίαν ἐσέρπεν ἐν
ὁποίαι κα ἄνθρωπος ἀποθάνηι ἁμερᾶν τριῶν ἀφ᾽ ἇς κα ἁμέρας ὁ νεκρὸς
ἐξενιχθῆι, μηδὲ τῶν θνασιδίων μηδενὸς ἅπτεσθαι, μηδὲ τῶν σφιγκτῶν μηδενὸς
ἔσθεν· τούτων τῶν μυσαρῶν αἴ τι κα τᾶι ἱερεία συμβᾶι, ὥστε παραμαρτεῖν, αἰ
μέγ κά τι τῶμ μυσαρῶν ἔσθηι, περιταμέσθω χοίρωι θηλείαι καὶ ἀπὸ χρυσίου
(cup) προσπερμείας καθαράσθω καὶ περιρανάσθω· αἰ δέ τί κα τῶν ἄλλων
τῶγ γεγραμμένων παραμάρτηι, ἀπὸ χρυσίου καὶ προσπερμείας περιρανάσθω
[–]

---

[20] τός > ὅς.
[21] κάρυκας > κήρυκας.
[22] τᾶι τελετᾶι > τῇ τελετῇ.
[23] Prior to the slaying of the animal, the priest and each of the participants would take a handful of oats from a reed basket (in which lay concealed the sacrificial knife) and raise their arms in the air. The priest would then recite a prayer, invocation, petition, and vow, and all who looked on would signify their "Amen" by hurling the grain at the animal (Dionysios of Halicarnassus, *Roman Antiquities*, 7.72.15). Thus, while only one person wielded the knife, this ritual of assent made the slaying a corporate act.

Vocabulary
Ἰσθμός, ὁ, Isthmos

SELECT BIBLIOGRAPHY

Nilsson, M. P. *Geschichte der Griechischen Religion*, 3rd ed., 2 vols. Munich: C. H. Beck,
    1955–1967, I, 91–110; II 70–71.
Wächter, Theodor. *Reinheitsvorschriften im griechischen Kult*. Giessen: A. Töpelmann,
    1910, 33, 46, 49, 60, 116.

7.8.

The Sacred Redemption (Manumission) of Slaves to Apollo in Delphi

(GDI II/2, 2171, 2170)

The redemption, or "manumission," of slaves was one of the most important social and legal institutions of the Greco-Roman world. One of the mechanisms for formally freeing a slave was to dedicate the slave to a god. This method was notably practiced at Delphi, where the manumissions took place in the Temple of Pythian Apollo. Sacred manumission provided a safeguard to the liberty of manumitted slaves by giving the process a public forum and by investing the transaction with a sacred authority, since the slave, in effect, became consecrated by the process to Apollo himself.

The original document was written on papyrus or a wooden tablet. It was then deposited in the temple archives and copies were given to a citizen of Delphi or to a citizen from the slave's hometown, his name being cited on the document. A copy of this document was engraved on the polygonal wall of the sanctuary. Delphic manumission contracts were inscribed to publicize the freed slave's new legal status. In fact, more than one thousand Delphic manumission inscriptions have survived dating from 200 BCE to 74 CE. These inscriptions are engraved on the polygonal stones lining the road of a 90-meter retaining wall leading up to the Temple of Apollo.

The slave transacted his manumission through the god Apollo, who contracted the sale of the slave through the mediation of his priests. The money for the ransom was actually provided by the slave himself. Upon completion of the sale, the slave was deemed to be the property of Apollo, even though he was in fact a freedman. The fictive character of this sale is made explicit by the formula "just as the slave entrusts the god with the purchase price (καθὼς ἐπίστευσε ὁ δεῖνα τῶι θεῶι τὰν ὠνάν)."

CONDITIONAL MANUMISSION

The granting of full manumission was often a two-stage process. Many slaves were permitted to purchase their freedom on the condition that they would remain under obligation to work for their original masters until the death of the master. In legal terms, this was termed a *paramone* (παραμονή) clause. Though the master retained the right to punish the slave, he could not sell the slave because the slave was legally no longer his property. In most cases, this *paramone* contract remained in effect until the death of the master.

Other conditions could also be connected with the *paramone* clause, such as responsibility for arranging the master's funeral and annual commemorative rites. The premature release from this *paramone* clause was possible, either at the discretion of the master or by the payment of a second ransom, the amount of which was sometimes agreed upon in the original manumission contract. If this amount was not specified in the original contract, a second contract could be drawn up that superseded the previous agreement.

The Structure of Delphic Manumission Inscriptions: The Delphic manumission records are very formulaic and often include the following information:

(1) The date, the name of the eponymous Archon of Delphi in the genitive case (ἄρχοντος τοῦ δεῖνος), and the month are specified, along with the names of town councilors in office at the time (βουλευόντων τοῦ δεῖνος, κ.τ.λ.). The name of the secretary or treasurer might also be added. If the slave's master was not from Delphi, the inscription is also dated according to the eponymous official of the master's hometown.

(2) The text continues with the verb ἀπέδοτο ("to hand over"), followed by the name of the master (nom.) of the slave, a reference to Pythian Apollo (dat.) as recipient (τῶι Ἀπόλλωνι τῶι Πυθίωι), and then an identification of the slave in terms of gender, age, name, and descriptor of background (γένος, race/sort/kind of slave). Male and female slaves are referred to as a σῶμα ἀνδρεῖον ("male body") and σῶμα γυναικεῖον ("female body") respectively.

(3) Next follows the ransom price (τιμή) for manumitting the slave. The average price for manumitting a male slave (between the years 80 and 30 BCE) was about 4 silver minas (400 drachmae). Sometimes the additional phrase καθὼς ἐπίστευσε ὁ δεῖνα τὰν ὠνὰν τῶι θεῶι ("just as so-and-so entrusted contract for purchase to the god") is added.

(4) Following the price is a statement confirming that the master had received the ransom in full and naming the slave and the god as his intermediary in the sale: καὶ τὰν τιμὰν ἀπέχει/ἔχει πᾶσαν ("and he has received the entire payment").

(5) The guarantor(s) (βεβαιωτήρ, βεβαιωτῆρες) of the purchase is then named. The guarantor was liable for the freedom of the slave. If the master was not

from Delphi, there were normally two guarantors; the first was a native of Delphi and the second was from the hometown of the master.

(6) If the manumission is deferred (παραμένω), this condition is inserted at this point (*paramone* clause).

(7) Next follows a statement of the legal obligation of the owner and guarantor to protect the slave against anyone attempting to take away his freedom: εἰ δέ τις (ἐφ)άπτοιτο τοῦ δεῖνος (slave) ἐπὶ καταδουλισμῶι ("if anyone should claim as his property So-and-so [slave] with a view to enslavement ..."). The master (κύριος), being present (παρατυχών) at the time, should rescue (συλάω) the slave, "on the grounds that he is free" (ὡς ἐλεύθερον ὄντα) and is "not deserving of punishment" (ἀζήμιος) and "not liable to further punishment and penalty" (ἀνυπόδικος δίκας καὶ ζαμίας).

(8) Next may follow a statement concerning the slave's new legal status: ἐφ᾽ ὧιτε (> ὧτε > ὥστε) ἐλεύθερος εἶμεν (> εἶναι) ("on the condition that he be free").

(9) Finally, various witnesses are listed, beginning with the priest(s) of Apollo, followed by private citizens.

Dialect: The dialect of these texts is Phokean of the NW group (cf. IG X/2, 255, §7.18). In contrast to Ionic and Attic (H-dialects), North West is an Â-dialect, which is to say, it has retained (like Doric) the proto-Greek long ᾱ (e.g., ά > ή, τᾶς > τῆς, τάν > τήν, αὐτάς > αὐτῆς). The 3rd declension gen. pl. ending is -ιος (e.g., πόλιος > πόλεως), and κα is used in place of Attic ἄν. Note also the use of *iota*-adscript (e.g., τᾶι οἰκίαι > τῇ οἰκίᾳ, cf. IV, 16).

(a) The Conditional Manumission of a Female Slave

(GDI II/2, 2171)

Provenance: Delphi (cf. Fig. 2).
Date: Second to first century BCE.[1]

LINES 1-7

(Ἐπί) ἄρχοντος Φιλονίκου,[2] μηνὸς Θεοξενίου, βουλευόντων Πάτρωνος,[3] Δάμωνος, Εὐκλείδα, Στράτωνος, ἀπέδοτο Φίλαγρος[4] Ἀρχύτα τῶι Ἀπόλλωνι τῶι Πυθίωι

---

[1] The standard work on the dating of these inscriptions is that of Georges Daux, *Chronologie delphique* (Paris: E. de Boccard, 1943).

[2] Philonikos.

[3] Here follows the names (gen.) of the city councilors at the time of the manumission: Patron, Damon, Efkleidas, and Straton.

[4] Philagros (name of the master), followed by ethnic (place of origin),

σῶμα γυναικεῖον ἇι[5] ὄνομα Διόκλεια[6] τὸ γένος[7] οἰκογενές, τιμᾶς[8] ἀργυρίου μνᾶν[9] τριῶν, καὶ τὰν τιμὰν ἀπέχει πᾶσαν,[10] βεβαιωτὴρ κατὰ τοὺς νόμους τᾶς πόλιος·[11] Βαβύλος.[12]

Vocabulary

ἀπέχω, receive; receive a payment

βεβαιωτήρ, -ῆρος, ὁ, guarantor

βουλεύομαι, plan, resolve, decide; be a member of the City Council (βουλή)

γυναικεῖος, -α, -ον, of a woman, female

ἐφάπτω, mid. claim somebody (w. gen.) as one's property

Θεοξένιος, Theoxenios[13]

μνᾶ, ἡ, μνᾶς (gen.), μνῆν (acc.); pl. μναῖ, μνέων (gen. pl. > NW μνᾶν), mina (= 100 drachmae)

οἰκογενής, -ές, born in the house, homebred (slave)

Πύθιος, -α, -ον, Pythian (i.e., of Delphi), epithet of Apollo

τιμή, ἡ, price

LINES 7–11

παραμεινάτω δὲ Διόκλεια παρὰ[14] Κλεοπάτραι[15] τῆι ματρὶ Φιλάγρου ποιοῦσα τὸ ἐπιτασσόμενον πᾶν τὸ δυνατόν, ἐξουσίαν δὲ (Kleopatra) ἐχέτω ἐπιτιμοῦσα καὶ διδέουσα (commands) τρόπωι ὧι κα θέληι πλὰν[16] μὴ πωλέουσα (her).

Vocabulary

ἐπιτάσσω, instruct/order somebody to do something

ἐπιτιμάω, warn, speak seriously; rebuke

παραμένω, remain (in a place); remain/stay (of slaves whose manumission was deferred)

---

[5] ἇι > ἧι > ᾗ (dat. of poss.).

[6] Διόκλεια (fm.), name of the slave.

[7] τὸ γένος, "kind/type."

[8] τιμᾶς > τιμῆς.

[9] μνᾶν, NW > μνέων.

[10] τιμὰν…πᾶσαν.

[11] τᾶς πόλιος > τῆς πόλεως.

[12] Babulos.

[13] The names of the Delphic months are as follows: (1) Ἀπελλαῖος, (2) Βουκάτιος, (3) Βοάθοος, (4) Ἡραῖος, (5) Δαιδαφόριος, (6) Ποιτρόπιος, (7) Ἀμάλιος, (8) Βύσιος, (9) Θεοξένιος, (10) Ἐνδυσποιτρόπιος, (11) Ἡράκλειος, (12) Ἰλαῖος.

[14] παρά (w. dat.), "with," "at the house of."

[15] Kleopatra.

[16] πλὰν, NW > πλήν.

LINES 11–16

ἐπεί κά¹⁷ τι πάθοι¹⁸ Κλεοπάτρα, ἐλευθέρα ἔστω Διόκλεα καὶ ὑπαγέτω πᾶι κα θέληι. εἰ δέ τις ἐφάπτοιτο Διοκλέας ἐπὶ καταδουλισμῶι, κύριος ἔστω ὁ παρατυχὼν¹⁹ συλέων (her) ὡς²⁰ ἐλευθέραν οὖσαν ¹⁵ ἀζάμιος ὢν καὶ ἀνυπόδικος πάσας δίκας²¹ καὶ ζαμίας²² καὶ ὁ βεβαιωτὴρ βεβαιούτω.

Vocabulary

ἀζάμιος > ἀζήμιος, -ον, not deserving of punishment

ἀνυπόδικος, -ον, not liable to (w. gen.)

ἐφάπτω, mid. claim somebody (w. gen.) as one's property

καταδουλισμός, ὁ, enslavement

πᾶι (Dor.) > πῆι > πῇ, anywhere

συλέω > συλάω, to rescue

ὑπάγω, bring under one's power, induce somebody to do something; bring before a court of law; go away, depart

LINES 11–23

εἰ δέ τι²³ γένοιτο ἐγ²⁴ Διοκλέας τέκνον ἐν τῶι τᾶς παραμονᾶς χρόνωι, εἴ κα μὲν θέληι ἀποπνεῖξαι (it) Διόκλεα, ἐξουσίαν ἐχέτω, εἰ δὲ θέλοι τρέφειν, ἔστω τὸ τρεφόμενον ἐλεύθερον. εἴ κα μὴ αὐτὸ θέληι, πωλῆσαι δὲ τὸ γενηθέν,²⁵ μὴ ἐχέτω ἐξουσίαν Διόκλεα μηδὲ ἄλλος μηθείς.²⁶ μάρτυροι·²⁷ ὁ ἱερεὺς τοῦ Ἀπόλλωνος, Ἐμενίδας, Εὐάγγελος, Λαιάδας, Δάμων, Καλλίας.

Vocabulary

ἀποπνεῖξαι > ἀποπνίξαι, s.v. ἀπογνίγω, to choke, throttle

παραμονή, ἡ, the obligation (of a slave) to continue to serve (i.e., a deferment of manumission)

---

¹⁷ κα, NW > Att. ἄν.

¹⁸ S.v. πάσχω, i.e., when she dies.

¹⁹ S.v. παρατυγχάνω.

²⁰ ὡς, "on the grounds that."

²¹ πάσας δίκας > πάσης δίκης.

²² ζαμίας > ζημίας.

²³ τι...τέκνον.

²⁴ ἐγ > ἐν.

²⁵ S.v. γίνομαι.

²⁶ μηθείς > μηδείς.

²⁷ μάρτυρος = μάρτυς.

(b) The Manumission of a Young Man in Delphi

(GDI II/2, 2170)

Provenance: Delphi.
Date: Second to first century BCE.

LINES 1-6

(Ἐπί) ἄρχοντος Φιλονίκου,²⁸ μηνὸς Ἡρακλείου, βουλευόντων²⁹ Πάτρωνος, Δάμωνος, Στράτωνος, Εὐκλίδα, ἀπέδοντο Πάσων καὶ Διόδωρος³⁰ οἱ Ὀρέστα τῶι Ἀπόλλωνι τῶι Πυθίωι (for) παιδάριον ὧι ὄνομα Ἀλέξιππος³¹ ἐπ' ἐλευθερίαι, τιμᾶς ἀργυρίου μνᾶν δύο, καὶ τὰν τιμὰν ἔχοντι³² πᾶσαν,³³ καθὼς ἐπίστευσε³⁴ Ἀλέξιππος τὰν ὠνὰν³⁵ τῶι θεῶι,⁵ ἐφ' ὧιτε³⁶ ἐλεύθερος εἶμεν³⁷ καὶ ἀνέφαπτος ἀπὸ πάντων τὸν πάντα βίον. βεβαιωτὴρ κατὰ τοὺς νόμους· Καλλίας³⁸ Εὐκλίδα.

Vocabulary
ἀνέφαπτος, -ον, not to be claimed as a slave
ὠνή, ἡ, contract for purchase, price

LINES 6-11

εἰ δέ τις ἐφάπτοιτο Ἀλεξίππου ἐπὶ καταδουλισμῶι, βέβαιον παρεχέτωσαν τῶι θεῶι τὰν ὠνὰν οἵ τε ἀποδόμενοι καὶ ὁ βεβαιωτὴρ βεβαιούτω. ὁμοίως δὲ καὶ ὁ παρατυχὼν κύριος ἔστω συλέων   Ἀλέξιππον ὡς ἐλεύθερον ἀνυπόδικος ὢν καὶ ἀζάμιος πάσας δίκας καὶ ζαμίας.³⁹ μάρτυροι·¹⁰ Ἀμύντας, Πάτρων, Εὐκλίδας, Βαβύλος, [– – –], Πρωτογένης.

Vocabulary
ἀζάμιος > ἀζήμιος, -ον, not deserving of punishment
ἀνυπόδικος, -ον, not liable to (w. gen.)

---

²⁸ Philonikos.
²⁹ Here follow the names of city councilors.
³⁰ Πάσων and Διόδωρος (names of the masters); οἱ Ὀρέστα, ethnic.
³¹ Alexippos (slave's name) (cf. *ll.* 5–6).
³² ἔχοντι > ἔχουσι.
³³ τιμὰν…πᾶσαν.
³⁴ Here "entrusted."
³⁵ ὠνάν > ὠνήν.
³⁶ ὧιτε > ὧτε > ὥστε.
³⁷ εἶμεν, NW > εἶναι.
³⁸ Kallias (name of guarantor) + ethnic.
³⁹ ζαμίας > ζημίας.

βέβαιος, -ον, steady, secure, reliable; subst. security, guarantee, βέβαιον παρέχειν τὴν ὠνήν, confirm/guarantee the contract for purchase; superl. βεβαιότατος, most reliable; βεβαίως, with certainty

Ἡράκλειος, Herakleios (month name, cf. table 9.19)

καταδουλισμός, ὁ, enslavement

συλέω > συλάω, to rescue

SELECT BIBLIOGRAPHY

Fitzgerald, William. *Slavery and the Roman Literary Imagination.* Cambridge: Cambridge University Press, 2000.

Tucker, C. Wayne. "Women in the Manumission Inscriptions at Delphi." Transactions of the American Philological Association 112 (1982), 225–236.

7.9.

The Hellenistic Healing Testimonials of Epidauros

(LiDonnici A1–5, 8, B12, C21)

Provenance: Epidauros (Epidavros, see Fig. 2), located on the Saronic Gulf of the Peloponnese. This city was the site of the most renowned Asklepieion (healing center) of Asklepios, the god of healing.

Date: ca. 300–250 BCE.

Text: Lynn R. LiDonnici, *The Epidaurian Miracle Inscriptions: Text, Translation and Commentary* (Atlanta: Scholars Press, 1995), 84–93, A1–5, A18, B12, C21.

The gods of Greco-Roman antiquity were often associated with specific places. Asklepios was linked with healing shrines (Asklepieia), which were dedicated to him throughout the ancient world in places such as Pergamon, Athens, and Thelpoussa (Arkadia) and on the islands of Kos and Chios. The most famous of these healing shrines was the Asklepieion in Epidauros. The sick and injured from far and wide would make a pilgrimage to Epidauros to sleep, or "incubate," in the sanctuary's *abaton* (the innermost room of the temple), located near the Temple of Asklepios. During the night, the god Asklepios would communicate with the patient, either through a direct epiphany or indirectly through a dream or by an intermediary such as a snake or dog.

Archaeologists have discovered six columns inscribed with "healing testimonials" (*iamata*), dating to the early Hellenistic period. These testimonials attest to the intervention of Asklepios, who would cure people by performing various kinds of medical procedures (cf. Paus. *Graec. Descr.* 2.27.3). The healing testimonial inscriptions are quite concise and formulaic (though not every testimonial includes every element of the general structure): (1) they begin with a citation of the name of the suppliant, sometimes followed by his or her place of origin; (2) the testimonials then diagnose the medical condition (sometimes followed by a remark about the suppliant's lack of faith, skepticism, or even mocking attitude);

(3) next the testimonials tell of the act of divine healing of Asklepios in the *aba-ton*, which he performed either by appearing to the suppliant in a vision or dream and giving instructions or by acting directly; (4) the testimonials cite the demonstration of a successful cure; (5) finally, they sometimes narrate the thanksgiving and praise given by the suppliant to Asklepios and the offering or payment given in appreciation for the divine healing. These events are later recorded on a votive plaque. The votive plaques themselves were subsequently inscribed on stone columns as tokens of thanksgiving to the god.

Dialect: The dialect of the testimonials is Argolic, in the family of West Greek (see footnotes).[1] Note also the use of *iota*-adscript and the frequent use of infinitives (cf. IV, 16).

Related Texts: The healing testimonial of Marcus Julius Apellas (§7.21); the healings of Jesus as recorded in the Synoptic Gospels (cf. §1.12).[2]

ΘΕΟΣ ΤΥΧΑ ΑΓΑΘΑ[3]
ΙΑΜΑΤΑ ΤΟΥ ΑΠΟΛΛΩΝΟΣ[4] ΚΑΙ ΤΟΥ ΑΣΚΛΑΠΙΟΥ
A1 (LINES 3–9)

Κλεὼ[5] πένθ᾽ [6] ἔτη ἐκύησε. Αὕτα πέντ᾽ ἐνιαυτοὺς ἤδη κυοῦσα ποὶ[7] τὸν   θεὸν (as) ἱκέτις ἀφίκετο καὶ ἐνεκάθευδε ἐν τῶι ἀβάτωι· ὡς δὲ τάχιστα[8] ἐξῆλθε ἐξ αὐτοῦ[9] καὶ ἐκ[10] τοῦ ἱαροῦ[11] ἐγένετο, κόρον ἔτεκε, ὅς εὐθὺς γενόμενος αὐτὸς ἀπὸ τᾶς κράνας ἐλοῦτο[12] καὶ ἅμα τᾶι ματρὶ περιῆρπε. τυχοῦσα δὲ τούτων ἐπὶ τὸ ἄνθεμα[13] ἐπεγράψατο· οὐ μέγεθος πίνακος θαυμαστέον, ἀλλὰ τὸ θεῖον, πένθ᾽ ἔτη ὡς ἐκύησε ἐγ[14] γαστρὶ Κλεὼ βάρος, ἔστε ἐγκατεκοιμάθη (her) καὶ μιν (the god) ἔθηκε ὑγιῆ.

---

[1] Cf. Buck 154–155, 162–64 (§§223–225, 249–251).
[2] On similarities in structure see Martin Debelius, *From Tradition to Gospel* (London: I. Nicholson and Watson, 1934), 164–172.
[3] Literally "God. Good Luck."
[4] Epidauros was also the site of the hilltop sanctuary of the god Apollo Maleatas. In point of fact, only Asklepios accomplished the works of healing, but according to myth, Apollo was his father.
[5] Kleo.
[6] πένθ᾽ > πέντε.
[7] ποί, Dor. > πρός, cf. 2.15, 4.34, 5.44 (Buck §135.6).
[8] τάχιστα (superl. of ταχύς), "as soon as."
[9] I.e., the *abaton*.
[10] "Outside."
[11] ἱαρόν > ἱερόν (cf. 2.10, 21, 4.35, 39, 5.42, 8.124).
[12] Contr. impf. mid. forms of λούω such as ἐλούμην and ἐλοῦτο belong to λόω.
[13] ἄνθεμα > ἀνάθεμα.
[14] Assim.: ν before γ becomes γ.

Vocabulary

ἄβατον, τό, *abaton* (sleeping chamber of the sanctuary of Asklepios)

βάρος, -ους, τό, a weight, load, burden

ἐγκατακοιμάομαι (= ἐγκοιμάομαι), aor. pass. (dep.) ἐγκατεκοιμάθην, aor. fem. ptc. ἐγκατακοιμαθεῖσα: sleep in a *enkoimeteria* (sleeping hall) seeking prophetic dreams to obtain a cure from a disease, "to incubate"

ἔστε, until (cf. 2.14)

θαυμαστέος, -α, -ον, be wondered at

ἱκέτης, -ου, ὁ / ἱκέτις, -ιδος, ἡ, suppliant, one who comes seeking help or protection

κόρος, ὁ, **boy**; κόρα, ἡ, a girl; pl. pupils (of the eyes)

κράνας > κρήνης, s.v. κρήνη, ἡ, spring, fountain

κυέω, aor. inf. κυῆσαι: be pregnant; conceive a child

μιν, him, her, it, 3rd pers. pron. (acc. sg.) in Ep. and Ion.

περιέρπω, walk about

πίναξ, πίνακος, ὁ, flat wooden plaque (plastered or primed, then painted and inscribed)

ὑγιής, -ές, healthy; τίθημι ὑγιή, make well

A2 (LINES 9–22)

Τριέτης φορά... Ἰθμονίκα[15] Πελλανὶς ἀφίκετο εἰς τὸ ἱαρὸν ὑπὲρ γενεᾶς.[16] ἐγκατακοιμαθεῖσα δὲ ὄψιν εἶδε· ἐδόκει αἰτεῖσθαι τὸν θεὸν κυῆσαι κόραν, τὸν δ' Ἀσκλαπιὸν φάμεν[17] ἔγκυον ἐσσεῖσθαί[18] νιν,[19] καὶ εἴ τι ἄλλο (else) αἰτοῖτο,[20] καὶ τοῦτο οἱ ἐπιτελεῖν, αὐτὰ δ' οὐθενὸς φάμεν[21] ἔτι ποιδεῖσθαι. ἔγκυος δὲ γενομένα ἐγ γαστρὶ ἐφόρει τρία ἔτη, ἔστε παρέβαλε ποὶ τὸν θεὸν ἱκέτις[22] ὑπὲρ τοῦ τόκου· ἐγκατακοιμαθεῖσα δὲ ὄψιν εἶδε· ἐδόκει ἐπερωτῆν[23] νιν τὸν θεόν, εἰ οὐ γένοιτο αὐτᾶι[24] πάντα ὅσσα[25] αἰτήσαιτο καὶ ἔγκυος εἴη·[26] ὑπὲρ δὲ τόκου ποιθέμεν[27]

---

[15] Ithomika of Pellene.

[16] "For a family."

[17] φάμεν, inf. > φάναι, s.v. φημί (cf. 2.20, 3.31–32).

[18] ἐσσεῖσθαι, Dor. fut. inf. of εἰμί.

[19] Subj. of inf. (ἐσσεῖσθαί).

[20] Opt. cf. table 9.3.3.

[21] φάμεν, inf. > φάναι (s.v. φημί).

[22] Acc. of spec. ("as").

[23] ἐπερωτῆν > ἐπερωτᾶν (cf. 3.39).

[24] αὐτᾶι > αὐτῆι > αὐτῇ.

[25] ὅσσα > ὅσα.

[26] Cf. opt. of εἰμί, cf. Table 9.13.3.

[27] ποιθέμεν Dor. > ²aor. inf. προσθεῖναι (s.v. προστίθημι) (Buck §154.3).

νιν οὐθέν, καὶ ταῦτα πυνθανομένου αὐτοῦ,[28] εἴ τινος καὶ ἄλλου δέοιτο, λέγειν, ὡς[29] ποιησοῦντος καὶ τοῦτο. ἐπεὶ δὲ νῦν ὑπὲρ τούτου παρείη[30] ποτ᾽ [31] αὐτὸν ἱκέτις, καὶ τοῦτό οἱ φάμεν ἐπιτελεῖν. μετὰ δὲ τοῦτο σπουδᾶι[32] ἐκ τοῦ ἀβάτου ἐξελθοῦσα, ὡς ἔξω τοῦ ἱαροῦ ἦς,[33] ἔτεκε κόραν.

Vocabulary

αἰτέω/έομαι, ask, beg; make a request

ἔστε, until

μιν, him, her, it, 3rd pers. pron. (acc. sg.) in Ep. and Ion.

νιν (encl.), Dor. acc. of 3rd pers. for αὐτός, αὐτήν

οὗ (encl. οὑ), him, her (acc.); **οἷ** (dat., encl. οἱ)

παραβάλλω, throw to (esp. of fodder to animals); venture to (do something)

ποιδέομαι > **προσδέομαι** (cf. ποί, Dor. > πρός), be in need of something in addition

πυνθάνομαι (older form πεύθομαι), 3. ἐπυθόμην, ²aor. mid. ptc. πυθόμενος: learn something from somebody (gen.), inquire concerning something; subst. a question

σπουδή, ἡ, diligence, concern, attention; haste, hurry; **ἐν σπουδῇ**, in concern

τόκος, ὁ, birth; offspring; interest (on money owed)

τριέτης, -ες, lasting three years

φορά, ἡ, pregnancy

A3 (LINES 22–33)

Ἀνὴρ τοὺς τᾶς[34] ξηρὸς δακτύλους ἀκρατεῖς[35] ἔχων πλὰν[36] ἑνὸς ἀφίκετο ποὶ τὸν θεὸν ἱκέτας· θεωρῶν δὲ τοὺς ἐν τῶι ἱαρῶι[37] πίνακας (was) ἀπίστει τοῖς ἰάμασιν καὶ ὑποδιέσυρε τὰ ἐπιγράμματα. ἐγκαθεύδων δὲ ὄψιν εἶδε· ἐδόκει ὑπὸ τῶι ναῶι ἀστραγαλίζοντος[38] αὐτοῦ καὶ μέλλοντος βάλλειν τῷ ἀστραγάλωι,[39] ἐπιφανέντα τὸν θεὸν ἐφαλέσθαι ἐπὶ τὰν χῆρα[40] καὶ ἐκτεῖναί οὑ τοὺς δακτύλους· ὡς δ᾽

---

[28] Gen. absol.

[29] ὡς + ptc. in gen. here expresses purpose or intention.

[30] Cf. εἴη in 2.17.

[31] ποτ᾽ > ποτί > πρός.

[32] σπουδᾶι > σπουδῆι > σπουδῇ.

[33] ἦς (Dor.) > 3rd sg. impf. of εἰμί.

[34] τᾶς > τῆς.

[35] ἀκρατεῖς is in 2nd pred. pos. (cf. IV, 19).

[36] πλάν > πλήν.

[37] ἱαρῶι > ἱερῶι > ἱερῷ.

[38] Gen. absol.

[39] Instr. dat.

[40] τὰν χῆρα > τὴν χεῖρα (acc.) (cf. 3.28).

ἀποβαίη,[41] δοκεῖν συγκάμψας τὰν χῆρα καθ' ἕνα[42] ἐκτείνειν τῶν δακτύλων· ἐπεὶ δὲ πάντας (fingers) ἐξευθύναι, ἐπερωτῆν νιν τὸν θεόν, εἰ ἔτι ἀπιστησοῖ τοῖς ἐπιγράμμασι τοῖς ἐπὶ τῶμ[43] πινάκων τῶν κατὰ[44] τὸ ἱερόν, αὐτὸς δ' οὐ φάμεν·[45] Ὅτι τοίνυν ἔμπροσθεν ἀπίστεις αὐτοῖς οὐκ ἐοῦσιν[46] ἀπίστοις, τὸ λοιπὸν ἔστω τοι,[47] φάμεν, Ἄπιστος ὄνομα. ἀμέρας δὲ γενομένας[48] ὑγιὴς ἐξῆλθε.

Vocabulary

ἀκρατής, -ές, powerless
ἀπιστέω, disbelieve
ἀποβαίνω, alight, move off
ἀστραγαλίζω, play with knucklebones (ἀστράγαλοι) as dice[49]
ἀστράγαλος, knucklebone
ἐξευθύνω, straighten
ἐπίγραμα, -ματος, τό, inscription
ἐφάλλομαι, ἐφηλόμην: to leap/spring upon
ἴαμα, -ματος, τό, healing, cure
νιν (encl.), Dor. acc. of 3rd pers. for αὐτός, αὐτῆ
οὕ (encl. οὐ), him, her (acc.); οἵ (dat., encl. οἱ)
ξηρός, -ά, -όν, dry; paralyzed
οὕ (encl. οὐ), him, her (acc.)
πλήν, nevertheless; but only, except
συγκάμπτω, to bend
τοίνυν, indeed, then; therefore; δὴ τοίνυν, "I suggest/submit (that)"
ὑποδιασύρω, sneer, disparage

A4 (LINES 33–41)

Ἀμβροσία[50] ἐξ[51] Ἀθανᾶν[52] ἀτερόπτιλλος. αὕτα ἱκέτις ἦλθε ποὶ τὸν θεόν· περιέρπουσα δὲ κατὰ τὸ ἱαρὸν τῶν ἱαμάτων τινὰ διεγέλα ὡς (being) ἀπίθανα καὶ ἀδύνατα ἐόντα,[53] χωλοὺς καὶ τυφλοὺς ὑγιεῖς γίνεσθε ἐνύπνιον ἰδόντας μόνον. ἐγκαθεύδουσα

---

[41] 3rd sg. opt.
[42] καθ' ἕνα, distributive κατά, "one by one."
[43] Assim.: ν before μ becomes μ (τῶμ πινάκων, 3.30).
[44] "Around."
[45] φάμεν inf. (poet.) > φάναι, s.v. φημί.
[46] ἐοῦσιν, Dor. > οὖσιν; here concessive adv. ptc. ("although").
[47] τοι> σοι (dat. of poss.).
[48] Gen. absol.
[49] Dice were typically used for divination at oracular shrines.
[50] Ambrosia (fm. proper name).
[51] Prep. ἐκ freq. used with the names of women to indicate their hometown.
[52] Ἀθανᾶν, Dor. 1st decl. gen. pl. > Ἀθηνῶν.
[53] ἐόντα, Dor. > ὄντα.

δὲ ὄψιν εἶδε· ἐδόκει οἱ ὁ θεὸς ἐπιστὰς[54] εἰπεῖν, ὅτι ὑγιῆ μέν νιν ποιησοῖ, μισθὸμ[55] μάντοι[56] νιν δέοι[57] ἀναθέμεν[58] εἰς τὸ ἱαρὸν ὖν ἀργύρεον[59] ὑπόμναμα[60] τᾶς ἀμαθίας. εἴπαντα δὲ ταῦτα ἀνσχίσαι οὔ τὸν ὄπτιλλον[61] τὸν νοσοῦντα καὶ φάρμακόν τι ἐγχέαι· ἀμέρας δὲ γενομένας[62] ὑγιὴς ἐξῆλθε.

Vocabulary

ἀδυύατος, -ον, impossible; weak, crippled

ἀμαθία, ἡ, stupidity

ἀνασχίζω, aor. inf. ἀν(α)σχίσαι, open up, cut open

ἀπίθανος, -ον, incredible, unbelievable

ἀτερόπτιλλος, -ον, Dor. > ἑτερόφθαλμος, one-eyed (i.e., blind in one eye)

διαγελάω, ridicule something/somebody

ἐγχέω, pour in/over

ἐγκαθεύδω, sleep in temple in order to seek prophetic dreams and obtain a cure from a disease, i.e., "incubate"

ἐνύπνιον, τό, a dream

μέντοι, Dor. μάντοι, yet, nevertheless

νοσέω, be ill, sick

ὑπόμνημα, -ματος, τό, reminder; memorandum

ὗς, ὑός, ὁ/ἡ, pig (known for their reputed stupidity)

A5 (LINES 41–48)

Παῖς ἄφωνος. οὗτος ἀφίκετο εἰς τὸ ἱαρὸν ὑπὲρ φωνᾶς·[63] ὡς δὲ προεθύσατο καὶ ἐποίησε τὰ νομιζόμενα, μετὰ τοῦτο ὁ παῖς ὁ τῶι θεῶι πυρφορῶν ἐκέλετο (him), ποὶ τὸμ[64] πατέρα τὸν τοῦ παιδὸς ποτιβλέψας, ὑποδέκεσθαι[65] ἐντὸς ἐνιαυτοῦ,[66] τυχόντα ἐφ' ἃ πάρεστι, ἀποθυσεῖν τὰ ἴατρα.[67] ὁ δὲ παῖς ἐξαπίνας·[68] Ὑποδέκομαι,

---

[54] S.v. ἐφίστημι.

[55] μισθὸμ νιν, assim. (ν before μ becomes μ).

[56] μάντοι, Dor. > μέντοι.

[57] S.v. δεῖ, opt. δέοι.

[58] ἀναθέμεν, Dor. > ²aor. inf. ἀναθεῖναι (s.v. ἀνατίθημι).

[59] ἀργύρεον > ἀργύριον.

[60] ὑπόμναμα > ὑπόμνημα, acc. of spec. ("as").

[61] ὄπτιλλον = ὀφθαλμόν.

[62] Gen. absol.

[63] φωνᾶς > φωνῆς.

[64] Assim. (ν before π, β. φ, ψ, becomes μ), cf. τὸμ πατέρα, 5.44.

[65] ὑποδέκεσθαι > ὑποδέχεσθαι + inf. (ἀποθυσεῖν).

[66] Gen. of time.

[67] Acc. of spec. ("as").

[68] ἐξαπίνας, Dor. > ἐξαίφνης.

ἔφα·⁶⁹ ὁ δὲ πατὴρ ἐκπλαγεὶς πάλιν ἐκέλετο αὐτὸν εἰπεῖν· ὁ δὲ ἔλεγε πάλιν· καὶ
ἐκ τούτου ὑγιὴς ἐγένετο.

Vocabulary
ἀποθύω, offer up a votive sacrifice
ἄφωνος, -ον, voiceless, mute
ἴατρα, τά, thank offering for a cure
κέλομαι, command, bid
ποτιβλέψας > προσβλέψας, s.v. προσβλέπω, look at
προθύω, sacrifice on somebody's behalf; perform an opening sacrifice
πυρφορέω, carry a sacrificial fire; subst. ptc., somebody appointed to bear the fire
    for Asklepios
ὑποδέχομαι, entertain as a guest, provide hospitality for; to promise

A18 (LINES 120-122)

Ἀλκέτας⁷⁰   Ἁλικός. οὗτος τυφλὸς ἐὼν⁷¹ ἐνύπνιον εἶδε· ἐδόκει οἱ ὁ θεὸς ποτελθὼν⁷²
τοῖς δακτύλοις διάλεγειν τὰ ὄμματα καὶ (the man) ἰδεῖν τὰ δένδρη⁷³ πρᾶτον⁷⁴ τὰ
ἐν τῶι ἱαρῶι.⁷⁵ ἀμέρας δὲ γενομένας⁷⁶ ὑγιὴς ἐξῆλθε.

Vocabulary
ἐνύπνιον, τό, a dream

B12 (LINES 63-68)

Ἀντικράτης⁷⁷ Κνίδιος ὀφθαλμούς. οὗτος ἔν τινι μάχαι⁷⁸ ὑπὸ δόρατος πλαγεὶς⁷⁹ δι
ἀμφοτέρων τῶν ὀφθαλμῶν τυφλὸς ἐγένετο καὶ τὰν λόγχαν παροῦσαν ἐν τῶι
προσώπωι περιέφερε· ἐγκαθεύδων δὲ ὄψιν εἶδε· ἐδόκει οὐ τὸν θεὸν ἐξελκύσαντα

---

⁶⁹ ἔφα > ἔφη.
⁷⁰ Alketas of Halieis.
⁷¹ ἐών, Dor. > ὤν.
⁷² ποτελθών > προσελθών.
⁷³ δένδρεον, τό, older form of δένδρον.
⁷⁴ πρᾶτον > πρῶτον.
⁷⁵ **τὰ** δένδρη...**τὰ** ἐν τῷ ἱαρῶι (> ἱερῳ), 2nd attrib. pos. (cf. IV, 4.2).
⁷⁶ Gen. absol.
⁷⁷ Antikrates of Knidos.
⁷⁸ μάχαι > μάχηι> μάχῃ.
⁷⁹ πλαγείς > πληγείς.

τὸ βέλος εἰς τὰ βλέφαρα τὰς καλουμένας[80] κόρας πάλιν ἐναρμόξαι· ἁμέρας δὲ γενομένας ὑγιὴς ἐξῆλθε.

Vocabulary
βέλος, -εος, τό, missile (esp. arrow, dart)
βλέφαρα, τά, eyelids
δόρυ, -ατος, τό, spear
ἐναρμόζω, fit back into (εἰς)
ἐξέλκω, [1]aor. ptc. ἐξελκύσας: pull out
λόγχη, ἡ, spearhead
περιφέρω, carry around

C21 (LINES 123-129)

Δαμοσθένης[81] [from (ethnic)], ἀκρατὴς τῶν σκελέων. οὗτος ἀφίκετο εἰς τὸ ἱαρὸν ἐπὶ κλίνας[82] καὶ ἐπὶ βακτηρίας ἀπερειδόμενος περιεπορεύετο· ἐγκοιμαθεὶς δὲ ὄψιν εἶδε· ἐδόκει οἱ ὃν θεὸς ποιτάξαι[83] τετράμηνον ἐν τῶι ἱαρῶι παραμένειν, ὅτι ἐν τῶι χρόνωι τούτωι ὑγιὴς ἐσσοῖτο·[84] μετὰ τοῦτο ἐντὸς τετραμήνου ἐν ταῖς τελευταίαις ἁμέραις εἰσελθὼν εἰς τὸ ἄβατον μετὰ δύο βακτηριᾶν ὑγιὴς ἐξῆλθε.

Vocabulary
ἀπερείδω, to support
βακτηρία, ἡ, staff, cane
ἔγκυος, -ον, pregnant
παραμένω, remain (in a place); remain/stay (of slaves whose manumission was deferred)
περιπορεύομαι, walk about
τελευταῖος, -α, -ον, last (esp. of time)
τετράμηνος, -ον, for four months

SELECT BIBLIOGRAPHY

Burford, Alison. *The Greek Temple Builders at Epidauros*. Liverpool: Liverpool University Press, 1969.

---

[80] καλουμένας, "so-called," used by medical writers to introduce a new medical term such as "girls." According to LSJ, the pupils of the eyes were termed "girls" because a little image appears in them.
[81] Damosthenes.
[82] κλίνας > κλίνης.
[83] ποιτάξαι > προστάξαι.
[84] ἐσσοῖτο > εἴη, 3rd sg. opt. (cf. table 9.13.3).

Edelstein, E. J., and L. Edelstein (eds.). *Asclepios: Testimonies*. Baltimore: Johns Hopkins University Press, 1945.

Petsalis-Diomidis, Alexia. "The Body in Space: Visual Dynamics in Graeco-Roman Healing Pilgrimage." In Jaś Elsner and Ian Rutherford *Pilgrimage in Graeco-Roman & Early Christian Antiquity: Seeing the Gods*, 183–218. Oxford: Oxford University Press, 2005.

Wells, Louise. *The Greek Language of Healing from Homer to New Testament Times*. Berlin: Walter de Gruyter, 1998, 276 (app. 2.4).

7.10.

The Delphic Oracle Commands the Importation of Maenads

(IMagn-Mai 215)

Provenance: Magnesia on the Meander, Karia (cf. Fig. 2); inscribed on a stele, which was originally attached to a supporting base (βωμός).

Date: This inscription is a Roman copy (ca. 150 CE) of a (now lost) Hellenistic inscription, which quoted a Delphic oracle in twelve dactylic hexameters.[1] The events recounted in the text occurred in the mid-third century BCE.

Text: IMagn-Mai 215; H.W. Parke and D. E. Wormell, *The Delphic Oracle*, vol. 2: *The Oracular Responses* (Oxford: Basil Blackwell, 1956), 137–138; Albert Henrichs, "Greek Maenadism from Olympias to Messalina," *HSCP* 82 (1978), 121–160.

The inscription in this section tells of how the Magnesians consulted the Delphic oracle on the occasion of a miracle: a plane tree was struck by lightning, and a cloven tree had grown up in its place, in the midst of which appeared an image of the god Dionysos![2]

The Magnesians sent messengers to the Delphic oracle to inquire about the meaning of this miracle. The oracle explained that Dionysos was displeased with them for not having built him a sanctuary when they founded the city. To avoid future punishment, the Magnesians were directed to build a temple for Dionysos and to import three maenads from Thebes, who would bring the "maenadic rites" (τὰ ὄργια) and establish three Dionysian associations

---

[1] For other examples of dactylic hexameters see the metrical epigram of Bishop Aberkios (§7.11) and "the Klarian Oracle on Pagan Monotheism" (§7.23).

[2] Cf. the epiphany of Artemis and a Delphis oracle in *IMagnMai* 16, *ll.* 24ff.

(θίασοι).[3] The Magnesians did as they were instructed and imported the maenads and charged them to establish and oversee three Dionysian associations. The membership of these associations consisted of both men and women. This inscription is of particular interest because it demonstrates the interrelation between the civic administration, maenads (which Euripides' *Bacchae* would suggest were beyond the control of the city), and mixed private Dionysian associations.

Dialect: Ionic (see footnotes).

Dactylic Hexameter: Greek epigrams are of the "stichic" type of verse, which is to say, the lines of verse are short, of uniform length, and repeat themselves in a regular fashion (e.g., repeating hexameters). Each line consists of an orderly sequence of syllables, with each syllable counting long or short for the purpose of meter. By definition a dactylic hexameter is made up of six metra. A metron is the basic unit of a line of verse, with each metron consisting of two "feet." The first five metra may be either dactyl (a metron consisting of a long–short–short pattern, ‾ ˘ ˘) or spondee (a metron consisting of a long–long pattern, ‾ ‾), though a spondee is rare in the third and fifth metra. The sixth metron is a spondee, or in the case of a final anceps (i.e., a doubtful syllable whose quantity can be either long or short), a trochee (a metron consisting of a long–short pattern) is permitted. There must be a caesura (i.e., a break between two words in the middle of a metron), indicated by | either after the first or second syllable of the third metron or after the first syllable of the fourth metron.[4]

1	2	3	4	5	6	(feet)
‾ ˘ ˘	‾ ˘ ˘	‾ | ˘ | ˘	‾ | ˘ | ˘	‾ ˘ ˘‾	*x*	
or	or	or	or	or		
‾ ‾	‾ ‾	(‾ | ‾)	‾ | ‾	(‾ ‾)		

Related Texts: Dionysian associations, IG II² 1368 (§7.4), IMilet VI, 22 (§7.14), IG IX/1² 670 (§7.15), MAMA VI, 239 (§7.20).

---

[3] See Albert Henrichs's discussion and defense of the historical reliability of this oracle ("Greek Maenadism from Olympias to Messalina," 126–130).

[4] *x* represents an anceps (a doubtful syllable whose quantity can be either long or short), ‾ represents a long syllable, and ˘ represents a short syllable. For a summary of the rules for the determination of vowel quantity see Ezekiel the Tragedian (§6.6, n. 184). For a detailed explanation of the rules of Greek prosody see M. L. West, *Introduction to Greek Metre* (Oxford: Clarendon Press, 1987); Paul Maas, *Greek Metre*, trans. Hugh Lloyd-Jones (Oxford: Clarendon, 1962); D. S. Raven, *Greek Metre: An Introduction* (London: Faber and Faber, 1962).

LINES 1–11

Ἀγαθῇ τύχῃ. ἐπὶ πρυτάνεως⁵ Ἀκροδήμου⁶ τοῦ Διοτείμου ὁ δῆμος ὁ Μαγνήτων ἐπερωτᾷ τὸν θεὸν⁷ περὶ τοῦ σημείου τοῦ γεγονότος (namely) ὅτι πλατάνου κατὰ⁸ τὴν πόλιν κλασθείσης⁹ ὑπὸ ἀνέμου εὑρέθη ἐν αὐτῇ¹⁰ ἀφείδρυμα Διονύσου. τί αὐτῷ σημαίνει ἢ τί ἂν ποιήσας ἀδεως¹¹ διατελοίη·¹² δἰ ὃν θεοπρόποι ἐπέμφθησαν¹³ ἰς Δελφοὺς Ἑρμῶναξ¹⁴ Ἐπικράτους, Ἀρίσταρχος¹⁵ Διοδώρου.

Vocabulary

ἀφείδρυμα > ἀφίδρυμα, something that is set up, a statue

Διόνυσος, ὁ, god Dionysos

θεοπρόπος, ὁ, public messenger sent to inquire of an oracle

Μάγνης, -ητος, ὁ, Magnesian, citizen of Magnesia on the Meander (cf. *ll.* 14, 39)

πλάτανος, ἡ, plane tree (*Platanus orientalis*)

πρύτανις, -εως, ὁ, member of the tribe presiding in the Council or Assembly; pl. πρυτάνεις, οἱ, *prytaneis*, one of the ten (or twelve) rotating executive committees of the Council and Assembly¹⁶

---

⁵ On dating by means of prytany see note 19

⁶ Akrodemos, son of Dioteimos.

⁷ I.e., Pythian Apollo of Delphi.

⁸ κατά (w. acc.), "opposite."

⁹ Gen. absol. (s.v. κλάω.)

¹⁰ I.e., in the city.

¹¹ ἀδέως > ἡδέως, s.v. ἡδύς.

¹² διατελοίη > διατέλοι, cf. table 9.1.3(a).

¹³ S.v. πέμπω.

¹⁴ Hermonax, son of Epikrates.

¹⁵ Aristarchos, son of Diodoros.

¹⁶ The term ὁ πρύτανις specifies one member of a tribe presiding in the Council. The corresponding plural term, οἱ πρυτάνεις, specifies one of the ten (later twelve) rotating executive committees of the Council. In Athens, there were as many executive committees as there were "tribes," with each executive committee consisting of fifty councilors selected from the same tribe. The civil year was divided into a corresponding number of equal periods, with each period being known as one "prytany" (πρυτανεία) or "presidency period." Each *prytaneis* took a turn as the governing committee, serving in rotation for the period of one prytany. The days within each prytany (πρυτανεία) were numbered in succession using ordinal numbers (first day, second day, third day, etc.). Before each meeting of the Council, the president of the *prytaneis* would chose by lot one member from each of the non-prytanizing tribes to serve as "presiding officers" (πρόεδροι), one of whom served as a "president of the presiding officers" (ἐπιστάτης τῶν προέδρων). The presiding officers presided in the Council and were responsible for putting forth motions.

The Delphic Oracle (Lines 12–30)

Θεὸς ἔχρησεν·
Μαιάνδροιο λαχόντες[17] ἐφ᾽ ὕδασιν[18]
ἱερὸν ἄστυ, Μάγνητες κτεάνοις[19]
15   ἐπαμύντορες ἡμετέροισιν,
ἤλθετε πευσόμενοι[20] στομάτων[21] ἀπ᾽ ἐ-
μεῖο,[22] τίς (means) ὑμεῖν[23] μῦθος,[24] ἐπεὶ Βάκχος θάμνῳ ἔνι κείμενος ὤφθη.

Vocabulary

ἄστυ, -εως, τό, pl. ἄστη, city, town
Βάκχος, ὁ, Bacchus (an alternate name for the god Dionysos)
γενεά, -ᾶς, ἡ (Ion. γενεή, -ῆς), race, offspring
Δελφοί, -ῶν, οἱ, Delphi
ἐπαμύντωρ, -ορος, ὁ, defender
ἐκφάινω, 6. ἐξεφάνην: bring light, reveal; pass. show oneself
ἐσθός, -ή, -όν, good, morally good, faithful
θάμνος, ὁ, bush, shrub
Θῆβαι, αἱ, Thebes (var. Θήβη) in Boeotia
κτῆμα, -ματος, τό, anything gotten; pl. possessions
λαγχάνω, 2aor. ἔλαχον, subj. λάχην: receive (an inheritance); obtain something
    (e.g., an office) by lot; be chosen by lot
Μαιάνδροιο, gen. sg. (Ionic) > Μαιανδροίου, s.v. Μαίανδρος, ὁ, Meander river
μῦθος, ὁ, story, narrative
ὄφρα, in order that
πέδον, τό, plain

ἐξεφάνη δὲ ἔτι κοῦρος,[25] ἐπεὶ πτολί-
20   αιθρα τιθέντες, νηοὺς[26] οὐκ ᾠκίσ-
σατ᾽ ἐϋτμήτους[27] Διονύσῳ. ἀλλὰ
καὶ ὥς,[28] ὦ δῆμε μεγάσθενες, ἵδρυε

---

[17] Gen. absol. (s.v. λαγχάνω).
[18] S.v. ὕδωρ (i.e., river); ἐφ᾽ ὕδασιν...Μαιάνδροιο.
[19] κτεάνοις (> κτήμασι)...ἡμετέροισιν (> ἡμετέροις); the cryptic meaning of *ll.* 14–15 is explained by IMagn-Mai 46, *ll.* 8–10 (SIG³ 560), which refers to a Celtic raid on Delphi in 279/278 BCE.
[20] S.v. πυνθάνομαι.
[21] Pl. of στόμα is sometimes used for sg.
[22] ἐμεῖο, gen. sg. (Ion.) > ἐμοῦ.
[23] ὑμεῖν > ὑμῖν.
[24] τίς...μῦθος.
[25] κοῦρος > κόρος.
[26] νηούς > ναούς (cf. *l.* 23).
[27] νηοὺς...ἐϋδμήτους.
[28] ὥς = οὕτως, καὶ ὥς, "even so," "nevertheless."

νηοὺς θυρσοχαροῦς· ἱερῆα²⁹ τίθει³⁰
δὲ εὐ ἄρτιον ἀγνόν. ἐλθέτε δὲ

25   ἐς³¹ Θήβης ἱερὸν πέδον, ὄφρα λάβετε
Μαινάδας, αἳ (are) γενεῆς Εἰνοῦς ἄπο Κα-
δμηείης, αἳ δ᾽ ὑμεῖν³² δώσουσι καὶ
ὄργια καὶ νόμιμα ἐσθλά, καὶ θιά-
σους Βάκχοιο³³ καθειδρύσουσιν³⁴

30   ἐν ἄστει.

Vocabulary

ἄρτιος, -α, -ον, suitable, suited

Εἰνοῦς > Ἰνόος, s.v. Ἰνώ, Ἰνόος (gen.) (contr. Εἰνοῦς), Ino, Queen of Thebes, who was worshipped as a goddess following her death and transfiguration; she was one of the nurses of the infant Dionysos³⁵

εὔτμητος (Ep. ἐΰτμητος,), -ον, well-built, well-hewn

θίασος, ὁ, private religious association

θυρσοχαρής, -ές, delighting in the *thyrsos*³⁶

ἱδρύω, 2. ἱδρύσομαι, 3. ἵδρυσα/ἱδρυσάμην, 5. ἵδρυμαι: found, dedicate; mid. establish (a temple); dedicate; set up something (e.g., altar, statue)

Καδμηείη < Καδμείη, s.v. Καδμεῖος, -η, -ον, Kadmean, of Kadmos (Κάδμος, the legendary founder of Thebes)

μαινάς, -άδος, ἡ, maenad, female bacchante³⁷

μεγάσθενης > μεγαλοσθενής, -ές, of great strength

---

²⁹ ἱερῆα > ἱερέα (s.v. ἱερεύς); ἱερῆα…εὐάρτιον ἀγνόν

³⁰ Cf. table 9.12.2(c).

³¹ ἐς > εἰς.

³² ὑμεῖν > ὑμῖν.

³³ Βάκχοιο, gen. sg. (Ionic) > Βάκχου.

³⁴ καθειδρύσουσιν > καθιδρύσουσιν.

³⁵ Ino was a primordial Dionysian maenad and nurse to the god Dionysos (cf. Karl Kerenyi, *Dionysus: Archetypal Image of Indestructible Life* [Princeton, NJ: Bollingen, 1976], 246).

³⁶ A *thrysos* is staff of giant fennel, covered with ivy vines and leaves, carried by Dionysos and his followers.

³⁷ "Maenads" (literally "mad women") is essentially a poetic term that alludes to the ecstasy or wild possession that "mad" Dionysos (Homer, *Il.* 6.132) incited in his female followers (*Hymnus Homericus ad Cererem*, 386; Aesch., *fr.* 382; Soph., *Oedipus Tyrannus*, 212; Eur., *Ion*, 552; Ar., *Lysistrata*, 1283). In the *Bacchae*, the term is generally used pejoratively (cf. G. S. Kirk, *The Bacchae of Euripides*, 2d ed. [Cambridge: Cambridge University Press, 1979], note on 1295). According to Philo of Alexandria, the term "maenads" was a discriminatory designation for *bakchai*, alluding to the fact that wine makes women "mad" (*De plantatione*, 148). It is on account of the literary provenance of the term "maenads" that it rarely occurs in epigraphical sources. Albert Henrichs thinks that the occasional use of "maenad" in inscriptions reflects an attempt either to emulate poetic usage or to archaize the language. In epigraphical sources, the customary term for these devotees is Βάχαι (bacchants) for women and βουκολικός (cowherd) for men, appropriately named after the bull god, Βάκχος ("Greek Maenadism from Olympias to Messalina," 155– 156).

ὄργια, -ίων, τά, secret religious rites, religious mysteries

πτολίαιθρα > πτολίεθρα, s.v. πτολίεθρον, τό (Ep.), lengthened form of πόλις

Postscript (Lines 31–41)

Κατὰ τὸν χρησμὸν διὰ τῶν θεοπρόπων ἐδόθησαν ἐκ Θηβῶν Μαινάδες τρεῖς, Κοσκώ, Βαυβώ, Θετταλή·[38] καὶ ἡ μὲν Κοσκώ συνήγαγεν θίασον τὸν Πλατανιστηνῶν, ἡ δὲ Βαυβώ (συνήγαγεν τὸν θίασον) πρὸ πόλεως, ἡ δὲ Θετταλή (συνήγαγεν) τὸν (θίασον) τῶν Καταιβατῶν· θανοῦσαι[39] δὲ αὗται ἐτάφησαν[40] ὑπὸ Μαγνήτων, καὶ ἡ μὲν Κοσκώ[40] κεῖται ἐν Κοσκωβούνῳ, ἡ δὲ βαυβώ ἐν Ταβάρνει,[41] ἡ δὲ Θετταλή πρὸς[42] τῷ θεάτρῳ.

Altar

Θεῷ Διονυσῳ Ἀπολλώνιος Μοκόλλης[43] ἀρχαῖος μύστης[44] ἀρχαῖον χρησμὸν ἐπὶ στήλης ἀναγράψας σὺν τῷ βωμῷ ἀνέθηκεν (this).

Vocabulary

μύστης, ὁ / μύστις, ἡ, initiant

πλατανίστηνος, ἡ, earlier name for a "plane tree" (πλάτανος)

Καταιβάται, οἱ, *Kataibatai*, name of a *thiasos* dedicated to Dionysos[45]

Κοσκώβουνος, Hill of Kosko

---

[38] Kosko, Baubo, Thettale.

[39] S.v. θνήσκω.

[40] S.v. θάπτω.

[41] Tabarnis (fm.).

[42] πρός (ω. dat.), "near."

[43] Apollonios Mokolles.

[44] Thus the title ἀρχαῖος μύστης may be the rhetorical equivalent to ἀρχιμύστης, a common title for a high-ranking functionary of a Dionysian *thiasos*.

[45] Cf. Καταιβάτης, epithet of a god, who leads souls to the Netherworld.

7.11.

The Metrical Epigram of Bishop Aberkios: The Earliest Christian Epigram

(SEG 30.1479)

Provenance: Hieropolis (Koçhisar) in the Phrygian Pentapolis. Aberkios (Ἀβέρκιος) was the bishop of Hieropolis (Ἱερόπολις). After visiting Rome, he traveled along the Syrian coast, and then perhaps to Antioch, and then went to the Syrian city of Nisibis. He died before returning to his homeland.

Date: ca. 200 CE.

Text: SEG 30.1479; R. A. Kearsley, *NewDocs* VI, 177–181.

In 1882 William Ramsay discovered in Phrygia a sepulchre *cippus* with a Greek inscription concerning a Christian named "Alexander" and bearing the date 216 CE (300 Phrygian era). The inscription was made in imitation of the Aberkios inscription. Ramsay made a second visit to Phrygia in search of the original inscription and found a large portion of the second of three faces of the original text, not in Hierapolis, but rather in the neighboring town of Hieropolis, near Synnada. He reported that the inscription was found "in the interior of the passage leading to the men's bath-room of the hot springs near Hieropolis, on a small fragment of a marble *bomos*, complete at top and left, broken at right and bottom."[1]

This inscription is widely recognized as the earliest datable Christian inscription that communicates Christian belief.[2] The language of the inscription is

---

[1] The account of this can be found in Wm. Ramsay, "The Cities and Bishoprics of Phyrgia," *JHS* (1882), 424ff.; cf. W. M. Ramsay, "Les trois villes phrygiennes, Brouzos, Hierapolis et Otrous," *JHS* 6 (1882), 503–520. Ramsay argues that Hierapolis was frequently mistaken for Hieropolis. It was clear that the epitaph of Alexander had been copied from that of Aberkios.

[2] See M. Guarducci's defense of its Christian provenance (*Epigrafia greca* [Rome, 1967–1978], 4.380–386; cf. Guarducci, "L'iscrizione di Abercio e Roma," *Ancient Society*, 2 [1971], 174–203).

FIG. 17. Carved relief of a fish in incised panel, Apa, Turkey (IKonya 141).

couched in mystical and symbolic language, which served to conceal the mysteries of the Christian faith from those who were uninitiated. The text employs conventional phraseology, formulae, topoi, and vocabulary of traditional texts and epigrams but reapplies them to convey Christian ideas in a cryptic fashion.[3] The inscription is written in twenty-two dactylic hexameters (though some are flawed).[4] The inscription here concludes (*ll*. 17–22) with a dictation formula, a request for prayer, and finally an imprecation against disturbing the bishop's grave (*ll*. 20–22). These concluding verses have no poetic structure.

Ἐκλεκτῆς πόλεως ὁ πολείτης[5] τοῦτ' ἐποίησα
ζῶν ἵν'[6] ἔχω φανερὴν σώματος ἔνθα θέσιν,[7]
οὔνομ'[8] Ἀβέρκιος ὢν ὁ μαθητὴς ποιμένος ἁγνοῦ,
ὃς βόσκει προβάτων ἀγέλας (both) ὄρεσιν πεδίοις τε,
5   ὀφθαλμοὺς[9] ὃς ἔχει μεγάλους πάντη καθορῶντας·
Οὗτος (shepherd) γὰρ μ'[10] ἐδίδαξε [˘ / ‾ ‾] γράμματα πιστά.

Vocabulary
ἀγέλη, -ης, ἡ, herd, flock
βόσκω, feed/tend domestic animals, to graze (of cattle)
θέσις, -εως, ἡ, position, setting down, resting-place
καθοράω, look down upon
πεδίον, τό, plain
πολίτης, ὁ, citizen, countryman

7   εἰς Ῥώμην ὃς ἔπεμψεν ἐμὲν[11] βασιλιδ' ἀναθρῆσαι.
καὶ βασίλισσαν ἰδεῖν χρυσόστολον χρυσοπέδιλον.
Λαὸν δ' εἶδον ἐκεῖ λαμπρὰν σφραγεῖδαν[12] ἔχοντα
10   καὶ Συρίης[13] πέδον εἶδα καὶ (its) ἄστεα[14] πάντα, Νισῖβιν

---

[3] W. K. Wischmeyer, "Die Aberkiosinschrift als Grabepigramm," *JbAC* 23 (1980), 22–47; ed.pr. W. M. Ramsay, "The Cities and Bishoprics of Phyrgia," *JHS* 4 (1883), 424–427 (only *ll*. 7–15).

[4] On the rules of dactylic hexameters see the Delphic oracle inscription (§7.10; cf. "The Klarian Oracle on Pagan Monotheism," §7.23); for a summary of the rules for the determination of vowel quantity see Ezekiel the Tragedian (§6.6, n. 3).

[5] πολείτης > πολίτης.

[6] ἵν' > ἵνα.

[7] φανερὴν…θέσιν.

[8] οὔνομ' > ὄνομα.

[9] ὀφθαλμοὺς…μεγάλους.

[10] μ' > με.

[11] ἐμέν > ἐμέ.

[12] σφραγεῖδαν > σφραγῖδαν.

[13] Συρίης > Συρίας.

[14] ἄστεα > ἄστη.

Εὐφράτην διαβάς· πάντη δ᾽ ἔσχον συνομαίμους,
Παῦλον[15] ἔχων ἐπ᾽ ὄχῳ· Πίστις πάντη δὲ προῆγε
καὶ παρέθηκε τροφὴν[16] πάντη ἰχθὺν ἀπὸ πηγῆς
πανμεγέθη καθαρόν, οὗ ἐδράξατο παρθένος ἁγνή,
15   καὶ τοῦτον (faith) ἐπέδωκε φίλιοις ἐσθεῖν διὰ παντός,[17]
       (also) οἶνον χρηστὸν ἔχουσα, κέρασμα διδοῦσα μετ᾽ ἄρτου.

Vocabulary
ἀναθρέω, look at/upon
ἄστυ, -εως, τό, pl. ἄστη, city, town
βασιλιδ᾽ > βασιλιδα, s.v. βασιλιδίς, -ίδος, ἡ, imperial city
δράσσομαι, lay hold of (gen.), catch
Εὐφράτης, Euphrates River
κέρασμα, -ματος, τό, mixture; here "mixed wine" (i.e., wine diluted with water)
Νισῖβις, ἡ, Syrian city of Nisibis (mod. Nusaybin, Turkey)
ὄχος, ὁ, carriage
πανμεγέθης, -ες, immense
πάντη (adv.), in every way, on every side
παρατίθημι, serve up (food), provide
συνομαίμων, -ονος, ὁ / ἡ, brother, sister
φίλιος, -α, -ον, friendly; subst. friend
χρηστός, -ή, -όν, useful, good; pleasant to the taste; beloved; (adv.)
χρηστῶς, well
χρυσοπέδιλος, -ον, wearing golden sandals
χρυσόστολος, -ον, wearing a golden robe

17   Ταῦτα παρεστὼς εἶπον (to them) Ἀβέρκιος ὧδε γραφῆναι.
       ἑβδομηκοστὸν ἔτος καὶ δεύτερον ἦγον ἀληθῶς.
       Ταῦθ᾽ ὁ νοῶν εὔξαιτο[18] ὑπὲρ Ἀβερκίου πᾶς ὁ συνῳδός.[19]
20   Οὐ μέντοι τύμβῳ[20] τις ἐμῷ ἕτερόν τινα θήσει.
       Εἰ δ᾽ (somebody does) οὖν, Ῥωμαίων ταμείῳ θήσει δισχίλια χρυσᾶ
       καὶ χρηστῇ πατρίδι Ἱεροπόλει χίλια[21] χρυσᾶ.

---

[15] This reference to Paul may imply that Aberkios saw himself as following in Paul's footsteps (as recorded in Acts 18:23–21:16), on his way back to his country (namely visiting Issos, Tarsos, Derbe, Ikonion, Pisidian Antioch, and Apamea Kibotos).

[16] Acc. of spec.

[17] διὰ παντός, "continually."

[18] Cf. Table 9.2.3 (b).

[19] σύνῳδος > σύνοδος; ὁ νοῶν...πᾶς ὁ συνῳδός.

[20] τύμβῳ...ἐμῷ.

[21] χείλια > χίλια.

Vocabulary

ἀληθῶς, truly, actually, surely

δισχείλια > δισχίλια, s.v. δισχίλιοι, -αι, -α, two thousand

ἑβδομηκοστός, -ή, -όν, seventieth

σύνοδος, ἡ, civic meeting (at which motions are deliberated); community

ταμίας, ὁ, treasurer

ταμεῖον, treasury

τύμβος, ὁ, burial mound, grave

PART 8

Advanced-Level Hellenistic Greek: Atticizing and Literary Greek

Part 8 brings together a small selection of readings composed in literary Hellenistic Greek. Flavius Philostratus's *Life of Apollonios of Tyana* (§§8.1, 8.5) provides an example of "Atticizing" Greek, a style of Hellenistic Greek modeled on the standards of the Classical Greek of the great Attic authors of the fourth and fifth centuries BCE. This section also includes two samples of philosophical Greek, namely, excepts from Epicurus's *Letter to Menoeceus* (§8.2) and his *Letter to Herodotus* (§8.6) and an excerpt from the Stoic philosopher Epictetus (§8.3). The style and vocabulary of Epictetus are remarkably close to the Greek found in the New Testament. The final reading is taken from *Poimandres*, the first tractate of the well-known Hermetic Corpus (§8.4). The vocabulary lists of Part 8 have been compiled on the assumption that you have memorized all the (bolded) words listed for memorization in Parts 1–7 (excluding the online material).[1] But all vocabulary for memorization can also be found in the glossary (§10).

---

[1] §§1.1–10, 2.1–6, 3.1–9, 4.1–11, 5.1–10, 6.1–6, 7.1–11.

8.1.

Flavius Philostratus,
Life of Apollonios of Tyana

(*VA* 8.7.7–9)

Lucius Flavius Philostratus (172–250 CE) was a Greek Sophist. After study-ing in Athens, he settled in Rome. His earliest work tells the story of the life of Apollonios (ca. 40–120 CE), a wandering Neopythagorean religious teacher and miracle worker from Tyana (modern southwest Turkey). Apollonios was the sub-ject of several biographies.

However, the only surviving account of his life is that of Flavius Philostratus, who worked with these other biographies in writing his own work.

Apollonios of Tyana is one of many so-called divine men (θεῖοι ἄνδρες), who were worshipped as "gods," or "sons" of god, owing to their reputation for per-forming miracles, healing the sick, raising individuals from the dead, and even appearing to their followers after death.[1] According to his biography, Apollonios was born from the union of Apollo and a mortal virgin, named Karinus. At the end of his life, he was miraculously translated to heaven and, in a manner evocative of Christ's appearance to Paul on the road to Damascus (Acts 9:1–9), appeared to one of his disciples who had not accepted his teacher's instruction on the immortality of the soul.

Date: 217–238 CE.

Text: F. C. Conybeare, *Philostratus: Life of Apollonius of Tyana*, 2 vols. LCL 16–17 (Cambridge, MA, 1912); cf. Klauck, 168–177.

Related Texts: Philostratus: Life of Apollonios of Tyana (*VA* 4.17–18) (§8.5); like Jesus of Nazareth, Apollonios was charged with being a sorcerer and in league with demons (cf. Mark 3:20–30, §1.5).

---

[1] Adela Y. Collins, "Mark and His Readers: The Son of God among Greeks and Romans," *HTR* 93:2 (2000), 85–100; Charles Talbert, *What Is a Gospel?* (Philadelphia: Fortress, 1982); Barry Blackburn, *Theios Aner and the Markan Miracle Traditions* (Tübingen: Mohr Siebeck, 1991), 10–11, 229–230, 265.

8.7.7

Toward the end of his life, Apollonios was charged with being a sorcerer, someone who dealt with demons, and with falsely pretending to be a god. He defended himself before the emperor against these charges as follows:

265 (My accuser) Φησὶ γὰρ τοὺς ἀνθρώπους θεόν[2] ἡγεῖσθαί με καὶ δημοσίᾳ τοῦτ' ἐκφέρειν ἐμβεβροντημένους ὑπ' ἐμοῦ· καίτοι καὶ πρὸ τῆς αἰτίας ἐκεῖνα διδάσκειν (αὐτὸν) ἔδει, (namely) τί διαλεχθείς[3] ἐγώ, τί[4] δ' οὕτω[5] θαυμάσιον εἰπών ἢ πράξας ὑπηγαγόμην τοὺς ἀνθρώπους προσεύχεσθαί μοι; 270 οὔτε[6] γάρ, ἐς ὅ τι[7] ἢ ἐξ ὅτου[8] μετέβαλον ἢ μεταβαλεῖ μοι[9] ἡ ψυχή, (this) διελέχθην ἐν Ἕλλησι, καίτοι γιγνώσκων, οὔτε δόξας[10] περὶ ἐμαυτοῦ τοιαύτας ἀπέστειλα, οὔτ' ἐς λόγια καὶ χρησμῶν ᾠδὰς ἐξῆλθον, οἷα τῶν θεοκλυτούντων φορά, οὐδ' οἶδα (any) πόλιν οὐδὲ μίαν, 275 ἐν ᾗ ἔδοξε[11] ξυνιόντας[12] Ἀπολλωνίῳ θύειν. καίτοι πολλοῦ ἄξιος ἑκάστοις[13] ἐγενόμην, ὁπόσα ἐδέοντο μου, ἐδέοντο δὲ τοιαῦτα· (that) μὴ νοσεῖν οἱ νοσοῦντες, (might be) ὁσιώτεροι μύειν, (might be) ὁσιώτεροι θύειν, ὕβριν ἐκτετμῆσθαι νόμους ἐρρῶσθαι.[14] μισθὸς δ' ἐμοῦ μὲν τούτων (benefactions) ὑπῆρχε (that) τὸ βελτίους αὐτοὺς αὐτῶν φαίνεσθαι,[15] σοὶ δὲ ἐχαριζόμην ταῦτα·

Vocabulary

βελτίων, -ιον (comp. of ἀγαθός), better, better than (w. gen.); βελτίους...αὐτῶν (> ἑαυτῶν) (i.e., better than they were before)

ἐκτέμνω, 4. ἐκτέτμηκα, pf. pass. inf. ἐκτετμῆσθαι: cut out (of a diseased part), eliminate

ἐμβροντάω, pass. (lit.), be struck by lightning; be made insane/raving mad

θεοκλυτέω, call upon/invoke the gods

λόγιον, τό, a saying, oracle; omen

μεταβάλλω, to change; to turn/transform into something

---

[2]   Acc. of spec. ("as").

[3]   Note the three adverbial instrumental participles in a row ("by") (διαλεχθείς...εἰπών...πράξας ...).

[4]   τί...θαυμάσιον, "what (sort of) marvel/miracle."

[5]   οὕτω...εἰπών.

[6]   οὔτε...οὔτε...οὔτ"...οὐδ"...οὐδε....

[7]   ἐς ὅ τι (= εἰς ὅτι, s.v. ὅστις), referring to that into which his soul will transform in the future.

[8]   ὅτου (nt. gen. sg.), s.v. ὅστις, referring to an origin from which his soul transformed.

[9]   Dat. of poss.

[10]   δόξας (opinions)...τοιαύτας.

[11]   As in a decree structure, the infinitivess that follow (e.g., νοσεῖν) are all dependent on this verb.

[12]   ξυν- > συν-, s.v. σύνειμι (fr. εἶμι. cf. table 9.14).

[13]   Though the pl. of ἕκαστος is rare in the GNT, it is elsewhere commonly attested, meaning "all and each," "in every case."

[14]   S.v. ῥώννυμι.

[15]   Art. inf.

μυέω, initiate somebody (into the mysteries); pass. to have performed mysteries, to be initiated (into the mysteries)

ὁπόσος, -ον, as many as, as much as (like ὅσος)

χρησμός, -ον, oracular; subst. oracle

280 Ὥσπερ γὰρ οἱ τῶν βοῶν ἐπιστάται τὸ μὴ ἀτακτεῖν[16] αὐτὰς χαρίζονται[17] τοῖς κεκτημένοις τὰς βοῦς καὶ (ὥσπερ) οἱ τῶν ποιμνίων ἐπιμεληταὶ πιαίνουσιν αὐτὰ ἐς[18] τὸ τῶν πεπαμένων κέρδος νόσους τε 285 ἀφαιροῦσι μελιττῶν οἱ νομεῖς αὐτῶν, ὡς μὴ ἀπόλοιτο τῷ δεσπότῃ τὸ σμῆνος, οὕτως που καὶ ἐγὼ τὰ πολιτικὰ παύων[19] ἐλαττώματα[20] σοὶ διωρθούμην τὰς πόλεις, ὥστ᾽ εἰ καὶ θεὸν[21] ἡγοῦντό με, σοὶ κέρδος ἡ ἀπάτη εἶχε, ξὺν[22] προθυμίᾳ γάρ που ἠκροῶντό μου, δεδιότες[23] πράττειν,[24] ἃ μὴ δοκεῖ θεῷ. 290 ἀλλ᾽ οὐχὶ τοῦτο ᾤοντο, ὅτι δ᾽ ἐστί[25] τις[26] ἀνθρώπῳ πρὸς θεὸν ξυγγένεια,[27] δι᾽ ἣν μόνον ζώων θεοὺς οἶδε, φιλοσοφεῖ δὲ καὶ ὑπὲρ τῆς ἑαυτοῦ φύσεως καὶ ὅπη μετέχει τοῦ θείου. φησὶ μὲν οὖν καὶ (his) τὸ εἶδος αὐτὸ θεῷ ἐοικέναι, 295 ὡς ἀγαλματοποιΐα ἑρμηνεύει (it) καὶ χρώματα (of painters), τάς τε ἀρετὰς θεόθεν ἥκειν ἐπ᾽ αὐτὸν πέπεισται[28] καὶ τοὺς μετέχοντας αὐτῶν ἀγχιθέους τε εἶναι καὶ θείους.

Vocabulary

ἀγαλματοποιΐα, ἡ, sculpture

ἀγχιθεός, -όν, near to the gods

ἀκροάομαι, listen to, obey (+ gen.)

ἀτακτέω, neglect one's duties, neglect (animals)

δείδω, [2]pf. inf. δεδιέναι, [2]pf. ptc. δεδιώς: fear

διωρθόομαι, correct, improve

ἐλασσώμα (Att. ἐλαττώμα), -ματος, τό, defect

ἐπιστάτης, ὁ, overseer, manager; ἐπιστάτης τῶν βοῶν, cowherd, ἐπιστάτης τῶν ποιμνίων, shepherd

ἑρμηνεύω, interpret

θεόθεν, from the gods

---

[16] Cond. art. inf. ("if," cf. IV, 1.8).

[17] Pass. (not mid.).

[18] Telic ἐς > εἰς.

[19] Instr. adv. ptc. ("by," cf. IV, 1.6).

[20] τὰ πολιτικὰ...ἐλαττώματα.

[21] Acc. of spec. ("as").

[22] ξύν > σύν.

[23] S.v. δείδω, causal adv. ptc. ("because," cf. IV, 1.4).

[24] πράττειν > πράσσειν.

[25] Impers.

[26] τις...ξυγγένεια.

[27] ξυγγένεια > συγγένεια.

[28] S.v. πείθω.

μέλισσα (Att. μέλιττα), bee

νομεύς, ὁ, herdsman; νομεύς μελισσῶν, beekeeper

ὅπη, by which; ὅπη ἤ ὅπως, a way by which

πάομαι, to get/acquire; pl. subst. οἱ πεπάμενοι, owners

πιαίνω, fatten (animals)

πολιτικός, -ή, -όν, relating to citizens, civic

σμῆνος, -εος, τό, hive, swarm (of bees)

συγγένεια, ἡ, kinship, relationship with (πρός)

φιλοσοφέω, study philosophy, speculate about (ὑπέρ); subst. ptc. student of philosophy

8.7.8

Later in the narrative, Apollonios addresses the legal charge made against him by an Egyptian man and gives an account of how he really averted a plague from the city of Ephesos:

345 Ἔστω (me), βασιλεῦ, (address the) κατηγορία καὶ ὑπὲρ τῆς Ἐφέσου, ἐπειδὴ ἐσώθη, καὶ κρινέτω με ὁ Αἰγύπτιος, ὡς ἔστιν πρόσφορον τῇ γραφῇ[29] (αὐτοῦ). ἔστι γὰρ δήπου ἡ κατηγορία τοιαύτη· 350 (Let us suppose that) περὶ Σκύθας ἤ Κελτούς, οἵ (on) ποταμὸν Ἴστρον ἤ Ῥῆνον οἰκοῦσι, πόλις ᾤκισται μείων οὐδὲν Ἐφέσου τῆς ἐν Ἰωνίᾳ· ταύτην (πόλιν) ὁρμητήριον βαρβάρων οὖσαν,[30] οἵ μὴ ἀκροῶνταί σου, λοιμὸς μέν τις ἀπολεῖν ἔμελλεν, Ἀπολώνιος δὲ ἰάσατο (it). ἔστι μὲν γάρ τις καὶ πρὸς ταῦτα ἀπολογία[31] σοφῷ ἀνδρί, 355 ἤν[32] ὁ βασιλεὺς[33] (has) τὸ ἀντίξοον ὅπλοις, ἀλλὰ μὴ νόσοις αἱρεῖν (his enemies) βούληται, μὴ γὰρ ἐξαλειφθείη[34] πόλις μηδεμία, μήτε σοί, βασιλεῦ, μήτε ἐμοί, μήτε ἴδοιμι[35] πρὸς ἱεροῖς[36] νόσον, δὶ ἥν[37] οἱ νοσοῦντες ἐν[38] αὐτοῖς κείσονται, ἀλλὰ μὴ ἔστω ἐν (our) σπουδῇ τὰ (affairs) βαρβάρων, 360 μηδὲ τάττωμεν[39] (to restore) αὐτοὺς ἐς τὸ ὑγιαῖνον (our) πολεμιωτάτους ὄντας καὶ οὐκ ἐνσπόνδους τῷ περὶ[40] ἡμᾶς γένει.

---

[29] I.e., in a written accusation.

[30] ταύτην (πόλιν) is the direct object of ἔμελλεν.

[31] τις...ἀπολογία (i.e., with respect to having adverted a plague that would have destroyed one's enemies).

[32] ἤν (contr.) > εἰ ἄν ("unless").

[33] ὁ βασιλεύς...αἱρεῖν βούληται.

[34] Cf. table 9.3.3(b).

[35] S.v. ὁράω, table 9.1.3(a).

[36] πρὸς ἱεροῖς, "in temples."

[37] Antecedent is νόσον (fm.).

[38] "By."

[39] Hort. subj., τάττωμεν > τάσσωμεν.

[40] περί (+ acc.), "with respect to."

τὴν δὲ Ἔφεσον τίς ἀφαιρήσεται τὸ σώζεσθαι βεβλημένην μὲν τὰς⁴¹ ἀρχὰς τοῦ γένους ἐκ τῆς καθαρωτάτης Ἀτθίδος, (ἢ) ἐπιδεδωκυῖαν δὲ παρὰ πάσας (πόλεις), ὁπόσαι Ἰωνικαί τε καὶ Λύδιοι, 365 (ἢ) προβεβηκυῖαν δὲ ἐπὶ τὴν θάλατταν διὰ τὸ ὑπερήκειν τῆς γῆς, ἐφ' ἧς ᾠκίσθη, (ἢ) μεστὴν δὲ φροντισμάτων οὖσαν φιλοσόφων τε καὶ ῥητορικῶν, ὑφ' ὧν ἡ πόλις⁴² οὐχ ἵππῳ μυριάσι δὲ ἀνθρώπων ἰσχύει, (whose) σοφίαν (ἡ πόλιν) ἐπαινοῦσα; 370 τίς δ' ἂν⁴³ σοφὸς ἐκλιπεῖν σοι δοκεῖ τὸν⁴⁴ ὑπὲρ πόλεως τοιαύτης ἀγῶνα ἐνθυμηθεὶς μὲν (ὅτι) Δημόκριτον⁴⁵ ἐλευθερώσαντα λοιμοῦ ποτε Ἀβδηρίτας, ἐννοήσας δὲ Σοφοκλέα⁴⁶ τὸν Ἀθηναῖον, ὃς λέγεται καὶ ἀνέμους θέλξαι τῆς ὥρας πέρα πνεύσαντας, ἀκηκοὼς δὲ τὰ Ἐμπεδοκλέους,⁴⁷ ὃς νεφέλης ἀνέσχε φορὰν⁴⁸ ἐπ' Ἀκραγαντίνους ῥαγείσης;⁴⁹

Vocabulary

Ἀβδηρῖται, οἱ, people of Abdera, Thrace

αἱρέω, pres. inf. αἱρεῖν, ¹aor. ᾕρησα / εἷλον (√ ἑλ-), ²aor. mid. εἱλάμην/όμην: take by the hand; take away, remove; entrap, take captive; mid. take for oneself, choose; pass. be chosen

Ἀκραγάντινοι, people of Agrigentum, Sicily

ἀντίξοον, τό, opposition

ἀπολογία, ἡ, defense

Ἀτθίς, -ίδος, ἡ, Attic (i.e., of Attica)

βάρβαρος, -ον, barbarous (i.e., non-Greek-speaking, foreign); subst. barbarian

δήπου, doubtless; "I presume"

ἐλευθερόω, set free, liberate

ἐνθυμέομαι, 6. ἐνεθυμήθην, reflect; pass. (dep.), to have reflected

ἔνσπονδος, -ον, under treaty (i.e., at peace) with (+ dat.)

ἐξαλείφω, wipe out, obliterate

Ἐφέσιος, -ία, -ιον, Ephesian (adj.); subst. Ephesians

Ἔφεσος, ἡ, Ephesos

Ἴστρος, ὁ, Ister River (Danube)

Ἰωνικός, -η, -ον, of Ionia, Ionian; pl. subst., Ionian cities

κατηγορία, ἡ, accusation

Κελτοί, οἱ, Celts

λοιμός, ὁ, plague

---

⁴¹ Acc. of spec. ("as").
⁴² πόλις...ἰσχύει.
⁴³ τίς δ' ἂν > τίς δὲ ἂν.
⁴⁴ τὸν...ἀγῶνα.
⁴⁵ Demokritos, pre-Socratic philosopher born in Abdera.
⁴⁶ Sophokles, one of three great tragedians.
⁴⁷ Empedokles, pre-Socratic philosopher and a citizen of Agrigentum, Sicily.
⁴⁸ νεφέλης...φορὰν.
⁴⁹ S.v. ῥήγνυμι.

Λύδιος, -α, -ον, of Lydia, Lydian; pl. subst. Lydian cities

μείων (m.), μείον (nt.), of lesser importance (than) (+ gen.)

οἰκίζω, aor. ᾤκισα, poet. ᾤκισσα, 4. ᾤκικα, pf. pass. ᾤκισμαι: found a city/ colony; build

ὁρμητήριον, τό, military base of operations

πέρα, beyond (+ gen.); πέρα τῆς ὥρας, beyond the season (i.e., unseasonably)

προσφορός, όν, suitable, proper

Ῥῆνος, ὁ, Rhine River

ῥητορικός, -ή, -όν, oratorical, rhetorical; subt. rhetorician

Σκύθαι, οἱ, Scythians (people of the northeast of western Europe)

ὑγιαῖνος, -ον, relating to good health; subst. health

ὑπερήκω, to have outgrown (+ gen.)

φροντισμά, -ματος, τό, thought, idea

8.7.9

375 Ἐπικόπτει με ὁ κατήγορος· ἀκούεις (him) γάρ που καὶ σύ, ὦ βασιλεῦ, καί φησιν, οὐκ ἐπειδὴ σωτηρίας αἴτιος Ἐφεσίοις ἐγενόμην, γράφεσθαι[50] με, ἀλλ᾽ ἐπειδὴ προεῖπον (ὅτι) ἐμπεσεῖσθαι σφισι τὴν νόσον, τουτὶ[51] γὰρ ὑπὲρ (the powers of) σοφίαν εἶναι καὶ (is) τερατῶδες, 380 τῆς[52] δ᾽ ἐπὶ τοσόνδε ἀληθείας οὐκ ἂν ἐφικέσθαι με, εἰ μὴ γόης τε ἦν καὶ ἀπόρρητος. τί οὖν ἐνταῦθα ἐρεῖ Σωκράτης[53] ὑπὲρ ὧν ἔφασκε τοῦ δαιμονίου μανθάνειν; τί δὲ Θαλῆς[54] τε καὶ Ἀναξαγόρας, τὼ[55] Ἴωνε, ὁ μὲν τὴν εὐφορίαν τὴν τῶν ἐλαιῶν (προεῖπεν), 385 ὁ δὲ πολλὰ τῶν οὐρανίων παθῶν προεῖπεν; ἢ γοητεύοντε προειπεῖν ταῦτα; καὶ μὴν καὶ ὑπήχθησαν οὗτοι δικαστηρίοις ἐφ᾽ ἑτέραις αἰτίαις, καὶ οὐδαμοῦ τῶν αἰτιῶν εἴρηται[56] γόητας εἶναι σφᾶς, ἐπειδὴ προγιγνώσκουσι. 390 καταγέλαστον γὰρ τοῦτο ἐδόκει καὶ οὐδ᾽ ἐν Θετταλίᾳ (would it be) πιθανὸν κατ᾽ ἀνδρῶν[57] λέγεσθαι[58] σοφῶν, οὗ τὰ γύναια κακῶς ἤκουεν ἐπὶ[59] τῇ τῆς σελήνης ἕλξει.

---

[50] Pass. (s.v. γράφω), "to be indicted."

[51] In Attic, οὑτό, αὕτη, and τοῦτο are often strengthened by the addition of ι to form οὑτοσί, αὑτηί, τουτί.

[52] τῆς…ἀληθείας.

[53] Socrates (469–399 BCE).

[54] Thales of Miletos (624–546 BCE) and Anaxagoras (500–428 BCE), pre-Socratic philosophers.

[55] Here five dual forms appear in a row: τώ, Ἴωνε, προειπόντε, γοητεύοντε, γοητεύοντε (for dual paradigm see table 9.16.2).

[56] S.v. λέγω.

[57] ἀνδρῶν…σοφῶν.

[58] "To bring a charge against" (+ gen.).

[59] ἠκούω ἐπί, "to obey."

Vocabulary
ἀπόρρητος, -ον, unfit to be spoken, abominable; subst. detestable person
γόης, -ητος, ὁ, sorcerer
γοητεύω, be a sorcerer
γύναιον, τό, weak woman (term of contempt)
δικαστήριον, τό, court of justice
ἐλαία, ἡ, olive ἕλξις, -εως, ἡ, attraction, attractive power
ἐνταῦθα, here, there; then
ἐπικόπτω, reprove, censure
εὐφορία, ἡ, abundant crop
ἦ, is it the truth that … ?
Θεσσαλία, ἡ (Att. Θετταλία), Thessaly
Ἴων, -ωνος, pl. Ἴωνες, dual Ἴωνε (nom., acc., cf. table 9.16): Ionian
καταγέλαστος, -ον, ridiculous, absurd
κατήγορος, ὁ, accuser (cf. 390)
μανθάνω, ²aor. ἔμαθον,²aor. inf. μαθεῖν, 4. μεμάθηκα, pf. ptc. μεμαθηκώς: learn;
    learn something from (ἀπό / gen.) somebody
οὐδαμός, -ή, -όν, not anyone, not any; οὐδαμοῦ, nowhere
πάθος, -εος, τό, misfortune, calamity; pain; pl. τὰ πάθη, emotions, passions;
    οὐράνιος πάθος, meteorological disturbance
πιθανός, -ή, -όν, plausible
προγινώσκω (Att. προγιγνώσκω), foresee, have foreknowledge of
σφεῖς, σφέων (gen.), σφίσι(ν) (dat.), σφᾶς (acc.), they, them (pron.)
τερατῶδης, -ες, miraculous
τοσόσδε, τοσήδε, τοσόνδε, so great, so many; ἐπὶ τοσόνδε, to such a degree
φάσκω, declare, assert

390 πόθεν οὖν τοῦ περὶ τὴν Ἔφεσον πάθους ᾐσθόμην; ἤκουσας μὲν καὶ τοῦ κατηγόρου εἰπόντος, ὅτι μὴ κατὰ[60] τοὺς ἄλλους διαιτῶμαι, 395 κἀμοὶ[61] δὲ ὑπὲρ τῶν ἐμαυτοῦ σιτίων, ὡς λεπτὰ καὶ ἡδίω[62] τῆς ἑτέρων συβάριδος, (as) ἐν ἀρχῇ εἴρηται· τοῦτό (diet) μοι, ὦ βασιλεῦ, τὰς αἰσθήσεις (μου) ἐν αἰθρίᾳ τινὶ ἀπορρήτῳ φυλάττει κοὐκ[63] ἐᾷ θολερὸν περὶ αὐτὰς[64] οὐδὲν εἶναι, (καὶ ἐᾷ με) διορᾶν τε, ὥσπερ ἐν κατόπτρου αὐγῇ, πάντα γιγνόμενά τε καὶ ἐσόμενα.

Vocabulary
αἰθρία, ἡ (= ἄθρη), pure air, ether
ἀπόρρητος, -ον, indescribable

---

[60] κατά + acc., "in accordance with," "like."
[61] κἀμοί > καὶ ἐμοί ("and in my case").
[62] Cf. ἡδύς.
[63] κοὐκ > καὶ οὐκ.
[64] I.e., his senses.

αὐγή, ἡ, light of the sun; pl. (reflected) rays of the sun
διαιτάω, mid. lead/live one's life
διοράω, distinguish, discern
θολερός, -ον, foul; subst. foul thing
κάτοπτρον, τό, mirror
σιτίον, τό, food made from wheat, food; pl. diet, eating habits
σύβαρις, -εως, ἡ, luxury

400 οὐ γὰρ περιμενεῖ γε ὁ σοφὸς τὴν γῆν ἀναθυμιῶσαν ἢ τὸν ἀέρα διεφθορότα,
ἢν[65] τὸ δεινὸν ἄνωθεν ῥέῃ, ἀλλὰ ξυνήσει[66] αὐτῶν καὶ ἐπὶ θύραις ὄντων[67] ὕστερον
μὲν ἢ οἱ θεοί, θᾶττον[68] δὲ ἢ οἱ πολλοί, 405 θεοὶ μὲν γὰρ μελλόντων,[69] ἄνθρωποι δὲ
γιγνομένων, σοφοὶ δὲ προσιόντων αἰσθάνονται. λοιμῶν δ' αἰτίας ἰδίᾳ,[70] βασιλεῦ,
ἐρώτα,[71] (they are) σοφώτεραι[72] γὰρ ἢ ἐς τοὺς πολλοὺς λέγεσθαι· ἆρ οὖν (my)
τὸ οὕτως διαιτᾶσθαι λεπτότητα[73] μόνον ἐργάζεται τῶν αἰσθήσεων ἢ ἰσχὺν ἐπὶ[74]
(perceiving) τὰ μέγιστά τε καὶ θαυμασιώτατα;

Vocabulary
αἰτία, τό, cause; accusation, legal charge
ἀναθυμιάω, send forth vapor
ἄνωθεν, from above
ἆρα, then (marker of impatience when asking a question)
διαιτάσσω, lead one's life, live in a certain way
διαφθορέω (= διαφθείρω), ruin; pass. be corrupted, ruined
Ἰωνία, ἡ, Ionia (coastal region of west Anatolia)
περιμένω, wait (for)
πρόσειμι (fr. εἶμι, cf. table 9.14), approach

410 θεωρεῖν δ' ἔξεστιν, ὃ λέγω, καὶ ἀπ' ἄλλων μέν, οὐχ ἥκιστα δὲ κἀκ[75] τῶν[76]
ἐν Ἐφέσῳ περὶ τὴν νόσον ἐκείνην πραχθέντων·[77] τὸ γὰρ τοῦ λοιμοῦ εἶδος—
πτωχῷ δὲ γέροντι εἴκαστο – καὶ εἶδον καὶ ἰδὼν εἷλον[78] (it), οὐ παύσας νόσον,

---

[65] ἤν > εἰ ἄν ("if," "in case").
[66] ξυν- > συν-, s.v. συνίημι.
[67] Gen. absol. ("when").
[68] S.v. ταχύς.
[69] Ptc. of μέλλω, "(in the) future," "to come."
[70] ἰδίᾳ, "privately" (adv.).
[71] Cf. table 9.4.3(b).
[72] S.v. σοφός, comp. ("more clever," "subtle").
[73] λεπτότητα (subtleties) …τῶν αἰσθήσεων.
[74] ἐπί (+ acc.), "regarding."
[75] κἀκ > καὶ ἐκ.
[76] τῶν…πραχθέντων.
[77] S.v. πράσσω.
[78] S.v. αἱρέω.

ἀλλ᾽ ἐξελών,⁷⁹ (the god) ὅτῳ⁸⁰ δ᾽ εὐξάμενος, 415 δηλοῖ τὸ ἱερόν, ὃ ἐν Ἐφέσῳ ὑπὲρ τούτου (event) ἱδρυσάμην, (τὸ ἱερόν) Ἡρακλέους μὲν γὰρ Ἀποτροπαίου ἐστί, ξυνεργὸν⁸¹ (with me) δ᾽ αὐτὸν εἱλόμην, ἐπειδὴ (he is) σοφός τε καὶ ἀνδρεῖος ὢν ἐκάθηρε⁸² ποτε λοιμοῦ τὴν Ἦλιν τὰς ἀναθυμιάσεις ἀποκλύσας, ἃς παρεῖχεν ἡ γῆ κατ᾽ Αὐγέαν⁸³ τυραννεύοντα.⁸⁴

Vocabulary
ἀναθυμίασις, -εως, ἡ, foul exhalation
ἀνδρεῖος, -α, -ον, courageous, brave
ἀποκλύζω, wash off/clean
ἀποτρόπαιος, -ον, averting evil; subst.   Ἀποτρόπαιος, one who averts evil
εἰκάζω, ¹aor. inf. εἰκάσαι, 5. εἴκασμαι: represent by a likeness; liken; perceive something as something else; pass., take the form of
ἥκιστα (adv.), least; οὐχ ἥκιστα, not in the least, not only
Ἦλις, ἡ, city of Elis
Ἡρακλῆς, -έους, ὁ, Herakles (Lat. Hercules) (cf. 425)
συνεργός, -ον, working together, ὁ/ἡ συνεργός, helper
τυραννεύω, be an absolute ruler

420 τίς ἂν οὖν σοι, βασιλεῦ, δοκεῖ (as) φιλοτιμούμενος γόης φαίνεσθαι⁸⁵ θεῷ ἀναθεῖναι, ὃ αὐτὸς εἴργαστο; τίνας⁸⁶ δ᾽ ἂν κτήσασθαι θαυμαστὰς τῆς τέχνης (αὐτοῦ) θεῷ παρεὶς τὸ θαυμάζεσθαι; τίς δ᾽ ἂν Ἡρακλεῖ εὔξασθαι γόης ὤν; 425 τὰ γὰρ τοιαῦτα (wonders) οἱ κακοδαίμονες βόθροις (they dig) ἀνατιθέασι καὶ χθονίοις θεοῖς, ὧν τὸν Ἡρακλέα ἀποτακτέον, καθαρὸς γὰρ (he is) καὶ τοῖς ἀνθρώποις εὔους. ηὐξάμην αὐτῷ καὶ ἐν Πελοποννήσῳ ποτέ, λαμίας γάρ τι φάσμα κἀκεῖ,⁸⁷ περὶ τὴν Κόρινθον ἦλυε σιτούμενον τῶν νέων τοὺς καλούς, 430 καὶ (Heracles) ξυνήρατό μοι τοῦ ἀγῶνος (with her) οὐ θαυμασίων⁸⁸ δεηθεὶς δώρων, ἀλλὰ (only asking for) μελιττούτης καὶ λιβανωτοῦ καὶ τοῦ ὑπὲρ σωτηρίας τι ἀνθρώπων ἐργάσασθαι.⁸⁹

---

⁷⁹ S.v. ἐξαιρέω.
⁸⁰ ὅτῳ, Att. dat. (s.v. ὅστις).
⁸¹ ξυν- > συν- ; acc. of spec. ("as").
⁸² S.v. καθαίρω.
⁸³ Augeas, King of Elis/Eleia (on the Peloponnese).
⁸⁴ The fifth labor of Herakles was to clean the Augean stables, the horses of which produced an enormous quantity of dung. King Augeas had not had the stables cleaned for more than thirty years. Herakles accomplished this feat by rerouting the two rivers, the Alpheus and Peneus, to wash the filth from the stables.
⁸⁵ φαίνεσθαι...σοι.
⁸⁶ τίνας...θαυμαστάς.
⁸⁷ κἀκει > καὶ ἐκεῖ ("there also").
⁸⁸ θαυμασίων...δώρων.
⁸⁹ τοῦ ὑπὲρ... ἐργάσασθαι, art. inf. (expressing purpose).

Vocabulary

ἀλύω, wander, roam about (περί)

ἀποτακτέον, one must exclude

δῶρον, τό, gift

εὔοος (Att. contr. εὔους), -ον, well-disposed, kindly

θαυμαστής, ὁ, admirer

κακοδαίμων, -ονος, ὁ, poor devil, poor wretch

χθόνιος, -α, -ον, under the earth; χθόνιοι θεοί, gods of the underworld/Hades

Κόρινθος, ἡ, Corinth

λάμια, ἡ, evil spirit in the shape of a woman, which feeds on the flesh of men

λιβανωτός, ὁ, frankincense (gum of the λίβανος tree)

μελιττούτη, ἡ, honey cake (esp. used as a sacred offering)

ξυνήρατο > συνήρατο, s.v. συναίρω, 3. συνηράμην, provide assistance to some-
    body (dat.) with (gen.) some task

παρίημι, ²aor. ptc. παρείς, give up something to somebody else, give credit for
    something to somebody (cf. paradigm of ἵημι, table 9.15)

Πελοππόννησος, ὁ, Peloponnese

σιτέομαι, feed upon (+ acc.)

φάσμα, -ματος, τό, apparition, phantom

SELECT BIBLIOGRAPHY

Bowie, Ewen. *Philostratus*. Cambridge: Cambridge University Press, 2009.

8.2.

Epicurus, *Letter to Menoeceus*

(*Men.* 125–127)

Provenance: Athens.　　　*Date:* 341–270 BCE.

Epicurus founded the eponymous "Epicurean" school of philosophy, which was the most important school of naturalism in Hellenistic and Roman times. He was born on the Aegean island of Samos and later completed military service in Athens. He then moved to Kolophon, where he studied philosophy with Democritus. In 306 BCE Epicurus returned to Athens and founded his own philosophical school. This school was quaintly known as "the Garden," named after the garden of his house where he met with his students.

Among his surviving writings are three letters, the extracts of two of which are provided in this reader. The *Letter to Menoeceus* provides a summary of his ethical teachings, including his instruction on the nature of the gods, on the needless fear of death, and on the rational control of emotions and human appetites. His *Letter to Herodotus* summarizes his key teachings on nature (§8.6).

Text: Rainer Nickel, *Epikur: Wege zum Gluck* (Düsseldorf: Artemis & Winkler, 2003).

Related Texts: Epicurus, *Herodotos*, 38–42, 63–68 (§8.6).

ON DEATH (§§ 125–127)

125 Οὐθὲν γάρ ἐστιν ἐν τῷ ζῆν δεινὸν τῷ κατειληφότι[1] γνησίως (that) τὸ μηδὲν ὑπάρχειν ἐν τῷ μὴ ζῆν δεινόν. ὥστε μάταιος ὁ λέγων δεδιέναι τὸν θάνατον

---

[1] S.v. καταλαμβάνω, cf. table 9.1.6(d).

οὐχ ὅτι λυπήσει παρών,[2] ἀλλ᾽ ὅτι λυπεῖ μέλλων.[3] ὃ γὰρ παρὸν[4] οὐκ ἐνοχλεῖ, προσδοκώμενον κενῶς λυπεῖ. τὸ φρικωδέστατον οὖν τῶν κακῶν (namely) ὁ θάνατος (is) οὐθὲν πρὸς ἡμᾶς, ἐπειδήπερ[5] ὅταν μὲν ἡμεῖς ὦμεν, ὁ θάνατος οὐ πάρεστιν, ὅταν δὲ ὁ θάνατος παρῇ, τόθ᾽[6] ἡμεῖς οὐκ ἐσμέν.[7] οὔτε οὖν πρὸς τοὺς ζῶντάς (death) ἐστιν οὔτε πρὸς τοὺς τετελευτηκότας, ἐπειδήπερ περὶ οὓς μὲν[8] οὐκ ἔστιν, οἳ δ᾽ οὐκέτι εἰσίν. Ἀλλ᾽ οἱ πολλοὶ τὸν θάνατον ὁτὲ μὲν[9] ὡς μέγιστον τῶν κακῶν φεύγουσιν, ὁτὲ δὲ ὡς ἀνάπαυσιν τῶν ἐν τῷ ζῆν κακῶν αἱροῦνται. 126 ὁ δὲ σοφὸς οὔτε παραιτεῖται τὸ ζῆν οὔτε φοβεῖται τὸ μὴ ζῆν· οὔτε γὰρ αὐτῷ προσίσταται τὸ ζῆν οὔτε δοξάζεται κακὸν εἶναί τι τὸ μὴ ζῆν. ὥσπερ δὲ τὸ σιτίον οὐ τὸ πλεῖστον πάντως ἀλλὰ τὸ ἥδιστον αἱρεῖται, οὕτω καὶ χρόνον[10] οὐ τὸν μήκιστον ἀλλὰ τὸν ἥδιστον καρπίζεται. Ὁ δὲ παραγγέλλων τὸν μὲν νέον καλῶς ζῆν, τὸν δὲ γέροντα καλῶς καταστρέφειν, εὐήθης ἐστὶν οὐ μόνον διὰ τὸ τῆς ζωῆς ἀσπαστόν, ἀλλὰ καὶ διὰ τὸ τὴν αὐτὴν[11] εἶναι[12] (τὴν) μελέτην τοῦ καλῶς ζῆν καὶ τοῦ καλῶς ἀποθνήσκειν. πολὺ δὲ χείρων καὶ ὁ λέγων· (It is) καλὸν μὴ φῦναι, φύντα[13] δ᾽ ὅπως[14] ὤκιστα πύλας Ἀΐδαο[15] περῆσαι.[16]

Vocabulary

αἱρέω, pres. inf. αἱρεῖν, [1]aor. ἥρησα / εἷλον (√ ἑλ-), [2]aor. mid. εἱλάμην/όμην: take by the hand; take away, remove; entrap, take captive; mid. take for oneself, choose; pass. be chosen

ἀπελπίζω, despair

ἀσπαστός, -όν, gladly welcomed, desirable; τὸ ἀσπαστός, desirability

γνησίως, genuinely

δείδω, [2]pf. inf. δεδιέναι, [2]pf. ptc. δεδιώς: fear

εὐήθης, -ες, simple-minded, foolish

καρπίζω, enjoy the fruits (of something)

---

[2] Temp. adv. ptc. ("when," cf. IV, 1.1); s.v. πάρειμι.

[3] Causal adv. ptc. ("because," cf. IV, 1.4).

[4] Temp. adv. ptc. ("when").

[5] ἐπειδήπερ, intens. form of ἐπεί.

[6] τόθ᾽ > τότε.

[7] According to Epicurus, the body and soul (which are both compounds consisting of atoms) are born together and die together. Thus, when the soul separates from the body, it also dies. Likewise, when the body loses its soul, it decays.

[8] μέν...δέ... ("the former ... the latter ...").

[9] ὁτὲ μέν...ὁτὲ δέ... ("sometimes ... sometimes ...").

[10] Acc. of time.

[11] τὴν αὐτήν, "the same."

[12] Art. inf., w. τὴν...μελέτην functioning as the subj. of inf.

[13] Temp. adv. ptc. (cf. IV, 1).

[14] ὅπως + inf.

[15] Ἀΐδαο > Ἄδου.

[16] S.v. περάω.

καταστρέφω, come to an end (i.e., die)

μελέτη, ἡ, care

μήκιστος, -η, -ον, longest (time)

περάω, ¹aor inf. περῆσαι: pass through (a space)

προσίστημι, pass. προσίσταμαι: set against; pass. set oneself against something, encounter

φρικώδης, -ον, horrible, awful; superl. φρικωδέστατος, most horrible

φύω, ¹aor. inf. φῦναι: bring forth, be born

χείρων (m./fm.), **χεῖρον** (nt.), **-ονος:** worse, inferior to something (gen.); subst. the worst

ὠκύς, ὠκεῖα, ὠκύ, quick; superl. ὤκιστος, as quickly as possible

127 εἰ μὲν γὰρ πεποιθὼς τοῦτό φησιν, πῶς οὐκ ἀπέρχεται ἐκ τοῦ ζῆν; ἐν ἑτοίμῳ[17] γὰρ αὐτῷ τοῦτ᾽ (option) ἐστίν, εἴπερ ἦν βεβουλευμένον[18] αὐτῷ βεβαίως· εἰ δὲ μωκώμενος, (he is considered) μάταιος ἐν τοῖς οὐκ ἐπιδεχομένοις (his words). Μνημονευτέον δὲ ὡς τὸ μέλλον[19] οὔτε πάντως ἡμέτερον οὔτε πάντως οὐχ ἡμέτερον, ἵνα μήτε πάντως προσμένωμεν ὡς ἐσόμενον μήτε ἀπελπίζωμεν ὡς πάντως οὐκ ἐσόμενον. (continues ...)

Vocabulary

ἐπιδέχομαι, receive, welcome

μνημονευτέον (verbal adj. expressing necessity), "it must be remembered ... that (ὡς)"

μωκάομαι, speak in jest

προσμένω, expect

---

[17] ἐν ἑτοίμῳ, "at the ready," "at hand."

[18] Plpf. periphr. (cf. IV, 17).

[19] τὸ μέλλον (s.v. μέλλω), nt. subst. ptc., "the future."

8.3.

Epictetus, *Discourses*

(*Diatr.* 1.9.1–24)

Epictetus was one of the most influential philosophers of the Roman Stoics. He was born in Hierapolis (modern Pamukkale, Turkey) but was taken to Rome at an early age, as the slave of Epaphroditos, a wealthy freedman and secretary to Emperor Nero. While living in Rome he became an enthusiastic student of Stoicism under the tutelage of Musonius Rufus. When Domitian banished all philosophers from Rome in 93 CE, Epictetus fled to Nicopolis in southern Epiros, where he spent the remainder of his life teaching the Stoic way of life.

The style and vocabulary of his discourses, including a discussion of the fatherhood of God and what it means to be a "son of God," are remarkably close to the Greek of the Christian New Testament. Though he wrote nothing, his discourses were later compiled from his lecture notes and published by his most renowned pupil, Flavius Arrian, in 108 CE.

Date: Epictetus lived from 55 to 135 CE.

Text: Epictetus, *Dissertationes ab Arriani Digestae*, ed. Henricus Schenkl (Stuttgart: B. G. Teubner, 1965).

ΠΩΣ ΑΠΟ ΤΟΥ ΣΥΓΓΕΝΕΙΣ ΗΜΑΣ ΕΙΝΑΙ[1] ΤΩ ΘΕΩ ΕΠΕΛΘΟΙ ΑΝ ΤΙΣ ΕΠΙ ΤΑ ΕΞΗΣ

1.9.1 Εἰ ταῦτά ἐστιν ἀληθῆ τὰ[2] περὶ τῆς συγγενείας τοῦ θεοῦ καὶ ἀνθρώπων λεγόμενα ὑπὸ τῶν φιλοσόφων, τί ἄλλο ἀπολείπεται τοῖς ἀνθρώποις (to do) ἢ

---

[1] Art. inf. (cf. IV, 2).
[2] τα...λεγόμενα.

τὸ τοῦ Σωκράτους (did), μηδέποτε πρὸς τὸν πυθόμενον³ ποδαπός ἐστιν εἰπεῖν ὅτι (you are) Ἀθηναῖος ἢ Κορίνθιος, 2 ἀλλ᾽ (say) ὅτι (you are) κόσμιος; διὰ τί γὰρ λέγεις Ἀθηναῖον εἶναι σεαυτόν, οὐχὶ (say) δ᾽ ἐξ ἐκείνης μόνον τῆς γωνίας, εἰς ἣν ἐρρίφη⁴ γεννηθέν σου τὸ σωμάτιον; 3 ἢ (it is) δῆλον ὅτι ἀπὸ (place) τοῦ κυριωτέρου καὶ περιέχοντος οὐ μόνον αὐτὴν ἐκείνην τὴν γωνίαν, (ἀλλὰ) καὶ ὅλην σου τὴν οἰκίαν⁵ καὶ ἁπλῶς ὅθεν σου τὸ γένος τῶν προγόνων εἰς σὲ κατελήλυθεν ἐντεῦθέν ποθεν καλεῖς σεαυτὸν Ἀθηναῖον καὶ Κορίνθιον;

Vocabulary

ἀπολείπω, 2. ἀπολείψω: leave behind, desert, abandon; pass. be left behind, remain

γωνία, ἡ, corner

δῆλος, -η, -ον, clear, plain, evident; s.c., ἐστί (impers.), it is plain/evident

Κορίνθιος, -α, -ον, Corinthian (adj.); subst. a Corinthian person

κόσμιος (= κοσμοπολίτης), ὁ, citizen of the world (cf. 1.9.6)

κυρίως, with full authority; comp. κυριώτερος, greater authority; superl. κυριώτατος, supreme authority

ποδαπός, -ή, -όν, from what country?

πρόγονος, ὁ, forefather

συγγένεια, ἡ, kinship/relationship with/to (πρός),

1.9.4 ὁ τοίνυν τῇ διοικήσει⁶ τοῦ κόσμου παρηκολουθηκὼς καὶ μεμαθηκώς,⁷ ὅτι Τὸ μέγιστον καὶ κυριώτατον καὶ περιεκτικώτατον πάντων τοῦτό ἐστι τὸ σύστημα τὸ ἐξ ἀνθρώπων καὶ θεοῦ, ἀπ᾽ ἐκείνου δὲ τὰ σπέρματα καταπέπτωκεν οὐκ εἰς τὸν πατέρα τὸν ἐμὸν μόνον οὐδ᾽ εἰς τὸν πάππον, ἀλλ᾽ εἰς ἅπαντα μὲν τὰ ἐπὶ γῆς γεννώμενά τε καὶ φυόμενα, 5 προηγουμένως δ᾽ εἰς τὰ λογικά, ὅτι κοινωνεῖν μόνον ταῦτα πέφυκεν τῷ θεῷ τῆς συναναστροφῆς κατὰ τὸν λόγον ἐπιπεπλεγμένα, 6 διὰ τί μὴ εἴπῃ τις αὐτὸν κόσμιον; διὰ τί μὴ υἱὸν τοῦ θεοῦ; διὰ τί δὲ φοβηθήσεταί τι τῶν γιγνομένων ἐν ἀνθρώποις; 7 ἀλλὰ πρὸς μὲν τὸν Καίσαρα ἡ συγγένεια ἢ (πρὸς) ἄλλον τινὰ μέγα τῶν δυναμένων ἐν Ῥώμῃ ἱκανὴ παρέχειν ἐν ἀσφαλείᾳ διάγοντας καὶ ἀκαταφρονήτους καὶ δεδοικότας⁸ μηδ᾽ ὁτιοῦν,⁹ 8 τὸ δὲ τὸν θεὸν ποιητὴν¹⁰ ἔχειν καὶ πατέρα καὶ κηδεμόνα οὐκέτι ἡμᾶς ἐξαιρήσεται λυπῶν καὶ φόβων;

---

³ S.v. πυνθάνομαι.
⁴ S.v. ῥίπτω.
⁵ Here "family."
⁶ Dat. of resp.
⁷ S.v. μανθάνω.
⁸ S.v. δείδω.
⁹ S.v. ὅστις, ὅτι → ὁστισοοῦν, ὁτιοῦν, "anybody," "anything whatsoever."
¹⁰ Acc. of spec.

Vocabulary

ἀκαταφρόνητος, -ον, not despised, above contempt
διάγω, to cause to continue
διοίκησις, ἡ, administration, government
ἐπιπλέκω, interweave, combine, conjoin
καταπίπτω, pf. καταπέπτωκα: to fall, drop; descend
κηδεμών, -όνος, protector, guardian
παρακολουθέω, pf. ptc. παρηκολουθηκώς: follow, accompany; follow (in a course
    of events); follow in the mind, understand
περιεκτικός, -ή, -όν, containing; superl. περιεκτικώτατον, most comprehensive
ποιητής, ὁ, author, maker
προηγουμένως, particularly
συναναστροφή, ἡ, living with
σύστημα, -ματος, τό, composite whole, whole compounded of parts

1.9.8 Καὶ πόθεν φάγω, (Someone may) φησίν, μηδὲν ἔχων; Καὶ πῶς οἱ δοῦλοι,
πῶς οἱ δραπέται, τίνα πεποιθότες[11] ἐκεῖνοι ἀπαλλάττονται[12] τῶν δεσποτῶν; (Do
they rely) τοῖς ἀγροῖς. ἢ τοῖς οἰκέταις ἢ τοῖς ἀργυρώμασιν; (They rely) Οὐδενί,
ἀλλ᾽ ἑαυτοῖς· καὶ ὅμως οὐκ ἐπιλείπουσιν αὐτοὺς τροφαί. 9 τὸν δὲ φιλόσοφον ἡμῖν
δεήσει[13] ἄλλοις θαρροῦντα[14] καὶ ἐπαναπαυόμενον ἀποδημεῖν καὶ μὴ ἐπιμελεῖσθαι
αὐτὸν αὑτοῦ καὶ τῶν θηρίων[15] τῶν ἀλόγων εἶναι χείρονα καὶ δειλότερον,
ὧν ἕκαστον αὐτὸ αὑτῷ ἀρκούμενον οὔτε τροφῆς ἀπορεῖ τῆς οἰκείας[16] οὔτε
διεξαγωγῆς τῆς καταλλήλους καὶ κατὰ (its) φύσιν;

Vocabulary

ἀπορέω, be without something (gen.)
ἀργυρώματα, τά, silver vessels
δειλός, -ή, -όν, cowardly; comp. δειλότερος, more cowardly
διεξαγωγή, ἡ, way of living
ἐπαναπαύομαι, rely on somebody (+ dat.)
ἐπιλείπω, (of things) to fail one (acc.) (i.e., to run out)
ἐπιμελέομαι (w. gen.), pass. dep.: take care of something (gen.)
κατάλληλος, -ον, appropriate to (κατά), suitable for
ὅμως, nevertheless
χείρων (m./fm.), **χεῖρον** (nt.), **-ονος**: worse, inferior to something (gen.); subst.
    the worst

---

[11] Instr. adv. ptc. ("by," cf. IV, 1.6).
[12] ἀπαλλάττονται (Att.) > ἀπαλλάσσονται.
[13] S.v. δεῖ.
[14] θαρροῦντα (Att.) > θαρσοῦντα.
[15] Gen. of comp.
[16] τροφῆς...οἰκείας.

1.9.10 Ἐγὼ μὲν οἶμαι, ὅτι ἔδει καθῆσθαι τὸν πρεσβύτερον[17] ἐνταῦθα οὐ τοῦτο μηχανώμενον, ὅπως μὴ ταπεινοφρονήσητε μηδὲ ταπεινοὺς μηδ' ἀγεννεῖς τινας διαλογισμοὺς διαλογεῖσθε αὐτοὶ περὶ ἑαυτῶν, 11 ἀλλὰ μή τινες[18] ἐμπίπτωσιν τοιοῦτοι νέοι, οἳ ἐπιγνόντες τὴν πρὸς τοὺς θεοὺς συγγένειαν καὶ (ἐπιγνόντες) ὅτι δεσμά τινα ταῦτα – (which is to say) προσηρτήμεθα τὸ σῶμα καὶ τὴν κτῆσιν αὐτοῦ καὶ ὅσα τούτων ἕνεκα ἀναγκαῖα ἡμῖν γίνεται εἰς οἰκονομίαν καὶ ἀναστροφὴν τὴν ἐν τῷ βίῳ – ὡς βάρη τινὰ καὶ ἀνιαρὰ καὶ ἄχρηστα ἀπορρῖψαι θέλωσιν καὶ ἀπελθεῖν πρὸς τοὺς συγγενεῖς.

Vocabulary
ἀγεννής, -ές, base, sordid
ἀνιαρός, -ά, -όν, painful
ἀπορρίπτω, throw away, cast off
ἄχρηστος, -ον, useless, unprofitable
διαλογισμός, ὁ, debate, talk; estimation, consideration
πηδάω, leap
προσερωτάω, ask about in addition
ταπεινοφρονέω, be humble in mind, think of oneself as lowly

1.9.12 Καὶ τοῦτον[19] ἔδει τὸν ἀγῶνα ἀγωνίζεσθαι τὸν διδάσκαλον ὑμῶν καὶ παιδευτήν, εἴ τις[20] ἄρα ἦν· ὑμᾶς μὲν ἔρχεσθαι[21] λέγοντας· Ἐπίκτητε,[22] οὐκέτι ἀνεχόμεθα μετὰ τοῦ σωματίου τούτου δεδεμένοι καὶ τοῦτο τρέφοντες καὶ ποτίζοντες καὶ ἀναπαύοντες καὶ καθαίροντες, 13 εἶτα δι' αὐτὸ συμπεριφερόμενοι τοῖσδε[23] καὶ τοῖσδε. οὐκ ἀδιάφορα ταῦτα καὶ οὐδὲν πρὸς ἡμᾶς καὶ ὁ θάνατος οὐ κακόν; καὶ συγγενεῖς τινες τοῦ θεοῦ ἐσμεν κἀκεῖθεν[24] ἐληλύθαμεν; 14 ἄφες ἡμᾶς ἀπελθεῖν ὅθεν ἐληλύθαμεν, ἄφες λυθῆναί ποτε τῶν δεσμῶν τούτων τῶν ἐξηρτημένων καὶ βαρούντων. 15 ἐνταῦθα λῃσταὶ καὶ κλέπται καὶ δικαστήρια καὶ οἱ καλούμενοι τύραννοι δοκοῦντες ἔχειν τινὰ ἐφ' ἡμῖν ἐξουσίαν διὰ τὸ σωμάτιον καὶ τὰ τούτου κτήματα. ἄφες δείξωμεν αὐτοῖς, ὅτι οὐδενὸς ἔχουσιν ἐξουσίαν·

Vocabulary
ἀγωνίζομαι, to fight; struggle, strive
ἀδιάφορος, -ον, indifferent

---

[17] Epictetus here describes himself to Arrian as an old man (cf. 1.6.20, 2.6.23).
[18] τινες…τοιοῦτοι νέοι.
[19] τοῦτον…τὸν ἀγῶνα.
[20] εἴ τις, "whomever."
[21] Imperatival inf.
[22] Epictetus (voc.).
[23] S.v. ὅδε, ἥδε, τάδε.
[24] κἀκεῖθεν > καὶ ἐκεῖθεν.

βαρέω, pf. pass. ptc. βεβαρημένος: weigh down
ἐξαρτάω, pass. be furnished with, equipped with
λῃστής, ὁ, robber, pirate
παιδευτής, ὁ, instructor of youths
συμπεριφέρω, pass. accommodate/adapt oneself to

1.9.16 Ἐμὲ δ᾽ ἐν τῷδε λέγειν ὅτι Ἄνθρωποι, ἐκδέξασθε τὸν θεόν. ὅταν ἐκεῖνος σημήνῃ καὶ ἀπολύσῃ ὑμᾶς ταύτης τῆς ὑπηρεσίας, τότ᾽ ἀπολύεσθε πρὸς αὐτόν· ἐπὶ δὲ τοῦ παρόντος ἀνάσχεσθε ἐνοικοῦντες ταύτην τὴν χώραν, εἰς ἣν ἐκεῖνος ὑμᾶς ἔταξεν. 17 ὀλίγος ἄρα χρόνος οὗτος ὁ τῆς οἰκήσεως καὶ ῥᾴδιος τοῖς οὕτω διακειμένοις. ποῖος γὰρ ἔτι τύραννος ἢ ποῖος κλέπτης ἢ ποῖα δικαστήρια φοβερὰ τοῖς οὕτως παρ᾽ οὐδὲν[25] πεποιημένοις τὸ σῶμα καὶ τὰ τούτου κτήματα; μείνατε, μὴ ἀλογίστως ἀπέλθητε.

Vocabulary
ἀλογίστως, without reason
διακείμαι, be disposed in a certain manner, be well-disposed (cf. 1.9.21)
ἐνοικέω, dwell in
θηλυκός, -ή, -όν, female, woman-like, of feminine gender
οἴκησις, -εως, ἡ, dwelling
ὑπηρεσία, ἡ, service, labor

1.9.18 Τοιοῦτόν τι ἔδει γίνεσθαι[26] παρὰ[27] τοῦ παιδευτοῦ πρὸς τοὺς εὐφυεῖς τῶν νέων. 19 νῦν δὲ τί γίνεται; νεκρὸς μὲν ὁ παιδευτής, νεκροὶ δ᾽ ὑμεῖς. 20 ὅταν χορτασθῆτε σήμερον, κάθησθε κλάοντες περὶ τῆς αὔριον, πόθεν φάγητε. ἀνδράποδον, ἂν σχῇς[28] (it), ἕξεις (it)· ἂν μὴ σχῇς (it), ἐξελεύσῃ (from life)· ἤνοικται[29] ἡ θύρα. τί πενθεῖς; ποῦ ἔτι τόπος δακρύοις; τίς ἔτι (has) κολακείας ἀφορμή; διὰ τί ἄλλος ἄλλῳ φθονήσει; διὰ τί πολλὰ κεκτημένους θαυμάσει ἢ τοὺς ἐν δυνάμει τεταγμένους, 21 μάλιστ᾽ ἂν καὶ ἰσχυροὶ ὦσιν καὶ ὀργίλοι; τί γὰρ ἡμῖν ποιήσουσιν; ἃ δύνανται ποιῆσαι, τούτων οὐκ ἐπιστρεψόμεθα· ὧν ἡμῖν μέλει, ταῦτα οὐ δύνανται (to do). 22 τίς οὖν ἔτι ἄρξει τοῦ οὕτως διακειμένου;

Vocabulary
ἀνδράποδον, τό, slave, wretched creature
αὔριον (adv.), tomorrow
ἀφορμή, ἡ, starting point; occasion, pretext

---

[25] παρ᾽ οὐδέν, "as nothing," "of no value."
[26] γίνεσθαι, i.e., "to be said."
[27] παρά, "by."
[28] S.v. ἔχω.
[29] ἤνοικται > ἤνοιγται.

διάκειμαι, be well-disposed (in mind/attitude)
εὐφυής, -ές, naturally clever
κολακεία, ἡ, flattery
ποῦ, where?
φθονέω, be envious of somebody (dat.), be jealous
χορτάζω, feed/fatten (cattle); pass. eat one's fill

1.9.22 Πῶς Σωκράτης εἶχεν[30] πρὸς ταῦτα; πῶς γὰρ ἄλλως ἢ ὡς ἔδει τὸν πεπεισμένον[31] ὅτι ἐστὶ τῶν θεῶν συγγενής; 23 Ἄν μοι λέγητε, φησίν, νῦν ὅτι Ἀφίεμέν[32] σε ἐπὶ τούτοις, ὅπως μηκέτι διαλέξῃ τούτους τοὺς λόγους οὓς μέχρι νῦν διελέγου μηδὲ παρενοχλήσεις ἡμῶν τοῖς νέοις μηδὲ τοῖς γέρουσιν, 24 (and) ἀποκρινοῦμαι ὅτι Γελοῖοί ἐστε, οἵτινες ἀξιοῦτε, εἰ μέν με ὁ στρατηγὸς ὁ ὑμέτερος ἔταξεν εἴς τινα τάξιν, ὅτι ἔδει με τηρεῖν αὐτὴν καὶ φυλάττειν καὶ μυριάκις πρότερον αἱρεῖσθαι ἀποθνῄσκειν ἢ ἐγκαταλιπεῖν αὐτήν, εἰ δ᾽ ὁ θεὸς ἔν τινι χώρᾳ καὶ ἀναστροφῇ κατατέταχεν, ταύτην δ᾽ ἐγκαταλιπεῖν δεῖ ἡμᾶς. 25 τοῦτ᾽[33] ἔστιν ἄνθρωπος ταῖς ἀληθείαις[34] συγγενὴς τῶν θεῶν.

Vocabulary
αἱρέω, pres. inf. αἱρεῖν, [1]aor. ᾕρησα / εἷλον (√ ἑλ-), [2]aor. mid. εἱλάμην/όμην: take by the hand; take away, remove; entrap, take captive; mid. take for oneself, choose; pass. be chosen
κατατάσσω, place in
μυριάκις (adv.), ten thousand times
παρενοχλέω, annoy

---

[30] S.v. ἔχω, here "to understand."
[31] S.v. πείθω.
[32] For paradigm of ἵημι see table 9.15.
[33] I.e., Socrates.
[34] ταῖς ἀληθείαις (adv.), "in very truth."

8.4.

Poimandres: Hermetic Corpus

(*Poim.* 1–26)

Poimandres (Ποιμάνδρης) is the first tractate of the gnosticCorpus Hermeticum, a collection of fourteen to eighteen ancient Greek texts written in Egypt during the Greco-Roman period. The Corpus Hermeticum represents a form of pre-Christian gnosticism that shaped the religious, cultural, and philosophical milieus in which various forms of early Christianity emerged. But in contrast to the theology of Christian proto-orthodoxy, the creator god of hermetic gnosticism was believed to be distinct from, and an agent of, the highest God. Hermetic gnosticism was also radically dualistic, understanding the universe to be constituted by two irreducible elements, immateriality and materiality. The dualism of creation was also believed to be mirrored in both human beings and the godhead.

Date: First to third century CE.

Text: Paolo Scarpi (ed.), *Poimandres* (Venice: Masilio Editori, 1988).

SUMMARY OF THE MYTH

In order to facilitate the translation of this complex text, an overview of the story is warranted. *Poimandres* is essentially a myth of creation, which is set within another story, the story of the quest for salvation. The text begins with the narrator rejecting the material world in favor of a higher world (*Poim.*1). This narrator is evidently unfamiliar with the god who appears to him, for he must ask his name. The god's name is "Poimandres," who is also the god Hermes Trigmegistus. Having agreed to reveal the nature of reality to the narrator, Poimandres transforms himself into pure "Light" (φῶς), which is closely associated with the impersonal principle, the "Mind" (Νοῦς), which is also identical to the immaterial God. But Darkness (σκότος) is also present. It changes "into a kind of moist Nature" (εἰς ὑγρᾶν τινα φύσιν), or raw matter, from which the evil material world is formed (*Poim.* 4). Thus, Nature is opposed to Light, the former being described as "indescribably agitated" (ἀφάτως ταράσσω), "gloomy" (στυγνός), and "dreadful" (φοβερός) but the latter characterized as "serene" (εὔδιος) and happy (ἱλαρός, *Poim.* 4).

Divine "Light" (God) emanates the Logos (Λόγος), which is also the "Son of God" (υἱὸς θεοῦ, *Poim.* 6, cf. John 1:1–18) and the Son of the "Father" (who is also the "Mind," *Poim.* 6). In response to the Logos, Nature groans with an "inarticulate cry" (βοὴ ἀσυνάρθρως). Somehow the Logos enables Nature to release, or give birth to, the four elements: the first two of these elements, "Fire" (πῦρ) and "Air" (πνεῦμα), immediately ascend above the Logos and constitute a supra-lunar, material realm (*Poim.* 5). The remaining two elements, "Earth" (γῆ) and "Water" (ὕδωρ) – being too heavy to ascend – constitute a sub-lunar realm, being intermingled (συμμίγνυμι) until they are differentiated (*Poim.* 5, 11).

Next, Poimandres reveals that human beings share in both the heavenly Mind and the Logos. As such, they were originally not only closely associated with God, but actually in *union with* God (*Poim.* 16). By implication, the fall of humanity was the fall of God, and the salvation of humanity is an act of God saving God-self. Next, the narrator perceives Light becoming differentiated into "countless powers" (δύναμις ἀναρίθμητη, *Poim.* 7), each being an "archetypal form" (ἀρχέτυπον εἶδος) constituting the immaterial pattern of the material world (*Poim.* 8). The narrator also sees fire being subdued by a "great power" (δύναμις μεγίστος) (*Poim.* 7).

The "Will of God" (βουλὴ θεοῦ) – a feminine principle – sexually receives (λαμβάνει) the Logos (*Poim.* 22) and is thereby transformed into an active creator, bearing offspring. These offspring are probably the immaterial "souls" (ψυχαί) of human beings (*Poim.* 8). In contrast, the supreme God is hermaphroditic (i.e., both masculine and feminine) and sexually complete. The sexual union of masculine Logos with the feminine Will of God actually originates within God's very being (*Poim.* 24).

Following upon the emanation of the masculine Logos, God emanates the "Demiurge" (Δημιουργός, Poim. 9, cf. Heb. 11:10), who takes Fire and Air (which had previously ascended above the Logos) and fashions them into the seven "Governors" (διοικητεῖς), which is to say, the seven (known) planets, and places them in their spheres.[1] These planetary Governors encircle the material world and control it through their motion (*Poim.* 9, 11). The seven planets, being fixed at the boundary of the material world (which is the eighth sphere), also mark the beginning of the realm of God's immaterial world and the archetypal forms.

---

[1] I.e., the seven known planets: the moon, Mercury, Venus, the Sun, Mars, Jupiter, and Saturn.

It is the "government" (διοίκησις) of the earth by these Governors that constitutes human "Fate" (εἱμαρμένη). Moreover, their revolving motion "brings forth" (φέρει) a variety of "irrational" (ἄλογα) living beings (ζῷα), including birds, fish, and animals (*Poim.* 11, 37).

Notably, the text characterizes the Demiurge as "another Mind" (ἕτερος νοῦς) alongside God (Poim. 9). The Demiurge acts as the Mind of the material world, just as God acts as the Mind of the immaterial world. This Demiurge also functions as God's dutiful instrument on earth (*Poim.* 31). Following its birth, the Demiurge descends toward the material world and, in contrast to the Logos, subsists *under* Fire and Air. When the Demiurge descends, the Logos – owing to its "consubstantiality" with the Demiurge (*Poim.* 10) – "leaps up" (πηδᾷ) to unite with it (*Poim.* 10). Thus the Logos, which had been previously trapped, becomes freed through its attraction to the Demiurge (*Poim.* 33) and is now able to assist in creating the rest of the material world.

Next follows the creation of the "Primal Human" (Ἄνθρωπος, *Poim.* 12), who, being like God, is androgynous and sexually complete (*Poim.* 38). The Primal Human is created directly by God, not by the Demiurge. Like the Logos, the Primal Human is the "son of God" (υἱὸς θεοῦ) and is equal (ἴσος) to God in a way that the Demiurge is not (*Poim.* 12). At best, the Demiurge is the "brother" (ἀδελφός) of the Primal Human (Poim. 13) and "consubstantial" (ὁμοούσιος) with the Logos (*Poim.* 10). Thus, while God brought forth (ἀποκυέω) both the Demiurge and the Primal Human (*Poim.* 9), only the Primal Human "bears the image of the Father" (τὴν τοῦ πατρὸς εἴκονα ἔχων, *Poim.* 12, 40) and the "form" of God (μορφή), which is why God "loves" the Primal Human "as his own son" (ἠράσθη ὡς ἰδίου τόκου, *Poim.* 12, cf. Phil 2:1–16 [§4.14]). That which the Primal Human, Logos, and Demiurge have in common is that they are all (being emanations of God) inferior to God.

Next, God hands over (παραδίδωμι) all of creation to the Primal Human (*Poim.*13), who supplants the Demiurge. In order to take on this responsibility, the Primal Human must descend through several levels of the cosmos, beginning with the eighth sphere (the outer rim of the material world, where the Demiurge resides), through the remaining seven spheres (where the planets reside), finally arriving at the material world. When this happens, the seven Governors "fall in love" (ἔραμαι) with the Primal Human and, out of this love, grant the Primal Human a portion of their "position" (τάξις, *Poim.* 13). Having just "broken through" (ἀναρρήγνυμι) the "harmony" (ἁρμονία) of the spheres, the Primal Human "shows" (δείκνυμι) itself to Nature, who also falls in love with the Primal Human. We are told that Nature actually "smiles in love" (μειδιάω ἔρωτι), being attracted to Primal Human's "beauty" (κάλλος) and "power" (ἐνέργεια), as an expression of being attracted to "the beautiful form (μορφή) of God" (*Poim.* 14).

This brings us to the direct cause of the fall: the Primal Human "falls in love" (φιλῶ) with its own image. But it was incapable of fulfilling its own narcissism by having sexual intercourse *with itself*. But seeing its own beauty reflected in Nature, it decided to have sexual intercourse with Nature (*Poim.* 14). It is by virtue of this sexual union that the descendants of the Primal Human possess both a material "body" (σῶμα), which is "mortal" (θνητός), and an "essential" (οὐσιώδης) self, which is "immortal" (ἀθάνατος, *Poim.* 15). Thus, whereas these human bodies, being material, are subject to sexual desire and subject to Fate (ὑποκείμενος τῇ εἱμαρμένη),[2] their "essential" selves are beyond Fate and free of death, because they are "androgynous" (ἀρρενόθηλυς) and free of sexual desire (ἔρως) (*Poim.* 15). It is this "twofold" (διπλοῦς) nature of human beings that makes them "distinct from all (other) living beings on earth" (*Poim.* 15).[3]

After a period of time, the "bond" (σύνδεσμος) among all things "is loosened" and "all living beings," including human beings, become divided into males and females (*Poim.* 15). At this point, God orders all living creatures to "increase" (αὐξάνω, πληθύνω, *Poim.* 18), while at the same time (ironically) condemning the act of sexual intercourse (*Poim.* 18). Indeed, sexual intercourse is portrayed as both the cause and the consequence of mortality (*Poim.* 15). Human beings engage in sex because they are ignorant (*Poim.* 19–20), but when "thoughtful" (ἔννους), they "recognize" (ἀναγνωρίζω) that sexual intercourse is evil (*Poim.* 18–19, 21).

Conversely, human beings, being also immortal and divine through the Primal Human (*Poim.* 21, 26), possess the innate capacity to cultivate their unified-gender immateriality (*Poim.* 15) through sexual asceticism in life and then through separation from the body after death. By so doing, they gain the ability to actually reverse the fall of humanity in themselves (*Poim.* 24, cf. Acts Andr. 5–9 [§5.16]). The process of salvation of humanity consists of a kind of "stripping" (γυμνόω) off of the material somatic casings of human beings in order to liberate their *immaterial* selves (*Poim.* 26). Upon reaching the eighth sphere, which separates the immaterial from the material realm, these liberated human beings are transformed into one of the immaterial "beings" (τὸ ὄν), who praise God (*Poim.* 26). In essence, they become archetypal "powers" (δυνάμεις) of the primordial Light, and thus equal to God. Since human being are all descendants of the Primal Human, who originally emanated from God, this latter union is actually a *re*-union, a restoration of their former state, rendering the material world worthless.

---

[2] I.e., subject to the astrological determinism of the "harmony of the spheres" (*Poim.* 15).

[3] Thus between the Primal Human and its descendants is a significant gap. This may explain why the text speaks of a transitional stage of seven "post-primal" androgynes who reside on earth, corresponding to the seven Governors (*Poim.* 16–17).

A VISION OF POIMANDRES

The narrative begins with the awakened narrator's reflections on the nature of the world. Such reflections have been achieved by curbing the senses and rejecting the material world in favor of the immaterial world.

1 Ἐννοίας μοί ποτε γενομένης⁴ περὶ τῶν ὄντων καὶ μετεωρισθείσης⁵ μοι⁶ τῆς διανοίας σφόδρα, κατασχεθεισῶν⁷ μου τῶν σωματικῶν αἰσθήσεων, καθάπερ οἱ ὕπνῳ βεβαρημένοι ἐκ κόρου τροφῆς ἢ ἐκ κόπου σώματος, ἔδοξά τινα ὑπερμεγέθη μέτρῳ ἀπεριορίστῳ τυγχάνοντα καλεῖν μου τὸ ὄνομα καὶ λέγοντά μοι· Τί βούλει ἀκοῦσαι καὶ θεάσασθαι, καὶ νοήσας μαθεῖν καὶ γνῶναι; 2 Φημὶ ἐγώ· Σὺ γὰρ τίς εἶ; Ἐγὼ μέν, φησίν, εἰμὶ ὁ Ποιμάνδρης, ὁ τῆς αὐθεντίας νοῦς· οἶδα ὃ βούλει,⁸ καὶ σύνειμί σοι πανταχοῦ. 3 Φημὶ ἐγώ· Μαθεῖν θέλω τὰ ὄντα καὶ νοῆσαι τὴν τούτων φύσιν καὶ γνῶναι τὸν θεόν· τοῦτο, ἔφην, ἀκοῦσαι βούλομαι. Φησὶν ἐμοὶ πάλιν· Ἔχε νῷ σῷ ὅσα θέλεις μαθεῖν, κἀγώ σε διδάξω.

Vocabulary
ἀπεριόριστος, -ον, unlimited, infinite
αὐθεντίης, ὁ, master, absolute authority
βαρέω, pf. pass. ptc. βεβαρημένος: weigh down
κόρος, ὁ, one's fill of food; overeating
μετεωρίζω, to raise/soar to a height
μέτρον, τό, measure, size
σύνειμι (fr. εἰμί), 2. συνέσομαι, fut. inf. συνέσεσθαι: be with; join, catch up with
    somebody (dat.)
σωματικός, -ή, -όν, bodily, of the body
ὑπέρμεγας, -άλη, -α, immensely great/large

THE ABOVE AND THE BELOW

4 τοῦτο εἰπὼν ἠλλάγη⁹ τῇ ἰδέᾳ, καὶ εὐθέως πάντα μοι ἤνοικτο¹⁰ ῥοπῇ, καὶ ὁρῶ θέαν ἀόριστον, φῶς δὲ πάντα γεγενημένα, εὔδιόν τε καὶ ἱλαρόν, καὶ ἠράσθην ἰδών. καὶ μετ᾽ ὀλίγον σκότος κατωφερὲς ἦν, ἐν μέρει (of the light) γεγενημένον, φοβερόν τε καὶ στυγνόν, σκολιῶς ἐσπειραμένον, ὡς εἰκάσαι με· εἶτα μεταβαλλόμενον τὸ

---

⁴ Gen. absol.
⁵ Gen. absol.
⁶ Dat. of poss.
⁷ S.v. κατέχω, gen. absol.
⁸ βούλει > βούληι > βούλη.
⁹ S.v. ἀλλάσσω.
¹⁰ ἤνοικτο > ἤνοιγτο.

σκότος εἰς ὑγρὰν τινα φύσιν, ἀφάτως τεταραγμένην[11] καὶ καπνὸν ἀποδιδοῦσαν, ὡς ἀπὸ πυρός, καί τινα ἦχον ἀποτελοῦσαν ἀνεκλάλητον γοώδη· εἶτα βοὴ ἐξ αὐτῆς ἀσυνάρθρως ἐξεπέμπετο, ὡς εἰκάσαι φωνῇ πυρός.

Vocabulary
ἀνεκλάλητος, -ον, unutterable
ἀόριστος, -ον, limitless
ἀσυνάρθρως, inarticulately
ἀφάτος, -ον, unutterable; (adv.) ἀφάτως, indescribably
γοώδης, -ές, mournful
εὔδιος, -ον, clear, serene
θέα, ἡ, a vision (cf. *Poim.* 6)
ἱλαρός, -ον, joyful
καπνός, ὁ, smoke
κατωφερής, -ές, descending, downward (cf. *Poim.* 10–11, 14)
ῥοπή, ἡ, moment; (dat.), at once
σκολιός, -ά, -όν, curved, crooked, coiled; dishonest; σκολιῶς (adv.), coiling; σκολιόν, τό, intestine
στυγνός, -ή, -όν, gloomy, sullen (cf. *Poim.* 20)
ὑγρός, -ά, -όν, wet, moist; subst. liquid, the wet

5 ἐκ δὲ φωτός....λόγος ἅγιος ἐπέβη τῇ φύσει, καὶ πῦρ ἄκρατον ἐξεπήδησεν ἐκ τῆς ὑγρᾶς φύσεως ἄνω εἰς ὕψος· κοῦφον δὲ (the fire) ἦν καὶ ὀξύ, δραστικὸν δὲ ἅμα, καὶ ὁ ἀὴρ ἐλαφρὸς ὢν ἠκολούθησε τῷ πνεύματι, ἀναβαίνοντος[12] αὐτοῦ μέχρι τοῦ πυρὸς ἀπὸ γῆς καὶ ὕδατος, ὡς δοκεῖν κρέμασθαι αὐτὸν ἀπ᾽ αὐτοῦ· γῆ δὲ καὶ ὕδωρ ἔμενε καθ᾽ ἑαυτὰ συμμεμιγμένα, ὡς μὴ θεωρεῖσθαι τὴν γῆν (apart) ἀπὸ τοῦ ὕδατος· κινούμενα δὲ ἦν[13] διὰ τὸν ἐπιφερόμενον πνευματικὸν λόγον εἰς ἀκοήν. 6 ὁ δὲ Ποιμάνδρης ἐμοί· Ἐνόησας, φησί, τὴν θέαν ταύτην ὅ τι καὶ βούλεται; καί, Γνώσομαι, ἔφην ἐγώ. Τὸ φῶς ἐκεῖνο, ἔφη, ἐγὼ Νοῦς ὁ σὸς θεός, ὁ πρὸ φύσεως ὑγρᾶς τῆς ἐκ σκότους φανείσης. ὁ δὲ ἐκ Νοὸς φωτεινὸς Λόγος (is) υἱὸς θεοῦ. Τί οὖν; φημί. Οὕτω γνῶθι· τὸ ἐν σοὶ βλέπον καὶ ἀκοῦον, λόγος κυρίου, ὁ δὲ Νοῦς (is) πατὴρ θεός. οὐ γὰρ διΐστανται[14] ἀπ᾽ ἀλλήλων· ἕνωσις γὰρ τούτων ἐστὶν ἡ ζωή. Εὐχαριστῶ σοι, ἔφην ἐγώ. (And he replied) Ἀλλὰ δὴ νόει τὸ φῶς καὶ γνώριζε τοῦτο.

Vocabulary
ἄκρατος, -ον, pure
δραστικός, -ον, active

[11] S.v. ταράσσω.
[12] Gen. absol.
[13] Impf. periph.
[14] Cf. table 9.11.5(c).

ἐκπηδάω, leap out
ἐλαφρός, -ά, -όν, light (in weight)
πνευματικός, -ή, -όν, spiritual, spirit-like
ὕψος, -ους, τό, height
φωτεινός, -ή, -όν, shining, bright

7 εἰπόντος ταῦτα ἐπὶ πλείονα χρόνον ἀντώπησέ μοι, ὥστε με τρέμειν αὐτοῦ τὴν ἰδέαν· ἀνανεύσαντος δέ, θεωρῶ ἐν τῷ νοΐ μου τὸ φῶς (now was divided) ἐν δυνάμεσιν ἀναριθμήτοις ὄν, καὶ κόσμον ἀπεριόριστον γεγενημένον, καὶ περιίσχεσθαι[15] τὸ πῦρ δυνάμει μεγίστῃ, καὶ στάσιν ἐσχηκέναι[16] κρατούμενον· ταῦτα δὲ ἐγὼ διενοήθην ὁρῶν διὰ τὸν τοῦ Ποιμάνδρου λόγον. 8 ὡς δὲ ἐν ἐκπλήξει μου ὄντος,[17] φησὶ πάλιν ἐμοί· Εἶδες ἐν τῷ νῷ τὸ ἀρχέτυπον εἶδος, τὸ προάρχον τῆς ἀρχῆς τῆς ἀπεράντου·

Vocabulary
ἀνανεύω, raise one's head
ἀναρίθμητος, -ον, countless
ἀντωπέω (= ἀντοφθαλμέω), gaze at (dat.)
ἀπέραντος, -ον, infinite (cf. *Poim.* 11)
ἀπεριόριστος, -ον, limitless
ἀρχέτυπος, -ον, archetypal
διανοέω, have in mind; pass. understand
ἔκπληξις, ἡ, great astonishment
προάρχω, begin first
στάσις, -εως, ἡ, standing still; riot, rioting, uprising

THE FIRST EMANATION: THE DESCENT OF THE LOGOS

8 ταῦτα ὁ Ποιμάδρης (said) ἐμοι· Τὰ οὖν, ἐγώ φημι, στοιχεῖα τῆς φύσεως πόθεν ὑπέστη; Πάλιν ἐκεῖνος πρὸς ταῦτα· Ἐκ βουλῆς θεοῦ, ἥτις λαβοῦσα τὸν Λόγον καὶ ἰδοῦσα τὸν καλὸν (archtypal) κόσμον ἐμιμήσατο (it), κοσμοποιηθεῖσα διὰ τῶν ἑαυτῆς στοιχείων καὶ (out of her) γεννημάτων ψυχῶν. 9 ὁ δὲ Νοῦς ὁ θεός, ἀρρενόθηλυς ὤν, ζωὴν καὶ φῶς ὑπάρχων, ἀπεκύησε λόγῳ ἕτερον Νοῦν δημιουργόν, ὃς θεὸς τοῦ πυρὸς καὶ πνεύματος ὤν, ἐδημιούργησε διοικητάς τινας ἑπτά, ἐν κύκλοις περιέχοντας τὸν αἰσθητὸν κόσμον, καὶ ἡ διοίκησις αὐτῶν ἡ εἱμαρμένη[18] καλεῖται.

---

[15] S.v. περιέχω.
[16] S.v. ἔχω, here "to hold," "keep, "remain" in a certain way.
[17] Gen. absol.
[18] S.v. μείρομαι.

Vocabulary

αἰσθητός, -ή, -όν, perceptible, sensible

ἀποκυέω, bear young, bring forth

ἀρσενόθηλυς/ἀρρενόθηλυς, -εος, -υ, hermaphroditic, of both sexes

γέννημα, -ματος, το, offspring

δημιουγός, ὁ, builder; Creator, Demiurge

διοικητής, ἡ, administrator; financial administrator (Egypt); pl. (cosmic) Governors (i.e., the seven known planets: the moon, Mercury, Venus, Sun, Mars, Jupiter, Saturn)

διοίκησις, ἡ, administration, government

κοσμοποιέω, make a world

κύκλος, ὁ, circle; pl. heavenly bodies

μείρομαι, pf. pass. εἴμαρμαι, pf. fm. pass. ptc. εἱμαρμένος: be decreed by Fate; subst. ἡ εἱμαρμένη, Fate

μιμέομαι, imitate, copy

στοιχεῖον, τό, pl. components/elements into which matter is divisible

ὑφίστημι, [2]aor. ὑπέστην: come into existence

THE SECOND EMANATION: THE DEMIURGE

10 Ἐπήδησεν εὐθὺς ἐκ τῶν κατωφερῶν στοιχείων ὁ τοῦ θεοῦ Λόγος εἰς τὸ καθαρὸν (part) τῆς φύσεως δημιούργημα, καὶ ἡνώθη τῷ δημιουργῷ Νῷ (ὁμοούσιος γὰρ ἦν), καὶ κατελείφθη (behind) τὰ ἄλογα τὰ κατωφερῆ τῆς φύσεως στοιχεῖα, ὡς εἶναι ὕλην μόνην. 11 ὁ δὲ δημιουργὸς Νοῦς σὺν τῷ Λόγῳ, ὁ περιίσχων τοὺς κύκλους καὶ δινῶν ῥοίζῳ, ἔστρεψε τὰ ἑαυτοῦ δημιουργήματα καὶ εἴασε στρέφεσθαι ἀπ' ἀρχῆς ἀορίστου εἰς ἀπέραντον τέλος· ἄρχεται γάρ, οὗ λήγει· ἡ δὲ τούτων περιφορά, καθὼς ἠθέλησεν ὁ Νοῦς, ἐκ τῶν κατωφερῶν στοιχείων ζῷα ἤνεγκεν ἄλογα[19] (οὐ γὰρ ἐπεῖχε [to them] τὸν Λόγον), ἀὴρ δὲ πετεινὰ ἤνεγκε, καὶ τὸ ὕδωρ (ἤνεγκε) νηκτά· διακεχώρισται δὲ ἀπ' ἀλλήλων ἥ τε γῆ καὶ τὸ ὕδωρ, καθὼς ἠθέλησεν ὁ Νοῦς, καὶ ἡ γῆ ἐξήνεγκεν ἀπ' αὐτῆς ἃ εἶχε ζῷα τετράποδα καὶ ἑρπετά, θηρία ἄγρια καὶ ἥμερα.

Vocabulary

ἄγριος, -α, -ον, wild

δημιούργημα, -ματος, τό, piece of workmanship, creature

διαχωρίζω ἀπό, separate from

δινόω, spin something

ἑνόω, make one, unite with (dat.)

---

[19] ζῷα...ἄλογα.

ἥμερος, -ον, tame
κατωφερής, -ές, hanging down (cf. *Poim.* 11, 14)
λήγω, cease, end
νηκτός, -ή, -όν, swimming; subst. fish
ὁμοούσιος, -ον, consubstantial, co-essential
περιφορά, ἡ, revolution
πηδάω, leap
ῥοίζος, ὁ, whistling sound, whirl
τετράπουν, τό, quadruped

THE THIRD EMANATION: THE DESCENT OF THE PRIMAL HUMAN

12 Ὁ δὲ πάντων πατὴρ ὁ Νοῦς, ὢν ζωὴ καὶ φῶς, ἀπεκύησεν Ἄνθρωπον[20] αὐτῷ
ἴσον, οὗ ἠράσθη ὡς ἰδίου τόκου· περικαλλὴς γάρ, τὴν τοῦ πατρὸς εἰκόνα ἔχων·
ὄντως γὰρ καὶ ὁ θεὸς ἠράσθη τῆς ἰδίας μορφῆς, παρέδωκε τὰ ἑαυτοῦ πάντα
δημιουργήματα, 13 καὶ κατανοήσας δὲ τὴν τοῦ Δημιουργοῦ κτίσιν ἐν τῷ πυρί,
ἠβουλήθη καὶ αὐτὸς δημιουργεῖν, καὶ συνεχωρήθη ἀπὸ τοῦ πατρός· γενόμενος
ἐν τῇ δημιουργικῇ σφαίρᾳ, ἔξων[21] τὴν πᾶσαν ἐξουσίαν, κατενόησε τοῦ ἀδελφοῦ
τὰ δημιουργήματα, οἱ (Governors) δὲ ἠράσθησαν αὐτοῦ, ἕκαστος δὲ μετεδίδου
τῆς ἰδίας τάξεως· καὶ καταμαθὼν τὴν τούτων οὐσίαν καὶ μεταλαβὼν τῆς αὐτῶν
φύσεως ἠβουλήθη ἀναρρῆξαι τὴν περιφέρειαν τῶν κύκλων, καὶ τὸ κράτος τοῦ
ἐπικειμένου ἐπὶ πυρὸς κατανοῆσαι.

Vocabulary
ἀναρρήγνυμι, break through (cf. *Poim.* 14)
δημιουργικός, -ή, -όν, of the Demiurge, Demiurgical
ἐράω (act. only in pres. and impf.), pres. ptc. ἐρώμενος, 6. ἠράσθην: be in love with
    (+ gen.), fall in love; subst. pass. ptc. an object of love, a lover
καταμανθάνω, learn well, master
κράτος, -ους, τό, power; κατὰ κράτος, powerfully, mightily
μεταλαμβάνω, receive a share of something
περικαλλής, -ές, very beautiful
περιφέρεια, ἡ, curved boundary
συγχωρέω > συνχωρέω, 6. συνεχωρήθην: allow, grant consent
σφαίρα, ἡ, sphere, realm

---

[20] Here and below, the "Primal Human."
[21] S.v. ἔχω.

14 καὶ ὁ τοῦ τῶν θνητῶν κόσμου καὶ τῶν ἀλόγων ζῴων ἔχον πᾶσαν ἐξουσίαν διὰ τῆς ἁρμονίας (of the spheres) παρέκυψεν, ἀναρρήξας (already) τὸ κύτος, καὶ ἔδειξε τῇ κατωφερεῖ φύσει τὴν καλὴν τοῦ θεοῦ μορφήν, ὃν ἰδοῦσα ἀκόρεστον κάλλος καὶ πᾶσαν ἐνέργειαν ἐν ἑαυτῷ ἔχοντα τῶν (all seven) διοικητόρων τήν τε μορφὴν τοῦ θεοῦ ἐμειδίασεν ἔρωτι, ὡς ἅτε τῆς καλλίστης μορφῆς τοῦ Ἀνθρώπου τὸ εἶδος ἐν τῷ ὕδατι ἰδοῦσα καὶ τὸ σκίασμα ἐπὶ τῆς γῆς. ὁ δὲ ἰδὼν (in turn) τὴν ὁμοίαν αὐτῷ μορφὴν ἐν αὐτῇ οὖσαν ἐν τῷ ὕδατι, ἐφίλησε καὶ ἠβουλήθη αὐτοῦ οἰκεῖν· ἅμα δὲ τῇ βουλῇ ἐγένετο ἐνέργεια, καὶ ᾤκησε τὴν ἄλογον μορφήν· ἡ δὲ φύσις λαβοῦσα τὸν ἐρώμενον περιεπλάκη[22] ὅλη καὶ ἐμίγησαν·[23] ἐρώμενοι γὰρ ἦσαν. 15 καὶ διὰ τοῦτο (distinct) παρὰ πάντα (other) τὰ ἐπὶ γῆς ζῷα διπλοῦς ἐστιν ὁ ἄνθρωπος, θνητὸς μὲν διὰ τὸ σῶμα, ἀθάνατος δὲ διὰ τὸν οὐσιώδη ἄνθρωπον· ἀθάνατος γὰρ ὢν καὶ πάντων τὴν ἐξουσία ἔχων, τὰ θνητὰ πάσχει ὑποκείμενος τῇ εἱμαρμένῃ. ὑπεράνω οὖν ὢν τῆς ἁρμονίας (of the spheres) ἐναρμόνιος γέγονε δοῦλος. ἀρρενόθηλυς δὲ ὢν, ἐξ ἀρρενοθήλεος ὢν πατρὸς καὶ ἄϋπνος ἀπὸ ἀΰπνου (father)…κρατεῖται.

Vocabulary
ἀκόρεστος, -ον, insatiable
ἁρμονία, ἡ, harmony; framework of the universe, harmony of the seven Governors
αὔξησις, -εως, ἡ, growth, increase
ἄϋπνος, -ον, sleepless
διπλόος (contr. διπλοῦς), -η, -ον, twofold
ἐναρμόνιος, -ον, in harmony with
ἐνέργεια, ἡ, activity, (divine) action, force/energy
κύτος, -εος, τό, the starry vault of heaven
μειδιάω, to smile
οἰκέω, live with (gen.), inhabit/dwell in (acc.)
οὐσιώδης, -ες, essential
σκίασμα, -ματος, τό, shadow
ὑπεράνω (+ gen.), above

THE FIRST HUMAN BEINGS

16 Καὶ μετὰ ταῦτα· (I said) Νοῦς ὁ ἐμός· καὶ αὐτὸς γὰρ ἐρῶ τοῦ (your) λόγου.[24] ὁ δὲ Ποιμάνδρης εἶπε· Τοῦτό ἐστι τὸ κεκρυμμένον[25] μυστήριον μέχρι τῆσδε τῆς

---

[22] S.v. περιπλέκω.
[23] ἐμίγησαν > ἐμίχθησαν, s.v. μείγνημι.
[24] λόγος, here "discourse."
[25] S.v. κρύπτω.

ἡμέρας. ἡ γὰρ φύσις ἐπιμιγεῖσα τῷ Ἀνθρώπῳ ἤνεγκέ τι θαῦμα θαυμασιώματον·
ἔχοντος γὰρ αὐτοῦ τῆς ἁρμονίας τῶν ἑπτὰ (Governors) τὴν φύσιν,[26] οὓς ἔφην σοι
(are made) ἐκ πυρὸς καὶ πνεύματος, οὐκ ἀνέμενεν ἡ φύσις, ἀλλ᾽ εὐθὺς ἀπεκύησεν
ἑπτα ἀνθρώπους,[27] (corresponding) πρὸς τὰς φύσεις τῶν ἑπτὰ διοικητόρων,[28]
ἀρρενοθήλεας καὶ μεταρσίους. καὶ μετὰ ταῦτα (I said)· Ω Ποιμάνδρη, εἰς μεγάλην
γὰρ νῦν ἐπιθυμίαν ἦλθον καὶ ποθῶ ἀκοῦσαι· μὴ ἔκτρεχε. Καὶ ὁ Ποιμάνδρης
εἶπεν· Ἀλλὰ σιώπα. οὔπω γάρ σοι ἀνήπλωσα τὸν πρῶτον λόγον.[29] Ἰδοὺ σιωπῶ,
ἔφη ἐγώ.

Vocabulary
ἀναμένω, to delay
ἀναπλόω, explain, unravel
ἐκτρέχω, run away
ἐπιμ(ε)ίγνυμι, pass. have sexual intercourse with
μετάρσιος, -α, -ον, raised in the air
ποθέω, long for, have a great desire to do something

17 Ἐγένετο οὖν, ὡς ἔφην, τῶν ἑπτὰ τούτων ἡ γένεσις τοιῷδε τρόπῳ· Θηλυκὴ
γὰρ γῆ ἦν καὶ ὕδωρ ὀχευτικόν, τὸ δὲ ἐκ πυρὸς (ἡ φύσις ἐξήνεγκεν) πέπειρον.
ἐκ δὲ αἰθέρος τὸ πνεῦμα ἔλαβε καὶ ἐξήνεγκεν ἡ φύσις τὰ σώματα πρὸς τὸ εἶδος
τοῦ Ἀνθρώπου. ὁ δὲ Ἄνθρωπος ἐκ ζωῆς καὶ φωτὸς ἐγένετο εἰς ψυχὴν καὶ νοῦν,
ἐκ μὲν ζωῆς ψυχήν, ἐκ δὲ φωτὸς νοῦν, καὶ ἔμεινεν οὕτω τὰ πάντα τοῦ αἰσθητοῦ
κόσμου μέχρι περιόδου τέλους καὶ ἀρχῶν γενῶν. 18 (Poimandres) Ἄκουε λοιπόν
(point), ὃν ποθεῖς λόγον ἀκοῦσαι. τῆς περιόδου πεπληρωμένης[30] ἐλύθη ὁ πάντων
σύνδεσμος ἐκ[31] βουλῆς θεοῦ· πάντα γὰρ ζῷα ἀρρενοθήλεα ὄντα διελύετο ἅμα
τῷ ἀνθρώπῳ[32] καὶ ἐγένετο τὰ μὲν[33] ἀρρενικὰ ἐν μέρει, τὰ δὲ θηλυκὰ (ἐγένετο)
ὁμοίως. ὁ δὲ θεὸς εὐθὺς εἶπεν ἁγίῳ λόγῳ· Αὐξάνεσθε ἐν αὐξήσει καὶ πληθύνεσθε
ἐν πλήθει πάντα τὰ κτίσματα[34] καὶ δημιουργήματα, καὶ ἀναγνωρισάτω ὁ ἔννους
ἑαυτὸν ὄντα ἀθάνατον, καὶ (ὅτι) τὸν αἴτιον τοῦ θανάτου ἔρωτα, καὶ πάντα
τὰ ὄντα. 19 τοῦτο εἰπόντος, ἡ πρόνοια διὰ τῆς εἱμαρμένης καὶ ἁρμονίας (of
the spheres) τὰς μίξεις ἐποιήσαντο, καὶ τὰς γενέσεις κατέστησε, καὶ ἐπληθύνθη
κατὰ γένος τὰ πάντα καὶ ὁ ἀναγνωρίσας ἑαυτὸν ἐλήλυθεν εἰς τὸ περιούσιον

---

[26] τῆς ἁρμονίας...τὴν φύσιν (= τὴν φύσιν τῆς ἁρμονίας).
[27] Here the term ἄνθρωποι refers to "human beings" as transitional figures between the Primal Human
and earthly human beings.
[28] διοικήτωρ = διοικητής.
[29] λόγος, "discourse."
[30] Gen. absol.
[31] ἐκ, "by."
[32] Dat. of time.
[33] μέν...δέ....
[34] κτίσμα = κτίσις.

ἀγαθόν, ὁ δὲ ἀγαπήσας τὸ ἐκ³⁵ πλάνης ἔρωτος σῶμα, οὗτος μένει ἐν τῷ σκότει πλανώμενος, αἰσθητῶς πάσχων τὰ τοῦ θανάτου.

Vocabulary

αἰθήρ, -έρος, ὁ/ἡ, ether, upper air (as opposed to lower air), the divine element in the human soul; Αἰθήρ, personified ether

αἰσθητῶς, through the (physical) senses

ἀρρενικός, -ή, -όν, of masculine gender ἔννοος (contr. ἔννους, -ον), thoughtful (cf. *Poim.* 21)

διαλύω; dissolve into elements; break up, separate

θηλυκός, -ή, -όν, female, woman-like, of feminine gender

μίξις, -εως, ἡ, coupling, esp. sexual intercourse

ὀχευτικός, -ή, -όν, filled with sexual desire

πέπειρος, -ον, ripe; subst. ripeness

περίοδος, ἡ, period (cf. *Poim.* 18)

περιούσιος, -ον, overabundant

σύνδεσμος, ὁ, (irreg.), pl. σύνδεσμα, bond, anything for tying and fastening things together]] (+ gen.)

τοιόσδε, τοιάδε, τοιόνδε, such as this, such

THE WAY OF DEATHLESSNESS

20 Τί τοσοῦτον ἁμαρτάνουσιν, ἔφην ἐγώ, οἱ ἀγνοοῦντες, ἵνα στερηθῶσι τῆς ἀθανασίας; (And Poimandres replied) Ἔοικας, ὦ οὗτος,³⁶ τούτων μὴ πεφροντικέναι ὧν ἤκουσας. οὐκ ἔφην σοι νοεῖν; (And I, the narrator, replied) Νοῶ καὶ μιμνήσκομαι, εὐχαριστῶ δὲ ἅμα. (And Poimandres replied) Εἰ ἐνόησας, εἰπέ μοι, διὰ τί ἄξιοί εἰσι τοῦ θανάτου οἱ ἐν τῷ θανάτῳ ὄντες; (I replied) Ὅτι προκατάρχεται τοῦ οἰκείου σώματος τὸ στυγνὸν σκότος, ἐξ οὗ (came) ἡ ὑγρὰ φύσις, ἐξ ἧς τὸ σῶμα συνέστηκεν ἐν τῷ αἰσθητῷ κόσμῳ, ἐξ οὗ θάνατος ἀρδεύεται.

21 (Poimandres replied) Ἐνόησας ὀρθῶς, ὦ οὗτος. κατὰ τί δὲ Ὁ νοήσας ἑαυτὸν εἰς αὐτὸν χωρεῖ, (which is) ὅπερ³⁷ ἔχει ὁ τοῦ θεοῦ λόγος; φημὶ ἐγώ· Ὅτι ἐκ φωτὸς καὶ ζωῆς συνέστηκεν ὁ πατὴρ τῶν ὅλων,³⁸ ἐξ οὗ γέγονεν ὁ Ἄνθρωπος. (Poimandres) Εὖ φῂς λαλῶν· φῶς καὶ ζωή ἐστιν ὁ θεὸς καὶ πατήρ, ἐξ οὗ ἐγένετο ὁ Ἄνθρωπος. ἐὰν οὖν μάθῃς αὐτὸν³⁹ (composed) ἐκ ζωῆς καὶ φωτὸς ὄντα καὶ

---

³⁵ ἐκ, "through."
³⁶ ὦ οὗτος, "O you, yourself" (cf. *Poim.* 21–22).
³⁷ S.v. ὅσπερ.
³⁸ τὰ ὅλα, "universals."
³⁹ I.e., the Primal Human.

ὅτι ἐκ τούτων τυγχάνεις, εἰς ζωὴν πάλιν χωρήσεις. ταῦτα ὁ Ποιμάνδρης εἶπεν. (And I said) Ἀλλ᾽ ἔτι μοι εἰπέ, πῶς εἰς ζωὴν χωρήσω ἐγώ, ἔφην, ὦ Νοῦς ἐμός; φησὶ γὰρ ὁ θεός· Ὁ ἔννους ἄνθρωπος ἀναγνωρισάτω ἑαυτόν. 22 (And I replied) Οὐ πάντες γὰρ ἄνθρωποι νοῦν ἔχουσιν; (Poimandres:) Εὐφήμει, ὦ οὗτος, λαλῶν· παραγίνομαι αὐτὸς ἐγὼ ὁ Νοῦς τοῖς ὁσίοις καὶ ἀγαθοῖς καὶ καθαροῖς καὶ ἐλεήμοσι, τοῖς εὐσεβοῦσι, καὶ ἡ παρουσία μου γίνεται βοήθεια (to them), καὶ εὐθὺς τὰ πάντα γνωρίζουσι καὶ τὸν πατέρα ἱλάσκονται ἀγαπητικῶς καὶ εὐχαριστοῦσιν εὐλογοῦντες καὶ ὑμνοῦντες τεταγμένως πρὸς αὐτὸν τῇ στοργῇ, καὶ πρὸ τοῦ παραδοῦναι[40] τὸ σῶμα ἰδίῳ θανάτῳ μυσάττονται τὰς αἰσθήσεις, εἰδότες αὐτῶν τὰ ἐνεργήματα· μᾶλλον δὲ οὐκ ἐάσω αὐτὸς ὁ Νοῦς τὰ προσπίπτοντα ἐνεργήματα τοῦ σώματος ἐκτελεσθῆναι. (ὁ) πυλωρὸς ὢν ἀποκλείσω (all) τὰς εἰσόδους τῶν κακῶν καὶ αἰσχρῶν ἐνεργημάτων, τὰς ἐνθυμήσεις ἐκκόπτων.[41]

Vocabulary

αἰσχρός, -ά, -όν, shameful, base ἀγαπητικός, -ή, -όν, affection; (adv.) μυσάττομαι, loathe

ἀγαπητικῶς, affectionately

ἀθανασία, ἡ, immortality

ἀποκλείω, shut, close

ἀρδεύω (= ἄρδω), to water; pass. be watered

ἐκκόπτω, cut off/out

ἐκτελέω, accomplish, achieve; pass. be accomplished, reach an end

ἐνέργημα, -ματος, τό, effect

ἐνθύμησις, -εως, ἡ, imagination

εὐφημέω, observe a religious silence; impv. "hush!" "be still!"

ἱλάσκομαι, appease, conciliate

προκατάρχω, begin, cause; pass. be prior to, be the root cause of (gen.)

πυλωρός, ὁ, gatekeeper

στερέω, deprive of something

στοργή, ἡ, love

τεταγμένως, regularly

ὑμνέω, sing hymns, celebrate in a hymn

23 τοῖς δὲ ἀνοήτοις καὶ κακοῖς καὶ πονηροῖς καὶ φθονεροῖς καὶ πλεονέκταις καὶ φονεῦσι καὶ ἀσεβέσι πόρρωθέν εἰμι, τῷ τιμωρῷ ἐκχωρήσας δαίμονι,[42] ὅστις τὴν ὀξύτητα τοῦ πυρὸς προσβάλλων θρῴσκει αὐτὸν αἰσθητικῶς καὶ μᾶλλον ἐπὶ τὰς ἀνομίας αὐτὸν ὁπλίζει, ἵνα τύχῃ[43] πλείονος τιμωρίας, καὶ οὐ παύεται ἐπ᾽ ὀρέξεις

---

[40] Art. inf.
[41] Instr. adv. ptc. ("by," IV, 1.6).
[42] τῷ τιμωρῷ...δαίμονι.
[43] S.v. τυγχάνω.

ἀπλέτους τὴν ἐπιθυμίαν ἔχων, ἀκορέστως σκοτομαχῶν, καὶ τοῦτον βασανίζει (him), καὶ ἐπ᾽ αὐτὸν πῦρ ἐπὶ τὸ πλεῖον αὐξάνει.

Vocabulary
αἰσθητικῶς, through the senses
ἀκόρεστος, -ον, insatiate; (adv.) ἀκορέστως, insatiably
ἀνόητος, -ον, lacking understanding, foolish
ἄπλετος, -ον, immense, inordinate
ἐκχωρέω, give up a place to, give way to
θρώσκω, leap upon, attack
ὀξύτης, -ητος, ἡ, sharpness προσβάλλω, sharpen
πλεονέκτης, -ες, greedy, grasping
πόρρωθεν, Att. > πρόσωθεν, from afar
σκοτομαχέω, fight in the darkness
τιμωρός, -όν, avenging
ὁπλίζω, prepare somebody for (ἐπί)
ὀρέξις, -εως, ἡ, craving
φθονερός, -ά, -όν, envious

THE ASCENT OF THE SOUL TO THE EIGHTH SPHERE

24 (I said) Εὖ μοι πάντα, ὡς ἐβουλόμην, ἐδίδαξας, ὦ Νοῦς, ἔτι δέ μοι εἰπὲ περὶ τῆς ἀνόδου τῆς γινομένης. πρὸς ταῦτα ὁ Ποιμάνδρης εἶπε· Πρῶτον μὲν ἐν τῇ ἀναλύσει τοῦ σώματος τοῦ ὑλικοῦ παραδίδως αὐτὸ τὸ σῶμα εἰς ἀλλοίωσιν, καὶ τὸ εἶδος ὃ εἶχες ἀφανὲς γίνεται, καὶ τὸ ἦθος τῷ δαίμονι ἀνενέργητον παραδίδως, καὶ αἱ αἰσθήσεις τοῦ σώματος εἰς τὰς ἑαυτῶν πηγὰς ἐπανέρχονται, μέρη (of them) γινόμεναι καὶ πάλιν συνανιστάμεναι εἰς τὰς ἐνεργείας. καὶ ὁ θυμὸς καὶ ἡ ἐπιθυμία εἰς τὴν ἄλογον φύσιν χωρεῖ.

Vocabulary
ἀλλοίωσις, -εως, ἡ, alteration, change
ἀνάλυσις, -εως, ἡ, dissolving (into elements)
ἀνενέργητος, -ον, inactive
ἄνοδος, ἡ, the way up, ascent (of the soul)
ἀφανής, -ές, invisible
ἐπανέρχομαι, to return
ἦθος, -ους, τό, customs and manners, way of life
συνανίστημι, to make rise together; pass. rise at the same time
ὑλικός, -ή, -όν, belonging to matter, material

25 καὶ οὕτως ὁρμᾷ λοιπὸν ἄνω (ὁ ἄνθρωπος) διὰ τῆς ἁρμονίας, καὶ τῇ πρώτῃ ζώνῃ δίδωσι (up) τὴν αὐξητικὴν ἐνέργειαν καὶ τὴν μειωτικὴν (ἐνέργειαν), καὶ τῇ δευτέρᾳ (ζώνῃ δίδωσι) τὴν μηχανὴν τῶν κακῶν, δόλον (now) ἀνενέργητον,

καὶ τῇ τρίτῃ (ζώνῃ δίδωσι) τὴν ἐπιθυμητικὴν ἀπάτην (now) ἀνενέργητον, καὶ τῇ τετάρτῃ (ζώνῃ δίδωσι) τὴν ἀρχοντικὴν προφανίαν (now) ἀπλεονέκτητον, καὶ τῇ πέμπτῃ (ζώνῃ δίδωσι) τὸ θράσος τὸ ἀνόσιον καὶ τῆς τόλμης τὴν προπέτειαν (ἀνενέργητον), καὶ τῇ ἕκτῃ (ζώνῃ δίδωσι) τὰς ἀφορμὰς τὰς κακὰς τοῦ πλούτου (now) ἀνενεργήτους, καὶ τῇ ἑβδόμῃ ζώνῃ (δίδωσι) τὸ ἐνεδρεῦον ψεῦδος (ἀνενέργητον).

Vocabulary
ἀνενέργητος, -ον, inactive, powerless
ἀνόσιος, -ον, unholy, profane προπέτεια, ἡ, rashness, haste
ἀπλεονέκτητος, -ον, free of avarice
ἀρχοντικός, -ή, -όν, domineering
αὐξητικός, -ή, -όν, of growth
ἀφορμή, ἡ, starting point; occasion, pretext
ἐνεδρεῦω, ensnare, obstruct
ἐπιθυμητικός, -ή, -όν, lustful
ζώνη, ἡ, belt, zone (e.g., of the terrestrial sphere, of the planetary spheres)
θράσος, -ους, τό, arrogance
μειωτικός, -ή, -όν, diminishing, decrease
μηχανή, ἡ, machine, a device
ὁρμάω, to rush
προφανεία, ἡ, pride
τόλμα/τόλμη, ἡ, audacity, recklessness

26 καὶ τότε γυμνωθεὶς ἀπὸ τῶν τῆς ἁρμονίας ἐνεργημάτων γίνεται ἐπὶ τὴν ὀγδοατικὴν φύσιν,[44] τὴν ἰδίαν δύναμιν ἔχων, καὶ ὑμνεῖ σὺν τοῖς οὖσι τὸν πατέρα· συγχαίρουσι δὲ οἱ παρόντες τῇ τούτου (person's) παρουσίᾳ, καὶ ὁμοιωθεὶς τοῖς συνοῦσιν ἀκούει καί τινων δυνάμεων ὑπὲρ τὴν ὀγδοατικὴν φύσιν[45] φωνῇ τινι ἡδείᾳ[46] ὑμνουσῶν τὸν θεόν· καὶ τότε τάξει ἀνέρχονται πρὸς τὸν πατέρα, καὶ αὐτοὶ εἰς δυνάμεις ἑαυτοὺς παραδιδόασι, καὶ δυνάμεις γενόμενοι ἐν θεῷ γίνονται.[47] τοῦτό ἐστι τὸ ἀγαθὸν τέλος τοῖς γνῶσιν ἐσχηκόσι,[48] θεωθῆναι. λοιπόν, τί μέλλεις;[49] οὐχ ὡς πάντα παραλαβὼν καθοδηγὸς γίνῃ τοῖς ἀξίοις, ὅπως τὸ γένος τῆς ἀνθρωπότητος διὰ σοῦ ὑπὸ θεοῦ σωθῇ;

Vocabulary
ἀνθρωπότης, -ητος, ἡ, humanity, human race
γυμνόω, strip somebody naked

---

[44] I.e., zone.
[45] I.e., zone.
[46] S.v. ἡδύς.
[47] Perhaps "enter into (ἐν)."
[48] S.v. ἔχω.
[49] μέλλω w/o inf., "to delay," "wait."

θεόω, make into god, deify
καθοδηγός, ὁ, guide
ὀγδοατικός, -ή, -όν, eighth
συγχαίρω, rejoice with/at

SELECT BIBLIOGRAPHY

Barnstone, Willis. *Essential Gnostic Scriptures*. Boston: Shambhala, 2010.

Copenhaver, Brian P. *Hermetica: The Greek Corpus Hermeticum and the Latin Asclepius in a New Translation*. Cambridge: Cambridge University Press, 1992.

Scott, Walter (ed. and trans.). *Hermetica: The Ancient Greek and Latin*, 4 vols. Boulder, CO: Hermes House, 1982–1985.

Segal, Robert A. *The Poimandres Myth: Scholarly Theory and Gnostic Meaning*. Berlin: W. de Gruyter, 1986.

PART 9

Summary of Verbal Paradigms

CONTENTS

9.1 THEMATIC Ω-VERBS: ACTIVE INDICATIVE

Pres.   *Impf.*   *Fut.*   *1 Aor.*   *Perf.*   *Plpf*

9.1.1 Indicative

(a)	(b)	(c)	(d)	(e)	(f)
λύω	ἔλυον	λύσω	ἔλυσα	λέλυκα	(ἐ)λελύκειν
λύεις	ἔλυες	λύσεις	ἔλυσας	λέλυκας	(ἐ)λελύκεις
λύει	ἔλυε(ν)	λύσει	ἔλυσε(ν)	λέλυκε(ν)	(ἐ)λελύκει
λύομεν	ἐλύομεν	λύσομεν	ἐλύσαμεν	λελύκαμεν	(ἐ)λελύκειμεν
λύετε	ἐλύετε	λύσετε	ἐλύσατε	λελύκατε	(ἐ)λελύκειτε
λύουσι(ν)	ἔλυον	λύσουσι(ν)	ἔλυσαν	λελύκασι(ν)	(ἐ)λελύκεισαν

9.1.2 Subjunctive

(a)	(b)
λύω	λύσω
λύῃς	λύσῃς
λύῃ	λύσῃ
λύωμεν	λύσωμεν
λύητε	λύσητε
λύωσι(ν)	λύσωσι(ν)

9.1.3 Optative

(a)	(b)
λύοιμι	λύσαιμι
λύοις	λύσαις or -ειας
λύοι	λύσαι or -ειε(ν)
λύοιμεν	λύσαιμεν
λύοιτε	λύσαιτε
λύοιεν	λύσαιεν or -ειαν

9.1.4 Imperative

(a)	(b)
λῦε	λῦσον
λυέτω	λυσάτω
λύετε	λύσατε
λυέτωσαν, or -όντων	λυσάτωσαν or -σάντων

| Pres. | Fut. | 1 Aor. | Perf. |

9.1.5 Infinitive

(a)	(b)	(c)	(d)
λύειν	λύσειν	λῦσαι	λελυκέναι

9.1.6 Participle

(a)	(b)	(c)	(d)
λύων[1]	λύσων[2]	λύσας[3]	λελυκώς[4]
λύοντος	λύσοντος	λύσαντος	λελυκότος
λύοντι	λύσοντι	λυσαντι	λελυκότι
λύοντα	λύσοντα	λύσαντα	λελυκότα
λύοντες	λύσοντες	λύσαντες	λελυκότες
λυόντων	λυσόντων	λυσάντων	λελυκότων
λύουσι(ν)	λύσουσι(ν)	λύσασι(ν)	λελυκόσι(ν)
λύοντας	λύσοντας	λύσαντας	λελυκότας

9.2 THEMATIC Ω-VERBS: MIDDLE INDICATIVE

| Pres. | Impf. | Fut. | 1 Aor. | Perf. | Plpf |

9.2.1 Indicative

(a)	(b)	(c)	(d)	(e)	(f)
λύομαι	ἐλυόμην	λύσομαι	ἐλυσάμην	λέλυμαι	(ἐ)λελύμην
λύῃ	ἐλύου	λύσῃ	ἐλύσω	λέλυσαι	(ἐ)λέλυσο
λύεται	ἐλύετο	λύσεται	ἐλύσατο	λέλυται	(ἐ)λέλυτο
λυόμεθα	ἐλυόμεθα	λυσόμεθα	ἐλυσάμεθα	λελύμεθα	(ἐ)λελύμεθα
λύεσθε	ἐλύεσθε	λύσεσθε	ἐλύσασθε	λέλυσθε	(ἐ)λέλυσθε
λύονται	ἐλύοντο	λύσονται	ἐλύσαντο	λέλυνται	(ἐ)λέλυντο

---

[1] λύων, λύουσα, λύον.
[2] λύσων, λύσουσα, λύσον.
[3] λύσας, λύσασα, λῦσαν.
[4] λελυκώς, λελυκυῖα, λελυκός.

9.2.2 Subjunctive

(a)   (b)
λύωμαι   λύσωμαι
λύῃ   λύσῃ
λύηται   λύσηται

λυώμεθα   λυσώμεθα
λύησθε   λύσησθε
λύωνται   λύσωνται

9.2.3 Optative

(a)   (b)
λυοίμην   λυσαίμην
λύοιο   λύσαιο
λύοιτο   λύσαιτο
λυοίμεθα   λυσαίμεθα
λύοισθε   λύσαισθε
λύοιντο   λύσαιντο

Pres.   *Fut.*   *1 Aor.*   *Perf.*

9.2.4 Imperative

(a)   (b)
λύου   λῦσαι
λυέσθω   λυσάσθω
λύεσθε   λύσασθε
λυέσθωσαν, or -έσθων   λυσάσθωσαν or –σάσθων

9.2.5 Infinitive

(a)   (b)   (c)   (d)
λύεσθαι   λύσεσθαι   λύσασθαι   λελύσθαι

9.2.6 Participle

(a)   (b)   (c)   (d)
λυόμενος[5]   λυσόμενος[6]   λυσάμενος[7]   λελυμένος[8]

---

[5] λυόμενος, λυομένη, λυόμενον.
[6] λυσόμενος, λυσομένη, λυσόμενον.
[7] λυσάμενος, λυσαμένη, λυσάμενον.
[8] λελυμένος, λελυμένη, λελυμένον.

λυομένου	λυσομένου	λυσαμένου	λελυμένου
λυομένῳ	λυσομένῳ	λυσαμένῳ	λελυμένῳ
λυόμενον	λυσόμενον	λυσάμενον	λελυμένον

λυόμενοι	λυσόμενοι	λυσάμενοι	λελυμένοι
λυομένων	λυσομένων	λυσαμένων	λελυμένων
λυομένοις	λυσομένοις	λυσαμένοις	λελυμένοις
λυομένους	λυσομένους	λυσαμένους	λελυμένους

9.3 THEMATIC ω-VERBS: PASSIVE INDICATIVE

Pres.   *Impf.*   *Fut.*   *1 Aor. Perf.   Plpf*

9.3.1 Indicative

(a)	(b)	(c)	(d)	(e)	(f)
λύομαι	ἐλυόμην	λυθήσομαι	ἐλύθην	λέλυμαι	(ἐ)λελύμην
λύῃ	ἐλύου	λυθήσῃ	ἐλύθης	λέλυσαι	(ἐ)λέλυσο
λύεται	ἐλύετο	λυθήσεται	ἐλύθη	λέλυται	(ἐ)λέλυτο

λυόμεθα	ἐλυόμεθα	λυθησόμεθα	ἐλύθημεν	λελύμεθα	(ἐ)λελύμεθα
λύεσθε	ἐλύεσθε	λυθήσεσθε	ἐλύθητε	λέλυσθε	(ἐ)λέλυσθε
λύονται	ἐλύοντο	λυθήσονται	ἐλύθησαν	λέλυνται	(ἐ)λέλυντο

9.3.2 Subjunctive

(a)	(b)
λύωμαι	λυθῶ
λύῃ	λυθῇς
λύηται	λυθῇ

λυώμεθα	λυθῶμεν
λύησθε	λυθῆτε
λύωνται	λυθῶσι(ν)

9.3.3 Optative

(a)	(b)
λυοίμην	λυθείην
λύοιο	λυθείης
λύοιτο	λυθείη
λυοίμεθα	λυθεῖμεν, or -θείημεν
λύοισθε	λυθεῖτε, or θείητε
λύοιντο	λυθεῖεν, or -θείησαν

9.3.4 Imperative

(a)   (b)
λύου   λύθητι
λυέσθω   λυθήτω

λύεσθε   λύθητε
λυέσθωσαν, or -εσθων   λυθήτωσαν

9.3.5 Infinitive

(a)   (b)   (c)
λύεσθαι   λυθήσεσθαι   λυθῆναι

Pres.   *Fut.*   *1 Aor.*   *Perf.*

9.3.6 Participle

(a)   (b)   (c)   (d)
λυόμενος[9]   λυθησόμενος[10]   λυθείς[11]   λελυμένος[12]
λυομένου   λυθησομένου   λυθέντος   λελυμένου
λυομένῳ   λυθησομένῳ   λυθέντι   λελυμένῳ
λυόμενον   λυθησόμενον   λυθέντα   λελυμένον

λυόμενοι   λυθησόμενοι   λυθέντες   λελυμένοι
λυομένων   λυθησομένων   λυθέντων   λελυμένων
λυομένοις   λυθησομένοις   λυθεῖσι(ν)   λελυμένοις
λυομένους   λυθησομένους   λυθέντας   λελυμένους

9.4 THEMATIC VERBS: CONTRACT VERBS

Present Active

9.4.1 Present Active Indicative

(a)   (b)   (c)   (d)
ποιῶ   ἀγαπῶ   πληρῶ   ζῶ

---

[9] λυόμενος, λυομένη, λυόμενον.
[10] λυθησόμενος, λυθησομένη, λυθησόμενον.
[11] λυθείς, λυθεῖσα, λυθέν.
[12] λελυμένος, λελυμένη, λελυμένον.

ποιεῖς	ἀγαπᾷς	πληροῖς	ζῇς
ποιεῖ	ἀγαπᾷ	πληροῖ	ζῇ
ποιοῦμεν	ἀγαπῶμεν	πληροῦμεν	ζῶμεν
ποιεῖτε	ἀγαπᾶτε	πληροῦτε	ζῆτε
ποιοῦσι(ν)	ἀγαπῶσι(ν)	πληροῦσι(ν)	ζῶσι(ν)

9.4.2 Imperfect Active Indicative

(a)	(b)	(c)	(d)
ἐποίουν	ἠγάπων	ἐπλήρουν	ἔζων
ἐποίεις	ἠγάπας	ἐπλήρους	ἔζης
ἐποίει	ἠγάπα	ἐπλήρου	ἔζη
ἐποιοῦμεν	ἠγαπῶμεν	ἐπληροῦμεν	ἐζῶμεν
ἐποιεῖτε	ἠγαπᾶτε	ἐπληροῦτε	ἐζῆτε
ἐποίουν	ἠγάπων	ἐπλήρουν	ἔζων

9.4.3 Present Active Imperative

(a)	(b)	(c)	(d)
ποίει	ἀγάπα	πλήρου	ζῇ
ποιείτω	ἀγαπάτω	πληρούτω	ζήτω
ποιεῖτε	ἀγαπᾶτε	πληροῦτε	ζῆτε
ποιείτωσαν	ἀγαπάτωσαν	πληρούτωσαν	ζώντων

9.4.4 Present Active Subjunctive

(a)	(b)	(c)	(d)
ποιῶ	ἀγαπῶ	πληρῶ	ζῶ
ποιῇς	ἀγαπᾷς	πληροῖς	ζῇς
ποιῇ	ἀγαπᾷ	πληροῖ	ζῇ
ποιῶμεν	ἀγαπῶμεν	πληρῶμεν	ζῶμεν
ποιῆτε	ἀγαπᾶτε	πληρῶτε	ζῆτε
ποιῶσι(ν)	ἀγαπῶσι(ν)	πληρῶσι(ν)	ζῶσι(ν)

9.4.5 Present Active Infinitive

(a)	(b)	(c)	(d)
ποιεῖν	ἀγαπᾶν	πληροῦν	ζῆν

9.4.6 Present Active Participle

(a)	(b)	(c)	(d)
m.ποιῶν	ἀγαπῶν	πληρῶν	ζῶν
fm. ποιοῦσα	ἀγαπῶσα	πληροῦσα	ζῶσα
nt.ποιοῦν	ἀγαπῶν	πληροῦν	ζῶν

Present Passive

9.4.7 Present Passive Indicative

(a)	(b)	(c)
ποιοῦμαι	ἀγαπῶμαι	πληροῦμαι
ποιῇ or -εῖ	ἀγαπᾶσαι	πληροῖ
ποιεῖται	ἀγαπᾶται	πληροῦται
ποιούμεθα	ἀγαπώμεθα	πληρούμεθα
ποιεῖσθε	ἀγαπᾶσθε	πληροῦσθε
ποιοῦνται	ἀγαπῶνται	πληροῦνται

9.4.8 Imperfect Passive Indicative

(a)	(b)	(c)
ἐποιούμην	ἠγαπώμην	ἐπληρούμην
ἐποιοῦ	ἠγαπῶ	επληροῦ
ἐποιεῖτο	ἠγαπᾶτο	επληροῦτο
ἐποιούμεθα	ἠγαπώμεθα	επληρούμεθα
ἐποιεῖσθε	ἠγαπᾶσθε	επληροῦσθε
ἐποιοῦνται	ἠγαπῶντο	επληροῦντο

9.4.9 Present Passive Imperative

(a)	(b)	(c)
ποιοῦ	ἀγαπῶ	πληροῦ
ποιείσθω	ἀγαπάσθω	πληρούσθω
ποιεῖσθε	ἀγαπᾶσθε	πληροῦσθε
ποιείσθωσαν	ἀγαπάσθωσαν	πληρούσθωσαν

9.4.10 Present Passive Subjunctive

(a)	(b)	(c)
ποιῶμαι	ἀγαπῶμαι	πληρῶμαι

ποιῇ   ἀγαπᾷ   πληροῖ
ποιῆται   ἀγαπᾶται   πληρῶται
ποιώμεθα   ἀγαπώμεθα   πληρώμεθα
ποιῆσθε   ἀγαπᾶσθε   πληρῶσθε
ποιῶνται   ἀγαπῶνται   πληρῶνται

9.4.11 Present Passive Infinitive

(a)   (b)   (c)
ποιεῖσθαι   ἀγαπᾶσθαι   πληροῦσθαι

Present Middle

9.4.12 Present Middle Indicative

δέομαι   χρῶμαι
δέῃ   χρᾶσαι
δεῖται   χρᾶται
δεόμεθα   χρώμεθα
δεῖσθε   χρᾶσθε
δέονται   χρῶνται

9.4.13 Imperfect Middle Indicative

ἐδεόμην   ἐχρῶμην
ἐδέου   ἐχρῶ
ἐδεῖτο   ἐχρᾶτο
ἐδεόμεθα   ἐχρώμεθα
ἐδεῖσθε   ἐχρᾶσθε
ἐδέοντο   ἐχρῶντο

9.4.14 Present Middle Imperative

δέου   χρῶ
δείσθω   χράσθω

δεῖσθε   χρᾶσθε
δείσθωσαν   χράσθωσαν

9.5 THEMATIC VERBS: οἶδα

9.5.1 Indicative

(a)	(b)
Pf.	*Pfpf.*
οἶδα	ᾔδειν
οἶδας	ᾔδεις
οἶδε(ν)	ᾔδει
οἴδαμεν or ἴσμεν	ᾔδειμεν
οἴδατε or ἴστε	ᾔδεῖτε
οἴδασι(ν) or ἴδασιν	ᾔδεισαν

9.5.2 Subjunctive

εἰδῶ
εἰδῇς
εἰδῇ
εἰδῶμεν
εἰδῆτε
εἰδῶσι(ν)

9.5.3 Infinitive

εἰδέναι

9.5.4 Participle

m.	*fm.*	*nt.*
εἰδώς	εἰδυῖα	εἰδός
εἰδότος	εἰδυίας	εἰδότος
etc.		

9.6 THEMATIC VERBS: γινώσκω

9.6.1 Indicative

(a)	(b)[13]	(c)	(d)	(e)	(f)
pres.	*2 aor.*	*fut.*	*pf.*	*plpf.*	*impf.*
γινώσκω	ἔγνων	γνώσομαι	ἔγνωκα	ἐγνώκειν	ἐγινώσκον

---

[13] γινώσκω is athematic in the ²aor.

γινώσκεις   ἔγνως
γινώκει   ἔγνω
γινώσκομεν   ἔγνωμεν
γινώσκετε   ἔγνωτε
γινώσκουσι(ν)   ἔγνωσαν

9.6.2 Optative

γνοίην
γνοίης
γνοίη
γνοῖμεν or γνοίημεν
γνοῖτε or γνοίητε
γνοῖεν or γνοίσαν

9.6.3 Subjunctive

γνῶ
γνῷς
γνῷ or γνοῖ
γνῶμεν
γνῶτε
γνῶσι(ν)

9.6.4 Infinitive

γνῶναι

9.6.5 Imperative

9.6.6 ²Aor act. participle

γνῶθι   N. γνούς
γνώτω   G. γνόντος
     D. γνόντι
γνῶτε   A. γνόντα
γνώτωσαν   etc.

9.7 ATHEMATIC VERBS: δύναμαι

9.7.1 Present Middle Indicative

(a)	(b)
δύναμαι	κάθημαι
δύνασαι or δύνῃ	κάθῃ
δύναται	κάθηται
δυνάμεθα	καθήμεθα
δύνασθε	κάθησθε
δύνανται	κάθηνται

9.8 ATHEMATIC VERBS: δίδωμι, τίθημι, ἵστημι – ACTIVE INDICATIVE

9.8.1 Present

(a)	(b)	(c)
δίδωμι	τίθημι	ἵστημι
δίδως	τίθης	ἵστης
δίδωσι(ν)	τίθησι(ν)	ἵστησι(ν)
δίδομεν	τίθεμεν	ἵσταμεν
δίδοτε	τίθετε	ἵστατε
διδόασι(ν)	τιθέασι(ν)	ἱστᾶσι(ν)[14]

9.8.2 Imperfect

(a)	(b)	(c)
ἐδίδουν	ἐτίθην	ἵστην
ἐδίδους	ἐτίθεις	ἵστης
ἐδίδου	ἐτίθει	ἵστη
ἐδίδομεν	ἐτίθεμεν	ἵσταμεν
ἐδίδοτε	ἐτίθετε	ἵστατε
ἐδίδοσαν	ἐτίθεσαν	ἵστασαν

---

[14] The α of the stem contracts with the α of the ending.

9.8.3 Future

(a)	(b)	(c)
δώσω	θήσω	στήσω
δώσεις	θήσεις	στήσεις
δώσει	θήσει	στήσει
δώσομεν	θήσομεν	στήσομεν
δώσετε	θήσετε	στήσετε
δώσουσι(ν)	θήσουσι(ν)	στήσουσι(ν)

9.8.4 Aorist

		Transitive	*Intransitive*
(a)	(b)	(c)	(d)
ἔδωκα	ἔθηκα	ἔστησα[15]	ἔστην[16]
ἔδωκας	ἔθηκας	ἔστησας	ἔστης
ἔδωκε(ν)	ἔθηκε(ν)	ἔστησε(ν)	ἔστη
ἐδώκαμεν	ἐθήκαμεν	ἐστήσαμεν	ἔστημεν
ἐδώκατε	ἐθήκατε	ἐστήσατε	ἔστητε
ἔδωκαν	ἔθηκαν	ἔστησαν	ἔστησαν

9.8.5 Perfect

(a)	(b)	(c)
δέδωκα	τέθεικα	ἕστηκα
δέδωκας	τέθεικας	ἕστηκας
δέδωκε(ν)	τέθεικε(ν)	ἕστηκε(ν)
δεδώκαμεν	τεθείκαμεν	ἑστήκαμεν
δεδώκατε	τεθείκατε	ἑστήκατε
δεδώκασι(ν)	τεθείκασι(ν)	ἑστήκασι(ν)

---

[15] Transitive use: "I set up, I caused to stand."
[16] Intransitive form: "I stood."

9.9 ATHEMATIC VERBS: δείκνυμι, φημί, ἔφην – ACTIVE INDICATIVE

9.9.1		9.2
Pres.	*Pres.*	*Impf.*
δείκνυμι or δεικνύω	φημί	ἔφην
δεικνύεις	φής	ἔφης
δείκνυσι(ν)	φησί(ν)	ἔφη (and ²aor)
δείκνυμεν	φαμέν	ἔφαμεν
δείκνυτε	φατέ	ἔφατε
δεικνύασι(ν)	φασί(ν)	ἔφασαν

9.10 ATHEMATIC VERBS: δίδωμι, τίθημι, ἵστημι – MIDDLE INDICATIVE

9.10.1 Present

(a)	(b)	(c)
δίδομαι	τίθεμαι	ἵσταμαι
δίδοσαι	τίθεσαι	ἵστασαι
δίδοται	τίθεται	ἵσταται
διδόμεθα	τιθέμεθα	ἱστάμεθα
δίδοσθε	τίθεσθε	ἵστασθε
δίδονται	τίθενται	ἵστανται

9.10.2 Imperfect

(a)	(b)	(c)
ἐδιδόμην	ἐτιθέμην	ἱστάμην
ἐδίδοσο	ἐτίθεσο	ἵστασο
ἐδίδοτο	ἐτίθετο	ἵστατο
ἐδιδόμεθα	ἐτιθέμεθα	ἱστάμεθα
ἐδίδοσθε	ἐτίθεσθε	ἵστασθε
ἐδίδοντο	ἐτίθεντο	ἵσταντο

9.10.3 Future

(a)	(b)	(c)
δώσομαι	θήσομαι	στήσομαι

δώσῃ	θήσῃ	στήσῃ
δώσεται	θήσεται	στήσεται

δωσόμεθα	θησόμεθα	στησόμεθα
δώσεσθε	θήσεσθε	στήσεσθε
δώσονται	θήσονται	στήσονται

9.10.4 Aorist

(a)	(b)	
ἐδόμην	ἐθέμην	(no middle forms)
ἔδου	ἔθου	
ἔδοτο	ἔθετο	

ἐδόμεθα	ἐθέμεθα
ἔδοσθε	ἔθεσθε
ἔδοντο	ἔθεντο

9.10.5 Perfect

(a)	(b)	(c)
δέδομαι	τέθειμαι	ἕσταμαι
δέδοσαι	τέθεισαι	ἕστασαι
δέδοται	τέθειται	ἕσταται

δεδόμεθα	τεθείμεθα	ἑστάμεθα
δέδοσθε	τεθεῖσθε	ἕστασθε
δέδονται	τεθεῖνται	ἕστανται

9.11 ATHEMATIC VERBS: δίδωμι, τίθημι, ἵστημι– PASSIVE INDICATIVE

9.11.1 Present

(a)	(b)	(c)
δίδομαι	τίθεμαι	ἵσταμαι
δίδοσαι	τίθεσαι	ἵστασαι
δίδοται	τίθεται	ἵσταται

διδόμεθα	τιθέμεθα	ἱστάμεθα
δίδοσθε	τίθεσθε	ἵστασθε
δίδονται	τίθενται	ἵστανται

9.11.2 Imperfect

(a)	(b)	(c)
ἐδιδόμην	ἐτιθέμην	ἱστάμην
ἐδίδοσο	ἐτίθεσο	ἵστασο
ἐδίδοτο	ἐτίθετο	ἵστατο
ἐδιδόμεθα	ἐτιθέμεθα	ἱστάμεθα
ἐδίδοσθε	ἐτίθεσθε	ἵστασθε
ἐδίδοντο	ἐτίθεντο	ἵσταντο

9.11.3 Future

(a)	(b)	(c)
δοθήσομαι	τεθήσομαι	σταθήσομαι
δοθήσῃ	τεθήσῃ	σταθήσῃ
δοθήσεται	τεθήσεται	σταθήσεται
δοθησόμεθα	τεθησόμεθα	σταθησόμεθα
δοθήσεσθε	τεθήσεσθε	σταθήσεσθε
δοθήσονται	τεθήσονται	σταθήσονται

9.11.4 Aorist

(a)	(b)	(c)
ἐδόθην	ἐτέθην	ἐστάθην
ἐδόθης	ἐτέθης	ἐστάθης
ἐδόθη	ἐτέθην	ἐστάθη
ἐδόθημεν	ἐτέθημεν	ἐστάθημεν
ἐδόθητε	ἐτέθητε	ἐστάθητε
ἐδόθησαν	ἐτέθησαν	ἐστάθησαν

9.11.5 Perfect

(a)	(b)	(c)
δέδομαι	τέθειμαι	ἔσταμαι
δέδοσαι	τέθεισαι	ἔστασαι
δέδοται	τέθειται	ἔσταται
δεδόμεθα	τεθείμεθα	ἐστάμεθα
δέδοσθε	τέθεισθε	ἔστασθε
δέδονται	τέθεινται	ἔστανται

9.12 ATHEMATIC VERBS: δίδωμι, τίθημι, ἵστημῑ NON-INDICATIVE MOODS

δίδωμι (√ δο)   τίθημι (√ θε)   ἵστημι (√ στα)

9.12.1 Subjunctive – Active

(a) Pres.	(b) Aor.	(c) Pres.	(d) Aor.	(e) Pres.	(f) Aor.
διδῶ	δῶ	τιθῶ	θῶ	ἱστῶ	στῶ
διδῶς	δῷς	τιθῇς	θῇς	ἱστῇς	στῇς
διδῷ	δῷ	τιθῇ	θῇ	ἱστῇ	στῇ
διδῶμεν	δῶμεν	τιθῶμεν	θῶμεν	ἱστῶμεν	στῶμεν
διδῶτε	δῶτε	τιθῆτε	θῆτε	ἱστῆτε	στῆτε
διδῶσι(ν)	δῶσι(ν)	τιθῶσι(ν)	θῶσι(ν)	ἱστῶσι(ν)	στῶσι(ν)

9.12.2 Imperative – Active

(a) Pres.	(b) Aor.	(c) Pres.	(d) Aor.	(e) Pres.	(f) Aor.
δίδου	δός	τίθει	θές	ἵστη	στῆθι[17]
διδότω	δότω	τιθέτω	θέτω	ἱστάτω	στήτω
δίδοτε	δότε	τίθετε	θέτε	ἵστατε	στῆτε
διδότωσαν	δότωσαν	τιθέτωσαν	θέτωσαν	ἱστάτωσαν	στήτωσαν

9.12.3 Infinitive

9.12.3.1 Active Inf.

(a) Pres.	(b) Aor.	(c) Pres.	(d) 2Aor.	(e) Pres.	(f) 2 Aor.
διδόναι	δοῦναι	τιθέναι	θεῖναι	ἱστάναι	στῆσαι/στῆναι

---

[17] But ἀνίστημι has the alternate form, ἀνάστα.

9.12.3.2 Middle Inf.

(a)	(b)	(c)	(d)	(e)	(f)
δίδοσθαι	δόσθαι	τίθεσθαι	θέσθαι	ἵστασθαι	στήσασθαι

9.12.3.3 Passive Inf.

(a)	(b)	(c)	(d)	(e)	(f)
δίδοσθαι	δοθῆναι	τίθεσθαι	τεθῆναι	ἵστασθαι	σταθῆναι

9.12.4 Participle – Active

(a)	(b)	(c)	(d)	(e)	(f)
Pres.	*Aor.*	*Pres.*	*Aor.*	*Pres.*	*Aor.*
διδούς[18]	δούς[19]	τιθείς[20]	θείς[21]	ἱστάς[22]	στάς[23]
διδόντος	δόντος	τιθέντος	θέντος	ἱστάντος	στάντος
διδόντι	δόντι	τιθέντι	θέντι	ἱστάντι	στάντι
διδόντα	δόντα	τιθένταν	θέντα	ἱστάντα	στάντα
διδόντες	δόντες	τιθέντες	θέντες	ἱστάντες	στάντες
διδόντων	δόντων	τιθέντων	θέντων	ἱστάντων	στάντων
διδοῦσι(ν)	δοῦσι(ν)	τιθεῖσι(ν)	θεᾶσι(ν)	ἱστᾶσι(ν)	στᾶσι(ν)
διδόντας	δόντας	τιθέντας	θέντας	ἱστάντας	στάντας

9.12.5 Perfect Active Participle of ἵστημι

Sg.		*m.*	*fm.*	*nt.*
	N	ἑστώς	ἑστῶσα	ἑστός
	G	ἑστότος	ἑστώσης	ἑστότος
	D	ἑστότι	ἑστώσῃ	ἑστότι
	A	ἑστότα	ἑστῶσαν	ἑστός
Pl.	N	ἑστότες	ἑστῶσαι	ἑστότα
	G	ἑστότων	ἑστωσῶν	ἑστότων
	D	ἑστόσι(ν)	ἑστώσαις	ἑστόσι(ν)
	A	ἑστότας	ἑστῶσας	ἑστότα

---

[18] διδούς, διδοῦσα, διδόν.
[19] δούς, δοῦσα, δόν.
[20] τιθείς, τιθεῖσα, τιθέν.
[21] θείς, θεῖσα, θέν.
[22] ἱστάς, ἱστᾶσα, ἱστάν.
[23] στάς στᾶσα, στάν.

9.12.6 Pres. and Aor. Middle Participle

(a)	(b)	(c)	(d)	(e)	(f)
Pres. [24]	*Aor.*[25]	*Pres.* [26]	*Aor.*	*Pres.*[27]	*Aor.*
διδόμενος	δόμενος	τιθέμενος	θέμενος[28]	ἱστάμενος	στάμενος[29]

9.12.7 Aor. Passive Participle

m.	δοθείς	τεθείς	σταθείς
fm.	δοθεῖσα	τεθεῖσα	σταθεῖσα
nt.	δοθέν	τεθέν	σταθέν

9.13 ATHEMATIC VERBS: εἰμί

9.13.1 Indicative

(a)	(b)	(c)
Pres.	*Impf.*	*Fut.*
εἰμί	ἤμην	ἔσομαι
εἶ	ἦς	ἔσῃ
ἐστί(ν)	ἦν	ἔσται
ἐσμέν	ἦμεν or ἤμεθα	ἐσόμεθα
ἐστέ	ἦτε	ἔσεσθε
εἰσί(ν)	ἦσαν	ἔσονται

9.13.2 Subjunctive   9.13.3 Optative

ὦ	εἴην
ᾖς	εἴης
ᾖ	εἴη
ὦμεν	εἴημεν / εἶμεν
ἦτε	εἴητε / εἶτε
ὦσι(ν)	εἴησαν / εἶεν

---

[24] διδόμενος, -η, -ον.
[25] δόμενος, -η, -ον.
[26] τιθέμενος, -η, -ον.
[27] ἱστάμενος, -η, -ον.
[28] θέμενος, -η, -ον.
[29] στάμενος, -η, -ον.

9.13.4 Imperative

ἴσθι
ἔστω or ἤτω

ἔστε
ἔστωσαν or ἔστων

9.13.5 Infinitive

εἶναι

9.13.6 Participle

m.	fm.	nt.
ὤν	οὖσα	ὄν
ὄντος	οὔσης	ὄντος
ὄντι	οὔσῃ	ὄντι
ὄντα	οὖσαν	ὄν
ὄντες	οὖσαι	ὄντα
ὄντων	οὐσῶν	ὄντων
οὖσι(ν)	οὔσαις	οὖσι(ν)
ὄντας	οὔσας	ὄντα

9.14 ATHEMATIC VERBS: εἶμι

Pres.	Subj.	Opt.	Impv.	Impf.
εἶμι	ἴω	ἴοιμι/ ἰοίην	☒	ᾖα/ ᾖειν
εἶ	ἴῃς	ἴοις	ἴθι	ᾔεισθα/ᾔεις
εἶσι	ἴῃ	ἴοι	ἴτω	ᾔειν/ᾔει
ἴμεν	ἴωμεν	ἴοιμεν	-	ᾖμεν
ἴτε	ἴητε	ἴοιτε	ἴτε	ᾖτε
ἴασι	ἴωσι	ἴοιεν	ἰόντων/ἴτωσαν	ᾖσαν/ᾔεσαν

Infinitive ἰέναι

Present Participle
nom. ἰών, ἰοῦσα, ἰόν
gen. ἰόντος, ἰούσης, ἰόντος

9.15 ATHEMATIC VERBS: ἵημι

Active Indicative			*Subjunctive* Hyphenated endings only occur in compound forms of the verb.	
Pres.	*Impf.*	*²Aor.*	*Pres.*	*²Aor.*
ἵημι	ἵην	ἧκα	ἱῶ	- ὧ
ἵης/ἱεῖς	ἵεις	ἧκας	ἱῆς	- ἧς
ἵησι	ἵει	ἧκε	ἱῆ	- ῆ
ἵεμεν	ἵεμεν	- εἷμεν	ἱῶμεν	- ὧμεν
ἵετε	ἵετε	- εἷτε	ἱῆτε	- ῆτε
ἱᾶσι	ἵεσαν	- εἷσαν	ἱῶσι	- ὧσι

Infinitive

ἱέναι   - εἷναι

Pres. Participle	*²Aor. Ptc.*
ἱείς (m.), ἱέντος (gen.)	εἵς, ἕντος
ἱεῖσα (fm.)	εἷσα
ἱέν (nt.)	ἕν
ἱέντες (m. pl.)	ἕντες

ἵημι – *Passive (only occurs in compound forms)*

Future	Aorist	
-εθήσομαι	Ind.	-ειθην
	Subj.	-εθῶ
	Infin.	-εθῆναι
	Ptc.	-εθείς

9.16 DUAL FORMS

9.16.1 Definite Article (All Genders)

N/V τώ
G τοῖν
D τοῖν
A τώ

9.16.2 Present and ²Aorist Participial Endings

	m.	*fm.*	*nt.*
N/V	-οντε	-ούσα	-οντε
G	-όντοιν	-ούσαιν	-όντοιν
D	-όντοιν	-ούσαιν	-όντοιν
A	-οντε	-ούσα	-οντε

9.16.3 Dual (2nd and 3rd pers.) Forms of εἰμί

Ind.   ἐστόν
Subj.   ἦτον
Opt.   2nd pers. εἴητον/εἶτον, 3rd pers. εἰήτην/εἴτην

9.17 CARDINAL AND ORDINAL NUMBERS

	Cardinal Numbers	*Ordinal Numbers*
1.	εἷς (m.), μία (fm.), ἕν (nt.)	πρῶτος, -η, -ον
2.	δύο, δυσί(ν) (dat.)	δεύτερος, -α, -ον
3.	τρεῖς (m., fm.), τρία (nt.)	τρίτος, -η, -ον
4.	τέσσαρες (m./fm.), τέσσαρα (nt.)	τέταρτος, -η, -ον
5.	πέντε	πέμπτος, -η, -ον
6.	ἕξ	ἕκτος, -η, -ον
7.	ἑπτά	ἕβδομος, -η, -ον
8.	ὀκτώ	ὄγδοος, -η, -ον
9.	ἐννέα	ἔνατος, -η, -ον
10.	δέκα	δέκατος, -η, -ον
11.	ἕνδεκα	ἑνδέκατος, -η, -ον
12.	δώδεκα	δωδέκατος, -η, -ον
20.	εἴκοσι(ν)	εἰκοστός, -η, -ον
100.	ἑκατόν	ἑκατοστός, -η, -ον

9.18 ALPHABETIC NUMERALS

The alphabetic system for writing numerals became widely used alongside the acrophonic system in the Hellenistic period. This is a quasi-decimal system that requires twenty-seven letters, nine for the numbers 1–9, nine for the tens (10–90), and nine for the hundreds (100–900). In Attica, the symbol ι was used for 6, replacing the earlier form ϝ (digamma), which was not used in Attica in the Roman period. By convention, editors identify alphabetic numerals for numbers up to 999 by marking them with an oblique stroke to the upper right of the number (e.g., α′) above the line.

α′	1	ια′	11	κα′	21	μ′	40	φ′	500
β′	2	ιβ′	12	κβ′	22	ν′	50	χ′	600
γ′	3	ιγ′	13	κγ′	23	ξ′	60	ψ′	700
δ′	4	ιδ′	14	κδ′	24	ο′	70	ω′	800
ε′	5	ιε′	15	κε′	25	π′	80	↑ or ⅄′	900

𝈖/ ϛ'/F	6	ις'	16	κϛ'	26	ϙ'	90	,α	1000
ζ'	7	ιζ'	17	κζ'	27	ρ'	100	,β	2000
η'	8	ιη'	18	κη'	28	σ'	200	,γ	2000
θ'	9	ιθ'	19	κθ'	29	τ'	300		
ι'	10	κ'	20	λ'	30	υ'	400		

9.19 MONTH NAMES

	Attic	*Macedonian*	*Egyptian*
1	Ἑκατομβαιών[30]	Δῖος	Θώθ
2	Μεταγειτνιών	Ἀπελλαῖος	Φαωφί
3	Βοηδρομίων[31]	Αὐδναῖος'	Ἀθύρ
4	Πυανοψιών, -ῶνος	Περίτιος	Χοιάκ
5	Παιμακτηριών	Δύστρος	Τυβί
6	(Ποσειδεών β'/ ὕστερος)[32]	Ξανθικός	Μεχίρ
7	Γαμηλιών	Ἀρεμίσιος	Φαμενώθ
8	Ἀνθεστηριών	Δαίσιος	Φαρμουθί
9	Ἐλαφηβολιών	Πάνημος	Παχών
10	Μουνυχιών	Λώος	Παῦνί
11	Θαργηλιών	Γορπιαῖος	Ἐπιφί
12	Σκιροφοριών	Ἡπερβερεταῖος	Μεσορί

9.20 GREEK CURRENCY

1 drachma	δραχμή	= 1 denarius
1 stater		= ¾ denarius (15 staters = 22 ½ denarii)
8 chalkoi	(χαλκοί)	= 1 obol
6 obols	(ὀβολοί)	= 1 drachma
100 drachmae	(δραχμαι)	= 1 mina
60 minas	(μναῖ)	= 1 talent

---

[30] First month until early first century CE (approx. July).
[31] First month from early first century CE.
[32] Or Ἀδριανιών, intercalary month.

9.21 CURRENCY EQUIVALENTS

8 chalkoi	(χαλκοί)	= 1 obol
6 obols	(ὀβολοί)	= 1 drachma
100 drachmae	(δραχμαί)	= 1 mina
60 minas	(μναῖ)	= 1 talent

9.22 TERMS EMPLOYED TO NARRATE THE APPROVAL OF DECREES

γνώμη	preliminary resolution/motion
ἐπειδή / ἐπεί	"whereas" / "since"
προσαγαγεῖν (s.v. προσάγω)	"to introduce a proposal to Council"
εἶπεν	"he proposed (the motion that)"
ἐπεψήφιζεν (s.v. ἐπιψηφίζω)	"he put (an approved proposal as) a formal motion to a vote (that)," "to decree"
δεδόχθαι	"be it resolved that"
ἔδοξεν/δοκεῖ	"it was/is resolved (by)"
ἐψήφισθαι (s.v. ψηφίζω)	"be it resolved that"
χρηματίσαι (s.v. χρηματίζω)	"to deliberate on (committee business)"
συνβάλλεσθαι (s.v. συμβάλλω)	"to communicate (a preliminary resolution)"

PART 10

Glossary

ἄβατον, τό, *abaton* (sleeping chamber of the sanctuary of Asklepios)

ἀγαθός, -ή, -όν, good

ἀγαθωσύνη, ἡ, generosity, goodness

ἀγαλλιάομαι, to rejoice exceedingly

ἀγαπάω, ἀγαπήσω, ἠγάπησα, ἠγάπηκα, ἠγάπημαι, ἠγαπήθην: love

ἀγάπη, ἡ, love

ἀγαπητός, -ή, -όν, beloved, dear(est)

ἄγγελος, ὁ, messenger, angel

ἀγέλη, -ης, ἡ, herd, flock

ἁγιάζω, to make sacred, sanctify, consecrate to

ἁγίασμα, -ματος, τό, sanctuary

ἅγιος, -ια, -ιον, holy

ἁγνεία, ἡ, chastity, a sexually unmolested state

ἁγνεύω, to keep pure from (w. gen.); mid. to keep oneself pure from

ἀγνοέω, to not know something, be ignorant of; pass. to not be known/recognized

ἄγνοια, ἡ, ignorance

ἁγνός, -ή, -όν, pure, chaste (of women), holy

ἀγρός, ὁ, field, countryside

ἀγορά, ἡ, marketplace (of a city); meeting, assembly; ἀγορὰν ἄγω/συνάγω, to convene a meeting

ἀγοράζω (w. gen.), to buy (with); to ransom (with)

ἀγορανόμος, ὁ, clerk of the market (responsible for regulating buying and selling)

ἄγω, ἄξω, ἤγαγον, ἦχα, ἦγμαι, ἤχθην: to lead, bring

ἀγωγή, ἡ, policy; love spell

ἀγών, -ῶνος, ὁ, contest, game, race; struggle; legal trial, test; athletic games

ἀγωνίζομαι, to fight, struggle, strive

ἀγωνοθέτης, -ου, ὁ, president of the games

ἄδηλος, -ον, invisible/not evident to the senses

Ἅδης, -ου (uncontr.   Ἀίδης,   Ἀίδαο), ὁ, Hades, She'ol, the Netherworld

ἀδελφή, ἡ, sister, fellow believer

ἀδελφός, ὁ, brother

ἀδικέω, to do wrong; pass. to be wronged by somebody

ἀδίκημα, -ματος, τό, wrongdoing, offense

ἀδικία, ἡ, wrongdoing, injustice

Ἀδρίας, -ου, ὁ, Adriatic Sea (btw. Crete and Sicily)

ἀδύνατος, -ον, impossible; weak, crippled

ᾄδω, 2. ᾄσω/ᾄσομαι, 3. ᾖσα, ¹aor. inf. ᾆσαι: to sing

ἀεί, ever, constantly, eternal; (adv.) eternally; at that time

ἀένναος, -ον, ever-flowing, everlasting

ἀήρ, ὁ, ἀέρος (gen.), air; atmosphere

ἀθάνατος, -ον, immortal

ἀθεώρητος, -ον, invisible

Ἀθῆναι, -ῶν, αἱ (Dor. Ἀθᾶναι, -ᾶν): Athens

Ἀθηναῖος, -α, -ον, Athenian (adj.); subst. ὁ Ἀθηναῖος, Athenian

Ἀθήνη, ἡ, goddess Athene

ἄθροισμα, τό, assemblage of atoms, organism

αἰ, Dor. > Att. εἰ

Αἰγύπτιος, -ία, -ιον, Egyptian (adj.); subst. ὁ Αἰγύπτιος; Αἰγυπτία, ἡ, Egyptian woman

Αἴγυπτος, ἡ, Egypt

αἰθήρ, -έρος, ὁ/ἡ, ether, upper air (as opposed to lower air), the divine element in the human soul; personified Αἰθήρ

αἷμα, -ματος, τό, blood

αἰνέω, to praise

αἱρέω, pres. inf. αἱρεῖν, pres. act. impv. αἱρείσθω/θωσαν, pres. mid. impv. αἱρείσθωσαν, ¹aor. ᾕρησα / εἷλον (√ ἑλ-), ²aor. mid. εἱλάμην/όμην: to take by the hand; to take away, remove; to entrap, take captive; mid. to take for oneself, choose; pass. to be chosen

αἴρω, ἀρῶ, ᾖρα/ἦρα, αἴρω, ἀρῶ, ἦρα, ἦρκα, ἦρμαι, ἤρθην: to lift, take up/away, carry, pick up, hoist up; to take (away), remove; to weigh anchor; to put an end to, destroy, kill

αἴσθησις, ἡ, perception, sensation; pl. (physical) senses

αἰσθάνομαι, impf. ᾐσθόμην, ²aor. ᾐσθόμην: to have the sense/perception of (gen.); to perceive by the senses

αἰσθητός, -ή, -όν, perceptible, sensible

αἰσχύνη, ἡ, shame, disgrace

αἰσχύνω (only mid. and pass. in NT), mid. to be ashamed

αἰτέω/έομαι, to ask for, beg; to make a request

αἰτία, τό, cause; accusation, legal charge

αἴτιον, τό, cause, reason

αἴτιος, -ία, -ιον, responsible for, guilty of; subst. the accused, the one who is the cause

αἰχμαλοτεύω, to take prisoner, lure away; pass. to be taken prisoner

αἰχμαλωτίζω = αἰχμαλοτεύω

αἰών, -ῶνος, ὁ, period, age

αἰώνιος, -ον, eternal

ἀκαθαρσία, ἡ, physical and ritual impurity; moral impurity

ἀκάθαρτος, -ον, unclean, impure; τὰ ἀκάθαρτα, impurities, filth

ἀκέραιος, -ον, innocent

ἀκοή, ἡ, (faculty of) hearing; act of hearing; ear; account, report; obedience; pl. αἱ ἀκοαί, ears; chamber where the voice of Aklepios is heard

ἀκολουθέω, follow

ἀκόλουθος, -ον, following, later; (adv.) ἀκολοῦθως, following, next; according to

ἀκοσμέω, to be disorderly; pl. subst. disorderly people

ἀκρατής, -ές, powerless

ἄκρατος, -ον, pure, unmixed

ἀκριβῶς, accurately, carefully

ἀκροάομαι, to listen to, obey (w. gen.)

ἀκροβυστία, ἡ, foreskin; fig. state of being uncircumcised

ἀκούω, hear

ἄκρον, τό, high point, top (of a mountain, staff); outermost edge; end, edge (of the earth); peel (of fruit)

ἀκρόπολις, -εως, ἡ, citadel, castle; the (Athenian) Acropolis

ἀλήθεια, ἡ, truth

ἀληθής (m. and fm.), -ές (nt.), true, truthful

ἀληθινός, -ή, -όν, real, genuine, true, dependable

ἀληθῶς, truly, actually, surely

ἁλίσκομαι (defective pass., act. supplied by αἱρέω), subj. ἁλῶ, -ῶς (2), -ῷ (3): to be caught doing something

ἀλλά, but, except

ἀλλάσσω, 2. ἀλλάξω, 6. ἠλλάγην: to change, alter; to exchange one thing for another

ἀλλήλων, each other, one another

ἄλλος, -η, -ον, other, another

ἀλλότριος, -ία, -ιον, belonging to another; foreign; ὁ ἀλλότριος, stranger

ἀλόγος, -ον, irrational

ἅλς, ὁ, ἁλος, salt

ἅμα, together with (w. dat.); (adv.) at the same time, when; all at once

ἁμαρτάνω, ²aor. ἥμαρτον (but oft. ἁμαρησ- in non-ind. moods), 4. ἡμάρτηκα: to sin, commit a sin

ἁμάρτημα, τό, sin, transgression

ἁμαρτία, ἡ, sin

ἁμαρτωλός, -όν, sinful; subst. a sinner

ἀμελέω, to disregard, neglect

ἄμεμπτος, -ον, blameless, faultless

ἀμήν, amen, truly, indeed

ἀμήχανος, -ον, unmanageable; impossible

ἄμμα, -ματος, τό, knot; βάλλω ἄμμα, to tie a knot in something (gen.)

ἀμπελών, -ῶνος, ὁ, vineyard

ἀμύνω, to defend; mid. to defend oneself against; to keep from, ward off from

ἀμφότεροι, -αι, -α, both, all

ἄμωμος, -ον, faultless, above reproach

ἄν, particle that renders a statement contingent

ἀνά, each, apiece; ἀνὰ μέσον, between, within (w. gen.)

ἀναβαίνω, ἀναβήσομαι, ἀνέβην, ἀναβέβηκα: to go/come up

ἀναβλέπω, to look up/above at (w. acc.), regain sight

ἀναβοάω, cry out

ἀναγγέλλω, tell, proclaim; to report, inform

ἀναγινώσκω, to read

ἀναγκάζω, to force, compel, urge

ἀναγκαῖος, -α, -ον, necessary, indispensable, essential; (ἐστιν) ἀναγκαῖον + inf., it
    is necessary to, one must

ἀνάγκη, ἡ, necessity, obligation; tribulation, calamity; pl. calamities; μετὰ ἀνάγκης,
    by force, through compulsion

αναγνωσις, ἡ, reading

ἀναγνωρίζω, to become reacquainted; to learn to recognize

ἀναγορεύω, to proclaim publicly

ἀναγραφή, ἡ, inscription; inventory

ἀναγράφω, to engrave and publicly set up; to record in a public register

ἀνάγω, 3. ἀνήγαγον, 6. ἀνήχθην: to lead up; pass. to be brought to/up; to be
    restored to an original condition; to sail away, put out to sea

ἀναδέχομαι, to accept, receive, undertake

ἀνάθεμα, -ματος, τό, votive offering (ἄνθεμα); the object of a curse

ἀνάθημα, -ματος, τό, votive plaque

ἀναιρέω, 2. ἀναιρήσω/ἀνελῶ, 3. ἀνεῖλον/ἀνεῖλα: to destroy; to execute, kill; mid.,
    to take up for oneself

ἀνακλίνω, 6. ἀνεκλίθην: to lay down; pass. to lie down, recline at a meal

ἀνακράζω, to cry out, scream, shout

ἀναλαμβάνω, 6. ἀνελήφθην: to take up, carry; to resolve; to take up (a discourse);
    to take over, carry away

ἀναλίσκω, see ἀναλόω

ἀναλόω (also ἀναλίσκω), to use up; to spend, pay a fee; pass. to be used,
    consumed

ἀνάλωμα, -ματος, τό (oft. pl.), cost, expense

ἀναμένω, to wait for/until

ἀνάπαυσις, ἡ, relief, rest

ἀναπαύω, ¹aor. mid. ἀνεπαυσάμην, fut. mid. ἀναπαήσομαι: to cause to rest; to end, finish; mid. to rest

ἀναπλέω, 3. ἀνέπλευσα: to sail up (a river)

ἀνάστασις, -εως, ἡ, resurrection (of the dead); erection (of a building)

ἀναστρέφω, 6. ἀνεστράφην, fut. pass. ἀναστραφήσομαι: to overturn something; pass. to behave, conduct oneself; to associate with

ἀναστροφή, way of life, conduct, behavior

ἀνατέλλω, 2. ἀνατελῶ, 3. ἀνέτειλα: to cause to spring/grow up

ἀνατίθημι, 3. ἀνέθηκα, aor. mid. ἀνεθέμην, ²aor. inf. ἀναθεῖναι: to refer, attribute something (acc.) to something (dat.), ascribe, attribute; to set something up; to dedicate something (to a god); mid. to confer, lay something (acc.) before somebody (dat.) for consideration

ἀνατολή, ἡ (poet. ἀντολίη), east; κατὰ ἀνατολάς, eastward; εἰς τὴν ἀνατολήν, πρὸς ἀνατολάς, toward the east

ἀνατρέφω, 3. ἀνέθρεψα, 6. ἀνετράφην: to care for, bring up, raise

ἀναφέρω, 2. ἀνοίσω, 3. ἀνήνεγκον: to take up, carry away; to offer up; to bring back, 1 Esd 1:36; to refer to (ἐπί)

ἀνδρεία, ἡ, courage

ἀνδρεῖος, -α, -ον, courageous, brave

ἄνειμι (fr. εἶμι) (this verb provides the fut. and impf. forms of ἀνέρχομαι): to go up (to a city)

ἄνεμος, ὁ, wind

ἀνεπίληπτος, -ον, free from seizure

ἄνεσις, -εως, ἡ, rest, relaxation; relief

ἄνευ, without (w. gen.)

ἀνέχω, to hold/lift up, detain/delay something; mid. to tolerate, endure

ἀνήρ, ἀνδρός, ὁ, man, husband

ἀνθρώπινος, -η, -ον, belonging/suited to humans, common to humanity, human

ἄνθρωπος, ὁ, human being, man

ἀνθύπατος, ὁ, proconsul

ἀνίστημι, ²aor. act. ptc, ἀναστάς, ²aor. act. impv. ἀνάστηθι/ἀνάστα: (trans.) to raise up something, (intrans.) rise, get up; ἀνίστημι ἐπί, to rise up against

ἀνόητος, -ον, lacking understanding, foolish

ἀνοίγω, ἀνοίξω, ἀνέῳξα/ἤνοιξα/ἠνέῳξα, ἀνέῳγα, ἀνέῳγμαι/ἠνέῳγμαι/ἤνοιγμαι, ἀ νεῴχθην/ἠνοίχθην/ἠνεῴχθην: open

ἀνομέω, to sin, act lawlessly; subst. ὁ ἀντικείμενος, opponent, adversary

ἀνομία, ἡ, lawless deed; lawlessness

ἄνομος, -ον, lawless; subst. lawless man

ἀντέχομαι, to cling to, be devoted to something (gen.)

ἀντιλαμβάνω (w. gen.), to receive in turn, take part in; to help, support; to perceive/notice something

ἀντιλέγω (w. dat.), ²aor. ptc. ἀντειπών: to contradict somebody/something

Ἀντιόχεια, ἡ, Antioch; Syrian Antioch (on the Orontes River); Pisidian Antioch

ἀντολίη, s.v. ἀνατολή

ἄνω, above; upward

ἄνωθεν, from above

ἄξιος, -α, -ον, worthy, deserving; proper, fitting; ἀξίως (adv.), worthily

ἀξιόω, impf. ἠξίουν: to make somebody worthy of something; to think/deem worthy/fit, deem suitable; to entreat/ask somebody; pass. to be permitted

ἀξίωμα, -ματος, τό, honor, rank

ἀόρατος, -ον, unseen, invisible

ἀόριστος, -ον, unlimited, limitless

ἀπαγγέλλω, to tell, inform, proclaim

ἀπάγω, 3. ἀπήγαγον: to lead away by force; to bring before, bring by force to (εἰς / acc. of goal) somebody/something; to lead somebody somewhere

ἀπαιτέω, to demand something

ἀπαλλάσσω (Att. ἀπαλλάττω), 6. ἀπηλλάγην, ²aor. pass. ptc. ἀπαλλαγείς, fut. pass. ἀπαλλαγήσομαι: to make something go away; pass. to be released/separated from (ἀπό); to be cured of

ἀπαντάω, 3. ἀπήντησα, ¹aor. inf. ἀπαντῆσαι: to meet somebody (w. dat.); to attend a meeting; to go (somewhere) to meet somebody (dat.)

ἀπάντησις, -εως, ἡ, meeting, greeting (esp. of the public welcome of an official)

ἀπαρνέομαι, to deny somebody; ἀπαρνέομαι ἑαυτόν, to deny oneself (i.e., to be without regard for one's own advantage or convenience)

ἅπας, ἅπασα, ἅπαν, alternate form of πᾶς, πᾶσα, πᾶν

ἀπατάω, to deceive, cheat

ἀπάτη, ἡ, deception, deceitfulness

ἀπειθέω, 3. ἠπείθησα, ¹aor. ptc. ἀπειθήσας: to disobey, be disobedient

ἀπειλή, ἡ, threat

ἄπειμι (fr. εἶμι), ptc. ἀπιόντος, impf. ἀπῄειν: to leave, depart

ἄπειρος, -ον, boundless, limitless; inexperienced

ἀπεκδέχομαι, to await eagerly

ἀπελεύθερος, ὁ, freedman (i.e., emancipated slave)

ἀπελπίζω, to despair

ἅπερ s.v. ὅσπερ

ἀπέρχομαι, to go away, depart

ἀπέχω, to receive; to receive a payment; mid. to stay away from

ἀπιστέω, to disbelieve

ἀπιστία, ἡ, unbelief, incredibility

ἄπιστος, -ον, unbelieving, faithless; unbelievable; subst. unbelievers

ἁπλῶς, sincerely, with integrity; absolutely; generally; οὔτε ἁπλῶς, not at all, not so much as

ἀπό, ἀπ᾽, ἀφ᾽ (w. gen.), from, away from

ἀπογράφω, to register with (παρά) somebody; to file a report

ἀποδείκυνμι, to nominate somebody; to reserve for somebody; to demonstrate; to mark out an area (of asylum, market, etc.)

ἀποδέχομαι, to receive favorably, welcome (w. gen.)

ἀποδημέω, to travel abroad

ἀποδίδωμι, ²aor. impv. ἀπόδος: to give; to give back, return; to hand over; to deliver a letter; to pay; to repay; to reimburse; to reward; ἀποδοῦναι λόγον, to give account, render financial accounts; to grant; to give off (smoke)

ἀποδοκιμάζω, to reject

ἀποθνήσκω, ἀποθανοῦμαι, ἀπέθανον: to die

ἀποκαθίστημι, ¹aor. ἀπεκατέστησα / ²aor. ἀπεκατέστην: to re-establish, restore, cure; to depose (a king)

ἀποκαλύπτω, 6. ἀπεκαλύφθην, to reveal, disclose

ἀποκάλυψις, ἡ, revelation

ἀποκόπτω, to cut off/away; castrate

ἀποκρίνομαι, to answer

ἀποκρύπτω, to hide from, keep hidden

ἀπόκρυφος, -ον, hidden away; τὰ ἀπόκρυφα, hidden things

ἀποκτείνω, ἀποκτέννω (later form), fut. ἀποκτεννῶ, ¹aor. ἀπέκτεινα, ¹aor. pass. ἀπεκτάνθην: to kill

ἀποκυέω, to bear young, bring forth

ἀπολαμβάνω, to receive something; to regain, recover; mid. to take away/aside; to receive

ἀπολείπω, 2. ἀπολείψω: to leave behind; to desert, abandon; pass. to be left behind, remain

ἀπόλλυμι (s.v. ὄλλυμι), 2. ἀπολέσω/ἀπολῶ/ἀπολοῦμαι, ¹aor. ἀπώλεσα/²aor. ἀπωλόμην, 4. ἀπόλωλα, ²plpf. ἀπωλώλειν: to destroy; to lose; mid. to perish, be ruined; to die, be lost; to be destroyed

Ἀπόλλων, -ωνος, ὁ, Apollo

ἀπολογέομαι, to defend oneself; make a defense

ἀπολογία, ἡ, defense

ἀπολύω, to dismiss; to release; to relieve from; to be delivered out of (w. gen.); to divorce somebody (acc.) from oneself (gen.)

ἀπορέω, to be without something (gen.)

ἀποστέλλω, ἀποστελῶ, ἀπέστειλα, ἀπέσταλκα, ἀπέσταλμαι, ἀπεστάλην: to send, commission

ἀπόστολος, ὁ, messenger, apostle

ἀποστρέφω, ²aor. pass. ἀπεστράφην (dep.): to look back at (ἐπί) somebody; to look away; to revoke; to refrain from, turn back from doing something

ἀποτελέω, 3. ἀπετέλεσα, to produce; to bring about

ἀποτίνω, 2. ἀποτείσω, 3. ἀπέτεισα, ¹aor. inf. ἀποτεῖσαι, ¹aor. impv. ἀποτεισάτω: to pay a fine, pay what is due; mid. to exert oneself, strive ἀποτρέχω, to hurry away

ἀποφέρω, ²aor. inf. ἀπενεγκεῖν, aor. mid. inf. ἀποφέρεσθαι: to carry off/away; mid. to win a prize; to carry away from (ἀπό) somebody to (ἐπί) somebody

ἅπτομαι, 3. ἡψάμην, ¹aor. mid. impv. ἅψαι: to touch, take hold of (w. gen.); to strike, attack

ἀπώλεια, ἡ, destruction, annihilation

ἄρα, so, then

ἆρα, interrogative particle expecting negative response

ἀρά, curse, imprecation

ἀργύριον, τό, silver coin (= 1 drachma); money; a fine; silver (= ἄργυρος)

ἄργυρος, ὁ, silver

ἀρέσκω, to strive to please somebody, serve; (impers.) to be pleasing to somebody (w. dat.)

ἀρεστός, -ή, -όν, pleasing, acceptable to

ἀρετή, ἡ, virtue, excellence

ἀριθμέω, ¹aor. mid. ἠριθμησάμην: count, number

ἀριστερός, ά, ονί, best; euphem. (like εὐώνυμος) for "left"; ἀριστερά, on the left; ἀριστερά, ἡ, left hand; τὰ ἀριστερά (μέρη), on the left side

ἄριστος, -η, -ον, best; finest

ἀρκέω (w. dat.), to be enough/suffient for; to be satisfied with (w. dat.), be self-sufficient

ἄρκος, ὁ/ἡ, a bear

ἅρμα, -ματος, τό, chariot

ἁρμονία, ἡ, harmony; framework of the universe, harmony of the seven Governors (planets)

ἁρπάζω, 6. ἡρπάγην, ²aor. pass. ptc. ἁρπαγείς, fut. pass. ἁρπαγησόμαι: to snatch away, seize by force, take up (to heaven)

ἀρρωστέω, to be very sick

ἀρσενόθηλυς/ἀρρενόθηλυς, -εος, -υ, hermaphroditic, of both sexes

ἄρσην, ὁ, ἄρσενος, male, masculine (gram. gender)

Ἄρτεμις, -ιδος, ἡ, goddess Artemis (Roman Diana)

ἄρτι, now, at the present time, just now

ἀρτοκόπος, ὁ, baker

ἄρτος, ὁ, bread, food

ἀρχάγγελος, ὁ, archangel

ἀρχαῖος, -α, -ον, old, ancient; τὰ ἀρχαῖα, things of old

ἀρχή, beginning, origin; magistracy/office; pl. powers, heavenly powers

ἀρχιέρεια, ἡ, chief priestess

ἀρχιερεύς, -έως, ὁ, high/chief priest

ἀρχισυνάγωγος, ὁ, synagogue president

ἄρχω, to rule, govern (w. gen.); mid. to begin something (gen.)

ἄρχων, -οντος, ὁ, prince, ruler, leader; archon (title of a city magistrate) ἄρωμα, -ματος, τό, spice; spices and aromatic oils (esp. used for embalming the dead)

ἀσέβεια, ἡ, impiety, iniquity

ἀσεβέω, to act profanely/wickedly (against), commit sacrilege

ἀσεβής, -ές, irreverent to God or to the gods, impious, ungodly

ἀσθένεια, ἡ, weakness, illness

ἀσθενέω, to be weak, sick

Ἀσία, ἡ, Roman province of Asia

Ἀσκληπιός, ὁ, Asklepios (god of healing)

ἀσπάζομαι, to greet, welcome somebody; to take leave of

ἀσπίς, -ίδος, ἡ, shield; Egyptian asp/cobra

ἀστεῖος, -α, -ον, pleasing, beautiful; refined, honorable

ἀστήρ, -έρος, ὁ, star

ἄστυ, -εως, τό, pl. ἄστη, city, town

ἀσφάλεια, ἡ, safety; safeguarding/security of a structure,

ἀσφαλής, -ές, safe; subst. (τὸ) ἀσφαλές, safeguard; ἀσφαλῶς, safely; for certain, beyond doubt

ἅτε, just as, as if

ἀτελής, -ές, incomplete, imperfect; nt. subst. imperfection

ἀτενίζω, 2. ἀτενίσω: to stare at, look intently at (w. dat./ πρός)

ἄτομος, -ον, indivisible, Epicurus; subst. τὸ ἄτομος, atom

αὐγή, ἡ, light of the sun; pl. rays of the sun

αὐθαίρετος, -ον, self-chosen, voluntary; (adv.) αὐθαιρέτως, by free choice

αὖθις, again; (in a sequence) in turn

αὐλή, ἡ, court (of a temple, palace)

αὐλητης, ὁ, flute player

αὐξάνω / αὔξω, 3. ηὔξανον: to make grow/increase; pass. to grow/increase in size/ number/strength

αὔριον (adv.), tomorrow

αὐτογενέτωρ, -ορος, ὁ, self-generating

αὐτοκράτωρ, ὁ, absolute master of somebody; emperor

αὐτός, -ή, -ό, he/she/it, himself/herself/itself (intensifier)

ἀφαιρέω, 3. ἀφεῖλον, 2aor. inf. ἀφελεῖν, 1aor. mid. ἀφειλάμην: to take away from (gen.), remove; mid. to take away something from somebody/something

ἀφανίζω, to remove, get rid of; to destroy, ruin; pass. to vanish; to be ruined, be destroyed

ἄφεσις, -εως, ἡ, release (fr. captivity); the act of sending away, letting go; pardon (fr. punishment), forgiveness

ἀφίημι, impf. ἤφιον, 3. ἀφῆκα, 2aor. 2nd pers. sg. impv. ἄφες, 6. ἀφέθην, fut. pass. ἀφεθήσομαι, 2aor. pl. pass. ptc. ἀφέντες: to let, allow, permit; to leave behind; to forsake; to forgive somebody (dat.); to release (manumit) a slave to (ἐπί); to acquit of (ἐπί) charges

ἀφικνέομαι, 3. ἀφικόμην: arrive at (εἰς), to come to; to reach (a certain condition)

ἀφίστημι, ¹aor. ἀπέστησα/²aor. ἀπέστην, ²aor. subj. ἀποστῶ: to cause to stand away; to keep away from somebody (gen.); to withdraw something; mid. to go away, withdraw from (intrans.), abandon; to rebel, revolt

ἀφορίζω, to separate, divide; to set apart, appoint (for a purpose)

ἀφορμή, ἡ, starting point; occasion, pretext

Ἀφροδίτη, Aphrodite (goddess)

ἄφρων, -ονος (m./fm.), -ον (nt.), foolish, unlearned (contrasting φρόνιμος)

Ἀχαΐα, ἡ, Roman province of Achaia

ἄχρι, ἄχρις (w. gen.), as far as, up to; (conj), until

Βαβυλών, -ῶνος, ἡ, Babylon,

βαδίζω, 3. βάδισα: to go, walk, proceed; to go to visit at (παρά) a place

βάθρον, τό, bench, seat

Βακχεῖον, Bacchic society

Βάκχος, ὁ, Bakchos (Dionysos)

βαλανεῖον, τό, bathhouse

βαλανεύς, ὁ, bath attendant (who heats bathwater)

βάλλω, 2. βαλῶ, 3. ἔβαλον, 4. βέβληκα, 5. βέβλημαι, 6. ἐβλήθην: to throw; to put/place; mid. to lay down (as a foundation/beginning)

βαπτίζω, to wash, purify; to plunge, dip, baptize

βάπτισμα, -ματος, τό, baptism

βάρβαρος, -ον, barbarous (i.e., non-Greek-speaking, foreign); subst. barbarian

βαρέω, pf. pass. ptc. βεβαρημένος: to weigh down

βάρος, -ους, τό, a weight, load, burden

βαρύς, -εῖα, -ύ, heavy; fierce

βασανίζω, to torture, torment; ptc. subst. torturer

βάσανος, ἡ, torture, torment

βασιλεία, ἡ, kingship, royal power, royal reign (of God)

βασιλεύς, ὁ, king

βασιλεύω, to rule, reign; to become like a king

βασιλικός, -ή, -όν, royal

βασίλισσα, -ης, ἡ, queen

βαστάζω, to pick up; to carry a burden, bear a burden; to remove, take away

βάτος, ἡ, bramble bush, prickly shrub

βδέλυγμα, -ματος, τό, abomination

βέβαιος, -ον, steady, secure, reliable; subst. security, guarantee, βέβαιον παρέχειν τὴν ὠνήν, to confirm/guarantee the contract of purchase; superl. βεβαιότατος, most reliable; (adv.) βεβαίως, with certainty

βεβαιόω, to confirm

βεβαιωτήρ, -ῆρος, ὁ, guarantor

βία, ἡ, strength, force

βιάζω/ομαι, to force, use force, do something by force; to lay hands on, violate (a law); pass. to be forced

βίαιος, -α, -ον, violent

βίβλος/βύβλος, ὁ, Egyptian papyrus; a scroll of papyrus (book)

βίος, ὁ, life, mode of life

βιόω, to live (for a period of time), pass one's life

βλασφημέω, to slander, defame, speak impiously

βλασφημία, ἡ, slander, defamatory speech, impious speech

βλέπω, to see, look

βοάω, to cry, call out, shout

βοή, ἡ, shouting (of a crowd); outcry

βοήθεια, ἡ, help; (naut.) reinforcing cables

βοηθέω, to help, come to the aid of somebody (dat.), render assistance to somebody; to defend oneself

βοηθός, ὁ, helper; protector

βόθρος, ὁ, pit, trench

βόσκω, to feed/tend domestic animals, graze (cattle)

βουλεύομαι, to plan, resolve, decide; to be a member of the City Council (βουλή)

βουλή, ἡ, plan, decision; τίθημι βουλήν, to reach a decision, decide; City Council (βουλή) (which was subordinate to the ἐκκλησία [Assembly]); will (of God)

βούλομαι, 6. ἠβουλήθην (dep.): to will, wish, want; to mean (something)

βουνός, ὁ, hill; cf. Κοσκώβουνος, Hill of Kosko

βοῦς, βοός, ὁ/ἡ, ox, cow

βραβεῖον, τό, prize awarded by an adjudicator (βραβεύς)

βραχίων, -ονος, ὁ, arm; strength

βρέχω, to rain; to soak (in a liquid)

βροτός, ὁ, man (poet.)

βρῶμα, -ματος, τό, food (sg. and pl.)

βρῶσις, -εως, ἡ, eating/consumption; food

Βυζάντιον, τό, Byzantion

βωμός, ὁ, altar

Γαλῖος, ὁ, Galius (Roman praenomen)

γάλα, τό, γάλακτος, milk

γαμέω, Att. ¹aor. ἔγημα / HGr ¹aor. ἐγάμησα: to marry

γάμος, ὁ (oft. in pl. w. no difference in meaning), wedding; πρὸς γάμον, in marriage

γάρ, for (postpos. conj.)

γαστήρ, -τρος, ἡ, belly, stomach; womb

γέ, even, at least, indeed

γελάω, to laugh

γελοῖος, -α, -ον, ridiculous, absurd

γεμίζω, to fill with (w. acc.)

γέμω (w. gen.), to be full of something

γενεά, -ᾶς, ἡ (Ion. γενεή, -ῆς), race, offspring

γενέθλιος, -ον, belonging to one's birth; ἡμέρα γενέθλιος, birthday celebration

γένεσις, -εως, τό, generation, offspring, birth; beginning, origin

γενναῖος, -α, -ον, high-born; noble; subst., τὸ γενναῖον, nobility

γεννάω, to conceive a child; pass. to be born

γένος, -ους, τό, family; race; nation, people; offspring, descendants; sort, kind

γερουσία, ἡ, Council of Elders, Senate

γέρων, -οντος, ὁ, old man, elder, senator (who often were experts on religious matters)

γεύομαι, to taste/eat something (gen.); to experience

γεῦσις, ἡ, taste

γεωργός, ὁ, farmer

γῆ, ἡ, earth, dirt

γίνομαι, γενήσομαι, ἐγενόμην, γέγονα, γεγένημαι, ἐγενήθην: to become, come about, be

γινώσκω, γνώσομαι, ἔγνων, ἔγνωκα, ἔγνωσμαι, ἐγνώσθην: to know, come to know

γλυκύς, -εῖα, -ύ, sweet; comp. γλυκερός, -ή, -όν

γλῶσσα, ἡ, tongue, language

γνώμη, ἡ, intention, purpose; resolution, decision; preliminary resolution (of a City Council); opinion

γνωρίζω, 2. γνωριῶ: to make known; to gain knowledge of, recognize

γνῶσις, ἡ, knowledge; secret knowledge; personal acquaintance

γνωστός, -η, -ον, known; subst. knowledge

γογγύζω, to complain

γογγυσμός, ὁ, complainer; complaining

γόης, -ητος, ὁ, sorcerer

γονεύς, ὁ, pl. γονεῖς, parent

γόνυ, -νατος (Ep. and Ion. γούνατος, etc. nt. pl. γούνατα), τό, pl. γόνατα: knee

γοῦν, thus, then; at any rate

γράμμα, τό, letter, pl. τὰ γράμματα, literature, learning; letters

γραμματεύς, ὁ, secretary/registrar (of an association, council, civic council, etc.); expert in Torah, scribe

γραμματεύω, to serve as a secretary/clerk (of Assembly or Council)

γραφή, writing, written/engraved text, passage of scripture (sg.), Scriptures (pl.)

γράφω, γράψω, ἔγραψα, γέγραφα, γέγραμμαι, ἐγράφην: to write

γυνή, γυναικός, ἡ, woman, wife

γρηγορέω, to wake up; to be alert, watchful; to watch over (ἐπί)

γυμνάζω, mid. to exercise oneself, train

γυμνάσιον, τό, gymnasium, center for schooling in athletics and Greek culture (i.e., a school for educating ἔφηβοι) γυμνός, -ή, -όν, naked

γυμνόω, to strip somebody naked

γύμνωσις, -εως, ἡ, nakedness

γυναικεῖος, -α, -ον, of a woman, matters pertaining to women; nt. pl. τὰ γυναικεῖα, menstruation

δαιμονίζομαι, to be possessed by a demon/hostile spirit

δαιμόνιον, τό, semi-divine god/spirit; demon, evil spirit

δαίμων, -ονος, ὁ, δαίμων (voc.): lesser god/spirit, "demon"; semi-divine being

δάκνω, ¹aor. ἔδηξα/ ²aor. ἔδακον: to bite

δάκρυον, τό / pl. δάκρυα, -ύων, -ύοις: tear

δακρύω, to weep

δάκτυλος, ὁ, finger

Δαμασκός, ἡ, Damascus

δέ (postpos.), but, and

δεῖ (impers.), pres. act. inf. δεῖν, 3rd sg. fut. δεήσει, impf. ἔδει, opt. δέοιμι: it is nec-essary, one must (w. inf.), should/must do something

δεῖγμα, -ματος, τό, example

δείδω, ²pf. inf. δεδιέναι, ²pf. ptc. δεδιώς: to fear

δείκνυμι, δείξω, ἔδειξα, δέδειχα, ——, ἐδείχθην: to show, point out; reveal, explain, prove

δεῖνα, ὁ/ἡ, τοῦ δεῖνος, τῷ δεῖνι, τὸν δεῖνα: so-and-so

δεινός, -ή, -όν, terrible, fearful; τὸ δεινόν, evil

δεξιός, -ά, -όν, right; δεξιά, on the right; δεξιά, ἡ, right (hand), authority; right (leg); τὰ δεξιά (sc. μέρη), on the right side

δεῖξις, -εως, ἡ, calling up a god (gen.), making a god (gen.) appear

δειπνέω, to dine

δεῖπνον, τό, meal, dinner

δέκα, ten

δεκαπέντε, fifteen

δεκατέσσαρες, -ων, fourteen

δέκατος, -η, -ον, tenth; δέκατον μέρος, ten percent (10%)

δεκτός, -ή, -όν, acceptable, favorable

Δελφοί, -ῶν, οἱ, Delphi

δένδρον, τό, tree

δεξιός, -ά, -όν, right; δεξιά, on the right; δεξιά, ἡ, right (hand), authority; right (leg); τὰ δεξιά (sc. μέρη), on the right side

δέομαι, s.v. δέω (2)

δέρμα, -ματος, τό, skin; leather, hide

δερμάτινος, -η, -ον, leather (adj.)

δεσμός, ὁ, pl. δεσμοί/δεσμά: shackles/chains (of prison), sandal straps; (fig.) a hin-drance that deafens or physically handicaps

δεσμωτήριον, τό, prison

δεσμώτης, ὁ, prisoner

δεσπότης, master, lord, ruler; owner

δεῦρο (adv.), here; come here

δεύτερος, -α, -ον, second; secondary

δέχομαι, to receive, accept

δέω, 3. ἔδησα, pf. pass. δέδεμαι, pf. pass. ptc. δεδεμένος: to bind/tie, put in chains; to imprison; pass. to be bound, to be bound to somebody in marriage

δέομαι, ¹aor. pass. ptc. δεηθείς (dep.): to ask for (w. gen.), to plead for something (w. gen.), beg of somebody

δή, really, indeed; of course; then, therefore; now, at this point; τί δή; what is going on?

δηλονότι, it is plain that, clearly, of course

δῆλος, -η, -ον, clear, plain, evident; s.c., ἐστί (impers.), it is plain/evident

δηλόω, to reveal; to explain, make clear/evident; pass. to be announced

δημιουργέω, to create

δημιούργημα, -ματος, τό, piece of workmanship, created world

δημιουγός, ὁ, builder; Creator; Demiurge

Δημήτηρ, -τερος/-τρος, ἡ (Dor. Δαμάτηρ): Demeter

δῆμος, ὁ, people, crowd; the People (i.e., the full citizen body of a Greek *polis*, as represented by the ἐκκλησία)

δημόσιον, -α, -ον, public; nt. subt. τὸ δημόσιον, the state; ἡ δημοσία, public court; (adv.) δημοσίᾳ, publicly

δηνάριον, τό, denarius (Lat. loanw.)

διαβαίνω, ²aor. ptc. διαβάς: to cross over

διάβολος, ὁ, slanderer, adversary

διαβούλιον, τό, counsel, deliberation; debate

διάγραμμα, instructions, ordinances (containing specific directions or schedules rather than general legislation)

διάθεσις, ἡ, placing in order, arrangement

διαθήκη, ἡ, treaty, covenant; last will and testament

διακονέω (w. dat./gen.), to serve, render assistance to

διακονία, service; aid, support, distribution

διακόσιοι, -ίαι, -ία, two hundred

διακρίνω, to judge, decide; pass., to bring an issue to a decsion; to doubt

διαλέγω, aor. pass. ptc. διαλεχθείς (dep.): to examine, check; mid. to converse with (dat.), to discourse, instruct, lecture

διαλογίζομαι, to consider, ponder

διαλογισμός, ὁ, debate, talk; estimation, consideration

διαλύω, to dissolve into elements; to break up, separate

διαμένω, 3. διέμεινα: to persist, remain, continue unchanged, survive

διάνοια, ἡ, understanding, mind, thoughts

διανοίγω, 6. διηνοίχθην: to open; to explain, interpret

διαρρήγνυμι/ διαρρήσσω, 3. διέρρηξα, 6. διεράγην: to tear something; to tear something to pieces; to break (shackles)

διασπείρω, pf. pass. ptc. διεσπαρμένος: to disperse; pass. to be scattered

διαστρέφω, pf. pass. ptc. διεστραμμένος: to turn away; to pervert, distort

διασώζω, to bring safely through, convey to safety

διάταγμα, -ματος, edict, decree

διατάσσω, to direct, appoint; to put in order

διατελέω, to continue to do something

διατίθημι, mid. to establish a covenant

διαφέρω, to carry through, spread through; (impers.) διαφέρει τινί, it matters to somebody, it makes a difference; pass. to drift about in the sea

διαφόρον, τό, money; pl. revenues

διδασκαλία, ἡ, teaching

διδάσκαλος, ὁ, teacher

διδάσκω, διδάξω, ἐδίδαξα, —, —, ἐδιδάχθην: to teach

διδαχή, ἡ, teaching, instruction

δίδωμι, δώσω, ἔδωκα, δέδωκα, δέδομαι, ἐδόθην: to give

διέρχομαι, to go through; to come/go toward a destination; to cross over

διηγέομαι, 3. διηγησάμην: to recite, relate, tell

διήγησις, -εως, ἡ, narrative, story, account

διΐστημι, pres. pass. διΐσταμαι: to separate; pass. to be separated

δικαιόω, to declare somebody to be justified; pass. to be acquitted

δίκαιος, -α, -ον, just, righteous, upright; (adv.) δικαίως, uprightly; honestly, righteously; fairly, justly

δικαιοσύνη, ἡ, justice, uprightness, righteousness; honesty

δικαίωμα, -ματος, τό, statute; righteous act

δικαστήριον, τό, court of justice

δίκη, ἡ, judgment, punishment

διό, therefore, for this reason

διοίκησις, ἡ, administration, government

διοικητής, ἡ, administrator; financial administrator (Egypt); pl. (cosmic) Governors (i.e., the seven known planets)

Διόνυσος, ὁ, god Dionysos

διόπερ, therefore (emphatic for διό)

Διός, see Ζεύς

διότι, for, because; therefore

δίσκος, ὁ, disk; sun disk (i.e., sun); discus event

διψάω, to be thirsty

διωγμός, ὁ, persecution; persecution against (ἐπί)

διώκω, to pursue, chase; to persecute; to strive for; to recite (a spell)

δόγμα, -ματος, τό, statute

δοκέω, 3. ἔδοξα, pf. mid. inf. δεδόχθαι: to think, suppose, consider; to seem to (w. inf.), regard to be (something); δοκεῖ + inf., it seems (to somebody) that, he purportedly; εἰ δοκεῖ (w. dat.), if it pleases (somebody); ἔδοξε/δοκεῖ, it was/is resolved (by); to seem good/appropriate/best; to propose/make (a request); pass. to be decided; pass. mid. inf. δεδόχθαι, "be it resolved that (re a motion)"

δοκιμάζω, to approve for (membership)

δόλος, ὁ, cunning, deceit

δόξα, ἡ, glory, honor

δοξάζω, to think, imagine; glorify; mid. to display one's greatness; pass. to be supposed to be; to be held in honor

δόρυ, -ατος, τό, spear

δουλεία, ἡ, slavery

δουλεύω, to be a slave to somebody (dat.); to serve somebody (dat.)

δούλη, ἡ, female slave

δοῦλος, ὁ, slave, servant

δραπέτης, ὁ, runaway slave

δραχμή, ἡ, drachma (abbrev. δρ.), light drachma

δρόμος, ὁ, racing, running; the course of (one's) life/of a season (καιρός)

δύναμαι (dep.), impf. ἠδυνάμην/ἐδυνάμην, 6. ἐδυνήσθην: to be able

δύναμις, ἡ, power

δυνατός, -ή, -όν, strong, powerful; able, capable of; subst. ruler; δυνατώτερός, stronger

δύο, dat. pl. δυσί(ν), two

δύνω (also δύω), mid. δύομαι, 2. δύσομαι, ²aor. ἔδυν: to go down/set (of the sun); mid. set (of the sun); to sink

δώδεκα, twelve

δωρεάν, without payment, without reason/cause, in vain

δώρημα, τό, gift

δῶρον, τό, gift

ἐάν, if

ἑαυτου, him-/herself, his own

ἐάω, pres. mid. inf. ἐᾶσθαι, impf. εἴων, 2. ἐάσω, 3. εἴασα: to allow, permit; to leave, let go; mid. to be left to oneself

ἑβδομήκοντα, seventy

ἕβδομος, -η, -ον, seventh

Ἑβραῖος, -ου, ὁ, Hebrew person

ἐγγίζω, to approach, come near (in either a spatial or temporal sense)

ἐγγύς (adv.), near, close to; on the verge of

ἐγείρω, ἐγερῶ, ἤγειρα, —, ἐγήγερμαι, ἠγέρθην: to raise up; intrans., rise

ἐγκαθεύδω, to sleep in a temple (seeking prophetic dreams and a cure for a disease), "to incubate"

ἐγκαλέω, to bring a charge against somebody (dat.); pass. to be charged with (w. gen.)

ἐγκατακοιμάομαι (= ἐγκοιμάομαι), aor. pass. (dep.), ἐγκατεκοιμάθην, ¹aor. fem. ptc. ἐγκατακοιμαθεῖσα to sleep in a temple (seeking prophetic dreams and a cure for a disease), "to incubate"

ἐγκαταλείπω, ¹aor. ἐγκατέλιψα/²aor. ἐγκατέλιπον: to forsake, abandon, desert

ἐγκρατεία, ἡ, self-control, esp. withdrawal from sexual activity, sexual abstinence

ἔγκυος, -ον, pregnant

ἐγώ (pron.), I

εἶδος, -ους, τό, form, appearance

ἔθνος, -ους, τό, people, nation; pl. gentiles

ἔθος, -ους, τό, custom(s)

ἔθω, to be accustomed to (pres. only in ptc.), εἴωθα (pf. used in place of pres.), to be in the habit of doing something (w. inf.)

εἰ, if

εἰμί, to be

εἰδωλολατρία, -ας, ἡ, idolatry

εἰκάζω, ¹aor. inf. εἰκάσαι, 5. εἴκασμαι: to represent by a likeness; to liken to; to perceive something as something else; pass., to take the form of

εἴκοσι, twenty

εἴκω, ¹aor. act. inf., εἶξαι: to yield to somebody; to give way to (a passion or impulse)

εἰκών, -όνος, ἡ, image; statue

εἶλον, s.v. αἱρέω

εἱμάτιον, s.v. ἱμάτιον

εἶμι, inf. ἰέναι: to come/go, go into, come into contact with

εἴπερ, since; if really/indeed

εἰρήνη, ἡ, peace

εἴργω, s.v. ἔργω

εἰς (w. acc.), into, to, as; for (expressing the goal of an action)

εἷς, μία, ἕν, one

εἰσέρχομαι, εἰσελεύσομαι, εἰσῆθον, εἰσελήλυθα: to go/come in, enter

εἰσάγω, to lead in, bring in; to introduce

εἰσακούω (w. gen.), to hear, obey

εἴσειμι (fr. εἶμι), impf. εἰσῆειν, inf. εἰσιέναι: to enter; to come before, enter before

εἰσέρπω, to go into, enter

εἴσοδος, -ου, ἡ, entrance; entrance door, entrance hall; entering, access

εἰσοράω (also ἐσοράω), pres. ptc. εἰσορῶν, εἰσορῶντος: to look upon (w. admiration), gaze toward (πρός)

εἰσπλέω (Att. ἐσπλέω), 3. εἴσπλευσα: to sail in/into

εἰσπορεύομαι, to go in(to), enter; to have sexual intercourse with

εἰσφέρω, to bring in/to (εἰς); to introduce; to enter into (πρός) the presence of a high official; mid. to contribute/pay, provide

εἶτα, then, next; and so, therefore

εἴωθα (pf. of obsol. pres. ἔθω; pf. w. pres. meaning), ²pf. ptc. εἰωθώς, -υῖα, -ός: to be accustomed to; nt. ptc. subst., τὸ εἰωθός, custom

ἐκ, ἐξ, out of, from

ἕκαστος, -η, -ον, each, every

ἑκατόν, one hundred

ἑκατοντάρχης, ὁ, centurion (cf. κεντυρίων)

ἑκατοστός, -ή, -όν, hundredth

ἐκβάλλω ἐκβαλῶ, ἐκέβαλον, ἐκβέβληκα, ἐκβέβλημαι, ἐκεβλήθην, to throw out, cast out

ἔκβασις, -εως, ἡ, result, outcome; a way out, escape

ἐκβοάω, to call out, shout out

ἐκδέχομαι, to expect, look forward to, wait for somebody (acc.); to take/receive

ἐκδίδωμι, to surrender; to pay for something

ἐκδύω, 6. ἐξεδύθην: to strip, take off; mid. to strip/undress oneself; pass. to be stripped (of one's clothing)

ἐκεῖ, there

ἐκεῖθεν, from there

ἐκεῖνος, -η, -ο, that

ἐκζητέω, to seek out, require

ἐκκλησία, assembly, community, congregation

ἐκλάμπω, 2. ἐκλάμψω, 3. ἐξέλαμψα: to blaze up; to shine, beam forth

ἐκλέγω, ¹aor. mod. ἐξελέξαμαι: to collect revenue (money); mid. to choose, select

ἐκλείπω, 3. ἐξέλιπον, 4. ἐκλέλοιπα: to forsake; to remain, be left; to pass away (die); to abandon, quit

ἐκλεκτός, -ή, -όν, chosen, elect; precious

ἐκπέμπω, to send out; to issue an edict (ἄκτον)

ἐκπίπτω, impf. pass. ἐξεπεμπόμην, 3. ἐξέπεσον: to fall off; to lose, forfeit; to run off course, run aground; to be issued/published (of a decree); to resolve that (w. inf.); pass. to come forth from

ἐκπλήσσω, impf. ἐξεπλησσόμην, 6. ἐξεπλάγην, aor. pass. ptc. πλαγείς: to amaze; pass., to be amazed

ἐκπορεύομαι, to go away, come out (of gods/evil spirits)

ἔκστασις, ἡ, a spell; ecstasy

ἐκτείνω, ¹aor. inf. ἐκτεῖναι, pf. ptc. ἐκτετακώς: to stretch out, lay out, spread out; to hold out

ἐκτέμνω, 4. ἐκτέτμηκα, pf. pass. inf. ἐκτετμῆσθαι: to cut out (trees, a diseased part) ἕκτος, -η, -ον, sixth

ἐκτός (w. gen.), out of

ἐκφαίνω, 6. ἐξεφάνην: to bring light, reveal; pass. to show oneself

ἐκφέρω, 3. ἐξήνεγκον, 6. ἐξηνέχθην, aor. pass. subj. ἐξενέχθω: to lead out, take out; to produce; to carry out (the dead for burial); to declare one's opinion

ἐκφεύγω, ²aor. ἐξέφυγον: to escape

ἔλαιον, τό, olive oil

ἐλάσσων, -ονος (m./fm.), ἔλασσον (nt.), smaller, less

ἔλεγχος, ὁ, proof, legal argument; accusation

ἐλέγχω, to reprove, reproach

ἐλεάω/έω, to be merciful; to feel pity; pass. to be shown mercy

ἐλεήμων, -ον, -ονος (gen.), merciful, compassionate

ἔλεος, -ους, τό, mercy, compassion

ἐλευθερία, ἡ, freedom

ἐλεύθερος, -έρα, -ον, free; subst. freeman/freewoman

ἐλευθερόω, to set free, liberate

ἕλκω, ¹aor. εἵλκυσα: to pull an object/person; to attract; to stretch something; to spin thread

Ἕλλην, -ηνος, ὁ, / pl.   Ἕλλησι (dat.): Greek (person), Gentile

Ἑλληνικός, -ή, -όν, Hellenic, Greek (adj.); τὰ Ἑλληνικά, Greek customs

ἐλπίς, ἐλπίδος, ἡ, hope

ἐμαυτοῦ, – ῆς, (reflexive pron.) myself; (poss. pron.) my own

ἐμβαίνω, 4. ἐμβέβηκα, pf. ptc. ἐμβεβηκώς: to embark (in a boat); to plunge into water; to march/process

ἐμβάλλω, to throw in/against

ἐμβλέπω, to look at (dat.), gaze on; to consider

ἔμμενω, ¹aor. ἐνέμεινα: abide in, persevere in, stay fixed in; abide by, stand by, be true to

ἐμός, -ή, -όν, mine, my

ἐμπίπλημι/ἐμπιπλάω (w. gen.), pres. ptc. ἐμπιπλῶν, 2. ἐμπλήσω, ¹aor. mid. impv. ἔπλησαι: to fill full of something

ἐμπίπτω, 2. ἐμπέσουμαι, ²aor. ἐνέπεσον, ²aor. inf. ἐμπεσεῖν: to fall into (a state/condition); to intrude into/among

ἐμπνέω, ἐνέπνευσεν, ¹aor. ptc. ἔμπνευσας, ¹aor. pass. ptc. ἐμπνευσθείς: to blow/breathe upon

ἔμπροσθεν (w. gen.), before, in front of; previously

ἐμφανίζω, to explain; to inform, make a report; to present evidence, show plainly

ἐμφυσάω, 3. ἐνεφύσησα: to blow in, breathe into

ἐν (w. dat.) in, among, with; when, while, during

ἔναντι, in the sight of, before (w. gen.)

ἐναντίος, -α, -ον (w. gen.), contrary, against, opposed; ἐναντίον, before; τὸ ἐναντίον, on the other hand; subst. οἱ ἐναντίοι, τὰ ἐναντία, the opposites ἐνάρετος, -ον, virtuous, excellent

ἐνάρχομαι, to begin, make a beginning

ἔνατος, -η, -ον, ninth

ἔνδεκα, eleven

ἐνδέκατος, -η, -ον, eleventh

ἔνδον, inside, within

ἔνδοξος, -ον, held in honor, of high repute; glorious; subst. glorious features; (adv.) ἐνδόξως, gloriously

ἔνδυμα, τό, clothing; garment

ἐνδύω, aor. inf. ἐνδῦσαι: to dress, put on (clothing); mid. to clothe (oneself), wear

ἐνειλέω, 3. εἴλησα: to wrap in something; to roll up something

ἔνειμι (fr. εἰμί), 3rd pers. impf. ἐνῆν, to be possible, in one's power

ἕνεκα/ἕνεκεν (w. gen.), because of, for the sake of, on account of; in honor of; for this reason; τίνος ἕνεκα, why?

ἐνενήκοντα (indecl.), ninety

ἐνέπω (also ἐννέπω), impf. ἔννεπον: to tell, pronounce that

ἐνέργεια, ἡ, activity, (divine) action, force/energy

ἐνεργέω/έομαι (w. impers. subject): to be at work (in something), be operative, to activate

ἐνέργημα, -ματος, τό, effect

ἔνθα (adv.), here, where

ἐνθάδε (adv.), here, in this place

ἐνιαυτός, ὁ, year; κατὰ ἐνιαυτόν, annual, yearly

ἐνίστημι, ²pf. act. ptc. ἐνεστώς, ἐνεστῶσα, ἐνεστός: to be present, to be impending (at the time of writing)

ἐννέα, nine (indecl.)

ἐννοέω, to reflect on, occupy one's mind with

ἔννοια, ἡ, thought, insight

ἐνοχλέω, to trouble, annoy; pass. to be disturbed, troubled

ἐνταῦθα, here, there; then

ἐντέλλω/ομαι (w. dat.), 2. ἐντελεῖμαι, 3. ἐνετειλάμην, 5. ἐντέταλμαι: to command somebody

ἐντεῦθεν, from there/here (of place); from then (of time), from that (of cause); ἐντεῦθεν...ἐντεῦθεν..., on this side ... on that side

ἐντολή, ἡ, commandment, instruction

ἐντός (w. gen.), within, among; within (a period of time); inside

ἐντρέπω, 6. ἐνετράπην: to show deference to, respect

ἐντυγχάνω, 3. ἐνέτυχον, ²aor. inf. ἐντυχεῖν: to bring a charge against; to appeal, petition; to happen to meet with/run into somebody; to happen to read

ἐνύπνιον, τό, a dream

ἔνωσις, -εως, ἡ, union

ἐνώπιον (w. gen.) before, in the presence of

ἕξ, six

ἐξάγω, to lead out, bring

ἐξαιρέω, 3. ἐξεῖλον (fr. √ ἐξελ-), ²aor. mid. ἐξειλόμην, ²aor. ptc. ἐξελών: to remove; mid. to take away, destroy, bring to naught; to rescue, deliver, save

ἐξαίφνης (adv.), suddenly (Dor. ἐξαπίνας)

ἐξανίστημι, mid. ἐξανίσταμαι: to raise up; to establish; to arise, get up, awake

ἐξαποστέλλω, to send somebody off/away; to send on a mission, commission a senator

ἐξεγείρω, to awaken; to raise from the dead; pass. to be awakened, wake up; to be raised up

ἔξειμι (fr. εἶμι), inf. ἐξιέναι, ptc. ἐξιών, -οῦσα, -όν: to go out, leave, depart from a place

ἐξέρχομαι, to come or go out or forth, get out

ἐξηγέομαι, to tell (in detail), report

ἑξήκοντα (indecl.), sixty

ἑξῆς (adv.), next, following; τὰ ἑξῆς, the following things; that which follows, the consequences

ἐξίστημι, 2. ἐκστήσω/ομαι, 3. ἐξέστησα: (trans.), to amaze; (intrans.) to be amazed/astonished; to be out of one's mind

ἐξομολογέομαι, to confess, acknowledge

ἐξορκίζω (= ἐξορκόω), to make somebody swear/taken an oath; to conjure by (κατά) a god

ἐξουδενόω (= ἐξουδενέω), to despise, treat with contempt

ἐξουθενέω, s.v. ἐξουδενόω

ἐξουσία, ἡ, authority, right

ἔξω, out, outside; (prep. w. gen.) out of, outside; ὁ ἔξω, outsider, unbeliever

ἔοικα (pf. w. pres. sense), pf. inf. ἐοικέναι, ptc. ἐοικώς: to be like, resemble (w. dat.)

ἑορτή, ἡ, festival, feast

ἐπαγγελία, ἡ, a promise

ἐπαγγέλλω, ¹aor. mid. ἐπηγγειλάμην, ¹aor. ptc. ἐπαγγειλάμενος: to promise

ἐπαινέω, to commend somebody, praise; approve (statutes)

ἐπαίνος, ὁ, praise, commendation of something

ἐπαίρω, 3. ἐπῆρα, ¹aor ptc. ἐπάρας: to lift up something, hoist

ἐπαισχύνομαι, to be ashamed

ἐπακούω, to hear, listen to; to heed

ἐπάνω, above, over; on top of; onward

ἐπαοιδη, s.v. ἐπῳδή

ἐπαρχία, ἡ, province (Lat. provincia)

ἐπαύριον (adv.), the next day

ἐπεγείρω, to awaken; to excite, rise up against, assault; pass. to wake up

ἐπεί, when, after; because, since; ἐπειδήπερ, intensive form of ἐπεί

ἐπείγω, to hasten on, press on; pass., to hurry oneself toward (ἐπί) ἐπειδή, since, because; after

ἔπειτα/ἔπειτεν, then, next

ἐπέρχομαι, to come upon, against; to arrive at

ἐπερωτάω, to ask a question, question somebody; to put the question (with respect to a formal motion); to consult a god/oracle about something

ἐπέχω, 2aor. act. impv. ἐπίσχες: to hold firmly to; to stay, halt; to stay on (for a period of time); to offer, extend

ἐπί, ἐπ᾽, ἐφ᾽ (w. gen.) on, at the time of; (w. dat.) on, on the basis of; (w. acc.) on, around

ἐπιβαίνω, to set foot on, walk on; to get upon, mount on; to embark (in a ship)

ἐπιβάλλω, to lay on; to put on something; to board a ship

ἐπιβλέπω, to look at/upon (gen.); to consider

ἐπιγινώσκω, to recognize

ἐπίγραμα, -ματος, τό, inscription

ἐπιγράφω, to write on/in; to inscribe on

ἐπιδείκνυμι/ἐπιδεικνύω, pres. mid. inf. ἐπιδείκνυσθαι, 3. ἐπέδειξα, ¹aor mid. ἐπεδειξάμην: to show, point out, discuss; to prove that (ὅτι)

ἐπιδημέω, to come to stay in a city, reside temporarily in a place; to live at home; to stay at home

ἐπιδίδωμι, 6. ἐπεδόθην, pf. ptc. ἐπιδεδωκώς: to give into one's hands; to give somebody one's hand; to surrender, give up control; to give back/return; to increase/grow in size

ἐπιζητέω, to seek after, desire

ἐπιθυμέω, to desire; pass. to attract

ἐπιθυμητός, -ή, -όν, desirable; costly, precious

ἐπιθυμία, ἡ, desire for good things (longing); negative desire (lust, covetousness, craving)

ἐπιθύω, to offer a sacrifice/spell for (acc. / ἐπί) something

ἐπικαλέω, to call upon; mid. to call in as a helper; pass. to be called

ἐπικατάρατος, -ον, accursed

ἐπίκειμαι, to set over (w. dat.), to set/lay upon; to adorn with; (of an impersonal force) to confront

ἐπικρατέω, to have power/mastery over (w. gen.)

ἐπιλαμβάνω, 5. ἐπείλημμαι: to take hold of something, overtake, seize; pass. to be imprisoned

ἐπιλανθάνομαι (w. gen.), 2. ἐπιλήσομαι, 3. ἐπελαθόμην, pf. pass. ptc. ἐπειλημμένος: to forget; to neglect, overlook

ἐπιλέγω, 3. ἔπειπον, to utter a spell/magical word

ἐπίλεκτος, -ον, chosen, choice

ἐπιμαρτυρέω/ομαι, to bear witness to something; mid. to call upon somebody (acc.) to witness to somebody (dat.)

ἐπιμέλεια, ἡ, care, attention; responsibility

ἐπιμελέομαι (w. gen.) pass. (dep.): to take care of something (gen.)

ἐπιμελής, -ές, careful, attentive; (adv.) ἐπιμελῶς, diligently

ἐπιμένω, 3. ἐπέμεινα: to stay on, remain

ἐπιπίπτω, 4. ἐπιπέπτωκα: to fall on/over

ἐπιπληρόω, to fill up with

ἐπιποθέω, to long for somebody (acc.), earnestly desire

ἐπισκέπτομαι (= ἐπισκοπέω), to inspect/examine something; to visit somebody (acc.)

ἐπισκευάζω, to repair, restore (a building)

ἐπισκοπέω, to watch over, inspect, observe

ἐπίσκοπος, ὁ, bishop

ἐπισπάω, to be responsible for bringing something on/making something happen; to pull the foreskin over the head of the penis (in order to hide the marks of circumcision)

ἐπίσταμαι, to know, understand

ἐπιστάτης, ὁ, overseer, manager; ἐπιστάτης τῶν βοῶν, cowherd; ἐπιστάτης τῶν ποιμνίων, shepherd

ἐπιστήμη, ἡ, knowledge

ἐπιστολή, ἡ, letter

ἐπιστρέφω, to return; to turn (in religious/moral sense), turn around/back; pass. (dep.), to pay attention to, care about

ἐπιτάσσω (Att. ἐπιτάττω), pres. ptc. ἐπιτασσόμενος, ¹aor. inf. ἐπιτάξαι, aor. pass. ptc. ἐπιταχθείς: to instruct/order somebody to do something; to impose regulations; subst. ptc. regulations, things decreed

ἐπιτελέω, to complete; to perform, accomplish; to perform a ritual; to celebrate (a birthday)

ἐπιτίθημι, ²aor. ptc. ἐπιθείς: to lay/put something (acc.) on (ἐπί) somebody/something (acc.); to give something (acc.) to somebody (dat.)

ἐπιτιμάω, to warn, speak seriously; to rebuke

ἐπιτίμιον, τό, assessment of damages, penalty, punishment

ἐπιτρέπω, to allow somebody (dat.) to do something (inf.); to permit somebody to do something; to tolerate, put up with; pass. to be entrusted as a legal guarantor

ἐπιφαίνω, ²aor. pass. ptc. ἐπιφανείς: to show, appear; to divinely manifest

ἐπιφανής, -ές, appearing, manifest (of a god); used as title by Antiochus IV Epiphanes; notable, distinguished

ἐπιφέρω, ¹aor ptc. ἐπενέγκας: to lay upon; to hover over; to carry (on one's person); to bring on/about; to bring legal action (κρίσιν) against (κατά) somebody; to compel; pass. to be hovering over

ἐπιχωρέω, to move over/toward; to grant somebody permission to do something

ἐπιψηφίζω, 3rd sg. ¹aor. ἐπεψήφιζεν, aor. mid. inf. ἐψήφισθαι: to put (a motion) to a vote

ἔπος, ὁ, word; speech

ἐπουράνιος, -ον, heavenly

ἑπτά, seven

ἐπῳδή (= ἐπαοιδη), enchantment, spell

ἐράω (act. only in pres. and impf.), pres. ptc. ἐρώμενος, 6. ἠράσθην: to be in love with (w. gen.), fall in love; subst., pass. ptc., an object of love, a lover

ἐργάζομαι, 3. εἰργασαμην, ¹aor. mid. inf. ἐργάσασθαι: to work, labor, till; to produce an effect, be productive; to bring about

ἐργασία, ἡ, production; business

ἐργάτης, ὁ, worker, a worker in a trade

ἔργον, τό, work, deed, task

ἔργω / εἴργω, to shut out; pass. to be shut out of (gen.)

ἐρευνάω, see ἐραυνάω

ἐρίζω, to quarrel; to engage in philosophical disputation

ἔριον, τό, wool

ἑρμηνεία, ἡ, interpretation

ἑρμηνεύω, to interpret

Ἑρμῆς, -οῦ, ὁ, Hermes (messenger of the gods); Mercury (planet)

ἑρπετόν, τό, reptile

ἔρρωσο, s.v. ῥώννυμι

ἐρύω, mid. ἐρύομαι/ῥύομαι, 2. ῥύσομαι, 3. ἐρρυσάμην: mid. to rescue, save, deliver

ἔρχομαι, ἐλεύσομαι, ἦλθον, ἐλήλυθα: to come/go

ἔρως, -ωτος, ὁ, love; Ἔρως, god of love

ἐρωτάω, to ask (a question), request, beg

ἐσθίω, 2. φάγομαι, 3. ἔφαγον: to eat

ἐσθός, -ή, -όν, good, morally good, faithful

ἔσχατος, -η, -ον, last, final; lowest, most insignificant

ἔσω, inside, within (adv.)

ἑταῖρος, ὁ, a companion, friend; ἑταίρα, ἡ, prostitute

ἕτερος, -η, -ον, another, different, one of two

ἔτι, still, yet (adv.)

ἑτοιμάζω, to prepare; pass., to be ready

ἕτοιμος, (-η), -ον, prepared, ready; at hand; at hand

ἔτος, ἔτους, τό, year

εὖ (adv.), well

εὐαγγελίζω/ομαι, to announce good news, make a joyful announcement

εὐαγγέλιον, a joyful announcement, good news

εὐγενής, -ές, of noble birth, high social status

εὐδοκία, ἡ, goodwill, purpose; desire

εὐδοκέω, to take pleasure in, be pleased with; be pleased (to do something), consider somebody/something good

εὕδω, to sleep, rest

εὐεργεσία, ἡ, benefaction

εὐεργετέω, to confer (benefits)

εὐεργέτης, ὁ, benefactor

εὔθετος, -ον, fit, suitable, qualified

εὐθύς, εὐθεῖα, εὐθύ, straight; (adv.) εὐθύς, immediately, at once

εὐλαβής, -ές, prudent; reverent, pious; comp. εὐλαβέστερος; adv. εὐλαβῶς, cautiously, piously keeping clean from

εὐλογέω, to bless

εὐλογητός, -ή, -όν, blessed, praised

εὐλογία, ἡ, blessing

εὔνοια, ἡ, affection, enthusiasm; goodwill

εὑρίσκω, εὑρήσω, εὗρον, εὕρηκα, ——, εὑρέθην: to find, discover

εὐσέβεια, ἡ, reverence toward the gods, piety

εὐσεβέω, to worship/reverence (the gods)

εὐσεβής, -ές, discharging sacred duties; pious, devout; superl. εὐσεβέστατα, most pious

εὐτυχέω, to be prosperous, have good fortune; εὐτύχει, "farewell"

εὐφραίνω, to make glad; pass. to rejoice, celebrate

εὐφροσύνη, ἡ, joy, cheerfulness

εὐχαριστέω, to do a favor for somebody (dat.); to give thanks

εὐχή, ἡ, prayer; vow, oath; εὐχῆς ἕνεκεν, in fulfillment of a vow

εὔχομαι, 3. ηὐξάμην, ¹aor. mid. impv. εὖξαι: to pray; to vow

εὐωδία, ἡ, aroma, fragrance; perfume

εὐώνυμος, -α, -ον, honored; euphem. for "left"

ἐφάλλομαι, ἐφηλόμην: to leap/spring upon

ἐφάπτω, mid. to claim somebody (w. gen.) as one's property

Ἐφέσιος, -ία, -ιον, Ephesian; subst. Ephesians

Ἔφεσος, ἡ, Ephesos (Ionia)

ἐφέστιον, τό, household, family

ἔφηβος, ὁ, an ephebe/adolescent enrolled in a system for educating young men for citizenship and military service

ἐφικνέομαι, ²aor. ἐφικόμην: to reach (to); to attain (to)

ἐφίστημι, pres. mid. ἐφίσταμαι, 3. ἐπέστησα/ἐπέστην, aor. ptc. ἐπιστάς, -άντος, 4. ἐφέστηκα: to stand on; to stand near, stand beside (w. παρά); to approach somebody (w. dat.); to come upon, attack; mid. (intrans.), to come upon somebody (w. dat.), overtake somebody

ἔχθρα, ἡ, hatred, enmity

ἐχθρός, -ά, -όν, enemy, hated; ὁ ἐχθρός, an enemy

ἔχω, ἕξω, ἔσχον, ἔσχηκα: trans. to have, hold; intrans. to be, feel

ἕως, (1) conj. until (w. any tense); while (w. pres. ind. only); (2) prep. (w. gen.) to, until, as far as

ζάω (√ζη), ζήσω / ζήσομαι, ἔζησα: to live

Ζεύς, Διός (gen.), Διΐ (dat.), Δία (acc.), Ζεῦ (voc.), Zeus

ζῆλος, ὁ, also ζῆλος, -ους, τό, jealousy; zeal
ζηλόω, to strive; to be filled with envy or jealousy
ζημία, ἡ, loss, damage; fine, financial penalty
ζημιόω, to fine somebody (dat.); pass. to suffer a loss, forfeit
ζητέω, to seek, look for
ζμύρνα, s.v. σμύρνα
ζωή, ἡ, life
ζῷον, τό, animal, living creature
ζῳοποιέω, to give life to, make alive

ἤ, or, than
ἡγεμών, -όνος, ὁ, leader; imperial governor (of a Roman province)
ἡγέομαι (w. inf.), to lead the way; to consider, regard; to regard as necessary;
    subst. ptc. leader, chief; pass. to be led
ἤδη, now, already
ἡδονή, ἡ, enjoyment, pleasure
ἡδύς (m.), -εῖα (fm.), -ύ (nt.), pleasant; pleasant to the taste/sweet, welcome; comp.
    ἡδίων (nom.), ἡδίω (acc.); superl. ἥδιστος, -η, -ον, pl. ἥδιστα, most gladly, most
    delicious (food); most pleasant to the taste; ἥδιστα μᾶλλον, all the more; (adv.)
    ἡδέως, with pleasure, gladly
ἠθικός, -ή, -όν, ethical; (adv.) ἠθικῶς, ethically
ἦθος, -ους, τό, customs and manners, way of life
ἥκω, pres. inf. ἥκειν, 2nd sg. pres. impv. ἥκε, 2. ἥξω: to have come/arrived, be
    present
ἡλικία, ἡ, life span, years of age; maturity, εἰς ἡλικίαν, to one's life span; ἐπέρχομαι
    εἰς ἡλικία, to come of age; παρὰ καιρὸν ἡλικίας, past the normal age
ἥλιος, ὁ, sun; Ἥλιος, ὁ, Helios (sun god)
ἡμεῖς, we
ἡμέρα, ἡ, day
ἡμέτερος, -α, -ον, our
ἥμισυς, -εια, -υ, half; μέχρι τοῦ ἡμίσους, up to the middle (of one's body)
ἠρεμέω, to be quiet, to not speak with (ἐκ)
ἡρῷον, τό (uncontr. ἡρῶιον), grave/shrine of a hero (ἥρως)
ἡσσάομαι (Att. ἡττάομαι), 6. ἡσσήθην: to overcome; pass. to give way to, give into
    (w. dat.), succumb to
ἥσσων, -ον (Att. ἥττων, -ον), lesser, inferior, weaker; (adv.) nt. ἧσσον, less
ἡσυχάζω, to keep quiet; to find rest
ἡσυχία, ἡ, quietness, silence; decorum; rest
ἦχος, ὁ, echo; sound

θάλλασσα, ἡ, sea, lake
θάλπω, to keep warm, inflame (the passions), comfort
θάμνος, ὁ, bush, shrub

θάνατος, ὁ, death

θάπτω, 2. θάψω, 3. ἐτάφησα, ¹aor. inf. θάψαι, pf. pass. ptc. τεθαμμένος, 6. ¹aor. ἐθάφθην/²aor. ἐτάφην: to bury somebody; to provide a funeral for (πρὸς) somebody (dat.)

θαρσέω (Att. θαρρέω), to be of good courage

θάσσων (Att. θάττων), s.v. ταχύς

θαῦμα, τό, a wonder

θαυμάζω, intrans. to marvel, wonder, be amazed; trans. to marvel or wonder at, admire

θαυμάσιος, -α, -ον, wonderful, excellent; superl. θαυμασιώτατος, -η, -ον, most admirable/excellent/wonderful; τὰ θαυμάσια, marvels, wonders

θαυμαστός, -ή, -όν, wonderful, marvelous

θεά, ἡ, goddess

θεάομαι, 3. ἐθεασάμην: to see, look at, notice, observe

θέατρον, τό, theater

θεῖος, θεία, θεῖον, divine; τὸ θεῖον, deity, the Divinity, divine substance; τὰ θεῖα, acts of the gods; (adv.) θείως, divinely

θέλγω, 3. ἔθελξα, ¹aor. inf. θέλξαι: to bewitch, enchant

θέλημα, το, will, desire

θέλω, impf. ἤθελον, 2. θελήσω, 3. ἠθέλησα: to wish, want, desire

θεμέλιος, ὁ, foundation

θεοπρόπος, ὁ, public messenger sent to inquire of an oracle

θεός, ὁ, God, god

θεοσεβής, -ές, pious; subst. god fearer

θεραπεία, ἡ, worship of a god; pl. divine services; medical treatment, healing

θεραπεύω, to serve a deity, perform a ritual for a god; to heal

θερμός, -ή, -όν, hot; τὸ θερμός (= θερμότης), heat

θέσις, -εως, ἡ, position, setting down; resting place

θεσπέσιος, -α, -ον, divine, oracular

θεωρέω, to see, watch, observe

Θῆβαι, αἱ (var. Θήβη), Thebes

θηλυκός, -ή, -όν, female, woman-like, feminine (gram. gender)

θῆλυς, -λεια, -λυ, female; she- ; subst. woman

θηρεύω, to hunt, catch

θηριομαχία, ἡ, to fight with wild beasts (as a spectator event) (Lat. venatio)

θηρίον, τό / θηρσί (dat. pl.): wild animal

θησαυρός, ὁ, treasury, storehouse; pl. treasures

θίασος, ὁ, private religious association

θιασώτης, ὁ, member of a θίασός

θιγγάνω, ²aor. ἔθιγον: to touch (w. gen.), take hold of; pass. to be touched

θλίβω, pf. pass. ptc. τεθλιμμένος: push; to oppress, afflict; pass. to be oppressed, experience pain

θλῖψις, ἡ, distress, affliction, tribulation (apocalyptic term) θνῄσκω, 3. ἔθανον, ²aor. ptc. θανών, pf. act. inf. θνηκέναι: to die, be dead; subst. the deceased

θνητός, -ή, -όν, mortal; subst. a mortal; stillbirth (when the fetus has died in the uterus); τὰ θνητά, things affecting mortals

θορυβέω, to trouble/bother somebody; to create a disturbance, clamor for somebody (acc.); pass. to be troubled, distressed

θόρυβος, ὁ, uproar, public disturbance

θρεπτός, ὁ / θρεπτή, ἡ, house slave

θρίξ, -τριχός, ἡ, hair

θρόνος, ὁ, chair, seat, throne

θυγάτηρ, -τρος, ἡ, daughter; female descendant

θῦμα, -ματος, τό, sacrificial victim, sacrifice

θυμός, ὁ, soul/spirit (as the principle of life); soul/heart (as shown by feelings and passions, esp. joy and grief); passion, desire; anger, rage

θυμόω, to make angry, provoke; pass. to be angry

θύρα, ἡ, door, doorway (of a house); entrance (of cave/tomb); ἐπὶ θύραις, lit. "at the doors" (i.e., impending)

θυρίς, -ίδος, ἡ, window

θυσία, ἡ, sacrifice

θυσιαστήριον, τό, altar of burnt offerings (in the forecourt of the Jerusalem temple)

θύω, to sacrifice (a victim)

θώραξ, -ακος, ὁ, (soldier's) breastplate, coat of mail

ἴαμα, -ματος, τό, healing, cure

ἰάομαι, 2. ἰάσομαι, 3. ἰασάμην, 6. ἰάθην: to heal/cure; to find a remedy

ἰατρός, ὁ, physician

ἴδε, ἴδου, ἴδετε, look! see!

ἰδέα, ἡ, idea, kind, form

ἰδίᾳ (adv. of ἴδιος), -α, -ον, privately

ἴδιος, -α, -ον, one's own, belonging to one, personal

ἱδρύω, 2. ἱδρύσομαι, 3. ἵδρυσα/ἱδρυσάμην, 5. ἵδρυμαι: to found, dedicate; to set up something (altar, statue); mid. to establish (a temple); to dedicate

ἱέρεια, ἡ, priestess

ἱερόν, temple, temple precincts

ἱερεύς, -έως, ὁ, pl. ἱερῆς (later ἱερεῖς), priest; ἐπὶ ἱρέως, during the priesthood of so-and-so

ἱεροποιός, ὁ, magistrate who oversees the temples and sacred rites

ἱερός, -ά, -όν, sacred, holy

Ἱεροσόλυμα, -ματος / Ἱερουσαλήμ, Jerusalem

ἱερόσυλος, -ον, sacrilegious; subst. temple robber, sacrilegious person

ἱκανός, -ή, -όν, sufficient, considerable; many, a number of; (adv.) ἱκανῶς, sufficiently, adequately ἱκέτης, -ου, ὁ / ἱκέτις, -ιδος, ἡ, suppliant (i.e., one who comes seeking help or protection)

Ἰκόνιον, τό, Ikonion (Lat. Iconium)

ἱλάσκομαι, to appease, conciliate

ἵλεως (adv.), merciful, gracious, kindly

ἱμάς, -άντος, ὁ, strap

ἱμάτιον, τό, outer garment, cloak, robe; pl. clothes; grave clothes, funeral shroud

ἱματισμός, ὁ, clothing

ἵνα, in order that (w. subj.), that (introducing an indirect statement)

ἰόβακχος, ὁ, Iobakchos, member of the Bakcheion

ἰός, ὁ, poison

Ἰουδαῖος, -α, ον, Jewish/Judean (adj.); Jew/Judean (noun)

Ἰούλιος, Julius (Roman nomen)

ἱππεύς, -έως, ὁ, horseman, cavalryman (as a collective noun)

ἵππος, ὁ, horse; cavalry (collective noun); pl. ἵπποι, bouncers (in a men's drinking club)

Ἴσις/ Εἶσις, ἡ, Ἴσιδος (gen.), goddess Isis

Ἰσραήλ, ὁ, Israel

ἴσος, -η, -ον, same, equal, equivalent; nt. pl., on an equality; (adv.) ἴσως, equally

ἵστημι, στήσω, ἔστησα ἔστην, ἔστηκα, ἔσταμαι, ἐστάθην: trans. to set, establish; intrans. to stand

ἱστορέω, to visit somebody, get to know somebody; pass. to be recorded

ἱστορία, ἡ, story, account

ἰσχυρός, -ά, -όν, strong, powerful; comp. ἰσχυρότερος, stronger

ἰσχύς, -ύος, ἡ, strength, might

ἰσχύω, to be able/strong; to defeat, overcome; to prevail against (κατά); to be valid, be in force; to be able to, have the power to (w. inf.); subst., something strong; dissolution, breaking up

Ἰταλία, ἡ, Italy

ἰχθύς, -ύος, ὁ, fish

Ἰωνία, ἡ, Ionia (coastal region of west Anatolia)

καθαιρέω, to tear down, destroy; pass. to suffer loss of (w. gen.)

καθαίρω, ¹aor. ἐκάθηρα, to wash, clean; to purge, perform a purification

καθάπερ (= καθά), just as, in the same way, in accordance with

καθαρεύω, to be pure, clean; to be free from

καθαρίζω, to purify from (ἀπό), cleanse

καθαρμός, cleansing, ritual to remove defilement (once it has been contracted)

καθαρός, -ά, -όν, pure, clean, innocent; superl. καθαρώτατος, purest

καθέδρα, ἡ, chair, seat

καθέζομαι, ¹aor pass. ptc. καθεσθείς, -θεῖσα, -θέν: to sit, sit down; to sit by (w. ἐπί); to sit as a suppliant (in a sacred service)

καθεύδω, to sleep; to die; to have sex with (πρός) somebody

καθηγέομαι, to lead, command (w. gen.)

καθῆκω, to be appropriate, suitable, proper; nt. ptc. (τὸ) καθῆκον, what is appropriate

κάθημαι, to sit, sit down

καθιδρύω, to consecrate, dedicate; to found/establish something

καθίζω, (instrans) to sit down, take one's seat; stay; (trans.) to cause to sit, set

καθίστημι, 3. κατέστησα, 6. κατεστάθην, ¹aor. pass. ptc. καθεσθείς: to appoint somebody; to constitute, make

καθότι, to swear (an oath) that; because (= διότι)

καθώς, just as

καί, and; also, even (adv.)

καινός, -ή, -όν, new; strange; comp. καινότερος

καιρός, ὁ, period of time, favorable/proper time, fixed time (for an event)

καίπερ, although (w. ptc.)

Καῖσαρ, -αρος, ὁ, emperor, caesar; Caesar (as a name of a month in the Province of Asia)

καίτοι, although, and yet

καίω (Att. κάω), 3. ἔκαυσα: to light something, kindle a fire, burn

κακία, ἡ, wickedness, evil

κακόω, to do evil, hurt/harm

κακῶς (adv.), wrongly, wickedly; κακῶς ἔχειν, to be sick/ill

κάλλιστος, -η, -ον (superl. of καλός), best, especially noble/fine

κάλλος, -ους, τό, beauty

καλύπτω, pf. pass. ptc. κεκαλυμμένος: to cover, hide, conceal

καλέω, καλέσω, ἐκάλεσα, κέκληκα, κέκλημαι, ἐκλήθην: to call, name, invite

καλός, -ή, -όν, useful, praiseworthy, excellent, fine; beautiful

καλῶς, rightly, well; καλῶς ἂν ποιήσαις/ποιήσεις, lit. "you would do well (to)"; fig. "please" (epistolary formula expressing a polite request); hurrah for, bravo for (to approve the words of a speaker)

καπνός, ὁ, smoke

καρδία, ἡ, the center of physical, spiritual, and mental life; fig. heart

καρπός, ὁ, fruit, grain, harvest

καρτερέω, to be steadfast, persist

κασίγνητος, ὁ / κασιγνήτη, ἡ, brother, sister

κατά, (w. acc.) according to; (w. gen.) against, down from

καταβαίνω, καταβήσομαι, κατέβην, καταβέβηκα: to go down, descend

καταβάλλω, to lead/bring down; to contribute something to

καταγγέλλω, to announce, preach

κατάγω, 3. κατήγαγον, 6. κατήχθην: to bring down; to carry in procession; pass. (naut.) to call in at a port, put into shore

καταισχύνω, to humiliate, shame, disgrace

κατακαίω (Att. κατακάω), impf. κατέκαιον, 2. κατακαύσω: to burn completely, burn up κατάκειμαι, to lie down in/on (dat. / εἰς)

κατακλίνω, to make somebody lay down; pass. to recline at table, to banquet

κατακολουθέω, to obey (commandments) (dat.)

κατάκριμα, τό, condemnation, punishment, penalty

κατακρίνω, to condemn; to sentence somebody to do something

καταλαμβάνω, to obtain, attain, seize; to catch up to somebody (acc.), overtake; to understand; to fall (of night)

καταλλάσσω, 6. κατηλλάγην, aor. pass. subj. καταλλαγῶ, aor. pass. ptc. καταλλαγείς: to reconcile; pass. to become reconciled

καταλείπω / καταλιμπάνω, 3. κατέλιπον, ²aor. ptc. καταλι(μ)πών, 6. κατελείφθην, aor. pass. inf. κατελείφθηναι: to leave behind; to abandon, forsake; to have remaining; to leave alone

καταλιμπάνω, see καταλείπω

κατάλυσις, ἡ, disruption

καταλυσμός, ὁ, flood, deluge

καταλύω, to destroy, abolish; to eradicate

κατανοέω, to observe; to gaze at

καταντάω, to come to, arrive at, reach; to attain to something

καταξιόω, to consider somebody worthy

καταπίπτω, pf. καταπέπτωκα: to fall, drop; to descend

καταργέω, to deactivate, render ineffective, make powerless (contrasting ἐνεργῶ); to release from, estrange from

κατασείω, to wave one's hand, signal

κατασκευάζω, to construct, build; to prepare

καταφεύγω, ¹aor. κατέφυγα/²aor. κατέφυγον: to flee; to take refuge

καταφιλέω, to kiss, caress; to kiss somebody in greeting/farewell

καταφρονέω, to despise, treat with contempt

καταφυγή, ἡ, place of refuge

καταφυτεύω, to plant

καταχράομαι, to make full use of something, have full ownership of something (dat.)

κατεργάζομαι, 3. κατειργασάμην: to bring about, accomplish; to prepare; to work out

κατέρχομαι, 4. κατελήλυθα: to go down; to derive from, descend from; (naut.) to put into port

κατεσθίω, impf. κατήσθιον, 3ʳᵈ pl. impf. -θοσαν, 3. κατέφαγον: to eat, devour

κατέχω, ²aor. κατέσχον, ¹aor. pass. ptc. κατασχεθείς: to possess, occupy; to hold back, bind, confine; to understand that (ὅτι); to hold (a ship) on a certain course

κατηχέω, 3. κατήχησα: to teach, instruct

κατισχύω, to overpower; prevail over (acc.), become master of

κατοικέω, to settle, dwell in; subst. inhabitants

κατοικία, ἡ, dwelling place; territory (for habitation)

κατοικίζω, to settle, establish; pass. to be settled, dwell

κάτω, down (adv.)

καυχάομαι, to boast, take pride in

καύχημα, -ματος, τό, boast; a ground for boasting, object of boasting

κεῖμαι, 2. κείσομαι: to stand/be standing; to recline; to lie sick; to lie buried; to be appointed, established; subst. (τά) κείμενα, something established/existing

κελεύω, to command (officially) + inf. to order that

κενός, -ή, -όν, empty, void (space); τὸ κενόν, the void; no purpose; κενῶς / διὰ κενῆς / εἰς κενόν, in vain, to no purpose

κεντυρίων, -ωνος, ὁ, centurion (Lat. loanw., cf. ἑκατοντάρχης)

κέρας, -ατος, τό, horn (of an animal), container made from the horn of an animal

κερδαίνω, 3. ἐκέρδησα/ἐκέρδανα: to gain, profit; to spare oneself, avoid

κέρδος, -ους, τό, gain, profit

κεφαλή, ἡ, head

κῆδος (Aeol. κᾶδος), -εος, τό, performing funeral rites for the dead

κῆπος, ὁ, garden

κηρύσσω, κηρύξω, ἐκήρυξα, κακήρυχα, κεκήρυγμαι, ἐκηρύχθην: to proclaim, make known, preach

κῆρυξ, -υκος, ὁ, herald, public messenger; trumpet shell (seashell with sharp edges used in torture)

κιβωτός, ἡ, chest, treasure chest; sacred depository, Ark (of the Covenant); boat, ark (barge)

κιθαριστής, ὁ, kithara player

Κιλικία, ἡ, province of Cilicia

κινδυνεύω (impers.), there is a danger/risk that + inf.

κινέω, to move; to stir up; pass. to be moved/resolved (of an inward personal disposition)

κίνησις, -εως, ἡ, motion, movement

κλαίω, pres. ptc. κλάων, 3. ἔκλαυσα: to weep (for), cry

κλάω, 6. ἐκλάσθην: to break, break off; pass. to be damaged

κλείω, 6. ἐκλείσθην: to close up, shut up

κλέπτης, -ου, ὁ, thief

κλέπτω, to steal

κληρονομέω, to inherit, acquire possession of something

κληρονομία, inheritance

κληρονόμος, ὁ, heir, inheritor

κληρόω, to obtain by lot, appoint by lot; pass. to be assigned

κλῆρος, ου, ὁ, that which is assigned by lot, a share, portion; inheritance, inheritable estate

κλῆσις, ἡ, calling, vocation

κλητός, -ή, -όν, called

κλίνη, ἡ, couch, bed

κλίνω, 3. ἔκλινα: to bend down; κλίνω τὴν κεφαλήν, to bow one's head; ἔκλινεν τὰ γόνατα, to fall on one's knees

κλύω, aor. impv. κλῦθι: to hear, attend to

κοιλία, ἡ, belly, womb

κοιμάομαι, ¹aor. pass. ptc. κοιμηθείς (dep.): to fall asleep; to sleep; subst. one who has fallen asleep; (fig.) to die

κοινός, -ή, -όν, common, shared; public; κοινῇ σωτηρίᾳ, for common safety; subst. τὸ κοινόν, treasury; religious association; τὰ κοινά, common funds, public money; κοινῇ (adv.), in common, as a group; in public

κοινωνέω, to have a share of something (w. gen.)

κοινωνία, ἡ, fellowship, partnership; sexual intercourse with (πρός)

κοίτη, ἡ, bed

κοιτών, -ῶνος, ὁ, bed chamber

κόκκινος, -η, -ον, scarlet, red; τὸ κόκκινον, scarlet cloth,

κολάζω, to punish, chastise; to punish for (ἐπί)

κολακεία, ἡ, flattery

κόλασις, ἡ, punishment, torture

κολυμβάω, to swim

κομίζομαι, to get back, recover; to bring into (ἐν) a place, introduce

κοπιάω, ¹aor. ἐκοπίασα: to work hard, labor

κόπος, ὁ, labor, work; reward for labor; produce/harvest

κόπτω, 3. ἔκοψα: to cut, beat (one's breast); to strike somebody, fight; mid. to mourn

Κορίνθιος, -α, -ον, Corinthian; subst. a Corinthian person

Κόρινθος, ἡ, Corinth

κόρος, ὁ, boy; κόρα, ἡ, girl; pl. pupils (of the eyes)

κοσμέω, to put in order, arrange; to adorn, dress

κοσμικός, -ή, -όν, earthly, worldly

κόσμος, ὁ, world (as a place of habitation); good order; ornament, ornamentation

κουφίζω, to lighten

κοῦφος, -η, -ον, light (in weight), airy

κράζω, to scream, screech; to call out, cry out, shout

κρᾶσις, -εως, ἡ, mixing, blending of things (that form a compound)

κραταιός, -ά, -όν, powerful, mighty

κρατέω, to attain something; to conquer, master, rule over (w. gen.), subdue; take possession of (w. gen.); to take custody of; to hold something (w. gen.)

κράτιστος, -η, -ον, most excellent, noblest; most excellent; "his Excellency" (official title given to senators and magistrates)

κράτος, -ους, τό, power; κατὰ κράτος, powerfully, mightily

κρέας, ὁ, κρέως, meat/flesh

κρείσσων (Att. κρείττων), -ον, gen. –ονος (comp. of ἀγαθός): stronger, better, of higher rank/value ; subst. τὸ κρεῖσσον, something better

κρεμάννυμι/κρεμάζω, 1. pres. mid. κρέμαμαι, pres. mid. ptc. κρεμάμενος, 3. ἐκρέμασα, aor. mid. inf. κρέμασθαι, aor. pl. ptc. κρεμάσαντες, 6. ἐκεμάσθην: to hang up something, hang something from (gen.); to hang somebody in execution; mid. to hang, be suspended; pass. to be hung up, suspended

κρημνός, ὁ, cliff, precipice

Κρήτη, ἡ, Crete

κρίμα, τό, legal case; judgment

κρίνω, κρινῶ, ἔκρινα, κέκρικα, κέκριμαι, ἐκρίθην: to judge, reach a decision, decide; pass. to be decided

κρίσις, -εως, ἡ, judgment, judging; condemnation

κρίσμα, see κρίμα

κρυπτός, -ή, -όν, hidden

κρύπτω, impf. pass. ἐκρυβόμην, 3. ἔκρυψα, 6. ἐκρύβην, ²aor. pass. inf. κρυβῆναι, pf. pass. ptc. κεκρυμμένος: to cover, hide, conceal; pass. to be hiding

κτάομαι, 3. ἐκτησάμην, ¹aor. mid. inf. κτήσασθαι, pf. κέκτημαι, plpf. pass. ἐκέκτημην: to get, acquire; to possess; subst. οἱ κεκτήμενοι, owners

κτῆμα, -ματος, τό, anything gotten; pl. possessions,

κτῆνος, -ους, τό, domestic animal; mostly pl. τὰ κτήνεα, herds, cattle, livestock

κτήσις, -εως, ἡ, property, possessions

κτίζω, to found, create, make; to build; pass. to be created, constructed

κτίσις, -εως, ἡ, creation, that which is created; creature, created thing

κυβερνήτης, ὁ, shipmaster (who is responsible for the crew)

κυέω, ¹aor. inf. κυῆσαι: to be pregnant; to conceive a child

κύκλος, ὁ, circle; pl. heavenly bodies

κυκλόω, to encircle, surround

κύκλῳ, in a circle, around; all around

κυλίω, to roll something up/down; mid., to roll oneself upon something; to pour down

κῦμα, -ματος, τό, wave (of the sea)

Κύπρος, ἡ, Cyprus

κυρία, ἡ, lady

κυριακός, -ή, -όν, belong to the Lord, the Lord's

κυριεύω (w. gen.), to have power over, rule over; to gain mastery over; to control

κύριος, earthly master or lord; Lord (as title of God and Christ)

κύριος, -α, -ον, valid/good (re law and statutes); ἀγορά κυρία, regular meeting/ assembly

κυρίως (adv.), with full authority; comp. κυριώτερος, greater authority; superl. κυριώτατος, supreme authority

κύων, ὁ, κυνός (gen.), κύνα (acc.): dog

κωλύω, to hinder, prevent; to prohibit

κώμη, ἡ, village; pl. countryside

κῶμος, ὁ, carousing, wild partying

κωφός, -ή, -όν, deaf, unable to speak

λαγχάνω, ²aor. ἔλαχον, subj. λάχην, ptc. λαχών: to receive (an inheritance/honor); to obtain an office; to choose by lot

λάθρᾳ, secretly (adv.)

λαμβάνω, λήμψομαι, ἔλαβον, εἴληφα, εἴλημμαι, ἐλήμφθην: to take, take hold of, receive

λαμπρός, -ά, -όν, bright, shining; superl. λαμπρότατος, -η, -ον, brightness, splendor; most excellent (w. titulature)

λάμπω, 3. ἔλαμψα: to shine, shine forth; to shine upon somebody (dat.)

λανθάνω (also λήθω), ²aor. ἔλαθον, ²pf. ptc. λεληθότως: to escape notice, be unknown to somebody (acc.); pf. ptc. as adv., secretly

λαός, ὁ, people, nation

λατρεύω (w. dat.), to serve somebody (as a religious duty), worship

λέγω, ἐρῶ, εἶπον, εἴρηκα, εἴρημαι, ἐρρέθην/ἐρρήθην: to speak, say

λειτουργέω, to provide service (during sacrifices)

λειτουργία, ἡ, public service, public liturgical service; priestly ministry

λεπτός, -ή, -όν, light (in weight); light (diet), thin; fine, delicate, subtle; τὸ λεπτόν δρ., light drachma (= 1 obol); superl. λεπτότητος

λευκός, -ή, -όν, white; comp. –τερος, whiter

λέων, -οντος, ὁ / λέαινα, ἡ, lion, lioness

λήθη, ἡ, forgetfulness

λῃστής, ὁ, robber, pirate

λίαν, very, exceedingly

λιθάζω, ¹aor. ptc. λίθασας: to stone somebody (as a means of execution)

λίθινος, -α, -ον, made of stone

λίθος, ὁ, stone; precious stones, jewels

λιμήν, -μένος, ὁ, harbor

λίμνη, ἡ, lake

λογίζομαι εἰς (w. acc.), to estimate, reckon; to have regard for, esteem

λογικός, -ή, -όν, rational; τὰ λογικά, rational beings

λόγιον, τό, saying, oracle; omen

λογισμός, ὁ, deliberation, reasoning; reasoning (as a faculty of the mind); λογισμοί, financial accounts

λόγος, ὁ, statement, saying, utterance, discourse; proposal; complaint; (magical) spell, formula

λοιδορέω, to rebuke, abuse somebody

λοιμός, ὁ, plague

λοιπός, -ή, -όν, remaining, rest; (τὸ) λοιπόν, from now on, finally; (adv.); οἱ λοιποί/τὰ λοιπά the rest/others

λούω/λόω, to bathe, wash; mid. to bathe oneself (the contr. impf. mid. forms, ἐλούμην and ἐλοῦτο, to belong to λόω); to bathe (as a baptism)

λύπη, ἡ, sorrow; affliction; pl. pains, labor pains

λυπέω, to cause pain/grief; pass. to be sorrowful, distressed

λύσις, ἡ, a releasing; divorce; breaking (of spells); interpretation; solution (of a riddle)

λυτρόω, mid. to release by payment of a ransom, redeem

λύχνος, lamp (of metal or clay)

μαγικός, -ή, -όν, magical; pl. subst. works of sorcery

μάγος, ὁ, magician

μαθητής, ὁ, pupil, disciple

μαῖα, ἡ, midwife

μαινάς, -άδος, ἡ, maenad, female bacchante

μακαρίζω, 2. μακαριῶ: to call/consider blessed; to pronounce blessed for (w. gen.)

μακάριος, -α, -ον, blessed, happy

Μακεδονία, ἡ, Macedonia

Μακεδών, -όνος, ὁ, Macedonian person

μακράν (adv.), far (away)

μακροθυμέω, to be long-suffering, patient

μάλα, very; comp. μᾶλλον, more, all the more; instead of/rather than; by all means; μᾶλλον ἤ, more than; μᾶλλον...ἤ...; πολλῷ μᾶλλον, much more; superl. μάλιστα, most of all, above all, especially

μάλιστα, most of all, above all, especially

μᾶλλον, more, rather; μᾶλλον...ἤ, more...than, cf. μάλα

μανθάνω, ²aor. ἔμαθον,²aor. inf. μαθεῖν, 4. μεμάθηκα, pf. ptc. μεμαθηκώς: to learn; to learn something from (ἀπό / gen.) somebody

μαραίνω, to quench; pass. to die out (of a flame); to waste/wither away

μαρτυρέω, to bear witness, testify; to speak favorable of; to approve of somebody (dat.); to approve of somebody; pass. to gain approval for something, be approved of by somebody

μαρτυρία, ἡ, evidence; martyrdom

μαρτύριον, τό, testimony, proof; martyrdom

μάρτυς, -υρος, ὁ, witness; martyr

μαστιγόω, to whip, flog

μαστίζω, to strike with a whip, scourge

μαστός, ὁ, woman's breast; man's breast

μάταιος, -α, -ον, empty, useless, powerless; foolish

μάχαιρα, ἡ, sword, dagger

μάχη, ἡ, a fight/fighting, quarrel, dispute; battle

μάχομαι, to quarrel, dispute; to fight; μάχομαι ἐν, fight with (ἐν/dat.), be in conflict with; οἱ μαχόμενοι, those who fight, combatants

μεγαλύνω, to praise, glorify, exalt

μέγας, μεγάλη, μέγα, large, great

μέγεθος, -ους, τό, size, magnitude, greatness

μέγιστος, -η, -ον (superl. of μέγας, μεγάλη, μέγα): best, extraordinary; topmost, foremost; mighty

μεθερμηνεύω, to translate

μεθίστημι, 3. μετέστησα: to remove; to seduce (to apostasy), shift somebody over to (a particular way of life)

μεθύσκω, 3. ἐμέθυσα: to make somebody drunk; pass. to become drunk

μεθύω, to be drunk

μ(ε)ίγνημι, 3. ἔμ(ε)ιξα, ¹aor impv. μῖξον,¹aor. pass. ἐμ(ε)ίχθην, more oft. ²aor. pass. ἐμ(ε)ίγην: to mix; to bring together; pass. to be brought into contact with, be intermingled

μειδιάω, to smile

μείρομαι, pf. pass. εἵμαρμαι, pf. pass. ptc. εἱμαρμένος: pass. to be decreed by Fate; fm. ptc. ἡ εἱμαρμένη, Fate

μέλαν, -ανος, τό, ink

μέλας, -αινα, -αν, black, dark

μελέτη, ἡ, care

μέλι, -ιτος, τό, honey

μέλλω (w. inf.), to be about to, intend to

μέλος, -ους, τό, melody, music; bodily frame (usually pl.)

μέλω, (impers.) μέλει τινι, it is a care/concern to somebody; pass. to be of special interest to somebody (dat.)

μέντοι (Dor. μάντοι), yet, nevertheless

μένω, μενῶ, ἔμεινα, μεμένηκα: to remain, stay

μερίζω, 2. μεριῶ, 6. ἐμερίσθην: to divide; to assign

μεριμνάω, to be anxious to do something

μέρος, -ους, τό / nom. and acc. pl., τὰ μέρη: part, piece; one's part/role; place; a separate part (in contrast to the whole)

μέσος, -η, -ον, middle, in the middle/midst; ἀνὰ μέσον, between, within (w. gen.)

μεστός, -ή, -όν, filled with, full of (gen.); subst. something that is full/filled

μετά, (w. gen.), with; (w. acc.), after, behind

μεταβάλλω, to change; to turn/transform into (εἰς) something

μεταβολή, ἡ, change, changing

μεταδίδωμι, to give a share, impart

μετανοέω, to repent

μετανοία, ἡ, repentance

μεταξύ (w. gen.), between

μεταπέμπω, to send for, summon; to arrest somebody

μεταστρέφω, to change, turn (somebody's mind) to; to pervert something

μετατίθημι, to put in another place, transfer to another place; mid. to change one's mind, turn away

μετέχω, to partake of (gen.), participate in

μετουσία, ἡ, participation, partnership

μέτρον, τό, measure; size

μέχρι(ς), (prep. w. gen.) until, to; to the extent; (conj.) until

μή, not (w. non-ind. verbs)

μηδαμῶς, by no means, not at all

μηδέ, nor, but not, not even (with non-indicative moods)

μηδείς, μηδεμία, μηδέν (w. non-ind.), no one, nothing; μηδέν (adv.), not at all, in no way

μηδέποτε, never

μηδέπω, not yet (w. non-ind. moods)

μήκιστος, -η, -ον, longest (time)

μήν (= εἰ μήν), surely, indeed (used in combination w. various particles); καὶ μήν, furthermore

μήν, ὁ, μηνός, month

μηνύω, 3. ἐμήνησα, ¹aor. pass. ptc. μηνυθείς: to disclose a secret, report

μήποτε, that … not, lest

μήπως, that perhaps, lest somehow

μήτηρ, -τρός, ἡ, mother

μηχανάομαι, to plot against, contrive against somebody

μιαίνω, 3. ἐμίανα, 5. μεμίαμμαι: to defile, contaminate; mid. to defile oneself

μίγνημι, s.v. μείγνημι

μικρός, -α, -ον, little, small, of little importance

μιμνήσκομαι (w. gen.) (also μνήσκομαι), 3. ἐμνήσθην, 4. μέμνημαι, 6. ἐμνήσθην: to remember somebody, recollect; to make mention of (w. gen.); pass. (dep.) remembered/to be remembered

μισέω, hate, despise

μισθός, ὁ, wages, pay; physician's fee

μνᾶ, ἡ, μνᾶς (gen.), μνῆν (acc.) / pl. μναῖ, μνέων (gen. pl. > NW μνᾶν), mina (= 100 drachmae)

μνῆμα, -ματος, τό, grave, tomb

μνημεῖον, τό, tomb, sepulchre

μνημονεύω (w. gen.), to remember, think of; to make mention of (περί); μνημονευτέον (verbal adj. expressing necessity), must be remembered, must be kept in mind

μνημόσυνον, τό, memorial, remembrance, legacy

μνηστεύω, to betrothe; pass. to be betrothed, engaged

μοῖρα, ἡ, portion, share; ἱερὰ μοῖρα, sacred share (that is rightfully due); destiny, fate

μοιχεία, ἡ, adultery

μόλις, with difficulty, scarcely; only rarely, not readily

μονογενής, -ές, only, unique

μόνος, -η, -ον, only, alone

μορφή, ἡ, form, outward appearance

μουσικός, -ή, -όν, musical

μυέω, to initiate somebody (into the mysteries); pass. to have performed myster-ies, be initiated into the mysteries; subst. ceremony of initiation into the mysteries

μῦθος, ὁ, story, narrative

μυριάς, -άδος, ἡ, ten thousand; a myriad; (mostly pl.) countless thousands

μυσαρός, -ά, -όν, foul, dirty; subst. polluted thing

μυστήριον, τό, mystery, secret knowledge; pl., secret rituals

μύστης, ὁ, / μύστις, ἡ, an initiate

μωρία, -ας, ἡ, foolishness

μωρός, -ά, -όν, foolish, stupid; subst. foolish thing

ναός, ὁ, temple, inner part of Jewish temple, sanctuary

ναῦς, ἡ, ναός (gen., Att. νεώς), ναῦν (acc.), ship (of larger vessels)

ναύτης, ὁ, sailor

νεανίσκος, ὁ, a youth, young man; servant

νεκρός, -ά, -όν, dead, lifeless; pl. the dead

νέος, -α, -ον, new; ὁ νεός, boy/young man; ἡ νέα νουμηνία, New Year

νεότης, -ητος, ἡ, youth, state of youthfulness

νεύω, to nod, beckon with the hand

νεφέλη, ἡ, cloud

νεώτερος, ὁ (comparative of νέος), young man

νή, by (particle of strong affirmation, w. acc. of divinity being invoked)

νῆσος, ἡ, island

νηστεία, ἡ, day of fasting, esp. the Day of Atonement

νηστεύω, to fast, observe a fast

νικάω, to defeat; to win a court case

νίκη, victory; Νίκη, goddess Nike

νιν (encl.), Dor. acc. of 3rd pers. pron. for αὐτός/αὐτή (him /her)

νοερός, -ή, -όν, intellectual

νοέω (w. acc.), aor. pass. ptc. νοηθείς: to perceive, understand (that); mid. to bear in mind, think; pass. to be thought of, be perceived

νομίζω, to think, suppose, assume; to institute a custom; pass. ptc. customary; subst. (nt. pl. ptc.), customary things

νόμιμος, -η, -ον, to conform to the law, legal; pl. τὰ νόμιμα, laws, statutes

νόμος, ὁ, law, Torah

νοσέω, to be ill, sick

νόσος, ἡ, disease, illness

νουθεσία, ἡ, warning, instruction, admonition

νουθετέω, to instruct; to warn, admonish

νουμηνία, ἡ, new moon; first day of the lunar month; ἡ νέα νουμηνία, the New Year

νοῦς ὁ, νοός, (gen.), νοΐ/νῷ (dat.), νοῦ (gen.), νοῦν (acc.): mind, understanding; κατὰ νοῦν, in one's mind

νύμφη, ἡ, bride, young wife

νυμφίος, ὁ, bridegroom

νῦν, now, at the present

νυνί, strengthened form of νῦν, now, at this time

νύξ, νυκτός, ἡ, night

ξενίζω, to entertain/host as a guest; to surprise, startle; subst. (nt. pl. ptc.), strange things/notions

ξένιος, -α, -ον, hospitable; epithet of Zeus, "protector of the rights of hospitality"

ξένος, -η, -ον, strange, foreign; subst. a stranger, foreigner; guest

ξύλον, τό, wood, tree (collective, trees); cross

ξηρός, -ά, -όν, dry; paralyzed

ὁ, ἡ, τό, the

ὀβολός, ὁ, pl. ὀβολοι: obol

ὀγδοήκοντα, eighty

ὄγδοος, -η, -ον, eighth

ὀγκόω, pass. to swell (through pregancy); to be pregnant

ὅδε, ἥδε, τάδε, this

ὁδεύω, to travel

ὁδηγέω, to guide, lead; to lead to (πρός/εἰς)

ὁδός, ἡ, way, road, journey

ὀδούς, -όντος, ὁ, pl. teeth

ὅθεν (adv. of place), from where, from which; for which reason

οἶδα, fut. εἰδήσω, plpf. ᾔδειν: to know, understand, perceive

οἰκεῖος, -α, -ον, of a household; belonging to the same kin/family; proper to a thing, suitable; individual; οἱ οἰκεῖοι, family members

οἰκέτης, household slave

οἰκέω, to live with (gen.); to inhabit/dwell (acc.)

οἰκίζω, ¹aor. ᾤκισα, poet. ᾤκισσα, 4. ᾤκικα, pf. pass. ᾤκισμαι: to found a city/colony; to build (a temple)

οἰκοδομέω, pf. pass. ᾠκοδόμημαι: to build/construct; to form/fashion; (fig.) to build up, encourage

οἰκονομία, ἡ, management of a household; administration of an office; economy; arrangement, structure (of parts), "anatomy"

οἶκος, ὁ, also οἰκία, ἡ, house, home

οἰκουμένη, ἡ, inhabited world

οἶνος, ὁ, wine

οἴομαι (also οἶμαι), impf. ᾤμην: to think that, suppose; to feel like (w. inf.)

οἷος, -α, -ον, what kind (of), such as; οἷον + inf. (impling fitness, possibility), it is possible

ὀκνέω, 3. ὤκνησα: to hesitate

ὄλεθρος, -ου, ὁ, destruction

ὀλίγος, -η, -ον, little, few; pl. δι᾽ ὀλίγων, in a few (words), briefly; (πρὸς) ὀλίγον, a short while; μετ᾽ ὀλιγον, after a brief (time)

ὁλοκαυτώμα, -ματος, τό, a whole burnt offering

ὅλος, -η, -ον, whole, all

ὁμιλία, ἡ, conversation

ὄμμα, -ματος, τό, eye

ὄμνυμι (later ὀμνύω), 2. ὀμοῦμαι, 3. ὤμοσα, aor. subj. ὀμόσω: to swear/confirm an oath, swear by (ἐν or + acc.) a god

ὅμοιος, -α, -ον (w. dat.), like, similar to (w. dat. or gen.); subst. τὰ ὅμοια, the same things

ὁμοιόω, to make like, become like (w. dat.)

ὁμοίωμα, -ματος, τό, likeness, form, appearance

ὁμοίως (adv.), likewise, in the same way

ὁμοῦ (adv.), in the same place/time, together

ὅμως, nevertheless

ὀνειδίζω, to mock, insult, heap insults upon

ὀνειδισμός, ὁ, reproach, contempt

ὄνειρος, ὁ, a dream

ὄνομα, -ματος, τό, name

ὀνομάζω, to name/call something (by a certain name); to utter a name (acc.) (for magical purposes) on (ἐπι)

ὄντως, actually, really

ὀξύς, -εῖα, -ύ, sharp; swift, quick (of spirit/mind); comp. -τερος

ὅπερ, s.v. ὅσπερ

ὅπῃ, by which; ὅπῃ ἢ ὅπως, a way by which

ὁπλίται, s.v. ὅπλον

ὅπλον, τό, tool, large shield; pl. τὰ ὅπλα, weapons, arms

ὁποῖος, -α, -ον, of what sort, such as

ὁπόσος, -ον, as much/many, how much/many

ὅπου, where (non-interogative)

ὅπως, that, in order that

ὅραμα, -ματος, τό, a vision

ὅρασις, ἡ, seeing, sight; apearance; pl. eyes

ὁράω, ὄψομαι, εἶδον, ἑόρακα / ἑώρακα, —, ὤφθην: to see

ὀργάνον, τό, tool, bodily organ, device; musical instrument

ὀργή, ἡ, anger, wrath

ὄργια, -ίων, τά, secret religious rites, religious mysteries ὀργίζω, pass. to become angry

ὀργίλος, -η, -ον, inclined to anger, quick-tempered; subst. hot temper; one of violent temper

ὀρθός, -ή, -όν, upright, erect; straight, true, correct; ὀρθῶς, correctly, rightly, strictly; normally, in good order

ὀρθόω, to set upright; pass. to be erected

ὁρίζω, to set limits; to appoint, set; to administer an oath; pass. to be fixed/determined; to be limited

ὅριον, τό, boundary, τὰ ὅρια, region, district

ὁρκίζω: to make somebody swear an oath to somebody (acc.), swear by the name (τῷ ὀνόματι τοῦ) of somebody; conjure by (acc.), magically invoke by (acc.)

ὅρκος, ὁ, oath

ὁρμάω, to rush

ὄρος, -ους, τό, mountain, hill

ὅς, ἥ, ὅ, who, which, what

ὀσμή, ἡ, smell, fragrance

ὅσος, -η, -ον, as much as; pl. as many as, all; + ἄν (or ἐάν), whoever, whatever

ὅσπερ, ὅνπερ (acc.) / ἥπερ (fm.) / ὅπερ (nt.) / ἅπερ (nt. pl.): the very man/woman/thing(s); which indeed/exactly; ὅνπερ τρόπον, in the same way

ὅστις, ἥτις, ὅτι, who, which, whoever

ὀστοῦν, τό (uncontr. ὀστέον), pl. ὀστᾶ, ὀστῶν (uncontr. ὀστέων), bone

ὄστρακον, τό, potsherd

ὅταν, when, whenever

ὅτε, when, while

ὅτι, that, because

οὗ, where

οὗ, whose (gen. of relative pronoun ὅ)

οὐ, οὐκ, οὐχ, not, no

οὐαί (w. dat.), woe/alas; concerning, by reason of (dat.)

οὐδαμός, -ή, -όν, not anyone, not any; οὐδαμοῦ, nowhere, not anywhere

οὐδέ, not even; οὐδέ… οὐδέ…neither … nor …

οὐδείς, οὐδεμία, οὐδέν, no one, nothing, no

οὐδέποτε, never

οὐκέτι (adv.), no longer, no more

οὖν, then (temporal), therefore (in a discourse or line of argument)

οὔπω, not yet

οὐράνιος -ον, heavenly, from heaven; meteorological

οὐρανός, ὁ, sky, heaven

οὖς, τό, ὠτός (gen.), ὠτί (dat.) / pl. τὰ ὦτα: dim. ὠτίον: hearing

οὐσία, ἡ, being, essence; substance

οὐτέ, not, nor; οὐτέ… οὐτέ…, neither…nor…

οὗτος, αὕτη, τοῦτο, this

οὕτω, οὕτως, (1) adv. in this way, thus, so; (2) adj. such; (3) as follows

οὐχί, not, not so, no indeed

ὀφειλέτης, ὁ, a debtor, one who is under obligation, one who is guilty/liable for

ὀφείλω (and –έω), 2. ὀφειλήσω, 3. ὠφείλησα: to owe somebody something, be indebted to somebody; to be obligated to, should/must (w. inf.); ἁμαρτίαν ὀφείλω (w. dat.), to incur sin against

ὀφθαλμός, ὁ, eye

ὄφις, -εως, ὁ, serpent, snake

ὄφρα, that, in order that

ὄχλος, ὁ, crowd; army; pl. peoples

ὀψέ (adv.), late, late in the evening; as prep. (w. gen.), late for something

ὀψιά, ἡ, evening

ὄψις, -εως, ἡ, appearance, countenance, face; vision, apparition

πάθος, -ους (uncontr. -εος), τό, misfortune, calamity; emotions, passions; pain; pl. τὰ πάθη, feelings; οὐράνιος πάθος, meteorological disturbance

παιδάριον, young man; small boy

παιδεία, ἡ, teaching, education; discipline, correction

παιδευτής, ὁ, instructor of youths

παιδεύω, to teach, instruct; to correct, discipline

παιδίον, τό, child, infant

παιδίσκη, ἡ, female slave, maidservant

παῖς, παιδός, ὁ/ἡ, child (in relation to parents); slave/servant (in relation to a master/God); ἐκ παιδός, from childhood

παλαιός, -ά, -όν, old, former

πάλιν, again, once more

πανταχοῦ, everywhere

πάντη (adv.), in every way, on every side

παντοκράτωρ, -ορος, ὁ, almighty one

πάντοτε, always (adv.)

πάντως (adv.), certainly, doubtless; strictly

πάππος, ὁ, grandfather

παρά, (w. gen.) from, by, (w. dat.) with, in the presence of; (w. acc.) beside, along

παραβολή, ἡ, parable, proverb; discourse

παράγγελμα, τό, commandment

παραβαίνω, 3. παρέβην: to transgress

παραβάλλω, to throw to (esp. of fodder to animals); to venture to (do something)

παράβασις, -εως, ἡ, disobedience, violation of a boundary or norm

παραγγέλλω, to command, instruct somebody (dat.); subst. ptc. instructions, things announced

παραγίνομαι, to be beside, be present with, visit with (πρός); to come to one's side/aid; to arrive at/in/from (εἰς/ἐν/ἐκ)

παράγω, to march by; to introduce; to (make) pass by

παράδεισος, -ου, ὁ, garden, orchard (in Eden); a place of blessedness above the earth, "Paradise"

παραδέχομαι, to accept, receive

παραδίδωμι, to hand over to another, transmit

παραιτέομαι, to ask for, entreat, beg, request; to excuse oneself (παραιτοῦμαι, "excuse me")

παρακαλέω, to beg, request; to urge, encourage; to console, comfort; to appeal to; to summon

παράκειμαι, to be ready; to have available, have in stock

παράκλησις, -εως, ἡ, encouragement, comfort

παρακολουθέω, pf. ptc. παρηκολουθηκώς: to follow, accompany; to follow (in a course of events); to follow in the mind, understand

παρακούω, to ignore, pay no attention to; to disobey

παραλαμβάνω, to receive, accept; to take, take charge of; to take over/receive somebody as a prisoner; to inherit sacred objects; to succeed to an office

παραμένω, to remain (in a place); to remain/stay (of slaves whose manumission was deferred)

παραμονή, ἡ, obligation of a slave to continue to serve his or her master after manumission

παράνομος, -ον, lawless, unlawful

παράπτωμα, τό, an offense, wrongdoing

παρασκευάζω, to provide, prepare for somebody/something (dat.)

παρασπείρω, to be interspersed/dispersed in

παρατίθημι, to serve up (food), provide

παρατυγχάνω, ²aor. ptc. παρατυχών: to be somewhere by chance, be present at

παραχρῆμα, immediately, instantly; recently

πάρειμι (fr. εἰμί), pres. ptc. παρών, -οῦσα, -όν, impf. παρῆν, opt. παρείην: to be present, be here; (impers.) to come to/upon, arrive; πάρειμι + inf., to be possible to (do something); subst. ptc. the present; bystander

παρεμβολή, ἡ, army; battalion

παρέρχομαι, pf. inf. παρεληλυθέναι: to walk past, pass by; to pass away; (of time) to be past; (of a past) to be over; to disobey

παρέχω, 3. παρέσχον, ²aor. ptc. παρασχών, ²aor. mid. impv. παράσχου: to provide/give; + inf., to allow somebody (dat.) to do something

παρθένος, ἡ, virgin, unmarried girl

παρίστημι (also παριστάνω), pf. ptc. παρεστώς: to stand before (w. dat.); to approach, come near; to render, present oneself, offer, supply; to show

παρό > παρ᾽ ὅ, for what reason

παρουσία, ἡ, coming, arrival; technical term for the second "coming" of Christ; (personal) presence

παροχή, ἡ, supply of something

παρρησία, ἡ, confidence, boldness; (adv.) παρρησίᾳ, freely, openly, plainly παρρησιάζομαι, to speak openly/freely

πᾶς, πᾶσα, πᾶν, (w/o article) each, every (pl. all); (w. article) entire, whole, all; everyone, everything

πάσχω, πείσομαι, ²aor. ἔπαθον, ptc. παθών, πέπονθα: to suffer, endure, undergo; to experience

πατάσσω, ¹aor. inf. πατάξαι: to strike, slay

πάτηρ- τρός, ὁ, father

πάτριος, -α, -ον (= πατρικός), derived from one's fathers, hereditary; customary; subst. τὸ πάτριον, tradition; τὰ πάτρια, ancestral customs

πατρίς, -ίδος, ἡ, homeland; hometown

πατρῷος, -α, ον, of one's father(s), hereditary (privileges/honors)

παύω, to make to end, bring to an end; mid. to stop doing something, cease

πεδίον, τό, plain

πέδον, τό, ground, plain

πείθω, πείσω, ἔπεισα, πέποιθα, πέπεισμαι, ἐπείσθην: to persuade, convince; (pass.) to obey; (pf. act. and pass.) to trust, rely on, have confidence

πεινάω, to be hungry

πειρασμός, ὁ, period/process of tempting, trial, test

πέμπτος, -η, -ον, fifth

πέμπω, πέμψω, ἔπεμψα, —, —, ἐπέμφθην: to send, appoint

πένης, -ητος, ὁ, poor person

πενθέω, to be sad, grieve, mourn; πενθῶ ἐπί, to mourn over

πένθός, -ους, τό, mourning, sorrow

πεντήκοντα, fifty

πεντακόσιοι, -αι, -α, five hundred

πέρα, beyond (w. gen.); πέρα τῆς ὥρας, beyond the season (i.e., unseasonably)

πέραν, on the other side, across; τὸ πέραν, the opposite side

πέρας, -ατος, τό, limit, end (of the earth), boundary; (adv.) πέρας, finally, in conclusion; as a result

περάω, ¹aor inf. περῆσαι: to pass through

περί (w. gen.), about, concerning; (w. acc.) around, near

περιάγω, ²aor. ptc.: περιαγαγόντες: to go about; to lead around/about

περιαιρέω, aor. inf. περιελεῖν, ptc. περιελών, impf. 3rd sg. περιῃρεῖτο: to take away, remove; to cut away (of anchors)

περιβάλλω, ²aor. περιέβαλον, pf. ptc. περιβεβλημένος: to lay something around, put around; to clothe with something; to encircle; mid. to throw around oneself, Acts 98:6; to embrace, clothe oneself

περίβολος, ὁ, enclosing wall of a temple

περιεργάζομαι, to meddle in

περιέρπω, to walk about

περιέχω, ²aor. ptc. περίσχων, ²aor. pass. inf. περισχέσθαι: to include; to encompass, surround; to come upon, befall

περίλοιπος, -ον, remaining, surviving; οἱ περίλοιποι, remnant (of Joseph)

περιμένω, to wait (for)

περιπατέω, to walk about, go about, live

περιπλέκω, pf. inf. περιπλακῆναι, 6. περιεπλάκην: to embrace; pass. to be embraced

περισσεύω, to be present in abundance, increase, overflow

περισσός (Att. περιττός), -ή, -όν, abundant, profuse; comp. περισσότερος, -α, -ον, abundantly, still more

περισσότερον, see περισσός

περιστερά, ἡ, dove

περιτέμνω (Dor. περιτάμνω), pf. ptc. περιτετμηκώς, -κυῖαι, -κός, pf. pass. ptc. περιτετμημένος: to cut off; to circumcise a man, circumcise a woman

περιτίθημι, to put around, wrap around

περιτομή, -ῆς, ἡ, circumcision

περίχωρος, -ον, neighboring, surrounding; subst. τὸ περίχωρον, surrounding region

πετεινός, -ή, -όν, winged; τὸ πετεινόν, bird

πέτρα, -ας, ἡ, rock

πεύθομαι, see πυνθάνομαι

πηγή, ἡ, running water; a spring source, fountain; source

πήγνυμι, 3. ἔπηξα, ¹aor. ptc. πήξας, 6. ἐπάγην: to pitch a tent; pass. to become stiff, congealed

πηδάω, to leap

πιάζω, to catch (of an animal); to seize, arrest (a person)

πικρός, -ά, -όν, bitter, harsh; fierce (animal); πικρῶς, bitterly, fiercely

πίμπλημι, 3. ἔπλησα, ¹aor. inf. πλάσαι, ¹aor. impv. πλῆσον, 6. ἐπλήσθην, fut. pass. πλησθήσομαι: to fill, fulfill; pass. to be filled with (w. gen.)

πίναξ, ὁ, πίνακος, flat wooden plaque (plastered or primed, then painted and inscribed)

πίνω, πίομαι, ἔπιον, πέπωκα, ——, ἐπόθην: to drink

πιπράσκω, 3. πέπρακα, 6. ἐπράθην: to sell something

πίπτω, πεσοῦμαι, ἔπεσον, πέπτωκα: to fall, fall down

πιστεύω, to believe in, have confidence in; to entrust oneself to, entrust something to somebody, trust

πίστις, -εως, ἡ, confidence, faithfulness, belief

πιστός, -ή, όν, trustworthy, faithful; this term is related to the practice of making oaths; it refers to one who can be "trusted" to take an oath and is "faithful" to the agreement undertaken.

πλανάω, to lead astray; pass. to wander, be led astray

πλάνη, ἡ, error, deceit

πλάσμα, τό, anything formed; a body, molded thing

πλάσσω (Att. πλάττω), 3. ἔπλασα, pf. pass. inf. πεπλάσθαι: to form, mold, fashion πλατεῖα, ἡ, street

πλατύς, -εῖα, -ύ, wide

πλεῖστος, -η, -ον, most, greatest, chief

πλείων (m./fm.), πλείονα (m./fm. acc.), πλεῖον/πλέον (nt.); pl. πλείονες (nom.), πλειόνων (gen.), πλείοσιν (dat.), πλείους (m. acc.): more; more (than + gen.); better/greater; ἐπὶ (τὸ) πλεῖον, all the more; ἐπὶ πλεῖον, at greater length; ἐπὶ πλείονα χρόνον, for a long time; adv. (nt. pl.), πλείονα, all the more; (superl.), πλεῖστος, -η, -ον, most; subst., πλεῖστοι, the majority

πλεονάζω, ¹aor. ἐπλεόνασα: (trans.) to increase, cause to grow, multiply, (intrans.) become more/abundant

πλευρά, -ᾶς, ἡ, side; rib

πλέω, inf. πλεῖν, 3. ἔλευσα: to sail, travel by ship

πληγή, ἡ, a blow, wound; plague; ἔρχομαι πληγῶν, to come to blows; sudden calamity

πλῆθος, -ους, τό, great number, multitude; abundance, great quantity

πληθύνω, to multiply, increase, grow in number

πλήν, nevertheless; but only, except

πλήρης, -ες / pl. -εις (m.), -ες (nt.): full; solid

πληρόω, to fill, fulfill

πλησίον (w. gen.), near, nearby; ὁ πλησίον, neighbor; ἡ, female companion

πλήσσω, ²aor. pass. ptc. πληγείς: to wound, strike; to sting (of bees); to bite

πλοῖον, τό, boat

πλόος (contr. πλοῦς), ὁ, πλοός (gen.) / pl. πλοῖ (nom.), πλῶν (gen.): sailing, voyage; "voyage" (of life)

πλούσιος, -α, -ον, rich, wealthy; ὁ πλούσιος, rich man; comp. πλουσιώτερος, -ον, richer

πλοῦτος, ὁ, wealth, riches

πνεῦμα, τό, breath, human spirit, one's inner self, ghost, Spirit/Breath (of God)

πνευματικός, -η, -ον, spiritual

πνέω, 3. ἔπνευσα: to blow (of wind)

πνοή, ἡ, wind, breath

πόθεν (interog. adv.), from where? how? in what way? why?

ποθέω, to long for, have a great desire (to do something)

ποιέω, to do, make

ποιητής, ὁ, author, maker

ποικίλος, -η, -ον, various, various kinds

ποιμαίνω, to herd, tend flocks

ποιμήν, -ένος, ὁ, herd

ποίμνιον, τό, flock (of sheep/goats)

ποῖος, -α, -ον, what? which? what sort/kind of? (interr. pronoun)

πολεμέω, to wage war, go to war with

πολεμίος, -α, -ον, hostile; subst. enemy; superl. πολεμιώτατος, most bitter enemy

πόλεμος, ὁ, war, battle

πόλις, -εως, ἡ, city

πολιτεία, ἡ, citizenship; way of life, conduct

πολιτεύω (often mid.), mid. inf. πολιτεύεσθαι: to conduct one's life in a particular
   way; to live under a certain set of laws; to deal with in one's private affairs

πολίτης, ὁ, citizen, countryman

πολλάκις, often, repeatedly

πολύς, gen. πολλοῦ, πολλή, πολύ, much, many; πολυ (adv.), often

πομπεύω, to walk in a procession

πομπή, ἡ, solemn procession

πονηρός, -ά, -όν, evil, bad

πόνος, ὁ, hard labor; pain, affliction

πορεύομαι, to go, proceed

πορνεία, ἡ, unlawful sexual practice, sexual promiscuity/immorality

πορνεύω, to engage in prohibited sexual activity, commit sexual immorality; (fig.)
   to practice idolatry

πόρ΄νη, ἡ, prostitute, whore

πόρρω (= πόρσω) (adv.), far away, far off

πορφύρα, ἡ, purple dye; purple cloth; purple stripe

πόσος, -η, -ον, how great? how much/many?

ποταμός, ὁ, river

πότε, when? (in direct question); when (in indirect question); ἕως πότε,
   how long?

ποτέ (encl.), once, former, formerly, sometimes, ever; at last; ὅσον ποτέ, whatever; whenever, ὅταν ποτέ

πότερον, whether

ποτήριον, τό, cup

ποτί, Dor. > πρός

ποτίζω, 2. ποτιῶ, 3. ἐπότισα: to give somebody a drink

ποτόν, τό, drink

πού (enclit.), (adv. of place) somewhere; "I suppose," "perhaps"

ποῦ, where?

πούς, ποδός, ὁ, foot

πρᾶγμα, matter, event, affair; thing

πρᾶξις, -εως, ἡ, way of acting/conducting; action/deed; (magical) ritual

πράσσω (Att. πράττω), 3. ἔπραξα, ¹aor. ptc. πράξας, ¹aor pass. ptc. πραχθείς:
   to do something; to commit an act; to achieve, accomplish, be busy with; τὰ
   περίεργα πράσσειν, to practice magic; to charge somebody money for something; pass. to take place, happen

πραΰς, πραεῖα, πραΰ, mild, soft, gentle; meek, unassuming

πρεσβεία, ἡ, embassy, mission

πρεσβύτερος, -α, -ον, older: ὁ πρεσβύτερος, old man; elder/official; ancestor

πρεσβυτής, ὁ, old man; ambassador

πρίν (ἤ), before, until

προάγω, to draw near to, approach; to bring up to; to lead forward

προβαίνω, pf. ptc. προβεβηκώς: to advance, make progress; to pass (of time)

πρόβατον, τό, sheep

προγινώσκω (Att. προγιγνώσκω), to foresee, have foreknowledge of

πρόγνωσις, -εως, ἡ, foreknowledge, ability to know beforehand,

προγράφω, to write above; to set forth as a public notice, advertise; to exhibit in a public place; to register/record (names)

προεδρία, ἡ, front seat (i.e., seat of honor)

πρόεδροι, οἱ, presiding officers

πρόειμι (fr. εἶμι): to go forward; proceed, continue

προέρχομαι, to go forward, approach; to come/go before; to come/go forth; to go (read) forward

πρόθεσις, -εως, ἡ, plan, purpose; offering, "(the Bread of) Presence"

προθυμία, ἡ, willingness, eagerness

πρόθυμος, -ον, ready, eager; (adv.) προθύμως, zealously, earnestly

προθύω, to sacrifice on somebody's behalf; to perform an opening sacrifice

προΐστημι, pf. act. ptc. προεστηκώς, 6. προεστάθην > προΰστην: to set over, choose as one's leader; pass. to be leader of, preside over something (gen.); subst. ptc. leader

προλαμβάνω, to take something on one's own; anticipate

προλέγω, 3. προεῖπον, 4. προείρηκα: to warn in advance; say beforehand/above

πρόνοια, ἡ, Providence

πρός (w. acc.), toward, with (prep.)

προσάγω, to bring to; to put in; to bring forward (committee business); to come near, approach, to draw near

προσδέχομαι, to accept, receive; to welcome; to admit into membership; to wait for

προσδοκάω (Ion. -έω), to wait in suspense; to anticipate

προσέρχομαι, to come or go to, approach

προσευχή, ἡ, prayer; (Jewish) prayer house

προσεύχομαι, pray

προσέχω, to pay attention to, notice; to take care of; mid. to cling to something (w. dat.); προσεχω τὸν νούν (w. dat.), to turn one's attention/mind to

προσήλυτος, proselyte, convert to Judaism (i.e., fully entitled members of the Jewish religious community)

πρόσθεν, (τό), before, in front of; τὸ πρόσθεν, earlier, formerly

προσίστημι, mostly pass. (dep.), προσίσταμαι: to set against; to set oneself against something, encounter

προσκαλέω/έομαι (mostly mid.), 6. προσεκλήθην: to summon, entreat; to call to a special task; to encourage

προσκαρτερέω, to provide service to (w. dat.)

προσκεφάλαιον (NW ποτικεφάλαιον), pillow, head cushion

προσκόπτω, 2. προσκόψω, 3. προσέκοψα: to hit against; offend

προσκυνέω, worship, kneel

προσκύνημα, -ματος, τό, act of obeisance to (παρά) a god on behalf of somebody (gen.)

προσλαλέω, to speak to

προσλαμβάνω, mid. to take somebody aside; to partake of food

πρόσοδος, ἡ, access, approach; revenue, public revenue

προσπίπτω, to fall upon; to prostrate oneself before, fall down before (πρός)

προστάγμα, -ματος, τό, command

προστάσσω (Dor. ποιτάσσω), pf. pass. ptc. προστεταγμένος: to command, order (w. dat.); pass. to be fixed, determined

προστίθημι, aor. subj. προσθῶ, ²aor. inf. προσθεῖναι: to add to something; to continue, repeat (an action)

πρόστιμον, τό, penalty, fine

προσφέρω, 3. προσένεγκον: to bring to somebody; to offer something as a sacrifice; to offer/reach out one's hand

πρόσωπον, τό, face

πρότερος, -α, -ον, former, earlier, past; πρότερον/πρότερον ἤ (adv.), before, previously

προτιμάω, inf. προτιμᾶν: to prefer

πρόφασις, -εως, ἡ, motive, pretext, excuse; προφάσει ὡς, as a pretext, under the pretext of

προφήτης, ὁ, prophet

πρυτανεία, ἡ, period during which the *prytaneis* (πρυτάνεις) of each tribe (φυλή) presided in the Council and Assembly

πρύτανις, -εως, ὁ, member of the tribe presiding in the Council or Assembly; pl. πρυτάνεις, οἱ, *prytaneis*, one of the ten (or twelve) rotating executive committees of Council and Assembly

πρωΐ (adv.), early, early in the morning

πρωτεύω, to be pre-eminent, be first among

πρῶτος, -η, -ον, first, foremost, before; πρῶτον (adv.), first, before, earlier, to begin with; (adv.) πρώτως, for the first time

πτωχεία, ἡ, poverty, Gos. Thom. 3

πτωχός, -ή, -όν, poor

Πύθιος, -α, -ον, Pythian (i.e., of Delphi), epith. of Apollo

πύλη, ἡ, gate

πυλών, -ῶνος, ὁ, city gate; gateway, door

πυνθάνομαι (older form πεύθομαι), 2. πεύσομαι, 3. ἐπυθόμην, ²aor. mid. ptc. πυθόμενος: to learn something from somebody (gen.), inquire concerning something (gen.); subst. a question

πῦρ, πυρός, τό, fire

πυρόω, to burn with fire; to heat to red hot: pass. to be set on fire, be purified by fire (of metals) πυρρός, -ά, -όν, yellowish-red, red; comp. –τερος

πωλέω, to sell, offer for sale; pass. to be for sale; subst. ptc. vendor

πώς (encl.), somehow, in some way

πῶς, interrog. particle how? in what way?

ῥάβδος, ἡ, rod, staff

ῥᾴδιος, -α, -ον, easy; (adv.) ῥᾴδιον, a light manner

ῥάπτω, 3. ἔρραψα: to sew (a garment); to alter (a garment)

ῥέω, 3rd pl. ¹aor. impv. ῥευσάτωσαν: to flow, stream, waft

ῥήγνυμι/ῥήσσω, fut. ῥήξω, aor. impv. ῥῆξον, aor. ptc. ῥήξας, ²aor. pass. ptc. ῥαγείς, -εῖσα, -έν, 3rd sg. ²aor. pass. impv. ῥαγήτω, fut. pass. ῥαγήσομαι: to tear, tear in pieces; pass. to break out, burst, break in two

ῥῆμα, -ματος, what is said, a word, a saying

ῥίζα, ἡ, root

ῥίπτω, 3. ἔρριψα, ¹aor. impv. ῥῖψον, 6. ἐρρίφην: to throw, cast away; to lay/put something down

ῥόδον, τό, rose

ῥομφαία, ἡ, sword

ῥύομαι, s.v. ἐρύω

ῥυπαρός, -ά, -όν, filthy, dirty

Ῥωμαῖος, -α, -ον, of the Romans, Roman; subst. Roman person

Ῥώμη, ἡ, Rome

ῥώννυμι, 4. ἔρρωμαι, pf. mid. inf. ἐρρῶσθαι, pf. mid. ptc. ἐρρωμένος, pf. mid. impv. ἔρρωισο: to be in good health/well; ἔρρωσο, "farewell"; pass. to be strengthened

σαββατίζω, 2. σαββατιῶ: to keep the Sabbath; σαββατίζω τὸ σάββατον, to keep the Sabbath as a Sabbath

σάββατον, τό (often in pl.), the Sabbath

σάλπιγξ, -ιγγος, ἡ, trumpet

Σάραπις, ὁ, god Sarapis

σαρκοφάγος, -ον, flesh eating; subst. flesh eater; sarcophagus

σάρξ, σαρκος, ἡ, flesh, physical body

σατανᾶς, -α (gen.), ὁ, adversary, Satan (w. article), enemy of God

σβέννυμι, 3. ἔσβεσα, aor. inf. σβέσαι, aor. pass. impv. σβέσθητι: to extinguish, put out (a fire); pass. to be extinguished

σεαυτοοῦ, -ῆς (reflexive pron.), yourself

Σεβαστός, -ή, -όν, Augustan (adj.); Σεβαστός for Lat. Augustus; pl. Augusti

σέβω/ομαι, to worship, reverence; mid. ptc. subst. σεβόμενοι, god fearers (i.e., Gentiles who took part in synagogue services without becoming full προσήλυτοι); subst. θεὸν σέβων, god fearer

Σεινᾶ, see Σινᾶ

σείω, to shake

σελήνη, ἡ, moon

σεμνός, -ή, -όν, solemn, reverent; honorable, above reproach; superl. σεμνότατος, -η, -ον, most solemn/holy; (adv.) σεμνῶς, reverently

σημαίνω, 2. σημανῶ, 3. ἐσήμηνα, aor. impv. σήμανον: to give a sign/signal, indicate something (acc.) with a sign; to report, make known

σημεῖον, τό, sign, token, distinguishing mark, portent; a marking (on approved sacrificial animals); pl. stripes

σήμερον, τό, today; (adv.), today

σιγάω, to be silent

σιγή, ἡ, silence, quiet

σίδηρος, ὁ, iron, anything made of iron

Σιδών, -ῶνος, ἡ, Sidon

Σινά/Σεινᾶ (indecl.), Sinai; Σίναιον ὄρος, Mount Sinai

σιτίον, τό, food made from wheat, food; pl. diet, eating habits

σιωπάω, to keep silent, say nothing, become quiet

σκανδαλίζω, to cause to be caught/to fall; pass. to be led into sin

σκάνδαλον, -ου, τό, obstacle, that which causes stumbling

σκέλος, -εος, τό, leg (fr. the hip downward)

σκέπη, ἡ, protection, shelter, shade

σκεῦος, -ους, τό, vessel, container; instrument; kedge, driving anchor; τὰ σκευή, equipment, ship's tackle, possessions

σκηνή, ἡ, tent, tabernacle

σκήνωμα, -ατος, τό, tent, dwelling, tabernacle

σκληρός, -ά, -όν, hard, difficult

σκολιός, -ά, -όν, curved, crooked, coiled; dishonest; σκολιῶς, coiling; τὸ σκολιόν, intestine

σκοτεινός, -ή, -όν, dark

σκότος, -ους, τό, darkness; sin, evil

σκῦλον, τό, pl. σκύλα: spoils, booty

σκώληξ, -ηκος, ὁ, worm

σμύρνα, ἡ (also ζμύρνα), myrrh (gum from an Arabian tree used for embalming the dead, as incense, and as a salve)

σοφία, ἡ, wisdom

σοφιστής, ὁ, master, expert

σπείρω, 3. ἔσπειρα, ¹aor. mid. ptc. ἐσπειραμένος, pf. pass. ptc. ἐσπαρμένος, 6. ἐσπάρην: to sow seed; to scatter, spread, extend

σπέρμα, τό, seed, offspring, children; descendants

σπεύδω, 3. ἔσπευσα: to hurry; to take an interest in somebody

σπήλαιον, τό, cave

σπλάγχα, τά, inward parts, entrails (esp. heart, lungs, liver, kidneys); fig. affection, love σπλαγχνίζω (= σπλαγχνεύω), to eat the entrails of a sacrificial victim

σπονδή, ἡ, drink offering, libation; donation of wine

σπουδάζω, to pay serious attention to; to study; to hurry, be in a hurry to do something

σπουδαῖος, -α, -ον, good, excellent

σπουδή, ἡ, diligence, concern, attention; haste, hurry; ἐν σπουδῇ, in concern

στάδιον, τό, stadium, arena

στάσις, -εως, ἡ, standing still; riot, rioting, uprising

στατήρ, -ῆρος, ἡ, stater (coin)

σταυρός, ὁ, cross

σταυρόω, to crucify

στεγάζω, to contain, enclose; subst. ptc., enclosure

στεῖρα, ἡ, incapable of bearing children, infertile, barren

στενάζω, to groan, sigh

στέργω, to feel affection for somebody, show affection to

στέφανος, ὁ, wreath; crown; crowing

στεφανόω, to crown; to honor somebody; pass. to be crowned with; to be honored by (ὑπό) somebody for (some virtue [acc.]) with a crown (dat.)

στῆθος, -ους (uncontr. -εος), τό, (breast of both sexes)

στήλη, ἡ, stele, (inscribed) stone slab

στηρίζω, to set up, establish, strengthen

στοιχεῖον, τό, pl. components/elements into which matter is divisible

στοιχέω, to correspond to, coincide

στολή, ἡ, robe, garment

στολίζω, to dress, adorn, decorate

στόμα, -ματος, τό, mouth

στρατηγός, ὁ, *strategos*, military commander; *strategos*, Egyptian (Ptolemaic) governor of a *nome* (administrative unit)

στρατιώτης, ὁ, soldier

στρέφω, 6. ἐστράφην: to turn, turn around; to change into (w. εἰς) something; to make revolve, turn something around; mid. to turn oneself around in circles; pass (dep.), to turn toward

σύ, you (sg.)

συγγένεια, ἡ, kinship/relationship with/to (πρός)

συγγενής, -ές, related to (gen.) somebody, akin to; subst. a relative, kinsman

συγγίνομαι, pf. συγγεγενημαι, to associate with (w. dat.); to mingle with, have sexual intercourse with; to be a companion

συγκαθεύδω, to have sex with somebody (dat.)

σύγκρισις, -εως, ἡ, a compound, aggregate substance

συγχαίρω, to rejoice with/at

συζητέω (w. dat.), to dispute, debate

συκῆ, ἡ, fig tree

συλλαμβάνω, 3. συνέλαβον, ²aor act. inf. συλλαβεῖν, ²aor. mid. impv. συλλαβοῦ, 6. συνελήμφθην: to lay hold of, seize; comprehend; to conceive a child; mid. to take part in something with somebody

συμβαίνω, 3. συνέβην, 4. συμβέβηκα, pf. ptc. συμβεβηκώς: to happen; συνέβη (w. acc. + inf.), it happened that (impers.); συμβαίνω τί τινι, something happens to somebody; subst. τὸ συμβεβηκός, a contingent attribute ("accident") of something

συμβάλλω, impf. συνέβαλλον: to converse with (dat.), engage in an argument; to communicate (a preliminary resolulion)

συμβουλεύω, to recommend

συμβούλω, to advise, counsel

συμμείγνυμι, pf. pass. ptc. συμμεμιγμένος: to mix together, mingle with; mid. to associate with; to be joined sexually with (gen.)

συμπάθεια, ἡ, affinity

σύμπας, σύμπασα, σύμπαν, all together (w. collective nouns); ἡ σύμπασα, the whole (world)

συμπτώμα, -ματος, τό, attribute; faculty

συμφέρω, to help, be advantageous; to bring together, collect; (impers.) it is useful/good/best; subst. nt. ptc. (τὸ) συμφέρον, what is useful/best/beneficial; the welfare

συμφορά, ἡ, misfortune, calamity

σύμφωνος, -ον, harmonious, in agreement (with)

σύν (w. dat.) with, in company with

συνάγω, gather together, assemble

συναγωγή, synagogue

συνδειπνέω, to dine with somebody

συνδοκέω, to seem good also

συνέδρος, ὁ, member of the Council (συνέδριον)

συνείδησις, ἡ, conscience

σύνειμι (fr. εἰμί) (1), 2. συνέσομαι, fut. inf. συνέσεσθαι: to be with; to join, catch up with somebody (dat.)

σύνειμι (fr. εἶμι) (2), ptc. συνιών, συνιοῦσα, συνιόν, 3rd pl. pres. impv. συνίτωσαν: to meet together (on), assemble

συνεργέω, to work together with somebody (attain something or bring about something), assist

συνεργός, -ον, working together, ὁ/ἡ συνεργός, helper

συνέρχομαι, to assemble, gather together

σύνεσις, -εως, ἡ, understanding, discernment

συνετός, -ή, -όν, intelligent, discerning

συνέχω, to keep closed; to seize, torment

συνίημι (fr. ἵημι), ptc. συνιείς, -εντος, pl. συνιέντες, 2. συνήσω, 3. συνῆκα, ¹aor. subj. συνῶ: to understand something (gen.); subst. wise ones συνίστημι/συνιστάνω, fut. συστήσω, ²aor. act. inf. συστῆναι, ²aor. mid. inf. συστήσασθαι, ²aor. pass. subj. συστηθῶ: to demonstrate, show; to introduce/recommend somebody to somebody; to be composed of (gen.); mid. to establish; to join (in battle)

σύνοδος, ἡ civic meeting (at which motions are deliberated); community

συνουσία, ἡ, being with/together with; sexual intercourse

συντάσσω, to arrange for something to be done, command; to prescribe (a medical treatment)

συντέλεια, ἡ, completion, consumation

συντελέω, ¹aor. pass. ptc. συντελεσθείς: to bring to an end, finish, carry out, accomplish; to arrange, agree upon; to pay (toward common expenses); pass. to be brought to perfection

συντίθημι, aor. mid. συνεθέμην: mid. to agree to/on, consent to

Συρία, ἡ, Syria

συστέλλω, mid. inf. συστέλλεσθαι, ¹aor. συνέστειλα, pf. pass. ptc. συνεσταλμένος: to humiliate; (naut.) to fold up, furl a sail; mid. to be discouraged; pass. (of time), to grow shorter

σύστημα, -ματος, τό, the whole compounded of parts

σφάγιον, mostly pl. σφάγια, victims, offerings, sacrifices

σφάλλω, 6. ἐσφάλην: to make fall; pass. to stumble/fall over something (acc.), transgress; to fail

σφεῖς, σφέων (gen.), σφίσι(ν) (dat.), σφᾶς (acc.) (pl. pron.): they, them

σφόδρα, very (much), extremely, greatly (adv.)

σφραγίζω, to seal (for security), seal by impressing a seal with a signet ring

σφραγίς, -ῖδος, ἡ, (wax) seal

σχεδόν, adv. nearly, almost

σχῆμα, -ματος, τό, bodily form, shape; looks, outward appearance; a way of life; the character or property of a thing; style

σχίζω, to split, divide

σχίσμα, τό, crack, cleft; dissension, schism

σχοινίον, τό, rope

σῴζω, σώσω, ἔσωσα, σέσωκα, σέσῳσμαι / σέσωμαι, ἐσώθην: to save, rescue, deliver

σῶμα, -ματος, τό, body, physical body

σωματικός, -ή, -όν, bodily, of the body

σωμάτιον, τό, poor body (dim. of σῶμα)

σωτήρ, -ῆρος, ὁ, savior

σωτηρία, ἡ, deliverance, rescue, salvation

σωφροσύνη, ἡ, prudence, discretion; self-control, esp. sexual self-restraint

τάλαντον, τό, a talent (measure of weight ranging from 108 to 130 pounds)

ταμίας, ὁ, treasurer

τάξις, -εως, ἡ, arrangement; (official) appointment; position, order

ταπεινός, -ή, -όν, humble, lowly; undistinguished

ταπεινόω, to humble, humiliate; to bring low, be made low

ταπείνωσις, -εως, ἡ, humiliation, humility

ταράσσω, pf. pass. ptc. τεταραγμένος: to agitate physically, pervert something; (fig.) to stir up, disturb mentally, throw into confusion; pass. to be troubled, vexed; to be thrown into disorder/confusion

τάσσω (Att. τάττω), pf. pass. τέτακμαι, pf. pass. ptc. τεταγμένος: to station, post somebody before; to set; to appoint; to determine; to undertake (a task); to restore; pass. to be ordained that (w. acc. + inf.); τὰ ταταγμένα, instructions

ταφή, ἡ, burial, burial place

ταφικόν, τό, burial fee

τάφος, grave, tomb

τάχα, quickly; perhaps

τάχηλος, ὁ, neck

ταχύς, -εῖα, -ύ, swift, quick, soon; ταχέως (adv.), quickly; comp. θάσσων (Att. θάττων), θᾶσσον, quicker, sooner than (ἤ); superl. τάχιστος, -η, -ον, most quickly, as quickly as possible, as soon as

τέ, and; τέ...δέ..., both ... and ... (usually follows the word it coordinates)

τείνω, 3. ἔτεινα: to stretch, reach out, extend; to apply

τεῖχος (>τοῖχος), -ους, τό, city wall

τεκμαίρομαι, 3. ἐτεκμηράμην, 6. ἐτεκμήρθην: to conjecture, guess; pass. to be indicated

τέκνον, τό, child

τέλειος, -α, -ον, complete, perfect; mature, full-grown (of persons); τὰ τέλεια, mature animals; superl. τελειότατος, -η, -ον, most perfect

τελειόω, to fulfill; pass. to be accomplished (of promises, prophecies); to become mature, perfect

τελετή, ἡ, initiation rite into sacred mysteries

τελευταῖος, -α, -ον, last (of time)

τελευτάω, pres. impv. 2nd sg. τελεύτα: to die, pass away

τελέω, 6. ἐτελέσθην, pf. pass. ptc. τετελεσμένος: to finish, complete, fulfill; to perfect; to initiate (into a mystery religion), pass. to be accomplished

τέλος, -ους, τό, end; outcome, resolution, conclusion

τέμενος, -εος, τό, precincts of a temple

τέρας, -ατος, τό, portentous sign, a wonder

τεσσαράκοντα (Att. τετταράκοντα), forty

τέσσαρες, nt. τέσσαρα, gen. τεσσάρων, four

τέταρτος, -η, -ον, fourth

τέχνη, ἡ, trade, skill, craftsmanship

τεχνίτης, -ου, ὁ, craftsman, artisan, skilled worker; musician τηρέω, to keep, observe

τίκτω, 2. τέξομαι, 3. ἔτεκον, 4. τέτοκα, pf. pass. τέτεγμαι, fm. pf. pass. ptc. τετοκυῖα, 6. ἐτέχθην: to give birth (to)

τίθημι, θήσω, ἔθηκα, τέθεικα, τέθειμαι, ἐτέθην: to put, set, lay

τιμάω, ¹aor. ἐτίμησα, ¹aor. ptc. τιμάς: to honor

τιμή, -ῆς, ἡ, honor, pl. honors; price/cost, value; (gen.), at a price of

τίμιος, -α, -ον, precious, valuable; superl. τιμιώτερος, -α, -ον, more precious

τιμωρία, ἡ, retribution, vengeance

τίνω, 2. τίσω (also τείσω), 3. ἔτ(ε)ισα, to pay a penalty, undergo something (acc.) as a punishment

τίς, τί, who? which? what?

τις, τι (encl.), anyone, anything

τοίνυν, indeed, then; therefore; δὴ τοίνυν, "I suggest/submit (that)"

τοιοῦτος, -αύτη, -οῦτον, of such a kind, such as this, for example; τὰ τοιαῦτα, similar/related things

τοῖχος, s.v. τεῖχος

τόκος, ὁ, birth; offspring; interest (on money owed)

τόλμα/τόλμη, ἡ, audacity, recklessness

τολμάω, to dare to, be bold enough to (w. inf.); to show boldness toward (ἐπί)

τόπος, ὁ, place, location

τοσοῦτος, -αύτη, -οῦτον, so much/great/large, etc.; pl. so many

τότε, then, at that time

τράπεζα, ἡ, table; τράπεζα τῆς προθέσεως, table of the Bread of Presence; offering table (for a god)

τράχηλος, ὁ, neck

τράγος, ὁ, goat

τραχύς, -εῖα, -ύ, rough, rocky

τρεῖς, τρία, three

τρέμω: to tremble at (w. acc.), shake in fear, be in awe of

τρέπω, 3. ἔτρεψα/ἔτραπον, ²aor. pass. ἐτρέπην: to incline/turn somebody toward (εἰς); to turn back to, go back to; mid. to turn/take oneself to (εἰς)

τρέφω, ¹aor. ἔθρεψα, pf. pass. ptc. τεθραμμένος: to rear/raise a child; to feed

τρέχω, 2. δραμέομαι, 3. ἔδραμον: to run

τριάκοντα, thirty

τριακόσιοι, -αι, -α, three hundred

τρίς (adv.), three times

τρίτος, -η, -ον, third

τρόμος, ὁ, trembling

τρόπος, ὁ, way, manner; ὃν τρόπον, (just) as; καθ᾽ ὃν τρόπον, in the manner that

τροφή, ἡ, food

τρώγω, to eat

τυγχάνω, pres. ptc. τυχών, τυχόντος / τυχοῦσα / τυχόν, ²aor. ἔτυχον, ²aor. 3rd sg. subj. τήχῃ, inf. τυχεῖν, pf. τέτ(ε)υχα, pf. ptc. τετ(ε)υχώς: to gain, experience; to happen, turn out (as a result), happen to be; to gain/receive something (gen.); to attain to (ἐπί); to obtain one's request (w. gen.); ἔτυχεν δέ, and it came to pass that (w. acc.); adj. ptc. ordinary

τύμβος, ὁ, sepulchral mound, grave

τύπος, ὁ, image, form; type, prototype, pattern; pl. details

τυπόω, to stamp a shape into something

τύπτω, ἔτυψα: to beat, strike

τύραννος, ὁ, tyrant, king, prince

τύχη, ἡ, luck; ἀγαθῇ τύχῃ, "for good fortune"; Τύχη Ἀγαθή, Agathe Tyche (goddess)

ὑβρίζω, to insult, mistreat

ὕβρις, -εως, ἡ, damage; acts of insolence, insolence; pl. insults

ὑγιαίνω, to be in good health

ὑγίεια, ἡ, health;   Ὑγίεια, goddess Hygeia (daughter of Asklepios)

ὑγιής, -ές, healthy; τίθημι ὑγιή, to make well

ὑγρός, -ά, -όν, wet, moist; subst. liquid, the wet/water

ὕδωρ, -ατος, τό, water

ὑετός, ὁ, rain

υἱός, ὁ, son, descendant

ὕλη, ἡ, matter

ὑλικός, -ή, -όν, belonging to matter, material

ὑμεῖς, you (pl.)

ὑμέτερος, -α, -ον, your

ὑμνέω, to sing hymns, celebrate in a hymn

ὕμνος, ὁ, hymn

ὑπάγω, to bring under one's power, induce somebody to do something; to bring before a court of law; to go away, depart

ὑπακοή, ἡ, obedience; answer

ὑπακούω, to obey (w. dat.); to be subject to

ὑπάρχω, impf. ὑπῆρχον: to exist, be present; to belong to; to possess; subst. ptc. τὰ ὑπάρχοντα, possessions, property

ὑπέρ, with: (w. gen.) for, in behalf of; about, concerning; (w. acc.) over and above, beyond

ὑπερβάλλω, to exceed, surpass

ὑπερβολή, ἡ, excess, extraordinary character, superiority, surpassing; surpassing quality, greatness; καθ᾽ ὑπερβολήν, to an extraordinary degree

ὑπερέχω, to be of more value, better than; to excel; ptc. subst. great value; to rise above; transcend

ὑπερηφανία, ἡ, arrogance, pride

ὑπεροράω, ²aor. ptc. ὑπεριδών: to overlook, disregard

ὑπεροχή, ἡ, pre-eminence, dignity; state of superiority, καθ᾽ ὑπεροχή, with superior (w. gen.)

ὑπερῷον, τό, upper part of a house, upper portico

ὑπηρέτης, -ου, ὁ, assistant, attendant; helper

ὕπνος, ὁ, sleep; καθ᾽/κατὰ (τὸν) ὕπνον, in a dream

ὑπνόω, to sleep

ὑπό, ὑπ᾽, ὑφ᾽ (w. gen.), by, by means of; (w. acc.), under, below

ὑπογράφω, to write below

ὑποδείκνυμι/ὑποδεικνόω, 3. ὑπέδειξα: to show, reveal, indicate

ὑποδέχομαι, to entertain as a guest; to provide hospitality for; to promise

ὑπόδημα, pl. -ματα, sandal, shoe

ὑπόθεσις, -εως, ἡ, general theory

ὑπόκειμαι, to lie under, below; to be subject to somebody/something

ὑποκρίνομαι, aor. pass. inf. ὑποκριθῆναι: to play a part; to pretend, deceive

ὑπόκρισις, ἡ, hypocrisy

ὑπολαμβάνω, to reply; to believe, assume, suppose; to undertake to

ὑπομένω, to remain, await; to endure, stand one's ground, hold out; bear an ordeal, put up with

ὑπόμνημα, -ματος, τό, reminder; memorandum

ὑπομονή, ἡ, endurance, perseverance

ὑπόστασις, -εως, ἡ, basis; frame of mind

ὑποστρέφω, to return, turn back

ὑποτάσσω, to make subject; to append; pass. to be subjected to

ὑποτίθημι, aor. mid. ptc. ὑποθέμενος: to suggest, advise

ὑποφέρω, fut. ὑποίσω: to bear up, endure

ὕστερος, -α, -ον, coming after; last; (adv.) ὕστερον, after, finally, later than (ἤ)

ὑψηλός, -ή, -όν, tall, high; proud, haughty

ὕψιστος, -η, -ον, highest; ὁ ὕψιστος, the Most High (God)

ὕψος, -ους, τό, height

ὑψόω, to lift up, raise; (fig.) to exalt

φαίνω, pres. pass. inf. φαίνεσθαι, 2. φανῶ/οῦμαι, 3. ἔφανα, 6. ἐφάνην, ²aor. fm. pass. ptc. φανείς, -εῖσα, -έν, aor. pass. impv. φάνηθι: to shine, give light; mid. to make one's appearance, attend (a meeting); pass. to appear, be seen, become visible, appear to be, be apparent (that)

φανερός, -ά, -όν, known, visible; evident, notable; (adv.) φανερῶς, openly, publicly

φανερόω, to make known, show, manifest, reveal

φαντασία, ἡ, fantasy; appearance, presentation

Φαρισαῖος, Pharisee

φαρμακεία, ἡ, sorcery

φάρμακον, τό, drug, medicine; magic potion; spell cast using a magic potion

φέγγος, -ους, τό, light, radiance, flash

φείδομαι, ¹aor. mid. ἐφεισάμην: to refrain from, spare somebody (gen.) from something

φέρω, οἴσω, ἤνεγκα, ἐνήνοχα, ἐνήνεγμαι, ἠνέχθην: to bring, bring along, carry; to endure, bring against (of charges); to establish, validate

φεύγω, 2. φεύξομαι, 3. ἔφυγον: to flee, escape; to avoid, turn from

φήμη, ἡ, good report, fame

φημί, 3rd sg. φησίν, 3rd pl. φασίν, impf. 3rd sg. ἔφη: say; (impers.) it is said

φθάνω, 2. φθήσομαι, 3. ἔφθασα, 4. ἔφθακα: to attain, reach; to arrive, come/go first, come/go before (others)

φθαρτός, -ή, -όν, perishable

φθείρω, fut. pass. φθαρήσομαι: to sexually seduce; to be dissolved

φθονέω, to be envious of somebody (dat.), be jealous

φθορά, ἡ, depravity, moral corruption; miscarriage

φιάλη, ἡ, phial (shallow bowl from which wine was poured onto an altar while prayers were recited and then the remainder of the wine was consumed)

φιλάνθρωπος, -ον, humane; τὰ φιλάνθρωπα, humane concessions (technical term for privileges given to ethinic communities); (adv.) φιλανθρώπως, humanely, kindly

φιλέω, to love; to kiss

φιλία, ἡ, friendship

φίλιος, -α, -ον, friendly; subst. friend

φιληδονία, ἡ, love of pleasure

φιλόδωρος, -ον, generous, bountiful

φίλος, -η, -ον, beloved, pleasant; popular; subst. friend

φιλοσοφέω, to study philosophy, speculate about (ὑπέρ); subst. ptc. student of philosophy

φιλοσοφία, ἡ, philosophy

φιλόσοφος, ὁ, philosopher; adj. φιλοσόφος, -ον; superl. φιλοσοφώτατος, most philosophical

φιλοστορία, ἡ, tender love, strong affection

φιλοτιμέομαι (pass. dep.): to strive after honor, be ambitious; make a sincere effort

φιλοτιμία, ἡ, love of honor, generosity

φίλτρον, τό, love potion

φλέγω, to burn with fire; pass. to be on fire; to be filled w. (intense emotion)

φλόξ, ἡ, φλογός, flame; πῦρ φλογός, flaming fire

φοβέομαι (pass. dep.), to fear, be afraid of

φοβερός, -ά, -όν, terrible, horrifying, dreadful

φόβος, ὁ, fear, fright

φοιτάω, to come in, go about

φονεύς, -έως, ὁ, φονέα (acc. sg.) / φονέας (acc. pl.): murderer

φονεύω, to murder, kill

φόνος, ὁ, murder

φορά, ἡ, payment, (membership) dues; tribute; rapid motion

φορέω, to wear (clothing/armor); to bear, suffer

φορτίον, τό, a load, cargo; burden

φρονέω, to think, have in mind, set one's mind on, be concerned about

φρόνησις, -εως, ἡ, practical wisdom

φρόνιμος, -ον, prudent, wise; superl. -τατος, wisest

φροντίζω, to consider, ponder; to be concerned about somebody (gen.); to pay attention to something (gen.)

φύω, 4. πέφυκα: to bring forward, produce/form; to create, put forth

φυλακή, ἡ, prison

φύλαξ, -ακος, ἡ, guard; guardian, protector

φυλάσσω (Att. φυλάττω), to keep; to guard, protect; to observe, follow; pass. to be kept

φυλή, ἡ, tribe

φύλλον, τό, leaf

φυσικός, -ή, -όν, natural, inborn; comp. φυσικώτερος, more natural; (adv.) φυσικῶς, naturally, physically

φύσις, ἡ, circumstance; nature (of something), natural condition; substance; natural being, creature; female genitalia

φυτεύω, to plant something

φύω, ¹aor. ἔφυσα/²aor. ἔφυν, aor. inf. φῦναι: to bring forth, be born

φωνέω, to speak; to give (a speech)

φωνή, ἡ, sound, voice, language

φώς, φωτός, ὁ, man

φῶς, φωτός, τό, light

φωστήρ, -ῆρος, ὁ, star

χαίρω, fut. χαρήσομαι, ²aor. pass. ἐχάρην: rejoice; χαῖρε, greetings (spoken address), good day; (in letters) inf., χαίρειν (w. dat.), greetings; πολλὰ χαίρειν, many greetings

χαλάω, to lower, let down

χαλεπός, -ή, -όν, difficult; cruel, harsh; χαλεπῶς, with difficulty, with great discomfort

χάλκεος, -έα, -εον (later form, χαλεῖος, -α, -ον; Att. contr. χαλκοῦς, -ῆ, -οῦν), (of) bronze

χαλκός, ὁ, bronze; anything made of metal; χαλκός, a chalkos (copper coin; 8 chalkos = 1 obol)

χαλκοῦς, -ῆ, -οῦν, see χάλκεος

χαρά, ἡ, joy, happiness

χαρακτήρ, -ῆρος, ὁ, outward appearance; distinctive features χαρίζομαι, impf. ἐχαριζόμην, 5. κεχάρισμαι: to show a favor/kindness to somebody; to freely grant, give, bestow favor upon somebody; to be pleasing/beloved; pass. to be given freely

χάριν (w. gen.), because of, by reason of (oft. follows the noun it modifies); ὧν χάριν, for which

χάρις, -ιτος, ἡ, gratuitous service (free from contractual obligations or counterservice), beneficient disposition, goodwill toward someone, sign of favor, benefaction

χάρισμα, τό, gift, something freely given

χαριτόω, to bestow favor upon

χορτάζω, to feed/fatten (cattle); pass. to eat one's fill

χεῖλος, -ους, τό / pl. τὰ χείλη: lips; edge, shore (of the sea), bank (of a river)

χειμάζομαι, to be tossed/battered by a storm

χειμών, -ῶνος, ὁ, storm

χείρ, χειρός, ἡ, hand

χείρων (m./fm.), χεῖρον (nt.), -ονος: worse; inferior to something (gen.); subst. the worst

Χερουβ, τό / χερουβιν/ειν/ιμ (pl.): cherub, cherubim, winged creatures (like the Egyptian sphynx), half human, half lion

χήρα, ἡ, widow

χθές, yesterday

χθόνιος, -α, -ον, under the earth; χθόνιοι θεοί, gods of the underworld/Hades

χιλιάς, -άδος, ἡ, thousand

χίλιοι, -αι, -α, thousand

χιτών, -ῶνος, ὁ, tunic

χλωρός, -ά, -όν, greenish-yellow; subst. green plant

χορτάζω, to feed/fatten (cattle); pass. to eat one's fill

χόρτος, ὁ, grass; χόρτος τοῦ ἀγροῦ, wild grass, hay

χοῦς, τό, χοός (gen.), dust, clay

χράω, pres. mid. inf. χρῆσθαι, ¹aor. mid. inf. χρήσασθαι: to proclaim (by gods in oracles); to direct by an oracle (w. inf.); mid. to make use of something (dat.); to treat somebody with (w. dat. / ἐν); to be subject to, suffer from sickness; w. adv. to treat somebody (dat.) in a particular way (e.g., well/badly); to warn somebody (dat.)

χρεία, ἡ, the need, necessity

χρή (impers. or subject in acc.), impf. ἐχρῆν: it is necessary for somebody (acc.) to do something (inf.)

χρηματίζω (w. dat.), to deliberate on (committee business); to give ear to (an oracle), make known a divine injunction/warning; to issue instructions to somebody; pass. to be warned

χρῆσις, -εως, ἡ, use, employment of something

χρησμός, ὁ, oracular response, oracle

χρηστός, -ή, -όν, useful, good; pleasant to the taste; beloved; (adv.) χρηστῶς, well

χριστός, ὁ, messiah, anointed one; ὁ Χριστός, the annointed one, the Christ

χρόνος, ὁ, time (chronological), period of time

χρίω, 3. ἔχρισα, 4. κέχρικα, 5. κέχριμαι: to anoint (with); to rub/smear with

χρύσεος, -α, -ον (contr. χρυσοῦς, -ῆ, -οῦν), golden, gold

χρυσίον, τό, gold, money, anything made of gold, gold vessel

χρυσός, ὁ, gold, gold coin

χρυσοῦς, s.v. χρύσεος

χρῶμα, -ματος, τό, color

χωλός, -ή, -όν, lame, unable to walk

χώρα, ἡ, country, countryside; a place; land (as opposed to sea)

χωρέω, to go forward, make progress; (of money) to be spent; subst. ptc. payment; to hold, contain something (gen.)

χωρίζω, to divide, separate; to depart, go away from

χωρίον, τό, plot of land, property; place (to sit)

χωρίς, also χωρὶς ἤ (w. gen.), except for, apart from

ψαλμός, ὁ, psalm, song of praise

ψεύδομαι, to lie, tell a falsehood

ψεῦδος, -ους, τό, lie, lying

ψηφίζω, freq. mid. ψηφίζομαι (for citation of formal motion), aor. mid. inf. ἐψηφίσθαι, aor. mid. inf. ἐψηφίσθαι: to approve a motion, to decree; aor. mid. inf. "be it resolved that"

ψήφισμα, -ματος, τό, decree

ψῆφος, ἡ, vote

ψυχή, ἡ, soul, life, person, one's inmost being

ψυχόω, to give a soul to, to "be-soul"

ψυχρός, -ή, -όν, cold

ὧδε, here; now, at this point; in this way

ᾠδή, ἡ, song, ode

ὠδίν, -ῖνος, ἡ / pl. ὠδῖνες: labor pains

ὠδίνω, to suffer labor pains

ὠκύς, ὠκεῖα, ὠκύ, quick; superl. ὤκιστος, as quickly as possible,

ὠνή, ἡ, contract for purchase

ὥρα, ἡ, moment, time, short indefinite period of time

ὡραῖος, -α, -ον, beautiful; gracious

ὡς, as, like, about (with numbers/time), when (with expressions of time)

ὡσεί, like, as if, about, approximately

ὥσπερ, as, just as, even as; like

ὥστε, so that, with the result that

ὠφελέω, to gain, profit, achieve (something); to help, benefit

Made in the USA
Middletown, DE
21 September 2017